Intimacy, Family, and Society

Intimacy, Family, and Society

Arlene Skolnick
Jerome H. Skolnick
University of California, Berkeley

Little, Brown and Company   *Boston*

For Michael and Alexander

Preface

Intimacy, Family, and Society is a follow-up to our earlier *Family in Transition*. In *Family in Transition* our major efforts were devoted to challenging the then prevailing view that the nuclear family was universal, built into human nature, and the backbone of society. We tried to show that there was considerable variability in family form, function, and ideology, that variations from nuclear family norms were not necessarily pathological or unworkable, and that the realities of nuclear family life did not conform to the idealized images of social science and popular thought. We noted mass-media challenges to conventional views on sex, marriage, and the family, and lamented the relative backwardness of social science literature, much of which seemed unchanged since the 1950s.

During the early 1970s, however, a large assortment of well-written and well-researched scholarly articles appeared, either challenging previous theoretical approaches to the family or examining some of the new patterns of familial and sexual behavior.

As materials became available and as our own ideas developed (see Arlene Skolnick's *The Intimate Environment*), we found that we were able to put together a virtually brand-new set of readings which complemented and developed, but did not render obsolete, the readings in *Family in Transition*. In *Family in Transition*, we emphasized the structural problems of the nuclear family in modern society. In *Intimacy, Family, and Society*, there is a greater emphasis on personal experience and interpersonal relations in the family. Thus we have included a new section on the masculine role in the family and society, and we have expanded our material on the variety of life styles—for example, remaining single. Also, we have tried to make the readings even more teachable and learnable by including a brief introduction to each article.

Finally, criticism of the nuclear family has become so commonplace that it seems necessary to emphasize, once again, that the nuclear family also has a place in the pluralistic assortment of life styles, and that it is the *ideology* of the nuclear family that needs again to be questioned, along with any other ideology that proclaims itself the sole or best answer for the domestic relationships of every human being.

It is especially difficult to make acknowledgments for this volume. Both of us have done much reading, discussing, and attending of conferences on the family, with so many colleagues that to name only a few would be inaccurate. The Center for the Study of Law and Society provided, as always, a congenial and stimulating environment and was especially helpful in our consideration of legal controls on the family. We are most grateful to Cecilia Tighe, Kelly Lee, Emily Knapp, and Gary Lee for research and secretarial assistance. Our friends, editor Christopher Hunter, and production supervisor Kenneth Burke made useful suggestions and were fun to work with. And we certainly appreciate Mary Woodcock's patience and persistence in dealing with the permissions file.

Jerome and Arlene Skolnick

Contents

Domestic Relations
and Social Change

Around the turn of the century, the institution of the family was believed to be in a state of decline. Significant developments such as the movement of population from country to city, the shift of manufacturing from home to factory, and the emergence of the kindergarten and day nursery convinced scholars and laymen that the family had outlived its usefulness. For the first time in history, men and women could find work and satisfy basic needs without family ties of blood or marriage. On the whole, scholars lamented the passing of the family, while feminists applauded it.

Succeeding generations of family scholars scoffed at the gloomy predictions of their predecessors. While acknowledging that the family no longer served as workplace, school, or hospital, they judged its remaining functions to be more important than ever. The family nurtured and raised children, and provided refuge for adults from the impersonality and competition of public and industrial life.

The social realities of post-World War II rendered obsolete earlier notions of family decline. Statistics showed more people than ever marrying and re-marrying; they were marrying younger and producing record numbers of babies. Few women were choosing childless careers, or any careers at all. The single-family dwelling dominated the housing market and the life styles of family members.

A 1954 survey revealed that at 6:00 P.M. of any working day, three-quarters of American males from ages 20 to 59 had returned home from work, to stay for the rest of the evening (De Grazia, 1964, p. 173). Even within cities, few lived up to either the cosmopolitan or fragmented version of the urban stereotype:

> The picture that emerges [from studies of metropolitan areas in the 40's and 50's] is of a society in which the conjugal family is extremely power-ful among all types of population. . . . By and large, the conjugal family keeps to itself; outside is the world—formal organizations, work, and the communities. . . . The family retires to its domain . . . to work in the

1

garden, listen to radio or television, care for children, and read the products of the mass media (Greer, 1962, pp. 93–94).

During this period, the "keep to itself" life style of the conjugal family meshed with a general mood of satisfaction with America as an affluent and bountiful society. For the first time since the great depression, the majority of American families were able to afford life's basic necessities plus such luxuries as an automobile and a TV. The general prosperity overshadowed in both popular awareness and the social sciences the poverty of a considerable portion of the population. The focus of attention was the middle class and its patterns of consumption. America was thought of as a "middle class society where some people were simply more middle class than others" (Bottomore, 1966, p. 105). Family textbooks could state unapologetically that they were based on the middle class family because that was the goal everyone was striving toward. Deviation from the prevailing family patterns was attributed to poverty, bad luck, or mental illness, but rarely, if ever, to choice.

By the early 1970s, everything had changed. The media were no longer talking about "togetherness," but about the present crisis and shaky future of the family. In one of the magazine's last issues, *Life* declared the nuclear family one of the most maligned institutions of 1972. A business-oriented weekly featured as its lead story an article which asked, "Is the American Family in Danger?" (*U.S. News and World Report,* April 16, 1973). Obviously, a content analysis of the media cannot be taken as an indicator of what is actually happening in real life. Still, the media do reflect public moods and concerns, even as they reinforce and amplify these. Thus, the 1970s heralded a widespread sense of profound change in the values and assumptions of family life.

What had happened? Somehow, the unanticipated social turbulence of the sixties had boiled over onto the institution of the family. In the tranquility of the fifties, no one had foreseen the rise of student dissent, public protests, and the emergence of a counterculture. Even more unlikely in those days than widespread political protest was a politics of the family. At the beginning of the 1960s, the discovery of poverty had only called into question the *prevalence* of middle class family patterns, not their *validity*. By 1970 assumptions about the good and the right family life were being challenged by rebellious students, the commune movement, women's liberation, gay liberation, and new patterns of sexual expression and openness. The family patterns of the previous decade were challenged not only by sexual and cultural revolutionaries. The emergence of public concern about overpopulation and pollution posed a still deeper challenge. The four and five child family, the three car garage, the all electric home, the suburban way of life itself, were suddenly revealed as hidden menaces to the environment. On the whole, family scholars not only failed to predict the changes in family attitudes and behavior, they also failed to acknowledge the changes after they occurred.

On the Uses and Limits of Statistics

The classical stance of the family sociologist, confronted by the claim that something is happening to marriage and the family, is to point in the direction of demographic statistics. He (and it usually is a he) will point out that the majority of marriages still end in death rather than divorce, that divorced people often remarry, that most people live in nuclear family households, that in the overwhelming majority of marriages the man is the major breadwinner, that the wife is still moving to where her husband's job is, rather than the reverse.

The following excerpts typify social-science conclusions of stability in the family:

> Each new generation smiles with amusement at the courtship patterns of the preceding generation, and each generation of parents looks with some consternation on the innovations introduced by its children. In this way, intergenerational change calls attention to itself so that our interests are focussed on the differences. . . . The similarity from one generation to the next is ignored. . . . Yet studies of attitudes and behavior covering all the generations of the century show only relatively minor changes in basic patterns between contiguous generations. Each generation introduces some new twist on an old theme: Statistical averages change slightly: A few more girls have intercourse with their fiances before marriage, men get married a fraction of a year younger on the average, a few more couples practice contraception, a few more women are employed in outside jobs. (Udry, 1966, pp. 25–26)

> The popular notion that America is undergoing a sexual "revolution" is a myth. The belief that our more permissive sexual code is a sign of a general breakdown of morality is also a myth. (Reiss, 1970, p. 43)

> The available data indicate that since World War II, there has not been a mass retreat from chastity standards among the advantaged groups. (Pope and Knudson, 1965, p. 315)

There are three difficulties with these arguments. First, they assume that future predictions may be soundly made on the basis of prior regularities. Thus, many sociologists argued in the late sixties that there really was no sexual revolution because sexual patterns hadn't changed that much from the 1920s. Kinsey had found little change between women born 1920–29 and their mothers. It was assumed that girls born after World War II would show the same pattern as their mothers, and indeed the surveys of the early 1960s did not show much change. Marked changes were going on, however, particularly in regard to teen-age sex (see Sorenson, 1973), but there was a delay between the behavior and the collection and reporting of data concerning that behavior.

A second, and more serious, limitation of statistics is their interpretive subjectivity. There are many ways to calculate divorce rates and other indicators of family change. For example, Scanzoni (1972) recently argued that it is a "misuse and abuse" (p. 5) of divorce data to predict that one-third to one-half of this year's marriages are "destined" to end in a divorce court. Scanzoni points out that in any *given* year, "when comparing the chances for divorce anytime throughout the first twenty-six years of marriage, the annual percentage probability of divorce *in the first marriage* ranges from less than 1 percent to about 2 percent for whites and up to 3 percent for blacks." Scanzoni's data, even if correct, lead to an essentially trivial conclusion. It is difficult to imagine that anyone entering a first marriage is interested in "the annual percentage probability" of dissolution by divorce for a *given* year. The relevant question for most persons newly married or contemplating marriage is, What are the chances my marriage is "destined" for divorce? The answer to that question is found, over a 26-year period, by a *cumulative* percentage over time. Assuming Scanzoni is correct, if you are white and you marry this year the chances that you will be divorced in any *given* year are around 1.5 percent. Over 26 years, the chances would be roughly 39 percent. If you are black, double this figure. White or black, the statistics are consistent with a prediction that one-third to one-half of all marriages contracted this year are *destined* to end in divorce.

A third limitation of demographic statistics is their failure to capture changes in attitudes, values, and social climate. For example, the observation that marriages continue to occur fails to see that marriage has changed as a normative institution; it has lost its taken-for-granted, lifelong quality. In a sense, the Catholic view of marriage generated an emotional if not a doctrinal validity for most people until recently, and *this* is what has changed. Divorce is an unspoken but significant possibility for the newly married today. And as one writer suggests, both partners remain permanently available on the marriage market, no matter how long they are married. The statistics fail to record the sense of wonder and exceptionalism that surrounds the couple who have stayed married for more than a decade—the increasing public recognition that staying married to the same person is an unusual feat, not something to be taken for granted.

Moral Contexts and Plausible Deviance

Arguments back and forth about numbers—how many college women are having intercourse with how many men, how many homosexuals there are, how many married couples are exchanging roles—obscure a vital point;

namely, behavior is a form of communication where the same act can have different meanings according to its moral context. Thus an unmarried woman's affair with a man may be seen by her and others in a context of sin and remorse—as in the standard confession magazine story. This expression of deviance serves to reinforce conventional morality. Alternatively, the "deviants" may not actually adhere to conventional standards, but still respect them outwardly by keeping variant behavior discreet. This second approach undermines conventional morality, but does not really challenge it. Furthermore, the "deviant" sexuality is carried out under conditions of pluralistic ignorance; each violator wonders if others have acted this way. The third alternative is to defy conventional standards openly, as happens when college women live openly with young men, unwed movie actresses publicize their pregnancies, homosexuals picket in support of gay liberation, or women's liberationists denounce marriage and advocate masturbation.

The open violation of conventional norms affects even the most conservative elements of society. As Sumner (1960) pointed out in 1907, much of the force of moral rules rests in their being taken for granted, in the unthinkability of their being questioned, and in the assumption, sometimes unconscious, that terrible consequences will follow their violation. The failure of public sinners to suffer either guilt or the wrath of God further undermines the authority of the rules. Furthermore, once a rule becomes the subject of debate, no matter how the debate comes out, it can scarcely maintain its sacred character.

Although the open flaunting of unconventional behavior in the name of alternative standards is perhaps the most dramatically different feature of the present time, social change may occur even in the absence of large numbers of new recruits to the "deviant" ranks. As Gagnon and Simon comment:

> Significant social change does not come about only when there have been changes in overt behavior patterns. The moment of change may simply be the point at which new forms of behavior appear plausible. An example of this phenomenon of the increased plausibility of a behavior without behavioral change is the current status of homosexuality as a public topic. There is no evidence that there has been a growth in the proportion of the population with homosexual preferences. . . . [The homosexual] still faces the risks of arrest, conviction, or imprisonment, and the more frequent costs of rejection by friends, family, or loss of employment.
>
> Nevertheless, in recent years homosexuality has become one of the standard fares on the frontiers of the American cultural scene. (Gagnon and Simon, 1970, pp. 10–12)

The notion of *plausibility* suggests that whether or not there has been revolutionary change in the family, sex, and childrearing behavior, such change now appears possible to increasingly large numbers of people, especially young people.

The plausibility of deviance also influences traditional family values and patterns. Even the most traditionally inclined middle class man or woman finds it increasingly difficult to regard marriage and family matters as the unquestioned and inevitable progression of life's stages. The college woman who drops out of school to get married, the female graduate student who drops out of school because of pregnancy, or the couple who opt to have a third or fourth child may find themselves the objects of disapproval or at least be asked to justify their behavior.

The New Moralities

Although those who see signs of family disintegration and those social scientists who see an unbroken continuity are on opposite sides of the issue, they are both alike in this: they fail to give much weight to the emergence of new ideologies of sex, marriage, and family. The breakdown theorist sees only the breaking of old rules, while the continuity theorist sees a continuation of the old ones. Both ignore the possibility that moral redefinition is taking place in ways that do not and perhaps cannot show up in demographic studies. More may be involved than changes in the rules. We may be witnessing the emergence of new cultural definitions of sex and marriage.

There is an analogy here with what happens when one scientific theory challenges and then replaces another. As Thomas Kuhn has pointed out, new scientific theories do not merely offer new explanations of old facts and findings. Rather, new theories change the meanings of the old facts—scientists "see new and different things" when looking in the same place. For example, when the theory that the earth revolved around the sun replaced the theory that the earth was the center of the universe, the concept of the earth itself changed. Under the old theory, people perceived the earth as an immovable object—part of the definition of the earth was something that couldn't move. In the same way, Einstein's concept of curved space violates our sense of what space is.

Similar kinds of redefinition now seem to be emerging with regard to sex, sex roles, and family life. More seems to be involved than changing evaluations concerning the rightness or wrongness of particular acts. For example, the "old" concepts of sex and family were based on definitions of these matters as essentially natural. Thus, heterosexuality was defined as a natural life force. Male and female sex roles, including the division of labor in the family, were thought to be determined by anatomic and physiological differences.

Such challenge to traditional family and sex role patterns as are emerging from women's liberationists, people in communes, and homosexuals involve fundamental changes in the concept of the "natural." Thus, such groups are apt to point out that strong and independent women, the communal family or group marriage, the homosexual or bisexual inclination are as "natural" as their traditional counterparts. We take traditional social patterns for granted and see them as "natural" only because they have existed unchallenged. The concept of the natural in itself comes to be defined not as a matter of obvious fact but as a matter of cultural definition, and a political weapon in a contest between competing ideologies (see Pierce, 1971).

The articulation of alternative moralities of sex and family life means that family pluralism is replacing consensus. As Marvin Sussman points out in this volume, it is a rather curious fact that while in America there has been recognition of a variety of religious, ethnic, and political beliefs, with regard to sex and family, a single standard has tended to prevail. Variations from traditional sex and family patterns tended to be ignored, and where noticed were proclaimed to be immoral, unnatural, or sick.

The Nuclear Family Model

The turbulence of the 1960s left the social sciences in a state of self-doubt. Not only had they failed to predict the outbreak of militancy and protest, but the leading theorists of sociology, political science, and psychology had declared such events unlikely if not impossible in an advanced industrial democracy. Most social scientists had assumed that such societies were balanced social systems, with adjustive mechanisms to maintain themselves in a steady state. Harmony, relative lack of conflict, and gradual rather than abrupt change were considered to be the normal state of affairs. In such social theories, the family played a vital role in socializing children and maintaining the psychological adjustment of adults. Such assumptions about society and family made it difficult for social scientists to anticipate and explain the disruptions of the sixties and the family malaise that exists today in many segments of American society.

Let us look in more detail at the model of the family that prevailed in the social sciences as part of the balanced social system. The nuclear family model was constructed by the joint efforts of anthropology, psychoanalysis, and sociology. The leading proponents of the nuclear family model are Malinowski and Murdock in anthropology, Freud and Parsons in sociology. Its major assumptions are as follows:

1. The nuclear family—a man, a woman, and their children—is universally found in every human society, past, present, and future.
2. The nuclear family is the foundation of society, the key institution guaranteeing the survival and stability of the whole society.

3. The nuclear family is the building block, or elementary unit of society. Larger groupings—the extended family, the clan, the society—are combinations of nuclear families.

4. The nuclear family is based on a clear-cut, biologically structured division of labor between men and women, with the man playing the "instrumental" role of breadwinner, provider, and protector, and the woman playing the "expressive" role of housekeeper and emotional mainstay.

5. A major "function" of the family is to socialize children, that is, to tame their impulses and instill values, skills, and desires necessary to run the society. Without the nuclear family, the adequate socialization of human beings is impossible.

6. Other family structures, such as mother and children, or the experimental commune, are regarded as deviant by the participants, as well as the rest of the society, and are fundamentally unstable and unworkable.

Alternative Conceptions

Obviously, the nuclear family model is based on a core of truth, in that a woman and a man must unite sexually to produce a child. But neither kinship ties nor living arrangements necessarily follow from actual biological ties. The main problem with the nuclear family model is intellectual; it influences thinking in certain directions or, more precisely, it impedes us from considering alternative interpretations.

In looking at exotic cultures, the model leads us to assume that because one can find parents and their children in every society, their ideas and feelings about family life must also be like ours. In our own society, the nuclear model defines what is normal and natural both for research and "therapy," and subtly influences our thinking to regard deviations from the nuclear model as sick or perverse or immoral.

Actually, the concept of the universality of the family is misleading. It leads us to attribute our concept of the family—as a legally united couple living together in their own household and raising their children together—to humankind in general. But the definition of marriage is not the same across cultures. Although some cultures have marriage contracts, weddings, and notions of monogamy and permanence, most cultures lack one or more of these attributes. In some cultures, the West Indies, for example, although such definitions of marriage exist, the majority of people mate and have children without legal marriage and often without living together.

In many societies, husbands, wives, and children do not live together under the same roof. In some societies, husbands and wives live apart and belong to different economic units. In other societies, children live apart from their parents.

Still other attributes of the American family system set it apart. For example, our economic organization, with the husband as family breadwinner, is far from universal. In many cultures, wives raise their own crops and are partially or wholly self-supporting (Stephens, 1963, p. 15). Nor is our concept of fatherhood universal. A father, to us, is the biological creator of a child, its provider and legal guardian, and the husband of the child's mother. We expect these aspects of fatherhood to go together, although divorce creates conflict of roles. Among some peoples, however, the identity of the biological father is irrelevant; the child belongs to the husband of its mother who is said to experience all the emotions of fatherhood.

Variations in family form and function have been cited by anthropologists as exceptions which prove the universality of the nuclear family rule, rather than as interesting phenomena in their own right. This approach can be criticized not only on intellectual grounds for ignoring interesting issues, but has also had unfortunate practical consequences. As Suzanne Keller points out in this volume:

> The fallacy of universality has done students of human behavior a great disservice. By leading us to seek and hence to find a single pattern, it has blinded us to historical precedents for multiple legitimate family arrangements.

New Perspectives on the Family

Besides getting in the way of understanding diverse family arrangements, the assumptions surrounding the nuclear family model also obscure the workings of the nuclear family itself. It blinds us to problematic aspects of ordinary family life. The model assumes that the family at one and the same time serves the needs of society and of the individuals within the family, and overlooks the ways the three may be at odds. Problems such as illegitimacy, broken homes, mental illness, marital and parent-child conflict have always been recognized as family problems, but have been thought of as afflictions, alien growths feeding on the family, but separate from it. The source of family problems was traced to the individual family member whose psychological impairments prevented him or her from carrying out family and social roles. On the other hand, it is possible to look at some family problems as arising out of the structure and processes of the family itself, as well as out of the tensions between family and society. Such a perspective on the family can be found in two very different fields of family study: history and family psychiatry.

History and the Family

Historians have recently turned to the study of the family partly because of a new interest in the everyday life of ordinary people, and partly because new methods of studying such people became available. Such historical studies are of great significance not only for their intrinsic scholarly value, but also because historical accounts of actual behavior of men, women, and children challenge prevailing social science assumptions about the family.

Unfettered by the balanced, consensual model of society, historians have found great variability in family life. They have been able to treat such issues as premarital sexuality, illegitimacy, infanticide, and generational conflict as part of family life itself rather than as a separate category of deviance.

The division of families into a normal type and a pathological type is simply not applicable to the historical evidence. For example, Kessen's history of the field of child study observes:

> Perhaps the most persistent single note in the history of the child is the reluctance of mothers to suckle their babies. The running war between the mother, who does not want to nurse, and the philosopher-psychologists, who insist she must, stretches over two thousand years; the redundancy of the argument and its slow but discernible development form a model—and a somewhat amusing one—for the history of child study. (Kessen, 1965, pp. 1–2)

David Hunt (1970) in a study of childrearing practices in early modern France found what would be considered by today's standards widespread mistreatment of children, or as he puts it a "breakdown in parental care," although his study was limited to upper class families. Rather than being an instinctive trait, tender feelings toward infants—the sense that a baby is a precious individual—seem to emerge only under certain social conditions. Infants must have a decent chance of surviving, and adults must experience life conditions offering enough security to avoid the feeling that children are competing with them in a struggle for survival. Throughout many centuries of European history, both these conditions were lacking. In the allocation of scarce resources, European society, as one historian put it, preferred adults to children (Trexler, 1973, p. 110).

Perhaps the most shocking finding of the new historical studies is the prevalence of infanticide throughout European history. Infanticide has always been associated with primitive or Oriental peoples, or assumed to be the desperate act of an unwed mother. It now appears that infanticide provided a major means of birth control in all societies lacking reliable contraception, Europe included, and it was practiced by families on legitimate children. Historians now believe that rises and falls in fertility may actually reflect variations in infanticide rates (Shorter, 1973). For years, social scientists had assumed that the needs of society, the family, and the child were in fundamental harmony with each other. The findings of the recent historical studies, particularly those dealing with infanticide, show that these interests may sometimes be in conflict:

The West for centuries has assumed that its main cultural values were on the one side reason, calculation, order, balance, and harmony, and on the other, the sacredness of each individual life. For centuries the family was viewed as the source of balance *and* the seat of unlimited generativity. The two are at odds. . . . If fifteenth-century parents could not support the new infant without starving themselves or their older children, they had to act. Charity, said the medieval lawyers touching on the problem, begins at home. (Trexler, 1973, p. 110)

Psychiatry and the Family

In recent years there has been a conceptual revolution in the psychological understanding of family life. The changed view of the nature of family life came about when researchers and therapists began to observe whole families in live interaction with each other. Strange as it may seem, the study of the family had gone on for years and years without anyone trying to describe what goes on when family members get together. Family research had been carried out by interviewing individuals about their family lives, or asking them to fill out questionnaires. The first observational studies were carried out with the families of schizophrenics. It was thought that the patient's bizarre behavior might make sense if he or she could be seen in the natural habitat of the family. Researchers did find peculiar interaction patterns in the families of schizophrenics, such as: members saying contradictory things without realizing it; family myths and secrets; alliances between two family members; disagreements and quarrels; one family member singled out as a scapegoat to blame for the family's troubles. Many researchers began to speak of "schizophrenic families" rather than schizophrenic individuals. To learn more about family interaction, research was undertaken on families of other kinds of psychiatric patients, and even delinquents. These families, it turned out, showed similarly peculiar interaction patterns. Finally, when so-called "normal" families were studied, they also showed similar patterns, thus throwing into doubt the whole concept of the "normal" family as a separate and distinct type.

Predicaments of the Modern Family

The new studies of family history and family interaction reveal that previous thinking about the family had been too one-sided in emphasizing family harmony and adjustment, and the mutual benefits flowing between family and society. The studies of family interaction show that intimacy provides not only love and care, but often tension and conflict as well; and that these are inseparable parts of intimate relationships. The historical studies highlight the family's vulnerabilities to particular social, cultural, and economic contexts.

With these perspectives in mind, let us turn again to the question of the family in contemporary America. As we noted earlier, since the turn of the century family scholars have been debating the impact of modernization on the family. The older generation of scholars saw the family being undermined by its loss of economic functions in urban-industrial societies. Succeeding scholars argued that emotional functions of the family were more necessary than ever, as the family was the best institution for fostering child nurturance and adult intimacy. It now appears that both points of view may be correct: The conditions of modern life do undermine family ties *and* do generate exceptional needs for nurturant, intimate, and enduring relationships. This dilemma confronts us today.

The major changes creating the dilemma are: 1) loss of constraints and restrictions in work and marriage; 2) emotional and task overload; 3) contradictory demands and values; 4) demographic change.

1. Loss of Constraints and Restrictions in Work and Marriage

Modern family life in America and Europe contrasts sharply with family life in past eras in those societies, and also with the family systems of "traditional" or pre-modern societies. Although European family life has not been characterized by the large, organized kin groups found in non-Western societies, kinship ties exerted much stronger constraints over the individual before the modern era. In pre-industrial societies, work and marriage were not matters of individual choice. A person's economic and marital destiny was determined by hereditary status, tradition, and economic necessity. Continuity of marriages and conformity to prescribed behavior, within the family and outside, were enforced by severe economic, familial, and community sanctions.

Modernization liberates the individual from such restrictions. Goode, a leading student of family modernization, writes (1963) that whenever the modern pattern of work and family replaces the traditional one, it is accompanied by an ideology of liberation. Modernization promises freedom of opportunity to find work that suits one's talents, freedom to marry for love and dissolve the marriage if it fails to provide happiness, and greater equality in the family between husband and wife, and between parents and children.

The freedom of modern family life is bought at the price of fragility and instability in family ties. The removal of the kin group as a source of economic and social control means that the whole structure of family life comes to rest on a very fragile basis: the mutual feelings of two individuals. As Simmel (1950, pp. 118–144) has shown, the couple or dyad is not only the most intimate of social relationships, it is also the most unstable. In traditional systems, the inevitable tensions of marriage are "contained" by kin and community pressures, and also by low expectations concerning the romance or happiness to be found in marriage (Goode, 1966, p. 493).

2. Emotional and Task Overload

Even those family scholars who stress vital functions played by the family in modern societies acknowledge that societies also create strains on families. Parsons, for example, noted that when the family and the home no longer functioned as an economic unit, women, children, and old people were placed in an ambiguous position outside the occupational world. For children, the shift to industrial work, and the removal of the father from the home, also meant that the mother became a more central figure. Little boys could no longer observe and participate in father's work. This created a strain on both child and mother. Goode, who looks at family change in countries now undergoing modernization, does not stress the family's loss of economic functions so much as the separation of the nuclear unit from the extended kin group. He sees the emerging woman's role as particularly and paradoxically stressful; although "modernism" offers woman equality and liberation from the restrictions of the kin group, it leaves her in an isolated household with increased burdens of childrearing.

The male role in modern society is not free of strain either. Under constant pressure to produce, achieve, and support, most men spend their lives at work from which they derive little personal satisfaction. The assembly line operative provides the classic example of the alienated worker. At higher levels of the occupational scale, although work is often intrinsically rewarding, there are associated discontents. Goode writes:

> The modern technological system is psychologically burdensome on the individual because it demands an unremitting discipline. . . . Lower-level jobs give little pleasure to most people. However, in high-level professional, managerial and creative positions, the standards of performance are not only high but are often without clearly stated limits. The individual is under considerable pressure to perform better than he is able. The conjugal family again integrates with such a system by its emphasis on emotionality, especially in the relationship of husband and wife. . . . Of course, the family cannot succeed in this task. (Goode, 1963, p. 14)

As this suggests, the family is supposed to make up for the harsh, impersonal, competitive world outside the home by supplying warmth and intimacy. But, as Moore (1958) argues, the stripping away of work, education, and other functions from the nuclear family leaves members with little or nothing on which to base their relationships. It is difficult to provide emotional security in a vacuum. "Togetherness" is harder to achieve by itself than as a by-product of joint effort.

Furthermore, intimate relations generate their own tensions and frustrations, which require some kind of outlet away from the home. Moreover, the home may be the place where outside tensions are discharged explosively, rather than being soothed away. A father's hard day at the office or factory or a child's hard day at school may be dissolved in familial tenderness or be taken out on other family members around the dinner table. The outcome of the family drama is unpredictable. Its setting—a private dwelling—is not.

Besides the emphasis on emotional togetherness, modern family life differs from its traditional counterpart in being set off physically as well as psychologically from the social world outside the home. Some writers have argued that this privacy is the key to understanding the plight of the modern family. Anthropologists note that only among Eskimos is there a comparable degree of isolation in nuclear families as they go about their daily round (Stephens, 1963), and that isolation breeds tension and emotional instability, particularly in mothers (Minturn and Lambert et al., 1964). Looking at the American family in historical perspective, Barbara Laslett (1973) argues that family privacy is a relatively recent phenomenon. In the past, when families were larger, servants, boarders, and lodgers were common. Households were more open to the community, and the family possessed a more public character. Observation by outsiders implied more social control over family behavior, and also more social support. Thus, a husband and wife might be constrained from arguing with each other in front of outsiders; similarly the need to argue might arise less often than it does now, since a husband and wife are more apt to behave circumspectly in the presence of others. Like King Midas's touch, family privacy is a dream of affluence which turns out to have unexpected costs when fulfilled. Privacy is a form of solitariness, and solitariness can be lonely and threatening. The single nuclear family, writes Napier,

> is in trouble, almost everywhere. Its major burden is its rootlessness, its aloneness with its tasks. Parents are somewhere else; the business you can't trust; the neighbors you never see; and friends are a help, when you see them, but never enough. Sometimes, late at night, the parent wakes up and on a sea of silence hears the ship creak, feels it drift, fragile and solitary, with its cargo of lives. (Napier, 1972, p. 540)

3. Contradictory Demands and Values

In addition to the privacy dilemma, a variety of contradictory cultural instructions clash head-on in the modern family. As Goode notes, the ideology that goes along with the modern conjugal family emphasizes personal freedom, individualism, and sexual equality. Yet the realities of daily existence of most people fail to fulfill these values. Furthermore, both men's and women's roles contain a set of incompatible demands. Women are expected to experience the same education as men, and then retreat from the world of work and achievement. Yet, as Parsons notes (1949, p. 223), being a housewife is not quite enough as identity. Women are under pressure to be glamorous sexual partners, cultural companions, and above all, mothers of well-adjusted, high-achieving children.

For men, the demands of the modern occupational system often compete with the demands of family. Particularly àt the higher levels of professional and technical skill, the job is supposed to take precedence over the family. When the job calls for moving to a new community, traveling, evening and weekend meetings, its claims usually come first. Yet at the same time, the cultural script calls for the middle class man to be a devoted husband and father.

For all family members, there is the contradiction between a morality stressing enjoyment and self-fulfillment and a morality of duty, responsibility, work, and self-denial. The do-your-own-thing fun morality is expressed not only by the hippie counterculture, but also by the advertising industry, the credit card buy-now-pay-later philosophy, the spread of leisure time pursuits such as boating, skiing, photography, hi-fi music, and for men, the brand of sexual consumership represented by *Playboy* magazine, which has recently been translated into women's versions. The new morality of fun and games often reunites the family in activities that everyone can enjoy, but it also pulls family members apart in its emphasis on individual pursuit of enjoyment. Also, to the extent that fun morality teaches us that family life should be fun, it imposes a paradoxical demand: we are obligated to have a good time (see Wolfenstein, 1954). In the past, one could live up to demands of marriage and parenthood by doing one's duty. Now, duty is not enough. We are under obligation to enjoy all aspects of family life. As a result, pleasurable activities, even sex itself, become permeated by the work ethic: Am I a competent sexual performer? Is my spouse? Do I enjoy my children as much as I am supposed to?

4. Demographic Change

It was only about 50 years ago that death and birth hovered constantly over every household, essentially uncontrollable and unpredictable. It is hard to comprehend how profoundly family life has been affected by the reduction in mortality and spread of contraception during the past five or six decades. Although infant and child mortality rates had begun to decline a century earlier, the average family could not assume it would see all its infants survive to middle or old age. Death struck most often at children, but with an average life expectancy of about 50 years (Ridley, 1972), adults would often die in the prime of their productive years. The widow and

widower with young children were more familiar figures on the social landscape than the divorced person is today.

The reduction of infant and child mortality released women from the demands of constant childbearing, and the development of contraceptives made
it possible for them to control their fertility. Thus, women today are living
longer, having fewer children, and having them earlier than in previous generations. The result of these changes is the increase in the number of married women at work. In the past, with later marriage and more children,
the time the last child left home would be close to the end of the average
mother's life expectancy. Today the average woman can look forward to
three or four decades without maternal responsibilities. Since the prevailing
assumptions about women are based on the notion that they are constantly
involved with pregnancy, childrearing, and related domestic concerns, the
current ferment about women's roles may be seen as a way of bringing cultural attitudes in line with existing social realities.

The changes noted above also have profound implications for marriage.
With earlier marriage and longer life spans, the duration of marriage has
nearly doubled, from about 25 or 27 years, to about 50. With the decline in
the number of children, marriage becomes more of a personal relationship
between husband and wife, and less of a union of a mother and father pre-
occupied with the needs of their offspring. The prospect of 50 years with the
same person increases tensions in marriage and makes it more likely that
dissatisfaction will lead to divorce. Furthermore, in a rapidly changing society, the couple who seemed to be well-suited to each other in their early
twenties may find themselves growing in different ways and at different rates
later on.

Conclusion: Is the Family Dying?

The strains and dilemmas in contemporary family life do not mean that
the nuclear family is about to disappear from the social landscape. What we
are experiencing is not the death of the family so much as the demystification
of family life, the erosion of sentimental myths portraying the family as a
utopian retreat of peace and harmony sealed off from the tense impersonal
world outside the home. Nor does the emergence of alternative family styles,
such as communes, living together without marriage, single-parent families,
group marriage, remaining single, imply that the nuclear family is obsolete.
Rather, it is likely that the nuclear family will continue to be the major, but
not the only, living pattern. As we noted earlier, variability in family living,
even within the same society, is not new. What is new in the current scene is
the ideology of pluralism; in the past divergent family forms were considered
sick, immoral, or symptoms of social disorganization.

There is little reason to expect that the current social trends affecting family life will be reversed. It is not likely, for example, that divorce will again be regarded as an offense against public decency, that virginity will be considered the normal condition of unmarried women, that population pressures will reverse themselves and demand that women devote most of their lives to childbearing. Indeed, in a post-industrial society, some of the trends noted earlier can be expected to accelerate. Faster rates of social change, a more complex occupational structure, higher levels of education, more leisure —all of these tend to increase the personality trends associated with family strain, such as individualism, the pursuit of self-realization and enjoyment. There is little reason to expect a return to the "Protestant ethic" of hard work, self-denial, and sexual repression associated with the early stages of industrial development.

Some writers suggest that only the upper part of the middle class experiences family strains and discontents. Out in middle America, it is argued, in the blue collar and lower middle classes, among the "unmeltable" ethnics, life still centers around home, family, and the work ethic. Such a point of view makes the same mistake as the family theorists of the fifties: It freezes social reality to one historical moment, overlooking forces altering the present situation. The middle class family style that was celebrated in the fifties is best understood not as an end point, but as one phase of the process of family modernization. With increasing levels of affluence and education, the "silent majority," and most particularly its children, may be expected to show the symptoms of discontent similar to those found in upper and middle class families at present.

Despite the assumptions of the nuclear family model, the vital family functions of reproduction, child care, economic cooperation, and so forth can be carried out in a variety of ways. Many societies have higher rates of nuclear family instability than we do, but the breakup of a marriage is not so disruptive because kin groups are more important than the marital relationship. We lack such "back-up institutions" to carry on family functions when a nuclear family becomes troubled. The emergence of communes, crash pads, drop-in clinics, encounter groups, and crisis switchboards indicates the need for back-up or support systems outside the family, especially as religious and other institutional sources become less salient for a mobile and restless population.

There, however, is a real dilemma that will not be easy to solve. Throughout most of human history, intimacy and community were the by-products of kinship systems and economic necessity. The conjugal family—the freedom to choose one's spouse—was the first step in the liberation of family life from these restraints. In our own day, the conjugal family itself has come to be seen as oppressive by some, and difficult by many. Individual freedom in family matters has been extended to the right not to marry at all, or to choose from a variety of competing life styles. The change is a liberating one, but we should not lose sight of the costs. The need for intimacy and enduring commitment has outlasted the social institutions that provided for them in the past, and their replacements have not yet been invented.

References

1. Bottomore, T. B. *Classes in Modern Society*. New York: Pantheon, 1966.
2. De Grazia, S. *Of Time, Work, and Leisure*. Garden City: Doubleday, Anchor Books, 1964.
3. Gagnon, J. H., and W. Simon. *The Sexual Scene*. Chicago: Aldine, *Transaction*, 1970.
4. Goode, W. J. *World Revolution and Family Patterns*. New York: The Free Press, 1963.
5. Goode, W. J. "Family Disorganization." In *Contemporary Social Problems*, 2d ed., edited by R. K. Merton and R. A. Nisbet, pp. 493–522. New York: Harcourt, Brace, and World, 1966.
6. Greer, S. *The Emerging City: Myth and Reality*. New York: The Free Press, 1962.
7. Hunt, D. *Parents and Children in History: The Psychology of Family Life in Early Modern France*. New York: Basic Books, 1970.
8. Kessen, E. W. *The Child*. New York: John Wiley, 1965.
9. Laslett, B. "The Family as a Public and Private Institution." *Journal of Marriage and the Family*, in press, 1973.
10. Minturn, L., W. E. Lambert, et al. *Mothers of Six Cultures*. New York: John Wiley, 1964.
11. Moore, B. M., Jr. "Thoughts on the Future of the Family." In *Political Power and Social Theory*, Cambridge: Harvard University Press, 1958.
12. Napier, A. Introduction to Section Four in *The Book of Family Therapy*, edited by A. Farber, M. Mendelsohn, A. Napier, pp. 535–545. New York: Science House, 1972.
13. Parsons, T. *Essays in Sociological Theory: Pure and Applied*. Glencoe, Ill.: The Free Press, 1949.
14. Pierce, C. "Natural Law, Language, and Women." In *Women in Sexist Society*, edited by V. Gornick and B. K. Moran, pp. 242–258. New York: Basic Books, 1971.
15. Pope, H., and D. Knudson. "Premarital Sex Norms: The Family and Social Change." *Journal of Marriage and the Family*, August 1965, pp. 314–323.
16. Reiss, I. L. "How and Why America's Sex Standards are Changing." In *The Sexual Scene*, edited by J. H. Gagnon and W. Simon, pp. 43–58. Chicago: Aldine, *Transaction*, 1970.
17. Ridley, J. C. "The Effects of Population Change on the Roles and Status of Women." In *Toward a Sociology of Women*, edited by C. Safillios-Rothschild. Lexington, Mass.: Xerox College Publishing, 1972, pp. 372–386.
18. Scanzoni, J. *Sexual Bargaining*. Englewood Cliffs: Prentice-Hall, 1972.
19. Shorter, E. "Infanticide in the Past." *History of Childhood Quarterly*, Summer 1973, pp. 178–180.
20. Simmel, G. *The Sociology of Georg Simmel*. Edited by K. Wolf. New York: The Free Press, 1950.
21. Sorenson, R. C. *Adolescent Sexuality in Contemporary America*. New York: World, 1973.
22. Stephens, W. N. *The Family in Cross-Cultural Perspective*. New York: Holt, Rinehart and Winston, 1963.

23. Sumner, W. G. *Folkways.* New York: Mentor, 1960.

24. Trexler, R. C. "Infanticide in Florence: New Sources and First Results." *History of Childhood Quarterly,* Summer 1973, pp. 98–116.

25. Udry, J. R. *The Social Context of Marriage.* Philadelphia: Lippincott, 1966.

26. Wolfenstein, M. "Fun Morality: An Analysis of Recent American Child-Training Literature." In *Childhood in Contemporary Cultures,* edited by M. Mead and M. Wolfenstein. Chicago: University of Chicago Press, 1954, pp. 168–178.

1

Conceptions
of the Family

21

Introduction

"We speak of families," R. D. Laing has observed, "as though we know what families are. We identify, as families, networks of people who live together over time, who have ties of marriage or kinship to one another" (Laing, 1971, p. 3). Yet as Laing observes further, the more one studies the emotional dynamics of groups presently called "families," the less clear it becomes how these differ from groups not designated "families." Further, contemporary family patterns and emotional dynamics may not appear in other places and times.

As an object of study, the family is plagued with a unique set of problems. First, there is the assumption that family life, so familiar a part of everyday experience, is thus easily understood. But familiarity may breed a sense of destiny—what we experience is transformed into the "natural":

> One difficulty in the psychological sciences lies in the familiarity of the phenomena with which they deal. A certain intellectual effort is required to see how such phenomena can pose serious problems or call for intricate explanatory theories. One is inclined to take them for granted as necessary or somehow "natural." (Chomsky, 1968, p. 21)

Only in the past decade or so have family scholars come to recognize how problematic a subject "the family" is, and how hard it is to answer basic questions: Is there a definition of family that can apply to all places and times? What is the relationship between the family as an abstraction and particular families with their own idiosyncrasies and differences from each other? What "test" can we apply to distinguish between a family and a group that is not a family?

Familiarity also obscures the moral and legal implications of family study. It is difficult for the family scholar to escape deeply embedded notions of propriety, health, and legality in family life. Indeed, family research has often been motivated by a desire to understand how to "improve" family life, that is, to achieve conformity to purportedly ideal patterns. Yet, as Ball notes in Chapter 1, the definition of a problem family often rests on one's conception of the family as an institution.

Further difficulties complicate the study of the family. It does not fit neatly

22

within the boundaries of any single scholarly field; genetics, physiology, archeology, anthropology, sociology, and psychology all touch upon it. Religious and ethical authorities also claim a stake in the family. In addition, troubled individuals and families generate therapeutic demands on family scholarship. In short, the study of the family is interdisciplinary, controversial, and necessary for the formulation of social policy and practices.

Interdisciplinary subjects present certain characteristic problems. First, each discipline has its own assumptions and views of the world, which may not directly transfer into another field. For example, some biologists and physically oriented anthropologists tend to analyze human affairs in terms of individual motives and instincts; for them, society is a shadowy presence, serving mainly as the setting for biologically motivated individual action. Many sociologists and cultural anthropologists, in contrast, perceive the individual as an actor playing a role written by culture and society; according to this view, the individual has no wholly autonomous thoughts and impulses. An important school of psychologists sees man neither as a passive recipient of social pressures nor as a creature driven by powerful lusts, but as an information processor trying to make sense of his environment. There is no easy way of reconciling such perspectives. Scientific paradigms—characteristic ways of looking at the world—determine not only what answers will be found, but what questions will be asked.

The second problem with interdisciplinary subjects is that they demand competence in more than one field. At a time when competent scholars find it difficult to master even one corner of a field—say the terminology of kinship, or the physiology of sexual arousal—intellectual demands on students of the family become vast. Although writers on the family confront many issues, their professional competence is usually limited. Thus a biologist may cite articles in psychology to support a position, without comprehending the tentativeness with which psychologists regard the researcher and his work. Similarly, a psychologist or sociologist may draw upon controversial biological studies. Professional competence means more than the ability to read technical journals; it includes informal knowledge—being "tuned in" to verbal understandings and evaluations of research validity. Usually a major theory or line of research is viewed more critically in its own field than outsiders realize.

The distinction between tentativeness of research and the assertiveness of popular writings is illustrated by research on the prehistoric origins of the human family. Washburn and his associates have hypothesized a series of causal links relating hunting, tool use, brain size, dependency of the human infant, upright posture, and language to forms of human social organization, particularly the family. Within the field of anthropology, Washburn's theory was and is the subject of debate, particularly regarding the contention that when man was a hunter, he was genetically programmed to be aggressive, and hence is innately driven to warfare.

Washburn's theory, however, has been introduced to the public through the more sensationalized and exaggerated versions of Desmond Morris, Robert Ardrey, and Lionel Tiger. These writers take the most speculative and controversial aspects of the theory—the idea of man as a killer ape born with implacable instincts to make war on his fellows, seize and defend territory, and exclude and dominate females—and raise these aspects to the level of established scientific fact. Further, on the basis of these alleged facts they construct analyses of social problems and recommend political solutions.

Thus, besides the characteristic ideology of each field of study, there is the personal ideology each individual brings to the study of the family. No one can approach the subject without assumptions and preferences about reality, human nature, the social and political order—for example, the necessity of the nuclear family, the insatiability of human drives, the scarcity of goods, the fragility of society, and so on.

The study of the family has suffered because it has been a subtopic of other areas of study rather than a main topic. The fields that concern themselves with the family have as their primary focus either the individual, as in psychology or biology, or the larger society, as in sociology. Thus, the family is a "slippery" concept, as one writer puts it, that often seems less real than either individuals or the society. Only recently has the family come to be studied and observed in its own right as a natural group, with distinct social processes that cannot be inferred from the study of either individuals or societies.

The articles in this part present some of the diverse ways of looking at the family. The perspectives range from primate studies to history to family psychiatry. Each of the articles not only presents information about the family from the point of view of some particular field of study, but also challenges some basic assumption or widely held view about the nature of family life.

References

1. Chomsky, N. *Language and Mind.* New York: Harcourt, Brace, and World, 1968.
2. Laing, R. D. *The Politics of the Family.* New York: Random House, 1971.
3. Washburn, S. L., and I. DeVore. "Social Behavior of Baboons and Early Man." In *Social Life of Early Man,* edited by S. L. Washburn. Chicago: Aldine, 1961, pp. 96–100.

Chapter 1

The Nature of the Family

In this article, Ball raises a fundamental question: "Just what is a family?" He argues that you have to know what a family is before you can say what a family problem is, and that most family sociologists fail to come to grips with the definitional problem. For example, many writers on the family assume that families are groups of people related by blood or marriage, who live together, and who cooperate economically and in the rearing of children. Ball points out that these characteristics do not necessarily hang together. It is important to distinguish between kinship—ties of blood or marriage—and households—places where people live who may or may not be family members. Ball proposes as a definition of the family a group of people who live together in domestic and sexual relationships. However, the same objection can be raised against Ball's definition: domesticity and sexuality need not necessarily go together.

The "Family" as a Sociological Problem: Conceptualization of the Taken-for-Granted as Prologue to Social Problems Analysis

Donald W. Ball

The question of just what constitutes the generic category of "social problems" has continued to occupy the attention of sociologists, if not perplex them for an extended period (Mills, 1943; Bend and Vogelfanger, 1964; Merton, 1961; Douglas, 1971, and forthcoming). This definitional issue is

Reprinted by permission of the Society for the Study of Social Problems and the author from "The Family as a Sociological Problem: Conceptualization of the Taken-for-Granted as Prologue to Social Problems Analysis" by Donald W. Ball, *Social Problems*, 19, no. 3 (1972), pp. 295–305.

not merely trivial; such semantic problems are not, for they shape and structure the processes and the very outcome of systematic inquiry.

The following is in that tradition generally, while differing in the specifics. Here, we are concerned not so much with just what is a social problem. But more narrowly with a phenomenon frequently treated within a social problems frame of analysis—*Just what is a family?* Or, *What has been assumed to be a family*—and thus an object of family study? Similarly, *Just what is a household?* Or what has been assumed about them? Although a catalogue of unhappy people and their "family social problems" might be more interesting and readable, first things must come first—even if typically ignored.

I

It is a basic assumption, herein, that a meaningful analysis of the social problems associated with, affecting, or caused by a particular sociocultural process or structure cannot make any great headway until that specific process and/or structure has been both identified and adequately conceptualized and delineated. And it follows that whether or not particular issues will be dealt with—either analytically, or in terms of policy—as manifestations of family-related social problems, will be dependent upon conceptions of the former no less than those of the latter.

Therefore, a basic contention underlying the following analysis is: *A major source of those traditional social problems with families as their focal points are directly derivative from the concepts and definitions of the family itself,* as these constructs are held by laymen and professionals alike. Fundamentally, these social problems are seen in terms of empirical departures from those definitions which every man and social scientist hold as regards the family.

Thus, one of the first tasks must be the examination of these definitions as they relate to families as socially problematic phenomena. This might be thought of as "the family as a *sociological* problem" in contradistinction to "the family and *social* problems."

II

It is, of course, difficult to "get at" the content of, or the distribution of, lay definitions of the family. It is one of the social phenomena about which everyone knows (Schutz, 1962, 1964; Garfinkel, 1967). However, based upon members' knowledge (Schneider, 1968, pp. 8–14), it seems clear that in addition to kinship (Farber, 1968, pp. 1–45) and cohabitation or common residence, there are two moral dimensions which underlie most such definitions in North America: (1) religious perspectives, and (2) legalistic constructions (also see Nye and Berardo, 1966, pp. 269–316).

Although they form the basis for the formulation and execution of social policy, these versions of what the family is about speak to ideals, what the family should be, e.g., in Judaeo-Christian or Anglo-American common-law terms, rather than what families actually may be in terms of observable social conduct and social organization. Thus, such conceptions of the family define the desirable rather than necessarily the observable. And since these are ideals, actual families and their situations may fall far short of this bench mark, and, thereby, become perceived as problematic by policy makers and executors, not to mention social scientists whose conceptual schemes rely upon unexamined lay-based terms and their definition(s) (Cicourel, 1964).

While such primitive views may aid the flow of discourse, and thus ratify assumptions about reality (Berger and Luckmann, 1966; Berger and Kellner, 1964) by validating the taken-for-granted sharing of definitions of the world-out-there, they do little to aid in sociological analysis, and may actually mis-direct, if not retard, this task.

Not surprisingly, the professional social-scientific literature is no less hazy in many ways than the nonprofessional viewpoints. Examining a major theoretical contribution to scholarship on family by Nye and Berardo (1966) shows that the index to this collection of eleven theoretical essays to various approaches to the study of the family does not list even one definition of the family. Neither does the McIver award-winning work by Goode (1963). And looking at one of the most frequently cited definitions, that by Burgess (1926); also Turner (1970, pp. 4–5), which conceives of the family as "a unity of interacting personalities," does not in itself sufficiently differentiate families from bowling teams or delinquent gangs (cf. Whyte, 1943, 1955) to provide any analytical utility of conceptual specification. Most efforts ap-pear to employ some simplistic, unproblematic notions of either marriage or offspring, and let it go at that (cf. the efforts in Christensen, 1964).

Although such imprecision is generally the rule, the literature is not with-out exception. Thus, Farber combines kinship positions and their normative regulation in his attempt (1964, pp. 5–7; 1966, p. 8), and Parsons *posits* an "isolated nuclear family" as the proper object of sociological attention in North American society (for a review and bibliography of the Parsonian view, see Rodman, 1965, pp. 262–286). However, possibly the most thor-ough and elaborate effort has been that of Stephens (1963, pp. 1–32), toward whose thoughtful work on the problems of defining the family we may profitably turn. Since his work is cross-cultural, rather than restricted to the North American context (also see Stephens, 1962), he is unable to rely upon "members' knowledge" or intuitive understanding of just what the family is—or what is a family.

III

Marriage and the Family

By beginning with the perennial question "is the family universal?" Stephens is thus forced to confront the issue of whether or not the answer to this important and much debated question is not at least partially, if not totally, dependent upon just how a family is defined (cf. Spiro, 1960; Gough, 1959; Murdock, 1949).

In attempting to formulate an adequate, cross-culturally applicable definition of the family, Stephens begins by defining marriage:

> Marriage is a socially legitimate sexual union, begun with a public announcement and undertaken with some idea of permanence; it is assumed with a more or less explicit marriage contract, which spells out reciprocal rights and obligations between spouses, and between the spouses and their future children. (p. 5)

Stephens then breaks down this definition into its several constituent parts: (1) socially legitimate sexual union, (2) publicly announced, (3) with some idea of permanence, and (4) assumed with a contract (pp. 5-7). With marriage as a basis, Stephens then goes on *to define the family as:*

> A social arrangement based on marriage and the marriage contract, including recognition of the rights and duties of parenthood, common residence for huband, wife and children, and reciprocal economic obligations between husband and wife. (p. 8)

Besides marriage, this definition of the family rests upon three other subsidiary concepts: (1) reciprocal economic obligations, (2) common residence, and (3) the rights and duties of parenthood (pp. 8-10). Having interdependently defined both marriage and family, Stephens then proceeds to critically analyze these definitions.

Concerning *marriage* (pp. 10-12), he begins by noting that socially legitimate sexual unions exclude many sexual relationships which are permanent or nearly so, rewarding to the participants, but not positively sanctioned by either law or community. The criterion of a public announcement also excludes or makes marginal many social groups which otherwise might qualify as "families." Finally, the notion of some idea of permanence speaks to intent at time of union and does not speak to the realities of continued existence or dissolution. Similarly a marriage contract is perhaps most frequently an unspoken contract, without the obligations of either party explicitly specified, made clear, or provided with standards of accountability.

And regarding the concept of the *family* (pp. 12-19): reciprocal economic obligations, as do so many of these criteria, refer to an ideal, rather than actual practices, which are often at great variance with that norm. Common residence would rule out all those groups otherwise thought of as families in which one parent is absent (especially the mother), or alternatively where there are (or have been) no children. Similarly, the rights and duties of parenthood refer only to those families which have, or at least have had children in the past.

Such definitional attributes have been a fertile source for the generation of traditional family-based social problems. And intellectually, while thorough, they bear a large, albeit unacknowledged, debt to common-sense, taken-for-granted, lay conceptions of the family.

After Stephens: Family Defined	Some Traditional Familial Social Problems Generated by the Definition

1) Based upon marriage
  (a) socially legitimate sexual union
  (b) begun with a public announcement
  (c) idea of permanence
  (d) assumed with contract
	1) Common-law unions, and/or
	  (a) incest with cohabitation; under-age partners
	  (b) elopement; lack of state legitimation, e.g., license
	  (c) proxy marriages; term marriages
	  (d) violation of vows; misrepresentation by either party

2) Reciprocal economic obligations between spouses	2) Non-support; ambiguity and/or contention about division of labor
3) Common residence	3) Separation; desertion
4) Rights and duties of parenthood	4) Illegitimacy; non-support of offspring

Empirically then, we may observe many units which might approximate the notion of family but which fall short of the ideal as defined by Stephens, as well as those held by laymen and policy-makers. Thus, common-law spouses, one-parent families, stable homosexual relationships, and most recently communes, all fall beyond the purview of the family as it has been defined either by stipulation or tacit acceptance of lay views in the social scientific literature; even though they may conform to some of the definitional criteria—a list which omits (in part because it is not relevant in some cultures) any consideration of affection, emotion, home, or love (see Goode, 1959).

IV

A more recent, and a more cogent analysis speaking to these problems is that by Donald R. Bender (1967). Rather than assuming, as sociologists typically have, that the definition of the family is easy and/or obvious to professionals and laymen alike, anthropologists have treated the question as *problematic,* as potentially varying from context to context, as requiring an answer based upon empirical data rather than academic dictate. And in trying to develop a conceptualization which is not only faithful to particular cultures, but will also allow for comparisons and generalization between and across cultures, anthropologists have been much more alive to the possibility, if not probability, of departures from the norms of North American conceptualizations of the family.

Households and Families

In both scientific and commonsense usage the two terms, households and families, have often been used interchangeably and synonymously (see Glick, 1964, pp. 304, 307–308). However, in the past ten years, there has been a growing recognition that not all cases of one were necessarily cases of the other. Unfortunately, as Bender (1967) pointed out, recognition that families and households might be conceptually and empirically different speaks to what they are not—not what they are; points upon which the literature had not been clear. Thus, it was to such a clarification that Bender addressed himself. For in the (then) current confusion—which is still widespread,

> There is, as yet, no general consensus regarding the utility of conceptually distinguishing families from households. They are frequently treated as [identical], the terms being used interchangeably, and *a great many definitions of the "family" still incorporate common residence as an integral part.* (Bender, 1967, p. 493, emphasis added)

The fundamental distinction between families and household is twofold. First, they are analytically and conceptually differentiated. Families are groups of persons bound by ties of *kinship;* consanguineal and affinal relationships, obligations, instrumental and affectional bonds and ties (Turner, 1970). Households are groups of persons (or they can be a person) bound to a *place.* They are living together in residential propinquity. Secondly, they are also empirically differentiated. The members making up the roster of particular instances of each type of group may or may not correspond. Frequently, they do coincide, thus giving ratification to both lay assumptions and lay-assumption-based social-scientific conceptualizations and usages; but frequently they do not. Dispersion from a common residence does not ordinarily destroy kinship linkages, and thus a family (Adams, 1968; Reiss, 1965), although it may attenuate them. Similarly, mere common residence does not a family make. (In fact, Goode, 1964, p. 92, has pointed to "empty shell families" as a problematic type; here common residence persists, but kinship and affective ties are no longer honored.)

Logically, there are three relationships of empirically observable families to empirically located households. (1) Membership may coincide, i.e., all family members reside together. Here, the central question may be who is drawing the boundaries or delimiting the extent of the family, i.e., reckoning kin. Members will ordinarily have kin whose status is clear, both to themselves and/or any observer, lay and scientific alike. This is likely to be the case for parents, children, and siblings; grandparents and grandchildren; aunts and uncles; cousins, nieces and nephews—probably, in North American society, in about that order of clarity and consistency (cf. Schneider and Homans, 1965).

Complicating this, though, are what can be called *fictive* kin (Keesing, 1958, pp. 271–272), "pretend relatives," e.g., "Uncle Stan" who is actually a friend of the child's parents, and *discretionary* kin. These are persons ordinarily distant in kinship terms, who may or may not be included as family, the decision to do so being based upon member's inclination. Thus, in North American society: when siblings marry, whether or not their respective spouses are related to one another is a matter of their discretion (kinship experts say they are not); they are *or* may not be considered in-laws by one another (but probably not a scientific observer). I once asked a colleague whether his wife's sister's husband was his brother-in-law. He answered in the affirmative, and when asked why he considered him to be so, he replied, ". . . because I like him." However, I asked another similarly-situated colleague the same question and he answered no; even though he and the potential discretionary kin are good friends and professional collaborators.

One of the most elaborate examples of fictive kinship has been provided by Giallombardo in her description of a *Society of Women: A Study of a Women's Prison* (1966). Here, the basic structural unit in the inmate social system is a homosexual dyad cast as a "marriage alliance" (pp. 133–157). These units are elaborated and integrated into larger "family groups" (pp. 158–189), complete with conventional kinship terminology (pp. 214–217), e.g., mother, father, aunt, uncle, and so on.* Thus, in this case, an entire social system is based upon units of fictive kinship. The sketchy reports on communes suggest a similar kind of elaboration, although to a lesser and not necessarily homosexually-based extent.†

It follows then that, in the long run, definitions of particular "families" are discretionary for both members and observers; and the question of coincidence of household and family rests in part on how the family is bounded.

---

*We may note that of the 15 reported terms, 8 are consistent with female sex roles, 6 are ordinarily associated with males, while one is ambiguous as to sex (cousins, which may either be male or female).

†In North America, the attribution of fictive kinship frequently functions to allow children to demonstrate expressive solidarity *via* "first-naming," while still expressing generational distance and its implied respect. Thus, "Uncle Pete" as a term of address would allow for the assertion of solidarity *without* the implications of equality indicative in first name alone.

This will be the case whether the problem at hand is an insider's or an outsider's, e.g., the reckoning of kin.

In North American society, the usually sought coincidence by analyst and non-expert alike is between (1) household and nuclear family, not extended family. A lack of coincidence is ascribed to groups where parent(s) absence obtains (see (2) below), but not children away at boarding school, college or university, or grown and gone from home.

(2) Membership may not coincide, involving at least one multi-person group of commonly resident kin and at least one other household occupied by persons kin to the first group. Keeping in mind the "boundary problem" and the distinction between extended and nuclear families, this situation is most typically the socially problematic parent-absent household, especially likely to be viewed as problematic when divorce, desertion, death or prolonged separation, e.g., military service or prison terms, are involved.

A last possibility (3) involves the possibility of no household common to any kin. This is more an analytic than an empirical type, and is noted only for the sake of completeness.

The points of the above discussion are twofold. First, that families, both theoretically and empirically, are separate from the concept of household. Second, that families, in the broad sense, are constituted of three different kinds of kin: (a) *conventional* kin, those members directly tied to one another through blood and/or marriage; (b) *discretionary* kin, whose ties are similar but weaker, and who may or may not recognize one another as obligatory kinsmen—such decisions being made on personalistic grounds; and (c) *fictive* kin, whose actual kin ties are imaginary and "as if" (Vaihinger, 1925), what might be thought of as non-kin kin. Although part of the experienced reality of family members, these latter two types have gone virtually unrecognized as empirical family phenomena by both lay and professional students of the Western family.

Households. Just as conceptions of the family have tied its definition to households, so too has the reverse been true, with familial phenomena, e.g., kinship, typically being linked to the conceptualization of households and household-types. Thus, Solien de Gonzales roots her discussion of types of households in kinship (thereby excluding non-kin cohabitation of all kinds), distinguishing between *affinal* households, which are comprised of married couples only, and *consanguineal* households, these latter bring those which involve

> a co-residential kinship group which includes no regularly present male in the role of the husband-father. (1965, p. 1542)

Such distinction is a useful advance, but it exhausts neither the analytical nor the empirical realities, even those limited to kinship bases and excluding non-kin possibilities.

More complete, albeit still kinship-based, is the social-anthropological conceptualization by Bohannon (1963, pp. 86–99, esp. 93–98), which involves a typology based upon the most fundamental kinship relation characterizing a household. The "most fundamental" relationship is that dyad within the nuclear family

> which is the most stable and enduring, that which is the last to be broken in conflict situations. (Bender, 1967, p. 494)

There are eight such logical possibilities, involving the various combinations of father-husband, mother-wife, son-sibling, and daughter-sibling. And of these, five are the empirically observable, basic situations according to Bohannon (1963, p. 95):

> 1. Societies in which the households are based predominantly on the husband-wife relationship.
> 2. Those based upon the father-son relationship.
> 3. Those based upon the mother-daughter relationship.
> 4. Those based upon the father-daughter relationship.
> 5. Those based upon the sibling relationship.

V

Of course, as anthropologists are fond of reminding us, a great range of variation in household is both viable and empirically observable—even though their presence in North American society would, in many cases, be treated as an instance of a social problem. And furthermore, all of Bohannon's examples are of family-based households, even though *the two concepts, household and family, are not necessarily related to one another.*

Households may involve kin, but this is a correlative attribute, the presence or absence of which is problematic, not a defining one. The defining attributes of households are two: propinquity and function. For in addition to common residence, household

> implies a group of persons who carry out domestic functions. . . . In one sense "household" refers to those persons who reside together; in another sense, it refers to a group of people carrying out domestic functions.

Thus,

> In the former sense, a household need not carry out domestic functions.
> In the latter sense, a household need not reside together as a unit.

Therefore,

it is important, then, to distinguish between co-residential groups and domestic functions. *Co-residential groups have as their referent propinquity,* while *domestic functions have as their referent social* [activities and] *functions.* (Bender, 1967, p. 495, emphasis added)

Domesticity. Domestic activities and functions involve a variety of phenomena, particularly those associated with the basic subsistence problems of food and shelter, and the care and socialization of the young. Solien de Gonzales described these generally as "economic cooperation and the socialization of children" (1960, p. 106), while Bohannon designated them as providing "food and shelter," "bringing up children," and "consumption" of goods and services (1963, p. 98). Such a list comes close to being isomorphic with Murdock's enumeration of the universal functions of the nuclear family (1949, pp. 1–11).

It is with those groups exhibiting both characteristics that students of households and families should be concerned: both residential propinquity and domestic activities. These are those groups of persons who are *living together.**

Living together, for our purposes, however, involves a third defining attribute: *sexual consequentiality,* either in the form of (1) mutual sexual gratification, or (2) offspring. The conventionally defined nuclear family is an example of the first—but so are stable homosexual couples and unmarried cohabiting heterosexuals; similarly, while the conventional nuclear family also exemplifies the second, so too does the father-absent "family" and the unmarried mother who keeps her child.

We are now in a position to offer an alternative conception which embraces these familial, residential, and domestic phenomena of *living together* in ways that previous analyses have tended not to, and is based upon the empirical realities of the actual social arrangements of the contemporary everyday-anyday world: *these may be defined as any cohabiting domestic relationship which is* (or has been) *sexually consequential, i.e., gratification for members,* or the *production of offspring.* These are *the relationships most often associated with the emotions of love and the home,* whether members are conventionally situated or otherwise (Ball, forthcoming).

This is a household and behaviorally based definition of people "living together," one which says nothing about families *per se,* marriage, kinship, religion, or legality—about traditional "problems" such as divorce or unsanctified unions. If not completely universal, it does, however, include such unconventional relationships as stable homosexual couples, as well as the

---

*Co-residence without domesticity includes dormitories, barracks, and the like. Domesticity without co-residence is exemplified by communal food preparation, children's day-care centers, etc.

conventional or socially sanctioned family about which so much has been written; it speaks not to moral ideals, but to the empirical realities of people residing with one another in domestic and sexually consequential ways.

Essentially, this is the same position regarding the genesis, perpetuation, and perception of social problems as that of labelling theorists (cf. Lemert, 1967, pp. 1–64), which recognizes the *social* origin of social problems *qua* problems, phenomena to be responded to in terms evaluatively moral, and amelioratively as regards action. Such a persuasion has informed a large body of scholarly and lay analyses of social problems and the family. The easy availability of these conventional materials makes their review here unnecessary, even if they were not contrary to the stance urged here which emphasizes (1) co-habitation and domesticity, and (2) sexual consequentiality as defining criteria for families (and households) in contemporary society rather than the doctrinaire considerations of traditional analysis.

This is not to suggest that the various phenomena traditionally treated as social problems are not problematic for *some* of the persons so involved. It is, however, to suggest the very rule-situated and definitional nature of the concerns falling most often within the rubric of familial social problems— and their ready elimination by alteration or manipulation of law, custom, or the relativities of morality.

In fact I would argue for the abandonment of the kinship-based view of family as basic in favor of the notion of persons "living together." Unfortunately, the notion of family is ingrained in most lay and professional worldviews. In essence, I would suggest that the sociology of the family be supplemented by a sociology of *households.* Though the two overlap, they are yet discrete.*

This is not to advocate that by some simple social or sociological "tinkering," the family as a source of social problems can be eradicated. It is but a short leap, though, to a position which argues that the problems which are endemic to social organization more generally do not spare households and the family—even when minimally defined as *domestic and sexually consequential cohabitation.* Fundamentally, on a cross-cultural basis, the social problem faced by all social groupings is that of "the division of labor" (Durkheim, 1933): the differentiation of activities and the integration of their outcomes (a reader on the family, in this *genre,* is Skolnick and Skolnick, 1971).

---

*Such a focus would include single individuals adopting children; and companionate marriages of the elderly, which may have little to do with sexual consequentiality— both of which fit the above argument no more than marginally. I am indebted to an anonymous referee on this point.

VI

Postscript

A household or family is not a simple microcosm of the larger sociocultural environment; it is not simply "society writ small." It is, however, characterized in its organization by two dimensions of differentiation which are fundamental to social structural arrangements in all societies: age and sex, universals of social organization whether kinship-based societies or complex nations in a modern age.

Age and sex are two minimal ascribed statuses or positions by which all persons are structurally positioned or socially organized. By ascribed position is meant a structural location determined at—and for all future times— the birth of the person. Other ascribed positions include ethnicity and caste. But note: much more than age and sex, which are to some extent salient at all times, these other ascriptive locations are situated in terms of both their relevance and their meaning. Thus, ethnicity comes into play only *vis-à-vis* other ethnics, i.e., it is not meaningful if the social system is homogenous in terms of ethnicity; similarly, not all social systems have castes, birth-defined stratified inequality. But all social organization recognizes and differentiates on the basis of age and sex distinctions, if only on the basis of a principle of inclusion and exclusion regarding eligibility for membership (cf. Eisenstadt, 1956; D'Andrade, 1966).

While both age *via* generation and sex form axes by which kinship is reckoned and families defined, the former is much more socially variable than the latter. While for most people sex distinctions basically constitute a binary code—the two positions of male and female—age is ordinarily subject to much finer social distinction. It is a continuous variable, theoretically subject to an infinite number of distinctions. This differentiation may range from the precision of birth-date to the grossness of generation, this last named being the temporal fundamental of kinship organization and family definition. And reciprocally, as families (and households) are defined *via* age and generation, so too persons are age-defined (not only chronologically, e.g., date of birth) within the context of families: most broadly into *families of orientation*—into which they are born—and *families of procreation*—into which their offspring are born.

It would appear that most age grades* in North American society are primarily linked to the family and familial contexts, and only secondarily to nonfamilial roles such as occupation. Thus, categories (and terms) such

---

*This term has a more technical meaning among anthropologists. Here it is used to refer to socially recognized age-positions or categories, broadly defined (and often ill-defined) by society and/or its analyst.

as infant, toddler, pre-schooler, sub-teen, and the like, appear to outnumber less, but only less, domestic designations like middle-aged and senior citizen. Unfortunately, there is no census or survey of age-grades and the consensus, or lack thereof, surrounding them and their defiintion.

It should be noted that the number of such age-grades seems to be of recent proliferation, particularly the more youthful categories, and that in part at least they would seem to be a product of commercial merchandisers. For to create a new age-grade is to create a new market, and to increase the probabilities of obsolescence; e.g., pre-schoolers "shouldn't" be dressed like toddlers, thus toddler clothes become inappropriate and pre-schooler clothes must be purchased if the child is to be suitably turned-out. But again, lacking data this is only speculation—but hopefully worthy of further investigation. Such labels designate not merely the duration of time lived, but the familial and societal location of persons so designated; and collectively they make up one more index of increasing societal differentiation: at the highest level of abstraction the basic cause, consequence, and solution to society-wide social problems.

Age and sex are what Banton has called *basic roles* (Banton, 1965, pp. 33–34ff.); they are, according to him, the most basic roles.* Age and sex will or should: 1) affect responses to ego from others more than any other roles or attributes; and 2) influence the availability and performance of other roles for ego more than any others. Thus, age and sex will have more interdependent relationships with other roles, in that they are dependent upon these ascriptive attributes more than any other biographical characteristics (cf. Cumming, 1967).

Sex and generation are locations implying a high degree of commitment (Schelling, 1956, pp. 282–287, and 1960; Becker, 1960; Goffman, 1961a, pp. 88–89). To be sexually or generationally located is to predetermine and rule in or out other social locations, courses of action, experienced selves, and imputed identities. A distinction should be kept in mind between the concepts of *commitment* and the related one of *attachment*. Commitment, like basic role, refers to the degree to which occupancy of a particular structural location conditions the possibilities of other positions or lines of action—by one's self or one's others—while *attachment* refers to the psychic investment, the degree of positive self-evaluation related to such a structural location. The two may co-vary, either positively or negatively. To be an inmate, e.g., of a prison or a mental hospital (Goffman, 1961b), is to be highly committed, though not necessarily attached (probably negatively so, if at all).

---

*Banton's usage of role essentially conforms to what we have called structural location or ascriptive position (see Banton, 1965, pp. 2–3, 25–29), i.e., he uses role in a structural sense rather than as behavioral repertoire or actor's perspective.

Conversely, childless couples seeking to adopt have a high attachment to the parental role but may have been unable to generate such a commitment.

Within the context of a family or household, commitment is generally high (though variable), while attachment is completely variable, from highly positive to the reverse. For families and other households, perhaps the major potential internal social problem—save for economically-based ones of subsistence—is the possibility of gap between commitment and attachment. More than anything else, such a discrepancy would seem to be the heart of intrafamilial generational conflict. Certainly it is such a gap, albeit defined in lay terms, which is perceived by older generation members to be at the heart of their problematic relationships with youthful members. And it is a similar discrepancy which informs the ideology of the women's liberation movement: a desire to redefine the shape of current commitments and, thereby, alter the experiences of attachment (for a recent overview of "militant women," see Bell, 1971, pp. 357–394).

The character of both generational conflict and that regarding sex roles, both within families and households and beyond these units, i.e., the larger society, is fundamentally the same: questions of commitment and attachment. Though the particulars change—changes so rapid that newspapers, not books, are the best references to the specifics of the moment—the basics remain similar and constant. Any sociological and social problems analysis must begin by identifying the kinds of commitments, the characteristics of attachments, and the desired alterations in both. Unfortunately, space precludes any such attempt here. However, the sociological analysis of social problems cannot, we have argued, precede the analysis of sociological problems they inspire. If we have been detained by the latter, it is so that others may do a more useful job on the former.

References

Adams, Bert N. *Kinship in an Urban Setting.* Chicago: Markham, 1968.

Ball, Donald W. *Living Together: Families and Households in Contemporary Society.* New York: Random House, forthcoming.

Banton, Michael. *Roles: An Introduction to the Study of Social Relations.* London: Tavistock, 1965.

Becker, Howard S. "Notes on the Concept of Commitment," *American Journal of Sociology,* 66(July 1960): 32–40.

Bell, Robert R. *Social Deviance.* Homewood, Ill.: Dorsey, 1971.

Bend, Emil, and Martin Vogelfanger. "A New Look at Mill's Critique." In *Mass Society in Crisis,* edited by Bernard Rosenberg, Israel Gerver, and F. William Howton, pp. 111–122. New York: Macmillan, 1964.

Bender, Donald R. "A Refinement of the Concept of Household: Families, Co-residence, and Domestic Functions." *American Anthropologist,* 69 (October 1967): 493–504.

Berger, Peter L., and Hansfried Kellner. "Marriage and the Construction of Reality." *Diogenes,* 4(Summer 1964): 1–24.

Berger, Peter L., and Thomas Luckmann. *The Social Construction of Reality.* Garden City: Doubleday, 1966.

Biddle, Bruce J., and Edwin J. Thomas, eds. *Role Theory: Concepts and Theory.* New York: Wiley, 1966.

Bohannon, Paul. *Social Anthropology.* New York: Holt, Rinehart and Winston, 1963.

Burgess, Ernest W. "The Family as a Unity of Interacting Personalities." *The Family,* 7(March 1926): 3–9.

Christensen, Harold T., ed. *Handbook of Marriage and the Family.* Chicago: Rand McNally, 1964.

Cicourel, Aaron V. *Method and Measurement in Sociology.* New York: The Free Press, 1964.

Cumming, Elaine. "The Name Is the Message." *Transaction,* 4(July/August 1967): 50–52.

D'Andrade, Roy G. "Sex Differences and Cultural Institutions." In *The Development of Sex Differences,* edited by Eleanor E. Maccoby, pp. 174–204. Stanford: Stanford University Press, 1966.

Douglas, Jack D. *American Social Order: Social Rules in a Pluralistic Society.* New York: The Free Press, 1971.

Douglas, Jack D. *The Sociology of Social Problems.* New York: Appleton-Century-Crofts, forthcoming.

Durkheim, Emile. *The Division of Labor in Society.* Translated by George Simpson. New York: Macmillan, 1933.

Eisenstadt, S. N. *From Generation to Generation: Age Groups and Social Structure.* Glencoe, Ill.: The Free Press, 1956.

Farber, Bernard. *Family: Organization and Interaction.* San Francisco: Chandler, 1964.

Farber, Bernard. *Comparative Kinship Systems: A Method of Analysis.* New York: Wiley, 1968.

Farber, Bernard, ed. *Kinship and Family Organization.* New York: Wiley, 1966.

Garfinkel, Harold. *Studies in Ethnomethodology.* Engelwood Cliffs, N.J.: Prentice-Hall, 1967.

Giallombardo, Rose. *Society of Women: A Study of a Women's Prison.* New York: Wiley, 1966.

Glick, Paul C. "Demographic Analysis of Family Data." In *Handbook of Marriage and the Family,* edited by Harold T. Christensen, pp. 300–334. Chicago: Rand McNally, 1964.

Goffman, Erving. *Encounters: Two Studies in the Sociology of Interaction.* Indianapolis: Bobbs-Merrill, 1961.

Goffman, Erving. *Asylums: Essays on the Social Situation of Mental Patients and Other Inmates.* Garden City: Doubleday, Anchor, 1961.

Goode, William J. "The Theoretical Importance of Love." *American Sociological Review,* 24(February 1959): 38–47.

Goode, William J. *World Revolution and Family Patterns.* New York: The Free Press, 1963.

Goode, William J. *The Family.* Englewood Cliffs, N.J.: Prentice-Hall, 1964.

Gough, E. Kathleen. "The Nayars and the Definition of Marriage." *Journal of the Royal Anthropological Institute of Great Britain and Ireland,* 89(Part I); reprinted as "Is the Family Universal?—The Nayar Case," in *A Modern Introduction to the Family,* edited by Norman W. Bell and Ezra F. Vogel, pp. 76–93. Glencoe, Ill.: The Free Press, 1959.

Keesing, Felix M. *Cultural Anthropology: The Science of Custom.* New York: Rinehart and Co., 1958.

Lemert, Edwin M. *Human Deviance, Social Problems, and Social Control.* Englewood Cliffs, N.J.: Prentice-Hall, 1967.

Merton, Robert K. "Social Problems and Sociological Theory." In *Contemporary Social Problems,* edited by Robert K. Merton and Robert A. Nisbet, pp. 697–737. New York: Harcourt, Brace and World, 1961.

Mills, C. Wright. "The Professional Ideology of Social Pathologists." *American Journal of Sociology,* 49(September 1943): 165–180.

Murdock, George Peter. *Social Structure.* New York: Macmillan, 1949.

Nye, F. Ivan, and Felix M. Berardo, eds. *Emerging Conceptual Frameworks in Family Analysis.* New York: Macmillan, 1966.

Reiss, Paul J. "Extended Kinship Relationships in American Society." In *Marriage, Family, and Society,* edited by Hyman Rodman, pp. 204–210. New York: Random House, 1965.

Rodman, Hyman. "Talcott Parsons' View of the Changing American Family." In *Marriage, Family, and Society,* edited by Hyman Rodman, pp. 262–286. New York: Random House, 1965.

Schelling, Thomas C. "An Essay on Bargaining." *American Economic Review,* 46(June 1956): 281–306.

Schelling, Thomas C. *The Strategy of Conflict.* Cambridge, Mass.: Harvard University Press, 1960.

Schneider, David M. *American Kinship: A Cultural Account.* Englewood Cliffs, N.J.: Prentice-Hall, 1968.

Schneider, David M., and Homans, George C. "Kinship Terminology and the American Kinship System." *American Anthropologist,* 57(December 1955): 1194–1208.

Schutz, Alfred. *Collected Papers, I: The Problem of Social Reality.* The Hague, Netherlands: Martinus Nijhoff, 1962.

Schutz, Alfred. *Collected Papers, II: Studies in Social Theory.* The Hague, Netherlands: Martinus Nijhoff, 1964.

Skolnick, A. S., and J. H. Skolnick. *Family in Transition.* Boston: Little, Brown, 1971.

Solien de Gonzales, Nancie L. "Household and Family in the Caribbean." *Social and Economic Studies,* 9(No. 1, 1960): 101–106.

Solien de Gonzales, Nancie L. "The Consanguineal Household and Matrifocality." *American Anthropologist,* 67(December 1965): 1541–1549.

Spiro, Melford E. "Is the Family Universal?—the Israeli Case." In *A Modern Introduction to the Family,* edited by Norman W. Bell and Ezra F. Vogel, pp. 64–75. Glencoe, Ill.: The Free Press, 1960.

Stephens, William N. *The Oedipus Complex: Cross-Cultural Evidence.* New York: The Free Press, 1962.

Stephens, William N. *The Family in Cross-Cultural Perspective.* New York: Holt, Rinehart and Winston, 1963.

Turner, Ralph H. *Family Interaction.* New York: Wiley, 1970.

Vaihinger, Hans. *The Philosophy of "As If."* Translated by C. K. Ogden. New York: Harcourt, Brace and Co., 1925.

Whyte, William Foote. *Street Corner Society.* Chicago: University of Chicago Press, 1943; rev. and enlarged, 1955.

In recent years, the evolution of the family has become the subject of a debate. On the one hand, there is the man-as-ape school of pop anthropology, which argues that male dominance and aggression are programmed into human genes and therefore there is little possibility of change in the relations between the sexes. On the other hand, some feminists hold that prehistoric human societies were matriarchies in which women ruled over men. Kathleen Gough, a noted anthropologist, reviews the evidence in this article, and concludes that the pop anthropologists have exaggerated the extent of male dominance in prehistoric times. Both they and the matriarchy theorists, she argues, have underestimated the influence of practical necessity in determining the division of labor and relations between the sexes. In societies with high birth and death rates and primitive technology, the unalterable facts of pregnancy and child care determined both the division of labor and the relative inequality of women. She concludes that the family's past does not limit its future.

The Origin of the Family | *Kathleen Gough*

The trouble with the origin of the family is that no one really knows. Since Engels wrote *The Origin of the Family, Private Property and the State* in 1884, a great deal of new evidence has come in. Yet the gaps are still enormous. It is not known *when* the family originated, although it was probably between two million and 100,000 years ago. It is not known whether it developed once or in separate times and places. It is not known whether some kind of embryonic family came before, with, or after the origin of language. Since language is the accepted criterion of humanness, this means that we do not even know whether our ancestors acquired the basics of family life before or after they were human. The chances are that language and the family developed together over a long period, but the evidence is sketchy.

Although the origin of the family is speculative, it is better to speculate with than without evidence. The evidence comes from three sources. One is the social and physical lives of non-human primates—especially the New and Old World monkeys and, still more, the great apes, humanity's closest relatives. The second source is the tools and home sites of prehistoric humans and proto-humans. The third is the family lives of hunters and gatherers of wild provender who have been studied in modern times.

Each of these sources is imperfect: monkeys and apes, because they are *not* pre-human ancestors, although they are our cousins; fossil hominids, be-

Reprinted by permission from "The Origin of the Family" by Kathleen Gough, *Journal of Marriage and the Family,* November 1971, pp. 760–770.

cause they left so little vestige of their social life; hunters and gatherers, because none of them has, in historic times, possessed a technology and society as primitive as those of early humans. All show the results of long endeavor in specialized, marginal environments. But together, these sources give valuable clues.

Defining the Family

To discuss the origin of something we must first decide what it is. I shall define the family as "a married couple or other group of adult kinsfolk who cooperate economically and in the upbringing of children, and all or most of whom share a common dwelling."

This includes all forms of kin-based household. Some are extended families containing three generations of married brothers or sisters. Some are "grandfamilies" descended from a single pair of grandparents. Some are matrilineage households, in which brothers and sisters share a house with the sisters' children, and men merely visit their wives in other homes. Some are compound families, in which one man has several wives, or one woman, several husbands. Others are nuclear families composed of a father, mother and children.

Some kind of family exists in all known human societies, although it is not found in every segment or class of all stratified, state societies. Greek and American slaves, for example, were prevented from forming legal families, and their social families were often disrupted by sale, forced labor, or sexual exploitation. Even so, the family was an ideal which all classes and most people attained when they could.

The family implies several other universals. (1) Rules forbid sexual relations and marriage between close relatives. Which relatives are forbidden varies, but all societies forbid mother-son mating, and most, father-daughter and brother-sister. Some societies allow sex relations, but forbid marriage, between certain degrees of kin. (2) The men and women of a family cooperate through a division of labor based on gender. Again, the sexual division of labor varies in rigidity and in the tasks performed. But in no human society to date is it wholly absent. Child-care, household tasks and crafts closely connected with the household tend to be done by women; war, hunting, and government, by men. (3) Marriage exists as a socially recognized, durable, although not necessarily lifelong relationship between individual men and women. From it springs social fatherhood, some kind of special bond between a man and the child of his wife, whether or not they are his own children physiologically. Even in polyandrous societies, where women have several husbands, or in matrilineal societies, where group membership and property pass through women, each child has one or more designated "fathers" with whom he has a special social, and often religious, relationship.

This bond of *social* fatherhood is recognized among people who do not know about the male role in procreation, or where, for various reasons, it is not clear who the physiological father of a particular infant is. Social fatherhood seems to come from the division and interdependence of male and female tasks, especially in relation to children, rather than directly from physiological fatherhood, although in most societies, the social father of a child is usually presumed to be its physiological father as well. Contrary to the beliefs of some feminists, however, I think that in no human society do men, as a whole category, have *only* the role of insemination, and *no* other social or economic role, in relation to women and children. (4) Men in general have higher status and authority over the women of their families, although older women may have influence, even some authority, over junior men. The omnipresence of male authority, too, goes contrary to the belief of some feminists that in "matriarchal" societies, women were either completely equal to, or had paramount authority over, men, either in the home or in society at large.

It is true that in some matrilineal societies, such as the Hopi of Arizona or the Ashanti of Ghana, men exert little authority over their wives. In some, such as the Nayars of South India or the Minangkabau of Sumatra, men may even live separately from their wives and children, that is, in different families. In such societies, however, the fact is that women and children fall under greater or lesser authority from the women's kinsmen—their eldest brothers, mothers' brothers, or even their grown up sons.

In matrilineal societies, where property, rank, office and group membership are inherited through the female line, it is true that women tend to have greater independence than in patrilineal societies. This is especially so in matrilineal tribal societies where the state has not yet developed, and especially in those tribal societies where residence is matrilocal—that is, men come to live in the homes or villages of their wives. Even so, in all matrilineal societies for which adequate descriptions are available, the ultimate headship of households, lineages and local groups is usually with men. (See Schneider and Gough, 1961, for common and variant features of matrilineal systems.)

There is in fact no true "matriarchal," as distinct from "matrilineal," society in existence or known from literature, and the chances are that there never has been.* This does not mean that women and men have never had relations that were dignified and creative for both sexes, appropriate to the

---

*The Iroquois are often quoted as a "matriarchal" society, but in fact Morgan himself refers to "the absence of equality between the sexes" and notes that women were subordinate to men, ate after men, and that women (not men) were publicly whipped as punishment for adultery. Warleaders, tribal chiefs, and *sachems* (heads of matrilineal lineages) were men. Women did, however, have a large say in the government of the long-house or home of the matrilocal extended family, and women figured as tribal counsellors and religious officials, as well as arranging marriages. (Lewis H. Morgan: The League of the *Ho-de-ne Sau-nee or Iroquois,* Human Relations Area Files, 1954)

knowledge, skills and technology of their times. Nor does it mean that the sexes cannot be equal in the future, or that the sexual division of labor cannot be abolished. I believe that it can and must be. But it is not necessary to believe myths of a feminist Golden Age in order to plan for parity in the future.

Primate Societies

Within the primate order, humans are most closely related to the anthropoid apes (the African chimpanzee and gorilla and the Southeast Asian orang-utan and gibbon), and of these, to the chimpanzee and the gorilla. More distantly related are the Old, and then the New World, monkeys, and finally, the lemurs, tarsiers and tree-shrews.

All primates share characteristics without which the family could not have developed. The young are born relatively helpless. They suckle for several months or years and need prolonged care afterwards. Childhood is longer, the closer the species is to humans. Most monkeys reach puberty at about four to five and mature socially between about five and ten. Chimpanzees, by contrast, suckle for up to three years. Females reach puberty at seven to ten; males enter mature social and sexual relations as late as thirteen. The long childhood and maternal care produce close relations between children of the same mother, who play together and help tend their juniors until they grow up.

Monkeys and apes, like humans, mate in all months of the year instead of in a rutting season. Unlike humans, however, female apes experience unusually strong sexual desire for a few days shortly before and during ovulation (the oestrus period), and have intensive sexual relations at that time. The males are attracted to the females by their scent or by brightly colored swellings in the sexual region. Oestrus-mating appears to be especially pronounced in primate species more remote from humans. The apes and some monkeys carry on less intensive, month-round sexuality in addition to oestrus-mating, approaching human patterns more closely. In humans, sexual desires and relations are regulated less by hormonal changes and more by mental images, emotions, cultural rules and individual preferences.

Year-round (if not always month-round) sexuality means that males and females socialize more continuously among primates than among most other mammals. All primates form bans or troops composed of both sexes plus children. The numbers and proportions of the sexes vary, and in some species an individual, a mother with her young, or a subsidiary troop of male juveniles may travel temporarily alone. But in general, males and females socialize continually through mutual grooming* and playing as well as

*Combing the hair and removing parasites with hands or teeth.

through frequent sex relations. Keeping close to the females, primate males play with their children and tend to protect both females and young from predators. A "division of labor" based on gender is thus already found in primate society between a female role of prolonged child care and a male role of defense. Males may also carry or take care of children briefly, and non-nursing females may fight. But a kind of generalized "fatherliness" appears in the protective role of adult males towards young, even in species where the sexes do not form long-term individual attachments.

Sexual Bonds Among Primates

Some non-human primates do have enduring sexual bonds and restrictions, superficially similar to those in some human societies. Among gibbons a single male and female live together with their young. The male drives off other males and the female, other females. When a juvenile reaches puberty it is thought to leave or be expelled by the parent of the same sex, and he eventually finds a mate elsewhere. Similar *de facto,* rudimentary "incest prohibitions" may have been passed on to humans from their prehuman ancestors and later codified and elaborated through language, moral custom and law. Whether this is so may become clearer when we know more about the mating patterns of the other great apes, especially of our closest relatives, the chimpanzees. Present evidence suggests that male chimpanzees do not mate with their mothers.

Orang-utans live in small, tree-dwelling groups like gibbons, but their forms are less regular. One or two mothers may wander alone with their young, mating at intervals with a male; or a male-female pair, or several juvenile males, may travel together.

Among mountain gorillas of Uganda, South Indian langurs, and hamadryas baboons of Ethiopia, a single, fully mature male mates with several females, especially in their oestrus periods. If younger adult males are present, the females may have occasional relations with them if the leader is tired or not looking.

Among East and South African baboons, rhesus macaques, and South American woolly monkeys, the troop is bigger, numbering up to two hundred. It contains a number of adult males and a much larger number of females. The males are strictly ranked in terms of dominance based on both physical strength and intelligence. The more dominant males copulate intensively with the females during the latter's oestrus periods. Toward the end of oestrus a female may briefly attach herself to a single dominant male. At other times she may have relations with any male of higher or lower rank provided that those of higher rank permit it.

Among some baboons and macaques the young males travel on the outskirts of the group and have little access to females. Some macaques expel from the troop a proportion of the young males, who then form "bachelor troops." Bachelors may later form new troops with young females.

Other primates are more thoroughly promiscuous, or rather indiscriminate, in mating. Chimpanzees, and also South American howler monkeys, live in loosely structured groups, again (as in most monkey and ape societies) with a preponderance of females. The mother-child unit is the only stable group. The sexes copulate almost at random, and most intensively and indiscriminately during oestrus.

A number of well-known anthropologists have argued that various attitudes and customs often found in human societies are instinctual rather than culturally learned, and come from our primate heritage. They include hierarchies of ranking among men, male political power over women, and the greater tendency of men to form friendships with one another, as opposed to women's tendencies to cling to a man. (See, for example, Morris, 1967; Fox, 1967.)

I cannot accept these conclusions and think that they stem from the male chauvinism of our own society. A "scientific" argument which states that all such features of female inferiority are instinctive is obviously a powerful weapon in maintaining the traditional family with male dominance. But in fact, these features are *not* universal among non-human primates, including some of those most closely related to humans. Chimpanzees have a low degree of male dominance and male hierarchy and are sexually virtually indiscriminate. Gibbons have a kind of fidelity for both sexes and almost no male dominance or hierarchy. Howler monkeys are sexually indiscriminate and lack male hierarchies or dominance.

The fact is that among non-human primates male dominance and male hierarchies seem to be adaptations to particular environments, some of which did become genetically established through natural selection. Among humans, however, these features are present in variable degrees and are almost certainly learned, not inherited at all. Among non-human primates there are fairly general differences between those that live mainly in trees and those that live largely on the ground. The tree dwellers (for example gibbons, orang-utans, South American howler and woolly monkeys) tend to have to defend themselves less against predators than do the ground-dwellers (such as baboons, macaques or gorillas). Where defense is important, males are much larger and stronger than females, exert dominance over females, and are strictly hierarchized and organized in relation to one another. Where defense is less important there is much less sexual dimorphism (difference in size between male and female), less or no male dominance, a less pronounced male hierarchy, and greater sexual indiscriminacy.

Comparatively speaking, humans have a rather small degree of sexual dimorphism, similar to chimpanzees. Chimpanzees live much in trees but also partly on the ground, in forest or semi-forest habitats. They build individual nests to sleep in, sometimes on the ground but usually in trees. They flee into trees from danger. Chimpanzees go mainly on all fours, but sometimes on two feet, and can use and make simple tools. Males are dominant, but not very dominant, over females. The rank hierarchy among males is unstable, and males often move between groups, which vary in size from two to fifty individuals. Food is vegetarian, supplemented with worms, grubs or occasional small animals. A mother and her young form the only stable unit. Sexual relations are largely indiscriminate, but nearby males defend young animals from danger. The chances are that our pre-human ancestors had a similar social life. Morgan and Engels were probably right in concluding that we came from a state of "original promiscuity" before we were fully human.

Human Evolution

Judging from the fossil record, apes ancestral to humans, gorillas and chimpanzees roamed widely in Asia, Europe and Africa some twelve to twenty-eight million years ago. Toward the end of that period (the Miocene) one appears in North India and East Africa, Ramapithecus, who may be ancestral both to later hominids and to modern humans. His species were small like gibbons, walked upright on two feet, had human rather than ape corner-teeth, and therefore probably used hands rather than teeth to tear their food. From that time evolution toward humanness must have proceeded through various phases until the emergence of modern *homo sapiens,* about 70,000 years ago.

In the Miocene period before Ramapithecus appeared, there were several time-spans in which, over large areas, the climate became dryer and sub-tropical forests dwindled or disappeared. A standard reconstruction of events, which I accept, is that groups of apes, probably in Africa, had to come down from the trees and adapt to terrestrial life. Through natural selection, probably over millions of years, they developed specialized feet for walking. Thus freed, the hands came to be used not only (as among apes) for grasping and tearing, but for regular carrying of objects such as weapons (which had hitherto been sporadic) or of infants (which had hitherto clung to their mothers' body hair).

The spread of indigestible grasses on the open savannahs may have encouraged, if it did not compel, the early ground dwellers to become active hunters rather than simply to forage for small, sick or dead animals that came their way. Collective hunting and tool use involved group cooperation and helped foster the growth of language out of the call-systems of apes.

Language meant the use of symbols to refer to events not present. It allowed greatly increased foresight, memory, planning and division of tasks—in short, the capacity for human thought.

With the change to hunting, group territories became much larger. Apes range only a few thousand feet daily; hunters, several miles. But because their infants were helpless, nursing women could hunt only small game close to home. This then produced the sexual division of labor on which the human family has since been founded. Women elaborated upon ape methods of child care, and greatly expanded foraging, which in most areas remained the primary and most stable source of food. Men improved upon ape methods of fighting off other animals, and of group protection in general. They adapted these methods to hunting, using weapons which for millennia remained the same for the chase as for human warfare.

Out of the sexual division of labor came, for the first time, home life as well as group cooperation. Female apes nest with and provide foraged food for their infants. But adult apes do not cooperate in food getting or nest building. They build new nests each night wherever they may happen to be. With the development of a hunting-gathering complex, it became necessary to have a G.H.Q., or home. Men could bring meat to this place for several days' supply. Women and children could meet men there after the day's hunting, and could bring their vegetable produce for general consumption. Men, women and children could build joint shelters, butcher meat, and treat skins for clothing.

Later, fire came into use for protection against wild animals, for lighting, and eventually for cooking. The hearth then provided the focus and symbol of home. With the development of cookery, some humans—chiefly women, and perhaps some children and old men—came to spend more time preparing nutrition so that all people need spend less time in chewing and tearing their food. Meals—already less frequent because of the change to a carnivorous diet—now became brief, periodic events instead of the long feeding sessions of apes.

The change to humanness brought two bodily changes that affected birth and child care. These were head-size and width of the pelvis. Walking upright produced a narrower pelvis to hold the guts in position. Yet as language developed, brains and hence heads grew much bigger relative to body size. To compensate, humans are born at an earlier stage of growth than apes. They are helpless longer and require longer and more total care. This in turn caused early women to concentrate more on child care and less on defense than do female apes.

Language made possible not only a division and cooperation in labor but also all forms of tradition, rules, morality and cultural learning. Rules banning sex relations among close kinfolk must have come very early. Precisely how or why they developed is unknown, but they had at least two useful functions. They helped to preserve order in the family as a cooperative unit, by outlawing competition for mates. They also created bonds *between* families, or even between separate bands, and so provided a basis for wider cooperation in the struggle for livelihood and the expansion of knowledge.

It is not clear when all these changes took place. Climatic change with increased drought began regionally up to 28 million years ago. The divergence between pre-human and gorilla-chimpanzee stems had occurred in both Africa and India at least 12 million years ago. The pre-human stem led to the Australopithecenes of East and South Africa, about 1,750,000 years ago. These were pygmy-like, two-footed, upright hominids with larger than ape brains, who made tools and probably hunted in savannah regions. It is unlikely that they knew the use of fire.

The first known use of fire is that of cave-dwelling hominids (Sinanthropus, a branch of the Pithecanthropines) at Choukoutien near Peking, some half a million years ago during the second ice age. Fire was used regularly in hearths, suggesting cookery, by the time of the Acheulean and Mousterian cultures of Neanderthal man in Europe, Africa and Asia before, during and after the third ice age, some 150,000 to 100,000 years ago. These people, too, were often cave dwellers, and buried their dead ceremonially in caves. Cave dwelling by night as well as by day was probably, in fact, not safe for humans until fire came into use to drive away predators.

Most anthropologists conclude that home life, the family and language had developed by the time of Neanderthal man, who was closely similar and may have been ancestral to modern *homo sapiens*. At least two anthropologists, however, believe that the Australopithecenes already had language nearly two million years ago, while another thinks that language and incest prohibitions did not evolve until the time of *homo sapiens* some 70,000 to 50,000 years ago. (For the former view, see Hockett and Ascher, 1968; for the latter, Livingstone, 1969.) I am myself inclined to think that family life built around tool use, the use of language, cookery, and a sexual division of labor, must have been established sometime between about 500,000 and 200,000 years ago.

Hunters and Gatherers

Most of the hunting and gathering societies studied in the eighteenth to twentieth centuries had technologies similar to those that were widespread in the Mesolithic period, which occurred about 15,000 to 10,000 years ago, after the ice ages ended but before cultivation was invented and animals domesticated.

Modern hunters live in marginal forest, mountain, arctic or desert environments where cultivation is impracticable. Although by no means "primeval," the hunters of recent times do offer clues to the types of family found during that 99 percent of human history before the agricultural revolution. They include the Eskimo, many Canadian and South American Indian groups, the forest BaMbuti (p̃ygmies) and the desert Bushmen of Southern Africa, the Kadar of South India, the Veddah of Ceylon, and the Andaman Islanders of the Indian Ocean. About 175 hunting and gathering cultures in Oceania, Asia, Africa and America have been described in fair detail.

In spite of their varied environments, hunters share certain features of social life. They live in bands of about 20 to 200 people, the majority of bands having fewer than 50. Bands are divided into families, which may forage alone in some seasons. Hunters have simple but ingenious technologies. Bows and arrows, spears, needles, skin clothing, and temporary leaf or wood shelters are common. Most hunters do some fishing. The band forages and hunts in a large territory and usually moves camp often.

Social life is egalitarian. There is of course no state, no organized government. Apart from religious shamans or magicians, the division of labor is based only on sex and age. Resources are owned communally; tools and personal possessions are freely exchanged. Everyone works who can. Band leadership goes to whichever man has the intelligence, courage and foresight to command the respect of his fellows. Intelligent older women are also looked up to.

The household is the main unit of economic cooperation, with the men, women and children dividing the labor and pooling their produce. In 97 percent of the 175 societies classified by G. P. Murdock, hunting is confined to men; in the other three percent it is chiefly a male pursuit. Gathering of wild plants, fruits and nuts is women's work. In 60 percent of societies, only women gather, while in another 32 percent gathering is mainly feminine. Fishing is solely or mainly men's work in 93 percent of the hunting societies where it occurs.

For the rest, men monopolize fighting, although interband warfare is rare. Women tend children and shelters and usually do most of the cooking, processing, and storage of food. Women tend, also, to be foremost in the early household crafts such as basketry, leather work, the making of skin or bark clothing, and in the more advanced hunting societies, pottery. (Considering that women probably *invented* all of these crafts, in addition to cookery, food storage and preservation, agriculture, spinning, weaving, and perhaps even house construction, it is clear that women played quite as important roles as men in early cultural development.) Building dwellings and making tools and ornaments are variously divided between the sexes, while boat-building is largely done by men. Girls help the women, and boys play at hunting or hunt small game until they reach puberty, when both take on the roles of adults. Where the environment makes it desirable, the men of a whole band or of some smaller cluster of households cooperate in hunting or fishing and divide their spoils. Women of nearby families often go gathering together.

Family composition varies among hunters as it does in other kinds of societies. About half or more of known hunting societies have nuclear families (father, mother and children), with polygynous households (a man, two or more wives, and children) as occasional variants. Clearly, nuclear families are the most common among hunters, although hunters have a slightly higher proportion of polygynous families than do non-hunting societies.

About a third of hunting societies contain some "stem-family" households —that is, older parents live together with one married child and grandchildren, while the other married children live in independent dwellings. A still smaller proportion live in large extended families containing several married brothers (or several married sisters), their spouses, and children. (For exact figures, see Murdock, 1957; Coult, 1965; and Murdock, 1967. In the last-named survey, out of 175 hunting societies, 47 percent had nuclear family households, 38 percent had stem families, and 14 percent had extended families.) Hunters have fewer extended and stem families than do non-hunting societies. These larger households become common with the rise of agriculture. They are especially found in large, pre-industrial agrarian states such as ancient Greece, Rome, India, the Islamic empires, China, etc.

Hunting societies also have few households composed of a widow or divorcee and her children. This is understandable, for neither men nor women can survive long without the work and produce of the other sex, and marriage is the way to obtain them. That is why so often young men must show proof of hunting prowess, and girls of cooking, before they are allowed to marry.

The family, together with territorial grouping, provides the framework of society among hunters. Indeed, as Morgan and Engels clearly saw, kinship and territory are the foundations of all societies before the rise of the state. Not only hunting and gathering bands, but the larger and more complex tribes and chiefdoms of primitive cultivators and herders organize people through descent from common ancestors or through marriage ties between groups. Among hunters, things are simple. There is only the family, and beyond it the band. With the domestication of plants and animals, the economy becomes more productive. More people can live together. Tribes form, containing several thousand people loosely organized into large kin-groups such as clans and lineages, each composed of a number of related families. With still further development of the productive forces the society throws up a central political leadership, together with craft specialization and trade, and so the chiefdom emerges. But this, too, is structured through ranked allegiances and marriage ties between kin groups.

Only with the rise of the state does class, independently of kinship, provide the basis for relations of production, distribution and power. Even then, kin groups remain large in the agrarian state and kinship persists as the prime organizing principle within each class until the rise of capitalism. The reduction in significance of the family that we see today is the outgrowth of a decline in the importance of "familism" relative to other institutions, that began with the rise of the state, but became speeded up with the development of capitalism and machine industry. In most modern socialist societies, the family is even less significant as an organizing principle. It is reasonable to suppose that in the future it will become minimal or may disappear, at least as a legally constituted unit for exclusive forms of sexual and economic cooperation and of child-care.

Morgan and Engels (1942) thought that from a state of original promiscuity, early humans at first banned sex relations between the generations of parents and children, but continued to allow them indiscriminately between brothers, sisters and all kinds of cousins within the band. They called this the "consanguineal family." They thought that later, all mating within the family or some larger kin group became forbidden, but that there was a stage (the "punaluan") in which a group of sisters or other close kinswomen from one band were married jointly to a group of brothers or other close kinsmen from another. They thought that only later still, and especially with the domestication of plants and animals, did the "pairing family" develop in which each man was married to one or two women individually.

These writers drew their conclusions not from evidence of actual group-marriage among primitive peoples but from the kinship terms found today in certain tribal and chiefly societies. Some of these equate all kin of the same sex in the parents' generation, suggesting brother-sister marriage. Others equate the father's brothers with the father, and the mother's sisters with the mother, suggesting the marriage of a group of brothers with a group of sisters.

Modern evidence does not bear out these conclusions about early society. All known hunters and gatherers live in families, not in communal sexual arrangements. Most hunters even live in nuclear families rather than in large extended kin groups. Mating is individualized, although one man may occasionally have two wives, or (very rarely) a woman may have two husbands. Economic life is built primarily around the division of labor and partnership between individual men and women. The hearths, caves and other remains of Upper Palaeolithic hunters suggest that this was probably an early arrangement. We cannot say that Engels' sequences are completely ruled out for very early hominids—the evidence is simply not available. But it is hard to see what economic arrangements among hunters would give rise to group, rather than individual or "pairing" marriage arrangements, and this Engels does not explain.

Soviet anthropologists continued to believe in Morgan and Engels' early "stages" longer than did anthropologists in the West. Today, most Russian anthropologists admit the lack of evidence for "consanguineal" and "punaluan" arrangements, but some still believe that a different kind of group marriage intervened between indiscriminate mating and the pairing family. Semyonov, for example, argues that in the stage of group marriage, mating was forbidden within the hunting band, but that the men of two neighboring bands had multiple, visiting sex relations with women of the opposite band (Semyonov, 1967).

While such an arrangement cannot be ruled out, it seems unlikely because many of the customs which Semyonov regards as "survivals" of such group marriage (for example, visiting husbands, matrilineage dwelling groups, widespread clans, multiple spouses for both sexes, men's and women's communal houses, and prohibitions of sexual intercourse inside the huts of the village) are actually found not so much among hunters as among horticultural tribes, and even quite complex agricultural states. Whether or not such a stage of group marriage occurred in the earliest societies, there seems little doubt that pairing marriage (involving family households) came about with the development of elaborate methods of hunting, cooking, and the preparation of clothing and shelters—that is, with a fully-fledged division of labor.

Even so, there *are* some senses in which mating among hunters has more of a group character than in archaic agrarian states or in capitalist society. Murdock's sample shows that sex relations before marriage are strictly prohibited in only 26 percent of hunting societies. In the rest, marriage is either arranged so early that pre-marital sex is unlikely, or (more usually) sex relations are permitted more or less freely before marriage.

With marriage, monogamy is the normal *practice* at any given time for most hunters, but it is not the normal *rule*. Only 19 percent in Murdock's survey prohibit plural unions. Where polygyny is found (79 percent) the most common type is for a man to marry two sisters or other closely related women of the same kin group—for example, the daughters of two sisters or of two brothers. When a woman dies it is common for a sister to replace her in the marriage, and when a man dies, for a brother to replace him.

Similarly, many hunting societies hold that the wives of brothers or other close kinsmen are in some senses wives of the group. They can be called on in emergencies or if one of them is ill. Again, many hunting societies have special times for sexual license between men and women of a local group who are not married to each other, such as the "lights out" games of Eskimo sharing a communal snow-house. In other situations, an Eskimo wife will spend the night with a chance guest of her husband's. All parties expect this as normal hospitality. Finally, adultery, although often punished, tends to be common in hunting societies, and few if any of them forbid divorce or the remarriage of divorcees and widows.

The reason for all this seems to be that marriage and sexual restrictions are practical arrangements among hunters designed mainly to serve economic and survival needs. In these societies, some kind of rather stable pairing best accomplishes the division of labor and cooperation of men and women and the care of children. Beyond the immediate family, either a larger family group or the whole band has other, less intensive but important, kinds of cooperative activities. Therefore, the husbands and wives of individuals within that group can be summoned to stand in for each other if need arises. In the case of Eskimo wife-lending, the extreme climate and the need for lone wandering in search of game dictate high standards of hospitality. This evidently becomes extended to sexual sharing.

In the case of sororal polygyny or marriage to the dead wife's sister, it is natural that when two women fill the same role—either together or in sequence—they should be sisters, for sisters are more alike than other women. They are likely to care more for each others' children. The replacement of a dead spouse by a sister or a brother also preserves existing intergroup relations. For the rest, where the economic and survival bonds of marriage are not at stake, people can afford to be freely companionate and tolerant. Hence pre-marital sexual freedom, seasonal group-license, and a pragmatic approach to adultery.

Marriages among hunters are usually arranged by elders when a young couple are ready for adult responsibilities. But the couple know each other and usually have some choice. If the first marriage does not work, the second mate will almost certainly be self-selected. Both sexual and companionate love between individual men and women are known and are deeply experienced. With comparative freedom of mating, love is less often separated from or opposed to marriage than in archaic states or even than in some modern nations.

The Position of Women

Even in hunting societies it seems that women are always in some sense the "second sex," with greater or less subordination to men. This varies. Eskimo and Australian aboriginal women are far more subordinate than women among the Kadar, the Andamanese or the Congo Pygmies—all forest people.

I suggest that women have greater power and independence among hunters when they are important food-obtainers than when they are mainly processors of meat or other supplies provided by men. The former situation is likelier to exist in societies where hunting is small-scale and intensive than where it is extensive over a large terrain, and in societies where gathering is important by comparison with hunting.

In general in hunting societies, however, women are less subordinated in certain crucial respects than they are in most, if not all, of the archaic states, or even in some capitalist nations. These respects include men's ability to deny women sexuality or to force it upon them; to command or exploit their labor or to control their produce; to control or rob them of their children; to confine them physically and prevent their movement; to use them as objects in male transactions; to cramp their creativeness; or to withhold from them large areas of the society's knowledge and cultural attainments.

Especially lacking in hunting societies is the kind of male possessiveness and exclusiveness regarding women that leads to such situations as savage punishments or death for female adultery, the jealous guarding of female chastity and virginity, the denial of divorce to women, or the ban on a woman's remarriage after her husband's death.

For these reasons, I do not think we can speak, as some writers do, of a class-division between men and women in hunting societies. True, men are more mobile than women and they lead in public affairs. But class society requires that one class control the means of production, dictate its use by the other classes, and expropriate the surplus. These conditions do not exist among hunters. Land and other resources are held communally, although women may monopolize certain gathering areas, and men, their hunting grounds. There is rank difference, role difference, and some difference respecting degrees of authority, between the sexes, but there is reciprocity rather than domination or exploitation.

As Engels saw, the power of men to exploit women systematically springs from the existence of surplus wealth, and more directly, from the state, social stratification, and the control of property by men. With the rise of the state, because of their monopoly over weapons, and because freedom from child care allows them to enter specialized economic and political roles, some men —especially ruling-class men—acquire power over other men and over women. Almost all men acquire it over women of their own or lower classes, especially within their own kinship groups. These kinds of male power are shadowy among hunters.

To the extent that men *have* power over women in hunting societies, this seems to spring from the male monopoly of heavy weapons, from the particular division of labor between the sexes, or from both. Although men seldom use weapons against women, they *possess* them (or possess superior weapons) in addition to their physical strength. This does give men an ultimate control of force. When old people or babies must be killed to ensure band or family survival, it is usually men who kill them. Infanticide—rather common among hunters, who must limit the mouths to feed—is more often female infanticide than male.

The hunting of men seems more often to require them to organize in groups than does the work of women. Perhaps because of this, about 60 percent of hunting societies have predominantly virilocal residence. That is, men choose which band to live in (often, their fathers'), and women move with their husbands. This gives a man advantages over his wife in terms of familiarity and loyalties, for the wife is often a stranger. Sixteen to 17 percent of hunting societies are, however, uxorilocal, with men moving to the households of their wives, while 15 to 17 percent are bilocal—that is, either sex may move in with the other on marriage.

Probably because of male cooperation in defense and hunting, men are more prominent in band councils and leadership, in medicine and magic, and in public rituals designed to increase game, to ward off sickness, or to initiate boys into manhood. Women do, however, often take part in band councils; they are not excluded from law and government as in many agrarian states. Some women are respected as wise leaders, story tellers, doctors, or magicians, or are feared as witches. Women have their own ceremonies of fertility, birth and healing, from which men are often excluded.

In some societies, although men control the most sacred objects, women are believed to have discovered them. Among the Congo Pygmies, religion centers about a beneficent spirit, the Animal of the Forest. It is represented by wooden trumpets that are owned and played by men. Their possession and use are hidden from the women and they are played at night when hunting is bad, someone falls ill, or death occurs. During the playing men dance in the public campfire, which is sacred and is associated with the forest. Yet the men believe that women originally owned the trumpet and that it was a woman who stole fire from the chimpanzees or from the forest spirit. When a woman has failed to bear children for several years, a special ceremony is held. Women lead in the songs that usually accompany the trumpets, and an old woman kicks apart the campfire. Temporary female dominance seems to be thought necessary to restore fertility.

In some hunting societies women are exchanged between local groups, which are thus knit together through marriages. Sometimes, men of different bands directly exchange their sisters. More often there is a generalized exchange of women between two or more groups, or a one-way movement of women within a circle of groups. Sometimes the husband's family pays weapons, tools or ornaments to the wife's in return for the wife's services and later, her children.

In such societies, although they may be well treated and their consent sought, women are clearly the moveable partners in an arrangement controlled by men. Male anthropologists have seized on this as evidence of original male dominance and patrilocal residence. Fox and others, for example, have argued that until recently, *all* hunting societies formed out-marrying patrilocal bands, linked together politically by the exchange of women. The fact that fewer than two-thirds of hunting societies are patrilocal today, and only 41 percent have band-exogamy, is explained in terms of modern conquest, economic change and depopulation.

I cannot accept this formula. It is true that modern hunting societies have been severely changed, de-culturated, and often depopulated, by capitalist imperialism. I can see little evidence, however, that the ones that are patrilocal today have undergone less change than those that are not. It is hard to believe that in spite of enormous environmental diversity and the passage of thousands, perhaps millions of years, hunting societies all had band-exogamy with patrilocal residence until they were disturbed by western imperialism. It is more likely that early band societies, like later agricultural tribes, developed variety in family life and the status of women as they spread over the earth.

There is also some likelihood that the earliest hunters had matrilocal rather than patrilocal families. Among apes and monkeys, it is almost always males who leave the troop or are driven out. Females stay closer to their mothers and their original site; males move about, attaching themselves to females where availability and competition permit. Removal of the wife to the husband's home or band may have been a relatively late development in societies where male cooperation in hunting assumed overwhelming importance.* Conversely, after the development of horticulture (which was probably invented and is mainly carried out by women), those tribes in which horticulture predominated over stock raising were most likely to be or to remain matrilocal and to develop matrilineal descent groups with a relatively high status of women. But where extensive hunting of large animals, or later, the herding of large domesticates, predominated, patrilocal residence flourished and women were used to form alliances between male-centered groups. With the invention of metallurgy and of agriculture as distinct from horticulture after 4000 B.C., men came to control agriculture and many crafts, and most of the great agrarian states had patrilocal residence with patriarchal, male-dominant families.

---

*Upper Palaeolithic hunters produced female figurines that were obvious emblems of fertility. The cult continued through the Mesolithic and into the Neolithic period. Goddesses and spirits of fertility are found in some patrilineal as well as matrilineal societies, but they tend to be more prominent in the latter. It is thus possible that in many areas even late Stone Age hunters had matrilocal residence and perhaps matrilineal descent, and that in some regions this pattern continued through the age of horticulture and even—as in the case of the Nayars of Kerala and the Minangkabau of Sumatra—into the age of plow agriculture, of writing, and of the small-scale state.

Conclusions

The family is a human institution, not found in its totality in any pre-human species. It required language, planning, cooperation, self-control, foresight and cultural learning, and probably developed along with these.

The family was made desirable by the early human combination of pro-longed child care with the need for hunting with weapons over large ter-rains. The sexual division of labor on which it was based grew out of a rudi-mentary pre-human division between male defense and female child care. But among humans this sexual division of functions for the first time became crucial for food production and so laid the basis for future economic special-ization and cooperation.

Morgan and Engels were probably right in thinking that the human family was preceded by sexual indiscriminacy. They were also right in seeing an egalitarian group-quality about early economic and marriage arrangements. They were without evidence, however, in believing that the earliest mating and economic patterns were entirely group relations.

Togther with tool use and language, the family was no doubt the most sig-nificant invention of the human revolution. All three required reflective thought, which above all accounts for the vast superiority in consciousness that separates humans from apes.

The family provided the framework for all pre-state society and the fount of its creativeness. In groping for survival and for knowledge, human beings learned to control their sexual desires and to suppress their individual selfish-ness, aggression and competition. The other side of this self-control was an increased capacity for love—not only love of a mother for her child, which is seen among apes, but of male for female in enduring relationships, and of each sex for ever-widening groups of humans. Civilization would have been impossible without this initial self-control, seen in incest prohibitions and in the generosity and moral orderliness of primitive family life.

From the start, women have been subordinate to men in certain key areas of status, mobility and public leadership. But before the agricultural revolu-tion, and even for several thousands of years thereafter, the inequality was based chiefly on the unalterable fact of long child care combined with the exigencies of primitive technology. The extent of inequality varied according to the ecology and the resulting sexual division of tasks. But in any case it was largely a matter of survival rather than of man-made cultural imposi-tions. Hence the impressions we receive of dignity, freedom and mutual re-spect between men and women in primitive hunting and horticultural socie-ties. This is true whether these societies are patrilocal, bilocal or matrilocal, although matrilocal societies, with matrilineal inheritance, offer greater freedom to women than do patrilocal and patrilineal societies of the same level of productivity and political development.

A distinct change occurred with the growth of individual and family property in herds, in durable craft objects and trade objects, and in stable, irrigated farm-sites or other forms of heritable wealth. This crystallized in the rise of the state, about 4,000 B.C. With the growth of class society and of male dominance in the ruling class of the state, women's subordination increased, and eventually reached its depths in the patriarchal families of the great agrarian states.

Knowledge of how the family arose is interesting to women because it tells us how we differ from pre-humans, what our past has been, and what have been the biological and cultural limitations from which we are emerging. It shows us how generations of male scholars have distorted or over-interpreted the evidence to bolster beliefs in the inferiority of women's mental processes —for which there is no foundation in fact. Knowing about early families is also important to correct a reverse bias among some feminist writers, who hold that in "matriarchal" societies women were completely equal with or were even dominant over men. For this, too, there seems to be no basis in evidence.

The past of the family does not limit its future. Although the family probably emerged with humanity, neither the family itself nor particular family forms are genetically determined. The sexual division of labor—until recently, universal—need not, and in my opinion should not, survive in industrial society. Prolonged child care ceases to be a basis for female subordination when artificial birth control, spaced births, small families, patent feeding and communal nurseries allow it to be shared by men. Automation and cybernation remove most of the heavy work for which women are less well equipped than men. The exploitation of women that came with the rise of the state and of class society will presumably disappear in post-state, classless society— for which the technological and scientific basis already exists.

The family was essential to the dawn of civilization, allowing a vast qualitative leap forward in cooperation, purposive knowledge, love, and creativeness. But today, rather than enhancing them, the confinement of women in homes and small families—like their subordination in work—artificially limits these human capacities. It may be that the human gift for personal love will make some form of voluntary, long-term mating and of individual devotion between parents and children continue indefinitely, side by side with public responsibility for domestic tasks and for the care and upbringing of children. There is no need to legislate personal relations out of existence. But neither need we fear a social life in which the family is no more.

References

Coult, Allen D. *Cross Tabulations of Murdock's World Ethnographic Sample.* Columbia: University of Missouri Press, 1965.

Fox, Robin. *Kinship and Marriage.* London: Pelican Books, 1967.

Hockett, Charles F., and Robert Ascher. "The Human Revolution." In *Man in Adaptation: The Biosocial Background,* edited by Yehudi A. Cohen. Chicago: Aldine, 1968.

Livingstone, Frank B. "Genetics, Ecology and the Origin of Incest and Exogamy." *Current Anthropology,* February 1969.

Morris, Desmond. *The Naked Ape.* Jonathan Cape, 1967.

Murdock, G. P. "World Ethnographic Sample." *American Anthropologist,* 1957.

Murdock, G. P. *Ethnographic Atlas.* Pittsburgh: University of Pittsburgh, 1967.

Schneider, David M., and Kathleen Gough. *Matrilineal Kinship.* Berkeley and Los Angeles: University of California Press, 1961.

Semyonov, Y. I. "Group Marriage, Its Nature and Role in the Evolution of Marriage and Family Relations." In *Seventh International Congress of Anthropological and Ethnological Sciences,* Vol. IV. Moscow, 1967.

During the past fifteen or twenty years, psychiatry has undergone a conceptual revolution, brought about by researchers and therapists working with and observing whole families. These observations of live family interaction have led to new ways of looking at mental illness, interpersonal relationships, and most significantly, the nature of family life itself. The two main ideas of the new psychiatry are that individuals cannot be understood apart from their social and familial environments, and that families are systems of behavior whose nature cannot be inferred from individual psychology or the larger society. Unfortunately, there is no single article that sums up these developments for the general reader. Nor, indeed, is there consensus or even a common language among workers in this field. For example, some writers see the new family theories as an extension of psychoanalytic theory, others see it as a revolt against the latter. The present article is a review of the development of the family therapy field by one of its leading theoreticians. Haley is a partisan of the point of view that family psychiatry replaces individual psychiatry.

A Review of the Family Therapy Field

Jay Haley

The idea of trying to change a family appeared in the 1950's at the same time as other happenings in the social sciences in America. At midcentury the social sciences became more social: the study of small groups flourished, animals were observed in their natural environments instead of in the zoo or

Reprinted by permission of Grune & Stratton, Inc., and the author from "A Review of the Family Therapy Fields" by Jay Haley in *Changing Families: A Family Therapy Reader* (New York: Grune & Stratton, Inc., 1971), pp. 1–12.

laboratory, psychological experiments were seen as social situations in experimenter-bias studies, businesses began to be thought of as complex systems, mental hospitals were studied as total institutions, and ecology developed as a special field, with man and other creatures looked upon as inseparable from their environments. As part of this shift to a social view, research investigators and people-changers took the unprecedented step of bringing whole families under direct observation. Instead of depending upon what a person said about his family life, the investigator actually observed him interacting with his family. This kind of observation led to a breakthrough in thinking about human problems which has had many consequences. One consequence was the idea of a therapist's intervening to change the ways in which family members deal with one another.

Before observational family research and therapy, no one had tried to describe and measure the habitual behavior of a group of intimates who had a history together and would have a future association. Small group research had been carried out with artificial collections of strangers, and family research had depended upon opinion surveys of family members about their lives. Therapeutic intervention was focused upon changing individuals.

Then for unexplained reasons a number of therapists began to deal with whole families in the 1950's, often without knowing that anyone else was doing so. Many of these people did not write for professional journals or attend meetings, so their work was known only locally, if at all. Curiously, a decade later many experienced family therapists still had not met each other. If they had been introduced, they still had not sat down together to discuss their work and seek a common view on what changing a family is all about.

This movement toward therapy with whole families occurred just when the dynamic concept of the individual, and psychoanalytic treatment, had won power and prestige in the psychiatric establishment after a long struggle. Everyone who was respectable wished to practice psychoanalysis or at least to give psychoanalytically oriented treatment. Consequently, therapy was defined as a form of medical treatment and psychiatrists held the highest status. Social workers and psychologists tended to be thought of as auxiliary personnel (and lay therapists were outside the pale, despite Freud's efforts).

An essential part of the medical model was the idea that a person could be changed if he were plucked out of his social situation and treated individually in a private office or inside a hospital. Once changed, he would return to his social milieu transformed because he had been "cleared" of the intrapsychic problems causing his difficulties. In this model, primary change was effected by providing the "patient" with insight into his unconscious conflicts, thus eliminating the repressive forces which were incapacitating him. The real world of the patient was considered secondary since what was important was his perception of it, his affect, his attitudes, the objects he had introjected, and the conflicts within him programmed by his past. While a science of human behavior was being conceptualized in social terms under the influence of systems theory, the people who were trying to change people were determinedly disregarding the social environment.

Just why a few people-changers broke away from the established ideas about psychopathology and change in the 1950's is unclear. Often treating whole families caused them to be penalized by professional isolation. It would be comfortable to assume that such therapists turned to family treatment because they were not getting results with psychoanalytically oriented therapy, yet that fact has not persuaded other therapists to change their ways. Sometimes family treatment seems to have come about because a therapist brought family members together when he was puzzled by something said by his patient. Though the family was interviewed only to gain information to help one individual belonging to it, what the therapist saw happening among the family members caused him to arrive at a new concept of the cause of human problems. Or sometimes a therapist noticed that, when his patient did change in individual therapy, there were consequences within the family— someone else developed symptoms, or the family began to come apart. Concern over this kind of change forced the therapist to think of the social function of psychopathology.

Often the shift to a family orientation was caused by a combination of factors. In my own case, two sets of circumstances occurred at the same times. I was a member of Gregory Bateson's project on communication, and we were doing research on schizophrenia. We had brought a schizophrenic patient together with his parents to try to find out why the patient could not be with them on visiting day for more than a few minutes without collapsing in an anxiety state. It was an information-gathering session, not a family treatment interview. Yet what we observed so changed our views about treating schizophrenics that by the beginning of the next year we had started a systematic program of treating families of schizophrenics. Simultaneously, I was doing brief therapy in private practice, and it became impossible for me not to notice that rapid change of a severe symptom in a patient produced instability in a marriage and family. Looking back on that period now, everyone was groping not only toward the idea that the family had something to do with pathology in a patient but also toward the idea that one could attempt to change the family. We began to learn that a number of therapists in different parts of the country, quite independent of one another, were also treating families. They were gaining considerable experience in this new endeavor, were collecting disciples, and were becoming more confident about their results.

As family therapists began to see a psychiatric problem as an expression of a family, they found that they had to reconceptualize therapy. To change an individual required one way of thinking, and to change the interaction among family members required quite another. While groping toward a new notion of what therapy was about, some family therapists thought at first that individual therapy might be appropriate for some cases and family therapy for others. Family therapy was beginning to be defined as interviewing a whole family together, and individual therapy as the treatment of one person. However, as family therapists began to be more flexible in their practices and clearer in their ideas, they realized that traditional individual therapy was actually *one* way to intervene in a family, whether the therapist thought of it that way or not. It was the intrusion of an outsider into a family even if the therapist considered himself to be dealing only with one person's fantasies. Some family therapists developed this view when they had to deal with families after one member had been in long-term individual therapy with consequences to the whole family.

By the end of the 1950's it was becoming clearer that family therapy was a different concept of change, rather than merely an additional method of treatment to be added to individual and group therapy. The focus of family treatment was no longer on changing an individual's perception, his affect, or his behavior, but on changing the structure of a family and the sequences of behavior among a group of intimates. With this shift, it became clearer that neither traditional individual therapy nor group therapy with artificial groups was relevant to the goals and techniques of family therapists. The problem was to change the living situation of a person, not to pluck him out of that situation and try to change *him*.

In the process of thinking in new ways about a human problem, family therapists had to revise their views on the importance of the real world. Often this meant unlearning what they had been taught in training. Thinking that a person's problem was with his maternal introject was different from thinking his problem was with his wife. Although it seems strange now, a child with a school phobia might be diagnosed and treated with no concern for the real situation in his home or, for that matter, in his school. An adolescent acting out in a hospital was examined with no consideration of his situation in the hospital. It was necessary to discard many of the notions about the causes and cures of phobias when it was discovered that a wife who feared to leave her home alone had a problem with a marital relationship which was confining her. Previously it had been assumed that everyone faces much the same situation and that people could be classified as normal, neurotic, or psychotic on the basis of how they handled that situation. Now it was discovered that everyone does not face the same situation but is adapting to a unique one.

A theoretical framework for these new ways of thinking was difficult to conceptualize. Actually observing families and trying to change them produced information which had never been gathered before. Rather than family therapy's developing because of a theory, it appeared that people were struggling to find a theory to fit their practices. There was no theoretical model which could be used to describe behavior in natural, ongoing groups, and there was no language for describing their relationships.

Moreover, investigators in the 1950's faced a continually changing unit of observation. They first shifted from the individual to the dyad. But the dyad proved unsatisfactory, and they moved to the triad. This was the period of the emphasis upon the nuclear family. Then with the recognition of the importance of extended kin and the social context of the family, the unit shifted to an even larger ecological network.

With each of these steps both researchers and therapists sought an appropriate social model. Group theory based upon artificial groups seemed to be of no use, since it did not involve habitual behavior among intimates with a history and future together. Role theory was popular with some investigators, but others thought it was too much a characterization of individual positions and could not deal with sequences between people. Other investigators tried information theory, or explored the language of symbolic logic, or experimented with games theory or learning theory. The most consistently popular model was a systems theory derived from cybernetics. This model could deal with interacting elements responding to one another in a self-corrective way, which is the way family members seemed to behave. Communications terminology began to be part of the language of this field as it was of other social sciences, and slow-motion films of family behavior were analyzed for body movement communication as well as linguistic and verbal behavior. Yet at the end of the decade no particular theoretical model was accepted by all the various investigators and therapists in the field. This lack of consensus might have been because they came from different professional backgrounds, or it might have been because the investigators worked in different geographic areas and some had not even met each other. Everyone talked about the family, but in a mixture of tongues.

Despite these difficulties, by the 1960's, the early pioneers had established a secure enough beachhead for family therapy and research so that others could follow them. The family view had been either ignored or opposed by the general psychiatric field, but it was beginning to be taken up in the larger cities and even some universities. Quite a bit of observational family research literature was developing, but little was being written about family therapy technique. Often the therapists knew how to treat a family but did not know how to describe what they had done for the printed page.

It now seems apparent that the 1960's was the period when family therapy and research left the pioneering stage, consolidated a body of knowledge and technique, and began to intrude seriously in the general clinical field. Since it takes about twenty years for an idea to enter a university, the decade 1960-1970 brought about the introduction of family concepts to the clinical programs of many departments of psychiatry, psychology, and social work. Generally, it is the younger generation of clinicians who have become interested in family therapy, particularly psychiatric residents and graduate students in psychology. In many parts of the country such students are treating families while their teachers have no experience to help them. This generation of students seems less interested in esoteric explorations of pathology and more concerned with what can be done. Family therapy appeals to them because it is an action-oriented form of treatment.

The entrance of family therapy ideas in the respectable psychiatric arena had consequences which were not anticipated. We have begun to realize, for example, that the status and function of the disciplines in the helping professions are based on the idea that the individual is the focus of diagnosis and treatment. When the unit of treatment shifts from the individual to the family, the disciplines become undisciplined and no one quite knows what profession should be looked on as an authority on what is wrong and what should be done. The change is particularly painful to psychiatrists, who have had higher status for many years because the medical model was the basis for individual diagnosis.

Another problem which is both practical and theoretical has been the change in the definition of the family. By the beginning of the 1960's, many family therapists were widening their focus to include not only the nuclear family but also the extended kin in family treatment. Later in the 1960's the unit of treatment broadened still more. The "family" language began to be applied to all systems with a history and a future, whether blood relatives, business staffs, or political systems. In relation to family therapy, the context of the family began to be taken into account, so that at times the unit of treatment was a larger ecological one yielding network descriptions and network therapy. Some family therapists realized that they had been talking about a family in isolation much as they had once talked about the isolated individual. Now a wider area of concern is being considered, partly because of the explosive force of community problems and the needs of mental health centers, which are responsible for a wider group than the family, and partly as the result of a systems orientation, which inevitably forces an awareness of the influence of context. Over this brief ten-year period we have already developed a generation gap, with the older family therapist talking about "pure" and "deep" family therapy of the single family and the younger family therapist talking about treating ecological systems.

Also in the 1960's the conditioning therapists began to move to join the family therapists. From setting up reinforcement schedules with individuals, a few conditioners began to program parents to reinforce the behavior of their children differently. This brought them into the family therapy field. One curious difference between conditioners and family therapists is the unit focused upon. Unlike psychodynamic therapists, conditioners have moved from the individual to the dyad, but they do not think in larger units. Learning theory has only a dyadic framework. Conditioners do not describe a child in a triangle with his parents or in terms of his larger ecology. They think of the way the mother reinforces the child and the way the father does, but they do not describe the conflict between the parents about the child.

Attempts at formal training in family therapy also began in the 1960's. This brought questions, such as "What ideas about the family are relevant to therapy?" and "How can an experienced family therapist teach what he knows how to do but has difficulty in describing?" When it is recognized that family therapy is not a method of treatment but a new orientation to the human dilemma, it is clear that any number of methods might be taught and used. With experience, family therapists often shift from a method approach and become more problem oriented, adapting what they do to the problem that has come in the door. Since students like to have a "method" which they can learn, family therapy is difficult for them to grasp. They must absorb a new orientation which is different from the one taught them in school, and they must learn a problem approach which can only be learned from experience with different problems.

Aside from such practical difficulties, a diverse conglomeration of ideas in the field continues; the 1960's did not bring about more certainty over what body of theories would achieve primacy. In the discourse among family therapists, concepts drawn from communication theory, ethology, anthropology, sociology, and learning theory occur as frequently as traditional psychological concepts. Everyone hesitates to construct a new language.

The mystery of what causes change has been only slightly clarified. Many new therapists beginning to treat families could abandon the idea that transference interpretations or insight into unconscious processes cause change. (Often they abandoned these concepts without realizing that this could also mean abandoning the theory of repression.) But as former individual therapists began treating families, they learned that some experienced family therapists were even doubting that helping family members understand how they deal with each other is related to change. It is beginning to be argued by many family therapists that talking to family members about understanding each other is necessary because something must be talked about and families expect this form of discussion, but that change really comes about through interactional processes set off when a therapist intervenes actively and directively in particular ways in a family system, and quite independently of the awareness of the participants about how they have been behaving.

Research in the 1960's explored different types of families, which resulted in more uncertainty about whether a typology of families is possible. Rather than establishing a typology, the trend is toward greater appreciation of stages of family development as a crucial factor in the development of symptomatology. Differences between families are being examined in terms of family crisis points rather than just in terms of type of family. With this emphasis, there is increasing awareness of the relationship between the ecological context of the family and the way the family members respond to one another. To explain what is happening in a family, the context of treatment, whether hospital involvement or the intrusion of multiple helpers quarreling over territory in the family, is becoming a necessary part of the description. Family diagnosis now includes the therapist, or the researcher, since family members are evidently not only responding to each other but also, simultaneously, to the situation in which they are observed. Some family therapists now argue more confidently that a "type" of family does not produce a "type" of patient, but that a disturbance in a family at a certain stage *plus* an external intervention combine to produce the symptomatic behavior apparent in one or more family members. For example, adolescent schizophrenia can be seen as a product of a stage of family life, when the child is disengaging from his parents, *and* a particular kind of outside intervention, which brings about a failure in successful disengagement and therefore strange behavior.

Perhaps one of the major discoveries of the 1960's was that of the importance of treating families at a moment of crisis, since structural changes are most easily brought about in crisis. If a treatment program subdues and stabilizes the family, change is more difficult. The leisurely pace of information-gathering diagnostic interviews, long-term expectations of the therapist, or the use of drugs and hospitalization to calm the atmosphere is being seen as a handicap to effective treatment. To change a stabilized, miserable situation and create space for individual growth of family members, the therapist often must induce a crisis which creates instability. When hospitals are involved in the stabilization process, this is hardly possible.

Another important struggle for the field of family therapy has been the necessity of preventing the distortion of family therapy ideas as they become more widely accepted. Now that family therapy is becoming respectable and is being taken up by the establishment, it is apparent that much which has been gained can be lost. A new idea about treatment which is introduced into a traditional psychiatric department in a university not infrequently is transformed to look remarkably like an old idea. The current attempt to save psychoanalysis by broadening its concepts to include a family view may have an effect on family therapy similar to that of the air pollution of a large city on a fresh breeze. Watching what is done to family therapy in a number of psychiatric departments and social work schools, one sees a grand confusion of individual and family concepts and goals of treatment.

Often such places seem to take up family therapy not because of a concern for effective treatment, but rather because they see that the medical model is being abandoned by therapists in the field and are trying to catch up, or because their funds for training require them to emphasize community work, where the family approach is more relevant than traditional individual therapy. Perhaps the community endeavors might save some of the family ideas even when they have been put through the political process in a university or a psychiatric network in a large city. In time, social work schools might even give up training their clinicians to be psychoanalysts and teach them something about changing the family and the community, as some nursing schools are now doing.

The family view poses a difficult digestive problem for the established institutions training clinicians, particularly the traditional inpatient centers. Having tremendous personal and financial investments in psychodynamic theory and practice, the staff cannot be expected to like the idea that family therapy represents a discontinuous change in basic premises about treatment and requires acceptance of new ideas and new forms of therapeutic intervention. If this is so, they will have wasted years of training in a diagnostic system that is not relevant to therapy. It seems more reasonable to believe that family therapy is really a variation on something Freud proposed, to argue that family systems are easily explained by more sophisticated ego theory, and to pretend that family problems can be resolved with transference interpretations. The need to salvage the past and defend status positions forces such institutions to exclude and dilute what is new in the field and to obscure the important issues.

Let me offer an example of how different the family view is from the traditional psychiatric posture in an inpatient institution. Rather than emphasize the average state hospital, which is often a custodial dustbin run by people with no knowledge of therapy, let us take an inpatient unit in a university psychiatry department. Such places have a large staff, considerable funds, and supposedly sufficient knowledge of therapy to be accredited to train young psychiatrists. I have visited many such places recently, and an example from one of them illustrates how discontinuous the family, or ecological, view is from the psychiatric orientation still being perpetuated in the better universities.

A young man had been hospitalized because he was possibly schizophrenic, was acting helpless, was involved in a dependent homosexual relationship, had severe anxiety spells, was possibly suicidal, and had dropped out of graduate school before completing his academic requirements. It was generally agreed by the staff that he should be hospitalized for two or three years and receive intensive individual psychoanalytically oriented therapy. This therapy would transform him and he would return to society as a mature, responsible individual—the goal described in the case protocol. Despite the fact that this institution had never reported, or even examined, whether such treatment of similar cases ever produced mature, responsible individuals, everyone assumed this was the proper treatment. Because the staff was up to date, they also recommended that the young man's parents be placed in a parents' group, apparently thinking this would help in the treatment. There was no theory or rationale of how this would help. From a traditional psychiatric view, what was being offered was the treatment of choice and it was fortunate that the patient's family could afford the great expense of the best psychiatric treatment.

According to the family orientation that has developed these last two decades, this traditional treatment program is absolutely contraindicated. It is based on an ideology which assumes that the patient's problem is internal and his social situation is secondary. The family view adopts quite the opposite view—the young man's problem is his social situation and his internal dynamics are a response to that situation. These two points of view represent a discontinuous change in thinking about human problems and how to change them.

From the family therapy view, the kind of treatment recommended above should fail. (There is increasing evidence that it does; the cure rate of long-term psychoanalytically oriented therapy in inpatient institutions has not matched the record of spontaneous remission.) The logic of the family view derives from the idea that a person is responding to his social situation, which must change before he can change. If the artificial environment in which a person is placed not only encourages psychopathology but includes factors which prevent change, the problem is compounded for a patient. The goal of treatment was to change the young man to a mature, responsible individual. Yet the treatment placed him in an artificial hospital situation where such a response was not possible. To be mature and responsible, one must make decisions about how to deal with large and small events in daily life. In the hospital, the young man is not required, and does not have the opportunity, to support himself as a responsible person must. Nor can he continue his academic education to prepare to support himself. He is not responsible even for elementary decisions; he does not have to decide when to get up in the morning, what to eat at mealtime, when to have mealtimes, or when to go to bed at night. These daily events are all decided for him, along with all his other activities, by people supposedly helping him to learn to be mature. He does not have to, nor can he, choose the friends he will associate with, as other people do, because they are chosen by the hospital. He does not have to work out the problem of courtship behavior with other young people, either male or female, because sexual behavior on the ward is forbidden (or defined as acting out). He does not have to, nor can he, keep up with his peers in a rapidly changing contemporary society; each day in the hospital he is falling behind his contemporaries in the real world.

Perhaps most important is the enforced dependency. Young people usually achieve independence and maturity when they support themselves and are no longer financially dependent upon their parents. This is a major step toward emotional independence and maturity. By the nature of hospitalization, the young man is tied more tightly in a dependency relationship to his parents. His father and mother must pay several thousand dollars a month for his hospitalization and treatment, making a financial sacrifice and so increasing his obligation to them as well as his dependency upon them. Whatever benefit he receives in the hospital he must owe to them (while the hospital staff often imply that he should reject his parents because they treat him badly). Should the young man become fond of his individual therapist and establish a "deep" relationship with him, there is the constant threat that his parents will deprive him of that friend by cutting off the money for his treatment. In this way the movement toward closeness with someone outside the family— which is normally a move toward independence from the family—is done in a setting which drives the young man toward more dependence upon his parents.

The parents in this case were to be seen separately from the young man in a parents' group, where they apparently pass the time of day with other parents who have hospitalized children. There is no therapeutic intervention to resolve the entanglements of child and parents as they attempt to disengage from each other. In fact the total structure of the treatment situation forces financial entanglement whether the young man and parents like it or not. Within this peculiar, dependent setting, the staff encourages the young man to be more responsible and condemns him if he behaves childishly. Viewed from the family, or ecological, orientation, this is a Kafka-like treatment situation in which the goals of therapy cannot be achieved because of the nature of the social system set up to achieve them.

If a family therapist is brought into this situation as a consultant, what advice can he offer? No information is given him which he can use to understand the case; psychological tests or interviews with the individual patient provide little of use, and there is no data on how the parents and patient behave with each other. Besides having no information to help him understand the problem, the family therapist consultant cannot see how this kind of hospital situation could bring about change. If he suggests that the patient be immediately discharged and treated within his natural social setting, the hospital staff will inevitably protest that the patient might do something disastrous. The argument is offered that hospitalization saves the patient's life because he might commit suicide (even though hospitalization does not prevent suicide and sometimes does not even delay it). The problem is compounded when a virtue is made of interminable treatment by insisting that the patient should be hospitalized for two or three years no matter how he responds because that will be "deeper" therapy. If a family therapist attempts to work within this setting, he must either change his ideas so that they are palatable to the establishment or he must produce a change in the orientation of the entire staff of the hospital and the resident training program as well as in the patient's family.

The fact that traditional psychiatry has no way other than hospitalization to treat a difficult young man like the one described is a serious defect. What makes the problem worse is the fact that it is almost impossible for psychiatrists to innovate other modes of treatment, even if they acknowledged that hospitalization is a failure, because young psychiatrists are being trained within this kind of setting. Since they do not learn other modes of therapy for difficult young people, they must logically end up recommending hospitalization even if they suspect that such treatment is not usually successful. Within such a treatment structure, young psychiatrists learn to focus upon fantasies and to ignore the real world. They think in terms of crazy individuals rather than crazy situations. Such learning today is likely to make them ineffective therapists in the clinics and practices where they will face real life problems when they finish training. They get no experience in crisis treatment, since hospitalization stabilizes crisis, and they learn nothing about working with families. Despite (or because of) their thorough knowledge of diagnosis, their ability to estimate ego strength, their concern with organicity, and their understanding of the myths of etiology, they are handicapped when they attempt therapy. The young patient will also be handicapped when he leaves the hospital to face his real problems because he will carry the stigma of being a former mental patient along with his other unsolved social dilemmas.

Experienced family therapists often find themselves opposing a structure in which there are large financial investments, and debating with hospital staffs about psychodynamic concepts they had found irrelevant to therapy many years ago. It is becoming evident that the more respectable the field of family therapy becomes, the more problems it will meet. To maintain the diversity of ideas of family therapy, as well as their integrity, as they are absorbed and transformed by the establishment will be an increasingly difficult task. As I look back, the work seemed easier when the family field was more ignored and less popular. Looking forward, I experience a curious uncertainty about what will happen to family therapy technique and theory in the decades to come.

Most social theorists believe that physical force or its threat is both rare and ineffective as a way of running a society or a social institution, particularly the family. Goode challenges this view. He argues that the family is a power system, like any other social unit. He examines the role of force in maintaining "legitimate" family arrangements, such as the status of women and children, and also illegitimate force in the family such as assault, murder, and child abuse.

Force and Violence in the Family | *William J. Goode*

Like all other social units or systems, the family is a power system. All rest to some degree on force or its threat, whatever else may be their foundations. Perhaps many rulers have believed that their regimes did not, and that they used physical force only on those who were evil, but those at the bottom of the power and class system, the disadvantaged, the deprived, women, and children have always known better.

Our aim of applying this bit of folk wisdom to the family is handicapped because in no field of social science have systematic observations been made about how force or its threat affects day-to-day interaction among human beings. Sociologists have not filled this gap, since they have been mainly exploiting the fact that much of social behavior is determined by norms, attitudes, and values, by the evaluations people make, by what people want or dislike, approve or deprecate. However, observation of the phenomenon is difficult, and I cannot fill that gap here. At this stage, I shall rather examine the problem theoretically, and analyze the empirical data on only one sub-segment, which is expressed in overt force or violence. On the other hand, a theoretical statement will at least point to the sets of forces that I believe can be observed, and that if understood properly would interpret social behavior more adequately.

I should prefer to use the term "power" here, but unfortunately that has come to mean a ragbag of phenomena and forces, usually the ability to impose one's will upon another in spite of his resistance. Since one can impose one's will with a variety of resources, from love to murder, the term is too broad. (See, for example, the conceptual analysis in Cartwright, 1959.) Since all of us have *some* power, even when someone has imposed his will upon us, the term is also too narrow. The term is tempting, since it carries a penumbra of references to strength, force, and domination, and indeed is often used to suggest force. However, I shall forego the use of the term because of these objections, and shall use the phrase, "force and its threat."

Reprinted by permission from "Force and Violence in the Family" by William J. Goode, *Journal of Marriage and the Family,* November 1971, pp. 624–635.

For the sake of simplicity I shall use the term "force" as my substitute, and "overt force" when I want to refer specifically to the actual exercise of physical force.

Force or its threat is used in all social systems because it is one of four major sets of resources by which people can move others to serve their ends. Three of these have played a large role in grand social science theory because they are also the major bases of all stratification systems: i.e., economic variables, prestige or respect, and force and its threat, sometimes called power. A fourth can be called likability, attractiveness, friendship, or love. (All of these can be found, under one label or another, in most of the classical theorists. For a more recent use of them, see Etzioni, 1961.) All of these are major elements in all family systems, or any other social system. All are necessary social means for the ends of both individuals and groups. All can be acquired and expended; all can be exchanged to some degree for each other. Some people and groups possess more of these social resources than others do, and are thereby better able to achieve their goals.

Of these, force and its threat have been in poor repute among social philosophers, social analysts, and especially family counselors. However my aim is not to praise or condemn, but to explore their impact on human action. Napoleon is given credit for wisdom because he is supposed to have commented that one can do anything with a bayonet except sit upon it. However thoughtful, the remark must at least be qualified by the obvious historical fact that his regime was nevertheless founded on force and fell apart when he could no longer muster enough.

Rulers officially deplore force because they are convinced that their domination is based on justice, but they use force just the same. Philosophers deplore force because they see people are most tempted to apply it when they wish to gain more than others believe they ought to have, i.e., when they wish to impose injustice on others.

Social analysts often try to prove that force is simply an ineffective way of controlling others. This is partly incorrect, as thousands of years of conquest, imperialism, exploitation, and injustice prove amply. They also miss the main point, since no society is ever based on force *alone*. We pose the question falsely if we ask whether the family or any other system will survive if its sole foundation is force, since no such system is likely to occur or to last long if it does. Alone, it *is* ineffective.

But this is very different from asking how useful force is in getting things done, or where it is to be observed in the family system. This is the focus of my inquiry here.

In the analysis that follows, we wish to examine both the legitimate and the illegitimate applications of force in the family, i.e., both force and violence, and also the more subtle elements of family structure where force plays a role, though no overt use of force is actually visible. I believe these latter cases are much more important, but I want to explain all these patterns, both illegitimate and legitimate, violent and peaceable, by the same set of variables, within a framework of exchange theory.

Force is primarily thought of as a deterrent, i.e., it stops others from doing something we disapprove, either at the time they do it, or in the future because of a punishment in the past or a threatened punishment in the future. It is equally obvious, however, that force or its threat can persuade others to *do* something, not merely to avoid doing something. It is evident that we can at a minimum stop a weaker person from a disapproved act by holding him, or any one at all by killing him. Even if we never go so far, we can by the threat of force at least alter the other person's calculation of the anticipated gain from a specific action. In our effort to gain compliance we may offer both a reward—love, respect, or money—and a threat of force, and we know that the latter will be one of the variables influencing the decision. The threat may be unwise or ineffective at times, but it does alter the person's view of his possible cost/reward ratio. As an element in social exchange, it alters the perceived payoffs.

But this way of expressing the general relationship between force and compliance in the family still suggests, because its language is imprecise, that both parties in the social interaction are conscious of force, and that we presume the actual use of overt force will be visible. It also suggests that force only occurs when someone wants to prevent another from carrying out some deviant, improper, or wrong act, as when a child must be forced to obey. In fact, force may be used in favor of an act, and even one disapproved by the society.* And most force is not visible; we observe few acts of violence in any given day.

Because people have been socialized to accept the family structure in which they live, and because they take that social structure for granted, they do not test whether force would be applied if they challenged it. They know in advance they would fail. In most families, the structure is not overthrown, because it is viewed as inalterable or at best the only real alternative. Thus, force plays a role even when no deviant act is actually committed. The rebellious child or wife knows that the father or husband is stronger, and can call upon outsiders who will support that force with more force. Knowing the costs and the certainty of failure, the individual sees no likelihood of altering the terms of exchange.

Let us consider a few of such family patterns where we are unlikely to observe the application of force, but where its threat creates a relatively stable, unchallenged set of understandings, behaviors, and imbalances of in-

---

*E.g., parents may use the threat of force to persuade a child to finish his homework; a parent may whip a child to force him to lie to outside authorities.

fluence or dominance. For example, if in a patrilineal polygamous society an older woman were to announce that she is henceforth to be treated as the leader of her patriline, tried to sell its cattle, started to give orders, set dates for rituals, or choose a chief, very likely she would be beaten or treated as insane. Similarly, if a child in our own society were to claim the headship of his family, give orders to his parents or siblings, try to write checks on his father's account, to trade in the automobile for a new one, the same result would occur.* That is, not only can his parents overpower him physically as a rule, but even if he is physically stronger they can call on superior force from other members of the family, as well as from outsiders such as policemen and juvenile authorities. The force or threat they command is not only their own strength but that of the community, which will back up the traditional family patterns.

Similarly, the mother who abandons her children, the father who runs off with the children, the wife or husband who takes a second spouse, the child who beats up his mother, the adolescent girl who wishes to spend a weekend with her boyfriend against the will of her parents, the wife who wishes to change the family domicile without the consent of her husband, all can be and sometimes are restrained by either force or its threat, if not from family members then at their request by the community through its command over force.†

Such a list is not meant to be exhaustive. Rather it alerts us to the many and diverse mandates and restrictions on all of us in our family roles, which are ultimately backed by force. They include parental rights and obligations, laws of custody, property rights, traditions and laws about the freedom of children, the mutual rights and obligations of husbands and wives, and testamentary laws and traditions, among others, and they define to a considerable extent the institution of the family in our society. They do so in other societies as well. A recent summary of laws of this type may be found in Clark, 1968; the European case is stated in Boschan, 1963.

---

*Note that in some cases of this type, the son's physical possession of his father's credit cards or other documents does not give him the power to engage in such transactions: specifically, he would have no recourse if a clerk or salesman refused. On the other hand, ultimately the real owner of such documents can call upon the courts and other agencies (e.g., corporations which would not wish to lose his business) and thus obtain recognition of his rights. Since everyone knows all this, clerks and salesmen behave as they do, i.e., they will not ordinarily treat the son as a surrogate for the parent without parental authorization.

†An interesting illustration of this occurred when the Soviets tried to change the family structure of Soviet Central Asia through immediate liberation of the Moslem women. Husbands' control over wives, which had been absolute, was declared officially ended by a series of emancipation laws. Control by force remained the crucial variable, however, since husbands were able to prevent their wives physically from going to the civil authorities. See Massell, 1968.

They function to shore up those family patterns by imposing strong sanctions when an individual tries to reject them. They are often expressed in laws, and thus are ultimately backed by the courts and the police system. They are similar to the force that maintains the economic system: the individual cannot invade the monopoly of a public utility, import forbidden goods, take over another person's property, sell drugs without quality controls, and so on. We do not ordinarily *see* force applied in these situations, because most people take this structure for granted, as part of the cosmos; they know they are likely to lose if they challenge it.

But such family patterns are backed not only by the state, just as laws generally are not supported only by policemen. Friends, neighbors, members of the community, in-laws and relatives, and other members of the conjugal family are also likely to intervene.* They are most likely to intervene with their resources of friendship, prestige, or even economic services and goods, either as promises or threats. Nevertheless, they can and do intervene with force and its threat as well.†

We should also see a further distinction here, between the weakness of a family member because he cannot command as *much* force as another— the adolescent boy commands *some* because of his own strength and can also defend himself from brutality by calling on outsiders—and the weakness because of an inability to command others to move in the desired direction. Thus, a husband can no longer sell his wife's property, as he once could, because her signature is required. He cannot successfully command her to vote as he wishes, or even to stop having movie dates with a friend whether male or female. This distinction is not, of course, an analytic one, since ultimately they both center on relative amounts of force, but pragmatically they differ, since the person who is commanded does not ordinarily have to act, to fight back actively; he or she need only fail to comply, and outsiders will not act in support of the command.

I do not think it is necessary but I shall repeat, that individual families and family systems are not maintained by force alone, any more than other social systems are. Daily role interaction also rests upon the constant flow of respect, affection, and services or gifts each family member makes to the

---

*Where outside community controls are not effective, force is much more visible. Oscar Lewis' (1965) study of Puerto Rican slum dwellers provides an example: "In the Rios family, uncontrolled rage, aggression, violence and even bloodshed are not uncommon." Numerous specific instances of this are related throughout the long record of participant observation of this extended family.

†Note the control implicit in the common pattern of pounding on a common apartment wall, when a family (usually husband and wife) is having a violent argument. It is a threat to call in outside authorities such as the police; it is also a reprimand, since "nice people" do not engage in such arguments. When individuals are persuaded to lower the noise level of their quarrel, violence is less likely to occur.

others. We can nevertheless carry out the mental experiment of imagining away *all* the supports of force I have mentioned, or imagining entirely different ones.

If, for example, no husband were able to use his own force or that of family members, relatives, neighbors, or the community to press his children toward obedience at any age, to eject from his house a man who is courting his wife, to threaten his wife for welcoming flirtations or going on dates with another, to press her to stay in the domicile he has chosen, to persuade her not to abandon the children when she would like to go off alone, to take care of the home and children, to avoid running up bankrupting bills with their creditors, it is easy to see that a substantial part of the structural strength of the family would be undermined. This is comparable to the place of deterrence in criminal actions: we know not everyone would suddenly begin robbing and stealing, if no force were usable—but many *would,* and many others would soon follow, upon seeing that those who took this greater freedom were not punished or deterred.

Socialization

Of course, most people have not only been trained to know that these structures are real and strong, and must therefore be accepted, but they have also been socialized to believe they are both right and desirable. In addition, the day-to-day social exchanges, shaped as they are by the existing force-based structures, offer better payoffs to those who do comply. On the other hand, it is equally important to emphasize that force and its threat have perhaps even more impact on the process of socialization than in normal adult interaction within the family. In this process by which we transform infants into people, inculcating in them the values, norms, and role habits of the family and society, or more specifically by which children come to accept as right and desirable the family patterns we approve, not only do we use force and threat in order to socialize our children, we also teach them thereby that force is useful, and we do in fact train them in the use of force and violence.*

Observational studies of childrearing are understandably rare, but no very sharp eye is needed to know that American parents typically use force on their children from the earliest ages on. As against the widespread denunciations of permissiveness and love in childrearing over the past generation—Agnew is only the most recent, loud-mouthed, and ill-informed—and in

---

*It is in daily life, and especially in the life of children, that the human propensity for violence is founded; we now suspect that much of that excess of violence which distinguishes man from animals is created in him by those child-training methods which set one part of him against another." (Erikson, 1969, p. 234)

spite of a probable slow decline in violent beatings over the past half-century or more, in fact love and permissiveness have not displaced force as a prime basis for molding U.S. children. Indeed, since parents themselves were trained to use and especially to threaten force, they cannot easily cast off that lesson when they confront an unwilling child.

Like other animals, man learns quickly from punishment. Doubtless this is a genetic inheritance of great survival value in the evolution of the species. An animal that did not learn almost instantaneously that fire burns, falls kill or maim, or a powerful male will slash if opposed, would stand little chance of living long. Punishment also constricts, since the fear it generates inhibits exploration: as Twain remarked, the cat that sits on a hot stove won't sit on a hot stove again, but may never sit on a cold one, either. In any event, the learning is quick and powerful.

The learning is also not merely cognitive, not simply a prediction. It is also emotional. The child learns that punishment will follow, but he also acquires a revulsion against a wide range of forbidden acts, an anxiety when he thinks of doing them, a feeling that they are undesirable and not pleasant. This effect is most striking, perhaps, in the area of sex, where early punishments color and distort later expressions of love, sexuality, and trust throughout the adult's life. However, the effect is general, and accounts for the depth of our commitment to the norms by which we live and by which we judge others morally and ethically.

I want to emphasize, however, that I am not speaking only of beatings, spankings, or blows, but any form of force or its threat. To underscore this, childrearing among the Japanese may be noted in passing. By contrast with the United States, one almost never sees a youngster being hit, but many Americans have marveled at what they see as the docility and "good behavior" of Japanese children. On the other hand, the child is not left alone, is not typically commanded from several rooms away, is guided through ritual bowing and other movements, is severely restricted in his explorations —in short, he learns early that the social space in which he will not be deterred, confined, or moved is very small indeed. He will rarely be left alone.*

The Japanese case is especially instructive, since it points up the great difficulties in measuring force when it so rarely expresses itself in overt physical shoving, hitting, or hurting. In every social system, the same measure-

---

*A brief sketch of "Japanese Family Structure and System of Obligations" can be found in Caudill (1952). "The main teaching and disciplinary techniques are teasing and ridicule—physical punishment is seldom used" (p. 30). A field study of "Taira: An Okinawan Village" by Thomas and Hatsumi Maretzki (1963) corroborates this, adding that threats are much more common than the actual occurrence of spanking or other physical punishment. See also the studies reported in *Families East and West* (Hill and Konig, 1970).

ment problem faces us. For example, the captain of a modern ship has a great deal of power (e.g., he can order the confinement of a crewman or passenger), but only rarely does he feel called upon to express it by the actual use of physical force. In socialization, parents may only rarely spank a child, but the child at least knows that he can be overwhelmed. As the columnist Jimmy Breslin remarked, in a discussion of the modern student revolt, "Why shouldn't I have been afraid of my parents? They were bigger and stronger than I, and I didn't have a nickel in my pocket." The problem is intensified, as noted earlier, by the fact that compliance is elicited from others not only because of force or the threat of force, but also through the daily exchanges of services, gifts and money, deference and respect, and love or affection. Consequently, we cannot measure the amount of force by simply noting the amount of compliance or conformity.

On the other hand, we can at least note in passing two sets of relationships: 1) between the command of power or force and other social resources; and 2) between physical punishment in childrearing and various other family variables. These do not solve our problem, but at least give us some information with which to think more productively about the place of force in the family as it shapes the terms of exchanges there.

Within the family itself, the harsh fact must be faced that the member with the greater strength and willingness to use it commands more force than others do. This is usually the father,* and in most cases it will also be the parents as compared with the children.† Since more husbands and parents are willing to use overt force in the lower class, they possess thereby an advantage as compared to their counterparts in other classes.‡

On the other hand, they may be impelled to use overt force because they lack other resources that yield power or force to middle or upper class parents and husbands. Most people do not willingly choose overt force when

---

*Lewis (1965) reports in the lower class Puerto Rican case that "The women show more aggressiveness and a greater violence of language and behavior than men." The women are also more likely to have greater resources in jobs and control of their families' loyalty.

†A summary of studies of the relation of class differences in socialization to differences in childrearing practices can be found in Bronfenbrenner (1958). He concludes that middle-class parents tend to use less punishment and rely more on appeals to guilt and the threat of the withdrawal of love.

A more recent study of 709 mothers in the city of Nottingham, England, showed that 56 percent of the mothers of one-year-olds in the highest class studied claimed they never hit their children as opposed to 35 percent in the lowest class (Newson, 1963).

‡Note however that this relationship may change in late adolescence, when the boy may become bigger and stronger than either parent. In most nonindustrial societies, the boy was given some adult responsibilities then or earlier. In industrial societies, they are sent away to schools and colleges, or allowed to take jobs independently. This is also a period when severe challenges to parental authority occur, if youngsters stay at home.

they command other means, because the costs of using force are high in any social system, but especially in the family, where it may destroy the possibility of achieving other goals than mere conformity, e.g., spontaneous affection and respect. Consequently, it is a general rule that the greater the other resources an individual can command, the more force he *can* muster, but the less he will actually deploy or use force in an *overt* manner. The husband in the middle or upper class family commands more force, in spite of his lesser willingness to use his own physical strength, because he possesses far more other social resources. His greater social prestige in the larger society and the family, his larger economic possessions, and his stronger emphasis on the human relations techniques of counter-deference, affection and communication give him greater influence generally, so that he does not have to call upon the force or its threat that he can in fact muster if he chooses, through kin, neighbors, or the police and courts.

However, we can at least assert that the same variables generate a greater command of force in family relations as create more of what is usually called "influence" in the larger society: success, prestige, and position outside the family; age; being male; control over property, money, gifts, jobs and services; living up to the ideals of the family and thereby engendering trust and loyalty; skills in understanding and communicating with others; political authority; intelligence and relevant information; friendship, love and attractiveness; and so on. Such resources command force within the family and also yield more outside support (both force and other kinds) when a direct family confrontation takes place. Of course the family member who possesses more of them can also have greater impact on the socialization process when he chooses.

Because family analysts deplore the use of physical force on children, they have carried out many studies designed to ascertain its effects. Few studies have obtained data from children, and I know of none that have reported the opinions of children about its consequences. In any event, since measures of the amount and frequency of force used are lacking, the results could not be expected to be very consistent from one study to another. I shall at this time merely list in passing a number of the hypotheses that have described the relationship between physical, punitive, or harsh socialization practices and other family variables, including of course the effectiveness of socialization. Without discussing their meaning in great detail, I shall simply present them as correlations.

Firm discipline and harsh punishment by the father are associated with his lower I.Q., occupational level, and class.

Restrictiveness and firm discipline by the father are associated with higher scores on ethnocentrism, conservative political attitudes, and authoritarianism in the child.

3. Harsher discipline is used on the first-born child than on later-born children.

4. Boys are subjected to more physical punishment than are girls, who are more often disciplined by love-oriented techniques.

5. The use of physical punishment is associated with the development in the child of a moral orientation based on fear of authority.

6. The Oedipus complex is more likely to occur in a severe form in societies where physical punishment is used more often.

7. Aggressive boys are more likely than others to have been encouraged by their parents in their aggression.

8. Younger mothers are more likely than older mothers to urge their children to fight back when attacked by others.

Although I have abstracted many propositions on the relationship between aggression outside the home and aggression directed toward parents, the findings are highly contradictory. In general, however, high permissiveness for aggression toward parents is associated with aggression; lower class children are given less punishment for outside aggression and more for aggression against parents; mothers who accept the child's dependency are less likely to punish their children for aggression toward parents than other mothers are; mothers who permit their children to direct aggression against parents are more permissive; middle class boys are punished more by their mothers but not by their fathers for peer-directed aggression, than are lower and upper class boys. On the other hand, some authors have suggested that there is no relation between social class and the severity of parental punishment for parent-directed aggression.

Middle class parents are more likely to use psychological punishments than physical punishments, as compared with lower class parents.

When the social and economic bonds among members of a community are strong, children are more likely to be punished for peer-directed aggression. Catholic parents are more likely to use physical punishment than are Protestant parents; and Italians are less permissive of aggression toward parents than are Jews; in general, mothers are more permissive of aggression toward themselves than are fathers.

The ability of the child to resist temptation is not correlated with severity of punishment for the child's aggression. The use of physical punishment is correlated with authoritarian control by the father, the boy's identification with the father, and stricter sexual control.

When parents spend more time in explaining the family rules, the child is less aggressive.

When parents disagree on discipline, one being lax and the other punitive, the child is more likely to be aggressive.

The more controlling and punitive the discipline of the father over the son, the more likely the son is to become alcoholic; this type of discipline is also associated with other anti-social behavior such as stealing, lying, or truancy from school.

(3) Fathers are more likely to use physical punishment on boys if all their siblings are brothers than if their son has only sisters and no brothers.

(4) Large families are more likely to use physical punishment in socialization.

(5) Adolescents whose parents use less authoritarian or punitive childrearing patterns are more likely to be satisfied with those parental policies.

(6) Parents who use explanation more often as a childrearing technique are more likely to carry out their threat of physical punishment if such a threat is actually made. The use of praise is negatively associated with use of physical punishment.

(7) Parents of repeater criminals (recidivists) are more likely than those of ordinary criminals to have used physical methods of punishment. Mothers who use physical punishment are likely to have less warmth for and more hostility towards their husbands than mothers who do not.

(8) Mothers of homosexuals are likely to have been harder on their sons in matters of discipline, and to have given more physical punishment.

(9) The severity of parental punishment for disobedience is paralleled by a belief in supernatural punishment for disobedience to the gods.

(10) When parents of aggressive boys stress masculine behavior, they are less likely to be warm and acceptant of their spouses than those who do not stress such behavior.

(11) Husbands are, in general, inclined to believe that their wives are not strict enough with the children, and the wives tend to believe that their husbands are too strict.

(12) The father's approval of physical punishment correlates with marital conflict.

(All of these were abstracted from Goode, Hopkins, and McClure, 1971.)

Most of these are well-known. In spite of their inadequacy they suggest several general conclusions (apart from specific findings) about the use of force in socialization. 1) Although there are many restrictions on it, it is widely used, and it does seem to "work." At the worst, most children who have been subjected to physical punishment will in fact grow up to become adequately functioning adults in this society. 2) It is more likely than some alternative techniques to create some effects that are judged by our contemporary values to be less desirable as outcomes of childrearing: e.g., a lesser amount of emotional spontaneity and freedom, of creativity, of communication and even a lesser willingness to give love. 3) However, it will continue to be used, because those who have been so reared are likely to rear their own children similarly, and because in any family confrontation between parents and children, some parents will at times resort to what is after all one effective way of eliciting obedience.

My first emphasis in this paper was on force embodied in continuing family roles and structures, the traditions and laws, that are accepted because people come to understand (whether or not they believe in their rightness) that others will defend them successfully with force if they are challenged. Most family members rarely reject these elements of the family structure.

My second emphasis was not only on that type of force which does not often become immediately visible, but also on overt force, physical force actually applied, in the molding of children during the socialization process.

Violence

In the final section I wish to explore a third aspect of force which emerges into violence within the family, appearing as assault, murder, or child abuse. Here, too, I wish to utilize the same framework of exchange variables so as to illuminate further the pervasive effect of force in the family, without at all denying the impact of other causes.* I shall first comment on assault and homicide, although certainly the dynamics there also apply to child abuse.

As we know, man is not a killer by instinct, because in the technical sense he has no instincts. But equally he is not restrained at all, as other great predators are, by automatic, nearly reflex mechanisms that prevent him from killing when his opponent quits. He is socialized not to kill, but that very socialization makes him care deeply about principles and honor, fairness and possessions, fidelity and self-respect; indeed, these emotional commitments are so great that he will risk or even give his life for them. It cannot be so surprising that he will also murder for them.

As I have already emphasized, parents and other moral authorities constantly exhort young children against violence, but their own behavior belies that advice. We are all trained for violence. The child does learn that force is very effective at stopping others, and that force or its threat can change other people's calculations of profit and loss. They can be persuaded to obey when faced with such consequences. The child experiences this directly, and watches it in others—the fright of his mother when his father is furious, arguments and threats among neighbors, the battles with his own siblings, and so on.

The child also learns to make differentiated responses, depending upon the number of variables: he learns to gauge, however incorrectly, which

---

*In this section I shall draw upon my paper, "Violence Between Intimates" (1969).

people seem more willing and able to fight. He learns which kinds of situations call forth a greater amount of violence, within the family or outside it. For example, to challenge his father by aggressing against him is almost certain to elicit violence, but perhaps not a challenge against a playmate. A boy should not punch a girl, or a youngster or weaker boy, but he may punch a bigger boy, and especially if the other started the battle. He learns that some acts so dishonor a person that violence is the only appropriate answer. In former days, of course, some kinds of acts justified duels.

He also learns, as part of this training for violence, that others are more or less likely to justify his violence; that is, others may support his own evaluations. In a slum area, to back down in a violent argument is to lose more face than is tolerable. Violence to protect one's sister's honor is praised by family members. He also learns *when* force (as distinct from other controls that might be available) will be more or less effective. He learns in addition how to call on the help of outsiders, whether kin, friends, or policemen, which laws might support or punish his use of force, and so on.

Little of this training justifies homicide, but much does justify the kinds of feelings, responses, traditions, evaluations, and actions that lead to violent assault and even homicide. Thus it is that family processes set in motion many patterns that ultimately generate violence: they inculcate the evaluations that make people want to force others to act in certain ways even at the risk of danger; they present models of the use of force and violence; they teach the various gradations of violence for different occasions; and they teach a set of rationalizations and justifications for violence.

Implicit in these comments is also a notion which is only now beginning to receive systematic attention: the contribution of the *victim* to the dynamics of violence. Typically, neither the victim nor the attacker *wills* the total outcome, whether it is a murder or a simple beating, but both contribute to it through the ongoing actions and counteractions of their daily lives. This is obviously so within the family, where from 40 to 50 percent of all homicides are carried out, but it is not only the victim that contributes to his own demise. Other members of the family and the neighborhood contribute as well, since they create the field of forces that play upon the main participants in the drama.

These social linkages between evaluations, social pressures and propensity to assault also generate some of the major differences in assault and homicide rates that have been widely reported in the research on violence: rates are higher in the South than the North; younger adults are more prone to violence than older adults; men kill more than women; blacks than whites; the poor more than the middle class; and so on. However, we believe that the same variables operate in much of family violence, whether the rates are high or low.

Some part of that variance we have just discussed, by noting the extent to which training for violence occurs, how strong a field of violence exists within the family and neighborhood, how effective the family may be in training its members to solve problems through nonviolent techniques, or how deeply they are taught to care about certain ends, so that they might risk violence to achieve them.

Most of those variables are essentially socialization processes, i.e., the extent to which family members are taught as children to avoid or use force and violence, and which costs justify it in a set of social exchanges. Since the repression of violence in middle class families is much stronger, more consistent, and backed by more resources, middle class people *are* less likely to resort to homicide or assault. However, we also suppose that almost everyone is capable of violence. Almost every family member is from time to time enraged to murderous impulses by other family members. If so, we should look at the dynamics that generate such responses, whether or not they issue in murder or assault. For it is likely that these underlying processes operate in creating such lethal feelings at all class levels.

In any continuing family structure, people are bound to one another through an ongoing flow of transactions which may in part be viewed as exchanges. When family members fight about what one has done to the other, they are likely to refer to these actions as exchanges, and comment on what each owes the other. In the enraged family, very likely most members feel the others owe a great deal, and pay out little, whether it is love and deference, personal services, or gifts.

Even in the more harmonious family, of course, the objective observer might not always see that each person's contribution is equal. The wife works hard, but in economic terms contributes less than the husband; the children do not pay in as much love as the parents do; or the husband demands and gets much personal service, but gives none. On the other hand, if what each gives is valued by the others, and they agree roughly on these evaluations, over a period of time they may feel no necessity to count in close terms what each owes to the other. A husband knows he works hard, but enjoys the respect, loyalty, and love that others express; a child feels constricted, but enjoys the protection and affection he gets; and so on.

Over time, however, many family relations turn sour, what each values more or less will alter, and what each is willing to do for the other may diminish, so that one or more members feel a growing sense of anger and frustration, of being in fact cheated by the exchanges in which they engage. A wife's ability or willingness to give love may decline, and a child's willingness to obey or pay respect may lessen. A brother-in-law's success may lead him to demand respect that a man cannot easily give. Family members come to feel diminished, put upon, punished unjustly, or short-changed by others.

We are all exhorted to talk out such problems, to be wise in presenting our grievances and listening to those of others. Most of us are not wise, however, and in any event the underlying problem is that both sides may honestly feel that they are being cheated in the flow of family transactions. If both believe they are already paying out more than they should be, it is difficult to alter the terms without perpetrating more injustice.

At the same time, since both are already emotionally close, they know the other's weaknesses, and have acquired great skill at neatly hurting the other, or bludgeoning the other with a flood of counter-attacks. Moreover, they cannot easily retreat to the masks and formulas that mere acquaintances or business friends can use to pass over the conflict. As I have commented elsewhere,

> Locked in but suffering from it, couples may engage in fighting that is savage and even lethal. Many men and women have finally come to the conclusion that homicide is a cleaner, neater solution than the dragged-out acerbic destruction of ego and dignity that is inherent in breaking off. (Goode, 1969, p. 958)

These dynamics also create two additional traits of man that increase the risk of violence among family members: the unwillingness of human beings either to submit or to escape. In this, man is like some of his domestic creations, such as gamecocks, pit bulldogs, and fighting bulls. He does not willingly escape or submit, as does the wild animal when another wins a battle. Man does not submit because thereby all that gives meaning to his existence is lost, i.e., values, norms, traditions, and moral or ethical beliefs. It is especially in the family that he cannot or will not escape easily, because his emotional investment in these relations is great, the costs of leaving are high, and the social pressures to maintain his kin ties are strong.

Thus it is that many family members continue to take part in an ongoing set of social transactions in which they feel they are paying more than they get in return, but self-respect and commitment to what they believe is fair keeps them from submitting, while no satisfying alternatives emerge elsewhere.

Shrugging one's shoulders and accepting the loss is also a difficult action to take. Even if a family member sees that he is constantly losing, the odds are poor, and change is unlikely, from time to time pleasurable exchanges do happen, and once more the hope is kindled that the other person will see the light and alter his behavior. Meanwhile, as against the situation of some payoff, there may be few alternatives that look better. In addition, the peculiarity of family relations, like that between lovers and close friends, is that they are *unique*. No other person can exactly substitute.

In the immediate situation of conflict, the emotions aroused are often high enough, even among those who are pacifically inclined, to call for a strong resolution. The conflict as it finally appears in the war of words is so sharp, the feeling of betrayal and loss so great, that redress must be physical and destructive. This impulse is the stronger because the person who wins the war of words—often the woman, since she is perhaps ordinarily more facile verbally—is not necessarily the person with the greatest sense of outrage or even with the better case to present. The person who is least fair may be most competent in verbal attack.

A further general peculiarity of all conversations, emphasized by ethnomethodologists, exacerbates the conflict. Social customs dictate, often without explicit rules, how to end conversations of different kinds (see Schegloff and Sacks, 1969), but perhaps none exists for ending conflict interaction. Among intimate friends, the formula may call for specifying when and where the next meeting will occur. At a cocktail party, a gesture or stating the need for another drink may be sufficient.

Unfortunately, conflict calls for peaceful resolution as an ending, and often that is not possible. Fighting conversation, being so unsatisfactory because it exposes still more disagreements and hostility as it progresses, does not easily lend itself to a safe completion. As already noted, two possible resolutions for the entire relationship, running or submission, seem difficult, and this holds for the conflict conversation as well. Escalation to the point of attack *is* one kind of end to the conversation, and often seems easier than tediously working through to some new harmony. Crushing the other can become a more tempting resolution to the interaction than any alternative. And, as a consequence, as the family member reviews in his mind all his injuries in the past, hurting the other can be a life-affirming act.

These dynamics also explain in part why so much assault is never reported to the police, and why the outsider finds it difficult to reconstruct just what took place. Both parties have contributed to the violence, not only over the long run but also within the ultimate conflict situation.

The process analyzed here also suggests a basis for Wolfgang's finding that women commit homicide more often in the kitchen and secondly the bedroom in order of frequency, and one-third of female victims were killed in the bedroom. It is in the bedroom where unresolved conflicts can burst out because both husband and wife finally go there for the evening and cannot easily leave as a way of ending the conversation. To some degree this is also true for the kitchen, where in lower class homes many family members are likely to spend much of their time (Goode, 1969, p. 126). The high emotion generated may also be seen in the finding that husband-wife slayings are more common than any other category if we consider only murders that were accompanied by a great deal of violence, such as repeated shootings or beatings.

Although to discuss the general field of social forces that create different homicide and assault rates in different classes or ethnic groups takes us too far afield into the general problem of violence, we should at least note that people who grow up in such social settings acquire a higher predisposition to violence because the norms against it are less stringent, punishment for resorting to it is milder, and training for it is stronger. Males are reared to believe that backing down is to deny one's masculinity, and bystanders are more likely to egg the conflicting parties on to a higher level of conflict.

Perhaps of more importance in this analysis is the fact that family members in such settings typically have fewer alternative resources of any kind that will help them to redress the balance of exchanges with their relatives or family members, and fewer alternative sources of pleasure and contentment, as compared with, say, middle class family members. Lower class people have less prestige, money, and power, and consequently they suffer greater frustration and bitterness. They can make fewer decisions that do not depend upon their friends or spouses. They generally command fewer resources with which to achieve their aims, with outsiders or intimates. Receiving less respect during the day from their experiences outside the home, they have less ability to withstand hurt and frustration in the home. They have less ability in talking out difficulties or mediation, whether the problem is one of sexual adjustment or family budgets.

A major consequence of these class and ethnic differences is the greater resort to violence among the disadvantaged members of the lower social strata in this and other societies. However, it is clear that these broader differences express themselves in the imbalances of transactions within the family, and the greater difficulty of improving the flow of services or gifts, loyalty and deference, or love and affection. They are more likely to feel that no other alternative to the satisfying use of force exists, and thus to be more easily tempted by it as a resolution if not a solution.

Child Abuse

It is not possible here to review the growing literature on child abuse (see Gil, 1970), but it is evident that the foregoing analysis also applies to this type of fanatical violence, as well. Although most people view child abusers as little short of psychotic fiends or mad killers, such parents do not hurt casually, and are typically not sadists. Their behavior is not explained, of course, so much by social pressures of their daily lives, as by their prior socialization, in which they were deprived of motherliness or tenderness, from mothers or fathers.

Abusing parents demand far higher performances from their children than ordinary parents. What they demand is beyond the capacity of their children even to understand, much less perform. Typically they become angry because the child will not stop crying, eats poorly, urinates after being told not to do so, and so on. In fact, they feel righteous about the punishments they have inflicted on their children.* They avoid facing the degree of injury they have caused, but they justify their behavior because they feel their children have been "bad."

Essentially, they approach the task of child care with the wish to do something for the child, a deep need for the child to fill their own lacks, to salve their own hurt self-esteem, to give them love, and a harsh demand that the child behave in a certain way. Failing that, the child demonstrates thereby his lack of respect, love, affection, goodness, and so on. The parents' high standards—e.g., that a six months' child must stop crying if the parent commands him—create an inevitable failure on the part of the child to show his virtue, and thus his concern for the parent himself. The parent is thus, at a deeper level, asking that the child not merely learn to eat, drink, control his crying and urination, etc., as an older child would, but that the child satisfy the parent's need for counterpayments of devotion and concern.

Typically, such parents were themselves given little love or tenderness as children, so that their underlying hunger is for a response that will redress the imbalances of their past lives. They therefore force the child to engage in a set of transactions or exchanges in which they set a high price on what they do, and the child cannot pay back adequately. For this failure, the child is punished. Of course, violence of this kind is not effective in eliciting either the warmth the parents need, or the performance they require—though eventually, if the child lives, he may indeed try to meet at least the behavioral standards out of fear.

I am not suggesting here that such parents are healthy, happy people who feel they have received a poor bargain. They do suffer from emotional problems. However, what is striking is that those problems have usually been generated by precisely the experience of an unsatisfying imbalance in their own childhood transactions with their parents. In turn, their daily experience with the children they abuse takes that form once again, a form that parallels the dynamics of assault and murder among family members described in the previous section: nothing less than severe punishment will right the injustice they have experienced.

Final Comments

To analyze force or its threat in several of its guises is to emphasize those aspects of family life that violate not only our personal ideals but also, at times, the goals of family members themselves. Typically, family members

*In this section, I have drawn especially upon Brandt F. Steele and Carl B. Pollock (1968). See also David G. Gillan and John H. Noble (1969).

want spontaneous affection from each other, not calculated obedience or compliance. If a family member conforms to rules because of the force they embody, while resenting it, others are both hurt and angry. Each wants the others to *want* to offer services, pay respect, cooperate and help, give loyalty or obedience. If members discharge their role obligations because that is the best bargain they can get in the face of superior force, the foundations of the family are fragile and labile indeed.

But though I have reiterated the fact that family systems rest on customs and tradition, deeply held beliefs and values, and the constant exchange of *other* resources than force or its threat, we cannot on that account ignore this pervasive set of processes in family life and social actions generally. I have focused on three main faces of this power. First, the family structures that are ultimately backed by force, though few challenge them and instead accept them as given, not to be questioned. Ordinarily, force is not visible here unless some family member rejects part of the structure, whereupon one or more family members, kinsmen, neighbors, or the community in the form of court and police will intervene to reassert the rules. Most people have been socialized to believe the rightness and reality of these patterns, but it would fly in the face of fact to suppose, as we cannot for any other social patterns, that the removal of these supports would not reduce compliance, first among the antagonistic or less committed and eventually among others.

With references to that socialization itself, as a second theme, we have pointed out that from the start it is based on overt physical force or threat, since the child begins his life with no commitment at all to family values. He does not know them or believe in them. Here again, almost all parents use love and its withdrawal, the pleasure of food and other comforts, and gifts or money to inculcate those values in the child. But in no societies do parents find these to be enough. They use physical punishment or its threat, restrain the child by force from hurting himself, bring him back home if he runs away, and so on. As one result, he learns that violation of a wide range of rules will be met with force. The lesson is not lost on him and is rather extended to other social rules as well.

Finally, we have probed the dynamics of violence in the family, which here has referred to overt but illegitimate force. This we have placed in the same framework of exchanges within the family, specifically those which yield a continuing residue of resentment because of felt injustice.

These exchanges are made between family members on the basis of the evaluation each brings to or accepts within the family, so that in a harmonious domestic unit each feels the exchanges are more or less equal in value. The child brings in no income, but does pay loyalty, obedience, and respect to his parents. The mother gives affection, salves hurt egos and supervises or carries out household tasks, and so on. As long as each values what he gets as roughly equal to what he gives, all are fairly content, and their feelings are reinforced by outsiders, who share the same values. Most do not calculate the pay-offs and investments. When, however, one or more family members beings to feel a continuing imbalance, they start to engage in conflict about them, and for various reasons noted in the paper they may also feel they cannot submit, escape, or right the balance. Such conflicts can escalate to the point of violence because no simpler or easier resolution emerges. The dynamics outlined earlier go some distance toward explaining the variations of assault and homicide rate among different classes, ethnic groups, the two sexes, age groups, or neighborhoods.

With reference to child abuse, which has only recently begun to be studied carefully, because it was to some extent hidden from view, it seems likely that the processes sketched here also apply, though to an extreme degree.

Finally, although we do not believe it is possible to take seriously an imaginary utopia in which force would not play a role, we do not at all suppose the amount of force now applied in these various areas of family life or social life in general is either necessary or desirable. It is not only possible but we think likely, that some part of every social system is pervaded by force if only because some or many of its participants believe the system is unjust: therefore, those who dominate must use force to maintain it. Women, children, slaves, Colonials, lower castes, and other disadvantaged segments of any society are constrained more than others by force—although all are to some extent—or they are enjoined to refrain from its use, simply because the existing structures would change without these buttresses.

However, as the worldwide revolutionary temper of our era amply shows, when the disadvantaged learn how much of the social structure is not embedded unchangeably in the cosmos but is held in place by force wielded by human beings, they become less willing to comply with its traditional rules. Perhaps one could even say, as a challenge to superordinates everywhere, that we could test whether and where justice is to be found, by removing more and more physical force as a support. The system which needs least support of this kind would, I think, be a closer approximation of justice than any we now know.

References

Boschan, Siegfried. *Europaisches Familienrecht Handbuch.* Berlin: P. Vahlen, 1965.

Bronfenbrenner, Urie. "Socialization and Social Class through Time and Space." In *Readings in Social Psychology,* edited by E. E. Maccoby, T. M. Newcomb, and E. L. Hartley, pp. 400–424. New York: Henry Holt, 1958.

Cartwright, D. "Power: A Neglected Variable in Social Psychology." In *Studies in Social Power,* edited by Dorwin Cartwright, pp. 1–15. Ann Arbor: Research Center for Group Dynamics, 1959.

Caudill, W. "Japanese Structure and System of Obligations." In *Japanese-American*

Personality and Acculturation. Genetic Psychology Monographs, 45 (February 1952): 29–33.

Clark, H. H. *The Law of Domestic Relations in the United States.* St. Paul: The West Publishing Co., 1963.

Erikson, E. *Gandhi's Truth.* New York: W. W. Norton and Co., 1969.

Etzioni, A. *A Comparative Analysis of Complex Organizations.* New York: The Free Press, 1961.

Gil, David G. *Violence Against Children: Physical Child Abuse in the United States.* Cambridge: Harvard University Press, 1970.

Gil, David G., and Noble, John H. "Public Knowledge, Attitudes and Opinions about Physical Child Abuse in the United States." *Child Welfare,* 48 (No. 7, 1969): 395–401, 426.

Goode, William J. "Violence Between Intimates." In *Crimes of Violence,* by D. J. Mulvihill, Melvin M. Tumin, and Lynn A. Curtis, pp. 126, 941–979. Washington: United States Government Printing Office, 1969.

Goode, W. J.; Hopkins, Elizabeth; and McClure, Helen M. *A Propositional Inventory in the Field of the Family.* Indianapolis: Bobbs-Merrill, 1971.

Hill, Reuben, and Rene Konig, eds. *Families East and West.* Paris: Mouton, 1970.

Lewis, Oscar. *La Vida.* New York: Vintage Books, 1965.

Maretzki, Thomas and Hatsumi. "Taira: An Okinawan Village." In *Studies of Child Rearing,* edited by Beatrice Whiting, pp. 363–540. New York: John Wiley, 1963.

Massell, G. J. "Law as an Instrument of Revolutionary Change in a Traditional Milieu: The Case of Soviet Central Asia." *Law and Society Review,* 2 (October 1968): 179–228.

Newson, John and Elizabeth. *Infant Care in an Urban Community.* New York: International Universities Press, 1963, pp. 194–201.

Schegloff, Emmanuel A., and Harvey Sacks. "Opening Up Closings." Paper delivered to the American Sociological Association, San Francisco, September 1969.

Steele, Brandt F., and Carl B. Pollock. "A Psychiatric Study of Parents Who Abuse Infants and Small Children." In *The Battered Child,* edited by Ray E. Helfer and C. Henry Kempe, pp. 103–147. Chicago: University of Chicago, 1968.

Whiting, Beatrice, ed. *Six Cultures: Studies of Child Rearing.* New York: John Wiley, 1963, pp. 363–540.

Chapter 2

Social Organization
and the Family

Families in modern societies differ from those in the past in many ways. Some writers have emphasized changes in the economic functions of the family, others have emphasized the ideology of marriage or love as the major contrast between the modern family and its historical counterpart. The present paper suggests that a high degree of privacy in family life is a significant feature of the modern family. In the past, the author argues, when the home was a workplace and a meeting place, when families had more children, and when non-kin such as boarders, apprentices, and servants were part of the household, interaction between family members was more open to observation by outsiders than now. Other factors, such as the size and design of houses, the availability of conveniences such as radio and TV, and the decline in the use of streets and other public places for family relaxation, also have tended to increase family privacy. In short, the family of the past had more of a public character. The implications of the increased privacy are twofold—there is less social control over how family members behave toward each other, but also less social support for carrying out family roles. Thus, the author concludes, the loss of public observation may have made family life more troubling and problematic than in former times.

The Family as a Public and Private Institution: An Historical Perspective

Barbara Laslett

This paper attempts to specify some of the ways in which the modern family in the United States differs from its historical predecessor through a distinction between the public and private character of social institutions. Access to institutions and events that are considered private is more limited —both structurally and normatively—than is access to more public acts and activities. One consequence of this more limited access is that there is greater control over the audience of potential observers within private than within public institutions. To the extent that behavior is influenced by accountability to others, privacy is likely to reduce social control and publicness to increase it. If structural mechanisms which inhibit social control over the enactment of family roles have been reduced in the modern American family, then there is reason to expect greater variability in these behaviors in the more contemporary period than was true in the past.

The specific hypothesis being investigated here is that the private family— that is, an institution characterized by relatively limited access and greater control over the observability of behavior—is a modern development which has occurred only within this century in the United States.* This development, it will be argued, is one consequence of the separation of work and family activities, historically associated with industralization in the west and with the changing characteristics of the family setting which have followed from this differentiation. The role of norms in this process of change will also be explored.†

Reprinted by permission from "The Family as a Public and Private Institution: An Historical Perspective" by Barbara Laslett, *Journal of Marriage and the Family,* August 1973, pp. 480–492.

*This statement should not be taken as an assertion that privacy as a general phenomenon has increased in the United States. The hypothesis relates to privacy in the enactment of family roles only.

†Any essay-length presentation which discusses changes in the family over the whole of American history is bound to commit errors of oversimplification. While on a general level I believe the changes described here to be accurate, there are likely to be deviations from them along local, temporal, socioeconomic, and ethnic lines. Socioeconomic and ethnic variation in family structure and behavior has attracted considerable sociological attention, although an analysis of variations in privacy by social class or ethnicity still remains to be done. The absence of attention to these variables in the analysis presented here in no way signifies their lack of importance.

The main focus of this analysis is on the context in which family activities occur. An attempt will be made to describe the "audience" of family behavior, *i.e.*, the people who comprise the actual or potential observers of family life, and the demographic, spatial, and normative mechanisms which permit and prohibit observation as they have varied over historical time. If one is willing to accept the general sociological assumption that individuals are responsive to their surroundings, of which persons who share a given physical space with them are a part, then different consequences are likely to occur, both in the family as an institution as well as in the quality and character of the behavior which occurs within the family, when the interactional context varies.

Within the sociological literature, there have been three major themes in discussions of the family across time: (1) the development of the isolated nuclear family in the more recent period compared to an extended family structure in the past (part of what William Goode, 1963, has called "the classical family of Western nostalgia"); (2) the growth of the companionship compared to the traditional or institutional family (see Burgess and Locke, 1953); and (3) the loss of functions by the family in the modern period compared to the past (see Ogburn and Nimkoff, 1955). Each of these views relates changes in the family to the development of an urban, industrial, and highly mobile society, and thus dates its formation as following these developments.

Some historians (see for instance, Aries, 1962; O'Neill, 1967; Laslett, 1969, 1971; Lockridge, 1966; Demos, 1968, 1970; Greven, 1966, 1970) have, in contrast, argued that certain aspects of the modern family structure predate industrialization. To the extent that "modern" is defined in terms of nuclear or conjugal family structure, there are good demographic reasons to believe that the nuclear family form was predominant before the advent of industrialization, at least in western Europe and America, since in societies which have late marriage ages and low life expectancy, only a small proportion of households are likely to exhibit an extended structure at any one point in time. (Berkner (1972, p. 405), in an analysis of 651 peasant households in one Austrian manor in 1763, found that when the age of the male head of the household was 18 through 27, 60 per cent of the families were extended, while when the age of the male household head was 58 through 90, 15 per cent of the families were extended.)

Historians who have emphasized the importance of ideology in the development of the modern family also dispute whether its development was prior to or post industrialization. O'Neill (1967, p. 5) argues, as does Ariès (1962), that the development of the modern family is related to "the discovery of the child," *i.e.*, to the conception of the "child" as a social category separate from adults, requiring special concern and attention. O'Neill says (1967, p. 17):

> The emergence of the modern family has had very little to do with the industrial revolution, which it predated, but instead has been substantially influenced by ideology.

Goode (1963, p. 19) suggests that:

> The ideology of the conjugal family is likely to enter the society through some spokesman *before* the material conditions for its existence are present, but the ideology does prepare individuals for adjustment to the demands of the new society.

Thus, ideology cannot be used as evidence for the actual existence of the family form which it describes. Furthermore, despite Goode's contention, the material and structural conditions which actually develop do not necessarily produce the kind of family for which the ideology has prepared the individual. Consequences of changed structural conditions, which were unanticipated by the ideology, may lead to a disjunction between expectations and reality, rather than have a preparatory effect.

Privacy and Family Role Behavior

Privacy, in this analysis, then, refers to the structural mechanisms which prohibit or permit observability in the enactment of family roles. The hypothesis being investigated here will be supported if the institution of the family can be shown to exhibit greater privacy, *i.e.*, that people's activities in their family roles are observable to fewer and less varied others, and if the institution of the family has greater control over the character of that observation in the more recent period of American history than was the case in the past.

One of the structural changes which has been associated with industrialization has been the separation of home and work activities. The consequences of this differentiation are extremely varied, but one result for the family may be seen in terms of the potential audience of behavior in different roles. When the family was economically productive as a unit, the setting of activities which engaged work and family roles were often the same. For instance, Riis (1968, p. 182), describing conditions in the tenements of New York, in the last decade of the nineteenth century, reports:

> ... we found in such an apartment five persons making cigars, including the mother. Two children were ill with diphtheria. Both parents attended to the children; they would syringe the nose of each child and without washing their hands, return to their cigars.

Ariès (1962, p. 383), describing seventeenth-century life in France, at least among the professional classes, says:

> There were no professional premises, either for the judge or the merchant or the banker or the businessman. Everything was done in the same room where he lived with his family.

These examples illustrate structural conditions which would permit a hetero-genous audience and relatively low control over one's observability in the enactment of family roles.

Merton (1957) makes the general point in his discussion of the role set. Although various members of one's role set may have differing views about appropriate and desirable behavior on the part of the status occupant, spatial and temporal separation of interactions with different others can reduce potential conflict between their expectations. When such spatial differentia-tion occurs, the individual, in the enactment of family roles, is less account-able to varied others, since observability of behavior is reduced. Thus social control over family behavior declines when privacy is increased. It should be noted, though, that the audience of family behavior also affects the sources of social encouragement and reward for the maintenance of norma-tive behavior within the family.

Privacy permits variability based on individual preference and predilec-tion which public accountability might tend to discourage. But the very struc-tural conditions which may limit the sources of social control can also affect the availability and character of social support.* In statistical terms, this might lead one to expect that a distribution descriptive of some behavior or attitude related to the family would show greater deviation from the mean under conditions of privacy and greater concentration around the mean under conditions of publicness.†

Privacy and Household Composition

Different structural mechanisms are likely to affect the audience of family behavior composed of persons who are members of the household compared to those who are not. Although one's observability will vary, even within the household, by the amount and usage of space (the number of rooms and the behavior which is designated as appropriate to them, the design of rooms and the means of access to them, etc., some of which will be discussed in a later section), there is likely to be less control over the observability of be-

---

*The presence or absence of social support for and social control over the enact-ment of family roles may provide some insight into the impact of feminist movements in the United States on traditional definitions of appropriate female behavior in their family roles. The growth of a private family not only means that the sources of social control over women's behavior in their familial roles has declined, but that the sources of social support and satisfaction for the enactment of traditionally defined family be-havior for women has also been reduced.

†A further consequence, suggested in personal communication by Bonacich (stem-ming from his experimental work on Prisoner Dilemma problems; see, for instance, Bonacich, 1972) is that under conditions of privacy, the adherence to normative pre-cepts is likely to depend on whether norms have been internalized by the individual, since external pressures to conformity are reduced.

havior by persons who share a household than by those who do not. Therefore, household composition is relevant to an analysis of the audience of behavior in family roles. This section will look at the ways in which household composition has changed over the period of American history as a means of answering questions about the composition and character of the audience of family behavior within the household.

As already mentioned, recent research has shown that the dominant structure of the family in the pre-industrial household, both in England and in the American colonies, was nuclear. (Parish and Schwartz (1972, p. 170) conclude from their analysis of household complexity in nineteenth-century France "that nuclear families existed over most of northern France, if not most of Europe, before industrialization.") Laslett (1971), for pre-industrial England, and Demos (1970), Greven (1970), and Lockridge (1966) for colonial New England, all describe the predominantly nuclear character of the household. While demographic factors (particularly the link between age of marriage and expectation of life) are likely to account, in part, for this structure in England (see Laslett, 1971, pp. 94–97), these purely demographic factors are less likely to explain such a structure in the early American setting. Marriage ages, particularly for women (see Greven, 1970, p. 290; Demos, 1970, p. 193) were younger in the American colonies than in England at a similar time, but of greater importance for family structure was that life expectancy appears to have been higher in the New World than in the Old. (Laslett (1971) discusses mortality in seventeenth-century England, and Greven (1970), Demos (1970), Farber (1972a), and Vinovskis (1971) discuss mortality in the early American period. Vinovskis (1972) discusses some of the problems of working with mortality data before 1860, of making comparative statements based on them, and some of the sources of variation associated with differential mortality.)

The changed demographic conditions of the American colonies, compared to the England from which many of them had come, has led John Murrin (1972, p. 238) to suggest that:

> . . . New England might have been responsible for a simple but tremendously important invention, at least in terms of scale—grandparents—who became numerous enough by the 1660's to raise serious problems in a paternalistic social environment.

Yet the solution of this problem does not seem, to any great extent, to have been the proliferation of tri-generational households. Thus the potential audience of family behavior resident within the household in the colonial period was not often expanded to include grandparents or other kin, despite changes in the demographic capability of doing so.

Beyond the early colonial experience, the available evidence continues to support the conclusion that an extended kinship structure was in no way characteristic of a large proportion of American households. Pryor (1972), in a study of Rhode Island family structure, found that in 1875, 82 per cent of families were nuclear. (In 1960, 85 per cent of Rhode Island households were nuclear.) Bloomberg *et al.* (1971), in an analysis of southern Michigan families, show that in 1880, 7.1 per cent of rural households, 9.0 per cent of village and town households, and 6.6 per cent of Detroit households included parents of the household head.

In terms of the evidence now available, then, it seems legitimate to conclude that that part of the potential audience of family behavior which is made up of household residents does not, for the overwhelming majority of American families, include fewer grandparents or other kindred in the present than it did in the past. Thus, while the extended versus nuclear character of family structure cannot be used to support the hypothesized change of the family from a more public to a more private institution, other changes in family structure and household composition do provide such evidence. One part of this evidence relates to the structure of the household kindred group and the other relates to the nonkindred residents within the household.

One major change that has occurred in the household kindred group of American families is a decrease in the number of children born per family (see Coale and Zelnik, 1963, p. 36). The audience of family behavior has been the focus of this analysis because of its potential for social control over and support for the normative enactment of family roles. While young children are meaningful members of any family, and concern over their well-being may determine many activities of family members, they are not likely to be seen as the repositories of socially approved behavior. Their membership in the audience of family behavior is less likely to provide a source of control, support or companionship for their parents than might the presence of adult children or other adult observers.*

The number of children born will affect the age strcuture, and thereby the composition, of the household kin group, as Table 1 indicates. If children are likely to serve as meaningful sources of social control and support only when they are adults (or quasi-adults), then the larger family is likely to have such persons in its midst for a longer period of the family life cycle than will smaller families, and therefore experience less privacy. Privacy is increased in smaller families by the effect which fewer children have on the age distribution of potential audience members.

---

*While young children may not act as sources of social control and support for their parents, changes in the number of children are likely to have marked effects on the children themselves, since siblings are important sources of socialization for each other. Demos discusses some of the consequences of changes in the size, and therefore the age structure of the sibling group, for the development of children (1970, p. 69; 1972).

Table 1. Hypothetical Age Distribution of Children in Two- and Five-Child Families (Assuming No Child Mortality and a Constant Two-Year Birth Interval*)

Age Distribution of Children in		Age Distribution of Children in		Age Distribution of Children in	
TWO-CHILD FAMILY	FIVE-CHILD FAMILY	TWO-CHILD FAMILY	FIVE-CHILD FAMILY	TWO-CHILD FAMILY	FIVE-CHILD FAMILY
0	0	5	5	10	10
2	2	7	7	12	12
	4		9		14
	6		11		16
	8		13		18

*Birth intervals are, in fact, parity-specific, with longer intervals between each succeeding birth. The assumption of a constant 2-year birth interval leads to a conservative estimate of the age distribution of children in large families, which would tend to strengthen the argument presented in the text.

Although children may not serve as mechanisms of normative social control or support during their childhood, as adults they are likely to be particularly important members of the household audience to their parents.* Beresford and Rivlin's (1966) analysis shows that the proportion of grown children (in the age group 15 to 24)—both male and female—who were likely to be living in their parents' households declined markedly from 1940 to 1960. Although these changes have been occurring since the latter part of the nineteenth century,† Beresford and Rivlin (1966, p. 248) say:

> A dramatic change did occur between 1885 and 1960 in household relationships of young adults in Massachusetts, but most of the change seems to have taken place since 1940.

This removal of young adults from the households of their parents has the result not only of increasing the privacy from familial sources available to the young adults themselves, but also of increasing the privacy of the households which they have left, since their departure has decreased the observability of their parents' behavior. Thus, privacy at both older and younger

---

*When a child becomes an adult is, at least in part, a social question, and there has been considerable variation in the timing of this transition. Ariès (1962), Demos (1970), Demos and Demos (1971), and Hunt (1970) discuss this point in relation to western European and early American families.

†The authors present a detailed comparison of Massachusetts household relationships in 1885 and 1960, as well as 1940 through 1960 comparison for the whole of the United States. Pryor's (1972) analysis of Rhode Island households in 1875 and 1960 indicates a growth of one-person households within that state, which would confirm Beresford and Rivlin's general finding.

ages is increased by the removal of young adults from their parental house-holds. The finding that this change has occurred most markedly in the middle of the twentieth century is partial confirmation of the hypothesis that the development of the private family is a phenomenon which has taken place in the twentieth century. (Katz (1972a, 1972b) has shown, in some very inter-esting work on Hamilton, Ontario, in the nineteenth century, that a large proportion of young men and women (between the ages of 12 and 20) ex-perienced a period of semi-dependency, during which they lived as boarders and servants in other people's homes. When young adults move into the households of others, privacy will be affected in a different way than when they establish homes of their own. It is this latter phenomenon to which Beresford and Rivlin are referring.)

While variations in the audience of family behavior within the household is partly related to changes in the kindred group, there have also been marked changes in the nonkin group resident within the household which has affected the audience of family behavior within the home. In the distant as well as the recent past, categories of persons other than kin have had legiti-mate and normal access to the household as resident members of it. Such persons were likely to include servants, boarders and lodgers, apprentices, and the children who were received into the household as part of the prac-tice of "putting out" children. The presence of these persons, as resident members of the household, is likely to have affected the degree of privacy which was available within it. Their presence lessened the degree to which family members could control observation of their behavior in the enactment of their family roles, and their removal increased that control.*

Demos, in describing the practice of "putting out children" in Plymouth Colony, says (1970, p. 72):

> There was little formal schooling anywhere in the old Colony until the last quarter of the [seventeenth] century, and the practice of placing children out may have constituted a functional equivalent for at least some of its young people.

Morgan, on the other hand, suggests (1944, pp. 76, 77) that:

> Puritan children were frequently brought up in other families than their own, even when there was no apparent educational advantage in-volved. . . . Puritan parents did not trust themselves with their own children, they were afraid of spoiling them by too great affection.

---

*Any overall discussion of changes in American household composition that neglects the effects of slavery is certainly incomplete. Greven's (1972) analysis of household composition in South Carolina discusses this issue to some extent. While the presence of slaves will not be discussed here, their existence is likely to have had effects not wholly dissimilar to the presence of other nonkindred household residents in terms of privacy by providing potential members for the audience of family behavior.

Whichever explanation is correct (or if both of them are), the practice of "putting out children" and apprenticeship was widespread in the past.*

Neither apprenticeship, the "putting out" system, nor service was restricted to a single class, although the conditions and terms of the contract varied by social class. (See, among others, Morgan, 1944, p. 132; Farber, 1972a, pp. 50–52; Demos, 1970, p. 73; Katz, 1972a, 1972b, for some examples of the relationship between social class and residence in others' households.) While the association of these practices to the stratification system is not wholly clear, their effect on the family is. Although, as Laslett (1971) describes the relationship of apprentices and Demos (1970) and Ariès (1962) describe the relationship of servants to the heads of the households in which they lived, as similar to family members, differences also existed (see Farber, 1972a, p. 50), and the presence of such persons within the household restricted domestic privacy. Hecht (1956) discusses the constraint on privacy which servants imposed on household members in eighteenth-century England. Gilman (1910, p. 42) discusses the same issue in relation to turn-of-the-century homes in the United States when she says:

> With servants living in our home by day and night, confronted with our strange customs and new ideas, having our family affairs always before them, and having nothing else in their occupation to offset this interest, we find in this arrangement of life a condition as far removed from privacy as could be imagined.

The practice of "putting out children" and apprenticeship, the varied social characteristics of the servant class, and widespread use of servants throughout many sectors of the social hierarchy indicate that the public-private distinction is not associated with a single social class only.

The tasks which were performed by servants, as well as by other nonkindred within the household, included many activities other than the domestic chores which we tend to associate with servants today, especially those related to the demands of an agricultural and domestic economy. In return, the master or head of the household was responsible for the moral and educational, as well as the physical, well-being of the persons within his domain. (See, among others, Ariès, 1962; Demos, 1970; Morgan, 1944; Farber, 1972a.) But the guardian and/or educational role which was associated with the presence of nonkin within the household changed rather early in the American experience. Farber (1972a, p. 49) says:

---

*This argument may appear specious in that, having argued that larger families lead to less privacy, I now claim that children were not at home, but were reducing privacy in someone else's home. It is likely that social class, and other sources of differentiation in the society, led to the privacy of many families being affected by the number and circulation of children.

> By the end of the eighteenth century, the apprentice system, stripped of
> its role of socializing youths and controlling deviants, had become some-
> what rationalized.

Douglas (1921), in a discussion of the history of American apprenticeship, also dates the beginning of this decline with the end of the eighteenth
and the beginning of the nineteenth century, *i.e.*, with the development of
the factory system of production, although he indicates that the timing of
this change varied by industry and area of the country. Douglas (1921, p.
55) says:

> His [the apprentice's] home had formerly been at his master's. He had
> lived and worked familiarly with him, receiving his board and clothing
> in return for his services. Now, with the growth of industry, the master
> could no longer house all of his apprentices. He had to let them find their
> own shelter, and commute their former benefits into cash allowance. . . .
> In brief, master and apprentice had stood in the relation of father and
> son; they now stood in the relation of employer and employee.

The growth of the factory system and of machine production, therefore, removed a nonkin segment of the household population who had once been
included as quasi-family members.*

While the decline of apprenticeship may have reduced the proportion of
nonkin residents within the household, an alternate source was to be found
among boarders and lodgers, particularly in the growing urban centers.
Modell (1972) provides a detailed analysis of patterns of boarding and lodging, particularly in the late nineteenth and early twentieth centuries. Lodging
was more frequent for men than for women, was almost as common among
American-born as foreign-headed households, and, although less common
among affluent compared to poorer families, was not restricted to the poor
only.

Modell's analysis of household composition among working-class families
indicates the importance of life cycle factors for the practice of taking in
boarders. Among childless couples, 15.9 per cent took in boarders, while in
families in which the father was 45 years or older and had no child less than
four years old living at home, 41.2 per cent took in boarders. An even larger
percentage of this latter group (54.7 per cent) was found to include boarders
among the poorest, when economic factors were taken into account. Thus, a
sizeable proportion of families were likely to have boarders in their midst at
some points in their lives.

---

*The growth of schools is relevant to a discussion of the dispersion of those activities
which were once located in the home. Some relevant material may be found in Bailyn
(1960) and Cremin (1970) for the colonial period. Cremin (1951, 1961) discusses
educational thought and institutions through the middle of the twentieth century.

The decline of boarding as a widespread practice did not occur until well into the twentieth century. Modell (1972) says:

> Extensive if imperfectly representative data on working-class families collected in industrial areas by the Commissioner of Labor in 1903 found that about 22 percent of the native-born and 25 percent of foreign-headed families had some income from boarders and lodgers in the previous years. . . . By 1930, the proportion of all United States families in urban areas who kept a lodger was 11.4 percent, a figure perhaps somewhat inflated by the depression which apparently continued to keep the figure as high as 9.0 percent in 1940. . . . Prosperity, changes in housing availability, and changed tastes reduced the urbanized-areas figure to 3.0 percent in 1960.

While apprentices and other people's children may have declined as sources of nonkindred household members early in the nineteenth century, and servants decreased steadily as industrialization grew, boarders seem to have replaced these other groups as nonkin household residents. It is not until well into the middle of the present century that household composition became restricted to the nuclear kin group.

Privacy and the Usage of Space

The analysis of the audience of family behavior, so far, has concentrated on family activities and interactions within the household. Yet the house does not provide the only site for family activities, and the privacy associated with the enactment of family roles can be measured in at least two spatial contexts, one within the house and the other outside of it. Parks, streets, churches, ball parks, camp sites, etc., are also places where the family group may be seen together. Therefore, the usage and availability of space, both in- and outside the household, is relevant to a consideration of the ways in which spatial characteristics will affect the visibility of family behavior. (Smith, 1971, discusses ways in which household space is likely to affect family interactions.)

Demos' (1970, pp. 24–51) description of some of the residences in Plymouth Colony—a small house of few rooms, with limited sources of heating—exemplifies conditions in which spatial limitations contributed to a lack of privacy within the household. Furthermore, the absence of what Hall (1969, pp. 103–107) refers to as "fixed-feature space" as a characteristic of room organization in the past—even when crowding was less of a problem than in the colonial cottage—also contributed to a lack of privacy in the enactment of family roles. Flaherty (1972, pp. 25–84) argues that privacy was not only valued but attainable in the New England colonies, but his descriptions, too, support the view that crowding existed within the household and privacy was difficult to attain.

Changes in architectural styles and practices are also likely to have had considerable effect on within-family interaction, although further study is necessary to elaborate on the nature of these changes. Flaherty (1972, p. 40), discussing the design of eighteenth-century American homes, says:

> . . . the absence of hallways . . . remained a basic flaw in the floor plan of the central-chimney house. Movement from one part of the house to another required passage through adjacent rooms.

The development of the central hallway, with rooms opening onto it, permitted a degree of within-family privacy not previously available. Frank Lloyd Wright's development of the open floor plan, where only bedrooms were separated from the free and open access of all other parts of the house (see Wright, 1954) also had a great effect on family interactions within the house. But Wright's modern innovation occurred when household composition (according to the evidence presented in the preceding section) was more likely to be composed of nuclear family members only, contributing to different consequences in the "open plan" colonial house or cottage compared to the modern suburban house.

Handlin (forthcoming) claims that the development of the single-family detached house as an ideal setting of American domestic life took place at the beginning of the nineteenth century and has had great influence on the work of architects and designers in the field of domestic design. The increasing population density and visibility which accompanied the change from rural to urban living from the mid-nineteenth century onward may have motivated a search for privacy within the home which had been less necessary (and less available) in an earlier period. Lynd and Lynd (1929, p. 26) describe changes in the usage of space in Middletown in the following way:

> In the eighties, with their ample yards, porches were not urgently needed. Towards 1900, as smaller yards were driving the family closer to the house, people began to hear of porches . . . and the era of porch furniture began. Already, however, business class homes are leading the way in a reversion to porchless designs with glassed-in sun parlor and sleeping porch. . . . The trend is apparently to divert the money formerly put into front porches to sleeping porches, glassed-in dens, and other more private and more often used parts of the house.

Evidence that privacy continues as a twentieth-century ideal for home design can be found in a recent analysis of the urban environment in which Michelson (1970, p. 101) discusses "the ultimate desirability of single-family housing in today's technology."

Several discussions of the family in the past have emphasized the out-of-doors settings of family interactions. A report in the *Architectural Record* (1892, p. 56) describing middle-class apartment living in New York at the end of the nineteenth century, remarks on "the tendency of many tenants to make parlors of, and hold receptions on, the stoops." McLaughlin (1971) describes similar patterns among first-generation Italians in Buffalo, New York, at the beginning of the twentieth century, and it is precisely the decline in such patterns which Jane Jacobs (1961) discusses in her analysis of contemporary American cities. Sennett (1970) describes the importance of parks for the social life of upper-class families in Chicago in the early part of the nineteenth century. If and when family social life takes place in the open, the possibility of observability is increased: the number of observers is likely to be greater and there will be less control over who those observers are in such a setting.*

Evidence still remains to be collected to support the claim that the spatial characteristics of the setting in which family interactions occur in the more recent period of American history has contributed to less public scrutiny of the enactment of family roles than was true in the past. There are several reasons, though, to believe that further work will uncover such evidence.

The involvement of the federal government (through VA and FHA loan programs) and private banks and insurance companies in financing the construction of dwelling units is likely to have contributed to a decrease in room overcrowding. These same factors are likely to have contributed to the realization of the single-family detached home ideal in this century to a greater extent than was true of any earlier period in American history.

Changes in the amenities available within the home—those associated with comfort (central heating, indoor plumbing, air conditioning, etc.) as well as those associated with entertainment (radio, television, and phonographs)—are likely to have decreased the proportion of family activities which take place outside the home, where control over visibility is limited, and to have increased the proportion of such activities which take place within the home, where control over visibility is increased.

Each of these factors provides a background for hypothesizing that further research into architectural and housing data will provide supporting evidence for the thesis that the private family is a twentieth-century development.

Privacy and Norms

The previous sections of this analysis have considered some of the structural and material conditions which have affected the context of family role behavior in the past and in the present. This section will discuss changes in

---

*Some constraints on observability, particularly in this case, those associated with residential segregation by class, would nevertheless continue to operate.

the norms which are likely to have had an impact on behavior within these changing contexts.

Morgan (1944) describes the importance of religion for family relationships and behavior among the Puritans in seventeenth-century New England. Not only did religion specify the correct relationships between family members—their duties and responsibilities to each other—but it also made it a sacred duty of members of the church to see that these edicts were fulfilled. Laws were enacted to ensure that proper behavior within families took place, and punishments were meted out to those who defaulted.

The quality of family relationships was also subject to legal control. Demos (1970, p. 93) says:

> It was not enough that married persons should simply live together on a regular basis; their relationship must be relatively peaceful and harmonious.

And courts had jurisdiction to punish offenders who deviated from "peaceful and harmonious" behavior. According to Morgan (1944, pp. 39–40):

> The government was not satisfied with mere cohabitation but insisted that it be peaceful. Husbands and wives were forbidden by law to strike each other, and the courts enforced the provisions on numerous occasions.

Husbands and wives were fined for using "ill words" to each other or "railing" at each other or "striking and kicking."

Thus, the norms regulating family relationships in the earliest period of American history were heavily influenced by religion, and were enforced through law via the scrutiny of others who were empowered by those same religious beliefs to mind their neighbors' business. (Demos (1970, pp. 49–51) has suggested that the anger which crowded living conditions generated in Plymouth Colony was unconsciously displaced onto neighbors through a "chronic hostility" toward them. Such a dynamic may have been reinforced by the sense that neighbors acted as constant watchdogs over an institution that Flaherty (1972, p. 45) claims was "the primary place where colonists sought privacy.") The same norms which specified what family behavior should be also specified that others had the right to hold one accountable for its proper enactment. Thus, public accountability was built into the system of norms surrounding the performance of family roles.

Handlin (forthcoming) claims that the nineteenth century saw major changes in American domestic life. Horace Bushnell, "an influential minister, living in Hartford, Connecticut, but with a national audience through his published sermons," referred to these changes as a "transition from mother and daughter power to water and steam power." Mothers and daughters were being released from some of the drudgery which had characterized housekeeping in the past. Some greater freedom of choice was becoming available in the public world of work through the changing demands of an industrialized economy. The growing place of women in public life—through club, consumer, and reform groups—also provided alternatives in the realm of public activity for the mothers and daughters whose energies were being somewhat released by technological advance. But the ideology which accompanied the structural changes in family life into the twentieth century emphasized the traditional place of women in their family roles, which were enacted in settings that were increasingly private. In my view, an important aspect of this ideology for the modern family can be traced through the development of what was later to become an organized, institutional effort to "professionalize" domestic activities—*i.e.*, through the growth of the home economics movement in the United States.

The home economics movement, whose history can be traced back to the efforts of nineteenth-century women's clubs and other organizations (see Baldwin, 1949; Bevier, 1924) was formally organized in 1899 at the first Lake Placid Conference on Home Economics, and was replaced in 1908-09 by the still ongoing American Home Economics Association. The story of the development of home economics as a subject of interest and attention in America cannot be told here in any detail. Its relevance to this analysis is in terms of the norms about family life which it exhibited, the mechanisms by which these norms were circulated and the ways in which they interacted with the changing structural bases of family life at the beginning of the twentieth century.*

Although varied ideas were expressed by early members of the home economics movement, two seem particularly important: (1) the belief that family roles were not instinctual or natural, but were to be learned; and (2) that skills must be taught and learned, not in the home, but in the schools, from specially trained personnel. The emphasis was on the need for scientific management, efficiency, and economy within the home and on the role of the school in producing these desired ends. (An interesting account of the background to these concerns within the field of education can be found in Cremin (1961).)

The argument was put in various ways in the *Proceedings* of the early annual conferences, in the *Journal of Home Economics* (which began publication in 1909), and in other writings. Some examples follow:

---

*The relevant historical context must be kept in mind. These events occurred at a period in which young women and children continued to be a source of factory labor, when the availability of domestic servants was sharply declining, when problems of health, sanitation, overcrowded housing, immigration, and poverty in the rapidly growing urban centers were attracting the attention of many social and political reformers.

> A woman does not keep house by inspiration as formerly thought. She keeps house 'well' only by application of intelligence and technical training. Neither does a woman take care of her children by inspiration. (Lake Placid Conference, 1902, p. 50)

> Many think that home economics is an instinct, the same that leads young birds to nest building, and that no special training is required. The man that undertakes any business goes through some form of apprenticeship and becomes familiar with all the details of management, but to the majority of women housekeeping is a combination of accidental forces. . . . So we are working toward a more systematic method of carrying on home work. Women and girls should have special education and training in this subject. . . . (Lake Placid Conference, 1907, p. 84)

The principles of health, sanitation, and nutrition had to be taught. They were neither instinctual nor could the home, through maternal teaching or example, be expected to provide the technical knowledge which proper housekeeping required.

> To choose the food for a family and to prepare it properly are feats the successful accomplishment of which require a technical training. . . . She [the homemaker] can not afford to disregard this increasing knowledge of the dependence of health on food, she can not afford to deprive her family, her children, of any aid that science can give to equip them in the most efficient manner for the stress and strain of life. (Lake Placid Conference, 1904, pp. 42–43)

The new knowledge and skills had to be made available to middle-class families experiencing the decline in available servants, to immigrant peasant women who were ignorant of modern housekeeping tchniques and who could not, therefore, pass these skills on to their daughters, and to working girls whose labor force participation had deprived them of the opportunity of learning at home the old skills, if not the new.

The answer to the problem was clear—education. Julia Lathrop, first head of the Children's Bureau (founded in 1912), said, in a speech to a class reunion at Vassar College (Addams, 1935, pp. 40–41):

> . . . the present status of the education of women demands a new specialization to be signaled by the creation of centers of study and research in the service of family life. . . . It is no less than a revolution which is implied. Its aim is to give the work of the woman head of a household the status of a profession.

Isabel Bevier, one of the most active early members of the home economics movement and President of the American Home Economics Association in 1911 and 1912, wrote (1924, p. 161):

> The original Lake Placid group had distinguished itself by putting emphasis upon the educational phase of the question and, from the first, there had been committees commissioned to find ways and means so to

develop the subject-matter that it would find favor with public school boards and makers of college curricula.

And their efforts met with considerable success, from the federal government, which provided funding for home economics education (see Douglas, 1924, p. 294; Cremin, 1961, p. 56; Bevier, 1924, pp. 172–178) and from colleges, universities, and public school systems which, for a while at least, steadily increased their offerings and training facilities in the field of home economics. (See Bevier, 1924, pp. 142–143.)

The concerns and ideology of the home economics movement were also disseminated through other channels than the schools. The General Federation of Women's Clubs, with a membership of 800,000 women in 1907 and affiliates in 47 states (see Lake Placid Conference, 1907, p. 98) was also interested and active in this work. Mrs. C. S. Buell, President of the State Federation of Clubs in Madison, Wisconsin, said to the Ninth Lake Placid Conference (1907, pp. 97–98):

> . . . we of the Federated women's clubs may be of aid in bringing to the active homemaker the results of your studies. . . . We appeal to you for your best thought and effort, pledging you our loyal support and earnest endeavor to make your purposes as far-reaching as possible.

The home economics movement, then, can be seen as developing a modern ideology for the American family in general and for the woman in it in particular. The goal of scientific home management and efficiency, and the use of educational institutions to achieve this end through the training of girls to be modern homemakers, emphasized traditional views of women's place in the home and reinforced the sanctity and privacy of the individual family. Not only was there the old will, reinforced by a scientific ideology, but there was also the way, provided by the new structural characteristics of the family described in earlier sections. The privacy which the New England colonists had valued so highly more than two centuries earlier was finally attainable.

Conclusion

The argument made here is that an attempt to understand changes in the American family may fruitfully be pursued by attention to variations in the family as a public and private institution. When it is common practice for family life to occur elsewhere than within the confines of the domestic establishment, such as in parks or on front stoops, when it is common for nondomestic activities—such as political and economic—to be pursued within the domestic context, when it is common for nonfamily members—such as servants, apprentices, and boarders—to constitute part of the household, then the family can be described as having a public character.

Structural and normative support for privacy within the family is, I would suggest, a more accurate description of the twentieth-century family than it was of its historical predecessor, despite the potential for much variation in publicness and privacy along other lines. A setting in which most of the interactions of family members take place in the home and those activities defined as appropriate to the home are related primarily to domestic and familial activities, there is greater control over the composition of the audience of family behavior, and thus a greater degree of privacy.

To the extent that family privacy has increased, then, it is also likely that there has been a decrease in social control over and social support for a traditional definition of the performance of family roles. The consequences of this development (as well as the truth of the claim itself) remain to be studied and discussed further. One theme in current considerations of the family is about the viability and future of the nuclear family form. (See, for instance, Gordon, 1972, pp. 1–22; Skolnick and Soklnick, 1971, pp. 1–32.) These discussions often point to the strains of nuclear family living which have led to experimentation with alternative family styles, such as communal living, group marriages, and single-parent families. If social control declines as privacy increases, then there may be structural reasons for believing that the current variability in the styles of American family life will continue.* The point should be made, though, that an increase of alternate family living styles does not necessarily herald the death of the nuclear family, but rather a variability in which several types of family organization will exist simultaneously.

One further observation may be appropriate. Goode's (1963) analysis of changing family patterns throughout the world led him to conclude that the conjugal family unit will become predominant as the structural and ideological features associated with the western experience of industrialization occur elsewhere. This analysis, which focuses on privacy, rather than on nuclearity per se, suggests that the change in family patterns which Goode sees in the future of newly industrializing nations may be an historical phase within each culture, and not necessarily a permanent development. If the analysis presented here, of the American case, has any predictive value, it is in suggesting that change will continue to occur beyond the development of the conjugal family.

*A continuation and extension of such variability, though, assumes that external forces will not impose greater conformity. Farber's (1972b) analysis of recent changes in law relating to the family and privacy suggests that legal restrictions in "the interests of the state" may provide a basis for limiting privacy and variation. The authority of the state, therefore, may attempt to impose restrictions on family life in the modern period in a manner familiar in colonial New England. That such legal restrictions, though, may have different consequences for different social class groupings in the society, again indicates the importance of that variable in understanding the process and change being discussed.

References

Addams, Jane. *My Friend, Julia Lathrop*. New York: Macmillan, 1935.

Architectural Record, 1 (July-September 1892): 55–64.

Ariès, Philippe. *Centuries of Childhood: A Social History of Family Life*. New York: Knopf, 1962.

Bailyn, Bernard. *Education in the Forming of American Society*. Chapel Hill: University of North Carolina Press, 1960.

Baldwin, Keturah E. *The AHEA Saga*. Washington, D.C.: American Home Economics Association, 1949.

Beresford, John C., and Alice M. Rivlin. "Privacy, Poverty and Old Age." *Demography*, 3 (1966): 247–258.

Berkner, Lutz K. "The Stem Family and the Developmental Cycle of the Peasant Household: An Eighteenth-Century Austrian Example." *American Historical Review*, 77 (April 1972): 398–418.

Bevier, Isabel. *Home Economics in Education*. Philadelphia: Lippincott, 1924.

Bloomberg, Susan E., Mary Frank Fox, Robert M. Warner, and Sam Bass Warner, Jr. "A Census Probe into Nineteenth-Century Family History: Southern Michigan, 1850–1880." *Journal of Social History*, 5 (Fall 1971): 26–45.

Bonacich, Phillip. "Norms and Cohesion as Adaptive Responses to Potential Conflict: An Experimental Study." *Sociometry*, 35 (September 1972): 357–375.

Burgess, Ernest W., and Harvey J. Locke. *The Family: From Institution to Companionship*. New York: American Book Company, 1953.

Clark, Euphemia. "A Campaign for Home Making." *Journal of Home Economics*, 1 (April 1909): 167–170.

Coale, Ansley J., and Melvin Zelnik. *New Estimates of Fertility and Population in the United States*. Princeton: Princeton University Press, 1963.

Cremin, Lawrence A. *The American Common School*. New York: Teachers College, Columbia University, 1951.

Cremin, Lawrence A. *The Transformation of the School: Progressivism in American Education*. New York: Knopf, 1961.

Cremin, Lawrence A. *American Education: The Colonial Experience, 1607–1783*. New York: Harper and Row, 1970.

Demos, John. "Families in Colonial Bristol, R.I." *William and Mary Quarterly*, 25 (January 1968): 40–57.

Demos, John. *A Little Commonwealth*. New York: Oxford, 1970.

Demos, John. "Demography and Psychology in the Historical Study of Family Life: A Personal Report." In *Household and Family in Past Time,* edited by Peter Laslett, pp. 561–569. Cambridge: Cambridge University Press, 1972.

Demos, John, and Virginia Demos. "Adolescence in Historical Perspective." In *Readings on the Sociology of the Family,* edited by Bert N. Adams and Thomas Weirath, pp. 30–40. Chicago: Markham, 1971.

Douglas, Paul H. *American Apprenticeship and Industrial Education*. Studies in History, Economics and Public Law XCV. New York: Columbia University, 1921.

Farber, Bernard. *Guardians of Virtue: Salem Families in 1800*. New York: Basic Books, 1972.

Farber, Bernard. "Historical Trends in American Family Law." Paper read at a National Conference on the Family Social Structure and Social Change, April 27–29, 1972. Clark University, Worcester, Massachusetts.

Flaherty, David H. *Privacy in Colonial New England*. Charlottesville: University Press of Virginia, 1972.

Gilman, Charlotte Perkins. *The Home: Its Work and Influence*. New York: Charlton, 1910.

Goode, William J. *World Revolution and Family Patterns*. New York: Free Press, 1963.

Gordon, Michael, ed. *The Nuclear Family in Crisis: The Search for an Alternative.* New York: Harper and Row, 1972.

Greven, Philip. "Family Structure in 17th-Century Andover." *William and Mary Quarterly*, 23 (April 1966): 234–256.

Greven, Philip. *Four Generations: Population, Land, and Family in Colonial Andover, Massachusetts.* New York: Cornell University Press, 1970.

Greven, Philip. "The Average Size of Families and Households in the Province of Massachusetts in 1764 and in the United States in 1790: An Overview." In *Household and Family in Past Time*, edited by Peter Laslett, pp. 545–560. Cambridge: Cambridge University Press, 1972.

Hall, Edward T. *The Hidden Dimension.* New York: Anchor Books, 1969.

Handlin, David P. "The Detached House in the Age of the Object and Beyond." Chapter of a forthcoming book, *New Dimensions in Housing.*

Hecht, J. Jean. *The Domestic Servant Class in Eighteenth-Century England.* London: Routledge and Kegan Paul, 1956.

Hunt, David. *Parents and Children in History: The Psychology of Family Life in Early Modern France.* New York: Basic Books, 1970.

Jacobs, Jane. *The Death and Life of Great American Cities.* New York: Vintage Books, 1961.

Katz, Michael B. "Four Propositions about Social and Family Structures in Pre-industrial Society." A paper prepared for the Comparative Social Mobility Conference, Institute of Advanced Study, Princeton, New Jersey, June 15–17, 1972.

Katz, Michael B. "Growing-up in the Nineteenth Century." Working Paper #31. Canadian Social History Project, 1972.

Lake Placid Conference on Home Economics. *Proceedings of the Fourth Annual Conference.* Lake Placid, New York, 1902.

Lake Placid Conference on Home Economics. *Proceedings of the Ninth Annual Conference.* Lake Placid, New York, 1907.

Laslett, Peter. "Size and Structure of the Household in England over Three Centuries." *Population Studies*, 23 (July 1969): 199–223.

Laslett, Peter. *The World We Have Lost.* 2nd ed. London: University Paperbacks, 1971.

Lockridge, Kenneth A. "The Population of Dedham, Massachusetts, 1636–1736." *Economic History Review*, 19 (1966): 318–344.

Lynd, Robert S., and Helen Merrell Lynd. *Middletown.* New York: Harcourt Brace, 1929.

McLaughlin, Virginia Yans. "Working Class Immigrant Families: First Generation Italians in Buffalo, New York." Paper delivered before the Organization of American Historians, April 1971.

Merton, Robert K. "The Role Set: Problems in Sociological Theory." *British Journal of Sociology*, 7 (June 1959).

Michelson, William. *Man and His Urban Environment: A Sociological Approach.* Reading, Mass.: Addison-Wesley, 1970.

Modell, John. "Strangers in the Family: Boarding and Lodging in Industrial America." Paper read at a National Conference on the Family, Social Structure and Social Change, April 27–29, 1972. Clark University, Worcester, Massachusetts.

Morgan, Edmund S. *The Puritan Family.* New York: Harper, 1944.

Murrin, John. Review Essay. History and Theory. *Studies in the Philosophy of History*, 2, 1972.

Ogburn, W. F., and M. F. Nimkoff. *Technology and the Changing Family.* Boston: Houghton Mifflin, 1955.

O'Neill, William L. *Divorce in the Progressive Era.* New Haven: Yale University Press, 1967.

Parish, William L., and Moshe Schwartz. "Household Complexity in Nineteenth Century France." *American Sociological Review*, 37 (April 1972): 154–173.

Pryor, Edward T., Jr. "Rhode Island Family Structure: 1887–1960." In *Household and Family in Past Time,* edited by Peter Laslett, pp. 571–589. Cambridge: Cambridge University Press, 1972.

Riis, Jacob. *Jacob Riis Revisited: Poverty and the Slum in Another Era.* Edited with an introduction by Francesco Cordasco. New York: Doubleday, Anchor, 1968.

Sennett, Richard. *Families Against the City: Middle Class Homes of Industrial Chicago, 1872–1890.* Cambridge, Mass.: Harvard University Press, 1970.

Skolnick, Arlene S., and Jerome H. Skolnick, eds. *Family in Transition: Rethinking Marriage, Sexuality, Child Rearing, and Family Organization.* Boston: Little, Brown, 1971.

Smith, Dorothy E. "Household Space and Family Organization." *Pacific Sociological Review,* 14 (January 1971): 53–78.

Vinovskis, Maris A. "American Historical Demography: A Review Essay." *Historical Methods Newsletter,* 4 (September 1971): 141–148.

Vinovskis, Maris A. "Morality Rates and Trends in Massachusetts Before 1860." *Journal of Economic History,* 32 (March 1972): 184–213.

Wright, Frank Lloyd. *The Natural House.* New York: Horizon Press, 1954.

The author of this article takes issue wtih many of the assumptions that have prevailed among scholars of the family. She argues that the family as we know it is not universal, is not the pillar of society, and is not immune to change. She attributes the current public concern about the family to fundamenatl challenges to the social and psychological basis of the family: the problems of marriage in urban industrial society, trends in work and education that are changing relations between the sexes, and the biological revolution.

Does the Family Have a Future? | *Suzanne Keller*

Some thirty-five years ago, two venerable students of human behavior engaged in a six-session debate on marriage and the family over the B.B.C. Their names were Bronislaw Malinowski and Robert Briffault, the one a world-famous anthropologist best known for his studies of the Trobriand Islands, the other a social historian devoted to resurrecting the matriarchies of prehistory. Of the two, paradoxically, it was Briffault, the self-trained historian, who turned out to be the cultural relativist whereas Malinowski, a pioneer in crosscultural research, exhibited the very ethnocentrism his studies were designed to dispel.

Both men noted that the family was in trouble in their day. Both were

Reprinted by permission from Suzanne Keller, "Does the Family Have a Future?" *Journal of Comparative Family Studies,* Spring 1971.

distressed by this and sought to discover remedies if not solutions. Despite their common concern, however, they were soon embroiled in vivid and vociferous controversy about the nature of the crisis and its cure. (*Marriage: Past and Present,* ed. M. F. Ashley-Montagu, Boston, Porter Sargent, 1956)

Briffault concluded from his reading of the evidence that the family rests on sentiments rooted in culture and social tradition rather than in human nature. Unless one grasps these social and cultural essentials, one cannot hope to understand, much less cure, what ails it. No recourse to natural instinct or to the "dictatorship of tradition or moral coercion" could save the modern family from its destined decline.

Malinowski disagreed. The family, he admitted, might be passing through a grave crisis but the illness was not fatal. Marriage and the family, "the foundation of human society," and a key source of spiritual and material progress, were here to stay, though not without some needed improvements. Among these were the establishment of a single standard of morality, greater legal and economic equality between husband and wife, and greater freedom in parent-child relations.

The disagreement of these two men stemmed, as it so often does, not from different diagnoses but from different definitions of the phenomenon. Malinowski defined the family as a legal union of one man and one woman, together with their offspring, bound by reciprocal rights and duties, and cooperating for the sake of economic and moral survival. Briffault defined the family much more broadly as any association involving economic production and sexual procreation. In his sense, the clan was a family.

The two agreed on only one point: parenthood and above all maternity are the pivots in the anatomy of marriage and the family. If these change so must the familial organization that contained them. Thus if one can identify such pivotal changes their difficulties are overcome while ours may be said to be just beginning.

There is good reason to suppose that such changes are now upon us. The malaise of our time reflects not simply a temporary disenchantment with an ancient institution but a profound convulsion of the social order. The family is indeed suffering a seachange.

It is curious to note how much more quickly the popular press, including the so-called women's magazines, have caught on to changing marital, sexual, and parental styles. While many of the experts are still serving up conventional and tradition-bound idols—the hard-working, responsible, breadwinner husband-father, the self-effacing, ministering, wife-mother, the grateful, respectful children—these magazines tempt the contemporary reader with less standard and more challenging fare. Whether in New York or in Athens, the newsstands flaunt their provocative titles— "Is This the Last Marrying Generation?", "Alimony for Ex-Husbands,"

"Why We Don't Want to Have Children," "Are Husbands Superfluous?"—in nonchalant profusion. These and other assaults on our sexual and moral codes in the shape of the new theater, the new woman, the new youth, and TV soap operas akin to a psychiatrist's case files, persuade us that something seems to be afoot in the whole sphere of marriage and family relations which many had thought immune to change. In point of fact the question is not *whether* the family is changing but how and how much; how important are these changes, how permanent, how salutary? The answers depend largely on the way we ask our questions and define our terms.

The family means many things to many people but in its essence it refers to those socially patterned ideals and practices concerned with biological and cultural survival of the species. When we speak of the family we are using a kind of shorthand, a label for a social invention not very different, in essence, from other social inventions, let us say the Corporation or the University, and no more permanent than these. This label designates a particular set of social practices concerned with procreation and child rearing; with the heterosexual partnerships that make this possible and the parent-child relations that make it enduring. As is true of all collective habits, once established, such practices are exceedingly resistant to change, in part because they evoke strong sentiments and in part because no acceptable alternatives are offered. Since most individuals are unable to step outside of their cultures, they are unable to note the arbitrary and variable nature of their conventions. Accordingly, they ascribe to their folkways and creeds an antiquity, an inevitability, and a universality these do not possess.

The idea that the family is universal is highly misleading despite its popularity. All surviving societies have indeed found ways to stabilize the processes of reproduction and child care else they would not have survived to tell their tale. But since they differ greatly in how they arrange these matters (and since they are willing to engage in Hot and Cold Wars to defend such differences) the generalization does not help us explain the phenomenon but more nearly explains it away.

In truth there are as many forms of the family as there are forms of society, some so different from ours that we consider them unnatural and incomprehensible. There are, for example, societies in which couples do not share a household and do not have sole responsibility for their offspring; others in which our domestic unit of husband and wife is divided into two separate units, a conjugal one of biological parents and a brother-sister unit for economic sustenance. There are societies in which children virtually rear each other and societies in which the wise father does not know his own child. All of these are clearly very different from our twentieth century, industrial-urban conception of the family as a legally united couple, sharing bed and board, jointly responsible for bearing and rearing their children, and formally isolated from their next of kin in all but a sentimental sense. This product of a long and complicated evolutionary development from prehistoric times is no simple replica of the ancient productive and reproductive institutions from which it derives its name and some of its characteristic features. The contemporary family really has little in common with its historic Hebrew, Greek, and Roman ancestors.

The family of these great civilizations of the West was a household community of hundreds, and sometimes thousands, of members ("familia" is the Latin term for household). Only some of the members were related by blood and by far the larger part were servants and slaves, artisans, friends, and distant relations. In its patriarchal form (again culturally variable), this large community was formally held together by the role of eldest male who more nearly resembled the general of an army than a modern husband-father. In its prime, this household community constituted a miniature society, a decentralized version of a social organization that had grown too large and unwieldy for effective management. In this it resembles the giant bureaucracies of our own day, and their proposed decentralization into locally based, locally staffed subsystems, designed to offset the evils of remote control while nevertheless maintaining their connection with it. Far from having been universal, this ancient family type, with its gods and shrines, schools and handicrafts, was not even widely prevalent within its own social borders. Confined to the landed and propertied upper classes, it remained an unattainable ideal for the bulk of common men who made up the society.

The fallacy of universality has done students of human behavior a great disservice. By leading us to seek and hence to find a single pattern, it has blinded us to historical precedents for multiple legitimate family arrangements. As a result we have been rather impoverished in our speculations and proposals about alternative future arrangements in the family sphere.

A second common fallacy asserts that the family is *the* basic institution of society, hereby revealing a misunderstanding of how a society works. For as a social institution, the family is by definition a specialized element which provides society with certain needed services and depends on it for others. This means that you cannot tamper with a society without expecting the family to be affected in some way and vice versa. In the contemporary jargon, we are in the presence of a feedback system. Whatever social changes we anticipate, therefore, the family cannot be kept immune from them.

A final fallacy concerns the presumed naturalness of the family in proof of which a motley and ill-assorted grab bag of anecdotal evidence from the animal kingdom is adduced. But careful perusal of ethological accounts suggests that animals vary as greatly as we do, their mating and parental groupings including such novelties as the love death, males who bear children, total and guilt-free "promiscuity," and other "abnormal" features. The range of variation is so wide, in fact, that virtually any human arrangement can be justified by recourse to the habits of some animal species.

In sum, if we wish to understand what is happening to the family—to our family—in our own day, we must examine and observe it in the here and now. In so doing it would be well to keep in mind that the family is an abstraction at best, serving as guide and image of what a particular society considers desirable and appropriate in family relations, not what takes place in actual fact. In reality there are always a number of empirical family types at variance with this, though they usually pay lip service to the overarching cultural ideal.

Challenges to the Contemporary Industrial Family

In the United States, as in other industrial societies, the ideal family consists of a legally constituted husband-wife team, their young, dependent children, living in a household of their own, provided for by the husband's earnings as main breadwinner, and emotionally united by the wife's exclusive concentration on the home. Probably no more than one-third of all families at a particular moment in time, and chiefly in the middle and would-be middle classes, actually live up to this image. The remaining majority all lack one or more of the essential attributes—in lacking a natural parent, or in not being economically self-sufficient, or in having made other necessary modifications.

One contrasting form is the extended family in which the couple share household arrangements and expenses with parents, siblings, or other close relatives. The children are then reared by several generations and have a choice of models on which to pattern their behavior. This type, frequent in working class and immigrant milieus, may be as cohesive and effective as the ideal type but it lacks the cultural legitimacy and desirability of the latter.

A third family type, prevalent among the poor of all ethnic and racial backgrounds, is the mother-child family. Contrary to our prejudices this need not be a deviant or distorted family form, for it may be the only viable and appropriate one in its particular setting. Its defects may stem more from adverse social judgments than from intrinsic failings. Deficient in cultural resources and status, it may nevertheless provide a humane and spirited setting for its members, particularly if some sense of stability and continuity has been achieved. Less fortunate are the numerous non-families, ex-families, and non-intact families such as the divorced, the widowed, the unmarriageables, and many other fragmented social forms, who have no recognized social place. None of these, however, threaten the existing order since they are seen and see themselves as involuntarily different, imperfect, or unfortunate. As such they do not challenge the ideals of family and marital relations but simply suggest how difficult it is to live up to them. When we talk of family change or decline, however, it is precisely the ideal standards which we have in mind. A challenge to them cannot be met by simple reaffirmations of old truths, disapproval, shock, or ridicule of the challengers, or feigned indifference. Such challenges must be met head on.

Today the family and its social and psychological underpinnings are being fundamentally challenged from at least three sources: (1) from accumulated failures and contradictions in marriage; (2) from pervasive occupational and educational trends including the changing relations between the sexes, the spread of birth control, and the changing nature of work; and (3) from novel developments in biology. Let me briefly examine each.

It is generally agreed that even in its ideal form, the industrial-urban family makes great, some would say excessive, demands on its members. For one thing it rests on the dyadic principle or pair relationship which, as Georg Simmel observed long ago, is inherently tragic and unstable. Whether in chess, tennis, or marriage, two are required to start and continue the game but only one can destroy it. In this instance, moreover, the two are expected to retain their separate identities as male and female and yet be one in flesh and spirit. No wonder that the image of the couple, a major source of fusion and of schism in our society, is highly contradictory according to whether we think of the sexes as locked in love or in combat. Nor do children, the symbols of their union, necessarily unify them. Their own growing pains and cultural demands force them into mutually exclusive socio-sexual identities, thereby increasing the intimate polarity. In fact, children arouse parental ambivalence in a number of ways, not the least of which is that they demand all but give back all too little. And yet their upbringing and sustenance, the moral and emotional climate, as well as the accumulation of economic and educational resources needed for survival, all rest on this small, fragile, essential but very limited unit. Held together by sentimental rather than by corporate bonds, the happiness of the partners is a primary goal although no one is very sure what happiness means nor how it may be achieved and sustained.

To these potentials for stress and strain must be added the loss of many erstwhile functions to school, state, and society, and with it something of the glamour and challenge of family commitments. Few today expect the family to be employment agency, welfare state, old age insurance, or school for life. Yet once upon a time, not too long ago at that, it was all that and more. At the same time, however, with fewer resources, some new burdens have been added stemming from rising standards of child health, education, and welfare. This makes parents even more crucially responsible for the potential fate of their children over whom they have increasingly less exclusive control.

Like most social institutions in the throes of change, moreover, the modern family is also beset by numerous internal contradictions engendered by the conflict between traditional patterns of authority and a new egalitarianism between husbands and wives and parents and children. The equality of the spouses, for example, collides with the continuing greater economic responsibilities, hence authority, of the husband. The voluntary harness of love chafes under the constraint of numerous obligations and duties imposed by marriage, and dominance patterns by sex or age clash with new demands for mutuality, reciprocity, equity, and individualism. These, together with some unavoidable disillusionments and disappointments in marriage, set the stage for the influence of broader and less subjective social trends.

One such trend, demographic in nature but bound to have profound social implications, concerns the lengthened life expectancy and the shortened reproductive span for women. Earlier ages at marriage, fewer children per couple, and closer spacing of children means: the girl who marries at 20 will have all her children by age 26, have all her children in school by her early thirties, have the first child leave home for job, schooling, or marriage in her late thirties, and have all her children out of the home by her early forties. This leaves some thirty to forty years to do with as personal pleasure or social need dictate. The contrast with her grandmother is striking: later marriage, and more children spaced farther apart, meant all the children in school no earlier than her middle or late thirties and the last to leave home (if he or she ever did) not before her early fifties. At which time grandmother was probably a widow and close to the end of her own lifespan. The empty nest thus not only occurs earlier today but it lasts longer, affecting not this or that unfortunate individual woman but many if not most women. Hence what may in the past have been an individual misfortune has turned into a social emergency of major proportions. More unexpected free time, more time without a socially recognized or appreciated function, more premature retirements surely puts the conventional modern wife, geared to the domestic welfare of husband, home, and children, at a singular disadvantage relative to the never-married career woman. Destined to outlive her husband, stripped of major domestic responsibilities in her prime years, what is she to do with this windfall of extra hours and years? Surely we must expect and prepare for a major cultural shift in the education and upbringing of female children. If women cannot afford to make motherhood and domestic concerns the sole foci of their identities, they must be encouraged, early in life, to prepare themselves for some occupation or profession not as an adjunct or as a last resort in case of economic need but as an equally legitimate pursuit. The childrearing of girls must increasingly be geared to developing a feminine identity that stresses autonomy, non-dependency, and self-assertion in work and in life.

Some adjunct trends are indirectly stimulating just such a reorientation. When women are compelled, as they often are, to earn their own living or to supplement inadequate family resources necessitated by the high emphasis on personal consumption and the high cost of services increasingly deemed essential as national standards rise, conventional work-dependency patterns are shattered. For, since the male breadwinner is already fully occupied, often with two jobs, or if he cannot or will not work, his wife is forced to step in. Thus there is generated internal family pressure—arising from a concern for family welfare but ultimately not confined to it—for wives to be gainfully employed outside of the home. And fully three-fourths in the post-childbearing ages already are, albeit under far from ideal conditions. Torn between home and job, between the precepts of early childhood with its promise of permanent security at the side of a strong male and the pressures of a later reality, unaided by a society unaware or indifferent to her problems, the double-duty wife must manage as best she can.

That this need not be so is demonstrated by a number of modern societies whose public policies are far better meshed with changing social realities. Surely one of our more neglected institutions—the single-family household which, despite all the appliances, remains essentially backward and primitive in its conditions of work—will need some revamping and modernizing. More household appliances, more and more attractive alternatives to the individually run household, more nursery schools, and a total overhaul of work-schedules not now geared to a woman's life and interests cannot be long in coming. While these will help women in all of their multiple tasks, they may also of course further challenge the presumed joys of exclusive domesticity.

All in all, it would appear that the social importance of the family relative to other significant social arenas will, as Briffault among others correctly anticipated, decline. Even today when the family still exerts a strong emotional and sentimental hold its social weight is not what it once was. All of us ideally are still born in intact families but not all of us need to establish families to survive. Marriage and children continue to be extolled as supreme social and personal goals but they are no longer—especially for men—indispensable for a meaningful existence. As individual self-sufficiency, fed by economic affluence or economic self-restraint, increases, so does one's exemption from unwanted economic as well as kinship responsibilities. Today the important frontiers seem to lie elsewhere, in science, politics, and outer space. This must affect the attractions of family life for both men and women. For men, because they will see less and less reason to assume full economic and social responsibilities for four to five human beings in addition to themselves as it becomes more difficult and less necessary to do so. This, together with the continued decline of patriarchal authority and male dominance—even in the illusory forms in which they have managed to hang on—will remove some of the psychic rewards which prompted many men to marry, while the disappearance of lineage as mainstays of the social and class order will deprive paternity of its social justification. For women, the household may soon prove too small for the scope of their ambitions and power drives. Until recently these were directed first of all to their children, secondarily to their mates. But with the decline of parental control over children a major erstwhile source of challenge and creativity is removed from the family sphere. This must weaken the mother-wife complex, historically sustained by the necessity and exaltation of motherhood and the taboo on illegitimacy.

Above all, the move towards worldwide population and birth control must affect the salience of parenthood for men and women, as a shift of cultural emphasis and individual priorities deflates maternity as woman's chief social purpose and paternity as the prod to male exertions in the world of work. Very soon, I suspect, the cultural presses of the world will slant their messages against the bearing and rearing of children. Maternity, far from being a duty, not even a right, will then become a rare privilege to be granted to a select and qualified few. Perhaps the day is not far off when reproduction will be confined to a fraction of the population, and what was once inescapable necessity may become voluntary, planned, choice. Just as agricultural societies in which everyone had to produce food were once superseded by industrial societies in which a scant 6 per cent now produce food for all, so one day the few may produce children for the many.

This along with changing attitudes towards sex, abortion, adoption, illegitimacy, the spread of the pill, better knowledge of human behavior, and a growing scepticism that the family is the only proper crucible for child-rearing, creates a powerful recipe for change. World-wide demands for greater and better opportunities for self-development, and a growing awareness that these opportunities are inextricably enhanced or curtailed by the family as a prime determinant of life-chances, will play a major role in this change. Equal opportunity, it is now clear, cannot stop at the crib but must start there. "It is idle," commented Dr. Robert S. Morrison, a Cornell biologist, "to talk of a society of equal opportunity as long as that society abandons its newcomers solely to their families for their most impressionable years." (New York Times, October 30, 1966) One of the great, still largely unchallenged, injustices may well be that one cannot choose one's parents.

The trends that I have sketched would affect marriage, male-female, and parent-child relations even if no other developments were on the horizon. But there are. As yet barely discernible and still far from being applicable to human beings, recent breakthroughs in biology—with their promise of a greatly extended life span, novel modes of reproduction, and dramatic possibilities for genetic intervention—cannot be ignored in a discussion devoted to the future of the family.

Revolution in Biology

If the early part of this century belonged to physics and the middle period to exploratory ventures into outer space, the next few decades belong to biology. The prolongation of life to double or triple its current span seems virtually assured, the extension of female fertility into the sixties is more than a distinct possibility, and novel ways of reproducing the human species have moved from science fiction to the laboratory. The question then arises, What will happen when biological reproduction will not only be inadvisable for the sake of collective well-being but superseded by new forms and eventually by non-human forms of reproduction?

A number of already existing possibilities may give us a foretaste of what is to come. For example, the separation of conception from gestation means that motherhood can become specialized, permitting some women to conceive and rear many children and others to bear them without having to provide for them. Frozen sperm banks (of known donors) are envisioned from which prospective mothers could choose the fathers of their children on the basis of particularly admired or desired qualities, thereby advancing an age-old dream of selecting a distinguished paternity for their children based on demonstrated rather than potential male achievement. And it would grant men a sort of immortality to sire offspring long after their biological deaths as well as challenge the implicit equation now made between fathers and husbands. Finally, the as yet remote possibility to reproduce the human species without sexual intercourse, by permanently separating sex from procreation, would permit unmarried women (and men) to have children without being married, reduces a prime motive for marriage and may well dethrone—inconceivable as this may seem—the heterosexual couple. All of these pose questions of legal and social policy to plague the most subtle Solon. Who is the father of a child—the progenitor or the provider where these have become legitimately distinct roles? Who is the mother—the woman who conceives the child or the one who carries it to term? Who will decide on sex ratios once sex determination becomes routine? Along with such challenges and redefinitions of human responsibility, some see the fate of heterosexuality itself to lie in the balance. In part of course this rests on one's assumptions about the nature of sexuality and sexual identity.

Anatomy alone has never been sufficient for the classification of human beings into male and female which each society labors to develop and then calls natural. Anatomy is but one—and by no means always a reliable— identifying characteristic. Despite our beliefs, sex identification, even in the strictest physical sense, is by no means clear cut. Various endeavors to find foolproof methods of classification—for example, for participation in the Olympics—have been unsuccessful, as at least nine separate and often un- correlated components of sexual phenotype have been identified. But if we cannot count on absolute physical differentiations between the sexes, we do even less well when it comes to their social and psychological attributes. Several decades of research have shown beyond doubt that most of what we mean by the difference between the sexes is a blend of cultural myth and social necessity, which must be learned, painstakingly and imperfectly, from birth on. Once acquired, sexual identity is not fixed but needs to be reinforced and propped up in a myriad of ways of which we are quite un- aware.

In the past this complicated learning process was guided by what we may call the categorical reproductive imperative which proclaimed procreation as an unquestioned social goal and which steered the procreative and sexual capacities and aspirations of men and women toward appropriate channels virtually from birth on. Many other features strengthened these tendencies —symbolism and sentiment, work patterns and friendships, all kinds of subtle and not so subtle rewards and punishments for being a "real" man, a real woman. But once the reproductive imperative is transformed into a reproductive ban what will be the rationale for the continuance of the ex- clusive heterosexual polarity in the future? If we keep in mind that only two out of our forty-six chromosomes are sex-carrying, perhaps these two will disappear as their utility subsides. Even without such dramatic changes, already there is speculation that heterosexuality will become but one among several forms of sexuality, these having previously been suppressed by strong social sanctions against sexual deviation as well as their inability to repro- duce themselves in standard fashion. More than three decades ago, Olaf Stapleton, one of the most imaginative science fiction writers of the century, postulated the emergence of at least six subsexes out of the familiar ancient polarity. At about the same time, Margaret Mead, in the brilliant epilogue to her book on sex and temperament (*Sex and Temperament in Three Primi- tive Societies,* William Morrow and Co., New York, 1935), suggested a reorganization and recategorization of human identity not along but across traditional sex lines so as to produce a better alignment between individual capacity and social necessity. In our time we have witnessed the emergence of UniSex (the term is McLuhan's) and predictions which range from the disappearance of sex to its manifold elaboration.

Some are speculating about a future in which only one of the current sexes will survive, the other having become superfluous or obsolescent. Depending on the taste, temperament—and sex—of the particular writer, women and men have alternately been so honored (or cursed). It is not always easy to tell which aspect of sex—the anatomical, psychological, or cultural—the writer has in mind but as the following comment suggests, much more than anatomy is at stake.

> Does the man and woman thing have a future? The question may not be hypothetical much longer. Within 10 years . . . we may be able to choose the sex of our offspring; and later to reproduce without mating male and female cells. This means it will someday be possible to have a world with only one sex, woman, and thereby avoid the squabbles, confusions, and headaches that have dogged this whole business of sex down the centuries. A manless world suggests several scientific scenarios. The most pessimistic would have society changing not at all, but continuing on its manly ways of eager acquisition, hot competition, and mindless aggression. In which case, half the women would become "men" and go right on getting ulcers, shouting "charge" and pinning medals on each other. (George B. Leonard, "The Man and Woman Thing," *Look*, December 25, 1968)

Long before the demise of heterosexuality as a mainstay of the social order, however, we will have to come to terms with changing sexual attitudes and mores ushered in by what has been called the sexual revolution. This liberalization, this rejection of old taboos, half-truths, and hypocrisies, also means a crisis of identity as men and women, programmed for more traditional roles, search for the boundaries of their sexual selves in an attempt to establish a territoriality of the soul.

Confusion is hardly, of course, a novel aspect of the human condition. Not knowing where we have come from, why we are here, nor where we are headed, it could hardly be otherwise. There have always been dissatisfied men and women rejecting the roles their cultures have assigned them or the responsibilities attached to these. But these are the stuff of poetry and drama, grist for the analyst's couch or the priest's confessional, in other words private torments and agonies kept concealed from an unsympathetic world. It is only when such torments become transmuted into public grievance and so become publicly heard and acknowledged that we can be said to be undergoing profound changes akin to what we are experiencing today.

Returning now to our main question—Does the famliy have a future?—it should be apparent that I expect some basic and irreversible changes in the decades ahead and the emergence of some novel forms of human togetherness. Not that the current scene does not already offer some provocative variations on ancient themes, but most of these gain little public attention, still less approval, and so they are unable to alter professed beliefs and standards. Moreover, every culture has its own forms of self-justification and self-righteousness and in our eagerness to affirm the intrinsic superiority of our ways, we neglect to note the magnitude of variations and deviations from the ideals we espouse. What are we to make, for example, of such dubious allegiance to the monogamous ideal as serial marriages or secret adulteries? Or, less morally questionable, what of the quasi-organized part-time family arrangements necessitated by extreme occupational and geographic mobility? Consider for a moment the millions of families of salesmen, pilots, seacaptains, soldiers, sailors, and junior executives where the man of the house is not often *in* the house. These absentee husbands-fathers who magically re-enter the family circle just long enough to be appreciated, leaving their wives in charge of the homes they pay for and of the children they sired, are surely no more than part-time mates. If we know little about the adjustments they have had to make or their children's responses, this is because they clearly do not fit in with our somewhat outmoded stereotyped notions of what family relations ought to be. Or consider another home-grown example, the institution of governesses and boarding schools to rear upper-class children. Where is the upper-class mother and how does she spend her time between vacations and homecoming weekends? Then there are of course many countries around the world—Israel, Sweden, the Socialist countries, some of the African societies—where all or nearly all women, most of them mothers, work outside of the home as a matter of course. And because these societies are free from guilt and ambivalence about the working mother, they have managed to incorporate these realities more gracefully into their scheme of things, developing a number of useful innovations along the way. Thus even in our own day, adaptions and modifications exist and have not destroyed all notions of family loyalty, responsibility, and commitment.

In fact, people may be more ready for change than official pronouncements and expert opinions assume. The spread of contraceptive information and the acceptance of full birth control have been remarkable. The relaxation of many erstwhile taboos has proceeded at breakneck speed, and the use of public forums to discuss such vital but previously forbidden topics as abortion, homosexuality, or illegitimacy is dramatic and startling in a society rooted in Puritanism. A number of studies, moreover, show that the better educated are more open to re-examination and change in all spheres, including the family. Since these groups are on the increase, we may expect greater receptivity to such changes in the future. Even such startling proposed innovations as egg transplants, test-tube babies, and cloning are not rejected out of hand if they would help achieve the family goals most Americans prize. (See "The Second Genesis" by Albert Rosenfeld, and the Louis Harris Poll, *Life,* June 1969, pp. 31–46.)

Public response to a changing moral and social climate is of course hard to predict. In particular, as regards family concerns, the reactions of women, so crucially bound up with motherhood and childrearing in their self-definitions, are of especial interest. In this connection one study of more than 15,000 women college students attending four year liberal arts colleges in the United States is relevant for its findings on how such a nationwide sample of young coeds, a group of great future significance, feels about marriage, motherhood and career. (Charles F. Westoff and Raymond H. Potvin, *College Women and Fertility Values*, Princeton University Press, 1967) Selecting only those items on which there was wide consensus and omitting details of interest to the specialist, the general pattern of answers was unmistakable. The large majority of these would-be wives and mothers disapproved of large families (three or more children), did not consider children to be the most important reason for marriage, favored birth control and birth planning, and thought it possible for a woman to pursue family and career simultaneously. They split evenly on the matter of whether a woman's main satisfaction should come from family rather than career, or community activities, and they were virtually united in thinking that mothers with very young children should not work. The latter strongly identifies them as Americans, I think, where nursery schools and other aids to working mothers—including moral support—are not only lacking but still largely disapproved of.

Thus if we dare to speculate further about the future of the family we will be on safe ground with the following anticipations: (1) a trend towards greater, legitimate variety in sexual and marital experience; (2) a decrease in the negative emotions—exclusiveness, possessiveness, fear and jealousy—associated with these; (3) greater room for personal choice in the kind, extent, and duration of intimate relationships, which may greatly improve their quality as people will both give and demand more of them; (4) entirely new forms of communal living arrangements in which several couples will share the tasks of childrearing and economic support as well as the pleasures of relaxation; (5) multi-stage marriages geared to the changing life cycle and the presence or absence of dependent children. Of these proposals, some, such as Margaret Mead's, would have the young and the immature of any age test themselves and their capacities to relate to others in an individual form of marriage which would last only so long as it fulfilled both partners. In contrast to this, older, more experienced and more mature couples who were ready to take on the burdens of parenthood would make a deeper and longer lasting commitment. Other proposals would reverse this sequence and have couples assume parental commitments when young and, having discharged their debt to society, be then free to explore more personal, individualistic partnerships. Neither of these seems as yet to be particularly appealing to the readers who responded to Mead's proposal as set forth in Redbook Magazine. (Margaret Mead, "Marriage in Two Steps," *Redbook Magazine,* July 1966; "The Life Cycle and Its Variation: The Division of Roles," *Daedalus,* Summer 1967; "A Continuing Dialogue on Marriage: Why Just Living Together Won't Work," *Redbook Magazine,* April 1968)

For the immediate future, it appears that most Americans opt for and anticipate their participation in durable, intimate, heterosexual partnerships as anchors and pivots of their adult lives. They expect these to be freer and more flexible than was true in the past, however, and less bound to duty and involuntary personal restrictions. They cannot imagine and do not wish a life without them.

Speculating for the long-range future, we cannot ignore the potential implications of the emerging cultural taboo on unrestricted reproduction and the shift in public concern away from the family as the central preoccupation of one's life. Hard as it may seem, perhaps some day we will cease to relate to families just as we no longer relate ourselves to clans, and instead be bound up with some new, as yet unnamed, principle of human association. If and when this happens, we may also see a world of Unisex, Multi-sex, or Nonsex. None of this can happen, however, if we refuse to shed some of our most cherished preconceptions, such as that monogamy is superior to other forms of marriage or that women naturally make the best mothers. Much as we may be convinced of these now, time may reveal them as yet another illusion, another example of made-to-order truths.

Ultimately all social change involves moral doubt and moral reassessment. If we refuse to consider change while there still is time, time will pass us by. Only by examining and taking stock of what is can we hope to affect what will be. This is our chance to invent and thus to humanize the future.

2

The Social Organization of Sex

Introduction

People have been theorizing about sexuality for thousands of years, yet the scientific study and public discussion of sexual matters is barely 70 years old. Many of the questions that earlier generations puzzled over remain unanswered, the experts in disagreement. The study of sexuality illustrates many of the problems that beset the social sciences in general, and the family in particular.

The study of sexuality has been hampered by cultural attitudes surrounding sexuality with anxiety, making it a taboo topic for private or public discussion, and by patriarchal traditions defining women as the natural subordinates of men due to biological and intellectual inferiority. As John Stuart Mill as well as later feminists have argued, the history of relations between the sexes is analogous to those between different races, classes, and castes. All such relationships have involved the domination of one group, defined by birth, by members of another group, also defined by birth.

Such power arrangements are assumed to be natural and inevitable, and alternatives to them unthinkable. When religion is given as the major justification for behavior, subordination of one group by another is explained in religious terms. More recently, domination has usually been justified in terms of biological necessity, irrevocable instincts, and inherent inferiority. Thus, in approaching the study of either the physical or the social relations between the sexes, it is important to understand how male dominance may have influenced both popular and professional conceptions of sexuality and sex differences.

The conventional idea of sexuality, a view reinforced by Freudian theory, defines sex as a powerful biological drive continually struggling for gratification against restraints imposed by civilization. The notion of sexual instincts also implies a kind of innate knowledge: a person intuitively knows his own identity as male or female, he knows how to act accordingly, and he is attracted to the "proper" sex object—a person of the opposite gender. In other words, the view of sex as biological drive pure and simple implies "that sexuality has a magical ability, possessed by no other capacity, that allows biological drives to be expressed directly in psychological and social behaviors" (Gagnon and Simon, 1970, p. 24).

130

The whole issue of the relative importance of biological versus psychological and social factors in sexuality and sex differences has been obscured by polemics. On the one hand, there are the strict biological determinists who declare anatomy is destiny. On the other hand, there are those who argue that all aspects of sexuality and sex role differences are matters of learning and social conditioning.

There are two essential points to be made about the nature vs. nurture argument. The first is that extreme positions overlook the connection between biology and experience. Yet the most recent research into the development of sex differences suggests not an opposition between genetics and environment, but an interaction:

> In the theory of psychosexual differentiation, it is now outmoded to oppose or juxtapose nature vs. nurture, the genetic vs. the environmental, the innate versus the acquired, the biological vs. the psychological, or the instinctive vs. the learned. Modern genetic theory avoids these antiquated dichotomies. . . . (Money and Ehrhardt, 1972, p. 1)

The second and related point concerns a misconception about how biological forces work. Both biological determinists and their opponents assume that if a biological force exists, it must be overwhelmingly strong. But the most sophisticated evidence concerning both psycho-sexual development *and* erotic arousal suggests that physiological forces are gentle rather than powerful. Thus, acknowledging the possible effects of prenatal sex hormones on the brains of human infants, Stoller warns against "biologizing":

> While the newborn presents a most malleable central nervous system upon which the environment writes, we cannot say that the central nervous system is neutral or neuter. Rather, we can say that the effects of these biological systems, organized prenatally in a masculine or feminine directions, are almost always . . . too gentle in humans to withstand the more powerful forces in human development, the first and most profound of which is mothering. . . . (Stoller, 1972, p. 211)

Striking evidence of the independence of sexual identity and activity from biological determinants comes from studies of hermaphrodites, and other "sex errors of the body." A program of research into the psychological effects of such errors has been carried out by John Money and his associates (1961, 1965). Their most significant conclusion is that the sense of gender identity—I am a boy, or I am a girl—is a product of social learning, rather than of anatomy and physiology.

Money studied the life histories of people who had been born with ambiguous genitalia—boy babies with underdeveloped penises, and girl babies with overdeveloped clitorises. Today doctors can perform tests to determine whether such an infant is genetically a boy or a girl (a girl's cells have two X chromosomes, while a boy's have one X and one Y). In the past however, such children were randomly assigned to one sex or the other. Money found that a child could be assigned to the wrong genetic sex, and yet grow up a psychologically "normal" member of that sex:

> The test cases are matched pairs of hermaphrodites chromosomally, gonadally, and diagnostically the same, but antithetical in sex assignment, biological history, and gender identity. The contrast between two such young adult individuals in gender role and gender identity is so complete that the ordinary person meeting them socially or vocationally has no clues as to the remarkable contents of their medical histories. (Money and Ehrhardt, 1972, p. 18)

Money's ultimate conclusion is that life experiences determine whether the individual sees himself and acts like a "normal" male, a "normal" female, a homosexual (a person who prefers to have erotic relations with his or her own sex), or a transsexual (one who actually sees himself or herself as a member of the opposite sex, but with a mistaken anatomy). Moreover, learned gender identity has a powerful psychological impact and is rarely unlearned. Thus, people who identify with the "wrong" gender typically prefer surgery to relearning as the means of bringing about consistency between physiology and psychosocial sex identity.

Even in matters of sexual feelings, the role of biological factors is less direct and more complicated than the idea of instinct implies. That sex is not a simple biological drive is evident from a number of facts. First, some men and women can live with little or no sexual experience without showing evidence of strain or compensation. Second, as Ford and Beach (1951, pp. 250–257) note, in both man and the primates, sexual behavior may be performed in the service of needs other than those of sex—for example, as a sign of dominance or submission.

Those who believe in sex as largely biological emphasize the role of hormones in sexual arousal and capacity. Actually, however, human sexuality is characterized by the evolutionary trend away from hormonal control over sexual behavior and toward control by the higher centers of the brain—in other words, control by learning and by symbolic, social meaning. Further, studies of the actual effects of hormones reveal that there is no simple relation between the amount of sex hormones in a person's blood and erotic arousal; that is, high arousal is possible at low levels of the hormones, and high levels need not necessarily lead to arousal. Research emphasizes the importance of psychological factors in erotic arousal. Perhaps the most striking evidence on this point is a finding by Money and Ehrhardt. They found that the love affairs and erotic responsiveness of their hermaphrodite subjects were in accord with the sex they had been reared in, regardless of their physiological sex.

Female orgasm offers another illustration of how social and cultural definitions can influence biological facts. A first and most obvious point about the study of sexuality, male and female, is that until quite recently, such investigation was considered almost as improper for the scientist as for anybody else. A second important point is that many of the pioneers who first challenged the taboos against sex research and writing succeeded only in replacing ignorance with misinformation. Thus, most people used to believe, and many still do, that normal women do not have sexual feelings at all, and certainly nothing comparable to the orgasm in males.

Later, under the influence of psychoanalysis and certain other writers, sophisticated people came to believe that women were indeed capable of sexual arousal and climax, and that the normal female response was the exact counterpart of the male's: the same sexual acts that resulted in the male orgasm should lead to a simultaneous vaginal orgasm in the woman. That the majority of women appeared incapable of having orgasms in the prescribed way was attributed by Freud and his followers to frigidity: The woman had either totally repressed all sexual feeling, or she had neurotically failed to transfer her sexual sensitivity from the clitoris to the vagina. Susan Lydon's article reviews the findings of Masters and Johnson that disprove Freud's transfer theory and the notion of two different kinds of female orgasm.

In short, the view that sexuality represents the animal side of human nature opposed to the "higher" human qualities of thought and reason is simply untenable in the light of the evidence. Yet it is difficult for many people to accept the idea that human sexuality is anything other than a natural force that can never change. The articles in this part indicate, however, that sexuality and sex roles are capable of change, and are changing now.

References

Ford, C. S., and F. A. Beach. *Patterns of Sexual Behavior*. New York: Harper, 1951.

Gagnon, J. H., and W. Simon. *The Sexual Scene*. Chicago: Aldine, Transaction, 1970.

Money, J. "Sex Hormones and Other Variables in Human Eroticism." In *Sex and Internal Secretions*, 3rd ed., edited by W. C. Young. Baltimore: Williams and Wilkins, 1961.

Money, J. *Sex Research: New Developments*. New York: Holt, Rinehart, Winston, 1965.

Money, J., and Anke A. Ehrhardt. *Man and Woman, Boy and Girl*. Baltimore: John Hopkins Press, 1972.

Stoller, R. J. "The Bedrock of Masculinity and Femininity—Bisexuality." *Archives of General Psychiatry*, 26 (1972), pp. 207–212.

Chapter 3

The Development of Sexuality

Kohlberg's article provides detailed understanding of how a child learns gender identity. At about the time the child is learning to talk—eighteen months or so—children are also learning to label themselves and others as male or female. Thus begins a lifelong accumulation of memories and fantasies in which the appropriate roles are acted out. The learning is very gradual, and changes with the child's stage of thinking—that is, young children may think that one's sexual identity is something that can change, like one's age. Kohlberg also shows that genital anatomy plays a relatively small part in young children's thinking about sex differences. Haircuts and social role differences, such as the fact that males are policemen and firemen, are more impressive to children's minds. In short, learning to be male or female seems to be a process of learning the rules, both explicit and implicit, defining sex roles.

A Cognitive-Developmental Analysis of Sex-Role Concepts

Lawrence Kohlberg

Oddly enough, our approach to the problems of sexual development starts directly with neither biology nor culture, but with cognition. In this chapter we shall elaborate and document a theory which assumes that basic sexual attitudes are not patterned directly by either biological instincts or arbitrary cultural norms, but by the child's cognitive organization of his social world along sex-role dimensions. Recent research evidence suggests that there are important "natural" components involved in the patterning of children's sex-role attitudes, since many aspects of sex-role attitudes appear to be universal across cultures and family structures, and to originate relatively early in the child's development. This patterning of sex-role attitudes is essentially "cognitive" in that it is rooted in the child's concepts of physical things—the bodies of himself and of others—concepts which he relates in turn to a social order that makes functional use of sex categories in quite culturally universal ways. It is not the child's biological instincts, but rather his cognitive organization of social-role concepts around universal physical dimensions, which accounts for the existence of universals in sex-role attitudes.

While we are talking about cognitive organization, and universals common to all children in sexual cognitions, we must take into account the fact that basic modes of cognitive organization change with age. As Piaget and his followers have documented in depth and detail, the child's basic cognitive organization of the physical world undergoes radical transformations with age development. So, too, do the child's conceptions of his social world. We shall review research findings which suggest that not only do young children's sex-role attitudes have universal aspects, but also that these attitudes change radically with age development. These age changes do not seem to be the result of age-graded sex-role socialization, but rather to be "natural" changes resulting from general trends of cognitive-social development. There is little reason to accept Freud's and Gesell and Ilg's view that these age changes are directly related to the maturation of the body or of body instincts. Instead, we shall review evidence suggesting that these trends are the result of general experience-linked changes in modes of cognition. Sex-role concepts and attitudes change with age in universal ways because of universal age changes in basic modes of cognitive organization. Increasing evidence from studies in the Piaget tradition suggests culturally universal developmental shifts in conceptualizations of physical objects. Because children's sex-role concepts are essentially defined in universal physical, or body, terms, these concepts, too, undergo universal developmental changes. As an example, recent research indicates that children develop a conception of themselves as having an unchangeable sexual identity at the same age and through the same processes that they develop conceptions of the invariable identity of physical objects.

The basic claim of theories of sexual instinct like Freud's libido theory is that the basic patterning of sexual attitudes is instinctual and "natural" in its origins, but that the expressions of these patterns are eventually channeled, distorted, or influenced by cultural forces. In contrast, social-learning theories of sex-role development see the patterning of sexual attitudes as a reflection of the patterning, or sex-typing, of the culture.

In contrast to either of these views, we see the child's social and sexual attitudes neither as direct reflections of cultural patterns nor as direct re-flections of innate structures. Both research results and clinical observation indicate that much of the young child's thinking about sex roles is radically different from the adult's. His physical concepts of anatomical differences, birth, sexual relations, etc., are quite different, as are his concepts of the social attitudes and values of males and females. Following Piaget's argu-ment concerning physical concepts, we shall contend that these differences are due not to ignorance or inadequate teaching patterns, but to qualitative differences between the structure of the child's thought and the adult's. The child's sex-role concepts are the result of the child's active structuring of his own experience; they are not passive products of social training.

It appears to us that this interactional point of view best fits the clinical data on sexual psychopathology and its relationship to early experience. Ever since Freud's classic statement, it has been recognized that sexual ab-normalities are incomprehensible if one assumes that there is a single in-nate or "normal" pattern of sexuality. There is clear evidence that hormonal and genetic factors influence the level of sexual arousal, but there is no clear evidence that these factors determine the patterning of sexuality, i.e., its aims and objects. Money and Hampson find that hermaphrodites who are chromosomally and hormonally of one sex lead normal sex lives patterned in terms of the opposite sex if they have been reared as members of that sex.

At first, this and other evidence seems to support the social-learning assumption that basic sexual attitudes are directly patterned by cultural expectations and reinforcement. However, it is extremely difficult to ac-count for recurrent forms of adult sexual psychopathology in terms of the general mechanisms of social reinforcement or modeling, since abnormal sex-role behaviors are obviously highly resistant to both cultural expectations and social reinforcement. It was this double-edged problem of sexual psy-chopathology that led Freud to postulate that there are innate "abnormal" or deviant instinctual sexual patterns which unfold in early childhood, and which can be fixated through childhood experience. On the one hand, therefore, it is clear that human sexual behavior is not the product of a strict and fixed instinct, or there would be no sexual psychopathology. On the other hand, it is just as clear that sexual behavior is not simply culturally patterned, or there would be no recurrent and resistant forms of sexual psy-chopathology in cultures and families that strongly disapprove of them.

Freud's notions of definite and instinctively patterned sexual stages have not stood up well in the face of direct psychological observations of children, although such observations clearly suggest infantile sexual interests, con-cerns, and pleasures in various body zones. However, in modified forms the notion that an experience at a critical period in the unfolding of instinctive patterns can affect subsequent attitudes and behaviors has received considerable support from animal and clinical research. In ground-nesting birds, early exposure to a moving object leads to imprinting, not only of following responses but of later sexual ones. Money, Hampson, and Hampson report critical-period phenomena which suggest that there is something like sexual imprinting in humans. They suggest that the development of normal adult sexual behavior is contingent on having been socially assigned to a given sex before the age of three or four. Hermaphrodites assigned at birth to one sex because of external genital characteristics have sometimes been reassigned later to the other sex, so that their social sex identity will be more consistent with their internal sex characteristics. Money and Hampson report that if this is done before age three to four, the child's later sexual adjustment is normal. If it is done after this age, real maladjustment seems to result. Money and Hampson use the term imprinting to describe this critical-age-period phenomenon in sex-role attitudes, since it is obviously not the result of the usual social reinforcement mechanisms, which are in principle reversible. The critical-period phenomena described by Money and Hampson are, however, obviously not genuine imprinting phenomena. As observed in birds, imprinting takes place at a very early period through exposure to a definite object. In contrast, the "imprinting" described by Money and Hampson occurs throughout the first three or four years, and is not the result of exposure to a definite object. Instead it is the fixation of an "abstract" self-concept or identity. Rearing a person as a member of one sex rather than the other does not mean that there will be a difference in exposure to parents or other love objects; there will be, however, a difference in labeling of the self. Such labeling is perhaps irreversible because basic cognitive categorizations are irreversible. After a certain point, social reinforcement cannot readily reverse or change basic categorizations of constancies in the child's physical world, though such reinforcement can readily change categorizations at earlier cognitive stages before constancies are stabilized. In a similar way the child aged two to four is very uncertain of the constancy of his sexual identity, and the label "boy" is for him as arbitrary as the label "Johnny." Once his sexual identity has been cognitively stabilized in the Money and Hampson "critical period," it must become extremely difficult to change it by social sex-role reassignment.

In general, then, our theory accepts the notion that there are important linkages between childhood experiences and adult psychopathology. It does so without postulating either biologically based critical periods or biologically patterned childhood sexual instincts. Instead, these linkages are explained in terms of the cognitive distortions characteristic of childhood sexual concepts, distortions which may become "fixated" by certain interpersonal experiences that stabilize distorted conceptions of body interactions and body feelings.

Our stress upon the cognitive basis of sex-role attitudes and their development does not mean that we are shifting our attention away from the motivational and emotional aspects of sex-role attitudes. We shall argue, however, that motivational aspects of sex-role development are best understood in terms of a theory of the self and of identification that rests on general competence, effectance, and self-regard motives, rather than upon infantile sexual drives or attachment and dependency motivations unique to the early parent-child relationship. The child's sexual identity is maintained by a motivated adaptation to physical-social reality and by the need to preserve a stable and positive self-image. We shall argue that motives to love and identify with parental models in the critical childhood years derive primarily from the child's adaptation to this reality and from his self-maintaining motives, rather than from fixed instincts or primary drives. Accordingly, sexual identifications with parents are primarily derivatives of the child's basic sexual identity and his self-maintaining motives—not the reverse, which is what psychoanalysis and social-learning theories have held. Our chapter, then, will start with fundamental concepts and findings on the development of the child's basic sex-role concepts and sex-role identity, and will move on to a consideration of how this identity determines the development of parent identifications.

Sex-Role Identity as a Product of Cognitive Growth

The Money and Hampson data suggest to us the following points: (1) Gender identity, i.e., cognitive self-categorization as "boy" or "girl," is the critical and basic organizer of sex-role attitudes. (2) This "gender identity" results from a basic, simple cognitive judgment made early in development. Once made, this categorization is relatively irreversible and is maintained by basic physical-reality judgments, regardless of the vicissitudes of social reinforcements, parent identifications, etc. Claiming that a simple gender self-categorization organizes sex-role attitudes, we can postulate the following: (3) Basic self-categorizations determine basic valuings. Once the boy has stably categorized himself as male, he then values positively those objects and acts consistent with his gender identity. This assumption that there are tendencies toward cognitive consistency which lead to the formation of values consistent with self-conceptual cognitive judgments has been elaborated and documented by "clinical" self-theorists (Rogers, Lecky, Kelly) and by "experimental" cognitive-balance theorists (Festinger, Osgood and Tannenbaum, Newcomb, Rosenberg).

Our view of the importance of gender identity in psychosexual development is not shared by many social-learning theorists, including Walter Mischel. In Mischel's view, sex-typed behavior and attitudes are acquired through social rewards that follow sex-appropriate responses made by the child or by a relevant model. The social-learning syllogism is: "I want rewards, I am rewarded for doing boy things, therefore I want to be a boy." In contrast, a cognitive theory assumes this sequence: "I am a boy, therefore I want to do boy things, therefore the opportunity to do boy things (and to gain approval for doing them) is rewarding."

The Money and Hampson "critical period" data suggest that by age five children have a stable gender identity which determines the value—rather than being primarily instrumental in the achievement—of many social rewards. . . .

Gender identity is perhaps the most stable of all social identities. If an American adult is asked what social class he belongs to, he is very often "objectively" incorrect; and if he is asked whether he is a Jew or a German or a Catholic or a Californian, he may be uncertain and engage in a long discussion of the criteria for being placed in these categories. The only category of social identity that is as basic and clear as gender is age, but age, unlike gender, continually changes. As we know, children lie to themselves and others in order to appear older, and middle-aged women lie to themselves and others in order to appear younger.

Even though the psychology of adult personality may take gender identity for granted, the genesis of this identity is still of great interest for developmental psychology. We have pointed out that adult gender identity is a basic cognitive reality judgment, and not a derivative of social rewards, parent identifications, or sexual identifications. At the same time, however, this gender identity had to develop. As we shall now attempt to demonstrate, the reality judgment "I really am and always will be a boy (or girl)" is the result of a cognitive development which is quite independent of variations in social sex-role training, and which is central to the development of other aspects of sex-role attitudes.

Obviously, this process begins with the child's hearing and learning the verbal labels "boy" and "girl." The child's verbal learning of his own gender label occurs quite early, usually sometime late in the second year of life. Gesell et al. report that two-thirds to three-fourths of 3-year-olds answered correctly the question "Are you a little girl or a little boy?" while the majority of 2½-year-olds did not answer it correctly. At this early age, however, correct self-labeling does not imply correct self-classification in a general physical category. The label "boy" may be a name just like the name "Johnny." The child may recognize that there are other boys in the world, just as there may be other Johnnies, but this recognition need not imply a basic criterion for determining who is a boy any more than it does for determining who is a Johnny; nor does it necessarily imply that everyone in the world is either a boy or a girl, or a Johnny or a non-Johnny. In the second year, the child learns that "boy" is a name which may be applied to others, and he may even experience a vague pleasurable "identification" in such common labeling. But this extension of the label does not imply the ability to make categorizations. A 2½-year-old boy, Tommy, observed by the writer, would go around the family circle saying, "I'm boy," "Daddy boy," "Mommy boy," "Joey (brother) boy." After correction he eliminated his mother from the list, but did not label people outside the family correctly.

In the third year of life then, the child seems to know his own sex label, and to generalize it unsystematically to others on the basis of a loose cluster of physical characteristics. Rabban reports that about two-thirds of a group of sixty middle-class and working-class children aged thirty to forty-one months (with an average age of three years) were able to reply correctly to the questions "Which doll looks most like you?" and "Is it (the doll) a boy or a girl?" Such generalization of a correct self-label to a doll did not, however, imply generally correct discrimination of the sex of the doll. Rabban reports that only about half of his three-year-old group was able to label correctly six dolls (father, mother, two boys, two girls) as "boy" or "girl." By age four almost all of Rabban's children labeled themselves and the dolls correctly. By four, children tend to label gender by some general physical criteria, primarily clothing and hair-style.

The findings discussed so far merely suggest that children learn gender self-labeling early (age two to three), and in the next two years learn to label others correctly according to conventional cues. Obviously there is more to the development of a stable gender identity than this. Investigations of this "more" have started from two points of view: the psychoanalytic and the cognitive-developmental. Both recognize that the young child's use of gender identification depends upon the child's ability to classify a physical object, the body. Both agree that the development of a stable gender identification is an important psychosexual developmental task, but disagree about how this development takes place: the psychoanalytic view stresses the interaction between the child's wishes and the adult's provision or denial of anatomical information in this development, whereas the cognitive-developmental view holds that the child's difficulties in establishing gender definition closely parallel his difficulties in establishing stable definitions of physical concepts in general, and that the former are resolved as the latter are. While both theories point to a number of important developments in gender-identity concepts, the central focus of both is upon the constancy of gender identity. The child's gender identity can provide a stable organizer of the child's psychosexual attitudes only when he is categorically certain of its unchangeability.

The fact that the young child is not certain of the constancy of gender identity before the age of five to six has been demonstrated by Kohlberg. In the course of this study, children of four to eight were asked whether a pictured girl could be a boy if she wanted to, or if she played boy games, or if she wore a boy's haircut or clothes. Most four-year-olds said that she could be a boy if she wanted to, or if she wore the appropriate haircut or clothes. By age six to seven, most children were quite certain that a girl could not be a boy regardless of changes in appearance or behavior. These findings correspond to more anecdotal observations. The following comments were made by Jimmy, just turning four, to his 4½-year-old friend Johnny:

Johnny: I'm going to be an airplane builder when I grow up.
Jimmy: When I grow up, I'll be a Mommy.
Johnny: No, you can't be a Mommy. You have to be a Daddy.
Jimmy: No, I'm going to be a Mommy.
Johnny: No, you're not a girl, you can't be a Mommy.
Jimmy: Yes, I can.

Among other difficulties, it would seem that Jimmy does not recognize that the category "male" applies to both boys and fathers, and that while age changes occur, gender changes do not. As another example, Philip (aged three years, ten months) told his mother. "When you grow up to be a Daddy, you can have a bicycle, too (like his father)."

Rabban found that the majority of his three-year-olds did not correctly use generalized sex labels, and did not reply correctly to the question "When you grow up, would you like to be a mamma or a daddy?" In contrast, 97 percent of his five-year-olds replied correctly. In light of findings discussed later, it is likely that the change in responses to questions of desired future identity primarily reflects cognitive stabilization of sex-role categories rather than changes in role preference.

From the cognitive-developmental point of view, the stabilization of gender-identity concepts is only one aspect of the general stabilization of constancies of physical objects that takes place between the years three and seven. The development of such conceptual constancies has been discussed by Piaget in terms of the conservation of physical-object properties under apparent changes. Piaget and his followers have demonstrated that children below the age of six to seven do not view physical objects as retaining an invariable mass, number, weight, length, etc., when the perceptual configuration in which the objects appear varies. While Piaget has only considered and studied conceptual constancies involving conservation of an object's quantity along some dimension, it appears that qualitative constancies of category or generic identity develop in the same period and in parallel fashion. Thus a majority of four-year-old children said that a pictured cat could be a dog if it wanted to, or if its whiskers were cut off. By age six to seven, most children were firm in asserting that a cat would not change its identity in spite of apparent perceptual changes. Similar results have been found by DeVries, using a live cat that is covered by a dog mask within the child's view.

The results of Kohlberg and DeVries's developmental studies of constancy of species and gender identity can be questioned from two points of view. One is the commonsense point of view, which would question purely verbal evidence that young children do not believe in constancy of identity. The other is the psychoanalytic view, which sees the young child's unrealistic thoughts about sexual constancy as largely a product of his wishes and fears. In contrast, the Piaget view assumes, first, that there is a parallelism or correspondence between the cognitive-verbal and affective aspects of the development of reality orientations, and, second, that cognitive-structural changes, rather than affective changes, are the primary sources of development in reality orientations.

In Piaget's view, the infant is from the start motivationally oriented toward contacting, maintaining, and mastering objects rather than toward pure tension discharge. The child's gradual increase in reality orientation, his increased awareness of the constancy of the existence and identity of external objects, is the result of increased cognitive differentiation of the self and the world rather than the result of basic qualitative changes in motivational processes. Like Piaget, Freud also stressed the importance of the child's spontaneous processes in determining his basic reactions to the "reality," and viewed infantile and adult thought processes as structurally or qualitatively different from one another (primary and secondary processes). However, Freud stresses motivational changes as basic to the development of different modes of thought. Infantile thought has the structure of fantasy; it is governed by the pleasure principle and the desire for immediate gratification. Mature thought is governed by the reality principle, by the delay of gratification, and by stable attachments to external objects. In more mundane terms, psychoanalysis holds that the young child's unrealistic thoughts about sexual identity are the result of his wishes and fears. Where emotional preoccupations are strong, fantasy thought predominates over secondary-process thought.

An example suggesting this psychoanalytic interpretation of gender identity is a spontaneous response made by Jimmy, a boy just turned five: "I can be a girl, you know. I can. I can wear a wig and have my throat so I can talk like a girl." It would seem plausible to attribute the immature logic of this statement to the fact that the boy's wishes and conflicts in this area were strong enough to override his interests in being realistic or correct. On another occasion, however, the writer (experimenter) had the following conversation with Jimmy:

Experimenter: Do airplanes get small when they fly away in the sky?
Jimmy: Yes, they get real tiny.
Experimenter: Do they really get small, or do they just look small?
Jimmy: They really get small.
Experimenter: What happens to the people inside?
Jimmy: They shrink.
Experimenter: How can they shrink and get small?
Jimmy: They cut their heads off.

These statements might also be taken as motivationally determined, rather than as a reflection of Jimmy's general level of thinking. Obviously, in the second conversation, Jimmy doesn't care about being correct, and ends up making a "fantasy" response. Sometimes Jimmy may care too much (sex-role), sometimes too little (airplane query), but if his general level of thinking is the same, it is hard to maintain that this level is a product of affective rather than cognitive-structural factors.

In order to compare the cognitive-structural and the affective interpretations of gender-identity beliefs in young children, the Kohlberg study asked the correlational question: "To what extent is level of development of belief in constancy consistent from physical and emotionally neutral types of constancies to social and emotionally charged constancies?"

In addition to the gender-identity task, children aged four to six were given three other conservation tasks: constancy of the species identity of the cat, conservation of mass of a piece of clay under various shape changes, and conservation of length of a piece of gum. The age norms for the gender-identity and species-identity tasks were found to be similar, with constancy on both slightly preceding constancy on conservation of quantitative dimensions of the classical Piaget type. Not only was the age development of the various constancy tasks parallel, but the gender-identity task was found to correlate quite highly ($r = .52$ to $.73$) with the other tasks among children of a given age. Even with mental age partialed out, correlations of gender identity with the other conservation tasks were substantial ($r = .36$ to $.64$). This evidence of consistency clearly indicates the importance of general cognitive-structural features in the child's beliefs about gender identity.

In addition to affective factors, psychoanalytic theory holds that the adult's withholding of anatomical information plays an important role in the child's uncertainties about the constancy of gender identity. In fact, however, the Kohlberg study suggests that young children revealing early exposure to parental anatomical "enlightenment" were no more advanced in sex-role constancy than children who did not reveal such enlightenment. The children of four to seven who indicated anatomical awareness in explaining "how you could tell boys from girls when they had clothes on" and "when they had clothes off" were not more advanced in sex-role constancy than were those who did not indicate such anatomical awareness. In general, even the enlightened younger child does not use genital differences as the basic criterion for sex classification. The writer has recorded questions from enlightened children in their third and fourth year who wanted to know whether they would still be boys if they did not have a penis. These questions indicate that awareness of genital differences does not directly lead to their use as the primary criterion of gender categorization or of gender constancy.

The major implication of the Kohlberg study is that the process of forming a constant gender identity is not a unique process determined by instinctual wishes and identifications, but a part of the general process of conceptual growth.

The previous article dealt with the development of gender identity in the young child—the knowledge that "I am a girl" or "I am a boy." This article deals with the development of eroticism or sexual behavior, the sense of one's self as a sexual (or nonsexual) being. It argues against the notion that sex is a powerful force always ready to erupt at any time in "strange and costly ways." Rather, the authors describe sexual behavior as "scripted," shaped by social and cultural circumstance, as well as one's own fantasy life. Sexuality is subordinated to social and psychological factors even in adolescent boys, who are strongly turned on by high doses of hormones during puberty. The authors stress the interaction of physiological and cultural factors in shaping the differences between male and female sexuality in adolescence.

Psychosexual Development

William Simon and John H. Gagnon

Erik Erikson has observed that, prior to Sigmund Freud, "sexologists" tended to believe that sexual capacities appeared suddenly with the onset of adolescence. Sexuality followed those external evidences of physiological change that occurred concurrent with or just after puberty. Psychoanalysis changed all that. In Freud's view, libido—the generation of psychosexual

Reprinted by permission from William Simon and John H. Gagnon, *The Sexual Scene* (New Brunswick: Transaction, Inc., 1970).

energies—should be viewed as a fundamental element of human experience at least beginning with birth, and possibly before that. Libido, therefore, is essential, a biological constant to be coped with at all levels of individual, social, and cultural development. The truth of this received wisdom, that is, that sexual development is a continuous contest between biological drive and cultural restraint, should be seriously questioned. Obviously sexuality has roots in biological processes, but so do many other capacities including many that involve physical and mental competence and vigor. There is, however, abundant evidence that the final states which these capacities attain escape the rigid impress of biology. This independence of biological constraint is rarely claimed for the area of sexuality, but we would like to argue that the sexual is precisely that realm where the sociocultural forms most completely dominate biological influences.

It is difficult to get data that might shed much light on the earliest aspects of these questions: Adults are hardly equipped with total recall and the preverbal or primitively verbal child does not have ability to report accurately on his own internal state. But it seems obvious—and it is a basic assumption of this paper—that with the beginnings of adolescence many new factors come into play, and to emphasize a straight-line developmental continuity with infant and childhood experiences may be seriously misleading. In particular, it is dangerous to assume that because some childhood behavior appears sexual to adults, it must be sexual. An infant or a child engaged in genital play (even if orgasm is observed) can in no sense be seen as experiencing the complex set of feelings that accompanies adult or even adolescent masturbation.

Therefore, the authors reject the unproven assumption that "powerful" psychosexual drives are fixed biological attributes. More importantly, we reject the even more dubious assumption that sexual capacities or experiences tend to translate immediately into a kind of universal "knowing" or innate wisdom—that sexuality has a magical ability, possessed by no other capacity, that allows biological drives to be expressed directly in psychosocial and social behaviors.

The prevailing image of sexuality—particularly that of the Freudian tradition—is that of an intense, high-pressure drive that forces a person to seek physical sexual gratification, a drive that expresses itself indirectly if it cannot be expressed directly. The available data suggest to us a different picture—one that shows either lower levels of intensity, or, at least, greater variability. We find that there are many social situations or life-roles in which reduced sex activity or even deliberate celibacy is undertaken with little evidence that the libido has shifted in compensation to some other sphere.

A part of the legacy of Freud is that we have all become remarkably adept at discovering "sexual" elements in nonsexual behavior and symbolism. What we suggest instead (following Kenneth Burke's three-decade-old insight) is the reverse—that sexual behavior can often express and serve nonsexual motives.

We see sexual behavior therefore as *scripted* behavior, not the masked expression of a primordial drive. The individual can learn sexual behavior as he or she learns other behavior—through scripts that in this case give the self, other persons, and situations erotic abilities or content. Desire, privacy, opportunity, and propinquity with an attractive member of the opposite sex are not, in themselves, enough; in ordinary circumstances, nothing sexual will occur unless one or both actors organize these elements into an appropriate script. The very concern with foreplay in sex suggests this. From one point of view, foreplay may be defined as merely progressive physical excitement generated by touching naturally erogenous zones. The authors have referred to this conception elsewhere as the "rubbing of two sticks together to make a fire" model. It would seem to be more valuable to see this activity as symbolically invested behavior through which the body is eroticized and through which mute, inarticulate motions and gestures are translated into a sociosexual drama.

A belief in the sociocultural dominance of sexual behavior finds support in cross-cultural research as well as in data restricted to the United States. Psychosexual development is universal—but it takes many forms and tempos. People in different cultures construct their scripts differently; and in our own society, different segments of the population act out different psychosexual dramas—something much less likely to occur if they were all reacting more or less blindly to the same superordinate urge. The most marked differences occur, of course, between male and female patterns of sexual behavior. Obviously, some of this is due to biological differences, including differences in hormonal functions at different ages. But the significance of social scripts predominates; the recent work of Masters and Johnson, for example, clearly points to far greater orgasmic capacities on the part of females than our culture would lead us to suspect. And within each sex—especially among men—different social and economic groups have different patterns.

Let us examine some of these variations, and see if we can decipher the scripts.

Whether one agrees with Freud or not, it is obvious that we do not become sexual all at once. There is continuity with the past. Even infant experiences can strongly influence later sexual development.

But continuity is not causality. Childhood experiences (even those that appear sexual) will in all likelihood be influential not because they are intrinsically sexual, but because they can affect a number of developmental trends, *including* the sexual. What situations in infancy—or even early child-hood—can be called psychosexual in any sense other than that of creating potentials?

The key term, therefore, must remain potentiation. In infancy, we can locate some of the experiences (or sensations) that will bring about a sense of the body and its capacities for pleasure and discomfort and those that will influence the child's ability to relate to others. It is possible, of course, that through these primitive experiences, ranges are being established—but they are very broad and overlapping. Moreover, if these are profound experiences to the child—and they may well be that—they are not expressions of biological necessity, but of the earliest forms of social learning.

In childhood, after infancy there is what appears to be some real sex play. About half of all adults report that they did engage in some form of sex play as children; and the total who actually did may be half again as many. But, however the adult interprets it later, what did it mean to the child at the time? One suspects that, as in much of childhood role-playing, their sense of the adult meanings attributed to the behavior is fragmentary and ill-formed. Many of the adults recall that, at the time, they were concerned with being found out. But here, too, were they concerned because of the real content of sex play, or because of the mystery and the lure of the forbidden that so often enchant the child? The child may be assimilating outside information about sex for which, at the time, he has no real internal correlate or understanding.

A small number of persons do have sociosexual activity during pre-adolescence—most of it initiated by adults. But for the majority of these, little apparently follows from it. Without appropriate sexual scripts, the experience remains unassimilated—at least in adult terms. For some, it is clear, a severe reaction may follow from falling "victim" to the sexuality of an adult—but, again, does this reaction come from the sexual act itself or from the social response, the strong reactions of others? (There is some evidence that early sexual activity of this sort is associated with deviant adjustments in later life. But this, too, may not be the result of sexual experiences in themselves so much as the consequence of having fallen out of the social main stream and, therefore, of running greater risks of isolation and alienation.)

In short, relatively few become truly active sexually before adolescence. And when they do (for girls more often than boys), it is seldom immediately related to sexual feelings or gratifications but is a use of sex for nonsexual goals and purposes. The "seductive" Lolita is rare; but she is significant: She illustrates a more general pattern of psychosexual development—a commitment to the social relationships linked to sex before one can really grasp the social meaning of the physical relationships.

Of great importance are the values (or feelings, or images) that children pick up as being related to sex. Although we talk a lot about sexuality, as though trying to exorcise the demon of shame, learning about sex in our society is in large part learning about guilt; and learning how to manage sexuality commonly involves learning how to manage guilt. An important source of guilt in children comes from the imputation to them by adults of sexual appetites or abilities that they may not have, but that they learn, however imperfectly, to pretend they have. The gestural concomitants of sexual modesty are learned early. For instance, when do girls learn to sit or pick up objects with their knees together? When do they learn that the bust must be covered? However, since this behavior is learned unlinked to later adult sexual performances, what children must make of all this is very mysterious.

The learning of sex roles, or sex identities, involves many things that are remote from actual sexual experience, or that become involved with sexuality only after puberty. Masculinity or femininity, their meaning and postures, are rehearsed before adolescence in many nonsexual ways.

A number of scholars have pointed, for instance, to the importance of aggressive, deference, dependency, and dominance behavior in childhood. Jerome Kagan and Howard Moss have found that aggressive behavior in males and dependency in females are relatively stable aspects of development. But what is social role, and what is biology? They found that when aggressive behavior occurred among girls, it tended to appear most often among those from well-educated families that were more tolerant of deviation. Curiously, they also reported that "it was impossible to predict the character of adult sexuality in women from their preadolescent and early adolescent behavior," and that "erotic activity is more anxiety-arousing for females than for males," because "the traditional ego ideal for women dictates inhibition of sexual impulses."

The belief in the importance of early sex-role learning for boys can be viewed in two ways. First, it may directly indicate an early sexual capacity in male children. Or, second, early masculine identification may merely be an appropriate framework within which the sexual impulse (salient with puberty) and the socially available sexual scripts (or accepted patterns of sexual behavior) can most conveniently find expression. Our bias, of course, is toward the second.

But, as Kagan and Moss also noted, the sex role learned by the child does not reliably predict how he will act sexually as an adult. This finding also can be interpreted in the same two alternative ways. Where sexuality is viewed as a biological constant which struggles to express itself, the female sex role learning can be interpreted as the successful repression of sexual impulses. The other interpretation suggests that the difference lies not in learning how to handle a pre-existent sexuality, but in learning how to *be* sexual. Differences between men and women, therefore, will have consequences both for *what* is done sexually, as well as *when*.

Once again, we prefer the latter interpretation, and some recent work that we have done with lesbians supports it. We observed that many of the major elements of their sex lives—the start of actual genital sexual behavior, the onset and frequency of masturbation, the time of entry in sociosexual patterns, the number of partners, and the reports of feelings of sexual deprivation—were for these homosexual women almost identical with those of ordinary women. Since sexuality would seem to be more important for lesbians—after all, they sacrifice much in order to follow their own sexual pathways—this is surprising. We concluded that the primary factor was something both categories of women share—the sex-role learning that occurs before sexuality itself becomes significant.

Social class also appears significant, more for boys than girls. Sex-role learning may vary by class; lower-class boys are supposed to be more aggressive and put much greater emphasis on early heterosexuality. The middle and upper classes tend to tolerate more deviance from traditional attitudes regarding appropriate male sex-role performances.

Given all these circumstances, it seems rather naive to think of sexuality as a constant pressure, with a peculiar necessity all its own. For us, the crucial period of childhood has significance not because of sexual occurrences, but because of nonsexual developments that will provide the names and judgments for later encounters with sexuality.

The actual beginnings and endings of adolescence are vague. Generally, the beginning marks the first time society, as such, acknowledges that the individual has sexual capacity. Training in the postures and rhetoric of the sexual experience is now accelerated. Most important, the adolescent begins to regard those about him (particularly his peers, but also adults) as sexual actors and finds confirmation from others for this view.

For some, as noted, adolescent sexual experience begins before they are considered adolescents. Kinsey reports that a tenth of his female sample and a fifth of his male sample had experienced orgasm through masturbation by age 12. But still, for the vast majority, despite some casual play and exploration that post-Freudians might view as masked sexuality, sexual experience begins with adolescence. Even those who have had prior experience find that it acquires new meanings with adolescence. They now relate such meanings to both larger spheres of social life and greater senses of self. For example, it is not uncommon during the transition between childhood and adolescence for boys and, more rarely, girls to report arousal and orgasm while doing things not manifestly sexual—climbing trees, sliding down bannisters, or other activities that involve genital contact— without defining them as sexual. Often they do not even take it seriously enough to try to explore or repeat what was, in all likelihood, a pleasurable experience.

Adolescent sexual development, therefore, really represents the beginning of adult sexuality. It marks a definite break with what went on before. Not only will future experiences occur in new and more complex contexts, but they will be conceived of as explicitly sexual and thereby begin to complicate social relationships. The need to manage sexuality will rise not only from physical needs and desires, but also from the new implications of personal relationships. Playing, or associating, with members of the opposite sex now acquires different meanings.

At adolescence, changes in the developments of boys and girls diverge and must be considered separately. The one thing both share at this point is a reinforcement of their new status by a dramatic biological event—for girls, menstruation, and for boys, the discovery of the ability to ejaculate. But here they part. For boys, the beginning of a commitment to sexuality is primarily genital; within two years of puberty all but a relatively few have had the experience of orgasm, almost universally brought about by masturbation. The corresponding organizing event for girls is not genitally sexual but social: they have arrived at an age where they will learn role performances linked with proximity to marriage. In contrast to boys, only two-thirds of girls will report ever having masturbated (and, characteristically, the frequency is much less). For women, it is not until the late twenties that the incidence of orgasm from any source reaches that of boys at age 16. In fact, significantly, about half of the females who masturbate do so only after having experienced orgasm in some situation involving others. This contrast points to a basic distinction between the developmental processes for males and females: males move from privatized personal sexuality to sociosexuality; females do the reverse and at a later stage in the life cycle.

We have worked hard to demonstrate the dominance of social, psychological, and cultural influences over the biological; now, dealing with adolescent boys, we must briefly reverse course. There is much evidence that the early male sexual impulses—again, initially through masturbation—are linked to physiological changes, to high hormonal inputs during puberty. This produces an organism that, to put it simply, is more easily turned on. Male adolescents report frequent erections, often without apparent stimulation of any kind. Even so, though there is greater biological sensitization and hence masturbation is more likely, the meaning, organization, and continuance of this activity still tends to be subordinate to social and psychological factors.

Masturbation provides guilt and anxiety among most adolescent boys. This is not likely to change in spite of more "enlightened" rhetoric and discourse on the subject (generally, we have shifted from stark warnings of mental, moral, and physical damage to vague counsels against nonsocial or "inappropriate" behavior). However, it may be that this very guilt and anxiety gives the sexual experience an intensity of feeling that is often attributed to sex itself.

Such guilt and anxiety do not follow simply from social disapproval. Rather, they seem to come from several sources, including the difficulty the boy has in presenting himself as a sexual being to his immediate family, particularly his parents. Another source is the fantasies or plans associated with masturbation—fantasies about doing sexual "things" to others or having others do sexual "things" to oneself; or having to learn and rehearse available but proscribed sexual scripts or patterns of behavior. And, of course, some guilt and anxiety center around the general disapproval of masturbation. After the early period of adolescence, in fact, most youths will not admit to their peers that they did or do it.

Nevertheless, masturbation is for most adolescent boys the major sexual activity, and they engage in it fairly frequently. It is an extremely positive and gratifying experience to them. Such an introduction to sexuality can lead to a capacity for detached sex activity—activity whose only sustaining motive is sexual. This may be the hallmark of male sexuality in our society.

Of the three sources of guilt and anxiety mentioned, the first—how to manage both sexuality and an attachment to family members—probably cuts across class lines. But the others should show remarkable class differences. The second one, how to manage a fairly elaborate and exotic fantasy life during masturbation, should be confined most typically to the higher classes, who are more experienced and adept at dealing with symbols. (It is possible, in fact, that this behavior, which girls rarely engage in, plays a role in the processes by which middle-class boys catch up with girls in measures of achievement and creativity and, by the end of adolescence, move out in front. However, this is only a hypothesis.)

The ability to fantasize during masturbation implies certain broad consequences. One is a tendency to see large parts of the environment in an erotic light, as well as the ability to respond, sexually and perhaps poetically, to many visual and auditory stimuli. We might also expect both a capacity and need for fairly elaborate forms of sexual activity. Further, since masturbatory fantasies generally deal with relationships and acts leading to coitus, they should also reinforce a developing capacity for heterosociality.

The third source of guilt and anxiety—the alleged "unmanliness" of masturbation—should more directly concern the lower-class male adolescent. ("Manliness" has always been an important value for lower-class males.) In these groups, social life is more often segregated by sex, and there are, generally, fewer rewarding social experiences from other sources. The adolescent therefore moves into heterosexual—if not heterosocial—relationships sooner than his middle-class counterparts. Sexual segregation makes it easier for him than for the middle-class boy to learn that he does not have to love everything he desires, and therefore to come more naturally to casual, if not exploitative, relationships. The second condition—fewer social rewards that his fellows would respect—should lead to an exaggerated concern for proving masculinity by direct displays of physical prowess, aggression, and visible sexual success. And these three, of course, may be mutually reinforcing.

In a sense, the lower-class male is the first to reach "sexual maturity" as defined by the Freudians. That is, he is generally the first to become aggressively heterosexual and exclusively genital. This characteristic, in fact, is a distinguishing difference between lower-class males and those above them socially.

But one consequence is that although their sex lives are almost exclusively heterosexual, they remain homosocial. They have intercourse with females, but the standards and the audience they refer to are those of their male fellows. Middle-class boys shift predominantly to coitus at a significantly later time. They, too, need and tend to have homosocial elements in their sexual lives. But their fantasies, their ability to symbolize, and their social training in a world in which distinctions between masculinity and femininity are less sharply drawn, allow them to withdraw more easily from an all-male world. This difference between social classes obviously has important consequences for stable adult relationships.

One thing common in male experience during adolescence is that while it provides much opportunity for sexual commitment, in one form or another, there is little training in how to handle emotional relations with girls. The imagery and rhetoric of romantic love is all around us; we are immersed in it. But whereas much is undoubtedly absorbed by the adolescent, he is not likely to tie it closely to his sexuality. In fact, such a connection might be inhibiting, as indicated by the survival of the "bad-girl-who-does" and "good-girl-who-doesn't" distinction. This is important to keep in mind as we turn to the female side of the story.

In contrast to males, female sexual development during adolescence is so similar in all classes that it is easy to suspect that it is solely determined by biology. But, while girls do not have the same level of hormonal sensitization to sexuality at puberty as adolescent boys, there is little evidence of a biological or social inhibitor either. The "equipment" for sexual pleasure is clearly present by puberty, but tends not to be used by many females of any class. Masturbation rates are fairly low, and among those who do masturbate, fairly infrequent. Arousal from "sexual" materials or situations happens seldom, and exceedingly few girls report feeling sexually deprived during adolescence.

Basically, girls in our society are not encouraged to be sexual—and may be strongly discouraged from being so. Most of us accept the fact that while "bad boy" can mean many things, "bad girl" almost exclusively implies sexual delinquency. It is both difficult and dangerous for an adolescent girl to become too active sexually. As Joseph Rheingold puts it, where men need only fear sexual failure, women must fear both success and failure.

Does this long period of relative sexual inactivity among girls come from repression of an elemental drive, or merely from a failure to learn how to be sexual? The answers have important implications for their later sexual development. If it is repression, the path to a fuller sexuality must pass through processes of loss of inhibitions, during which the girl unlearns, in varying degrees, attitudes and values that block the expression of natural internal feelings. It also implies that the quest for ways to express directly sexual behavior and feelings that had been expressed nonsexually is secondary and of considerably less significance.

On the other hand, the "learning" answer suggests that women create or invent a capacity for sexual behavior, learning how and when to be aroused and how and when to respond. This approach implies greater flexibility; unlike the repression view, it makes sexuality both more and less than a basic force that may break loose at any time in strange or costly ways. The learning approach also lessens the power of sexuality altogether; all at once, particular kinds of sex activities need no longer be defined as either "healthy" or "sick." Lastly, subjectively, this approach appeals to the authors because it describes female sexuality in terms that seem less like a mere projection of male sexuality.

If sexual activity by adolescent girls assumes less specific forms than with boys, that does not mean that sexual learning and training do not occur. Curiously, though girls are, as a group, far less active sexually than boys, they receive far more training in self-consciously viewing themselves—and in viewing boys—as desirable mates. This is particularly true in recent years. Females begin early in adolescence to define attractiveness, at least partially, in sexual terms. We suspect that the use of sexual attractiveness for nonsexual purposes that marked our preadolescent "seductress" now begins to characterize many girls. Talcott Parsons' description of how the wife "uses" sex to bind the husband to the family, although harsh, may be quite accurate. More generally, in keeping with the childbearing and child-raising function of women, the development of a sexual role seems to involve a need to include in that role more than pleasure.

To round out the picture of the difference between the sexes, girls appear to be well-trained precisely in that area in which boys are poorly trained— that is, a belief in and a capacity for intense, emotionally-charged relationships and the language of romantic love. When girls during this period describe having been aroused sexually, they more often report it as a response to romantic, rather than erotic, words and actions.

In later adolescence, as dates, parties, and other sociosexual activities increase, boys—committed to sexuality and relatively untrained in the language and actions of romantic love—interact with girls, committed to romantic love and relatively untrained in sexuality. Dating and courtship may well be considered processes in which each sex trains the other in what each wants and expects. What data is available suggests that this exchange system does not always work very smoothly. Thus, ironically, it is not uncommon to find that the boy becomes emotionally involved with his partner and therefore lets up on trying to seduce her, at the same time that the girl comes to feel that the boy's affection is genuine and therefore that sexual intimacy is more permissible.

In our recent study of college students, we found that boys typically had intercourse with their first coital partners one to three times, while with girls it was ten or more. Clearly, for the majority of females first intercourse becomes possible only in stable relationships or in those with strong bonds.

The male experience does conform to the general Freudian expectation that there is a developmental movement from a predominantly genital sexual commitment to a loving relationship with another person. But this movement is, in effect, reversed for females, with love or affection often a necessary precondition for intercourse. No wonder, therefore, that Freud had great difficulty understanding female sexuality—recall the concluding line in his great essay on women: "Woman, what does she want?" This "error"—the assumption that female sexuality is similiar to or a mirror image of that of the male—may come from the fact that so many of those who constructed the theory were men. With Freud, in addition, we must remember the very concept of sexuality essential to most of nineteenth-century Europe—it was an elemental beast that had to be curbed.

It has been noted that there are very few class differences in sexuality among females, far fewer than among males. One difference, however, is very relevant to this discussion—the age of first intercourse. This varies inversely with social class—that is, the higher the class, the later the age of first intercourse—a relationship that is also true of first marriage. The correlation between these two ages suggests the necessary social and emotional linkage between courtship and the entrance into sexual activity on the part of women. A second difference, perhaps only indirectly related to social class, has to do with educational achievement: here, a sharp border line seems to separate from all other women those who have or have had graduate or professional work. If sexual success may be measured by the percentage of sex acts that culminate in orgasm, graduate and professional women are the most sexually successful women in the nation.

Why? One possible interpretation derives from the work of Abraham Maslow: Women who get so far in higher education are more likely to be more aggressive, perhaps to have strong needs to dominate; both these characteristics are associated with heightened sexuality. Another, more general interpretation would be that in a society in which girls are expected primarily to become wives and mothers, going on to graduate school represents a kind of deviancy—a failure of, or alienation from, normal female social adjustment. In effect, then, it would be this flawed socialization—not biology—that produced both commitment toward advanced training and toward heightened sexuality.

For both males and females, increasingly greater involvement in the social aspects of sexuality—"socializing" with the opposite sex—may be one factor that marks the end of adolescence. We know little about this transition, especially among noncollege boys and girls; but our present feeling is that sexuality plays an important role in it. First, sociosexuality is important in family formation and also in learning the roles and obligations involved in being an adult. Second, and more fundamental, late adolescence is when a youth is seeking, and experimenting toward finding, his identity—who and what he is and will be; and sociosexual activity is the one aspect of this exploration that we associate particularly with late adolescence.

Young people are particularly vulnerable at this time. This may be partly due to the fact that society has difficulty protecting the adolescent from the consequences of sexual behavior that it pretends he is not engaged in. But, more importantly, it may be because, at all ages, we all have great problems in discussing our sexual feelings and experiences in personal terms. These, in turn, make it extremely difficult to get support from others for an adolescent's experiments toward trying to invent his sexual self. We suspect that success or failure in the discovery or management of sexual identity may have consequences in personal development far beyond merely the sexual sphere—perhaps in confidence and feelings of self-worth, belonging, competence, guilt, force of personality, and so on.

In our society, all but a few ultimately marry. Handling sexual commitments inside marriage makes up the larger part of adult experience. Again, we have too little data for firm findings. The data we do have come largely from studies of broken and troubled marriages, and we do not know to what extent sexual problems in such marriages exceed those of intact marriages. It is possible that, because we have assumed that sex is important in most people's lives, we have exaggerated its importance in holding marriages together. Also, it is quite possible that, once people are married, sexuality declines relatively, becoming less important than other gratifications (such as domesticity or parenthood); or it may be that these other gratifications can minimize the effect of sexual dissatisfaction. Further, it may be possible that individuals learn to get sexual gratification, or an equivalent, from activities that are nonsexual, or only partially sexual.

The sexual desires and commitments of males are the main determinants of the rate of sexual activity in our society. Men are most interested in intercourse in the early years of marriage—woman's interest peaks much later; nonetheless, coital rates decline steadily throughout marriage. This decline derives from many things, only one of which is decline in biological capacity. With many men, it is more difficult to relate sexually to a wife who is pregnant or a mother. Lower-class adult men receive less support and plaudits from their male friends for married sexual performance than they did as single adolescents; and we might also add the lower-class disadvantage of less training in the use of auxiliary or symbolic sexually stimulating materials. For middle-class men, the decline is not as steep, owing perhaps to their greater ability to find stimulation from auxiliary sources, such as literature, movies, music, and romantic or erotic conversation. It should be further noted that for about 30 percent of college-educated men, masturbation continues regularly during marriage, even when the wife is available. An additional (if unknown) proportion do not physically masturbate, but derive additional excitement from the fantasies that accompany intercourse.

But even middle-class sexual activity declines more rapidly than bodily changes can account for. Perhaps the ways males learn to be sexual in our society make it very difficult to keep it up at a high level with the same woman for a long time. However, this may not be vital in maintaining the family, or even in the man's personal sense of well-being, because, as previously suggested, sexual dissatisfaction may become less important as other satisfactions increase. Therefore, it need seldom result in crisis.

About half of all married men and a quarter of all married women will have intercourse outside of marriage at one time or another. For women, infidelity seems to have been on the increase since the turn of the century—at the same time that their rates of orgasm have been increasing. It is possible that the very nature of female sexuality is changing. Work being done now may give us new light on this. For men, there are strong social-class differences—the lower class accounts for most extramarital activity, especially during the early years of marriage. We have observed that it is difficult for a lower-class man to acquire the appreciation of his fellows for married intercourse; extramarital sex, of course, is another matter.

In general, we feel that far from sexual needs affecting other adult concerns, the reverse may be true: adult sexual activity may become that aspect of a person's life most often used to act out other needs. There are some data that suggest this. Men who have trouble handling authority relationships at work more often have dreams about homosexuality; some others, under heavy stress on the job, have been shown to have more frequent episodic homosexual experiences. Such phenomena as the rise of sadomasochistic practices and experiments in group sex may also be tied to nonsexual tensions, the use of sex for nonsexual purposes.

It is only fairly recently in the history of man that he has been able to begin to understand that his own time and place do not embody some eternal principle or necessity, but are only dots on a continuum. It is difficult for many to believe that man can change, and is changing, in important ways. This conservative view is evident even in contemporary behavioral science; and a conception of man as having relatively constant sexual needs has become part of it. In an ever-changing world, it is perhaps comforting to think that man's sexuality does not change very much, and therefore is relatively easily explained. We cannot accept this. Instead, we have attempted to offer a description of sexual development as a variable social invention—an invention that in itself explains little, and requires much continuing explanation.

Orgasm is a prime example of a human physiological response which cannot be understood apart from the cultural and interpersonal context in which it occurs—or fails to occur. This article discusses what might be called "the politics of orgasm."

The author argues that Freud's concept of the vaginal orgasm served the interests of men, because it stated that a "normal" woman would receive satisfaction automatically as a result of the man receiving his. Masters and Johnson's findings on the physiology of sexual response established the falsity of Freud's hypothesis that there are two distinct kinds of orgasm.

Understanding Orgasm | *Susan Lydon*

Tiresias, who had been both man and woman, was asked, as Ovid's legend goes, to mediate in a dispute between Jove and Juno as to which sex got more pleasure from lovemaking. Tiresias unhesitatingly answered that women did. Yet in the intervening 2000 years between Ovid's time and our own, a mythology has been built up which not only holds the opposite to be true, but has made this belief an unswerving ideology dictating the quality of

From Susan Lydon, "Understanding Orgasm," *Ramparts,* December 14–28, 1968.

relations between the sexes. Women's sexuality, defined by men to benefit men, has been downgraded and perverted, repressed and channeled, denied and abused until women themselves, thoroughly convinced of their sexual inferiority to men, would probably be dumbfounded to learn that there is scientific proof that Tiresias was indeed right.

The myth was codified by Freud as much as anyone else. In *Three Essays on the Theory of Sexuality*, Freud formulated his basic ideas concerning feminine sexuality: for little girls, the leading erogenous zone in their bodies is the clitoris; in order for the transition to womanhood to be successful, the clitoris must abandon its sexual primacy to the vagina; women in whom this transition has not been complete remain clitorally-oriented, or "sexually anaesthetic," and "psychosexually immature." In the context of Freud's total psychoanalytic view of women—that they are not whole human beings but mutilated males who long all their lives for a penis and must struggle to reconcile themselves to its lack—the requirement of a transfer of erotic sensation from clitoris to vagina became a prima facie case for their inevitable sexual inferiority. In Freud's logic, those who struggle to become what they are not must be inferior to that to which they aspire.

Freud admitted near the end of his life that his knowledge of women was inadequate. "If you want to know more about femininity, you must interrogate your own experience, or turn to the poets, or wait until science can give you more profound and more coherent information," he said; he also hoped the female psychoanalysts who followed him would be able to find out more. But the post-Freudians adhered rigidly to the doctrine of the master, and, as with most of his work, what Freud hoped would be taken as a thesis for future study became instead a kind of canon law.

While the neo-Freudians haggled over the correct reading of the Freudian bible, watered-down Freudianism was wending its way into the cultural mythology via Broadway plays, novels, popular magazines, social scientists, marriage counselors and experts of various kinds who found it useful in projecting desired images of woman. The superiority of the vaginal over the clitoral orgasm was particularly useful as a theory, since it provided a convenient basis for categorization: clitoral women were deemed immature, neurotic, bitchy, and masculine; women who had vaginal orgasms were maternal, feminine, mature, and normal. Though frigidity should technically be defined as total inability to achieve orgasm, the orthodox Freudians (and pseudo-Freudians) preferred to define it as inability to achieve vaginal orgasm, by which definition, in 1944, Edmond Bergler adjudged between 70 and 80 percent of all women frigid. The clitoral vs. vaginal debate raged hot and heavy among the sexologists—Kinsey's writings stressed the importance of the clitoris to female orgasm and contradicted Bergler's statistics—but it became clear that there was something indispensable to society in the

Freudian view which allowed it to remain unchallenged in the public consciousness.

In 1966, Dr. William H. Masters and Mrs. Virginia E. Johnson published *Human Sexual Response*, a massive clinical study of the physiology of sex. Briefly and simply, the Masters and Johnson conclusions about the female orgasm, based on observation of and interviews with 487 women, were these:

1. That the dichotomy of vaginal and clitoral orgasms is entirely false. Anatomically, all orgasms are centered in the clitoris, whether they result from direct manual pressure applied to the clitoris, indirect pressure resulting from the thrusting of penis during intercourse, or generalized sexual stimulation of other erogenous zones like the breasts.

2. That women are naturally multiorgasmic; that is, if a woman is immediately stimulated following orgasm, she is likely to experience several orgasms in rapid succession. This is not an exceptional occurrence, but one of which most women are capable.

3. That while women's orgasms do not vary in kind, they vary in intensity. The most intense orgasms experienced by the research subjects were by masturbatory manual stimulation, followed in intensity by manual stimulation by the partner; the least intense orgasms were experienced during intercourse.

4. That there is an "infinite variety of female sexual response" as regards intensity and duration of orgasms.

To anyone acquainted with the body of existing knowledge of feminine sexuality, the Masters and Johnson findings were truly revolutionary and liberating in the extent to which they demolished the established myths. Yet two years after the study was published, it seems hardly to have made any impact at all. Certainly it is not for lack of information that the myths persist; *Human Sexual Response*, despite its weighty scientific language, was an immediate best seller, and popular paperbacks explicated it to millions of people in simpler language and at a cheaper price. The myths remain because a male-dominated American culture has a vested interest in their continuance.

Before Masters and Johnson, men defined feminine sexuality in a way as favorable to themselves as possible. If woman's pleasure was obtained through the vagina, then she was totally dependent on the man's erect penis to achieve orgasm; she would receive her satisfaction only as a concomitant of man's seeking his. With the clitoral orgasm, woman's sexual pleasure was independent of the male's and she could seek her satisfaction as aggressively as the man sought his, a prospect which didn't appeal to too many men. The definition of feminine sexuality as normally vaginal, in other words, was a part of keeping women down, of making them sexually as well as economically, socially, and politically subservient.

In retrospect, particularly with the additional perspective of our own times, Freud's theory of feminine sexuality appears an historical rationalization for the realities of Victorian society. A prisoner of the Victorian ethos, Freud had to play the paterfamilias. Freud's analysis implied that woman's low status had not been conferred upon her by men, but by God, who created her without a penis.

The superiority of the vaginal orgasm seems almost a demoniac determination on Freud's part to complete the Victorians' repression of feminine eroticism, to stigmatize the remaining vestiges of pleasure felt by women and thus make them unacceptable to the women themselves. For there were still women whose sexuality hadn't been completely destroyed, as evidenced by one Dr. Isaac Brown Baker, a surgeon who performed numerous clitoridectomies on women to prevent the sexual excitement which, he was convinced, caused "insanities," "catalepsy," "hysteria," "epilepsy," and other diseases. The Victorians needed to repress sexuality for the success of Western industrialized society; in particular, the total repression of woman's sexuality was crucial to ensure her subjugation. So the Victorians honored only that aspect of sexuality which was necessary to the survival of the species—the male ejaculation; made women submissive to sex by creating a mystique of the sanctity of motherhood; and, supported by Freud, passed on to us the heritage of the double standard.

When Kinsey laid to rest the part of the double standard that maintained women got no pleasure at all from sex, everyone cried out that there was a sexual revolution afoot. But such talk, as usual, was deceptive. Morality, outside the marriage bed, remained the same, and children were socialized as though Kinsey had never described what they would be like when they grew up. Boys were taught that they should get their sex where they could find it, "go as far" as they could. On the old assumption that women were asexual creatures, girls were taught that since they needed sex less than boys did, it was up to them to impose sexual restraints. In whatever sex education adolescents did manage to receive, they were told that men had penises and women vaginas; the existence of the clitoris was not mentioned, and *pleasure* in sex was never discussed at all.

Adolescent boys growing up begging for sexual crumbs from girls frightened for their "reputations"—a situation that remains unchanged to this day—hardly constitutes the vanguard of a sexual revolution. However, the marriage manual craze that followed Kinsey assumed that a lifetime of psychological destruction could, with the aid of a little booklet, be abandoned after marriage, and that husband and wife should be able to make sure that the wife was not robbed of her sexual birthright to orgasm, just so long as it was *vaginal* (though the marriage manuals did rather reluctantly admit that since the clitoris was the most sexually sensitive organ in the female body, a little clitoral stimulation was in order), and so long as their orgasms were *simultaneous.*

The effect of the marriage manuals of course ran counter to their ostensible purpose. Under the guise of frankness and sexual liberation, they dictated prudery and restraint. Sex was made so mechanized, detached, and intellectual that it was robbed of its sensuality. Man became a spectator of his own sexual experience. And the marriage manuals put new pressure on women. The swing was from repression to preoccupation with the orgasm. Men took the marriage manuals to mean that their sexuality would be enhanced by bringing women to orgasm and, again coopting feminine sexuality for their own ends, they put pressure on women to perform. The marriage manuals' endorsement of the desirability of vaginal orgasm insured that women would be asked not only, "Did you come?" but also, "Did you conform to Freud's conception of a psychosexually mature woman, and thereby validate my masculinity?"

Appearances notwithstanding, the age-old taboos against conversation about personal sexual experience haven't yet been broken down. This reticence has allowed the mind-manipulators of the media to create myths of sexual supermen and superwomen. So the bed becomes a competitive arena, where men and women measure themselves against these mythical rivals, while simultaneously trying to live up to the ecstasies promised them by the marriage manuals and the fantasies of the media ("If the earth doesn't move for me, I must be missing something"). Our society has made sex a sport, with its record-breakers, its judges, its rules, and its spectators.

As anthropologists have shown, woman's sexual response is culturally conditioned; historically, women defer to whatever model of their sexuality is offered them by men. So the sad thing for women is that they have participated in the destruction of their own eroticism. Women have helped make the vaginal orgasm into a status symbol in a male-dictated system of values. A woman would now perceive her preference for clitoral orgasm as a "secret shame," ignominious in the eyes of other women as well as those of men. This internalization can be seen in literature: Mary McCarthy and Doris Lessing's writings on orgasm do not differ substantially from Ernest Hemingway's, and Simone de Beauvoir, in *The Second Sex*, refers to vaginal orgasm as the only "normal satisfaction."

One factor that has made this possible is that female sexuality is subtle and delicate, conditioned as much by the emotions as by physiology and sociology. Masters and Johnson proved that the orgasm experienced during intercourse, the misnamed vaginal orgasm, did not differ *anatomically* from the clitoral orgasm. But this should not be seen as their most significant contribution to the sexual emancipation of women. A difference remains in the *subjective* experience of orgasm during intercourse and orgasm apart from intercourse. In the complex of emotional factors affecting feminine sexuality, there is a whole panoply of pleasures: the pleasure of being penetrated and filled by a man, the pleasure of sexual communication, the pleasure of affording a man his orgasm, the erotic pleasure that exists even when sex is not terminated by orgasmic release. Masters and Johnson's real contribution was to show this "infinite variety in female sexual response"; that one experience is not better than another, but merely different.

There is no doubt that Masters and Johnson were fully aware of the implications of their study to the sexual liberation of women. As they wrote, "With orgasmic physiology established, the human female now has an undeniable opportunity to develop realistically her own sexual response levels." Two years later this statement seems naive and entirely too optimistic. Certainly the sexual problems of our society will never be solved until there is real and unfeigned equality between men and women. This idea is usually misconstrued: sexual liberation for women is wrongly understood to mean that women will adopt all the forms of masculine sexuality. As in the whole issue of women's liberation, that's really not the point. Women don't aspire to imitate the mistakes of men in sexual matters, to view sexual experiences as conquest and ego-enhancement, to use other people to serve their own ends. But if the Masters and Johnson material is allowed to filter into the public consciousness, hopefully to replace the enshrined Freudian myths, then woman at long last will be allowed to take the first step toward her emanicpation: to define and enjoy the forms of her own sexuality.

Chapter 4

The Social Context of Sexuality

In recent years, marriage or sex manuals have become both best sellers and the leading sources of sexual instruction. A number of writers have questioned whether sex manuals bring more harm than enlightenment. Besides being guilty of sheer misinformation, such manuals have been accused of fostering a mechanical approach to lovemaking, more appropriate to the factory or the office. The present article examines eighteen best-selling marriage manuals of the past two decades to see if the portrayal of female sexuality in them reflects recent research findings. The authors find that the implications of such research are ignored, and the advice offered in marriage manuals is biased by traditional ideologies of sexuality.

Different Equals Less: Female Sexuality in Recent Marriage Manuals

Michael Gordon and Penelope J. Shankweiler

> Coitus can scarcely be said to take place in a vacuum; although of itself it appears a biological and physical activity, it is so deeply within the larger context of human affairs that it serves as a charged microcosm of the variety of attitudes and values to which the culture subscribes. (Millett, 1970, p. 23)

This quotation from Kate Millett's *Sexual Politics* reveals the theme of the present paper. We are in agreement with her thesis that what takes place between men and women in the bedroom has something to tell us about the relationship that prevails between them in the world at large. While Millett draws primarily upon the work of three major novelists to docu-

Reprinted by permission from "Different Equals Less: Female Sexuality in Recent Marriage Manuals" by Michael Gordon and Penelope J. Shankweiler, *Journal of Marriage and the Family*, August 1971, pp. 459–465.

ment this thesis we will use non-fictional sources, more specifically marriage manuals published in the last two decades.* This form of literature was chosen because we feel it contains the currently regnant views on human sexuality, and also because it receives reasonably wide circulation (e.g., David Reuben's *Everything You Always Wanted to Know About Sex* has already sold over a million copies in the hard-bound edition alone).† Furthermore, the experts, often self-proclaimed, who write these manuals influence the views of those who provide sexual counseling in our society. Whether these books influence behavior in any important sense is moot, but at the very least they do help create the sexual expectations of those directly or indirectly exposed to them.

We see this as a study in sexual ideology. As traditionally defined, ideology refers to the body of beliefs and values which legitimate the status quo, an important aspect of which may be a dominant group's position vis-à-vis other groups in a society. If women are conceived of as a "minority" group it then becomes important to explore the ideology which perpetuates this status. It is our contention that a significant dimension of this ideology is the manner in which women have had their sexuality *defined* for them. Women have had specific boundaries imposed on the expression of their sexuality. To be sure, the same is true of men, but the constraints have been looser and fewer. Moreover, these boundaries are the creations, for the most part, of male "experts," whose opinions and advice have reflected the interests of a patriarchal society. We will begin by examining the manner in which female sexuality has been depicted in the manuals published in the period between 1830 and 1950.‡

Female Sexuality, 1830–1950

Stereotypes do on occasion reflect a considerable degree of the reality they generally simplify and distort. The popular image of nineteenth century, middle-class society being one in which the professed values placed sex in the category of an unfortunate procreative necessity is for the most part substantiated by the contents of the marriage manuals published dur-

*We use the term marriage and sex manuals interchangeably in this paper, though a good argument can be made for the point that the term sex manuals is best left reserved for those books which focus almost exclusively on sex education, in contrast to marriage manuals which focus on a broader spectrum of domestic life. By this definition books used in this study are sex manuals.

†In order to understand just how impressive this figure is, one must realize that Van de Velde's *Ideal Marriage* (1930) has not in the American edition sold as many copies in the forty years it has been in print, and it is one of the most popular marriage manuals ever published.

‡For a more complete discussion of the literature of this period the reader is referred to Gordon (in press) and Gordon and Bernstein (1970).

ing this period. Such books generally advocate a policy of sex for reproduction only, as is attested to by continence being the most frequently recommended form of contraception. Women are granted any form of sexual desire so begrudgingly that for almost all intents and purposes it is nonexistent.

> As a general rule, a modest woman seldom desires any sexual gratification for herself. She submits to her husband, but only to please him; and, but for the desire of maternity, would far rather be relieved from his attentions. The married woman has no wish to be treated on the footing of a mistress. (Hayes, 1869, p. 227)

However, as the century draws to a close one can see the *beginnings* of an acceptance of non-procreative marital sexuality, as well as female sexual desire, in some of the manuals.

In the early years of the twentieth century what was hinted earlier becomes the prevailing view, *viz.,* sex in the context of marriage is not only right and proper, but an important aspect of married life as well. As one might expect, this point of view is tied to a reorientation toward female sexuality. Its existence is now recognized, but in a form which distinctly sets it apart from male sexuality:

> It is the complexity of woman's sex nature you have not understood. A wife needs the affection of attention, interest. With her it is not merely a craving for carnal pleasures; it is something deeper, something of a spiritual nature which sweetly blended with her physiological demands. (Howard, 1912, p. 22)

> To a great percentage of men a strictly monogamous life is either irksome, painful, disagreeable or an utter impossibility. While the number of women who are not satisfied with one mate is exceedingly small. (Robinson, 1917, p. 325)

These two excerpts, which are typical of the period, are related to one another in an important fashion. One might say that the ideas contained in one almost logically flow from the other. Women are presented with a definition of their sexuality that conveniently excludes the possibility of engaging in the kind of nonmarital sexual behavior men are granted. Here, then, we have one rationale for the "double-standard" that has been with us so long, and that is only now beginning to break down.

Another important dimension of the conception of female sexuality that arose at the beginning of the century is its alleged dormancy. That is to say, in contrast to the male who from puberty on is confronted by imperious sexual impulses, females supposedly do not experience strong desire until sex is initiated—in the marriage bed, of course.

> No doubt women differ greatly, but in every woman who truly loves there lies dormant the capacity to become vibrantly alive in response to her lover, and to meet him as a willing and active participant in the sacrament of marriage. (Gray, 1922, p. 145)

What is of significance here is that female sexuality becomes a male creation, without his intercession it remains incipient at best, and nonexistent at worse.

Once a woman's sexual desire has been "awakened" by her husband, its satisfaction, not surprisingly, falls on his shoulders, and in a specific way, *viz.,* coitus culminating, ideally, in simultaneous climax. Writing in 1926 Margaret Sanger had the following to say on this matter:

> Experience will teach the husband to watch for and recognize in his beloved the approach of the culminating ecstasy. Not until this point is attained may he release his own emotions from control so that both together at the same moment may yield themselves for the final ecstatic flight. (Sanger, 1926, p. 142)

Such statements are encountered as early as 1900; by the 1930s their number has reached such proportions that it has been described as "a cult of mutual orgasm" (Gordon, in press). This emphasis on a particular form of orgasmic ordering is noteworthy because it defines the appropriate mode for sexual satisfaction in terms of the male's orgasmic potential.*

Thus, while the very recognition of female sexuality at the beginning of the century was in itself revolutionary, it was presented in invidious terms: not only was it different and less clamorous than that of the male, but essentially dependent upon him for its arousal and satisfaction. We hope to show that new evidence and knowledge is beginning to lead to a reappraisal of female sexual potential, but that the idea of male domination continues to be as firmly entrenched in the sexual sphere as it is in male-female relationships in the society as a whole.

The Manuals

The eighteen manuals on which this study is based were for the most part the best sellers of the 1950–70 period.† This is not to say that all of them were first published during these two decades. Some appeared earlier in the century, e.g., Chesser's *Love Without Fear* (1947), but continued to sell

---

*Some people have seen Freudian influence in the development of "the cult of mutual orgasm." As we have indicated, there were writers advocating this well before Freud hnd written on any topic bearing on this subject. However, in the 1920s and 1930s his conception of "mature" female sexuality being vaginal sexuality probably was a factor accounting for the growth of those recommending this form of orgasmic ordering, and, of course, was the source of what Koedt has called "the myth of vaginal orgasm."

†In the first author's earlier studies the manuals were selected differently. Because of their small numbers an attempt was made to locate the total universe of nineteenth century manuals, and 63 were ultimately found to be usable. Twentieth century manuals were selected by means of a representative sample of manuals published in each decade of the century.

in large number through the sixties.* We have adopted this selection procedure rather than sampling systematically from the manuals published in this two decade interval because we were not concerned with the views that were most representative of this type of literature, but rather with the views the greater number of people were being exposed to, and which thus could be viewed as being the most influential. In discussing this material we shall first explore what we see as indications of a broad changing sexual ethic and then focus on the treatment of female sexuality in this context.

Findings

The New Sexual Ethic

One of the most notable shifts in the recent manuals is the growing acceptance, often implicit, of nonmarital sex for women. As we have already noted, men in the past have been granted more sexual license than women and it was expected that they would engage in a certain amount of pre- or extramarital sex. This view holds through the 1950s, with most writers appearing to direct their books to couples entering marriage with the wife a virgin and the husband furtively experienced. In the 1960s we notice not only a less critical attitude toward premarital sex for women but the appearance of books which provide instruction for its successful pursuit as well. Among the earliest of these, and certainly the most widely read, was Helen Gurley Brown's *Sex and the Single Girl* (1962).†

> Nice, single girls *do* have affairs, and they do not necessarily die of them! They suffer sometimes, occasionally a great deal. However, quite a few "nice" girls have affairs and do not suffer at all! (Brown, 1962, p. 225)

The cheering can stop. While Helen Gurley Brown did openly and approvingly discuss nonmarital sex she was committed to the status quo insofar as male-female relationships are concerned. The same holds true of *The Sensuous Woman,* a recent best seller that graphically explores the frontiers of sexual behavior while clinging to conventional notions of broader relationships between the sexes. This book might have been appropriately subtitled, *How to Get to a Man's Heart Through His Genitals.*

It should be stressed that the acceptance of premarital experience in the

---

*Furthermore, several of the books included in this study have gone through innumerable printings and several editions and revisions. The year given for a book is usually that of its most recent revision, where it was possible to establish this date.

†This book is not a sex or marriage manual and is thus not included in the enumeration of manuals in this study. Its discussion is felt to be warranted because of the radical character of its theme.

majority of the manuals is much less explicit than in the books discussed above. For the most part, even throughout the sixties, sex is assumed to take place within the social context of love and marriage, the latter being "the most precious and deeply satisfying relationship we know" (Calderone, 1960, p. 13). Even those writers most deeply committed to sensuality still subscribe to the idealized view of sex as a sacrament, a means of communicating love for another person and ideally in a marital setting.

In view of such a sentiment it is not surprising to find that extramarital affairs are almost overwhelmingly rejected in the books included in the study, and concomitantly, a major concern is with improving marital sex so as to avert this eventuality. Some authors assume that the basic recipes have been mastered and "a couple who will not be content with a static love, even if it is a satisfying love, will have to keep up a constant search for ways of introducing a freshness into their sexual experience" (Chartham, 1970, p. 27). Moreover, it is expected that the approach of old age will not mark the end of the couple's sexual life. Increasingly we are finding books containing sections on what we might call gerontological sex. Masters and Johnson's (1966) finding on the abilities of the elderly, when in good health, to function adequately sexually has lent support to this position.

Part of the concern with reinvigorating marital sex is manifested in the growing interest in what we might call "gourmet" sex as is indicated by the titles of books such as *Sex for Advanced Lovers* (1970) and *Sophisticated Sex Techniques* (1967). These books are usually less programmatic than earlier ones such as, for example, Van de Velde's *Ideal Marriage* (1930). While the latter, as did similar books in the 1930s and 1940s, presented a demanding sexual regimen involving the specification of appropriate behavior at all stages of the sex act, more recent books in general seem to place more emphasis on spontaneity and the willingness to experiment. Alternative forms of sexual expression such as oral-genital and anal-genital, while previously either ignored, or relegated to foreplay, are now beginning to be elevated to ends in their own right, and represent part of a generally freer orientation toward recreative sex. The boundaries of human sexuality are slowly being expanded. Hedonism within the context of marriage is the new norm.

An important illustration of the rejection of the stress on technique and rationality in sex and the new hedonism, as well, is the reappraisal of simultaneous climax in the past two decades. In the first half of the century and particularly since the 1930s, "mutual orgasm" had been presented as the ultimate in sexual bliss. Recently some voices have been raised in opposition to this view. On the one hand there are those who feel it has created standards that most couples find difficult to meet:

> In many books of sexual enlightenment, simultaneous orgasm or almost simultaneous orgasm is put forth as being the normal, common and desirable thing. It is, however, a lie that has caused much damage in the course of time because it has resulted in many couples feeling abnormal or 'no good' without reason. (Hegeler and Hegeler, 1963, p. 196)

Others criticize it on what we may call aesthetic grounds:

> Although there is certainly no denying that mutual simultaneous orgasm is very enjoyable, there is also something to be said for consecutive orgasm. Since the precise moment of orgasm usually brings on a lapse of consciousness, neither man nor woman is able to enjoy the orgasm of their partner. (Reuben, 1969, p. 56)

Still others raise questions which relate to female sexuality:

> This pursuit of a fanciful notion will operate to maintain a woman at a single-orgasm level, a loss of completion far more to be deplored than that resulting from separate orgasm. (Street, 1959, p. 67)

The last excerpt was written in the year that Masters and Johnson began their research. Ironically enough, in the years since their research has been published we have not seen similar critiques.

The Nature of Female Sexuality

In the context of a growing emphasis on pleasure and spontaneity there is occurring a gradual change in ideas about female sexuality. In the books published between 1950–1965 men are perceived as having greater sexual needs than women, whereas in those appearing in the 1965–70 period the predominant idea is that men and women are equal in sexual desire but the nature of their sexuality is, in a variety of ways, different. The latter is witnessed by statements such as the following: "Men can enjoy sex, in an animal sort of way, without love. Women can't, so remind her of your love often, in some way or another" (Hall, 1965, p. 12). Female sexuality is still seen as more emotional and idealized than its male counterpart, something which grows out of love rather than physical desire.

What is important here is the persistence of a restrictive definition of female sexuality. If one is continually told that one has to care for, if not love, a man in order to sleep with him, then it can act as a self-fulfilling prophecy, and lo and behold many women find truth in David Reuben's words ". . . Before a woman can have sexual intercourse with a man she must have social intercourse with him" (Reuben, 1969, p. 103).

Furthermore, women are portrayed as likely to be negative about sex. In discussions of sexual maladjustment and experimentation it is generally the woman who is seen as the problematic partner. While socialization is frequently viewed as the source of female inhibitions, other differences are seemingly attributed to biological factors. Thus, Greenblat maintains:

> . . . In many women, as a result of physical development and social training, the desire for actual sexual intercourse as distinct from kissing and petting may develop somewhat later than in young men. However, it is also true that the greater complexity of the woman's sexual organs makes possible a much deeper and more lasting physical emotional [sic] response. This response is not easy to sum up in a few words and not easy to achieve or to satisfy in the few seconds or minutes of sexual activity that would satisfy most males. (Greenblat, 1956, p. 8)

Here we see the persistence of the belief in the dormancy and slow development of female sexuality. In fact, women are believed to reach sexual "maturity" 10 to 12 years later than men, who are at the peak of their desire and performance at eighteen, a point to which we will return later in the paper.

In general, men are presented as simple creatures sexually whose desire is as easily satisfied as it is aroused. They are supposedly capable of responding to what they think, imagine or see, while women are thought to be "touch" creatures who have to be slowly stimulated by gentle kisses and caresses. One author expresses concern that men should not base their idea of what "normal" women are like sexually on their experiences with women who:

> because of their unusually high sex and endowments are prone to have many voluntary and nonprostitutional premarital affairs. Such females are frequently so easily aroused and satisfied sexually that their male partners receive the erroneous impression that all normal females are, or should be, the way the minority of females behave. (Ellis, 1966, p. 19)

Reservations such as these notwithstanding, the prevailing view is that once a woman is aroused her desire is as strong as a man's—some books even mention the female capacity for multiple orgasm, but almost all fail to discuss its implications.

It is important to assess the extent to which such views of female sexuality are based on ideology. The findings of Masters and Johnson (1966) lend support to the position that while there are differences in the sexual response cycles of men and women, with the exception of orgasmic capacity, they resemble each other more than they differ. That is to say, the excitement, plateau, orgasmic and resolution phases are essentially similar. One does, of course, have to consider the degree to which cultural overlay masks some of these similarities. For example, a recent study carried out by the Institute for Sex Research at the University of Hamburg found that when exposed to erotic photographs women tend to judge them to be less arousing than do men but "the women showed almost the same degree of sexual-physio-logical reactions and activation of sexual behavior as the men" (Sigusch *et al.*, 1970, p. 23). The importance of the Hamburg findings is that they indicate the extent to which women are responding to cues that define so-cially appropriate and inappropriate situations calling for a sexual response, rather than their own bodies.

The Masters and Johnson (1966) study has been iconoclastic in a num-ber of ways. Not only have their findings raised serious doubts about the differences between male and female response cycles, but, as is well known, they have also toppled the oft-proclaimed distinction between vaginal and clitoral orgasms, and with this have prepared the ground for the emergence of a new view of female sexuality.*

The impact of their work has not been strongly felt in the marriage man-uals. A number of recent manuals do discuss the findings on the clitoris and gerontological sex, but they generally fail to explore the implications of the findings on the multiorgasmic capacities of women not only for sexual tech-nique, but for the broader relations between men and women as well. Only one book even broaches the latter topic. In commenting on Masters and Johnson's findings on multiple orgasm Robert Chartham notes:

> If multiple-orgasm becomes a widespread experience, however, the whole sexual relationship with regard to the sensual content of swiving [coitus] is likely to go reverse. Whereas in the past men have taken it for granted that theirs was the superior experience, since they could never bring an episode of swiving to its natural ultimate conclusion without coming off, now though they will still have this advantage, their responses are bound to be inferior to the multiple-orgasm partner. (Chartham, 1970, p. 85)

Others have carried such ideas much further, most notably Mary Jane Sherfey in her masterful essay on female sexuality.

Dr. Sherfey reviews the findings of Masters and Johnson and concludes that:

> . . . The more orgasms a woman has, the stronger they become; the more orgasms she has, the more she *can* have. To all intents and purposes, *the human female is sexually insatiable in the presense of the highest degrees of sexual satiation.* (Sherfey, 1966, p. 99)

---

*It should be pointed out that Kinsey and his associates in *Sexual Behavior in the Human Female* (1953, pp. 582–583) discussed evidence that seriously if not irrefutably questioned the possibility of a "vaginal orgasm." Interestingly enough this was virtually ignored while other sections of the book such as the differential sexual "maturation" rate of the sexes was frequently commented upon by authors of marriage manuals. This would seem to be a case of facts being widely disseminated which can be reconciled with prevailing beliefs and those which cannot, dismissed or ignored.

Moreover, she views monogamous marriage as something which men have never fully accepted and women have been coerced into accepting: ". . . Women's inordinate orgasmic capacity did not evolve for monogamous, sedentary cultures" (Sherfey, 1966, p. 118).

Another point raised by Sherfey that is important for our understanding of prevailing views of female sexuality is that of the differential sexual "maturation" rate of males and females. That is to say, men and women reach the height of their responsiveness at different times. The source of this view is the Kinsey study:

> We have pointed out that the male's capacity to be stimulated sexually shows a marked increase with the approach of adolescence, and that the incidences of responding males and the frequency of response to the point of orgasm, reach their peak within three or four years after the onset of adolescence. . . . On the other hand, we have pointed out that the maximum incidences of sexually responding females are not approached until some time in the late twenties and in the thirties. . . . (Kinsey et al., 1953, p. 714–715)

This has been frequently commented upon in the marriage manuals and plays an important role in defining current notions of women's sexual uniqueness. In the words of Maxine Davis, woman "is an early-leafing but late-flowering plant" (Davis, 1963, p. 88). Sherfey explores what others had hinted at: The roots of this difference may be more social than biological.

> Less than one hundred years ago, and in many places today, women regularly had their third or fourth child by the time they were eighteen or nineteen, and the life span was no more than thirty-five to forty years. It could well be that the natural synchronization of the peak periods for sexual expression in men and women have been destroyed only in recent years. (Sherfey, 1966, p. 118–119)

One would have to interpret this to mean that with the postponed age of marriage in industrial societies and the differential sexual license granted men and women, natural synchronization has broken down. Or, to put it differently, the reason women are "maturing" more slowly than men is they have less opportunity to engage in heterosexual relations and perhaps more importantly they are socialized in such a way as to suppress rather than encourage the expression of their sexuality early in adolescence in autoerotic forms.

What makes all of this especially interesting is the new data that is becoming available on changes in rates of premarital intercourse for college students. The studies of Bell and Chaskes (1970) and Christensen and Gregg (1970) found that between 1958 and 1968 there was an increase in female premarital sex. Bell and Chaskes also found that the context in which sexual intercourse had first occurred had changed, with the dating and going steady settings increasingly replacing engagement. Moreover, there is in general a growing convergence of the rates for men and women, with this being especially notable in Denmark where Christensen and Gregg report 95 percent of the men and 97 percent of the women having had premarital coitus. Findings such as these suggest that as the differences between male and female premarital experience rates begin to decrease, we may also see a growing convergence in sexual "maturation" rates.

Male and Female Sexual Roles

Even the growing number of authors who are advocating an "equal but different" image of female sexuality still subscribe, for the most part, to a belief in the importance of male leadership and initiative. Brisset and Lewis in their study of sex manuals note that "between three and four times as many prescriptions for behavior are directed to the male as to the female" (1970, p. 42). Nevertheless, a common theme is the encouragement of female initiative as a means of improving the couple's sex life. "The bride should overcome her modesty and let him know which caresses are most desirable and the manner of their performance" (Levine, 1950, p. 5). What this and similar authors are trying to do is have women overcome the passivity they feel impedes sexual pleasure, but the focus is always on the man:

> In lovemaking your body is your instrument. You shouldn't settle for less than the best. An Arthur Rubenstein or Van Cliburn is not going to select a clunky, unresponsive, out-of-tune piano on which to perform his artistry. ("J," 1969, p. 28)

The metaphor here is a rather revealing one.

For a number of authors the importance of male control takes on the character of an imperative for general domestic as well as sexual adjustment:

> Manly self-assertion can be *tempered* with gentleness and consideration, but both your sex life and your marriage suffer if you allow it to be smothered or overrestrained by such qualities. Emotionally and physically, your wife needs the assertiveness of a masculine figure to make a good marital adjustment. The highest form of considerateness in the long run is to become such a figure in her eyes. (Eichenlaub, 1968, p. 82)

So we see that while the trend toward what we have earlier called "gourmet" sex may have contributed to the emergence of a more active conception of the woman's role, it has not altered more fundamental sexual behavior. There is nothing irreconcilable between the feminine mystique and a woman who plays a more active role in bed, as long as control resides with the man.

Conclusion

We trust that our discussion of the manner in which female sexuality has been depicted in the marriage manuals of the past two decades has revealed the ideological overtones of such literature. Women in this century have been granted the right to experience sexual desire and have this desire satisfied, but always with the man calling the tune. This we have suggested is a manifestation of the minority group status of women. Given their primary roles of wives and mothers, their sexuality is something which has been subject to masculine definitions of its purity, spoilage, ruination and so on. Women have been given the sop of sexual spirituality in return for the sexual freedom they have been denied. In short, they have been offered a conception of their sexuality that has not allowed it to follow its underlying physiology.

We see this as an ideology reflecting the prevailing social relations between the sexes. As James Coleman notes:

> . . . When [a woman's] status and ultimate position do not depend greatly on her husband she need not be so cautious. Her sexual activity may now be a pleasure to be enjoyed more nearly for its own sake, without regard for its loss in value through promiscuity and loss of 'reputation.' Her sexual activity is not so much a commodity by which she establishes her ultimate social position, and she need no longer withhold it for exchange purposes. She becomes more like the male in this regard, having less reason to maintain her sexual activity as a scarce good in a market, more reason to consume it for its direct enjoyment. (Coleman, 1966, p. 217)

Since women are not independent in this regard, it is not surprising that the changes that have occurred in recent sex manuals do not represent a dramatic reorientation toward female sexual roles. The new findings on female sexuality appear to be poured into the old bottles of male-female relationships. If women have been encouraged to take more initiative it is in order that they might give more pleasure to their husbands rather than achieve more autonomy in the sexual realm.

References

Roll, Robert R., and Jay B. Chunkee. "Premarital Sexual Experience Among Coeds, 1958 and 1968." *Journal of Marriage and the Family*, 32 (February 1970): 30–35.

Brissett, Dennis, and Lionel Lewis. "Guidelines for Marital Sex: An Analysis of Fifteen Popular Marriage Manuals." *The Family Coordinator*, 19 (January 1970): 41–48.

Brown, Helen Gurley. *Sex and the Single Girl*. New York: Bernard Geis, 1962.

*Butterfield, Oliver M. *Sexual Harmony in Marriage*. New York: Emerson Books, 1967.

*Calderone, Mary S. *Release from Sexual Tensions*. New York: Random House, 1960.

*Chartham, Robert, *Sex for Advanced Lovers*. New York: New American Library, 1970.

*Chesser, Eustace. *Love Without Fear*. New York: Roy Publishers, 1947.

*Chesser, Eustace. *Love and the Married Woman*. New York: New American Library, 1970.

Christensen, Harold T., and Christina Gregg. "Changing Sex Norms in America and Scandinavia." *Journal of Marriage and the Family,* 32 (November 1970): 616–627.

Coleman, James S. Letter to the editor. *American Journal of Sociology,* 72 (September 1966): 217.

*Davis, Maxine. *Sexual Responsibility in Marriage*. New York: Dial Press, 1963.

*Eichenlaub, John E. *The Marriage Art*. New York: Dell, 1961.

*Eichenlaub, John E. *New Approaches to Sex in Marriage*. New York: Dell, 1968.

*Ellis, Albert. *The Art and Science of Love*. New York: Bantam Books, 1966.

Gordon, Michael. "From an Unfortunate Necessity of a Cult of Mutual Orgasm: Sex in American Domestic Education Literature, 1830–1940." In *The Sociology of Sex*, edited by James Henslin. New York: Appleton-Century-Crofts, in press.

Gordon, Michael, and M. Charles Bernstein. "Mate Choice and Domestic Life in the Nineteenth-Century Marriage Manual." *Journal of Marriage and the Family,* 32 (November 1970): 665–674.

Gray, A. H. *Men, Women and God*. New York: Association Press, 1922.

*Greenblat, Bernard R. *A Doctor's Marital Guide for Patients*. Chicago: Budlong Press Company, 1956.

*Hall, Robert E. *Sex and Marriage*. New York: Planned Parenthood, 1965.

Hayes, A. *Sexual Physiology of Woman*. Boston: Peabody Medical Institute, 1869.

*Hegeler, Inge and Sten. *An ABZ of Love*. New York: Medical Press, 1963.

Howard, William Lee. *Facts for the Married*. New York: Edward J. Clode, 1912.

*"J." *The Sensuous Woman*. New York: Lyle Stuart, 1969.

Kinsey, Alfred *et al*. *Sexual Behavior in the Human Female*. Philadelphia: Saunders, 1953.

*Levine, Lena. *The Doctor Talks with the Bride and Groom*. New York: Planned Parenthood, 1950.

Masters, William H., and Johnson, Virginia E. *Human Sexual Response*. Boston: Little, Brown, 1966.

Millett, Kate. *Sexual Politics*. New York: Doubleday, 1970.

*Reuben, David. *Everything You Always Wanted to Know About Sex . . .* New York: David McKay, 1969.

Robinson, William J. *Woman: Her Sex and Love Life*. New York: Eugenics Publishing Company, 1917.

Sanger, Margaret. *Happiness in Marriage*. New York: Blue Ribbon Books, 1926.

Sherfey, Mary Jane. "The Evolution and Nature of Female Sexuality in Relation to Psychoanalytic Theory." *Journal of the American Psychoanalytic Association,* 14 (January 1966): 28–127.

Sigusch, Volkmar, *et al*. "Psychosexual Stimulation: Sex Differences." *Journal of Sex Research,* 6 (February 1970): 10–24.

*Stone, Hannah and Abraham. *A Marriage Manual*. New York: Simon and Schuster, 1953.

*Street, Robert. *Modern Sex Techniques*. New York: Lancer Books, 1959.

*Van de Velde, Th. H. *Ideal Marriage*. New York: Random House, 1930.

Woodward, L. T. *Sophisticated Sex Techniques in Marriage*. New York: Lancer Books, 1967.

*One of the 18 books on which the present study is based.

During the past decade, most family scholars scoffed at the idea that a sexual revolution was going on. The authors of this article argue that such a position may have reflected wishful thinking, a lack of adequate data, and a tendency to overgeneralize from data available. They present data showing that attitudes toward premarital intercourse have liberalized considerably for both sexes. Premarital sexual behavior did not change as dramatically, but there were sharp increases in the sexual behavior of women. Thus, college men and women are becoming more alike in their sexual attitudes and behavior, and for everyone, attitudes and behavior are coming more into line. Thus, the old double standard of sex behavior for men and women, and the patterns of defining sex as sinful while engaging in it, are becoming passé.

Changing Sex Norms in America and Scandinavia

Harold T. Christensen
and Christina F. Gregg

It has been popular of late to claim that the so-called *Sexual Revolution* which has been sweeping America during the recent fifties and sixties is little more than a liberalization of attitudes: that there has been no real or significant increase in nonmarital sexual behavior. No one disputes the more or less obvious facts of greater tolerance with respect to the sexual behavior of others or of greater freedom and openness in discussion, in dress and manners, in public entertainment, and throughout the mass media. But when it comes to the question of whether premarital coitus—the practice itself—is undergoing much of an increase, there tends to be either uncertainty or the suggestion that it is not. Part of this may be due to wishful thinking, part to a lack of adequate data, and part to a tendency among scholars to overgeneralize from the data available. At any rate, there is need for new data and for a reexamination of the problem.

Terman (1938, pp. 320–323) was one of the first to present solid evidence concerning incidence and trends in premarital coitus. He compared persons born in and subsequent to 1910 with persons born before 1890 and reported increases of premarital coitus for both men and women—though at a more rapid rate for the latter, signifying an intersex convergence.

Then came Kinsey. Kinsey and associates (1953, pp. 298–302) also compared incidence of premarital coitus by decade of birth and reported virtually no trend for males but a very significant increase for females, which likewise

Reprinted by permission from "Changing Sex Norms in America and Scandinavia" by Harold T. Christensen and Christina F. Gregg, *Journal of Marriage and the Family*, November 1970, pp. 616–627.

pointed to an intersex convergence. Yet even for females there appeared to be little difference in non-virginity among those born during the first, second and third decades of the present century. But non-virginity was more than twice as great for females born in these three decades after the turn of the century as compared with those born before 1900. Since approximately twenty years are required to reach maturity, the suggestion in this finding is that the big change in the liberalization of female sexual behavior took place during the decade following World War I and that the picture has not altered much since that time. It must be noted, however, that these data are not suitable for measuring trends that may have occurred during the 1950's and 1960's.

Nevertheless, Reiss (1969) and certain other scholars (for example, Bell, 1966, Gagnon and Simon, 1970), after drawing upon the Kinsey data, have moved beyond the reach of these findings by claiming that there has been little if any increase in non-virginity over the past twenty years or so. Reiss explains the widespread *belief* concerning an increase as being due largely to the liberalizing of attitudes, which makes people more willing to talk and so increases their awareness and anxiety. In support of his position of no significant trend in premarital coitus since the 1920's, he cites several studies made during the 1950's and 1960's (Ehrmann, 1959; Freedman, 1965; Kirkendall, 1961; Reiss, 1967; Schofield, 1965) which give somewhat similar incidence percentages as those reported earlier by Kinsey. But there is a question of comparability. Although these more recent studies do not show incidence percentages greatly different from Kinsey's, they each tap different populations and employ differing methodologies—so that the no-trend conclusion may be quite spurious. Furthermore, the reported research by Reiss himself deals almost exclusively with attitudes, largely ignoring behavior. It is to his credit though, that he recognized the tenuous nature of the evidence and because of this, states his position somewhat cautiously. He said simply that the common belief that non-virginity has markedly increased of late "is not supported by the research"; and concluded: "Thus, although the evidence is surely not perfect, it does suggest that there has not been any change in the proportion of non-virginity for the past four or five decades equal to that which occurred during the 1920's" (Reiss, 1969, p. 110).

But the message that has come across to the public and even some scholars is that research has established that a virtually static level of premarital coitus has maintained itself since the early post-World War I period. This has been the most usual interpretation given recently in the popular press, by radio and television, and in some high school and college textbooks.

Even so, not everyone has believed it. Some, like the authors of this paper, have held mental reservations, though, until recently, they have been without appropriate data to test it out. A few years ago Leslie (1967, pp. 387–

392) examined this question by classifying chronologically virtually all studies which had reported incidence of premarital coitus, starting with 1915 and ending with 1965. He observed that for both sexes percentages tend to be higher in the more recent studies. Similarly, Packard (1968, pp. 135–204, 491–511, 517–523) took a careful look at the reported findings of over forty studies, including one of his own, which elicited student responses from 21 colleges in the United States and five from other countries (Luckey and Nass, 1969). He compared these studies and their findings across time; conceding, of course, the lack of strict comparability due to differing samples and methods. His tentative general conclusion was that ". . . While coital experience of U.S. college males seemed comparable to that of males 15 or 20 years ago, the college females reported a quite significantly higher rate of experience" (Packard, 1968, p. 186).

The very latest information coming to our attention is a report by Bell and Chaskes (1970) wherein the earlier no-evidence-to-support-a-trend position of Bell (1966) is modified with the statement: "The writers believe that change *has* been occurring in the sexual experience of college girls since the mid-1960's" (Bell and Chaskes, 1970, p. 81). These authors report increases in the premarital coitus of coeds between 1958 and 1968: from 10 to 23 percent during the dating relationship, from 15 to 28 percent during the going-steady relationship, and from 31 to 39 percent during the engagement relationship. Since proportionate increase was greatest at the first two dating levels, they conclude that the commitment of engagement has become a less important condition for many coeds participating in premarital coitus. They also report significant reductions at each dating level in the guilt connected with coitus, and point to a suggestion from their data of an increase in promiscuity. Still additional findings—though ones less relevant to our present analysis—were that premarital coitus tends to be associated with non-attendance at church, starting to date at an early age, and dating or going steady with a larger than average number of boys.

The Bell and Chaskes study has an advantage over many of the previous ones in that it taps college students in the same institution with the same measuring instrument at two different points in time, which more clearly enables it to look at *trends*. It nevertheless is limited to females alone on one college campus, and so sees its conclusions as suggestive rather than conclusive of any national change. These authors argue, from what is known about the youth rebellion movement of very recent years, that the increase in the premarital coitus of coeds is a phenomenon of the mid-1960's. It should be noted, however, that there is nothing in their data to establish the change as occurring at that precise point in time as against the early 1960's or even the late 1950's.

Our own research about to be reported has some of the same limitations as certain of the earlier studies (including the small size and non-random character of its samples) but there are added features which we hope will enable us to carry the analysis a little farther. We have involved behavior as well as attitudes, studied males as well as females, compared three separate cultures against each other, and measured identical phenomena in the same manner in the same populations at two different points in time. The focus of this report is to be upon the time dimension, or social change. Nevertheless, by seeing change cross-culturally and in the context of male-female interaction and attitude-behavior interrelatedness, it should be possible to better understand what actually is taking place. There is an interplay among these and possibly other factors. We feel that it is important to try to see the premarital sex phenomenon as a network and to look for interrelationships and then build toward an empirically-based theory to explain it all. Our study is but one start in that direction.

The senior author initiated his cross-cultural research on premarital sex back in 1958, at which time questionnaires were administered to college samples in three separate cultures differing on a restrictive-permissive continuum: highly restrictive Mormon culture in the Intermountain region of western United States; moderately restrictive Midwestern culture in central United States; and highly permissive Danish culture which is a part of Scandinavia (Christensen, 1960; 1966; 1969; Christensen and Carpenter, 1962a; 1962b). The 1958 study involved both record linkage and questionnaire data, but it is only the latter that are of concern in the present writing. He then repeated the study in 1968, using the same questionnaire administered in the same three universities. Every effort was made to achieve comparability across the two years. The unchanged questionnaire was administered in the same way to similar classes in the identical universities. In most instances within both years social science classes were used; the only real change being in Denmark, where large proportions of medical and psychology students were used in 1958 as against an almost exclusively sociology student sample in 1968. The repeat, of course, was chiefly for the purpose of getting at changes which may have occurred during a period of time popularly described as experiencing a sexual revolution. Although the study dealt with all levels of intimacy—necking, petting, and coitus—this report is to be limited to permarital coitus alone. Furthermore, it is limited to only selected aspects of premarital coitus. This is because our analysis of data has just begun, plus the necessity to restrict the length of the article.

Respective sample sizes involved in calculations for the statistics now to be reported were: for the Intermountain, 94 males and 74 females in 1958, and 115 and 105 respectively in 1968; for the Midwestern, 213 males and 142 females in 1958, and 245 and 238 respectively in 1968; for the Danish, 149 males and 86 females in 1958, and 134 and 61 respectively in 1968.

Some Measures of the Liberal Attitude

Three items from the questionnaire have been selected to illustrate comparisons and trends in the attitudinal component. Table 1 has been constructed to show percentages of respondents holding liberal or permissive views regarding these matters.

Table 1.　Percentages Taking Liberal Positions on Sex Questions, 1958 and 1968 Compared*

Items and Years	Intermountain		Midwestern		Danish	
	MALES	FEMALES	MALES	FEMALES	MALES	FEMALES
	%	%	%	%	%	%
I. Opposition to Censorship						
1968	61	58	71	59	99	97
1958	42	54	47	51	77	81
Difference	19	4	24	8	22	16
II. Acceptance of Non-Virginity						
1968	20	26	25	44	92	92
1958	5	11	18	23	61	74
Difference	15	15	7	21	31	18
III. Approval of Premarital Coitus						
1968	38	24	55	38	100	100
1958	23	3	47	17	94	81
Difference	15	21	8	21	6	19

*Percentages are based on numbers answering the question. The number of cases leaving a question unanswered varied from 0 to 8 in the various groups.

Opposing the Censorship of Pornography

Presented first are percentages of respondents who indicated agreement with the statement: "It is best not to try to prohibit erotic and obscene literature and pictures by law, but rather to leave people free to follow their own judgments and tastes in such matters." The three comparisons of interest in this analysis are as follows:

(1) As one moves from left to right—from the restrictive Intermountain culture to the permissive Danish culture—percentages taking the liberal stance by agreeing with the statement are seen to increase. This is true for both sexes and with respect to both sample years (with the single exception of the 1958 female comparison between Intermountain and Midwestern).

(2) More females than males opposed the censorship of pornography in 1958, whereas ten years later the reverse was true. Furthermore, this shift in pattern occurred consistently in each of the three cultures, suggesting that it may be something of a general phenomenon.

(3) The time trend over the decade 1958–68 was consistently in the direction of increasing opposition to this kind of censorship. The trend held for each of the three cultures and for both sexes—although females liberalized on this point in *smaller* degree than did males, which accounts for the shift in the male-female pattern mentioned in the previous paragraph.

Since (as will be shown throughout the remainder of our paper) females generally have liberalized in a proportionately *greater* degree than have males, this contrary finding on censorship requires some attempt at explanation. Our speculation is that females, with their more sheltered life, have been less knowledgeable and realistic regarding pornography and also possibly less attracted by its appeal. This might explain their greater opposition to censorship than males in 1958, not seeing pornography as particularly threatening. But the new openness of recent years undoubtedly has given them greater sophistication in these matters, and they may now better understand the reality of hardcore pornography and its differential appeal to the male; which could explain their lower opposition to censorship than males in 1968.

Accepting the Non-Virginity of a Partner

In the second section of Table 1 are shown percentages of those who indicated *disagreement* with the statement: "I would prefer marrying a virgin, or in other words, someone who has not had previous coitus (sexual intercourse)." As with the statement on pornography, permissive attitudes increased for both sexes and in both sample years from lows in the restrictive Intermountain to highs in the permissive Danish; and increased between 1958 and 1968, for both sexes and in each of the three cultures. These trends are shown to be without exception. The male-female comparisons show *females* to be the most *permissive*, in both sample years and in each of the cultures (with the single exception of 1968 Danish respondents, where they were equal).

Since practically every other measure in our questionnaire—as well as virtually all studies now in the literature—show females to be more conservative than males in sexual matters, one must ask "Why this exception?" Two possible reasons occur to us: in the first place, the typical female attitude may represent a realistic acceptance that more males do have premarital sex, making her chances of actually marrying a virgin somewhat smaller; and in addition, some females, with a sheltered upbringing and more limited sexual expression, may feel inadequate and hence welcome an experienced male to help show them the way. In this connection, it is interesting to note also that in the Midwestern sample—which may approximately reflect the overall situation for United States—females moved away from insistence on a virginal partner at a much more rapid rate than did males.

Approving Coitus Among the Unmarried

Finally, Table 1 shows percentages of those approving premarital coitus. Respondents were asked: first, to consider an average or typical courtship "in which there is normal love development and mutual responsibility"; next, to assume that this hypothetical relationship progresses at a uniform rate of six months between the first date and the start of going steady, another six months to an engagement, and still another six months to the wedding (or a total courtship of eighteen months); and then to mark on a scale the earliest time they would approve the start of necking, then of petting, and then of coitus. The percentages shown are restricted to coitus and they represent approval at any point prior to the wedding.

This item on approval of premarital coitus is free of the kinds of irregularities mentioned for the previous two. It shows highly consistent results for all three comparisons: a movement toward greater approval from Intermountain to Midwestern to Danish, for both sexes and in both sample years; greater approval given by males than by females (except for a tie among 1968 Danish respondents where both sexes hit the ceiling), for both sample years and each of the three cultures; and a trend toward greater approval over the 1958–68 decade, for both sexes and in each of the three cultures.

In connection with this last point, it is important to note that in each of the cultures females moved toward approval more strongly than did males, which means a trend toward intersex convergence. Females still have more restrictive attitudes than males but the difference is less than formerly.

An additional observation which should not be missed is that, in both sample years, male-female percentages are closer together in Denmark than in the other two cultures. This suggests that norm permissiveness may operate to reduce differences between the sexes seen in cross-cultural comparisons as well as in liberalizing trends over time.

Trend Comparison with Relevant Variables Controlled

As a double check on this trend pattern—and to at least partially determine whether it is real or merely the result of differing compositions of the two samples drawn ten years apart—we made a supplementary analysis of matched data. This was done for the Midwestern culture only (the most representative of American society and the most feasible for matched testing because of the larger sizes of its samples) and was further limited to data on premarital coitus (the most central in our present analysis). The matching occurred on four variables: sex of respondent, cumulative number of years in school, frequency of church attendance, and level of courtship development. This had the effect of controlling these variables across the 1958–68 period, while the time trend was being examined. Successful matching was completed for 202 pairs of respondents (127 pairs were male, 75 female).

In Table 2 we show for the Midwestern culture two measures of premarital coital approval for both matched and total samples. The first consists of average (mean) scores computed from the approval timing scale introduced earlier. The scale had ten divisions, with the first representing time of first date and the last representing time of marriage. Scores ranged from 1 to 10 according to markings on the scale, and it is *average* coital scores (means) that are shown here. The lower the score, the farther from marriage is the approved timing of first coitus. It will be observed that, by this measure, both males and females showed up more permissive in 1968 than they did in 1958 and that the trend held for the matched as well as unmatched comparisons.

Table 2. Measures of Premarital Coital Approval on Matched and Total Samples, Midwestern Culture, 1958 and 1968 Compared

Measures of Coital Approval	Total Sample		Matched Sample	
	MALES	FEMALES	MALES	FEMALES
I. Average Score				
1968	8.10	9.02	8.10	9.47
1958	8.58	9.69	8.63	9.67
Difference	-.48	-.67	-.53	-.20
II. Percent Approving				
1968	55.4	37.7	55.1	30.7
1958	46.7	17.4	48.0	21.3
Difference	8.7	20.3	7.1	9.4

The second measure is simply percent approving premarital coitus. Unmatched percentages are shown here in juxtaposition to percentages from the matched cases. But again the picture is very clear: matching has not altered the general trend; in the uncontrolled and the controlled analyses the trend was found to be toward greater approval—which is the permissive stance. And this was true for males and females alike, but for the latter the trend was the stronger.

Relationship of Behavior to Attitude

Some might argue that most of our generalizations up to this point are obvious, that everyone accepts the fact that attitudes toward premarital coitus have been liberalizing in recent years. The more controversial questions have to do with trends in sexual *behavior* and with how these relate to attitude. Has incidence of premarital coitus remained virtually unchanged since the 1920's, with a decline in guilt brought about by an increasing acceptance of the behavior—which is the position arrived at by Reiss (1962), or has behavior changed with attitudes regarding it?

Incidence of Premarital Coitus

As a first approach to the behavioral component, we show percentages of respondents claiming the premarital coital experience (Table 3). Our percentages on incidence of premarital coitus do not, of course, give an accurate picture of total coitus before marriage but only of experience up to the time the questionnaire was administered. This fact should not influence our various comparisons, however, since all the data are the same kind and hence comparable. Percentages are given for males and females separately and for the three cultures and both sample years of our study. An added refinement in testing for a time trend is provided for the Midwestern culture by means of matched cases to control for intervening variables, as was done in the case of attitudes.

Table 3. Percentage with Premarital Coital Experience, Total and Matched Samples*

Samples and Years	Sample Culture					
	Intermountain		Midwestern		Danish	
	MALES	FEMALES	MALES	FEMALES	MALES	FEMALES
	%	%	%	%	%	%
I. Total Samples						
1968	37	32	50	34	95	97
1958	39	10	51	21	64	60
Difference	-2	22	-1	13	31	37
II. Matched Samples						
1958			49	32		
1968			55	25		
Difference			-6	7		

*Based upon number answering. The number who failed to answer in any one group varied from 0 to 4.

Before examining the time-trend data, let it be noted that these incidence figures are (1) higher for males than females and (2) higher for the Midwestern than the Intermountain and for the Danish than the Midwestern. These generalizations are consistent for all comparisons (except the one between 1958–68 Danish males and females) and are the same as our earlier ones regarding approval of premarital coitus. Furthermore, there is, as before, the phenomenon of greater male-female similarity in Denmark than the other two cultures, suggesting that norm permissiveness may induce a leveling of gender differences.

Comparisons of 1968 with 1958 produce three additional generalizations. (1) In the two American samples, male incidence of premarital coitus remained approximately the same. Actually the figures show that it decreased slightly, but our conjecture is that this is no more than random variation. (2) On the other hand, female incidence in the two American samples rose sharply, suggesting that, as with coital approval, there is a trend toward intersex convergence. (3) The Danish sample, while showing a slightly higher rise in premarital coitus for females than for males, demonstrated a sharp rise for *both* sexes. This brought incidence figures for that country close to the ceiling. Approximately 95 percent had engaged in premarital coitus; and it will be recalled that 100 percent of both sexes there approved of such activity. It may be, of course, that at least part of the dramatic liberalization shown for Danish respondents is to be explained by the greater weighting of the 1968 Danish sample with sociology students.

The introduction of controls through matched-sample comparisons in the Midwestern culture made no appreciable change in the outcome (Table 3, part II). Although males decreased their behavior more and females increased theirs less in the matched sample as compared with the total sample, the conclusion of greater female than male liberalization and of intersex convergence during the decade seems inescapable.

The Approval-Experience Ratio

It is important to know how approval of and experience in premarital coitus interrelate: to what extent practice corresponds with precept and what are the directions and magnitudes of discrepancies in this regard. The ratios of Table 4 have been calculated by dividing percentages approving premarital coitus (part III of Table 1 and part II of Table 2) by percentages having experienced it (Table 3). A ratio of 1.00 would mean that approval and experience coincide exactly. Ratios lower than this indicate that experience exceeds approval; and higher, that approval exceeds experience. With the sex drive as strong as it is, one may wonder how the approval-experience ratio could ever be above 1.00: why, if people approve premarital coitus, they don't engage in it. The primary explanation seems to be that the attitude percentages are for approval of coitus occurring *anytime prior to marriage*, and approving respondents may not be close enough to marriage to feel ready for the experience.

Table 4. Comparisons of Approval-Experience Ratios, Total and Matched Samples

Samples and Years	Sample Cultures					
	Intermountain		Midwestern		Danish	
	MALES	FEMALES	MALES	FEMALES	MALES	FEMALES
I. Total Samples						
1968	1.05	.73	1.10	1.10	1.06	1.04
1958	.59	.31	.92	.84	1.48	1.35
Difference	.46	.42	.18	.26	-.42	-.31
II. Matched Samples						
1968			1.13	.96		
1958			.87	.84		
Difference			.26	.12		

The following generalizations seem evident: (1) In 1958, the magnitude of the ratio varies directly with the permissiveness of the culture; which means that restrictive cultures have higher percentages of their offenders who are violating their own standards—though it must be remembered that restrictive cultures have fewer offenders to start with. (2) Except for Midwestern respondents in 1968, females showed up with lower ratios than males, which means that proportionately more of them violate their own standards when they engage in premarital coitus. However, this intersex difference is of large magnitude only within the highly conservative Intermountain culture. (3) The 1958–68 trend was toward a rise in the ratio for both the Intermountain and Midwestern samples, where it previously had been below 1.00, and a lowering of the ratio in Denmark where it previously had been above 1.00. Thus the time trend has been toward a leveling and balancing of the approval-experience ratios, bringing them closer to each other and to the value of 1.00. In 1968, all ratios except for Midwestern males were closer to 1.00 than was true ten years earlier, and Intermountain females represented the only group in the total sample with experience remaining greater than approval (although in the matched sample this was true for Midwestern females also). The evidence suggests that there is less of a gap today between one's values and his behavior; that, regardless of his sex or the culture he is in, a person is more likely now than formerly to follow his own internalized norms.

Again, the matching procedure has not altered the basic conclusion. With these data, as with the total sample, the trend is seen to be toward a rising ratio. Attitudes have liberalized more rapidly than has behavior, so that the overall pattern today seems not to be one of violating one's own value system. Some individuals do, of course, but in terms of group averages the evidence is against it.

Evidences of Value-Behavior Discrepancy

In an earlier article (Christensen and Carpenter, 1962b) the senior author has demonstrated from cross-cultural data for 1958 that—even more than the act itself—it is the discrepancy between what one values and what he then does that determines guilt, divorce, and related negative effects. The analysis was based upon both group and individual comparisons between permissiveness scores (measuring attitude) and behavioral percentages (measuring coital experience).

Here we wish to report a slightly different approach applied to the 1958 and 1968 Midwestern samples, first with the total respondents and then with the matched cases. In Table 5 are presented percentages of those with premarital experience who answered approvingly of coitus before marriage. These percentages, in other words, are based upon *individual* case-by-case comparisons between coitus and coital approval. They show the proportions of cases in which there was *no discrepancy* of this kind. By subtracting any percentage figure from 100.0, the reader can, if he prefers it that way, determine the corresponding discrepancy magnitude.

Table 5.   Percentages with Premarital Coitus Who Approved Such Experience, Midwestern Culture, 1958 and 1968 Compared

	Total Sample		*Matched Sample*	
	MALES	FEMALES	MALES	FEMALES
	%	%	%	%
1968	82	78	76	58
1958	65	41	65	37
Difference	17	37	11	21

It will be observed that the trend between 1958 and 1968 was toward larger approval percentages (or less value-behavior discrepancy). This is true with respect to both sexes and for the matched as well as the total samples. It supports a similar finding based upon grouped data reported in the previous section. In both instances the evidence suggests that attitudes have been catching up with behavior and that proportionally fewer people today violate their own values when they engage in premarital coitus. Nevertheless, some individuals still show this discrepancy—perhaps as many as one-fifth of the males and two-fifths of the females.

It will be observed also that the movement of premarital coital participants toward approving what one does was greater for females than males (consistently shown in both sets of comparisons). Females in 1968 still gave evidence of greater value-behavior discrepancy than did males but the intersex difference in this regard was less than in 1958. And here too, the finding of Table 5 stands in general support of the picture for grouped data shown in Table 4.

Using Attitudes to Predict Behavior

Since the overall evidence is that attitudes have been liberalizing at a greater rate than behavior, which is narrowing the gap between the two, it might be expected that the predictive power of attitudes is increasing. To test this out, we calculated Gammas on the interaction of two variables: approval of premarital coitus and experience with premarital coitus. The Gammas reported in Table 6 indicate that the expectation was supported: coital approval was a better predictor of coital behavior for males and females at the end of the decade than at the beginning.

Table 6.   Incidence of Premarital Coitus as Related to Approval of Premarital Coitus, Midwestern Sample

| Incidence of Premarital Coitus | Approval of Premarital Coitus | | | | | |
| | Males | | | Females | | |
	YES	NO	TOTAL	YES	NO	TOTAL
			1968			
Yes	98	22	120	63	18	81
No	35	83	118	26	128	154
Total	133	105	238	89	146	235
	Gamma = .83			Gamma = .89		
			1958			
Yes	68	37	105	12	17	29
No	30	73	103	12	95	107
Total	98	110	208	24	112	136
	Gamma = .63			Gamma = .69		

The Commitment Phenomenon

Reiss (1969), largely from analyses of his attitudinal data, has concluded that America is moving toward the traditional Scandinavian pattern of "permissiveness with affection." This phrase has been used by Reiss and others to also mean *permissiveness with commitment.* Our own data should permit us to check out this claim at the behavioral level.

Two indices of affection-commitment are presented in Table 7: percentages (of those experienced in premarital coitus) who had confined their overall experience to one partner; and percentages whose first experience was with a steady or fiance(e). It will be noted that the cross-cultural, cross-sex, and time-trend comparisons derived from these two measures are remarkably similar. In both cases (with very minor exceptions that become evident upon close inspection) rather consistent patterns show up: more American than Danish respondents, more female than male respondents, and more 1958 than 1968 respondents confined their total premarital coital experience to one partner and *also* had their first coitus in a commitment relationship. The other side of the coin, so to speak, is that Danes appear to be more promiscuous than Americans, males more promiscuous than females, and 1968 respondents more promiscuous than 1958 respondents. The term "promiscuity" is used here in a nonevaluative sense and merely to designate the opposite of "commitment." Our measures of these two concepts are indirect and imperfect, to be sure, but undoubtedly they tell something.

Table 7.   Percentage Distributions of Responses to Items Showing a Commitment in the Sexual Relationship*

Items and Years	Sample Cultures					
	Intermountain		Midwestern		Danish	
	MALES	FEMALES	MALES	FEMALES	MALES	FEMALES
	%	%	%	%	%	%
I. Experience Confined to One Partner						
1968	28.6	43.8	39.0	70.0	20.5	25.0
1958	35.1	57.1	33.7	65.5	40.9	42.9
Difference	-6.5	-13.3	5.3	4.5	-20.4	-17.9
II. First Experience with a Steady or Fiance(e)						
1968	53.8	78.1	52.9	86.3	46.3	55.4
1958	47.2	100.0	42.8	75.9	67.8	74.5
Difference	6.6	-21.9	10.1	10.4	-21.5	-19.1

*Based upon number answering. The number failing to answer in any one group varied from 0 to 4.

Not only were the Danish generally more promiscuous than the Americans (1958 Danish males being an exception), but the shift toward greater promiscuity during the decade under study was greater for them. Apparently, Denmark may be moving away from its traditional pattern of premarital sex justified by a commitment relationship, and sexual promiscuity is coming in to take its place. But without further testing, this observation must be re-

garded as highly speculative, since the two Danish samples lack strict comparability.

It also is worth noting that the Danish male-female differences in response
to both of these items tended to be smaller than in either of the other two
cultures, another example of the possible leveling effect of norm permissiveness.

Intermountain females also moved dramatically in the direction of greater
promiscuity as indicated by these two measures, possibly because, being so
near the "floor" at the beginning of the decade, there was opportunity for the
general trend toward permissiveness to affect them proportionately more.
Intermountain males did not change much by either measure and, with them,
direction of change was inconsistent.

In two important respects Midwestern respondents stood out from the
rest. In the first place, they tended to show higher proportions in a commitment relationship (1958 males being the most noticeable exception); and in
the second place, this was the only culture where both sexes on both measures
showed *higher* commitment percentages in 1968 than 1958 (1958 Intermountain males did on the item "first coitus with a steady or fiance"). Could
it be that a general trend toward sexual freedom, such as has occurred in recent years, encourages the development of promiscuity in *both* the commit-
ment-oriented permissive society (such as Denmark) and the ascetic-oriented
restrictive society (such as the Intermountain Mormon): the same trend but
for different reasons—in the first, to escape commitment; in the second, to
escape repression? The question needs further research.

At any rate, the time trend in our Midwestern culture seems clear. To the
extent that our sample is representative and our measures adequate, the
Reiss hypothesis is supported there. Although it must be said that the testing
of this important phenomenon has only begun, it probably can be tentatively
concluded that at least a major current in premarital sex trends within this
country is a movement toward permissiveness with commitment.

While the emerging American pattern seems to be toward the traditional
Danish norm of premarital sex justified by commitment, the emerging Danish
pattern may be away from both commitment and restriction, toward free
and promiscuous sex. Furthermore, in this one respect at least, the converging lines of the two cultures seem now to have passed each other. Today the
Danes appear to be less committed and more promiscuous in their premarital
sexual contacts than do Midwestern Americans.

Negative Accompaniments of Coitus

Considerable interest centers around the question of consequences. Does
premarital coitus affect everyone the same, or do the norms of the culture

and the values which the individual has incorporated into his personality make any difference? Our working hypothesis has been that values are relevant data; and following this, the consequences of premarital sex acts are to some extent relative to the alignment or misalignment of values and behavior, being most negative where the disjuncture is the greatest. In sociological circles this line of reasoning has been labeled "Theory of Cognitive Dissonance" (Festinger, 1957). Applied to the data of our present study, we would predict greater negative effects in America than Denmark, for females than males, and during 1958 as compared with 1968, since these are the categories showing disproportionately high value-behavior discrepancy.

Table 8 presents data for two negative accompaniments of premarital coitus. The first of these—yielding to force or felt obligation—means simply that there were pressures other than personal desire which were chiefly responsible for the experience. It will be observed that, in general, results turned out as expected: coitus because of pressure is seen to be higher in restrictive than permissive cultures, higher among females than males, and higher in 1958 than in 1968.

Table 8. Percentage Distributions of Responses to Items that Indicate Negative Feelings Accompanying First Premarital Coitus*

| Items and Years | Sample Cultures | | | | | |
| | Intermountain | | Midwestern | | Danish | |
	MALES	FEMALES	MALES	FEMALES	MALES	FEMALES
I. First Experience Either Forced or by Obligation						
1968	2.4	24.2	2.5	23.1	10.0	18.5
1958	13.5	42.9	9.3	37.9	4.4	35.6
Difference	-11.1	-18.7	-6.8	-14.8	5.8	-17.1
II. First Experience Followed Chiefly by Guilt or Remorse						
1968	7.1	9.1	6.6	11.1	1.6	0.0
1958	29.7	28.6	12.1	31.0	4.3	2.0
Difference	-22.6	-19.5	-5.5	-19.9	-2.7	-2.0

*In I, the percentages are based upon the number answering; the number failing to answer varying from 0 to 6.

In II, the total number of cases was used as the base of the percents.

One irregularity in the patterns just noted was introduced by an unexpected increase in pressured coitus among Danish males, which also had the effect of reversing the cross-cultural picture for 1968 males. Reasons for this reverse trend for Danish males are not known, but it will be remembered from Table 7 that it also was Danish males who showed the greatest increase in promiscuous coitus. There is at least the possibility that these two phenomena are connected.

Part II of Table 8 gives percentages of those who specified either guilt or remorse as their predominant feeling the day after first premarital coitus. Here again, the overall patterns were in expected directions: coitus followed by guilt or remorse is seen to be higher in restrictive than permissive cultures (although Midwestern females exceed the Intermountain), higher for females than males (although not uniformly and with Denmark being a major exception), and consistently higher in 1958 than 1968. Whether the exceptions noted represent anything more than random variation cannot be determined from our non-probability samples. But at least the broad patterns seem clear and the consistency between our two measures builds confidence in the general findings.

Thus, whether measured by a feeling of external pressure at the time or a subsequent feeling of guilt or remorse, the negative accompaniments of premarital coitus appear to be greatest where the sex norms are restrictive (and, significantly, also where value-behavior discrepancy is the greatest)—in the American cultures as compared with the Danish, with females as compared with males, and in 1958 as compared with 1968.

Conclusion

The design of our investigation has enabled us to compare premarital sexual attitudes and behavior against each other; and to compare them separately and in combination across a restrictive-permissive continuum of cultures, across the differing worlds of males and females, and across a recent decade in time. Although the primary concern of this paper has been with recent social changes in premarital sex values and practices, the additional involvement of intersex and cross-cultural variables has enabled us to see the phenomena in better perspective and to tease out certain meanings that otherwise may have remained obscure. Furthermore, we have been interested in going beyond mere description, to the discovery of relationships; and then to interconnect these relationships with each other and with relevant concepts and propositions, with theory building as the ultimate goal. To establish needed controls, we have in places made supplementary analyses of Midwestern data including the use of matched sampling techniques. Nevertheless, we regard our study as more exploratory than definite. We feel that some significant leads have been uncovered but at the same time regard our conclusions as tentative—as plausible for the present, perhaps, but as hypotheses for future research.

We call attention to the strong suggestion from our data that values and norms serve as intervening variables *affecting the effects* of behavior. For the explaining of consequences, it would seem that even perhaps more important than the sexual act itself is the degree to which that act lines up or fails to line up with the standards set. Whether the comparisons have been between males and females, across cultures, or over time, we have demonstrated two parallel and probably interrelated patterns: value-behavior discrepancy is associated with sexual restrictiveness; and certain negative effects of pre-marital intimacy are associated with sexual restrictiveness. The possibility—we think probability—is that it is primarily value-behavior discrepancy that is causing the difficulty. This facet of our theory has been explored at greater length in earlier writing (Christensen, 1966, 1969).

References

Bell, Robert R. *Premarital Sex in a Changing Society.* Englewood Cliffs, N.J.: Prentice-Hall, 1966.

Bell, Robert R., and Jay B. Chaskes. "Premarital Sexual Experience Among Coeds, 1958 and 1968." *Journal of Marriage and the Family,* 32 (February 1970): 81–84.

Christensen, Harold T. "Cultural Relativism and Premarital Sex Norms." *American Sociological Review,* 25 (February 1960): 31–39.

Christensen, Harold T. "Scandinavian and American Sex Norms: Some Comparisons, with Sociological Implications." *The Journal of Social Issues,* 22 (April 1966): 60–75.

Christensen, Harold T. "Normative Theory Derived from Cross-Cultural Family Research." *Journal of Marriage and the Family,* 31 (May 1969): 209–222.

Christensen, Harold T., and George R. Carpenter. "Timing Patterns in the Development of Sexual Intimacy." *Marriage and Family Living,* 24 (February 1962): 30–35.

Christensen, Harold T., and George R. Carpenter. "Value-Behavior Discrepancies Regarding Premarital Coitus in Three Western Cultures." *American Sociological Review,* 27 (February 1962): 66–74.

Ehrmann, Winston W. "Marital and Nonmarital Sexual Behavior." In *Handbook of Marriage and the Family,* edited by Harold T. Christensen, pp. 585–622. Chicago: Rand McNally, 1964.

Ehrmann, Winston W. *Premarital Dating Behavior.* New York: Holt, 1959.

Festinger, Leon. *A Theory of Cognitive Dissonance.* New York: Harper and Row, 1957.

Freedman, Mervin B. "The Sexual Behavior of American College Women: An Empirical Study and an Historical Survey." *Merrill-Palmer Quarterly of Behavior and Development,* 11 (January 1965): 33–48.

Gagnon, John H., and William Simon. "Prospects for Change in American Sexual Patterns." *Medical Aspects of Human Sexuality,* 4 (January 1970): 100–117.

Kinsey, Alfred C., Wardell Pomeroy, Clyde Martin and Paul Gebbard. *Sexual Behavior in the Human Female.* Philadelphia: Saunders, 1953.

Kirkendall, Lester A. *Premarital Intercourse and Interpersonal Relationships.* New York: Julian, 1961.

Leslie, Gerald R. *The Family in Social Context.* New York: Oxford University Press, 1967.

Luckey, Eleanore B., and Gilbert D. Nass. "A Comparison of Sexual Attitudes and Behavior in an International Sample." *Journal of Marriage and the Family,* 31 (May 1969): 364–379.

Packard, Vance. *The Sexual Wilderness: the Contemporary Upheaval in Male-Female Relationships.* New York: David McKay, 1968.

Reiss, Ira L. *The Social Context of Premarital Sexual Permissiveness.* New York: Holt, Rinehart and Winston, 1967.

Reiss, Ira L. "Premarital Sexual Standards." In *The Individual, Sex, and Society: A Siecus Handbook for Teachers and Counselors,* edited by Carlfred B. Broderick and Jessie Bernard. Baltimore: The Johns Hopkins Press, 1969.

Schofield, Michael. *The Sexual Behavior of Young People.* Boston: Little, Brown, 1965.

Terman, Lewis M. *Psychological Factors in Marital Happiness.* New York: McGraw-Hill, 1938.

3

Woman and Man

Chapter 7 Love and Pairing

Introduction

Within the past few years, the feminist movement has profoundly influenced both scholarship and the day-to-day relations of men and women. In this part, most of the papers discuss both the scholarly and interpersonal aspects of what some are now beginning to call the "sex-role revolution."

In terms of scholarship, the main effect of the "revolution" thus far is on awareness and consciousness. For example, much social science writing was suddenly revealed to have been based on sexist assumptions. Many sociologists and psychologists took it for granted that women's roles and functions in society reflected universal physiological and temperamental traits. Since in practically every society women are subordinate to men, inequality was interpreted to be an inescapable necessity of organized social life. Such analyses suffer from the same intellectual flaw as interpretations suggesting that discrimination against nonwhites implies their innate inferiority. All such explanations fail to analyze the social institutions and forces producing and supporting the observed differences.

What seems to account for the traditional organization of sex roles is biological difference, but not in the sense of a rigid and inescapable force. In societies where there are no contraceptives and no bottle feeding, women must bear and nurse children. From this one basic fact a number of important consequences follow. Women work in most societies, but as Judith Brown (1970) points out, their work is limited to the kinds of tasks that are compatible with child watching. Thus, a mother with children cannot travel far from home or engage in dangerous activities, such as hunting large animals. Nor can a mother engage in work that requires rapt and sustained attention; rather, her tasks must be able to be interrupted and resumed.

The traditional explanation of women's work is that women are temperamentally suited not only for child care, but also for dull and monotonous tasks. Rather than temperament causing the division of labor between the sexes, it seems more likely that the necessities of women's work are responsible for so-called feminine nature. Since men's work varies from one society to another, the kinds of personality traits encouraged in men vary also.

Woman's role as caretaker of children has profound implications for the psychological development of both sexes. There is a good deal of evidence that girls have an easier time learning their feminine identity than boys do learning a masculine one. Both sexes tend to model themselves on the person closest to them in infancy. The little boy must undo this early learning and realize he is a different kind of creature from his mother. In short, the little girl becomes a woman merely by growing up, but the little boy becomes a man by proving to himself and others that he isn't female. This push away from women in male socialization means that a tendency to disparage women and female things is built into masculinity. There is no comparable bias built into female socialization.

In recent years, there has been a growing awareness that the traditional pattern of sex-role differentiation has costs for men as well as women. For both sexes, it is a psychological strain having to act out a role which may not fit one's inner experience and feelings. Male roles are probably more demanding in this regard than women's. It is a strain for women to have to act weaker, more dependent and submissive, and less competent than they really are, but it's probably a greater strain to have to act tougher, stronger, more dominant, and more competent than one really feels inside. It is also a strain to have one's masculine status constantly dependent on success at work, and providing well for a family of dependents.

While there is an increasing trend for men to become more involved in child care and household responsibilities, particularly among fathers who are young and college educated, the major change in men's roles has to do with work. Business managers and economists have become concerned about "blue-collar blues" and "executive dropout" (see Pleck, 1973): an unwillingness on the part of many men to persist in work that is boring, oppressive, demeaning, or lacking in personal value. Ironically, as males are showing signs of becoming disillusioned with work, competition, and achievement, women are becoming more involved with these values.

Relations between men and women have always been complicated by the tendency of each sex to live in a culture alien to the other. The sexual revolution, as well as the sex-role revolution, has complicated male-female relations still further. One obvious source of tension is a difference on the issues of sex and sex roles. There have always been ideological differences about these subjects, but they have never been as salient intellectually and emotionally as they are now. For example, a few years ago a man's derogatory remarks about women would not necessarily detract from his attractiveness as a partner. Indeed, witty derogation might enhance his charm. Today, women are offended, or at least put off by such remarks, and are more inclined to reject such a man.

Problems remain even where couples agree with each other ideologically.

The articles by Komarovsky and Miller reveal that even when men believe in sexual equality, they find it hard to live with the implications of their beliefs. Komarovsky reports that "liberal" college men still find it difficult to relate to females as bright or brighter than they are. Miller describes his own personal dilemmas trying to work out an equal marriage. Although he was committed to sharing child care and housework with his wife, he found it extremely burdensome to do so. The result was a compromise satisfying nobody: He was doing more "woman's work" than years of traditional male experience had led him to expect, while his wife felt he was doing less than his own principles stated he should.

Couple relations, both before and after marriage, have also been complicated by the new openness with regard to social norms in general, and sexual behavior in particular. Once, a relationship between a man and a woman could be easily categorized: It was either "honorable" or "dishonorable." An "honorable" relationship went through several distinct stages of commitment: dating, keeping company, going steady, agreeing to be married, announcing the engagement, and finally, marriage, presumably for life. Divorce was regarded as a personal tragedy and social stigma. Sexual relations at any point before marriage were also shameful, especially for the woman, although the shamefulness decreased depending on the closeness to marriage.

Today the system of courtship has given way to a new pattern of couple relationships. The distinction between the different stages of courtship and between courtship and marriage have broken down. Thus couple relationships can be intensely personal and sexually intimate very early, yet even marital relationships are less stable because they are not expected to last if one of the partners becomes dissatisfied. Farber (1964) has argued that, in effect, we have a "permanent availability" system of marriage; every adult remains on the marriage market, available to every other potential partner, whether currently married or not.

The tension arising out of a relationship that is deeply intimate and yet not certain to last adds another strain to an institution that already contains many strains. The basic cause of divorce, William Goode once observed, is marriage:

> All marriage systems require that at least two people, with their individual desires, needs and values, live together, and all systems create some tensions and unhappiness. (1966, p. 493)

Traditional societies do not necessarily have happier marriages, or even lower divorce rates—some have higher rates than ours. But the strong kin groups in such societies either keep couples together regardless of how they feel, or else they make it easy for couples to break up without much disruption. Divorce is much less disruptive when it does not result in a broken home, as when households are organized around fathers and sons, or mothers and daughters (see Bohannon, 1971).

Despite all its difficulties, marriage is not likely to go out of style in the near future. We agree with Jessie Bernard, who after a devastating critique of marriage from the point of view of a sociologist who is also a feminist, has this to say:

> The future of marriage is as assured as any social form can be. . . . For men and women will continue to want intimacy, they will continue to want to celebrate their mutuality, to experience the mystic unity which once led the church to consider marriage a sacrament. . . . There is hardly any probability such commitments will disappear or that all relationships between them will become merely casual or transient. The commitment may not take the form we know today, although that too has a future. (Bernard, 1972, p. 301)

References

Bernard, Jessie. *The Future of Marriage.* New York: World, 1972.

Bohannon, P. "Dyad Dominance and Household Maintenance." In *Kinship and Culture,* edited by F.L.K. Hsu, pp. 42–65. Chicago: Aldine, 1971.

Farber, B. *Family Organization and Interaction.* San Francisco: Chandler, 1964.

Goode, W. J. "Family Disorganization." In *Contemporary Social Problems*, 2nd ed., edited by R. K. Merton and R. A. Nisbet, pp. 493–522. New York: Harcourt, Brace, and World, 1966.

Pleck, Joseph. "Psychological Frontiers for Men." *Rough Times,* June-July 1973, Vol. 3, No. 6.

Chapter 5

Woman in Society

This article argues that the psychological differences between men and women arise from socialization practices and the effects of women's having a lower social status than men. Raising boys to be aggressive and girls to be passive and domestic may have been functional under primitive technological conditions, but is dysfunctional in an advanced industrial society. Besides being socialized into "feminine" behavior, women's characters are shaped by their membership in an oppressed minority. While it is true that women are not a minority in a numerical sense, their social situation resembles that of racial or religious minorities in that they are excluded from positions of power and are held to be inferior to the group which does exercise power. Many of the personality traits attributed to women have also characterized other victimized groups.

The Social Construction of the Second Sex

Jo Freeman

> The passivity that is the essential characteristic of the "feminine" woman is a trait that develops in her from the earliest years. But it is wrong to assert a biological datum is concerned; it is in fact a destiny imposed upon her by her teachers and by society.
>
> Simone de Beauvoir

During the last thirty years social science has paid scant attention to women, confining its explorations of humanity to the male. Research has generally reinforced the sex stereotypes of popular mythology that women are essentially nurturant/expressive/passive and men instrumental/active/aggressive. Social scientists have tended to justify these stereotypes rather than analyze their origins, their value, or their effect.

In part this is due to the general conservatism and reluctance to question the status quo which has characterized the social sciences during this era of the feminine mystique. In part it is attributable to the "pervasive permeation of psychoanalytic thinking throughout American society" (Rossi, 1965, pp. 102–103). The result has been a social science which is more a mechanism of social control than of social inquiry. Rather than trying to analyze why, it has only described what. Rather than exploring how men and women came to be the way they are, it has taken their condition as an irremediable given and sought to justify it on the basis of "biological" differences.

Nonetheless, the assumption that psychology recapitulates physiology has begun to crack. Masters and Johnson shattered the myth of woman's natural sexual passivity—on which her psychological passivity was claimed to rest. Research is just beginning into the other areas. Even without this new research new interpretations of the old data are being explored. What these new interpretations say is that women are the way they are because they've been trained to be that way. As the Bems put it: "We overlook the fact that the society that has spent twenty years carefully marking the woman's ballot for her has nothing to lose in that twenty-first year by pretending to let her cast it for the alternative of her choice. Society has controlled not her alternatives, but her motivation to choose any but the one of those alternatives" (1970, p. 26).

This motivation is controlled through the socialization process. Women are raised to want to fill the social roles in which society needs them. They are trained to model themselves after the accepted image and to meet as individuals the expectations that are held for women as a group. Therefore, to understand how most women are socialized we must first understand how they see themselves and are seen by others. Several studies have been done on this. Quoting from one of them, McClelland stated that "the female image is characterized as small, weak, soft and light. In the United States it is also dull, peaceful, relaxed, cold, rounded, passive and slow" (1965, p. 173). A more thorough study which asked men and women to choose out of a long list of adjectives those which most closely applied to themselves showed that women strongly felt themselves to be uncertain, anxious, nervous, hasty, careless, fearful, dull, childish, helpless, sorry, timid, clumsy, stupid, silly, and domestic. On a more positive side, women felt that they were understanding, tender, sympathetic, pure, generous, affectionate, loving, moral, kind, grateful, and patient (Bennett and Cohen, 1959).

This is not a very favorable self-image but it does correspond fairly well with the social myths about what women are like. The image has some nice qualities, but they are not the ones normally required for that kind of achievement to which society gives its highest social rewards. Now one can justifiably question both the idea of achievement and the qualities necessary for it, but this is not the place to do so. Rather, because the current standards are the ones which women have been told they do not meet, the purpose here will be to look at the socialization process as a mechanism to keep them from doing so. We will also need to analyze some of the social expectations about women and about what they define as a successful *woman* (not a successful person) because they are inextricably bound up with the socialization process. All people are socialized to meet the social expectations held for them, and it is only when this process fails to do so (as is currently happening on several fronts) that it is at all questioned.

Let us further examine the effects on women of minority group status. Here, an interesting parallel emerges, but it is one fraught with much heresy. When we look at the *results* of female socialization we find a strong similarity between what our society labels, even extols, as the typical "feminine" character structure and that of oppressed peoples in this country and elsewhere.

In his classic study on *The Nature of Prejudice*, Allport devotes a chapter to "Traits Due to Victimization." Included are such personality characteristics as sensitivity, submission, fantasies of power, desire for protection, indirectness, ingratiation, petty revenge and sabotage, sympathy, extremes of both self and group hatred and self and group glorification, display of flashy status symbols, compassion for the underprivileged, identification with the dominant group's norms, and passivity (1954, pp. 142–161). Allport was primarily concerned with Jews and Negroes, but compare his characterization with the very thorough review of the literature on sex differences among young children made by Terman and Tyler (1954). For girls, they listed such traits as sensitivity, conformity to social pressures, response to environment, ease of social control, ingratiation, sympathy, low levels of aspiration, compassion for the underprivileged, and anxiety. They found that girls compared to boys were more nervous, unstable, neurotic, socially dependent, submissive, had less self-confidence, lower opinions of themselves and of girls in general, and were more timid, emotional, ministrative, fearful, and passive.

Girls' perceptions of themselves were also distorted. Although girls make consistently better school grades than boys until late high school, their opinion of themselves grows progressively worse with age and their opinion of boys and boys' abilities grows better. Boys, however, have an increasingly better opinion of themselves and worse opinion of girls as they grow older (Smith, 1939).

These distortions become so gross that, according to Goldberg, by the time girls reach college they have become prejudiced against women. He gave college girls sets of booklets containing six identical professional articles in traditional male, female, and neutral fields. The articles were identical, but the names of the authors were not. For example, an article in one set would bear the name John T. McKay and in another set the same article would be authored by Joan T. McKay. Each booklet contained three articles by "women" and three by "men." Questions at the end of each article asked the students to rate the articles on value, persuasiveness and profundity and the authors on writing style and competence. The male authors fared better in every field, even such "feminine" areas as Art History and Dietetics. Goldberg concluded that "Women are prejudiced against female professionals and, regardless of the actual accomplishments of these professionals, will firmly refuse to recognize them as the equals of their male colleagues" (1969, p. 28).

This combination of group self-hate and distortion of perceptions to justify that group self-hate are precisely the traits typical of a "minority group character structure" (Clark and Clark, 1947). It has been noted time and time again. The Clarks' finding of this pattern in Negro children in segregated schools contributed to the 1954 Supreme Court decision that outlawed such schools. These traits, as well as the others typical of the "feminine" stereotype, have been found in the Indians under British rule (Fisher, 1954), in the Algerians under the French (Fanon, 1963), and in black Americans (Myrdal, 1944). There seems to be a correlation between being "feminine" and experiencing status deprivation.

This pattern repeats itself even within cultures. In giving TATs to women in Japanese villages, De Vos (1960) discovered that those from fishing villages where the status position of women was higher than in farming communities were more assertive, not as guilt-ridden and were more willing to ignore the traditional pattern of arranged marriages in favor of love marriages.

In Terman's famous 50-year study of the gifted, a comparison in adulthood of those men who conspicuously failed to fulfill their early promise with those who did fulfill it showed that the successful had more self-confidence, fewer background disabilities, and were less nervous and emotionally unstable. But, they concluded "the disadvantages associated with lower social and home status appeared to present the outstanding handicap" (Miles, 1954, p. 1045).

The fact that women do have lower social status than men in our society and that both sexes tend to value men and male characteristics, values, and activities more highly than those of women has been noted by many authorities (see Brown, 1965, p. 162; Hill and Becker, 1955, p. 790; Goldberg, 1969, p. 28; Myrdal, 1944, appendix V; Goode, 1965, p. 70). What has not been done is to make the connection between this status and its accompanying personality.

The failure to extensively analyze the effects and the causes of lower social status is surprising in light of the many efforts that have been made to uncover distinct psychological differences between men and women to account for the tremendous disparity in their social production and creativity. The Goldberg study implies that even if women did achieve on a par with men it would not be perceived or accepted as such and that a woman's work must be of a much higher quality than that of a man to be given the same recognition. But these circumstances alone, or the fact that it is the male definition of achievement which is applied, are not sufficient to account for the lack of social production. So research has turned to male/female differences.

Most of this research, in the Freudian tradition, has focused on finding the psychological and developmental differences supposedly inherent in feminine nature and function. Despite all these efforts, the general findings of psychological testing indicate that: (1) Individual differences are greater than sex differences; i.e. sex is just one of the many characteristics which define a human being. (2) Most differences in ability in any field do not appear until elementary school age or later. "Sex differences become more apparent with increasing education even if it is co-education" (Tyler, 1968, pp. 207–213).

An examination of the literature of intellectual differences between the sexes discloses some interesting patterns. First, the statistics themselves show some regularity. Most conclusions of what is typical of one sex or the other are founded upon the performances of two thirds of the subjects. For example, two thirds of all boys do better on the math section of the College Board Exam than the verbal, and two thirds of the girls do better on the verbal than the math. Bales' studies (1958) show a similar distribution when he concludes that in small groups men are the task-oriented leaders and women are the social-emotional leaders. Not all tests show this two-thirds differential, but it is the mean about which most results of the ability test cluster. Sex is an easily visible, differentiable and testable criterion on which to draw conclusions; but it doesn't explain the one third that doesn't fit. The only characteristic virtually all women seem to have in common, besides their anatomy, is their lower social status.

Second, girls get off to a very good start. They begin speaking, reading, and counting sooner. They articulate more clearly and put words into sentences earlier. They have fewer reading and stuttering problems. Girls are even better in math in the early school years. Consistent sex differences in favor of boys do not appear until high-school age (Maccoby, 1966, pp. 26ff). Here another pattern begins to develop.

During high school, girls' performance in school and on ability tests begins to drop, sometimes drastically. Although well over half of all high-school graduates are girls, significantly less than half of all college students are girls. Presumably, this should mean that a higher percentage of the better female students go on to higher education, but their performance *vis-à-vis* boys' continues to decline.

Girls start off better than boys and end up worse. This change in their performance occurs at a very significant point in time. It occurs when their status changes, or to be more precise, when girls become aware of what their adult status is supposed to be. It is during adolescence that peer-group pressures to be "feminine" or "masculine" increase and the conceptions of what is "feminine" and "masculine" become more narrow (Neiman, 1954). It is also at this time that there is a personal drive for conformity (Milner).

One of the norms of our culture to which a girl learns to conform is that only men excel. This was evident in Lipinski's study of "Sex-Role Conflict and Achievement Motivation in College Women" (1965), which showed that thematic pictures depicting males as central characters elicited significantly more achievement imagery than female pictures. One need only recall Asch's experiments (1956) to see how peer-group pressures, armed only with our rigid ideas about "femininity" and "masculinity," could lead to a decline in girls' performance. Asch found that some 33 percent of his subjects would go contrary to the evidence of their own senses about something as tangible as the comparative length of two lines when their judgments were at variance with those made by the other group members. All but a handful of the other 67 percent experienced tremendous trauma in trying to stick to their correct perceptions.

When we move to something as intangible as sex-role behavior and to social sanctions far greater than the displeasure of a group of unknown experimental stooges, we can get an idea of how stifing social expectations can be. It is not surprising, in light of our cultural norm that a girl should not appear too smart or surpass boys in anything, that those pressures to conform, so prevalent in adolescence, should prompt girls to believe that the development of their minds will have only negative results. The lowered self-esteem and the denigration of their own sex noted by Smith (1939) and Goldberg (1969) are a logical consequence. These pressures even affect the supposedly unchangeable IQ scores. Corresponding with the drive for social acceptance, girls' IQs drop below those of boys during high school, rise slightly if they go to college, and go into a steady and consistent decline when and if they become full-time housewives (Bradway and Thompson, 1962).

These are not the only consequences. Negative self-conceptions have negative effects in a manner that can only be called a self-fufilling prophecy. They stifle motivation and channel energies into those areas that are likely to get some positive social rewards. Then those subject to these pressures are condemned for not having strived for the highest social rewards society has to offer.

A good example of this double bind is what psychologists call the "need for achievement." Achievement motivation in male college sophomores has been studied extensively. In women it has barely been looked at; women didn't fit the model social scientists set up to explain achievement in men. Girls do not seem to demonstrate the same consistent correlation between achievement and scores on achievement tests that boys do. For example, Stivers (1959) found that "non-motivated for college" girls scored higher on achievement motivation exams than "well-motivated for college" girls. There has been little inquiry as to why this is so. The general policy followed by the researchers was that if girls didn't fit, leave them out. Nonetheless some theories have been put forward.

Pierce postulated that part of the confusion resulted from using the same criteria of achievement for girls that were used for boys—achievement in school. Therefore, he did a study of marriage vs. career orientation in high-school girls which did show a small but consistent correlation between high achievement motivation scores and marriage orientation (Pierce and Bowman, 1960). In 1961 he did another study which showed a very strong correlation between high achievement scores and actual achievement of marriage within a year of high-school graduation. Those who went on to college and/ or did not get married had low achievement scores (Pierce, 1961).

Although he unfortunately did not describe the class origins and other relevant characteristics of his study it does seem clear that the real situation is not that women do not have achievement motivation but that this motivation is directed differently from that of men. In fact, the achievement orientation of both sexes goes precisely where it is socially directed—educational achievement for boys and marriage achievement for girls. Pierce suggested that "achievement motivation in girls attaches itself not to academic performance, but rather to more immediate adult status goals. This would be a logical assumption in that academic success is much less important to achievement status as a woman than it is for a man" (1961, p. 23).

He goes on to say that "girls see that to achieve in life as adult females they need to achieve in non-academic ways, that is, attaining the social graces, achieving beauty in person and dress, finding a desirable social status, marrying the right man. This is the successful adult woman. . . . Their achievement motivations are directed toward realizing personal goals through their relationship with men. . . . Girls who are following the normal course of development are most likely to seek adult status through marriage at an early age" (1961, p. 42).

Achievement for women is adult status through marriage, not success in the usual use of the word. One might postulate that both kinds of success might be possible, particularly for the highly achievement-oriented woman. But in fact the two are more often perceived as contradictory; success in one is seen to preclude success in the other.

Horner (1970) just completed a study at the University of Michigan from which she postulated a psychological barrier to achievement in women. She administered a TAT word item to undergraduates that said "After first term finals Anne finds herself at the top of her medical school class." A similar one for a male control group used a masculine name. The results were scored for imagery of fear of success and Horner found that 65% of the women and only 10% of the men demonstrated a definite "motive to avoid success." She explained the results by hypothesizing that the prospect of success, or situations in which success or failure is a relevant dimension, are perceived as having, and in fact do have, negative consequences for women. Success in the normal sense is threatening to women. Further research confirmed that fear of social rejection and role conflict did generate a "motive to avoid success."

Ability differences correlate strongly with interest differences (Terman and Tyler, 1954, p. 1104) and women have a definite interest in avoiding success. This is reinforced by peer and cultural pressures. However, many sex differences appear too early to be much affected by peer groups and are not directly related to sex-role attributes.

One such sex difference is spatial perception, or the ability to visualize objects out of their context. This is a test in which boys do better, though differences are usually not discernible before the early school years (Maccoby, 1966, p. 26). Other tests, such as the Embedded Figures and the Rod and Frame Tests, likewise favor boys. They indicate that boys perceive more analytically, while girls are more contextual. This ability to "break set" or be "field independent" also does not seem to appear until after the fourth or fifth year (Maccoby, 1966, p. 27).

According to Maccoby, this contextual mode of perception common to women is a distinct disadvantage for scientific production. "Girls on the average develop a somewhat different way of handling incoming information—their thinking is less analytic, more global, and more preservative—and this kind of thinking may serve very well for many kinds of functioning but it is not the kind of thinking most conducive to high-level intellectual productivity, especially in science" (Maccoby, 1963, p. 30).

Several social psychologists have postulated that the key developmental characteristic of analytic thinking is what is called early "independence and mastery training," or "whether and how soon a child is encouraged to assume initiative, to take responsibility for himself, and to solve problems by himself, rather than rely on others for the direction of his activities" (Maccoby, 1963, p. 31). (See also Sherman, 1967; Vernon, 1965.) In other words, analytically inclined children are those who have not been subject to what Bronfenbrenner calls "oversocialization" (1961, p. 260), and there is a good deal of indirect evidence that such is the case. Levy has observed (1943) that "overprotected" boys tend to develop intellectually like girls. Bing found that those girls who were good at spatial tasks were those whose mothers left them alone to solve the problems by themselves, while the mothers of verbally inclined daughters insisted on helping them (Maccoby, 1963, p. 31). Witkin similarly found that mothers of analytic children had encouraged their initiative, while mothers of nonanalytic children had encouraged dependence and discouraged self-assertion (Witkin et al., 1962). One writer commented on these studies that "this is to be expected, for the independent child is less likely to accept superficial appearances of objects without exploring them for himself, while the dependent child will be afraid to reach out on his own, and will accept appearances without question. In other words, the independent child is likely to be more *active*, not only psychologically but physically, and the physically active child will naturally have more kinesthetic experience with spatial relationships in his environment" (Clapp, 1968).

The qualities associated with independence training also have an effect on IQ. Sontag did a longitudinal study (1953) in which he compared children whose IQs had improved with those whose IQs had declined with age. He discovered that the child with increasing IQ was competitive, self-assertive, independent, and dominant in interaction with other children. Children with declining IQs were passive, shy, and dependent.

Maccoby commented on this study that "the characteristics associated with a rising IQ are not very feminine characteristics. When one of the people working on it was asked about what kind of developmental history was necessary to make a girl into an intellectual person, he replied, 'The simplest way to put it is that she must be a tomboy at some point in her childhood' " (1963, p. 33).

Likewise Kagan and Moss noted that "females who perform well on problems requiring analysis and complex reasoning tend to reject a traditional feminine identification" (1962, p. 275). They also observed that among the children involved in the Fels study "protection of girls was associated with the adoption of feminine interests during childhood and adulthood. Maternal protection apparently 'feminized' both the boys and the girls" (1962, p. 225).

However, analytic abilities are not the only ones that are valued in our society. Being person-oriented and contextual in perception are very valuable attributes for many fields where, nevertheless, very few women are found. Such characteristics are also valuable in the arts and some of the social sciences. But while women do succeed here more than in the sciences, their achievement is still not equivalent to that of men. One explanation of this, of course, is the Horner study that established a "motive to avoid success." But when one looks further it appears that there is an earlier cause here as well.

The very same early independence and mastery training that has such a beneficial effect on analytic thinking also determines the extent of one's achievement orientation (Winterbottom, 1965).

Although comparative studies of parental treatment of boys and girls are not extensive, those that have been made indicate that the traditional practices applied to girls are very different from those applied to boys. Girls receive more affection, more protectiveness, more control and more restrictions. Boys are subjected to more achievement demands and higher expectations (Sears, Maccoby, and Levin, 1957). In short, while girls are not always encouraged to be dependent *per se*, they are usually not encouraged to be *independent* and physically active. "Such findings indicate that the differential treatment of the two sexes reflects in part a difference in goals. With sons, socialization seems to focus primarily on directing and constraining the boys' impact on the environment. With daughters, the aim is rather to protect the girl from the impact of environment. The boy is being prepared to mold his world, the girl to be molded by it" (Bronfenbrenner, 1961, p. 260). The pattern is typical of girls, Bronfenbrenner maintains, and involves the risk of "oversocialization."

He doesn't discuss the possible negative effects such oversocialization has on girls, but he does express his concern about what would happen to the "qualities of independence, initiative, and self-sufficiency" of boys if such training were applied to them. "While an affectional context is important for the socialization of boys, it must evidently be accompanied by and be compatible with a strong component of parental discipline. Otherwise, the boy finds himself in the same situation as the girl, who, having received greater affection, is more sensitive to its withdrawal, with the result that a little discipline goes a long way and strong authority is constricting rather than constructive (Bronfenbrenner, 1961, p. 260).

That these variations in socialization result in variations in personality is corroborated by Schachter's studies (1959) of first and later-born children. Like girls, first children tend to be better socialized but also more anxious and dependent, whereas second children, like boys, are more aggressive and self-confident.

Bronfenbrenner concludes that the crucial variable is the differential treatment by the father and "in fact, it is the father who is especially likely to treat children of the two sexes differently." His extremes of affection, and of authority, are both deleterious. Not only do his high degrees of nurturance and protectiveness toward girls result in "oversocialization," but "the presence of strong paternal power is particularly debilitating. In short, boys thrive in a patriarchal context, girls in a matriarchal one" (1961, p. 267).

His observations receive indirect support from Douvan (1963) who noted that "part-time jobs of mothers have a beneficial effect on adolescent children, particularly daughters. This reflects the fact that adolescents may receive too much mothering."

The importance of mothers, as well as mothering, was pointed out by

Kagan and Moss. In looking at the kinds of role models that mothers provide for developing daughters, they discovered that it is those women who are looked upon as unfeminine whose daughters tend to achieve intellectually. These mothers are "aggressive and competitive women who were critical of their daughters and presented themselves to their daughters as intellectually competitive and aggressive role models. It is reasonable to assume that the girls identified with these intellectually aggressive women who valued mastery behavior" (1962, p. 222).

There seems to be some evidence that the sexes have been differentially socialized with different training practices, for different goals, and with different results. If McClelland (1961) is right in all the relationships he finds between child-rearing practices (in particular independence and mastery training), achievement-motivation scores of individuals tested, actual achievement of individuals, and indeed, the economic growth of whole societies, there is no longer much question as to why the historical achievement of women has been so low. In fact, with the dependency training they receive so early in life, the wonder is that they have achieved so much.

But this is not the whole story. Maccoby, in her discussion of the relationship of independence training to analytic abilities, notes that the girl who does not succumb to overprotection and develop the appropriate personality and behavior for her sex has a major price to pay: a price in anxiety. Or, as other observers have noted: "The universe of appropriate behavior for males and females is delineated early in development and it is difficult for the child to cross these culturally given frontiers without considerable conflict and tension" (Kagan and Moss, 1962, p. 270).

Some anxiety is beneficial to creative thinking, but high or sustained levels of it are damaging, "for it narrows the range of solution efforts, interferes with breaking set ,and prevents scanning of the whole range of elements open to perception" (Maccoby, 1963, p. 37). This anxiety is particularly manifest in college women (Sinick, 1956), and of course they are the ones who experience the most conflict between their current—intellectual—activities and expectations about behavior in their future—unintellectual—careers.

Maccoby feels that "it is this anxiety which helps to account for the lack of productivity among those women who do make intellectual careers." The combination of social pressures, role-expectations and parental training together tell "something of a horror story. It would appear that even when a woman is suitably endowed intellectually and develops the right temperament and habits of thought to make use of her endowment, she must be fleet of foot indeed to scale the hurdles society has erected for her and to remain a whole and happy person while continuing to follow her intellectual bent" (1963, p. 37).

The reasons for this horror story must be now be clearly evident. Traditionally, women have been defined as passive creatures, sexually, physically, and mentally. Their roles have been limited to the passive, dependent, auxiliary ones, and they have been trained from birth to fit these roles. However, those qualities by which one succeeds in this society are active ones. Achievement orientation, intellectuality, and analytic ability all require a certain amount of aggression.

As long as women were convinced that these qualities were beyond them, that they were inferior in their exercise and much happier if they stayed in their place, they remained quiescent under the paternalistic system of Western civilization. Paternalism was a pre-industrial scheme of life, and its yoke was partially broken by the industrial revolution (Myrdal, 1944, p. 1077). With this loosening up of the social order, the talents of women began to appear.

In the 18th Century it was held that no woman had ever produced anything worthwhile in literature with the possible exception of Sappho. But in the first half of the 19th Century, feminine writers of genius flooded the literary scene (Montagu, 1946). It wasn't until the end of the 19th Century that women scientists of note appeared, and it was still later that women philosophers were found.

Only since the industrial revolution shook the whole social order have women been able to break some of the traditional bounds of society. In pre-industrial societies, the family was the basic unit of social and economic organization, and women held a significant and functional role within it. This, coupled with the high birth and death rates of those times, gave women more than enough to do within the home. It was the center of production and women could be both at home and in the world at the same time. But the industrial revolution, along with decreased infant mortality, increased life-span, and changes in economic organization, have all but destroyed the family as the economic unit. Technological advances have taken men out of the home, and now those functions traditionally defined as female are being taken out also (Keniston and Keniston, 1964). For the first time in human history women have had to devote themselves to being full-time mothers in order to have enough to do (Rossi, 1965).

Conceptions of society have also changed. At one time, authoritarian hierarchies were the norm and paternalism was reflective of a general social authoritarian attitude. While it is impossible to do retroactive studies on feudalistic society, we do know that authoritarianism as a personality trait does correlate strongly with a rigid conception of sex roles, and with ethnocentrism (Adorno et al., 1950). We also know from ethnological data that there is a "parallel between family relationships and the larger social hierarchy. Autocratic societies have autocratic families. As the king rules his subjects and the nobles subjugate and exploit the commoners, so does husband tend to lord it over wife, father rule over son (Stephens, 1963).

According to D'Andrade, "another variable that appears to affect the distribution of authority and deference between the sexes is the degree to which men rather than women control and mediate property" (1966, p. 189). He presented data which showed a direct correlation between the extent to which inheritance, succession, and descent-group membership were patrilineal and the degree of subjection of women.

Even today, the equality of the sexes in the family is often reflective of the economic equality of the partners. In a Detroit sample, Blood and Wolfe (1960) found that the relative power of the wife was low if she did not work and increased with her economic contribution to the family. "The employment of women affects the power structure of the family by equalizing the resources of husband and wife. A working wife's husband listens to her more, and she listens to herself more. She expresses herself and has more opinions. Instead of looking up into her husband's eyes and worshipping him, she levels with him, compromising on the issues at hand. Thus her power increases and, relatively speaking, the husband's falls (Blood, 1965, p. 46).

Goode also noted this pattern but said it varied inversely with class status. Toward the upper strata, wives are not only less likely to work but when they do they contribute a smaller percentage of the total family income than is true in the lower classes (1965, p. 76). Hill went so far as to say "Money is a source of power that supports male dominance in the family. . . . Money belongs to him who earns it, not to her who spends it, since he who earns it may withhold it" (1955, p. 790). Hallenbeck feels more than just economic resources are involved but does conclude that there is a balance of power in every family which affects "every other aspect of the marriage— division of labor, amount of adaptation necessary for either spouse, methods used to resolve conflicts, and so forth" (1966, p. 203). Blood feels the economic situation affects the whole family structure. "Daughters of working mothers are more independent, more self-reliant, more aggressive, more dominant, and more disobedient. Such girls are no longer meek, mild, submissive, and feminine like 'little ladies' ought to be. They are rough and tough, actively express their ideas, and refuse to take anything from anybody else. . . . Because their mothers have set an example, the daughters get up the courage and the desire to earn money as well. They take more part-time jobs after school and more jobs during summer vacation" (1965, p. 47).

Barry, Bacon and Child did an ethnohistoriographic analysis that provides some further insights into the origins of male dominance. After examining the ethnographic reports of 110 cultures, they concluded that large sexual differentiation and male superiority occur concurrently and in "an economy that places a high premium on the superior strength and superior development of motor skills requiring strength, which characterize the male" (1957, p. 330). It is those societies in which great physical strength and mobility are required for survival, in which hunting and herding, or warfare, play an important role, that the male, as the physically stronger and more mobile sex, tends to dominate. This is supported by Spiro's analysis of sex roles in an Israeli kibbutz (1956). There, the economy was largely unmechanized and the superior average strength of the men was needed on many jobs. Thus, despite a conscious attempt to break down traditional sex roles, they began reasserting themselves, as women were assigned to the less strenuous jobs.

Although there are a few tasks which virtually every society assigns only to men or women, there is a great deal of overlap for most jobs. Virtually every task, even in the most primitive societies, can be performed by either men or women. Equally important, what is defined as a man's task in one society may well be classified as a woman's job in another (D'Andrade, 1966, p. 191). Nonetheless, the sexual division of labor is much more narrow than dictated by physical limitations, and what any one culture defines as a woman's job will seldom be performed by a man and vice versa. It seems that what originated as a division of labor based upon the necessities of survival has spilled over into many other areas and lasted long past the time of its social value. Where male strength and mobility have been crucial to social survival, male dominance and the aura of male superiority have been the strongest. The latter has been incorporated into the value structure and attained an existence of its own.

Thus, male superiority has not ceased with an end to the need for male strength. As Goode pointed out, there is one consistent element in the assignment of jobs to the sexes, even in modern societies: "Whatever the strictly male tasks are, they are defined as *more honorific* [emphasis his]. . . . Moreover, the tasks of control, management, decision, appeals to the gods—in short the higher-level jobs that typically do *not* require strength, speed or traveling far from home—are male jobs" (1965, p. 70).

He goes on to comment that "this element suggests that the sexual division of labor within family and society comes perilously close to the racial or caste restrictions in some modern countries. That is, the low-ranking race, caste, or sex is defined as not being *able* to do certain types of prestigious work, but it is also considered a violation of propriety if they do it. Obviously, if women really cannot do various kinds of male tasks, no moral or ethical prohibition would be necessary to keep them from it" (1965, p. 70).

Sex roles originated in economic necessities but the value attached to any one role has become a factor of sex alone. Even cross-culturally, these roles, and the attitudes associated with them, are ingrained by common socialization practices. Barry, Bacon, and Child discovered that "pressure toward nurturance, obedience and responsibility is most often stronger for girls, whereas pressure toward achievement and self-reliance is most often stronger for boys" (1957, p. 328). These are the same socialization practices traditionally found in Western society. As the Barry, Bacon, and Child study showed, these socializations serve to prepare children for roles as adults that require women to stay near the home and men to go out and achieve. The greater emphasis a society places on physical strength, the greater the sex-role differentiation and the sex differences in socialization.

These sex-role differences may have served a natural function at one time, but it is doubtful that they still do so. The characteristics we observe in women and men today are a result of socialization practices that were developed for survival of a primitive society. The value structure of male superiority is a reflection of the primitive orientations and values. But social and economic conditions have changed drastically since these values were developed. Technology has reduced to almost nothing the importance of muscular strength. In fact, the warlike attitude which goes along with an idealization of physical strength and dominance is proving to be positively destructive. The value of large families has also become a negative one. Now we are concerned with the population explosion and prefer that our society produce children of quality rather than quantity. The result of all these changes is that the traditional sex roles and the traditional family structures have become dysfunctional.

To some extent, patterns of child-rearing have also changed. Bronfenbrenner reports (1958) that at least middle-class parents are raising both boys and girls much the same. He noted that over a 50-year period middle-class parents have been developing a "more acceptant, equalitarian relationship with their children." With an increase in the family's social position, the patterns of parental treatment of children begin to converge (Bronfenbrenner, 1969). He likewise noted that a similar phenomenon is beginning to develop in lower-class parents and that equality of treatment is slowly working its way down the social ladder.

These changes in patterns of child-rearing correlate with changes in relationships within the family. Both are moving toward a less hierarchical and more egalitarian pattern of living.

As Blood has pointed out, "Today we may be on the verge of a new phase in American family history, when the companionship family is beginning to manifest itself. One distinguishing characteristic of this family is the dual employment of husband and wife. . . . Employment emancipates women from domination by their husbands and, secondarily, raises their daughters from inferiority to their brothers. . . . The classic differences between mascu-

linity and femininity are disappearing as both sexes in the adult generation
take on the same roles in the labor market. . . . The roles of men and women
are converging for both adults and children. As a result the family will be
far less segregated internally, far less stratified into different age generations
and different sexes. The old asymmetry of male-dominated, female-serviced
family life is being replaced by a new symmetry" (1965, p. 47).

All these data indicate that several trends are converging at about the
same time. Our value structure has changed from an authoritarian one to a
more democratic one, though our social structure has not yet caught up.
Social attitudes begin in the family; only a democratic family can raise children to be citizens in a democratic society. The social and economic organization of society which kept women in the home has likewise changed. The
home is no longer the center of society. The primary male and female functions have left it and there is no longer any major reason for maintaining
the large sex-role differentiations which it supported. The value placed on
physical strength which reinforced the dominance of men, and the male
superiority attitudes that this generated, have also become dysfunctional.
It is the mind, not the body, which must now prevail, and woman's mind
is the equal of man's. The "pill" has liberated women from the uncertainty
of childbearing, and with it the necessity of being attached to a man for
economic support. But our attitudes toward women, and toward the family,
have not changed concomitantly with the other developments. There is a
distinct "cultural lag." Definitions of the family, conceptions of women and
ideas about social function are left over from an era when they were necessary for social survival. They have persisted into an era in which they are
no longer viable. The result can only be called severe role dysfunctionality
for women.

The necessary relief for this dysfunctionality must come through changes
in the social and economic organization of society and in social attitudes
which will permit women to play a full and equal part in the social order.
With this must come changes in the family, so that men and women are
not only equal, but can raise their children in a democratic atmosphere.
These changes will not come easily, nor will they come through the simple
evolution of social trends. Trends do not move all in the same direction or
at the same rate. To the extent that changes are dysfunctional with each
other they create problems. These problems must be solved not by complacency but by conscious human direction. Only in this way can we have
a real say in the shape of our future and the shape of our lives.

References

Adorno, T. W., et al. *The Authoritarian Personality*. New York: Harper, 1950.
Allport, G. *The Nature of Prejudice*. Reading, Mass.: Addison-Wesley, 1954.

Asch, S. E. "Studies of Independence and Conformity. A Minority of One Against a Unanimous Majority." *Psychological Monographs,* 70 (1956), no. 9.

Bales, R. F. "Task Roles and Social Roles in Problem-Solving Groups." In *Readings in Social Psychology,* 3rd ed., edited by T. M. Newcomb, E. Maccoby, and E. L. Hartley. New York: Holt, Rinehart & Winston, 1958.

Barry, H., M. K. Bacon, and I. L. Child. "A Cross-Cultural Survey of Some Sex Differences in Socialization." *Journal of Abnormal and Social Psychology,* 55 (1957): 330.

Bem, S., and D. Bem. "We're All Nonconscious Sexists." *Psychology Today,* 4, (1970), no. 6.

Bennett, E. M., and L. R. Cohen. "Men and Women: Personality Patterns and Contrasts." *Genetic Psychology Monographs,* 59 (1959): 101–155.

Blood, R. O. "Long-Range Causes and Consequences of the Employment of Married Women." *Journal of Marriage and the Family,* 27 (1965), no. 1.

Blood, R. O., and D. M. Wolfe. *Husbands and Wives.* Glencoe, Ill.: The Free Press, 1960.

Bradway, K. P., and C. W. Thompson. "Intelligence at Adulthood: A Twenty-five Year Followup." *Journal of Educational Psychology,* 53 (1962): 1–14.

Bronfenbrenner, U. "Socialization and Social Class through Time and Space." In *Readings in Social Psychology,* 3rd ed., edited by T. M. Newcomb, E. Maccoby, and E. L. Hartley, New York: Holt, Rinehart & Winston, 1958.

Bronfenbrenner, U. "Some Familial Antecedents of Responsibility and Leadership in Adolescents." In *Leadership and Interpersonal Behavior,* edited by Luigi Petrullo and Bernard M. Bass. New York: Holt, Rinehart & Winston, 1961.

Bronfenbrenner, U. "The Effects of Social and Cultural Change on Personality." *Journal of Social Issues,* 17 (1969), no. 1: 6–18.

Brown, R. *Social Psychology.* New York: The Free Press, 1965.

Clapp, J. "Sex Differences in Mathematical Reasoning Ability." Unpublished paper, 1968.

Clark, K., and M. Clark. "Racial Identification and Preference in Negro Children." In *Readings in Social Psychology,* edited by T. M. Newcomb and E. L. Hartley. New York: Holt, Rinehart & Winston, 1947.

D'Andrade, R. "Sex Differences and Cultural Institutions." In *The Development of Sex Differences,* edited by E. Maccoby. Stanford: Stanford University Press, 1966.

De Vos, G. "The Relation of Guilt Toward Parents to Achievement and Arranged Marriage Among the Japanese." *Psychiatry,* 23 (1960): 287–301.

Douvan, E. "Employment and the Adolescent." In *The Employed Mother in America,* edited by F. Ivan Nye and Lois W. Hoffman. Chicago: Rand McNally, 1963.

Fanon, F. *The Wretched of the Earth.* New York: Grove Press, 1963.

Fisher, L. *Gandhi.* New York: Signet Key, 1954.

Goldberg, P. "Are Women Prejudiced Against Women?" *Transaction,* April 1969.

Goode, W. J. *The Family.* Englewood Cliffs, N.J.: Prentice-Hall, 1965.

Hallenbeck, P. N. "An Analysis of Power Dynamics in Marriage." *Journal of Marriage and the Family,* 28 (May 1966), no. 2.

Hill, Reuben, and Howard Becker, eds. *Family, Marriage and Parenthood.* Lexington, Mass.: D. C. Heath, 1955.

Horner, M. "Femininity and Successful Achievement: A Basic Inconsistency." In *Feminine Personality and Conflict,* Bardwick et al. Belmont: Brooks/Cole, 1970.

Kagan, J., and H. A. Moss. *Birth to Maturity: A Study in Psychological Development.* New York and London: Wiley, 1962.

Keniston, E., and K. Keniston. "An American Anachronism: The Image of Women and Work." *American Scholar,* 33 (Summer 1964), no. 3: 355–375.

Levy, D. M. *Maternal Overprotection.* New York: Columbia University Press, 1943.

Lipinski, B. "Sex-role Conflict and Achievement Motivation in College Women." Unpublished doctoral dissertation, University of Cincinnati, 1965.

Maccoby, E. "Woman's Intellect." In *The Potential of Women,* edited by Farber and Wilson. New York: McGraw-Hill, 1963.

Maccoby, E. "Sex Differences in Intellectual Functioning." In *The Development of Sex Differences*, edited by E. Maccoby. Stanford: Stanford University Press, 1966.

McClelland, D. C. *The Achieving Society.* Princeton: Van Nostrand, 1961.

McClelland, D. "Wanted: A New Self-Image for Women." In *The Woman in America*, edited by Robert J. Lifton. Boston: Beacon Press, 1965.

Miles, C. C. "Gifted Children." In *Manual of Child Psychology*, edited by Leonard Carmichael. New York: Wiley, 1954.

Milner, E. "Effects of Sex-role and Social Status on the Early Adolescent Personality." *Genetic Psychological Monographs,* 40: 231–325.

Montagu, A. "Anti-Feminism and Race Prejudice." *Psychiatry,* 9 (1946): 69–71.

Myrdal, G. *An American Dilemma.* New York: Harper, 1944.

Neiman, L. J. "The Influence of Peer Groups upon Attitudes toward the Feminine Role." *Social Problems,* 2 (1954): 104–111.

Pierce, J. V. "Sex Differences in Achievement Motivation of Able High School Students." *Co-operative Research Project No. 1097,* University of Chicago, December 1961.

Pierce, J. V., and P. H. Bowman. "The Educational Motivation Patterns of Superior Students Who Do and Do Not Achieve in High School." U.S. Office of Education Project #208, *Co-operative Research Monograph No. 2,* 33–66. Washington, D.C.: U.S. Printing Office, 1960.

Rossi, A. "Equality Between the Sexes: An Immodest Proposal." In *The Women in America*, edited by Robert J. Lifton. Boston: Beacon Press, 1965.

Schachter, S. *The Psychology of Affiliation.* Stanford: Stanford University Press, 1959.

Sears, R. R., E. Maccoby, and H. Levin. *Patterns of Child Rearing.* Evanston, Ill.: Row, Peterson, 1957.

Sherman, J. A. "Problems of Sex Differences in Space Perception and Aspects of Intellectual Functioning." *Psychological Review,* 74 (July 1967), no. 4: 290–299.

Sinick, D. "Two Anxiety Scales Correlated and Examined for Sex Differences." *Journal of Clinical Psychology,* 12 (1956): 394–395.

Smith, S. "Age and Sex Differences in Children's Opinion Concerning Sex Differences." *Journal of Genetic Psychology,* 54 (1939): 17–25.

Sontag, I. W., C. T. Baker, and V. A. Nelson. "Mental Growth and Personality Development: A Longitudinal Study." *Monographs of the Society for Research in Child Development,* 23 (1953), no. 68.

Spiro, M. E. *Kibbutz: Venture in Utopia.* Cambridge: Harvard University Press, 1956.

Stephens, W. N. *The Family in Cross-Cultural Perspective.* New York: Holt, Rinehart & Winston, 1963.

Stivers, E. N. "Motivation for College of High School Boys and Girls." Unpublished doctoral dissertation, University of Chicago, 1959.

Terman, L. M., and L. Tyler. "Psychological Sex Differences." In *Manual of Child Psychology*, edited by Leonard Carmichael. New York: Wiley, 1954.

Tyler, L. "Sex Differences." Under "Individual Differences" in *International Encyclopedia of the Social Sciences*, vol. 7, pp. 207–213. New York: Macmillan, 1968.

Vernon, P. E. "Ability Factors and Environmental Influences." *American Psychologist,* 20 (September 1965), no. 9: 723–733.

Winterbottom, M. "The Relation of Need for Achievement to Learning Experiences in Independence and Mastery." In *Basic Studies in Social Psychology,* edited by Harold Proshansky and Bernard Seidenberg. New York: Holt, Rinehart & Winston, 1965.

Witkin, H. A., R. B. Dyk, H. E. Paterson, D. R. Goodenough, and S. A. Karp. *Psychological Differentiation.* New York: Wiley, 1962.

Why is it that women have always been responsible for child care? How is it that in some societies they do not participate in the economy while in others they support the society almost completely? The author, an anthropologist, argues that the division of labor is not based on physiological or temperamental differences, but on the fact that women in pre-industrial societies are burdened by pregnancy, nursing, and the care of young children most of their lives. Whether or not women participate in the economy depends upon the compatibility of work with child care responsibilities. Societies that make extensive use of woman power must provide mother substitutes, such as nurses, relatives, or nurseries, or else they must provide work that a mother can do at the same time she is taking care of her children. Such work must be nondangerous, close to home, able to be interrupted, and able to be performed without concentrated attention.

A Note on the Division of Labor by Sex | *Judith K. Brown*

In spite of the current interest in the economic aspect of tribal and peasant societies, the division of labor by sex continues to elicit only the most perfunctory consideration. This paper attempts to reassess the scant theoretical literature dealing with this division of labor and to suggest a reinterpretation based on some of the available ethnographic evidence.

I will begin with Durkheim. According to his theory, among the very primitive (both in the distant past and today), men and women are fairly similar in strength and intelligence. Under these circumstances the sexes are economically independent, and therefore "sexual relations [are] preeminently ephemeral" (1893, p. 61). With the "progress of morality," women became weaker and their brains became smaller. Their dependence on men increased, and division of labor by sex cemented the conjugal bond. Indeed, Durkheim asserts that the Parisienne of his day probably had the smallest human brain on record. Presumably she was able to console herself with the stability of her marriage, which was the direct result of her underendowment and consequent dependence.

Unlike Durkheim, Murdock does not attempt to reconstruct history, but his explanatory principle is also naively physiological. He writes:

> By virtue of their primary sex differences, a man and a woman make an exceptionally efficient cooperating unit. Man, with his superior physical strength, can better undertake the more strenuous tasks. . . . Not handicapped, as is woman, by the physiological burdens of pregnancy and

Reproduced by permission of the American Anthropological Association from "A Note on the Division of Labor by Sex" by Judith K. Brown, *The American Anthropologist* 72 (5), 1970.

nursing, he can range farther afield to hunt, to fish, to herd, and to trade. Woman is at no disadvantage, however, in the lighter tasks which can be performed in or near home. . . . . All known human societies have developed specialization and cooperation between the sexes roughly along this biologically determined line of cleavage. (1949, p. 7)

This overly simple explanation is contradicted by numerous ethnographic accounts of heavy physical labor performed by women. The greater spatial range of male subsistence activities may also not be based on physiology as Murdock suggests. Recently, Munroe and Munroe (1967) have reported sex differences in environmental exploration among Logoli children. According to the authors, the greater geographical range of boys' activities in this society may result from learning, although innate sex-linked factors are suggested as a possible alternative explanation.

Lévi-Strauss also suggests the economic interdependence of the sexes as the basis for the conjugal (or nuclear) family. This interdependence does not so much arise from actual sex differences as from culturally imposed prohibitions that make it impossible for one sex to do the tasks assigned to the other. He writes of the division of labor by sex as "a device to make the sexes mutually dependent on social and economic grounds, thus establishing clearly that marriage is better than celibacy" (1956, p. 277).

Taking their cue from ethnographic descriptions that suggest that women often perform the dull and monotonous subsistence activities (for example, Pospisil, 1963), other authors have offered "psychologizing" theories concerning the division of labor by sex. Malinowski suggested that women, owing to their docility, are forced to do such work: "Division of labor is rooted in the brutalization of the weaker sex by the stronger" (1913, p. 287). Others have suggested that women are psychologically better fitted for dull work. Mead summarizes this view, stating "Women have a capacity for continuous monotonous work that men do not share, while men have a capacity for the mobilization of sudden spurts of energy, followed by a need for rest and reassemblage of resources" (1949, p. 164).

What facts have these theories tried to explain? First, division of labor by sex is a universal. Planned societies such as Israel and Communist China have attempted to implement an ideology that views men and women as interchangeable parts within the economy, but have done so with only mixed success (Spiro, 1956; Huang, 1961, 1963). Second, in spite of the physiological constants and the possible, but less well-substantiated, psychological ones, women may contribute nothing to subsistence—as among the Rajputs (Minturn and Hitchcock, 1963); or they may support the society almost completely—as among the Nsaw (Kaberry, 1952). This variation, briefly noted by Mead (1949), has never been fully explained.

I would like to suggest that the degree to which women contribute to the subsistence of a particular society can be predicted with considerable accuracy from a knowledge of the major subsistence activity. It is determined by the compatibility of this pursuit with the demands of child care. (Female physiology and psychology are only peripheral to this explanation.) This fact has been noted repeatedly by ethnographers, but it has never been articulated in the theoretical literature dealing with the division of labor by sex.

Nowhere in the world is the rearing of children primarily the responsibility of men, and in only a few societies are women exempted from participation in subsistence activities. If the economic role of women is to be maximized, their responsibilities in child care must be reduced or the economic activity must be such that it can be carried out concurrently with child care.

The former is the method familiar to us among industrial or industrializing societies. Whether in the United States or in Communist China, the working mother is separated from her child, who is in the care of specialists in the school or the residential nursery while the mother is in her place of employment. In our society, controversy over the presence of mothers in the labor force inevitably centers on the desirability and quality of this substitute care (Maccoby, 1960).

Tribal societies also resort to substitute care so that mothers may work. Among the Gusii, women are responsible for the cultivation on which the society depends, and young child nurses (usually girls) are in charge of younger children and infants. However, the mother must periodically supervise the young caretakers. Minturn and Lambert write:

> This does not mean that the Nyasongo [Gusii] mothers spend a great deal of time actually interacting with their children. They have domestic and agricultural duties that take up most of their time. . . . Older children are often left with no one to look after them directly, but are kept close to home and within earshot of their mothers. . . . The burden of such supervision is clear, for instance, with respect to infant care. Older children chiefly care for infants but mothers must, in turn, supervise older children. (1964, pp. 244, 252)

Among the Yoruba (Marshall, 1964) an intricate system of reciprocity makes possible the trade activities of the women. During the early years of marriage, when her children are very young, a woman carries on only limited commercial activities. At this time she is likely to take into her home an older child as a helper. When her children are older, they in turn are placed in the homes of women who are still in the previous stage, and the mother's market activities increase in scope.

I have greatly oversimplified both examples. They illustrate two contrasts with the substitute care patterns of our own society. First, the women are not freed as completely for their economic pursuits. Second, the ethnographic accounts suggest that such substitute care is viewed not only as desirable but as an absolute necessity. Finally, the two cases are similar to the cases that are the focus of this paper, in that the work the women perform is not incompatible with child watching, even though the supervision of children may be only sporadic.

My main concern is with those societies that, without the intercession of schools, child-care centers, or child nurses, nevertheless depend on the subsistence activities of working mothers. These societies are able to draw on womanpower because their subsistence activities are compatible with simultaneous child watching. Such activities have the following characteristics: they do not require rapt concentration and are relatively dull and repetitive; they are easily interruptible and easily resumed once interrupted; they do not place the child in potential danger; and they do not require the participant to range very far from home.

Anthropologists have long noted the narrow range of subsistence activities in which women make a substantial contribution: gathering, hoe agriculture, and trade (Lippert, 1886/87; Schmidt, 1955; Murdock, 1957; Aberle, 1961). Although men do gather, carry on hoe cultivation, and trade, no society depends on its women for the herding of large animals, the hunting of large game, deep-sea fishing, or plow agriculture. That women can be proficient at these activities [Jenness (1923) reports women seal hunters among the Copper Eskimo; Forde (1934) reports that women herd reindeer for parts of the year among the Tungus] is evidence that the division of labor by sex is not based entirely on immutable physiological facts of greater male strength and endurance. However, it is easy to see that all these activities are incompatible with simultaneous child watching. They require rapt concentration, cannot be interrupted and resumed, are potentially dangerous, and require that the participant range far from home.

Bogoras' report of the summer herding of the reindeer Chukchee provides an especially appropriate illustration of a subsistence activity that is incompatible with child watching. Bogoras suggests that the division of labor is not sexually determined; instead the population is divided according to child-watching and non-child-watching members. He writes:

> With the beginning of summer, when sledges become useless and tents cannot be moved around the country, the Chukchee herdsmen usually leave their families in camp, and move with the herd about twenty miles away, to the summer pastures. Boys and girls of more than ten years, and young women having no small children, usually go along for a time. While moving about with the herd, the herdsmen have to carry on their backs all necessaries, such as extra clothing, rifle and ammunition, kettles, and provisions. . . . The burdens are carried by girls and by men who are not very agile; while the best herdsmen must remain unencumbered for moving swiftly around the herd. (1904, p. 83)

The reindeer Chukchee lived by herding and hunting, both very incompatible with simultaneous child care, and the women of the society made a negligible contribution to subsistence. In contrast, the Azande, as described by De Schlippe, are hoe cultivators, and the contribution of women to subsistence is considerable. De Schlippe offers a very detailed description of the division of labor by sex. Only a portion will be cited here because it illustrates the compatibility of the women's activities with simultaneous child watching:

> In all those field types which are grouped around the homestead and to which the common name of garden has been applied, as a rule women work alone or with their children. This may be explained by the proximity to the homestead and accordingly by the nature of this work. It consists of a great variety of different small tasks, many of which can be packed into one single day. A woman, trained in household work, is capable of doing a great deal of minor independent tasks without losing the order of her day's work. (1956, p. 40)

Another account that demonstrates the compatibility of hoe agriculture with simultaneous child watching is offered in the early nineteenth-century biography of the adopted Indian captive Mary Jemison (Seaver, 1823). It is the only description of Iroquois agricultural activity given from the point of view of a participant. It runs as follows:

> Our labor was not severe; and that of one year was exactly similar, in almost every respect, to that of the others. . . . Notwithstanding the Indian women have all the fuel and bread to procure . . . their cares certainly are not half as numerous, nor as great [as those of white women]. In the summer season, we planted, tended and harvested our corn, and generally had all our children with us . . . we could work as leisurely as we pleased. (Seaver, 1823, p. 55)

The carefree tone of this account is deceptive. The agricultural activities of the Iroquois women were highly productive. Not only was the tribe well provided with food, but the harvested surplus was carefully preserved and constituted a considerable part of the tribe's wealth. Morgan (1851) had high praise for the industry of the Iroquois women. It is all the more remarkable that such high productivity was possible with simultaneous childcare responsibilities.

The relaxed atmosphere that characterized the agricultural-child-watching activities of the Iroquois women also characterized the gathering-child-watching activities of the Lunga women, inhabitants of the Kimberley District of Western Australia. Phyllis Kaberry writes of the Aborigine women, "If livelihood is sometimes precarious, it is belied by the absence of any feverish haste" (1939, p. 18). Children accompanied the small groups of women gatherers on their daily forays into the bush. Kaberry describes one of these forays in great detail, ending her account as follows:

They lie for a while in the shade, gossip, eat some of the fish and roots, sleep, and about three o'clock move homeward. For all their desultory searching, there is little that they miss, or fail to note for a future occasion. . . . In actual quantity, the woman probably provides more over a fixed period than the man, since hunting is not always successful. She always manages to bring home something, and hence the family is dependent on her efforts to a greater extent than on those of the husband. (1939, pp. 22, 25)

A more recent study, that by Rose of the Angus Downs Aborigines, focuses on the effects of White contact on Aborigine economic activity and kinship structure. Under precontact conditions, according to Rose, when women gathered nuts and seeds for grinding, they formed themselves into "collectives of co-wives for the purpose of sharing the burdens of caring for children" (1965, p. 99). With the introduction of white flour, the women's economic role became what Rose considers a passive one, "collectives" were no longer necessary, and polygyny decreased markedly.

The final ethnographic example I will offer is that of the Yahgan as described by Gusinde. This tribe was rated by Murdock (1957) as being supported mostly by the subsistence activities of its women. It was the only tribe that depended on fishing, marine hunting, and marine gathering that was so rated in the world sample of 565 societies. Gusinde writes:

Far beyond the limited participation of the man in procuring food, she makes a considerable, altogether independent contribution to the support of her family by means of an activity that she alone can carry out. This is gathering, for which she is equipped by nature and to which she can devote herself without jeopardizing her more important duties as mother and wife. (1937, p. 538)

His description of subsistence activities is extremely detailed. Only a small portion will be cited here:

Assuming that low tide set in during the day, one woman will make a date with another. . . . Each of them brings along her baby clinging to her back, and little girls run ahead, each with her own little basket. Sometimes a boy or two will run along out of curiosity and sheer pleasure, and they will watch for a while, but it would never occur to them to help because that is not their work. These women are only short distances apart. Walking slowly, they go from one spot to another, for the entire ocean floor is usually densely strewn with mussels. . . . They stop working only when their little baskets are full. (1937, pp. 541–542)

The ethnographers cited here have all addressed themselves to the relationship between women's economic activities and their child-rearing responsibilities. It is obvious that certain subsistence activities are extremely compatible with simultaneous child care and that societies depending on such subsistence bases invite considerable economic contribution by women.

In the past, theoretical considerations of the division of labor by sex have suggested that women do only certain kinds of work for physiological and psychological reasons. On the basis of the ethnographic evidence I have presented here, I would like to suggest a further explanation: in tribal and peasant societies that do not have schools and child-care centers, only certain economic pursuits can accommodate women's simultaneous child-care responsibilities. Repetitive, interruptible, non-dangerous tasks that do not require extensive excursions are more appropriate for women when the exigencies of child care are taken into account.

References

Aberle, David. "Matrilineal Descent in Cross-Cultural Perspective." In *Matrilineal Kinship*, edited by David M. Schneider and Kathleen Gough. Berkeley: University of California Press, 1961.

Bogoras, Waldemar. "The Chukchee. The Jesup North Pacfiic Expedition." *American Museum of Natural History Memoir*, 7(1). New York: Stechert, 1904.

De Schlippe, Pierre. *Shifting Cultivation in Africa: The Zande System of Agriculture*. London: Routledge and Kegan Paul, 1956.

Durkheim, Emile. *De la division du travail social. (The Division of Labor in Society.)* Translated by George Simpson. Glencoe: The Free Press, 1933.

Forde, C. Daryll. *Habitat, Economy and Society*. New York: Dutton, 1963.

Gusinde, Martin. *Die Yamana, vom leben und denken der wassernomaden am Kap Horn. (The Yamana: the life and thought of the water nomads of Cape Horn.)* 1937. Translated by Frieda Schutze. New Haven: Human Relations Area Files, 1961.

Huang, Jen Lucy. "Some Changing Patterns in the Communist Chinese Family." *Marriage and Family Living*, 23 (1961): 137–146.

Huang, Jen Lucy. "A Re-evaluation of the Primary Role of the Communist Chinese Woman: The Homemaker or the Worker." *Marriage and Family Living*, 25 (1963): 162–166.

Jenness, D. "The Copper Eskimo." *Report of the Canadian Arctic Expedition, 1913–18*, 12. Ottawa: Acland, 1923.

Kaberry, Phyllis. *Aboriginal Woman: Sacred and Profane*. London: Routledge, 1939.

Kaberry, Phyllis. "Women of the Grass Fields: A Study of the Economic Position of Women in Bamenda, British Cameroons." *Colonial Research Publication*, 14. London: Her Majesty's Stationery Office, 1952.

Lévi-Strauss, Claude. "The Family." In *Man, Culture, and Society*, edited by Harry L. Shapiro. New York: Oxford University Press, 1956.

Lippert, Julius. *The Evolution of Culture*. 1886/87. Translated and edited by G. P. Murdock. New York: Macmillan, 1931.

Maccoby, Eleanor E. "Effects upon Children of Their Mothers' Outside Employment." In *A Modern Introduction to the Family*, edited by Norman W. Bell and Ezra F. Vogel. Glencoe: The Free Press, 1960.

Malinowski, Bronislaw. *The Family Among the Australian Aborigines: A Sociological Study*. London: University of London Press, 1913.

Marshall, Gloria. "Women, Trade and the Yoruba Family." Unpublished doctoral dissertation, Columbia University, 1964.

Mead, Margaret. *Male and Female: A Study of the Sexes in a Changing World*. New York: William Morrow, 1949.

Minturn, Leigh, and John T. Hitchcock. "The Rājpūts of Khalapur, India. In *Six Cultures: Studies of Child Rearing*, edited by Beatrice B. Whiting. New York: Wiley, 1963.

Minturn, Leigh, and Lambert, William. *Mothers of Six Cultures: Antecedents of Child Rearing.* New York: Wiley, 1964.

Morgan, Lewis Henry. *League of the Iroquois.* 1851. Reprinted. New York: Corinth Books, 1962.

Munroe, Robert L., and Munroe, Ruth H. "Maintenance-System Determinants of Child Development among the Logoli of Kenya." Paper presented at the American Anthropological Association meetings, Washington, D.C., 1967.

Murdock, George Peter. *Social Structure.* New York: Macmillan, 1949.

Murdock, George Peter. "World Ethnographic Sample." *American Anthropologist,* 59 (1957): 664–687.

Pospisil, Leopold. "Kapauku Papuan Economy." Yale University Publications in Anthropology, 67. New Haven: Department of Anthropology, Yale University, 1963.

Rose, Frederick G. G. *The Wind of Change in Central Australia: The Aborigines at Angus Downs, 1962.* Berlin: Akademie Verlag, 1965.

Schmidt, Wilhelm S. V. D. "Das Mutterrecht." *Studia Instituti Anthropos,* 10. Vienna-Mödlingen: Missions-druckerei St. Gabriel, 1955.

Seaver, James E. *A Narrative of the Life of Mrs. Mary Jemison.* 1823. Reprinted New York: Corinth Books, 1961.

Spiro, M. E. *Kibbutz: Venture in Utopia.* Cambridge: Harvard University Press, 1956.

When the feminist movement was reborn in the late 60s, it was dismissed by many as a passing fad on the part of a small group of upper middle class radical women. The movement has since confounded its detractors and surprised even its supporters by its widespread popularity. Women's groups have sprung up all over the country. And surveys by women's magazines show that the ideas of women's liberation have had a pronounced effect on women who do not identify with "women's lib." The present article reports on the emergence of feminism in a group of middle-aged lower middle class women.

What Do I Do for the Next 20 Years?

Susan Jacoby

"I'm short, fat and 45."

Rose Danielli digs her fork into a large piece of Sara Lee cherry cheese-cake as she begins to describe herself at the first meeting of a women's consciousness-raising group last September. Twelve women are crowded into the living room of a small red-brick house in the East Flatbush section of Brooklyn; many are old friends who have shared senior proms, weddings, births, miscarriages, family deaths and all of the other minor and major

From "What Do I Do for the Next Twenty Years?" by Susan Jacoby, *The New York Times Magazine,* June 17, 1973. © 1973 by The New York Times Company. Reprinted by permission.

events of life in a close-knit working-class community where neighbors still care about one another. Now they are supporting one another in a new experience: an effort to expand their middle-aged lives beyond the comfortable roles of wife, mother and grandmother. No group of women seems further removed from the worlds of Gloria Steinem and Betty Friedan, *Ms.* magazine, marriage contracts, "alternative life-styles," sexual experimentation and all of the upper-middle-class paraphernalia frequently associated with the feminist movement.

"My mother-in-law asked me the other day if I was one of those 'women's libbers,' " continues Mrs. Danielli, "and I told her I had always been something of a 'libber' even though I like being called 'Mrs.' She said she guessed I was telling the truth, because she remembered how hard I fought for my girls to go to college. My husband and I never went to college, and everyone in the family thought our three girls would go to work to help put my son Johnny through.

"Way back when the kids were in grade school, I told my husband, 'Joe, if one of our kids is going to college, all of them are going. Your girls aren't gonna have 10 children like your mama—they've gotta do something with their lives just like our boy.'

"Both of our families were shocked when our oldest girl went off to college—Joe's papa kept asking if we didn't need the extra money she could bring in working as a typist. We needed money, all right, but I never gave in—even when times were toughest and we were eating spaghetti without meat sauce three nights a week."

There is a note of solid satisfaction in Rose Danielli's voice as she finishes both her story and the cheesecake. The women have agreed to begin their first session by describing the most significant failures and successes of their lives; they will start to talk about the future after evaluating the past. The old friendship and neighborly bonds give their discussion a more comfortable aura than the sort that usually prevails in Manhattan consciousness-raising sessions, which frequently reflect the fragmented and transient nature of affluent high-rise apartment living.

"I was going to break the rules and interrupt," admits Alice Martino, a construction worker's wife who grew up on the same block with Rose in East Flatbush. "I thought Rose might go on and on about being fat, as though there were nothing more to her story."

The life stories outlined by the women have many common elements. The women are all in their 40's; most grew up in first- and second-generation Italian or Jewish immigrant homes. A few have lived in East Flatbush since they were children, and the rest came from nearby blue-collar neighborhoods. Most of the women graduated from high school, went to work for a year or two at poorly paid jobs, married by age 20 and quickly started having children. Only two of the 12 had any education beyond high school. Rose Danielli's background is typical; she worked as a telephone operator for a year before marrying Joe, a telephone installer, when they were both 19.

The husbands are blue-collar union men or white-collar workers employed by the city government; their general income range is between $9,000 and $14,000 a year. Most of the families have at least three children. Homemade soups and clothes are a necessary economy for them rather than an expression of the "traditional female role." Their houses represent the only important financial investment of their lives and are maintained with appropriate care—postage-stamp lawns raked free of leaves, living-room sofas glazed with plastic slipcovers and reserved for company, starched kitchen curtains, home freezers stocked with the specials the women unearth in numerous grocery stores on Saturday mornings. They worry in equal measure about the rising price of ground chuck, the fact that so many of their grown children are leaving the old neighborhood, and how to get along with the blacks who are moving into the area. A movie and dinner in a local Chinese or Italian restaurant is a once-a-month event. Manhattan is "the city," a place to be visited on wedding anniversaries for dinner and a hotel floor show.

Whatever their problems, the women love their husbands and are not about to leave them. They do not expect to liberate themselves by living alone, although they understand why some younger women find marriage an unsatisfactory state. They have neither the education nor the work experience to be tapped as token women for high-powered jobs in high-powered companies. One woman in the group says she is waiting breathlessly for the day when the local 6 o'clock news will feature a broadcaster who is not only black and female but over 40, thereby providing on-screen representation for three oppressed groups instead of two.

Nevertheless, the women are convinced that they can build a future different from the traditional path laid out by their mothers and grandmothers. The feminist movement is responsible in large measure for their belief that they can change the course of their middle-aged lives.

The movement was gaining strength and national publicity at a time when the women who make up the East Flatbush group began to face the void most full-time mothers experience after their children grow up and leave home. Their comments in the group sessions indicate that two main concerns spurred their interest in feminism: the feeling that society in general, and their husbands in particular, no longer viewed them as sexually interesting or even sexually functioning women, and the realization that they were "out of a job" in the same sense as a middle-aged man who is fired by his employer of 20 years.

The idea of a formal consciousness-raising group was suggested last fall by Lillian Schwartz, the only one of the women with any extensive contacts outside the neighborhood. She had been active for many years in citywide organizations concerned with the public schools, and she was hearing more and more about the feminist movement from the women she met in the course of her volunteer work. At the same time, her three closest friends in East Flatbush were constantly mulling over the question of what to do with the next 20 or 30 years of their lives. They agreed that an organized group might help them figure out what to do and quickly recruited enough interested women to make up a manageable dozen. Lillian hunted down a copy of *Ms.* with advice on how to form a consciousness-raising group.

The most important decision at the first meeting was that the sessions would be held regularly on Tuesday nights. Except in emergencies, they would not be subject to interference by children and husbands who had other activities in mind. At the second session, several women reported with glee that the announcement of a regular meeting had caused a storm in their homes. "In our house, my husband expects me home every evening," explained one woman. "That is, unless he decides to go bowling. Then I can go to the movies by myself or out to a neighbor's."

Some of the husbands resented the decision to regularize the meetings because they had chosen to view the group as just another *Kaffeeklatsch*. The reactions of the men included bitter opposition, secret sabotage, amused resignation and quiet support. "My poor man asked what he should tell the neighbors if they called and asked for me on Tuesday night," recalled a woman whose husband is part-owner of a Jewish delicatessen. "I told him to tell anyone who called the truth, that I'm working out what to do with my life. He said the hell he would, he'd tell them I was doing something for the temple."

Sarah Thomas, the 40-year-old wife of a policeman, had the biggest problem: Every time she planned to leave the house for her women's group, her husband had a minor household accident requiring her attention. The women were appropriately sympathetic when she arrived an hour late for the second meeting because her husband's ankle needed soaking after he twisted it on the front stoop. Before the next meeting, Sergeant Thomas carved a deep slice in his thumb with a potato peeler. When he poured boiling water over his hand, Sarah and the other women began to suspect the accidents were not entirely accidental.

At the fifth meeting, Sarah reported that "I told him since he was an experienced police officer he was used to dealing with emergencies and I was sure he could take care of a slight burn by himself. I figure if I just sail out of the house anyway, he'll stop having these accidents." (She proved a poor prophet, because she continued to attend the women's group meetings and, as of June, her husband was still chalking up at least two accidents a month.)

Most of the women spent considerable time talking about personal sexual problems during the early weeks of the group. In this respect, they resemble the younger wives, single women and divorcees who make up the membership of most consciousness-raising groups. But they are of a more reserved and modest generation than the younger feminists. No one mentions foreplay or sexual positions. If the East Flatbush women are worried about orgasms, they do not talk about it. An occasional mention of premarital sex produces flushes of embarrassment. But they are all acutely aware of the unfulfilled sexual desires that seem to be the lot of many middle-aged women in American society. To a greater or lesser degree, most of the women reported the same problem: The frequency of sexual relations with their husbands diminished drastically after they entered their 40's. For the unluckiest women, sex—like a night out in "the city"—became an event reserved for birthdays and anniversaries. "It's more like a monument than an act of love," one commented.

"I just want to be recognized as a woman," said Ruth Levine, a mother of five whose 100-pound figure and short black hair make her look a decade younger than her 46 years. Her husband is a cab driver who has worked 14- to 16-hour days throughout most of their married life.

"I'm going to be alive for another 20 or 30 years," she observed. "My husband and I sleep together maybe once a month. Oh, it's not that he wants another woman—I don't think that at all. It's just that . . . I'm familiar. Men really don't think of women in their 40's that way, in a sexual way. I know it isn't the way I look—I'm prettier now than I was when I had five children under the age of 10 to run after all day. I don't feel like having orgies, but I'm too young for this . . . this . . . it's almost an end to sex. I don't know how to make my husband realize this without hurting him. I don't want him to feel I'm making demands he can't meet. And I don't even know if I have the courage to talk about it with him, after all these years of letting the man lead the way. . . ."

Another woman sadly recalled a night when she put her arms around her husband while he was watching television and he pushed her away. "He said, 'Help, I married a sex maniac.' He made it sound like a joke, but I knew he was only half-teasing. Then he said, 'You know, Debbie, we're really getting too old for much fooling around. Our kids are going to be getting married pretty soon.' "

Alice Martino mocked the sex advice offered by conventional women's magazines. "They tell you to be careful to keep up your looks, don't walk around in front of your husband in rollers, go out and buy a new black negligee. But those little gems are stupid, because most women who like men have been following them for years. My hair is combed and my fanny is still pretty firm and I don't wear flannel pajamas to bed. It's the idea of settling into a new role after you get past a certain age that's so hard to fight.

"You know, when you were 20 the thing to do was make love and have children. Our eldest boy is getting married next month. The other night Rick said to me, "Well, pretty soon I'll be able to call you grandma.' I said he would over my dead body, that I would have murdered him if he'd called me 'Ma' while our kids were growing up. He laughed and said he was a fool, because he'd forgotten the time I shut him out of the bedroom after he gave me a new baby carriage for my birthday. A baby carriage. For my birthday!"

With the exception of Rose Danielli, who correctly surmised that losing 60 pounds would make a major change in her own sense of physical well-being as well as her husband's sexual behavior, the women agreed that spending money on "a new look" was not the answer to a lagging sex life. As a group, they were somewhat more tolerant of the sexual insecurities of middle-aged males than the younger women in consciousness-raising groups. Some of them compared the fatigue of their husbands with the exhaustion they felt when they were looking after small children.

"Life plays a dirty trick on women," said Ann Nussbaum, whose husband is a bookkeeper with the city Finance Administration. "The men think you're gorgeous when you're too young to know anything about life. How well I remember how hard it was to take any interest in my husband when I had been changing diapers all day. Now I have much more time and interest for sex, but my husband is the one who's beat. He does tax returns to make extra money on the side—I know he just feels like rolling over and going to sleep at the end of the day.

"One of the things I feel I have to get across to him is that being physically affectionate with each other doesn't have to mean sex; he doesn't have to feel all this pressure that men seem to feel about performance. I agree with Ruth that it's hard to talk about these things after a lifetime of being silent, but I don't see how we can get anywhere unless we speak up about what's bothering us."

As the group sessions continued, most of the women reported considerable success in their attempts to talk about sex with their husbands. They began seeking out more sex information from medical studies and books on women's health by feminist writers. Several women said their husbands were especially impressed by the Masters and Johnson finding that normal men and women can continue to enjoy sex into their 60's. Said Rose Danielli: "Joe told me, 'You know, Rose, we were brought up in ignorance even if we did manage to have four kids. This Masters-Johnson thing you're telling me about—I thought a wife would think her husband was a dirty old man if he kept trying to take her to bed when they were 50 years old.' "

One woman who was going through menopause reported that her husband was greatly relieved to learn she could still function sexually. "Like most of us here, I never really talked about these things with my husband. When I finally got up the nerve to say something, I found out he thought the change of life meant that a woman would find it difficult—physically difficult, that is—to have sex. I told him I was looking forward to the change because it meant I wouldn't have to worry about getting pregnant anymore. He said he'd never looked at it that way."

Many members of the group linked their sexual plight with the more general emptiness of middle-aged women who have devoted their entire lives to their families. "My nights will take care of themselves if I have something to occupy my days," said one. By December—the third month of the group sessions—most of the discussions centered around the need to find some sort of work.

Ruth Levine, who had never worked outside her home, surprised the rest of the group by becoming the first to take the plunge into the job market. She applied for a job as a file clerk in a large advertising agency and was hired with a warning from the personnel department that "most of the girls on your floor will be 25 years younger than you are."

Feminist opponents of job discrimination are correct in their assertion that file clerking is a thankless, dead-end task reserved by large companies for women. However, the upper-middle-class, college-educated feminists often fail to realize that a woman with no training may look upon a mundane job as an opportunity rather than an insult. For Ruth Levine, who had rarely left her neighborhood for 25 years, the file clerk's job was an important step into a wider world.

"Well, I know it's not much of a job in the eyes of anyone else," she reported to her group after she had been working for a month. "Even the secretaries look down on file clerks—especially a file clerk in her 40's. And I agree with some of the stuff I read in *Ms.* these days—a man, even a dumb one, would never have to take one of these jobs. But to me the job is something. Someone has to do this kind of work. I never went to college, I never worked before I was married, and I don't really have the training for anything more. What do I get out of the job? For one thing, I get to meet a lot of different people who give me new things to think about.

"The young girls ask me, 'Mrs. Levine, why are you working at your age when you have a husband and children? We're just waiting to get married and out of this hole.' I tell them I'm working because it's better than sitting home and being a vegetable, and that they should get themselves some more training or they'll be file clerks 20 years from now, whether they get married or not. I don't see any practical advice for girls like this in any of the magazines, including *Ms.* and *Cosmopolitan*. Cosmo tells girls how to put rouge on their breasts and *Ms.* tells you how to start your own business, but no one tells file clerks that life will stretch into a big zero unless they improve their skills."

The other important thing Ruth gets out of her job is money: She brings home more than $90 a week after taxes and Social Security withholding. "It makes me feel both that I'm independent and that I'm contributing something to the household," she said.

Sarah, the wife of the accident-prone police sergeant, broke in: "Whenever I talk about getting a job, my husband says I'm contributing something by staying home and taking care of the house."

"I know, I know, I've heard it all," Ruth replied. "My Hal said exactly the same thing. He said it made him feel like a second-class man, that he couldn't take care of his family by himself. I said, 'Hal, our youngest kid is 16. What am I going to do with myself for the next 20 years?' I told him I'd feel like we were pulling together—the way we did when the kids were little —if I could bring in a little money to make our lives easier.

"At first we agreed the money would go into a special account in my name, so it would be clear he was still paying for everything. Finally Hal saw the money was piling up and it was crazy not to use it. We put part of it into the regular budget and are saving the rest for a vacation."

Ruth reported that her husband's attitude toward her job changed slowly but definitely. He became less concerned about the fact that she was making money of her own and began to cut down on his own 14-hour work days in his taxi. The most unexpected dividend was a significant improvement in their sex life.

"I can't believe it. We have a sex life again. For the first time in years Hal can go out with me once a week; he comes home at 7 o'clock instead of midnight. That little bit of extra money makes a big difference to us. We go to bed together more than we did for the last 10 years.

"Hal and I have never been much for talking about sex, but one night he turned to me in bed and said, 'You know, Ruthie, I was just too beat to pay attention to you this way. I didn't realize it until you went to work and took some of the money pressure off me.' I said, 'You know, Hal, I didn't realize it either.'"

Ruth is taking a shorthand course so that she can move into a better-paying secretarial job next fall. After she took the first step, four other women in the group found jobs. Two returned to the secretarial work they had done before they were married, one found an opening as a teacher aide in the Head Start program for preschool children, and another put her fluent Italian to work as an interpreter for older immigrants in their dealing with city agencies. Two women in the group decided they would go to college and were accepted in adult-education programs leading toward a bachelor's degree.

The women who plan to enter college are undergoing profound changes that have also made a deep impact on their husbands. "I don't think I could take file clerking," announced Alice Martino one night, "but I'm not prepared for anything else. I always wanted to go to college, and I think that's just what I'm going to do."

Unlike many of the women, Alice has no serious financial problems. Her husband, Rick, earns more than $16,000 a year as a construction worker; they live rent- and mortgage-free in a house Alice's mother left them when she died. Their children are between ages 18 and 24, and are either currently attending college or have graduated.

Alice is enrolling in the highly respected adult-education program at Brooklyn College. After considering several possibilities, she decided on teaching as a career because she felt it offered the easiest entree for an older woman. She plans to make a specialty of speech and reading therapy because there is a shortage of trained personnel in those areas despite an over-all teacher surplus.

Contradicting the hard-hat stereotype, Alice's husband turned out to be more favorably disposed toward the feminist movement than the other women's husbands. In fact, he decided to follow his wife's example. "He confessed he was jealous of my plans to go to college," Alice said, "and then he decided he was being stupid because he could do it too. College was never a possibility for him when he was younger—he was the oldest son and his parents needed money very badly. He's thought about architectural engineering for years; he always said he knew more about putting up buildings than the engineers on the job.

"Anyway, he said he always assumed a man couldn't change his life in midstream but he figured if women were trying to do it, why not him. It won't be easy for him trying to build a new career when he's over 40, but it won't be easy for me either. We have it planned. I'll be teaching before Rick gets his engineering degree, and he'll have a pension because he's been in the union since he was 18. We'll have plenty of money to get along on while he looks for an employer who doesn't think a man is a fossil when he gets to be 40. As far as my teaching goes, I'll be less of a fossil than the younger teachers."

One of the more conservative women in the group told Alice she sounded like a starry-eyed 18-year-old. "I feel like one," she replied. "I haven't been this optimistic about life since I was 18."

Joan Loewenstein, who is also entering Brooklyn College next fall, was equally optimistic. She hopes to become a statistician or a computer programer. "A lot of people have been telling me I'm out of my mind to be thinking about this big a change 'at your age.' Oh, they love to use that phrase—'at your age.' But I've been lucky like Alice—my husband has been wonderful. His partner in the deli started this business about my age, and he said, "What do you think she should do at her age, buy a cemetery plot?' Abe is convinced I have a talent for math because I've always helped him keep the books for the store, done our income-tax return, that sort of thing.

"You know, we had a joint checking account all of our lives, but Abe always gave me the household money every week. I never wrote a check for anything unless it was something like the mortgage payment. I would never have bought myself a new dress without checking with him first. Abe has been doing some thinking on his own about Women's Lib. He says it suddently hits him how stupid it was for him to be doling out household money to me when I keep the books better than he does.

"So the other night he tells me, 'Joan, I'm not giving you money for the house anymore, you take what you need. Here I am, a man who's been letting a woman keep his books for 20 years, and still telling her what to spend each week. I know what I got out of it, but what did you get? I never really wanted to be cheap, it was just the way my parents did things.'

"You know, I was surprised at all this from Abe. Then I started thinking about that question—what *did* I get out of it. Well, I told Abe I was able to save some money from my allowance on the sly. He said, 'So, now you'll save on the open.' I guess it was sort of comfortable, acting like a little girl about money. Anyway, it sure won't do for a college girl—oops, woman—who wants to program computers."

Not all the women have had as much success in changing their own lives or the attitudes of their husbands. Judith Katz, who worked as a secretary before her marriage 20 years ago, encountered stiff opposition when she went back to work in the counseling office of a Brooklyn junior high school. Her husband especially resents the fact that she wanted a job enough to take an opening in a ghetto school with a tough reputation. As an expression of his disapproval, he refuses to ride the subway with his wife in the morning. Another of the women, an accountant's wife who is already attending classes at Brooklyn College, did not speak to her husband for several weeks after he told her, "You're too feather-brained to finish cleaning the house, much less four years of college."

In general, the East Flatbush men who disapprove of feminism express their reactions more openly than the professional husbands of upper-middle-class women who are the most vocal and visible participants in the movement. College-educated men are often reluctant to attack women's liberation in principle, but their practical behavior is another matter. Judging from the wide variety of male reactions described by the Flatbush wives, Middle-American men are no more or no less disturbed than other American men when the women in their lives try to break out of the traditional female pattern.

The East Flatbush women have considerable difficulty identifying with the widely publicized leaders of the movement. Said one: "I confess I don't feel much of a sense of sisterhood when I see pictures of Gloria Steinem with her streaked hair and slinky figure. I feel somehow that these people don't know how it is to be getting older with very little money and education. They have it a lot better than we do—it's not true that we're all in the same boat."

Another woman disagreed: "Well, there's one thing we all have in common—we're all afraid of muggers and rapists when we walk down a dark street at night. And that's something we have in common with the colored women who live right here in East Flatbush, even though most of us are better off financially than they are."

The women do identify with the movement on a variety of specific issues— child day-care centers, equal pay for equal work, the right to abortion and contraceptive information, the need to educate young girls to think of themselves as individuals in their own right instead of viewing themselves only as future wives and mothers. Several of the women now spend considerable time trying to introduce these reformist ideas into the conservative social environment of East Flatbush. One of their immediate goals is a health information service for girls and women of all ages; they feel that most East Flatbush women are unlikely to use the referral services now available in Manhattan. Rose Danielli had hoped to organize such a service through her church but ran head-on into a clash with her priest over contraceptive information.

"My husband said, 'Oh, Rose, don't get into a battle with Father ———.' Then he said, 'I give up. If you were willing to do battle with my mama you won't stop with the priest.'

"But Joe doesn't really mind the way I feel—in fact, I think he's kind of proud. This year our oldest girl gets her doctor's degree from Stanford, our boy gets his master's and our second youngest girl graduates from Hunter College. Joe told his parents the other night that sending all of his kids through college was the proudest accomplishment of his life, and that he wouldn't have done it if I hadn't insisted.

"We had to fight our girls, too, until they were old enough to have some sense. They used to remind me that I got married when I was 19 and their dad and I were happy. I just told them their grandparents never finished high school and they were happy too, but it's not progress if the next generation lives the same way. To me, that's what Women's Lib is all about—progress. In small steps, maybe, but still progress."

Next fall, the East Flatbush group will take in five new women because several of the founding members will be too busy with jobs and college courses. All of the women call that progress.

Chapter 6

Man in Society

The recent ferment over women's place and roles has inspired new ways of thinking about what it means to be a man as well as what it means to be a woman. The authors of this article—both males—argue that in learning to be a man in American society, a little boy is taught to be tough and to avoid showing emotions, especially tenderness or sadness. This inexpressiveness comes in two versions: the cowboy and the playboy. The cowboy possesses tender feelings towards women, although he cannot express them, while the playboy is unfeeling as well as outwardly cool. Both forms of inexpressiveness can create difficulties in marriage, since companionship and affection are the main goals of marriage in contemporary society.

The Inexpressive Male: A Tragedy of American Society

Jack O. Balswick and Charles W. Peek

The problem of what it means to be "male" and "female" is a problem which is faced and dealt with in its own way in every society. Through cross-cultural research one now surmises that culture rather than "nature" is the major influence in determining the temperamental differences between the sexes. It may be no accident that a woman, Margaret Mead, did the classic study demonstrating that temperamental differences between the sexes are explained very little in terms of innateness, but rather in terms of culture. In her book, *Sex and Temperament*, Mead reported on the differences in sex roles for three New Guinea societies. Using ethnocentric western standards in defining sex roles, she found that the ideal sex role for both the male and female was essentially "feminine" among the Arapesh, "masculine" among

Reprinted by permission from "The Inexpressive Male: A Tragedy of American Society" by Jack O. Balswick and Charles W. Peek, *The Family Coordinator*, October 1971, pp. 363–368.

the Mundugumor, and "feminine" for the male and "masculine" for the female among the Tchambuli. The Tchambuli represents a society that defines sex roles in a complete reversal of the traditional distinctions made between masculine and feminine roles in the United States.

It is the purpose of this paper to consider a particular temperament trait that often characterizes the male in American society. As sex role distinctions have developed in America, the male sex role, as compared to the female sex role, carries with it prescriptions which encourage inexpressiveness. In some of its extreme contemporary forms, the inexpressive male has even come to be glorified as the epitome of a real man. This will be discussed later in the paper when two types of inexpressive male are examined.

The Creation of the Inexpressive Male

Children, from the time they are born, both explicitly and implicitly are taught how to be a man or how to be a woman. While the girl is taught to act "feminine" and to desire "feminine" objects, the boy is taught how to be a man. In learning to be a man, the boy in American society comes to value expressions of masculinity and devalue expressions of femininity. Masculinity is expressed largely through physical courage, toughness, competitiveness, and aggressiveness, whereas femininity is, in contrast, expressed largely through gentleness, expressiveness, and responsiveness. When a young boy begins to express his emotions through crying, his parents are quick to assert, "You're a big boy and big boys don't cry." Parents often use the term, "he's all boy," in reference to their son, and by this term usually refer to behavior which is an expression of aggressiveness, getting into mischief, getting dirty, etc., but never use the term to denote behavior which is an expression of affection, tenderness, or emotion. What parents are really telling their son is that a real man does not show his emotions and if he is a real man he will not allow his emotions to be expressed. These outward expressions of emotion are viewed as a sign of femininity, and undesirable for a male.

Is it any wonder, then, that during the most emotional peak of a play or movie, when many in the audience have lumps in their throats and tears in their eyes, that the adolescent boy guffaws loudly or quickly suppresses any tears which may be threatening to emerge, thus demonstrating to the world that he is above such emotional feeling?

The Inexpressive Male as a Single Man

At least two basic types of inexpressive male seem to result from this socialization process: the cowboy and the playboy. Manville (1969) has referred to the *cowboy type* in terms of a "John Wayne Neurosis" which stresses the strong, silent, and two-fisted male as the 100 percent American he-man. For present purposes, it is especially in his relationship with women that the John Wayne neurosis is particularly significant in representing many American males. As portrayed by Wayne in any one of his many type-cast roles, the mark of a real man is that he does not show any tenderness or affection toward girls because his culturally-acquired male image dictates that such a show of emotions would be distinctly unmanly. If he does have anything to do with girls, it is on a "man to man" basis: the girl is treated roughly (but not sadistically), with little hint of gentleness or affection. As Manville puts it:

> The on-screen John Wayne doesn't feel comfortable around women. He does like them sometimes—God knows he's not *queer*. But at the right time, and in the right place—which he chooses. And always with his car/horse parked directly outside, in/on which he will ride away to his more important business back in Marlboro country. (1969, p. 111)

Alfred Auerback, a psychiatrist, has commented more directly (1970) on the cowboy type. He describes the American male's inexpressiveness with women as part of the "cowboy syndrome." He quite rightly states that "the cowboy in moving pictures has conveyed the image of the rugged 'he-man,' strong, resilient, resourceful, capable of coping with overwhelming odds. His attitude toward women is courteous but reserved." As the cowboy equally loved his girlfriend and his horse, so the present-day American male loves his car or motorcycle and his girlfriend. Basic to both these descriptions is the notion that the cowboy does have feelings toward women but does not express them, since ironically such expression would conflict with his image of what a male is.

The *playboy type* has recently been epitomized in *Playboy* magazine and by James Bond. As with the cowboy type, he is resourceful and shrewd, and interacts with his girlfriend with a certain detachment which is expressed as "playing it cool." While Bond's relationship with women is more in terms of a Don Juan, he still treats women with an air of emotional detachment and independence similar to that of the cowboy. The playboy departs from the cowboy, however, in that he is also "non-feeling." Bond and the playboy he caricatures are in a sense "dead" inside. They have no emotional feelings toward women, while Wayne, although unwilling and perhaps unable to express them, does have such feelings. Bond rejects women as women, treating them as consumer commodities; Wayne puts women on a pedestal. The playboy's relationship with women represents the culmination of Fromm's description of a marketing-oriented personality in which a person comes to see both himself and others as persons to be manipulated and exploited. Sexuality is reduced to a packageable consumption item which the playboy can handle because it demands no responsibility. The woman, in the process, becomes reduced to a playboy accessory. A successful "love affair" is one in which the bed was shared, but the playboy emerges having avoided personal involvement or a shared relationship with the woman.

The playboy, then, in part is the old cowboy in modern dress. Instead of the crude mannerisms of John Wayne, the playboy is a skilled manipulator of women, knowing when to turn the lights down, what music to play on the stereo, which drinks to serve, and what topics of conversation to pursue. The playboy, however, is not a perfect likeness; for unlike the cowboy, he does not seem to care for the women from whom he withholds his emotions. Thus, the inexpressive male as a single man comes in two types: the inexpressive feeling man (the cowboy) and the inexpressive non-feeling man (the playboy).

The Inexpressive Male as a Married Man

When the inexpressive male marries, his inexpressiveness can become highly dysfunctional to his marital relationship *if* he continues to apply it across-the-board to all women, his wife included. The modern American family places a greater demand upon the marriage relationship than did the family of the past. In the typical marriage of 100 or even 50 years ago, the roles of both the husband and the wife were clearly defined as demanding, task-oriented functions. If the husband successfully performed the role of provider and protector of his wife and family and if the wife performed the role of homemaker and mother to her children, chances were the marriage was defined as successful, both from a personal and a societal point of view. The traditional task functions which in the past were performed by the husband and wife are today often taken care of by individuals and organizations outside the home. Concomitant with the decline of the task functions in marriage has been the increase in the importance of the companionship and affectionate function in marriage. As Blood and Wolfe (1960, p. 172) concluded in their study of the modern American marriage, "companionship has emerged as the most valued aspect of marriage today."

As American society has become increasingly mechanized and depersonalized, the family remains as one of the few social groups where what sociologists call the primary relationship has still managed to survive. As such, a greater and greater demand has been placed upon the modern family and especially the modern marriage to provide for affection and companionship. Indeed, it is highly plausible to explain the increased rate of divorce during the last 70 years, not in terms of a breakdown in marriage relationships, but instead, as resulting from the increased load which marriage has been asked to carry. When the husband and wife no longer find affection and companionship from their marriage relationship, they most likely question the wisdom of attempting to continue in their conjugal relationship.

When affection is gone, the main reason for the marriage relationship disappears.

Thus, within the newly defined affectively-oriented marriage relationship male inexpressiveness toward *all* women, wife included, would be dysfunctional. But what may happen for many males is that through progressively more serious involvements with women (such as going steady, being pinned, engagement, and the honeymoon period of marriage), they begin to make some exceptions. That is, they may learn to be *situationally rather than totally inexpressive,* inexpressive toward women in most situations but not in all. As the child who learns a rule and then, through further experience, begins to understand the exceptions to it, many American males may pick up the principle of inexpressiveness toward women, discovering its exceptions as they become more and more experienced in the full range of man-woman relationships. Consequently, they may become more expressive toward their wives while remaining essentially inexpressive toward other women; they learn that the conjugal relationship is one situation that is an exception to the cultural requirement of male inexpressiveness. Thus, what was once a double *sexual* standard, where men had one standard of sexual conduct toward their fiancee or wife and another toward other women, may now be primarily a double *emotional* standard, where men learn to be expressive toward their fiancee or wife but remain inexpressive toward women in general.

To the extent that such situational inexpressiveness exists among males, it should be functional to the maintenance of the marriage relationship. Continued inexpressiveness by married males toward women other than their wives would seem to prohibit their forming meaningful relationships with these women. Such a situation would seem to be advantageous to preserving their marital relationships, since "promiscuous" expressiveness toward other women could easily threaten the stability of these companionship-oriented marital relationships.

In short, the authors' suggestion is that situational inexpressiveness, in which male expressiveness is essentially limited to the marital relationship, may be one of the basic timbers shoring up many American marriages, especially if indications of increasing extramarital sexual relations are correct. In a sense, then, the consequences of situational inexpressiveness for marital relationships do not seem very different from those of prostitution down through the centuries, where prostitution provided for extra-marital sex under circumstances which discouraged personal affection toward the female partner strong enough to undermine the marital relationship. In the case of the situationally inexpressive husband, his inexpressiveness in relations with women other than his wife may serve as a line of defense against the possible negative consequences of such involvement toward marital stability. By acting as the cowboy or playboy, therefore, the married male may effectively rob extramarital relationships of their expressiveness and thus preserve his marital relationship.

The inexpressiveness which the American male early acquires may be bothersome in that he has to partially unlearn it in order to effectively relate to his wife. However, if he is successful in partially unlearning it (or learning a few exceptions to it), then it can be highly functional to maintaining the conjugal relationship.

But what if the husband does not partially unlearn his inexpressiveness? Within the newly defined expressive function of the marriage relationship, he is likely to be found inadequate. The possibility of an affectionate and companionship conjugal relationship carries with it the assumption that both the husband and wife are bringing into marriage the expressive capabilities to make such a relationship work. This being the case, American society is ironically shortchanging males in terms of their ability to fulfill this role expectation. Thus, society inconsistently teaches the male that to be masculine is to be inexpressive, while at the same time, expectations in the marital role are defined in terms of sharing affection and companionship which involves the ability to communicate and express feelings. What exists, apparently, is another example of a discontinuity in cultural conditioning of which Benedict (1938) spoke more than 30 years ago.

Conclusion and Summary

It has been suggested that many American males are incapable of expressing themselves emotionally to a woman, and that this inexpressiveness is a result of the way society socialized males into their sex role. However, there is an alternative explanation which should be explored, namely, that the learning by the male of his sex role may not actually result in his inability to be expressive, but rather only in his thinking that he is not supposed to be expressive. Granted, according to the first explanation, the male cannot express himself precisely because he was taught that he was not supposed to be expressive, but in this second explanation inexpressiveness is a result of present perceived expectations and not a psychological condition which resulted from past socialization. The male perceives cultural expectations as saying, "don't express yourself to women," and although the male may be capable of such expressiveness, he "fits" into cultural expectations. In the case of the married male, where familial norms do call for expressiveness to one's wife, it may be that the expectations for the expression of emotions to his wife are not communicated to him.

There has been a trickle of evidence which would lend support to the first explanation, which stresses the male's incapacity to be expressive. Several studies (Balswick, 1970; Hurvitz, 1964; Komarovsky, 1962; Rainwater, 1965) have suggested that especially among the lowly educated, it is the wife playing the feminine role who is often disappointed in the lack of emotional concern shown by her husband. The husband, on the other hand, cannot understand the relatively greater concern and emotional expressiveness which his wife desires, since he does not usually feel this need himself. As a result of her research, Komarovsky (1962, p. 156) has suggested that "the ideal of masculinity into which . . . (men are) . . . socialized inhibits expressiveness both directly, with its emphasis on reserve, and indirectly, by identifying personal interchange with the feminine role." Balswick (1970) found that males are less capable than females of expressing or receiving companionship support from their spouses. His research also supports the view that inadequacy of expressiveness is greatest for the less educated males. Although inexpressiveness may be found among males at all socioeconomic levels, it is especially among the lower class male that expressiveness is seen as being inconsistent with his defined masculine role.

There may be some signs that conditions which have contributed toward the creation of the inexpressive male are in the process of decline. The deemphasis in distinctiveness in dress and fashions between the sexes, as exemplified in the "hippy" movement, can be seen as a reaction against the rigidly defined distinctions between the sexes which have characterized American society. The sexless look, as presently being advanced in high fashion, is the logical end reaction to a society which has superficially created strong distinctions between the sexes. Along with the blurring of sexual distinctions in fashion may very well be the shattering of the strong, silent male as a glorified type. There is already evidence of sharp criticisms of the inexpressive male and exposure of him as constituting a "hangup." Marriage counselors, sensitivity group leaders, "hippies," and certainly youth in general, are critical of inexpressiveness, and seek candid honesty in interpersonal relations. Should these views permeate American society, the inexpressive male may well come to be regarded as a pathetic tragedy instead of the epitome of masculinity, and fade from the American scene. Not all may applaud his departure, however. While those interested in more satisfactory male-female relationships, marital and otherwise, will probably gladly see him off, those concerned with more stable marital relationships may greet his departure less enthusiastically. Although it should remove an important barrier to satisfaction in all male-female relationships via an increase in the male's capacity for emotional response toward females, by the same token it also may remove a barrier against emotional entanglement in relations with females outside marital relationships and thus threaten the stability of marriages. If one finds the inexpressive male no longer present one of these days, then, it will be interesting to observe whether any gains in the stability of marriage due to increased male expressiveness *within* this relationship will be enough to offset losses in stability emanating from increasing displays of male expressiveness *outside* it.

References

Auerback, Alfred. "The Cowboy Syndrome." Summary of research contained in a personal letter from the author, 1970.

Balswick, Jack O. "The Effect of Spouse Companionship Support on Employment Success." *Journal of Marriage and the Family*, 32 (1970): 212–215.

Benedict, Ruth. "Continuities and Discontinuities in Cultural Conditioning." *Psychiatry*, 1 (1938): 161–167.

Blood, Robert, and Donald Wolfe. *Husbands and Wives: The Dynamic of Married Living*. Glencoe, Ill.: The Free Press, 1960.

Cox, Harvey. "Playboy's Doctrine of Male." In *Witness to a Generation: Significant Writings from Christianity and Crisis (1941–1966)*, edited by Wayne H. Cowan. New York: Bobbs-Merrill Company, 1966.

Hurvitz, Nathan. "Marital Strain in the Blue-Collar Family." In *Blue-Collar World*, edited by Arthur Shostak and William Gomberg. Englewood Cliffs, N.J.: Prentice-Hall, 1964.

Komarovsky, M. *Blue-Collar Marriage*. New York: Random House, 1962.

Manville, W. H. "The Locker Room Boys." *Cosmopolitan*, 166 (1969), no. 11: 110–115.

Mead, Margaret. *Sex and Temperament in Three Primitive Societies*. New York: William Morrow and Company, 1935.

Popplestone, John. "The Horseless Cowboys." *Transaction*, 3 (1966): 25–27.

Rainwater, Lee. *Family Design: Marital Sexuality, Family Size, and Contraception*. Chicago: Aldine, 1965.

In her earlier work, the author analyzed the effects on college women of the contradictory demands on them to achieve academically and also to fulfill traditional feminine roles. In this article, the focus is on men's attitudes toward sex roles. Komarovsky finds that while there is abstract affirmation of the value of equality between the sexes in her sample of Ivy League male seniors, emotionally these young men are still attached to traditional attitudes and patterns of behavior. For example, many felt that the man should be the intellectual superior of his female companion. Attitudes toward working wives were ambivalent and inconsistent; the men interviewed expressed negative images of both housewives and career women. The article illustrates the complexities of achieving attitude change in an area laden with profound personal implications.

Cultural Contradictions and Sex Roles: The Masculine Case | *Mirra Komarovsky*

In a rapidly changing society, normative malintegration is commonly assumed to lead to an experience of strain. Earlier research (Komarovsky, 1946) on cultural contradictions and the feminine sex role showed that women at an eastern college suffered uncertainty and insecurity because the norms for occupational and academic success conflicted with norms for the traditional feminine role. A replication (Wallin, 1950) at a western university reported agreement in the questionnaire data, but the interview material led the investigator to conclude that the problem was less important to the women than the earlier study had suggested. However, Wallin pointed out that, in his replication, the respondents were oriented to marriage, while the Komarovsky study had included an appreciable number of women oriented to careers. This finding tended to support the view that women who were satisfied with the traditional female role would show less strain when confronted with contrary expectations than women who hoped to have both a rewarding career and a rewarding marriage.

Men are also confronted with contradictory expectations. For example, the traditional norm of male intellectual superiority conflicts with a newer norm of intellectual companionship between the sexes. This research investigated the extent of masculine strain experienced by 62 college males randomly selected from the senior class of an Ivy League male college. The study included a variety of status relationships, but the results reported here deal with intellectual relationships with female friends and attitudes toward working wives.

From Mirra Komarovsky, "Cultural Contradictions and Sex Roles: The Masculine Case," *The American Journal of Sociology* (January, 1973), pp. 873–884. © by The University of Chicago. All rights reserved.

Methods

Each of the 62 respondents contributed a minimum of three two-hour interviews and also completed a set of five schedules and two psychological tests, the California Personality Inventory and the Gough Adjective Check List. The psychological tests were interpreted by a clinical psychologist. The 13-page interview guide probed for data on actual role performance, ideal role expectations and limits of tolerance, personal preferences, perception of role partner's ideal expectations, and relevant attitudes of significant others. Direct questions on strains came only at the end of this sequence. Extensive use was made of quasi-projective tests in the form of brief episodes. The total response rate of the original sample ($N = 79$) was 78%.

Intellectual Relationships with Female Friends

When fewer women attended college, the norm of male intellectual superiority might have had some validation in experience. But today college women are more rigorously selected than men in terms of high school academic performance (*Princeton Alumni Weekly*, 1971). Nevertheless, social norms internalized in early childhood are resistant to change. The first question for this research was, How many men would show insecurity or strain in their intellectual relationships with women when confronted with both bright women and the traditional norm of male superiority?

The Troubled Third

Of the 53 men for whom the data were available (six did not date, three could not be classified reliably), 30% reported that intellectual insecurity or strain with dates was a past or current problem. This number included men who, having experienced stress, sought to avoid it by finding dates who posed no intellectual threat. The following excerpts from interviews illustrate the views of this troubled third:

> I enjoy talking to more intelligent girls, but I have no desire for a deep relationship with them. I guess I still believe that the man should be more intelligent.
>
> * * *
>
> I may be a little frightened of a man who is superior to me in some field of knowledge, but if a girl knows more than I do, I resent her.
>
> * * *
>
> Once I was seeing a philosophy major, and we got along quite well. We shared a similar outlook on life, and while we had some divergent opinions, I seemed better able to document my position. One day, by chance, I heard her discussing with another girl an aspect of Kant that

just the night before she described to me as obscure and confusing. But now she was explaining it to a girl so clearly and matter-of-factly that I felt sort of hurt and foolish. Perhaps it was immature of me to react this way.

The mode of strain exemplified by these men might be termed "a socially structured scarcity of resources for role fulfillment." Apart from the ever-present problem of lack of time and energy, some social roles are intrinsically more difficult to fulfill, given the state of technical skills, the inherent risks, or other scarcities of facilities. The strain of a doctor called upon to treat a disease for which modern medicine has no cure is another case in point.

Selective dating and avoidance of superior women solved the problem for some troubled youths, but this offered no solution for six respondents who yearned for intellectual companionship with women but dreaded the risk of invidious comparisons. The newly emerging norm of intellectual companionship with women creates a mode of strain akin to one Merton and Barber (1963) termed "sociological ambivalence." Universalistic values tend to replace sex-linked desiderata among some male undergraduates who now value originality and intelligence in female as well as in male associates. The conflict arises when, at the same time, the norm of masculine intellectual superiority has not been relinquished, as exemplified in the following case: "I am beginning to feel," remarked one senior about his current girl friend, "that she is not bright enough. She never says anything that would make me sit up and say, 'Ah, that's interesting!' I want a girl who has some defined crystal of her own personality and does not merely echo my thoughts." He recently met a girl who fascinated him with her quick and perceptive intelligence but this new girl made him feel "nervous and humble."

The problem of this youth is to seek the rewards of valued attributes in a woman without arousing in himself feelings of inferiority. It may be argued that in a competitive society this conflict tends to characterize encounters with males as well. Nonetheless, if similar problems exist between two males, the utility curve is shaped distinctively by the norm of male intellectual superiority because mere equality with a woman may be defined as a defeat or a violation of a role prescription.

The Adjusted Majority

The 37 students who said that intellectual relationships with dates were not a problem represented a variety of types. Eleven men felt superior to their female friends. In two or three cases, the relationships were judged equalitarian with strong emphasis on the rewards of intellectual companionship. In contrast, several men—and their dates—had little interest in intellectual concerns. In a few instances the severity of other problems overwhelmed this one. Finally, some eight men were happily adjusted despite the acknowledged intellectual superiority of their women friends. What makes for accommodation to this still deviant pattern?

In seven of the eight cases, the female friend had some weakness which offset her intellectual competence, such as emotional dependence, instability, or a plain appearance, giving the man a compensating advantage. A bright, studious, but relatively unattractive girl may be acceptable to a man who is not as certain of his ability to win a sexually desirable female as he is of his mental ability. In only one of the eight cases the respondent admitted that his steady girl was "more independent and less emotional, actually a little smarter than I. But she doesn't make me feel like a dunce." Her superiority was tolerable because she provided a supportive relationship which he needed and could accept with only mild, if any, emotional discomfort.

Another factor which may account for the finding that 70% of the sample reported no strain is the fact that intellectual qualities are no longer considered unfeminine and that the imperative of male superiority is giving way to the ideal of companionship between equals. This interpretation is supported by responses to two standard questions and by the qualitative materials of the interviews. A schedule testing beliefs on 16 psychological sex differences asked whether the reasoning ability of men is greater than that of women. Only 34% of the respondents "agreed" or "agreed somewhat," while 20% were "uncertain"; almost half "disagreed" or "disagreed somewhat."

Another question was put to all 62 respondents: what are for you personally the three or four most desirable characteristics in a woman (man) who is to be close to you? Of all the traits men desired in a woman, 33% were in the "intellectual" cluster, in contrast with 44% of such traits if the friend were male. The fact that the sex difference was not larger seems significant. The major difference in traits desired in male and female intimates (apart from sexual attractiveness and love) was the relative importance of "social amenities and appearance" for women.

The qualitative data amply document the fact that the majority of the respondents ideally hoped to share their intellectual interests with their female as well as their male friends. To be sure, what men occasionally meant by intellectual rapport with women was having an appreciative listener: "I wouldn't go out," declared one senior, "with any girl who wasn't sharp and perceptive enough to catch an intellectual subtlety." But for the majority a "meaningful relationship" with a woman included also a true intellectual interchange and sharing. As one senior put it, "A guy leaving a movie with his date expects her to make a stimulating comment of her own and not merely echo his ideas." Another man wanted a date with whom he could "discuss things that guys talk about," and still a third man exclaimed: "What I love about this girl is that she is on my level, that I can never speak over her head."

It is this ideal of intellectual companionship with women, we suggest, that may explain the relative adjustment of the men in this sphere. As long as the expectation of male superiority persisted, anything near equality on the part of the woman carried the threatening message to the men: "I am not the intellectually *superior* male I am expected to be." But when the ideal of intellectual companionship between equals replaces the expectation of male superiority, the pressure upon the man eases and changes. Now he need only reassure himself that he is not inferior to his date, rather than that he is markedly superior to her. Once the expectation of clear superiority is relinquished, varieties of relationships may be accommodated. Given a generally similar intellectual level, comparative evaluations are blurred by different interests, by complementary strengths and weaknesses, and occasionally by rationalizations ("she studies harder") and other devices.

One final explanation remains to be considered. May the intellectual self-confidence of the majority be attributed in part to women's readiness to play down their intellectual abilities? That such behavior occurs is attested by a number of studies (Komarovsky, 1946; Wallin, 1950).

When respondents were asked to comment upon a projective story about a girl "playing dumb" on dates, the great majority expressed indignation at such "dishonest," "condescending" behavior. But some three or four found the behavior praiseworthy. As one senior put it, "Her intentions were good; she wanted to make the guy feel important."

Although we did not interview the female friends of our respondents, a few studies indicate that such playing down of intellectual ability by women is less common today than in the 1940s. Questionnaires filled out at an eastern women's college duplicated earlier studies by Wallin (1950) and Komarovsky (1946). The 1970 class was a course on the family, and the 1971 class probably recruited a relatively high proportion of feminists. Table 1 indicates that the occasional muting of intellectual competence by women may have played some role in the adjustment of the men, but it would appear to be a minor and decreasing role.

The hypothesis that the emerging ideal of intellectual companionship serves as a buffer against male strain needs a test which includes (as our study did not) some index of intellectual ability as well as indices of norms and of strain. Of the 27 men who disagreed with the proposition that the reasoning ability of men is greater than that of women, only five reported in-

Table 1.   Readiness of Women to Play Down Intellectual Abilities (%)

	Wallin 1950 (N = 163)	Sociology Class 1970* (N = 33)	Advanced Sociology Class 1971* (N = 55)
When on dates how often have you pretended to be intellectually inferior to the man?			
Very often, often, or several times.	32	21	15
Once or twice.	26	36	30
Never	42	43	55
In general, do you have any hesitation about revealing your equality or superiority to men in intellectual competence?			
Have considerable or some hesitation.	35	21	13
Very little hesitation.	39	33	32
None at all.	26	46	55

*Mirra Komarovsky, unpublished study.

tellectual insecurity with women, whereas of the 34 men who believed in masculine superiority or were uncertain, nine experienced strain. Most troubled were the 12 men who were "uncertain"; four of them were insecure with women. Case analyses suggest that the interplay between a man's experience, personality, and beliefs is complex. For example, one traditional man, having confessed feelings of intellectual insecurity on dates, clung all the more tenaciously to the belief in superior male reasoning ability.

Some men took the "liberal" position on sex differences as a matter of principle. Of the nine black students, eight rejected the belief in male superiority, perhaps because they opposed group comparisons in intelligence. Again, in some cases, the direction of the causal relation was the reverse of the one we posited: men who felt in fact intellectually superior were hospitable to the "liberal" ideology. In view of these complexities, our suggestive results as to the positive association between egalitarian norms and the absence of strain remain to be tested in larger samples.

Attitudes Toward Future Wives' Occupational Roles

The ethos on the campus of this study clearly demanded that men pay at least lip service to liberal attitudes toward working wives. If the initial responses to structured questions were accepted as final, the majority would have been described as quite feminist in ideology. But further probing revealed qualifications which occasionally almost negated the original response. For example, an affirmative answer to a proposition, "It is appropriate for a mother of a preschool child to take a fulltime job," was, upon further questioning, conditioned by such restrictions as "provided, of course, that the home was run smoothly, the children did not suffer, and the wife's job did not interfere with her husband's career." The interview provided an opportunity to get an assessment of normative expectations, ideal and operative, as well as of actual preferences. The classification of attitudes to be presented in this report is based on the total interview. Preferences reported here assume that a wife's paycheck will not be an economic necessity. The overwhelming majority were confident that their own earnings would be adequate to support the family. Throughout the discussion of working, only two or three men mentioned the temptation of a second paycheck.

Four types of response to the question of wives' working may be identified. The "traditionalists," 24% of the men, said outright that they intended to marry women who would find sufficient fulfillment in domestic, civic, and cultural pursuits without ever seeking outside jobs. "Pseudo-feminists," 16% of the men, favored having their wives work, at least when the question was at a high level of abstraction, but their approval was hedged with qualifications that no woman could meet.

The third and dominant response included almost half (48%) of the respondents. These men took a "modified traditionalist" position which favored a sequential pattern: work, withdrawal from work for child rearing, and eventual return to work. They varied as to the timing of these stages and as to the aid they were prepared to give their wives with domestic and child-rearing functions. The majority saw no substitute for the mother during her child's preschool years. Even the mother of school-age children, were she to work, should preferably be at home when the children return from school. Though they were willing to aid their wives in varying degrees, they frequently excluded specific tasks, for instance, "not the laundry," "not the cleaning," "not the diapers," and so on. Many hoped that they would be "able to assist" their wives by hiring maids. The greater the importance of the wife's work, the more willing they were to help her. (One senior, however, would help only if his wife's work were "peripheral," that is, not as important to her as her home.)

The last, the "feminist" type, was the smallest, only 7% of the total. These men were willing to modify their own roles significantly to facilitate their future wives' careers. Some recommended a symmetrical allocation of tasks —"as long as it is not a complete reversal of roles." In the remaining 5% of the cases, marriage was so remote that the respondents were reluctant to venture any views on this matter.

The foregoing summary of types of male attitudes toward working wives fails to reveal the tangled web of contradictory values and sentiments associated with these attitudes. We shall presently illustrate a variety of inconsistencies. But underlying them is one basic problem. The ideological support for the belief in sharp sex role differentiation in marriage has weakened, but the belief itself has not been relinquished. Increasing skepticism about the innate character of psychological sex differences and some convergence in the ideas of masculinity and femininity (see McKee and Sherriffs, 1957, 1959) have created a strain toward consistency. The more similar the perceptions of male and female personalities (see Kammeyer, 1964), the more universalistic must be the principles of evaluation applied to both sexes. "If you could make three changes in the personality of the girl friend who is currently closest to you, what would they be?" we asked the seniors. Universalistic values were reflected in the following, as in many other responses: "I would like her to be able to set a goal for herself and strive to achieve it. I don't like to see people slacking off." Earlier cross-sex association in childhood and early adolescence (see Udry, 1966) has raised male expectation of enjoying an emotional and intellectual companionship with women. These expectations, however, coexist with the deeply rooted norm that the husband should be the superior achiever in the occupational world and the wife, the primary child rearer. One manifestation of this basic dilemma is the familiar conflict between a value and a preference. "It is only fair," declared one senior, "to let a woman do her own thing, if she wants a career. Personally, though, I would want my wife at home."

More interesting are the ambivalent attitudes manifested toward both the full-time homemaker and the career wife. The image of each contained both attractive and repellent traits. Deprecating remarks about housewifery were not uncommon, even among men with traditional views of women's roles. A conservative senior declared, "A woman who works is more interesting than a housewife." "If I were a woman," remarked another senior, "I would want a career. It must be boring sitting around the house doing the same thing day in, day out. I don't have much respect for the type of woman whom I see doing the detergent commercials on TV."

But the low esteem attached by some of the men to full-time homemaking coexisted with other sentiments and convictions which required just such a pattern for one's wife. For example, asked about the disadvantages of being a woman, one senior replied, "Life ends at 40. The woman raised her children and all that remains is garden clubs and that sort of thing—unless, of course, she has a profession." In another part of the interview, this young man explained that he enjoyed shyness in a girl and detested aggressive and ambitious women. He could never be attracted to a career woman. It is no exaggeration to conclude that this man could not countenance in a woman who was to be his wife the qualities that he himself felt were necessary for a fulfilling middle age.

A similar mode of contradiction, incidentally, was also disclosed by some seniors with regard to women's majors in college. "There are no 'unfeminine' majors," declared one senior: "I admire a girl who is premed or prelaw." But the universalistic yardstick which led this senior to sanction and admire professional goals for women did not extend to the means for their attainment, as he unwittingly revealed in another part of the interview. Questioned about examples of "unfeminine" behavior, this senior answered: "Excessive grade consciousness." If a premed man, anxious about admission to a good medical school, should go to see a professor about a C in chemistry, this senior would understand although he would disapprove of such preoccupation with grades. But in a woman premed he would find such behavior "positively obnoxious."

If the image of the full-time homemaker contained some alienating features, the main threat of a career wife was that of occupational rivalry, as illustrated in the following excerpt from the interviews. A senior speaks:

> I believe that it is good for mothers to return to fulltime work when the children are grown, provided the work is important and worthwhile. Otherwise, housewives get hung up with tranquilizers, because they have no outlet for their abilities. . . . Of course, it may be difficult if a wife becomes successful in her own right. A woman should want her husband's success more than he should want hers. Her work shouldn't interfere with or hurt his career in any way. He should not sacrifice his career to hers. For example, if he is transferred, his wife should follow—and not vice versa.

In sum, work for married women with grown children is approved by this young man, provided that the occupation is of some importance. But such an occupation is precisely one which carries a threat to the husband's pride.

The expectation that the husband should be the superior achiever appears still to be deeply rooted. Even equality in achievement of husband and wife is interpreted as a defeat for the man. The prospect of occupational rivalry with one's wife seems intolerable to contemplate. "My girl friend often beats me in tennis," explained one senior. "Now, losing the game doesn't worry me. It is no way reduces my manhood. But being in a lower position than a woman in a job would hurt my self-esteem."

Another student, having declared his full support for equal opportunities for women in the occupational world, added a qualification: "A woman should not be in a position of firing an employee. It is an unpleasant thing to do. Besides, it is unfair to the man who is to be fired. He may be a very poor employee, but he is still a human being and it may be just compounding his unhappiness to be fired by a woman."

In sum, the right of an able woman to a career of her choice, the admiration for women who measure up in terms of the dominant values of our society, the lure but also the threat that such women present, the low status attached to housewifery but the conviction that there is no substitute for the mother's care of young children, the deeply internalized norm of male occupational superiority pitted against the principle of equal opportunity irrespective of sex—these are some of the revealed inconsistencies.

Such ambivalences on the part of college men are bound to exacerbate role conflicts in women. The latter must sense that even the men who pay lip service to the creativity of child rearing and domesticity reserve their admiration (if occasionally tinged with ambivalence) for women achievers who measure up in terms of the dominant values of our society. It is becoming increasingly difficult to maintain a system of values for women only (Komarovsky, 1953).

Nevertheless, to infer from this account of male inconsistencies that this is an area of great stress for them would be a mistake. It is not. By and large, the respondents assumed that the women's "career and marriage" issue was solved by the sequential pattern of withdrawal and return to work. If this doomed women to second-class citizenship in the occupational world, the outcome was consistent with the conviction that the husband should be the superior achiever.

Men who momentarily worried about the fate of able women found moral anchorage in their conviction that today no satisfactory alternative to the mother's care of young children can be found. Many respondents expressed their willingness to help with child care and household duties. Similarly, many hoped to spend more time with their own children than their fathers had spent with them. But such domestic participation was defined as assistance to the wife who was to carry the major responsibility. Only two or three of the men approved a symmetrical, rather than a complementary, allocation of domestic and occupational roles. An articulate senior sums up the dominant view:

> I would not want to marry a women whose only goal is to become a housewife. This type of woman would not have enough bounce and zest in her. I don't think a girl has much imagination if she just wants to settle down and raise a family from the very beginning. Moreover, I want an independent girl, one who has her own interests and does not always have to depend on me for stimulation and diversion. However, when we both agree to have children, my wife must be the one to raise them. She'll have to forfeit her freedom for the children. I believe that, when a woman wants a child, she must also accept the full responsibility of child care.

When he was asked why it was necessarily the woman who had to be fully responsible for the children, he replied:

> Biology makes equality impossible. Besides, the person I'll marry will want the child and will want to care for the child. Ideally, I would hope I'm not forcing her to assume responsibility for raising the children. I would hope that this is her desire and that it is the happiest thing she can do. After we have children, it will be her career that will end, while mine will support us. I believe that women should have equal opportunities in business and the professions, but I still insist that a woman who is a mother should devote herself entirely to her children.

The low emotional salience of the issue of working wives may also be attributed to another factor. The female partners of our respondents, at this particular stage of life, did not, with a few exceptions, force the men to confront their inconsistencies. Apparently enough women will freely make the traditional-for-women adjustments—whether scaling down their own ambitions or in other ways acknowledging the prior claims of the man's career. This judgment is supported by the results of two studies of female undergraduates done on the same campus in 1943 and 1971 (Table 2). The big shift in postcollege preferences since 1943 was in the decline of women undergraduates who opted for full-time homemaking and volunteer activities. In 1971, the majority chose the sequential pattern, involving withdrawal from employment for child rearing. The proportion of committed career women who hope to return to work soon after childbirth has remained constant among freshmen and sophomores.

Table 2. College Women's Attitudes toward Work and Family Patterns (%)

	Random Sample of Sophomore Class at Women's Liberal Arts College, 1943 (N = 78)	Class in Introductory Sociology, Same College 1971 (N = 44)
Assume that you will marry and that your husband will make enough money so that you will not have to work unless you want to. Under these circumstances, would you prefer:		
1. Not to work at all, or stop after childbirth and decide later whether to go back.	50	18
2. To quit working after the birth of a child but definitely to go back to work.	30	62
3. To continue working with a minimum of interruption for childbearing.	20	20

Source: Mirra Komarovsky, unpublished studies.

If women's attitudes have not changed more radically in the past 30 years, it is no doubt because society has failed to provide effective supports for the woman who wishes to integrate family life, parenthood, and work on much the same terms as men. Such an option will not become available as long as the care of young children is regarded as the responsibility solely of the mother. In the absence of adequate child care centers, an acceptance of a symmetrical division of domestic and work responsibilities, or other facilitating social arrangements, the attitudes of the majority of undergraduates reflect their decision to make some kind of workable adjustment to the status quo, if not a heroic struggle to change it.

Summary

Role conflicts in women have been amply documented in numerous studies. The problem underlying this study was to ascertain whether recent social changes and consequent malintegration with regard to sex roles have created stressful repercussions for men as well as for women. In a randomly selected sample of 62 male seniors in an eastern Ivy League college, nearly one-third experienced some anxiety over their perceived failure to live up to the norm of masculine intellectual superiority. This stressful minority suffered from two modes of role strain: scarcity of resources for role performance and ambivalence. The absence of strain in the majority may be explained by a changed role definition. Specifically, the normative expectation of male intellectual superiority appears to be giving way on the campus of our study to the ideal of intellectual companionship between equals. Attitudes toward working wives abounded in ambivalences and inconsistencies. The ideological supports for the traditional sex role differentiation in marriage are weakening, but the emotional allegiance to the modified traditional pattern is still strong. These inconsistencies did not generate a high degree of stress, partly, no doubt, because future roles do not require an immediate realistic confrontation. In addition, there is no gainsaying the conclusion that human beings can tolerate a high degree of inconsistency as long as it does not conflict with their self-interest.

References

Kammeyer, Kenneth. "The Feminine Role: An Analysis of Attitude Consistency." *Journal of Marriage and the Family*, 26 (August 1964): 295–305.

Komarovsky, Mirra. "Cultural Contradictions and Sex Roles." *American Journal of Sociology*, 52 (November 1946): 182–189.

Komarovsky, Mirra. *Women in the Modern World, Their Education and Their Dilemmas*. Boston: Little, Brown, 1953.

McKee, John P., and Alex C. Sherriffs. "The Differential Evaluation of Males and Females." *Journal of Personality*, 25 (March 1957): 356–363.

McKee, John P., and Alex C. Sherriffs. "Men's and Women's Beliefs, Ideals, and Self-

Concepts." *American Journal of Sociology*, 64 (1959), no. 4: 456–363.
Merton, Robert K., and Elinor Barber. "Sociological Ambivalence." In *Sociological Theory, Values and Socio-cultural Change*, edited by E. A. Tiryakian. Glencoe, Ill.: Free Press, 1963.
Princeton Alumni Weekly, February 23, 1971, p. 7.
Udry, J. Richard. *The Social Context of Marriage*. Philadelphia: Lippincott, 1966.
Wallin, Paul. "Cultural Contradictions and Sex Roles: A Repeat Study." *American Sociological Review*, 15 (April 1950): 288–293.

This autobiographical statement by a well-known sociologist describes the complexities and ambiguities of his own experience as a partner in an "egalitarian" marriage. Although he considers himself a long-time supporter of women's liberation, he found that his family life did not look so different from that of the average American male. Mainly, it was the coming of children, and the enormous amounts of time, attention, and emotion demanded by modern middle class standards of child care, that led to the lapse of his egalitarian ideals. Among his conclusions are the following: equality is not won once and for all, but must continually be striven for; equality in marriages where there are children requires a restructuring of attitudes toward children on the part of both men and women as well as institutional aids such as child care; sex equality is most easily achieved in bed—not in the kitchen.

On Men: The Making of a Confused Middle-Class Husband

S. M. Miller

When I was in my twenties, I would try to convince marriage-oriented women to become involved with me by predicting, on the basis of experience, that within six months of such involvement they would very likely be getting married—though not to me—because the association with me seemed to drive women to marriage. In my forties, I find that young women's work association with me seems to correlate highly with their movement into women's lib. Irrespective of whether proximity to me induces a liberation spirit or whether this spirit could possibly be due to larger cultural forces, my female co-workers have led me to think much more of late about sexism,

From S. M. Miller, "On Men: The Making of a Confused Middle-Class Husband," *Social Policy* (July/August 1971), 2:2, pages 33–39. Reprinted by permission of the Social Policy Corporation, New York, New York 10010. © SOCIAL POLICY.

and to review my own experiences over the decades within that framework.

Two interchanges with my colleagues particularly struck me. One wrote me a strong note asking why I was not publicly active in fighting sexism if I thought that I was so good on the question. I was somewhat stung by this passionate indictment, and in cool, clear, parsimonious prose replied that I did not consider myself to be very good on the sex issue, but that, looking around at most men of my own and perhaps younger ages, I was constantly surprised to find myself much better in my attitudes and behavior than they, though not good enough, etc.

But a nagging vision persisted despite my measured rejoinder. True, my wife worked, and always had worked, and I pushed her to do more professional writing, to establish herself solidly in her professional life; true, I had played a major role in bringing up our children, especially when they were young and my wife was going to school; true, in arguments with friends I had always taken pro-liberation positions. For decades I had argued against the then-fashionable *Kinder-Küche* motif of suburban existence and had counseled students against it. I advised husbands whose wives were diffusely unhappy that they should drive their talented and educated, if unsure, spouses into work, for staying home all day and taking care of a household made for a malcontentment that was compounded by social disapproval of the expression of unhappiness in mothering and wifing. Yes, all that was true. But how different was the present pattern of my own family life from that of a family with a more obviously backward husband than I?

Another female colleague, more disposed to be kindly toward me, told me, when I questioned a particular emphasis of women's lib, that I did not realize how backward young men now in their twenties and thirties were: they had been brought up in the suburban sadness in which their mothers played the required "good mother-wife" role, in which their sisters and their dates accepted the necessity of catering to men in order to make a "good catch." She went on to say that these men had not been confronted on sexist issues (this conversation preceded the mass media's elevating women's lib to celebrity status); indeed, they were largely unaware that there might be some injustice in the present ordering of the world.

My experience, I replied, had been different. In the left-wing ambience of New York City in the '40s and '50s, "male supremacy" and "male chauvinism" were frequently discussed. True, my male friends and I discussed the issues with our female friends and then often proceeded to exploit them, but a dextrous awareness we did have. (But I add, in order to avoid a reassuring self-debasement, that we did encourage our women friends and wives to think and to develop themselves; and I even believe that I was less exploitative than most.)

Yet I am dogged by the feeling expressed in the notion "If you're so smart, how come you're not rich?" Where is the egalitarian family life one would reasonably expect from my sophistication about women's lib issues and my personal experience with them in my younger manhood?

Way Back When

I have never had an intellectual problem with sexism. One reason may well have been the women who surrounded me as a child—my father's mother, my mother, and two considerably older sisters—although I know it sometimes goes quite the other way. My father slept, and my mother dominated—partly out of force of character and partly, one sister informed me fairly recently, because of the occupational and other failures of my father. He had tried to make it in America—and could not. His was the immigrant's rags-to-rags story. He started as a factory worker, and became a small businessman, only to be wiped out by the 1921 depression. He worked again as a machine operator, and then started a dress store, where he did the alterations and my mother was chief saleswoman. Again, his enterprise was rewarded by a depression—this time, that of the 1930s. He went back to working at a machine in the lowest-paid part of the garment industry, where he stayed until he retired in his early seventies. From the depression days on, my mother worked as a saleslady. I was a "latchkey kid" from an early age, warming up the meals that were left for me by my mother.

My mother was very smart and witty, and so was my older sister. They were obviously intellectually well endowed, although not well educated. My mother had a few years of formal schooling; my sister just managed to graduate from high school. (I think I developed my repugnance for credentialism because I recognized that these were two very smart though not well-educated women.)

From this experience, I grew up regarding women as competent and capable of making family and economic decisions. (By contrast, my mother disliked cooking; and it was a shock to me when I began to eat away from home to discover what a bad cook she was.) Women worked and ran things well. On the other hand, there was a notion that people frowned on women's working, so we tried to hide the fact that my mother worked. I think I felt both ashamed that my mother worked and irritated that "society" thought that it was wrong for women to work, especially when their incomes were needed.

Furthermore, sexism was, in principle, alien to the egalitarian and participatory circles in which my closest friends and I were passionately involved. We were out of step with the intellectual climate of the '40s and '50s because of our egalitarian, populist, antielitist spirit. We criticized Stalinist democratic centralism and American Celebration-style pluralist democracy because of their inadequate attention to equality and participation for all. We could no more subscribe to intellectual rationalizations of a low status for females than we could condone the miseries of oppression and deprivation among other parts of the population.

A third reason I see myself as intellectually escaping sexism has more manifest emotional roots. Looking back, I don't believe that I could have accepted a woman who would center her life completely on me and devote herself to making me happy. (Children were not part of my purview.) At one level, the intellectual, how could one individual be worthy of such dedication by another? At a deeper and, I suspect now, more significant level, I rejected or stayed away from easily giving or male-centered women because I did not consider myself worthy of another person's total devotion or capable of evoking the sentiments that would sustain it beyond the initial impulse. Furthermore, such devotion would demand an emotional response that I possibly could not make. In short, I did not think so well of myself that I could live with (overwhelming) devotion. As a consequence, I was usually involved with young women with strong career goals who were seeking their identity through work, not through family. They were my intellectual equals, if not superiors.

Thus I had a good beginning, it seems to me, for having a marriage that did not embody sexist currents. But I don't see that my current life is very different from that of men who espoused or expounded more sexist values. Years ago a good friend told me that I had the reputation among the wives in our circle of being "an excellent husband"; and he said, "You know, that's not a good thing." I now have the feeling that families that openly embrace both bourgeous and sexist values don't live very differently from us. I sense that we are engaged in a "lapsed egalitarianism," still believing in our earlier commitments and concerns about equality, but having drifted from the faith in our daily life.

What Happened

Probably the most important factor in accounting for the direction we took was our amazing naivete about the impact of having children—a naivete, incidentally, that I see today having a similarly devastating effect on many young parents. We just had no idea how much time and emotion children captured, how they simply changed a couple's lives, even when the wife's working made it possible, as it did in our case, to afford a housekeeper.

The early years of childrearing were very difficult. Our first son was superactive and did not sleep through the night. We were both exhausted. My wife insisted that I not leave everything to her; she fought with me to get me to participate in care of our son and apartment.I took on 2 a.m. and 6 a.m.

feedings and changings, for our ideology would not allow me just to help out occasionally: I had to "share," "really participate," in the whole thing. I resented that degree of involvement; it seemed to interfere terribly with the work I desperately wanted to achieve in. Indeed, I have always felt put upon because of that experience of many months.

To make matters worse, I did not know of other work-oriented husbands who were as involved as I with their children. True, I realized that my sons and I had become much attached to each other and that a lovely new element had entered my life; but I resented the time and exhaustion, particularly since I was struggling to find my way in my work. I did not consider myself productive and was in the middle of struggling to clarify my perspective. I looked at the problem largely in terms of the pressure of my job, which required a lot of effort, and, more importantly, in terms of my personality and my inability to work effectively. Although I wrote memoranda with great ease, I wasn't writing professional articles and books.

In retrospect, I think that it was the influence of the McCarthy and Eisenhower years that was more significant in my lack of development. My outlook and interests were not what social science and society were responding to. That changed later, and I was able to savor in the '60s that infrequent exhilaration of having my professional work and citizen concerns merge and of gaining both a social science and popular audience and constituency. But I did not know in the 1950s that this would unfold, and I felt resentment.

What I experienced was that, unlike my friends, I was working hard to make things easier for my wife; and I did not see rewards. Yes, she told me she appreciated my effort; but my activities were never enough, my sharing was never full, in the sense that I equally planned and took the initiative in the care of child and house. She was tired, too, and irritated by child care; and, in turn, I was irritated by what seemed to be her absorption in taking care of children.

And there were always those male friends who did so little, compared with me. I could, and did, tell myself that at some point along the line they would be paying heavy "dues" for their current neglect of their wives' plight, but it was small balm at the time. I wondered if I was not rationalizing my irritation by an intellectualizing metaphor about how one pays prices sooner or later and by a plaintively reassuring injunction never to envy anyone else, for who knew what lurked behind the façade of family equanimity?

Things were further complicated by another factor—less typical of today's young marrieds—my incomplete early socialization as a family member. For example, since as an adolescent and pre-adolescent I had eaten meals by myself, I had developed the habit of reading while eating. (Indeed, I am a compulsive reader, a "print nut"; if there is nothing around to read, I will study the labels on ketchup bottles.) The result was that marriage required a resocialization: I had to learn to talk to someone at mealtimes, and not to turn inward to my own thoughts or to *The New York Times.*

Of course, the reading is only the personal tip of the iceberg of a larger problem of not closing myself to others and becoming inaccessible because of stress or intellectual absorption. I am now, again, in a conscious period of trying to make myself more accessible emotionally to my family, but it is a struggle. For example, when we vacation, I spend the first few days devouring three to four mysteries a day—"decompressing" I call it—hardly talking to anyone. And, of course, when I am at a deadline, or caught in my inability to work out an idea, or just unable to get to work (there are few other conditions for me than these three), I am rather inaccessible, to say the least. I work against this tendency, but don't do notably well. While I do the mundane tasks of the household, psychologically I am often not much there. I think that I am winning the struggle against withdrawal, but what is a giant step to the battler may appear as a wiggle of progress to the beholder.

My wife has accommodated to my dislike of fixing things and "wasting time" on such things—not great matters in themselves, but symptomatic of the process of my disengagement from the burdens of home and family.

From a narrow perspective, I have useful incompetences protecting me from diversions of my energy and focus. I don't like to fix things and don't do them well (or soon). In my youth, in my proletarian near-idealization, I felt Arthur Miller was right when he had Willy Loman say that a man isn't a man unless he can do things with his hands. So I tried adult education shop courses and the like for a brief time. I went in a "klutz" and came out a "klutz." Now, in a spirit of reactive arrogance or greater self-pride, I boldly assert the counterposition that I believe in the division of labor and prefer to pay for specialized labor. I do little around the house—and that usually long delayed. Since skilled labor is hard to get at any price, things are undone, or my wife does them; but my principle of specialization (for me) remains unimpaired.

Similarly, I have been relieved of the task of paying bills. With my usual speed and my disdain for trivia, I did this job very rapidly and made mistakes. Now my wife spends time doing this task. It is easier, in her view, for her to do it than to keep after me to do a competent job. Failure is its own reward: I have escaped another task. Of course, I have been after my wife to have a part-time secretary and bookkeeper and have located several people for her. But she resists, as they do not provide enough help to make it worthwhile. The result is that my personnel efforts reduce my feelings of guilt when she spends evenings writing checks. After all, I did try to get her out of that function. But I am still irritated by her doing the checks—for that act is another indication that she is failing me by not showing our true equality by spending more time on her professional writing and research.

I guess what dismays me and makes me see my marriage and family as unfortunately typically upper middle-class collegial, pseudo-egalitarian American—especially in light of my own continuing commitment to an egalitarian, participatory ethos—is that I assume no responsibility for major household tasks and family activities. True, my wife has always worked at her profession (she is a physician), even when our sons were only some weeks old. (I used to say that behind the working wife with young children, there stands a tired husband.) True, I help in many ways and feel responsible for her having time to work at her professional interests. But I do partial, limited things to free her to do her work. I don't do the basic thinking about the planning of meals and housekeeping, or the situation of the children. Sure, I will wash dishes and "spend time" with the children; I will often do the shopping, cook, make beds, "share" the burden of most household tasks; but that is not the same thing as direct and primary responsibility for planning and managing a household and meeting the day-to-day needs of children.

It is not that I object in principle to housekeeping and childrearing. I don't find such work demeaning or unmasculine—just a drain of my time, which could be devoted to other, "more rewarding" things. (Just as I don't like to shop for clothes for myself, even though I like clothes.) My energies are poised to help me work on my professional-political concerns, and I resist "wasting time" on other pursuits, even those basic to managing a day-to-day existence.

The more crucial issue, I now think, is not my specific omissions and commissions, but the atmosphere that I create. My wife does not expect much of me, which frees me for work and lessens the strain I produce when I feel blocked from working. Even our sons have always largely respected my efforts to work, feeling much freer to interrupt their mother at her work. The years have been less happy than they would have been if I had been more involved and attentive and my wife had not lowered her ambitions.

Outstanding academically from an early age, a "poor girl" scholarship winner to a prestige college and medical school, excelling in her beginning professional work, my wife expected, and was expected, to do great things. But with children, she immediately reduced her goals. Of course, medical schools don't pay much attention to faculty members who are part-time or female, and the combination of the two almost guarantees offhand treatment.

She is now realizing fuller professional development. I have always felt guilty about her not achieving more, so I have nagged her to publish, though I have not provided the circumstances and climate that would make serious work much easier. I have had the benefit of feeling relieved that I was "motivating" her by my emphasis on her doing more, but I have not suffered the demands on my time and emotions that making more useful time available to her would have required. In the long run, I have undoubtedly lost more by limited involvement, because she has been distressed by the obstacles to her professional work. But the long run is hard to consider when today's saved and protected time helps meet a deadline.

Some Lessons

What are the lessons of this saga of a well-meaning male?

One is that equality or communality is not won once and for all, but must continually be striven for. Backsliding and easy accommodation to the male (because it is less troublesome) are likely to occur unless there is, at least occasionally, effort to bring about or maintain true communality rather than peaceful adjustment.

From this it follows that women must struggle for equality—that it will not easily be won or rewon. (A male is not likely to bestow it—in more than surface ways. Some women are arguing that it is not worth the effort to have equality with men in close personal relations and that they should not bother with men, but equality and communality among women will not be automatic either.) The struggle does not necessarily mean nastiness, but it does require the perceptiveness and willingness to engage issues not only of prejudice and discrimination but also of subtle practices requiring female accommodation to males.

I know that the point I am about to make is often misused, and will open me to much criticism; but let me try to make it. A third lesson is that the bringing up of children must be changed, and that many women are lagging in this respect, although present day-care concerns suggest a possible change. For all of male reluctance, resistance, and avoidance, many women, particularly when they have young children, end up structuring life so that it is difficult to achieve a collegial relationship. Indeed, the concentration on, nay absorption with, children makes even a low-level decent relationship, let alone an egalitarian one, difficult. Yes, I realize that the subordinate group is never the main source of difficulty, that men make women embrace the mother-housemother syndrome; but cultural and personal history are involved as well as direct or more covert husbandly pressure and unwillingness to be a full partner. Overinvolvement with children may operate to discourage many husbands from full participation because they do not accept the ideology of close attention to children.

I am *not* saying that the problem is with women, but that this part of the problem shouldn't be ignored. Even for the young parents it is important to have some measure of agreement on the mode, the style of childcare. This is difficult to realize before actually becoming parents. Perhaps it will not be an issue for those in their twenties who may have a different and more relaxed attitude toward children. (And, of course, many no longer feel unfulfilled if they do not have children.) For some, yes; but I doubt if that will be true of most relatively "straight" parents. What is needed is a reconsideration of what is required in parenthood and in running a household.

Let me consider the household care first. The easy notion that in the right atmosphere housework is not so bad seems wrong to me. A lot of jobs can be stomached, treated as routine; that is the best one can say of them—that they are manageable, "do-able." But they are not exciting, stimulating, or satisfying except to the extent that they are completed or "accomplished," i.e., gotten rid of for the moment. This is especially so when one's other interests are high, for then these tasks become highly competitive with other ways of using one's time and thus are dissatisfying. Housework can be a full-time job if it is not guarded against. Some agreement on a minimum, satisfactory level of household care and some efficiency and sharing in performing it are important for a couple.

I have mentioned, verbally at least, the desirability of *alles für die Eltern* and "salutary neglect" (before Moynihan, incidentally). But it has been difficult for my generation, whose adolescence and early twenties were stirred by Freud and who have wallowed in the guilt of parental omniscience and ethnic parental concern, to erase the sense of responsibility and guilt for how our children develop. What if one's son doesn't graduate from college or becomes a bomb-thrower or a homosexual—isn't it the parents' fault? When a son or daughter is 18 or 20, it seems easier to deny the responsibility, since so many youths are also in troubled times that it is difficult to talk of Freudian acting-out rather than of a generational change in consciousness. But at earlier ages it is much more difficult to shake the feeling of parental responsibility for how an infant or child is developing. I don't advocate callous neglect; but some less constraining and demanding views of parenthood—and probably some additional institutional aids like day care—are needed.

The problem is not always in the mother's attitudes. Some studies show that working-class women are very interested in working, but that their husbands feel that it is important to the children for their mothers to be home. The issue is not so much that the mother or father is lagging but how to move toward new views on child development and new institutions to further these views.

A fourth lesson has to do with sex, and I am rather surprised by it. It turns out that the most easy acceptance of equality is in bed—not in the kitchen.

Few middle-class men, except those regarded as crude or brutes, would assert that women do not have a right to enjoyment in bed equal to that of their partners—although I doubt that female extramarital affairs are treated as casually by men as men think their own extramarital adventures should be regarded by women. Even if the male does not generally assume a great responsibility for a female's difficulty in achieving orgasm, he is expected by himself and others to try to help her gain at least some measure of fulfillment. "Biff, bang, thank you ma'am" is more of a joke than ever before.

This suggests that that most delicate of human relations—sex—isn't so central. Men are adjusting to new requirements and are incorporating them into their definition of maleness. But the other elements of equality are not so easily absorbed into the definition of maleness. The "male-ness" of many young females' attitudes toward sex—ready to go to bed without much emotional involvement with the partner; sex as kicks, not love—may be misleading them. "Good sex" doesn't necessarily mean real equality.

I suspect many young women today are being exploited by men just as my generation exploited women, with the notion that true freedom, both political and psychological, is demonstrated by an "uninhibited" attitude toward relatively casual intercourse. The phenomenal and depressing success of *Love Story*, as trite and sentimentalized a story of romance and sexism as has come along in a long while—truly a 1950-ish, Eisenhower romance—indicates that many young women, even when they use four-letter words, dream of the everlasting and all-satisfying flame of love, including the purity of death as its authentication. And, I fear, they think that equality in bed means equality in other things. They are much less liberated than they think, and are probably sexually exploited by their male friends. Both young men and young women seem unlikely to sustain for long untraditional forms of bedding and wedding, which is one of the reasons that I think my experiences still have relevance.

But all these "implications" are minor, except for the importance of struggle. What strikes me as the crucial concern, at least for the occupationally striving family, is the male involvement in work, success, and striving. This is the pressure that often molds the family. Accommodation to it is frequently the measure of being a "good wife"—moving when the male's "future" requires it, regulating activities so that the male is free to concentrate on his work or business. It isn't sexism or prejudice against women that is at work here—although they are contributing factors—but the compulsive concentration upon the objective of achievement and the relegating of other activities to secondary concern. Egalitarian relationships cannot survive if people are not somewhat equally involved with each other and if the major commitment is to things outside the relationship that inevitably intrude upon it.

So long as success or achievement burns bright for the male, it is going to be difficult to change drastically the situation of the family and the women.

However, although I am strongly of the mind that success drives should be banked and other more humanitarian urges encouraged, I don't accept that all of the drive for success or achievement is pernicious or undesirable. This drive is exciting, and can be fulfilling. But it is a great danger to be avoided when it becomes all-embracing or when the success is without a content that is both personally and socially satisfying or beneficial.

To do interesting and useful things, to feel a sense of accomplishment, should be made easier. As in military strategy, a "sufficient level" of achievement rather than a "maximum level" of security or position should be sought. Being "number one" should not be the goal; rather, high competence should be enough for both men and women. I have seen many talented people blighted in their work by "number-one-ism" when they probably would have done outstanding and useful work by adopting high competence-performance criteria.

If women accept "success" to the same extent and in the same way that many men do, the problems will be enormous. If women simply adopt the "number-one-ism" that dominates the workplace, the drive for achievement will probably lead them into the same narrowing and unpromising obsessions that destroy many men.

A more egalitarian society in terms of the distribution of income and social respect would, of course, make it easier to escape "number-one-ism." But, meanwhile, we shall have to struggle with the values that surround us and corrode true equality in the home.

Finally, men have to feel some gain in the growing equality in their relationship with women. Over the long run there may well be greater satisfaction for males in egalitarian relationships, but in the short run the tensions and demands may not lead to enjoyment and satisfaction. Some short-term gains for males will be important in speeding up the road to equality. But such gains are not easily or automatically forthcoming. Substitute satisfactions or gains for the male are needed to push out sexism rapidly. That is why I made the first points about the inevitability of struggle. But successful struggle requires modes of living and relationships to which the male can accommodate without total loss, which is hard to achieve without women's falling back again to accommodating to men.

I recognize that I concentrate upon the upper middle class and upon the experience of one male. I don't think either is the world—I really don't. But I do perceive that some of my experiences and interpretations are not solipsist pieces of life, that with things changing, others are experiencing similar shocks and stresses. I wonder whether the egalitarian changes I see in some young families will mean permanent changes, or "lapsed egalitarianism" once again. My hope is that the '70s will be different.

This article describes Swedish government attempts to promote greater equality between the sexes. The author argues that traditional sex roles negatively affect men as well as women and points out advantages for both sexes in emancipation from such roles. Like some of the other articles, however, this one also points to difficulties in putting sex role reforms into effect, even when government policies try to promote equality. For example, older people raised under traditional ideologies may be unwilling to change or unable to take advantage of new opportunities. The author is Prime Minister of Sweden.

The Emancipation of Man | *Olof Palme*

In your language man can mean two things—human being and adult male. What I wish to say today is therefore embodied in the title I have given my address, "The Emancipation of Man." We have talked long enough about the emancipation of women, of the problem of woman's role in society. But in order that women shall be emancipated from their antiquated role the men must also be emancipated. Thus, it is the human beings we shall emancipate.

In the long-term program of the party I represent, the Social-Democratic Party of Sweden, we say that the aim over the long run must be that men and women should be given the same rights, obligations, and work assignments in society. This fundamental idea is today embraced by almost all political parties in Sweden.

For our part we mean that the emancipation of men and women would imply considerable advantages from all points of view. The men should have a larger share in the various aspects of family life, for example, better contact with the children. The women should become economically more independent, get to know fellow-workers, and have contacts with environments outside the home. The greatest gain of increased equality between the sexes would be, of course, that nobody should be forced into a predetermined role on account of sex, but should be given better possibilities to develop his or her personal talents. The development of the children would also be positively affected by more contacts with both sexes. Equality also provides prerequisite conditions for better economic security in the family as a result of the double income. If the family is not wholly dependent on only one person's income one can more easily manage temporary reductions in income owing to illness, unemployment, studies, etc.—not to mention what increased equality means for security in connection with divorce or death. The inde-

Reprinted by permission from "The Emancipation of Man" by Olof Palme, *Journal of Social Issues*, 28, no. 2 (1972), pp. 237–246.

pendence of husband and wife can be protected and the strain on one or the other spouse can cease.

It was not until the 1960s, after a long and intensive debate, that this way of thinking became more commonly accepted in Sweden. It is still in strident contrast to the factual conditions. I shall first give a short account of the debate and then give a few examples of the practical measures we are taking to make reality move closer to the ideal.

The view of the roles of the woman and the man inside the family has gradually changed. Before industrialization, in the agrarian society, the family was to a larger extent than now a working community in which both parents had contact with the children. As a result of industrialization the men began to work far away from home and the most important tasks for a woman began to be regarded as care and upbringing of the children. The discrepancy between different groups was, of course, considerable. There were many women who were forced into productive activity for economic reasons, although the community had not arranged for any child care, although they maybe had hard household chores to attend to, and although conditions in the working life were difficult. But the ideal was that the woman should remain at home and take care of the children. The distance between the world of men and women increased. The men were principally looked upon as family supporters and their relationship to the children was impaired; the women got an increasingly dominating role in the upbringing of the children.

During the twentieth century, the women in Sweden were given voting rights. They were given the same educational possibilities as men. The standard of living was raised, dwellings became better, household work became easier by means of mechanical aids, more easily handled material, more finished products. School meals were introduced in all schools. Child allowances and other social benefits eased the situation of families with children. At the same time, instruction on family planning resulted in most families planning the size of their family. The average life span was raised. Modern labor market policy, which aims at maintaining full employment, was introduced.

These factors contributed to changing the views on the role of women. Childbearing and taking care of children took up an increasingly shorter period of the life of most women. After that they had many years ahead when they often experienced that they were no longer fully employed. Most of the functions which the individual household had to carry out earlier now took place outside the home. One therefore began to talk about woman's double role, as mother and as gainfully employed. It should be possible for women to have a new life style: first education and work, then childcare in the home while the children were small, then a return to gainful occupation.

In order to facilitate this life style, demands were raised for, amongst other things, improved service in the dwelling areas, and adult education for women who wished to return to the labor market after having been at home.

But towards the end of the 1950s public discussion on a large scale began in Sweden. There was a feeling that the development was going too slowly. The women had obtained practically all formal rights, but they were still considerably underrepresented in politics and the women on the labor market had, as a rule, low wages and subordinate positions. The women had turned to and were in demand by a limited sector of the labor market, principally lower positions in retail trade, offices, care, and service. Women trying to realize the double-role system often found themselves having double work— at home and on the labor market.

A young woman wrote an essay entitled, "The Conditional Emancipation of Woman," in which she drew attention to the absurdity that the woman had been permitted to compete with the man on the labor market on the condition that she maintain her traditional functions inside the family. "Why should a woman have two roles and the man only one?" she asked. "Is not the role of the father as important as the role of the mother? Should not the household work and the care of the children be shared by the parents, whilst the society simultaneously makes greater efforts for the children?" These views were provocative challenges to many people. Their arguments were based on their own situation which seldom tallied with this idea. They experienced themselves as being attacked, instead of seeing the whole as a problem for the society, a problem which demanded reflection, toilsome work, and long-term planning. They ridiculed the very idea. (Ridicule is probably the weapon which has been most commonly used in the resistance against equality between the sexes.) It was a very emotional debate. But during the 1960s a number of books were published which gave an account of inquiries made and contained facts which gradually made the discussion change its character. It became more matter-of-fact and less emotional.

An important part was played by a book, which is now also translated in large part into English, namely Dahlstrom, *The Changing Roles of Men and Women* (1967). Sociologists, psychologists, social scientists, and economists examined the problem critically from different aspects, for example, just the condition that the role of the woman could not be changed if that of the man was not also changed. They showed how tradition and the expectations of the environment teach the children from the beginning that boys and girls should behave differently and have different characteristics. The so-called "sex roles," i.e., the culturally conditioned expectations for an individual on account of sex, act as a sort of uniform which represses the individuality of the child. For example, in Sweden it is usual for parents to give mechanical toys to boys and dolls only to girls. This guidance is later on reflected in the sex-determined choice of profession. Although the female re-

serve of talents is needed in technology training, boys alone almost entirely
are to be found in this field of instruction. Both children and adults needing
care should benefit from being in an environment with both female and male
nurses, but few boys are attracted to the nursing profession. Women and
men are at an early stage directed towards different spheres of interest, different worlds. The same education and the same role for men and women
should not only achieve real equality between the sexes but also increase
communication between men and women and give them more in common.

Boy and Man

It is not just the traditional female role which has disadvantages. Sociologists remind us that, according to statistics, men have a higher criminal
record, more stress and illness due to strenuous work, higher suicide rates,
and, as a rule, die at an earlier age than women. In school it is the boys who
have the greatest adaption problems. Men who are divorced and living alone
have greater difficulties managing than do divorced women. The interpretation is that the social pressures on the man to assert himself, to fight his way
in life, to be aggressive, and not to show any feelings create contact difficulties and adaption difficulties. Sociologists consider that one should not speak
of "the problem of woman's role in society" but of "the sex-role problem,"
in order to emphasize that the problem also concerns the traditional male
role. This designation is now becoming generally accepted.

The greatest disadvantage with the male sex role is that the man has too
small a share in the upbringing of the children. The ability to show affection
and to establish contact with children has not been encouraged in the man.
Right from the beginning both boys and girls need to have good contacts
with adults of both sexes. Studies have revealed a common trait in the picture
of children and youths with different kinds of behavioral disturbances: They
have poor or no contact with the father or any other grown-up male person.

Sociologists and psychologists draw particular attention to the identification problem for boys. Already at the age of three the child has a need to
identify the self with somebody of the same sex. This process is easier for
girls because they have constant contact with women. It is more difficult for
boys. In modern society they grow up practically wholly in a female world.
At home they are as a rule taken care of by the mother. During the early
school years their teachers consist entirely of female teachers. There is a risk
that the boys, by means of TV, comic strips, and other mass media, create a
false and exaggerated picture of what it means to be a man: Men are tough
and hard-boiled wild-west heroes, agents, supermen, soldiers. Boys compensate for their lack of contact with ordinary men by looking upon the men
of the mass media as their ideal. It should be possible to counteract these
problems. Men should from the beginning have just as much contact with

their children as the women. And we should have both men and women as child nurses, kindergarten teachers, and primary school teachers.

Earlier we had a rather intense discussion in Sweden on whether mothers of small children should work outside the home or not. As a result of the new view, the problem will be instead whether the *parents* of infants should be employed. One solution is that parents work part time and take turns at looking after the child. Many young families with flexible working hours, for example, undergraduate students, now practice this arrangement in Sweden. But psychologists seem to agree that it is not injurious if the child is taken care of by somebody else during part of the day—*nota bene*, if the care is good care and the parents have regular contact with the child.

The new role of the man implies that he must reduce his contributions in the working life—and maybe also in politics—during the period when he has small children. This is what women always had to do alone earlier. From the point of view of national economies, we could manage this loss in production if we can instead stimulate women to make increased contributions in this area.

We therefore look upon the emancipation of the man as important for the development of our children and for equality between the sexes. Both men and women are working towards this end. The result has been programs, drawn up in the different parties, in which it is demanded that men and women should have the same roles. The big trade union organizations have prepared their own programs which will make it possible for men to share child care with women. The trade union organizations and the organization of the employers also have a joint collaboration body which works for equality between the sexes in accordance with this principle. These views, which first appeared to be shocking and were ridiculed, have now been officially accepted; they are to be found in the report on the status of women in Sweden which the Swedish government submitted to the United Nations in 1968.

Public opinion nowadays is so well informed that if a politician today should declare that the woman ought to have a different role than the man and that it is natural that she devotes more time to the children, he would be regarded to be of the Stone Age. The supporters of the emancipation of man have, in other words, won the battle and the ridicule is now directed the other way. In theory, that is; in reality the resistance is still hard. In practical life you find injustices and one-eyed sex-role thinking.

The effort to accomplish the ideas of equality between the sexes is concentrated in the trade union and the political field. We do not have any special government body dealing with this problem but regard it as an aspect of reform work in all fields—in taxation policy, social policy, etc.

Reform in Sweden

An important reform proposal was approved by the Riksdag (the Swedish Parliament) this spring, 1970, and will enter into force on January 1, 1971. It is an important taxation reform which implies a redistribution of the tax burden between higher and lower income earners. But it also implies a changeover from joint taxation to individual taxation and to a single table giving the rates of national income tax. Hitherto we have had double tables, one which hits unmarried persons rather heavily and one which is less severe for married persons. The married man had double privileges compared with his unmarried colleague. For one thing he was taxed at lower rates and was able to make a tax reduction for his wife. The principle behind the new proposal is that all people shall be regarded as economically independent individuals and that society shall adopt a neutral attitude to the form of cohabitation which people choose. The support of the society shall be given where there is a need—to children, to the aged, to the sick, to the handicapped, etc.

Now, one cannot carry out such a radical reform without transitional regulations. We have a large group of families where the woman has no possibility of entering into gainful employment even if she wanted to. She can be too old to receive training, living in a place where there are no job opportunities, etc. For this reason a tax support for these families will remain during a transitional period. But it will be given in the form of a reduction of the final tax instead of as earlier of the income. In this way we have avoided the problem that reduction on the basis of the progressive taxation would be of greater value to those who have a high income than to those who have low incomes.

The extent of gainful occupation among married women in Sweden is not particularly high compared with other industrialized countries, but it is now increasing rapidly. If one defines employment as at least part-time work, 26% of married women in Sweden worked in 1960. In 1965 this share had risen to 33%. It is estimated that in 1970 43% of the married women are employed. The differences between various parts of the country are considerable; in some localities more than half the married women are working.

Married women who have been at home and wish to return to the labor market have the right to receive training and a special allowance. The authority which is responsible for labor market policy has the duty of activating hidden manpower resources, and this is done, amongst other things, by assembling information about job opportunities for women. We regard female unemployment to be an equally serious problem as male unemployment. Labor market policy also encourages firms to discard irrational recruiting according to sex and give the same work to men and women.

In 1960 the Swedish Employers' Confederation and the Swedish Confederation of Trade Unions agreed that special female wages would be abolished by 1965 at the latest. But although the women in most fields now have the same wages for the same work, they have nevertheless lower wages than the men. This is because women and men do not do the same work and the work carried out by the women is more poorly paid. Among the employees in industry, women receive on an average 80% of the wages of the men. This nevertheless is an improvement; ten years ago they only received 70%.

A study carried out by the Swedish Central Organization of Salaried Employees revealed that full-time working members who in 1966 had a net income below $3600 consisted of 85% women and 15% men. In the public sector and in banks and insurance companies, the same wages have been introduced for the same type of work. In other fields, equalization of the wages to men and women has been recommended. Both the workers' and the salaried employees' trade unions regard female wages as part of the low-income problem in general. They pursue a trade union policy which aims at reducing the wage discrepancies between different wage earners. The government has appointed a special commission which is surveying the occurrence, reasons, and effects of low salaries.

In the field of social policy we are working for gradually introducing the principle that the same social benefits should be paid irrespective of sex and civil status. The man who chooses to share the care of children with his wife should not be discriminated against in the social insurance system.

In urban planning we are endeavoring to design dwelling areas with expanded service in different forms to facilitate household work. We want to have good collective communications in order to reduce traveling time and make it easier for both husband and wife to have gainful employment.

The most important form of service is the nursery school, where the children can be while their parents are working. We therefore plan strong expansion of nursery schools during the 1970s. The goal is that all children shall be able to go to a universal school. Some of the children may only stay for three hours, others for a longer period, dependent on whether the parents are working, studying, or prefer to be at home. We have become more and more conscious of how important the first few years of a child's life are for his emotional and intellectual development later in life. The nursery school can compensate those children who do not get as much cultural stimulus at home as they should have.

We should also like working hours to be shorter for parents with small children. We are now heading for a general reduction of the working hours. The 40-hour week will soon be generally in effect and developments point towards a further reduction. If the reduction in working hours is in terms of shorter daily working hours and not in a prolonged vacation over the week-ends, it will be easier for both men and women to combine work with the role of parents.

The old generation in Sweden may consider it correct to *plan* a society with equality between the sexes, but any drastic changes in their *personal* behavior cannot be counted upon. Sex-role attitudes are founded early and are in general too emotional to be changed by means of rational argumenta-tion. As far as the young generation is concerned one can, however, hope to soften up the tradition that some feelings, characteristics, interests, be-haviors, and working assignments are suitable only for men and others only for women. Educational policy is an important instrument to contribute to a more liberal attitude.

Boys and girls in Sweden now receive the same education and are in-structed together in all subjects except in physical training. This means that both boys and girls have compulsory training in textile handicraft and also in wood and metal handicraft. They have also compulsory training in domestic science and child care. One of the aims of the school is to contribute towards equality between the sexes in the family, on the labor market, and in the rest of the community. This aim is emphasized in the training and advanced training of teachers. Study guidance and occupational orientation will con-tribute towards a more liberal choice of profession irrespective of sex.

But even if the school treats boys and girls alike and has the same expecta-tions for them, they are nevertheless influenced by the environment, parents, mass media, the behavior of men and women outside the school, etc., to re-gard their roles as being different. It is then up to the school to make the pupils conscious that they are subjected to such influences and that it is necessary to break an established cultural pattern if one wants to achieve equality between the sexes. Pupils will be stimulated to question critically and discuss the conditions which exist in the society and to arrive at a per-sonal opinion which is based on knowledge of reasons for and effects of the present sex roles.

My review of some of the practical measures we have taken and plan to take to enable men and women to have the same roles has been sketchy. The problems are connected with other political problems which I cannot detail here. The work towards equality between the sexes must be achieved jointly by men and women and not in a struggle against one another. Be-cause it necessitates changing the society, it should be carried out within the framework of strong political and trade union organizations. Also, in Sweden there are small but loud-voiced groups who maintain that reforms are meaningless and that revolution is the first prerequisite condition for equality between the sexes. This is a romantic attitude. We are working against the pressure of thousand-year-old traditions. It necessitates everyday stubbornness, toughness, and patience in order to change attitudes and to accomplish reforms which gradually change conditions in a peaceful manner. It is in this way we have changed and are changing Swedish society in many fields. Maybe one can become a pessimist when one observes the big gap between utopia and reality as far as the roles of men and women are concerned. But the strong swing which occurred in public opinion in Sweden during the 1960s arouses hope that the emancipation of men and women will be possible.

References

Dahlstrom, E., ed. *The Changing Roles of Men and Women*. London: Duckworth, 1967.

Chapter 7

Love and Pairing

The author is an experimental social psychologist. She attempts to apply the findings of laboratory research to the phenomenon of passionate love, which she defines as a distinct emotional state, not to be confused with strong liking. Passionate love, she argues, is experienced as a result of two factors: being stirred up emotionally, and labeling one's emotional arousal as "love." One of the more surprising hypotheses in this article is that any source of excitement or arousal—fear, anger, frustration, even rejection—can facilitate passion. What does this analysis signify for long-term love relationships? Very little per se, although it does help to explain the difficulty of sustaining a high level of passion over many years and to understand how fights and other emotionally arousing events can serve to stimulate a couple's sexual interest.

Passionate Love | *Elaine Walster*

Definitions

Liking has been defined by a number of researchers (e.g., Newcomb, 1961; Homans, 1950) as "a positive attitude toward another, evidenced by a tendency to approach and interact with him." Theorists generally agree on the genesis of liking: individuals like those who reward them.*

Researchers have spent little time defining or investigating *passionate love.* Many theorists simply assume that passionate love is nothing more than very intense liking. We would argue, however, that passionate love is a distinct emotional state. We would argue that a person will experience love only if 1)

*We use the term *companionate love* to indicate unusually intense *liking* between two persons.

he is physiologically aroused, and 2) he concludes that love is the appropriate label for his aroused feelings.

Passionate Love: A Taboo Topic

Most of us would agree that passion is more fascinating than friendship. However, a multitude of researchers have conducted experiments on liking, while very few have explored passionate love.

What accounts for this imbalance?

1. First, scientists who wanted to investigate romantic attraction found it very difficult to secure research funds. Granting agencies, sensitive to the feelings of legislators and the public, were nervous about even considering proposals whose titles contained the offensive words "Love" or "Sex." Even today, whenever a researcher is ill-mannered enough to affix such a title to his proposal, alert bureaucrats quickly expurgate the offensive term and substitute the euphemism "social affiliation."

2. Psychologists did not themselves acknowledge the legitimacy of investigating passionate love. They often ridiculed colleagues who began conducting experiments on this taboo topic. To study love was to be "soft-headed," "unscientific," or to possess a flair for the trivial. It is interesting to note that early in their careers some of our most eminent social psychologists conducted one—and only one—study on romantic attraction. Professional reaction to their research uniformly led them to decide to investigate other topics.

3. Psychologists tend to assume that in the laboratory one can only study mild and quickly developing phenomena. Although poets argue that love may occur "at first sight," psychologists have had less confidence that one can generate passionate love in a two-hour laboratory experiment. Thus, many researchers erroneously assumed that passionate love could only be studied in the field.

Suddenly, the situation changed. The humanists invaded psychology, and the study of tender emotions became respectable. Masters and Johnson's (1966) impressive research demonstrated that even sex could be examined in the laboratory. (Ironically, these pioneers were attacked by the public for failing to investigate love as well as sex.) In the last five years more psychologists have begun to study romantic love than investigated the phenomenon in the history of psychology.

The problem now is not finding respectability but finding out some facts. Presently, when faced with requests for information about love and sex, chagrined psychologists must admit that "they really don't know love at all." Hopefully, in this conference we can gain a better understanding about this vital—and entertaining—topic. In this lecture, I will propose a theoretical framework which may give us a better understanding of passionate love.

"What Is This Thing Called Love?"

Interpersonal attraction and companionate love seem like sensible phenomena. One can predict quite well how much a person will like another, if he knows to what extent the other rewards or punishes the person. Reward has so predictable an impact on liking that Byrne et al. (1968) could with confidence propose an exact correspondence between reinforcement and liking: ("Attraction towards X is a positive linear function of the proportion of positive reinforcements received from X or expected from X.") Data support their formulation.

Sometimes passionate love seems to operate in a sensible fashion. Some practical people have been known to fall in love with those beautiful, wise, entertaining, and kind people who offer affection or material rewards to them. Generally, however, passionate love does not seem to fit so neatly into the reinforcement paradigm. Individuals do *not* always feel passionate about the person who provides the most rewards with the greatest consistency. Passion sometimes develops under conditions that would seem more likely to provoke aggression and hatred than love. For example, reinforcement theorists argue that "we like those who like us and reject those who dislike us." Yet individuals experience intense love for those who have rejected them.

> A woman discovers her husband is seeing another. The pain and suffering the jealous wife experiences at this discovery cause her to realize how much she loves her husband.
> Lovers pine away for the girls who spurn their affection. For example, a recent Associated Press release reports the desperate excuse of an Italian lover who kidnapped his former sweetheart: " 'The fact that she rejected me only made me want and love her more,' he tearfully explained."

Reinforcement theorists tell us that "frustration always breeds aggression." Yet, inhibited sexuality is assumed to be the foundation of romantic feelings. Freud (1912) even argued that:

> Some obstacle is necessary to swell the tide of libido to its height; and at all periods of history whenever natural barriers in the way of satisfaction have not sufficed, mankind has erected conventional ones in order to enjoy love.

The observation that passionate love flourishes in settings which would seem to thwart its development has always been puzzling to social scientists. Poets attribute such inexplicable phenomena to the essential illogic of love. Scientists, who refuse to acknowledge that anything is inexplicable, do not have such an easy way out.

Happily, we believe that a theoretical framework exists which makes the "illogical" phenomena of passionate love explicable and predictable.

Schachter's Two-Component Theory

On the basis of an ingenious series of experiments, Schachter (1964) proposed a paradigm for understanding human emotional response. He argues that in order for a person to experience true emotion, two factors must coexist: 1) The individual must be physiologically aroused, and 2) It must be reasonable to interpret his stirred-up state in emotional terms. Schachter argued that neither physiological arousal nor appropriate cognitions *alone* is sufficient to produce an emotional experience.

It is possible to manipulate an individual's physiological arousal artificially. A drug, adrenalin, exists whose effects mimic the discharge of the sympathetic nervous system. Shortly after one receives an injection of adrenalin, systolic blood pressure increases markedly, heart rate increases somewhat, cutaneous blood flow decreases, muscle and cerebral blood flow increase, blood sugar and lactic acid concentration increase, and respiration rate increases slightly. The individual who has been injected with adrenalin experiences palpitation, tremor, and sometimes flushing and accelerated breathing. These reactions are identical to the physiological reactions which accompany a variety of natural emotional states.

An injection of adrenalin will not, by itself, however, engender an emotional response in a person. When an individual is injected with adrenalin and asked to introspect, he will report either no emotional response or, at best, report feeling "as if" he might be experiencing some emotion (Marañon, 1924). Individuals make statements such as "I feel *as if* I were afraid." The person who has been injected with adrenalin perceives that something is not quite authentic about his reactions. Something is missing.

Schachter argues that what is missing is an appropriate label for the physiological reactions one is experiencing. If one could lead the drugged individual to attribute his stirred-up state to some emotion-arousing event (rather than attributing it to the injection of adrenalin which he received), Schachter argues that he would experience a "true" emotion.

The researcher who wishes to test the notion that physiological arousal and appropriate cognitions are separate and indispensable components of a true emotional experience, is faced with the challenging task of separately manipulating these two components. In a classic study, Schachter and Singer (1962) conceived of a way to do just that. Volunteers were recruited for an experiment which the experimenters claimed was designed to investigate the effects of a new vitamin compound, Suproxin, on vision.

Manipulating Physiological Arousal: Volunteers were injected with a substance which was identified as Suproxin. Actually, one half of the students were injected with epinephrine (½ cc of a 1:1000 solution of Winthrop Laboratory's Suprarenin). Such an injection causes the intense physiological reactions described earlier. One half received a placebo (½ cc of saline solution).

Manipulating an Appropriate Explanation: Schachter wished to lead some of the volunteers to correctly attribute their physiological state to a nonemotional cause (the injection). He wished to lead others to attribute their stirred-up state to an emotional cause.

Thus, in one condition (the *Non-Emotional Attribution* condition), individuals were given a complete explanation of how the shot would affect them. They were warned that in 15 to 20 minutes the injection of "Suproxin" would cause palpitation, tremor, etc. Presumably, when students began to experience these symptoms, they could properly attribute their stirred-up state to the shot and would *not* attribute their excitement to the activities in which they were engaging at the time the adrenalin began to take effect.

In the *Emotional Attribution* conditions, things were arranged to *discharge* students from attributing their stirred-up state to the shot. One group of volunteers was given no information about possible side effects of the shot. A second group of volunteers was deliberately misled as to the potential side effects of the shot. It was assumed that volunteers who received either no information or incorrect information would be unlikely to attribute their tremors and palpitations to the shot. After all, these symptoms took 20 minutes to develop. Instead, the authors hoped that volunteers would attribute their arousal to whatever they happened to be doing when the drug took effect. The authors then arranged things so that what volunteers "happened to be doing" was participating in either a gay, happy, social interaction or participating in a tense, explosive interaction.

If the subject had been assigned to the *Euphoria* condition, his fellow student (who was actually a confederate) had been trained to generate excitement while they waited 20 minutes for the experiment to begin. As soon as the experimenter left the room, the confederate began "acting up." He shot paper wads into the wastebasket, built a paper tower which he sent crashing to the floor and generally kidded around.

In the *Anger* setting, the confederate had been trained to make the subject angry. The confederate first complained about the experimental procedures. He became especially indignant on encountering the questionnaire they had been asked to fill out (and which admittedly asked stupid and offensive questions). Finally, the confederate slammed his questionnaire to the floor and stomped out.

The authors assessed subject's emotional reactions to the confederate's behavior in two ways. Observers stationed behind a one-way mirror assessed to what extent the subject caught the stooge's euphoric or angry mood; secondly, subjects were asked to describe their moods and to estimate how euphoric and angry they felt.

Schachter and Singer predicted that those subjects who had received an adrenalin injection would have stronger emotional reactions than would subjects who had received a placebo or had received an adrenalin injection but had been warned of exactly what physiological changes they should expect. The data supported these hypotheses. The experiment thus supported the contention that both physiological arousal and appropriate cognitions are indispensable components of a true emotional experience. Schachter and Wheeler (1962) and Hohmann (1962) provide additional support for this contention.

The Two-Component Theory and Passionate Love

The discovery that almost any sort of intense physiological arousal—if properly interpreted—will precipitate an emotional experience has intriguing implications. We were particularly intrigued by the possibility that Schachter's "two-component" theory might help explain a heretofore inexplicable phenomenon—passionate love.

As long as researchers were busily absorbed in figuring out how passionate love could be integrated into the reinforcement paradigm, we made little progress. The observation that negative experiences often lead to increased evaluation remained inexplicable.

A sudden insight solved our dilemma. Two components are necessary for a passionate experience: arousal and appropriate cognitions. Perhaps negative experiences do not increase love by somehow improving one's evaluation of the other (beneficially altering his cognitions). Perhaps negative experiences are effective in inducing love because they intensify the second component—arousal.

We would suggest that perhaps it does not really matter how one produces an agitated state in an individual. Stimuli that usually produce sexual arousal, gratitude, anxiety, guilt, loneliness, hatred, jealousy, or confusion may all increase one's physiological arousal, and thus increase the intensity of his emotional experience. As long as one attributes his agitated state to passion, he should experience true passionate love. As soon as he ceases to attribute his tumultuous feelings to passion, love should die.

Does any evidence exist to support our contention? Some early observers noticed that any form of strong emotional arousal breeds love (although not, of course, interpreting this relationship in Schachterian terms). Finck (1891), an early psychologist, concluded:

> Love can only be excited by strong and vivid emotion, and it is almost immaterial whether these emotions are agreeable or disagreeable. The Cid wooed the proud heart of Diana Ximene, whose father he had slain, by shooting one after another of her pet pigeons. Such persons as arouse

> in us only weak emotions or none at all, are obviously least likely to
> incline us toward them. . . . Our aversion is most likely to be bestowed
> on individuals who, as the phrase goes, are neither 'warm' nor 'cold';
> whereas impulsive, choleric people, though they may readily offend us,
> are just as capable of making us warmly attached to them. (p. 240)

Unfortunately, experimental evidence does not yet exist to support the
contention that almost any form of high arousal, if properly labeled, will
deepen passion. There are, however, a few studies designed to test other
hypotheses, which provide some minimal support for our contention.*

Since it was the juxtaposition of misery and ecstasy in romantic love that
we initially found so perplexing, let us first examine the relation between
negative experiences and love.

Unpleasant Emotional States: Facilitators of Passion?

That negative reinforcements produce strong emotional reactions in all
animals is not in doubt. There is some evidence that under the right conditions such unpleasant, but arousing, states as fear, rejection, and frustration
do enhance romantic passion.

Fear: A Facilitator of Passion

Frightening a person is a very good way of producing intense psychological arousal for a substantial period of time (see Ax, 1953; Wolf and Wolff,
1947; and Schachter, 1957).

An intriguing study by Brehm et al. (1970) demonstrates that a frightened
man is a romantic man. Brehm et al. tested the hypothesis that "a person's
attraction to another would be multiplied by prior arousal from an irrelevant
event." In this experiment, some men were led to believe that they would
soon receive three "pretty stiff" electrical shocks. Half of the men, "Threat"
subjects, were allowed to retain this erroneous expectation throughout the
experiment. Half of the men, "Threat-Relief," were frightened and then,
sometime later, were told that the experimenter had made an error; they had
been assigned to the control group and would receive no shock. The remainder of the men were assigned to a control group, in which the possibility
of their receiving shock was not even mentioned.

Men were then introduced to a young co-ed, and asked how much they
liked her.

The Threat subjects who expected to be shocked in the future should be
quite frightened at the time they meet the girl. The Threat-Relief subjects

---

*These studies are only "minimally supportive" because the authors investigate only
liking, not passionate loving—a phenomenon we have argued is unique. Whether or not
the same results would occur in a romantic context must yet be determined.

who had just learned they would not be shocked should be experiencing vast relief when they meet the girl. Both the frightened and the frightened-relieved men should be more aroused than are men in the control group. Brehm predicted, as we would, that Threat and Threat-Relief subjects would like the girl more than would control subjects. Brehm's expectations were confirmed; threatened men experienced more liking for the girl (and did not differ in their liking) than did control group men, who had never been frightened. An irrelevant frightening event, then, does seem to facilitate attraction.

Rejection: An Antecedent of Passion

Rejection is always disturbing. And generally when a person is rejected he has a strong emotional reaction. Usually he experiences embarrassment, pain, or anger. Although it is probably most reasonable for a rejected person to label his agitation in this way, if our hypothesis is correct, it should be possible, under the right conditions, to induce a rejected individual to label his emotional response as "love" as well as "hate."

Some slight evidence that passionate love *or* hate may emerge from rejection comes from several laboratory experiments designed to test other hypotheses (Dittes, 1959; Walster, 1965; and Jacobs et al., 1971).

Let us consider one of these experiments and the way a Schachterian might reinterpret these data.

The experiment of Jacobs et al. was designed to determine how changes in the self-esteem of college students affected their receptivity to love and affection. First, students took a number of personality tests (the *MMPI*, Rorschach, etc.). A few weeks later, a psychologist returned an analysis of his personality to each student. Half of the students were given a flattering personality report. The reports stressed their sensitivity, honesty, originality, and freedom of outlook. (Undoubtedly this flattering personality report confirmed many of the wonderful things the students already thought about themselves.) Half of the students received an insulting personality report. The report stressed their immaturity, weak personality, conventionality, and lack of leadership ability. This critical report was naturally most upsetting for students.

Soon after receiving their analyses, the males got acquainted individually with a young female college student (actually, this girl was an experimental confederate). Half of the time the girl treated the boy in a warm, affectionate, and accepting way. Under such conditions, the men who had received the critical personality evaluation were far more attracted to her than were their more confident counterparts. (Presumably, the previous irrelevant arousal engendered by rejection facilitated the subsequent development of affection.)

Half of the time the girl was cold and rejecting. Under these conditions, a dramatic reversal occurred; the previously rejected men disliked the girl more than did their more confident counterparts. (Presumably, under these conditions, the low self-esteem individual's agitation was transformed to hatred.)

An irrelevant, painful event, then, can incite various strong emotional reactions toward others. Depending on how he labels his feelings, the individual may experience either intense attraction or intense hostility.

Frustration and Challenge: Facilitators of Passion

Socrates, Ovid, Terence, the Kama Sutra and "Dear Abby" are all in agreement about one thing: the person whose affection is easily won will inspire less passion than the person whose affection is hard to win.

Vassilikos (1964) poetically elucidated the principle that frustration fuels passion while continual gratification dims it:

> Once upon a time there was a little fish who was a bird from the waist up and who was madly in love with a little bird who was a fish from the waist up. So the Fish-Bird kept saying to the Bird-Fish: "Oh, why were we created so that we can never live together? You in the wind and I in the wave. What a pity for both of us." And the Bird-Fish would answer: "No, what luck for both of us. This way we'll always be in love because we'll always be separated." (p. 131)

Some provisional evidence that the hard-to-get person may engender unusual passion in the eventually successful suitor comes from Aronson and Linder (1965). These authors tested the hypothesis that: "A gain in esteem is a more potent reward than invariant esteem." They predicted that a person would be better liked if his positive regard was difficult to acquire than if it was easily had.

This hypothesis was tested in the following way: Subjects were required to converse with a confederate (who appeared to be another naive subject) over a series of seven meetings. After each meeting, the subject discovered (secretly) how her conversation partner felt about her. How the confederate "felt" was systematically varied. In one condition the girl expressed a negative impression of the subject after their first meetings. (She described the subject as being a dull conversationalist, a rather ordinary person, not very intelligent, as probably not having many friends, etc.) Only after the partners had become well acquainted did she begin expressing favorable opinions of the subject. In the remaining conditions, from the first, the confederate expressed only positive opinions about the subject.

As Aronson and Linder predicted, subjects liked the confederate whose affection was hard to win better than they liked the confederate whose high opinion was readily obtained.

The preceding evidence is consistent with our suggestion that under the right conditions, a hard-to-get girl should generate more passion than the constantly rewarding girl. The aloof girl's challenge may excite the suitor; her momentary rejection may shake his self-esteem. In both cases, such arousal may intensify the suitor's feelings toward her.

The preceding analysis lends some credence to the argument that the juxtaposition of agony and ecstasy in passionate love is not entirely accidental. (The original meaning of "passion" was, in fact, "agony"—for example, as in Christ's passion.) Loneliness, deprivation, frustration, hatred, and insecurity may in fact supplement a person's romantic experiences. Passion requires physiological arousal, and all of the preceding states are certainly arousing.

Pleasant Emotional States: Facilitators of Passion?

We would like to make it clear that, theoretically, passion need not include a negative component. The positive reinforcements of discovery, excitement, companionship, and playful-joy can generate as intense an arousal as that stirred by fear, frustration, or rejection. For example, in many autobiographical accounts, entirely joyful (albeit brief) passionate encounters are described (e.g., Duncan, 1968).

Sexual Gratification: A Facilitator of Passion

Sexual experiences can be enormously rewarding and enormously arousing. Masters and Johnson (1966) point out that sexual intercourse induces hyperventilation, tachycardia, and marked increases in blood pressure. And, religious advisors, school counselors, and psychoanalysts to the contrary—sexual gratification has undoubtedly generated as much passionate love as has sexual continence.

Valins (1966) demonstrated that even the erroneous belief that another has excited one (sexually or aesthetically) will facilitate attraction. Valins recruited male college students for a study of males' physiological reactions to sexual stimuli. The sexual stimuli he utilized were ten semi-nude *Playboy* photographs. The subjects were told that while they scrutinized these photographs, their heart rate would be amplified and recorded. They were led to believe that their heart rates altered markedly to some of the slides but that they had no reaction at all to others. (Valins assumed that the subjects would interpret an alteration in heart rate as sexual enthusiasm.)

The subjects' liking for the "arousing" and "nonarousing" slides was then assessed in three ways. Regardless of the measure used, the men markedly preferred the pin-ups they thought had aroused them to those that had not affected their heart rate. 1) They were asked to rate how "attractive or appealing" each pin-up was. They preferred the pin-ups they believed were arousing to all others. 2) They were offered a pin-up in remuneration for participating in the experiment. They chose the arousing pin-ups more often than the nonarousing ones. 3) Finally, they were interviewed a month later (in a totally different context) and they still markedly preferred the arousing pin-ups to the others.

Need Satisfaction: A Facilitator of Passion

Although psychologists tend to focus almost exclusively on the contribution of sex to love, other rewards can have an equally important emotional impact. People have a wide variety of needs, and at any stage of life many of one's needs must remain unsatisfied. When any important unsatisfied need is recognized or met, the emotional response which accompanies such reinforcement could provide fuel for passion. To the adolescent boy who has been humored, coddled, and babied at home, the girl who finally recognizes his masculinity may be an over-powering joy. The good, steady, reliable, hard-working father may be captivated when an alert lady recognizes that he has the potential to be a playful and reckless lover.

To the person who has been deprived of such rewards, an intelligent, artistic, witty, beautiful, athletic, or playful companion may prove a passionate and absorbing joy.

Labeling

We are proposing a two-factor theory of passionate love. Yet the preceding discussion has focused almost exclusively on one factor. We have concentrated on demonstrating that physiological arousal is a crucial component of passionate love, and that fear, pain, and frustration as well as discovery and delight may contribute to the passionate experience.

We should now at least remind the reader that according to our theory an individual will be incapable of experiencing "love" unless he's prepared to define his feelings in that way.

Cultural Encouragement of Love

In our culture, it is expected that everyone will eventually fall in love. Individuals are strongly encouraged to interpret a wide range of confused feelings as love. Linton makes this point in a somewhat harsh observation:*

---

*From *The Study of Man: An Introduction,* by Ralph Linton. Copyright 1936. Copyright © 1964 by Meredith Corporation. Reprinted by permission of Appleton-Century-Crofts, Educational Division, Meredith Corporation.

All societies recognize that there are occasional violent emotional attachments between persons of the opposite sex, but our present American
culture is practically the only one which has attempted to capitalize on
these and make them the basis for marriage. The hero of the modern
American movie is always a romantic lover, just as the hero of an old
Arab epic is always an epileptic. A cynic may suspect that in any ordinary population the percentage of individuals with capacity for romantic
love of the Hollywood type was about as large as that of persons able
to throw genuine epileptic fits. (p. 175)

Individuals are often encouraged to interpret certain confused or mixed
feelings as love, because our culture insists that certain reactions are acceptable if one is madly in love. For example, the delightful experience of sexual
intercourse can be frankly labeled as "sexual fun" by a man. Such an interpretation of what she is experiencing is probably less acceptable to his partner. She (and her parents) are undoubtedly happier if she attributes her
abandoned behavior to love.

Margaret Mead interprets jealously in one way:

Jealousy is not a barometer by which the depth of love may be read.
It merely records the degree of the lover's insecurity. It is a negative,
miserable state of feeling, having its origin in a sense of insecurity and
inferiority.

Jealous people, however, usually interpret their jealous reactions in quite
another way; jealous feelings are taken as evidence of passionate love rather
than inferiority. Thus, in this culture, a jealous man is a loving man rather
than an embarrassed man.

Thus, whether or not an individual is susceptible to "falling in love"
should depend on the expectations of his culture and his reference groups.

Individual Expectations

An individual's own expectations should also determine how likely he is
to experience love.

The individual who thinks of himself as a nonromantic person should fall
in love less often than should an individual who assumes that love is inevitable. The nonromantic may experience the same feelings that the romantic
does, but he will code them differently.

Similarly, individuals who feel they are unlovable should have a difficult
time finding love. Individuals convey their expectations in very subtle ways
to others, and these expectations influence the way one's partner labels *his*
reactions. The insecure girl who complains to her boyfriend: "You don't love
me, you just think you do. If you loved me you wouldn't treat me this way,"
and then itemizes evidence of his neglect, may, by automatically interpreting
her boyfriend's actions in a damaging way, affect an alteration in his feelings

for her. Alternately, a girl with a great deal of self-confidence may (by her unconscious guidance) induce a normally unreceptive gentleman to label his feelings for her as love.

References

Aronson, E., and D. Linder. "Gain and Loss of Esteem as Determinants of Interpersonal Attractiveness." *Journal of Experimental Social Psychology*, 1 (1965): 156–171.

Ax, A. F. "Fear and Anger in Humans." *Psychosomatic Medicine*, 15 (1953): 433–442.

Brehm, J. W.; M. Gatz; G. Geothals; J. McCrimmon; and L. Ward. "Psychological Arousal and Interpersonal Attraction." Mimeographed, available from authors, 1970.

Byrne, D., O. London, and K. Reeves. "The Effect of Physical Attractiveness, Sex, and Attitude Similarity on Interpersonal Attraction." *Journal of Personality*, 36 (1968): 269–271.

Dittes, J. E. "Attractiveness of Group as Function of Self-Esteem and Acceptance by Group." *Journal of Abnormal and Social Psychology*, 59 (1959): 77–82.

Duncan, I. *Isadora*. New York: Award Books, 1968.

Finck, H. T. *Romantic Love and Personal Beauty: Their Development, Causal Relations, Historic and National Peculiarities*. London: Macmillan, 1891.

Freud, S. "The Most Prevalent Form of Degradation in Erotic Life." In *Collected Papers*, 4, edited by E. Jones, pp. 203–216. London: Hogarth, 1925.

Hohmann, G. W. "The Effect of Dysfunctions of the Autonomic Nervous System on Experienced Feelings and Emotions." Paper read at Conference on Emotions and Feelings at New School for Social Research, New York, 1962.

Homans, G. C. *The Human Group*. New York: Harcourt, Brace, and World, 1950.

Jacobs, L., E. Walster, and E. Berscheid. "Self-esteem and Attraction." *Journal of Personality and Social Psychology*, 17 (1971): 84–91.

Linton, R. *The Study of Man* (1936). New York: Appleton-Century, 1964.

Marañon, G. Contribution a l'etude de l'action emotive de l'andrenaline. *Revue Francaise Endocrinalogia*, 2 (1924): 301–325.

Masters, W. H., and V. E. Johnson. *Human Sexual Response*. Boston: Little, Brown, 1966.

Mead, M. In *The Anatomy of Love*, by A. M. Krich. New York: Dell, 1960.

Newcomb, T. N. *The Acquaintance Process*. New York: Holt, Rinehart and Winston, 1961.

Schachter, J. "Pain, Fear and Anger in Hypertensives and Normotensives: A Psychophysiological Study." *Psychosomatic Medicine*, 19 (1957): 17–24.

Schachter, S. "The Interaction of Cognitive and Physiological Determinants of Emotional State." In *Advances in Experimental Social Psychology*, I, edited by Berkowitz, pp. 49–80. New York: Academic Press, 1964.

Schachter, S., and J. Singer. "Cognitive, Social and Physiological Determinants of Emotional State." *Psychological Review*, 69 (1962): 379–399.

Schachter, S., and L. Wheeler. "Epinephrine, Chlorpromazine, and Amusement." *Journal of Abnormal and Social Psychology*, 65 (1962): 121–128.

Valins, S. "Cognitive Effects of False Heart-rate Feedback." *Journal of Personality and Social Psychology*, 4 (1966): 400–408.

Vassilikos, V. *The Plant; the Well; the Angel: A Trilogy*. Translated from Greek by Edmund and Mary Keeley (1st American ed.). New York: Knopf, 1964.

Walster, E. "The Effect of Self-Esteem on Romantic Liking." *Journal of Experimental Social Psychology*, 1 (1965): 184–197.

Wolf, S., and H. G. Wolff. *Human Gastric Function*. 2nd ed. London: Oxford University Press, 1947.

One product of the sexual revolution of the past decade is the "living together" arrangement between unmarried women and men. The present article is based on an exploratory study of current patterns of cohabitation among college students. The author suggests that living together is becoming an increasingly common part of campus courtship. Rather than being a form of trial marriage, she finds living together to be associated with the "going steady" phase of dating; the couples in this study did not see themselves as married, nor were they planning to be married. On the other hand, the couples were more concerned with getting to know each other as whole persons rather than with the sexual aspects of the relationships. The author reports on a variety of problems experienced by the couples, but most of them felt that the benefits of their relationships outweighed the costs. Yet she also points out that we don't really know how early commitments to total relationships influence a young person's personality development, particularly achieving a sense of his or her own identity. Does living together help or hinder this process?

Heterosexual Cohabitation Among Unmarried College Students

Eleanor D. Macklin

During the past five or six years there have been periodic allusions in the popular press to a developing pattern of cohabitation among unmarried youth (*Newsweek*, 1966; *Esquire*, 1967; Grant, 1968; McWhirter, 1968; Schrag, 1968; *Time*, 1968; Bloch, 1969; Karlen, 1969; Rollin, 1969; Sheehy, 1969; *Life*, 1970; Coffin, 1971), but little attempt has been made to explore this phenomenon in the professional literature. The majority of research has continued to dwell on questions regarding the sexual values and attitudes of college students, documenting their increased willingness to engage in and to approve of premarital sexual relations (Bell and Chaskes, 1970; Cannon and Long, 1971; Christensen and Gregg, 1970; Herr, 1970; Kaats and Davis, 1970; Mosher and Cross, 1971; Luckey and Nass, 1972), but providing little information about the changes in living patterns which are simultaneously occurring. Exceptions include a series of published interviews with cohabiting college couples (Ald, 1969), an unpublished master's thesis based on interviews with 28 cohabiting student couples at the University of Iowa (Johnson, 1969), the unpublished work on "unmarried college liaisons" ("unmalias") by sociologist Robert N. Whitehurst (1969), a study

Reprinted by permission from "Heterosexual Cohabitation Among Unmarried College Students" by Eleanor D. Macklin, *The Family Coordinator*, October 1972, pp. 463–471.

of student and parental attitudes with respect to the university's responsibility in the area of off-campus cohabitation at Michigan State University (Smith and Kimmel, 1970), and a call for further research and counseling facilities by emotional health consultant Miriam Berger (1971).

It was because so little was known about the current patterns of cohabitation among college youth that the present study was undertaken. This report summarizes the initial pilot phase of this research. In order to obtain a more complete picture of the various forms which living together might assume, a fairly inclusive definition of cohabitation was adopted: To share a bedroom ⎫ for at least four nights per week for at least three consecutive months with ⎭ someone of the opposite sex. Throughout this paper, the definition of cohabitation will be used.

The objectives of this phase of the research were to gain an estimate of the prevalence of this experience, and an understanding of the nature of the relationship, the reasons for involvement, and the problems and benefits experienced. A series of four-hour semistructured interviews was conducted in April 1971 with fifteen junior and senior female students at Cornell University, Ithaca, N.Y., who had experienced heterosexual cohabitation. In September 1971, a questionnaire based on the interview schedule was given to 104 junior and senior women in a course on adolescent development at Cornell. Of the 86 who responded, 29 had experienced cohabitation. The fifteen interviewees had been involved in a total of 20 such relationships (eleven had experienced one such relationship, three had had two, and one, three). The 29 questionnaire respondents had experienced a total of 35 cohabitation relationships (24 had had one, four had had two, and one had had three).

The following discussion will be based on the information obtained from the combined group of 44 cohabitants. Questionnaire data will serve as the basis for all quantitative reporting, but it should be understood that interview data were generally corroborative.

Prevalence

From the present data one can only surmise the frequency with which cohabitation currently occurs at Cornell. Of the 86 junior and senior women who completed the questionnaire,* 34 percent had already had such an experience by the beginning of the 1971 fall term. When these 86 students were asked to predict what percentage of Cornell undergraduates probably experience cohabitation prior to graduation, almost three-quarters predicted

---

*Of the 104 junior and senior women in the class, 86 completed the questionnaire. Of these, 58 handed it in on the due date and 28 after a follow-up request. Since the percentage of cohabitants was the same for the initial and the follow-up respondents, it is assumed that the percentage would be similar for the eighteen non-returnees.

that 40 percent or more would do so. When asked how many of their close friends had experienced or were experiencing cohabitation, only 7 percent said "none," and over 40 percent said "many" or "most."

Of the 57 respondents who had not experienced cohabitation as defined, almost two-thirds checked that they had stayed with someone but not for as long as indicated in the definition. When asked why they had not cohabited, the large majority indicated that it was because they had not yet found an appropriate person. A few checked that it would be unwise for them at present due to the stage of their relationship, their immaturity, the possibility of discovery, or physical impracticality. Only one person said she had not because it would be wrong to do so outside of marriage.

Further clues to the frequency of cohabitation come from the questionnaire pretest which was given to two undergraduate classes in April 1971. Of 150 underclassmen responding, 28 percent indicated having experienced cohabitation. From an upperclass seminar on delinquency taught by the author, 12 of the 20 students volunteered to be interviewed regarding their cohabitation experience. One is led to conclude from all available evidence that cohabitation is a common experience for students on this particular campus and is accepted by many as a "to-be-expected" occurrence.

Description of the Cohabitation Experience

A wide variety of types of cohabitation experiences were revealed: among them, living with a male roommate in a co-op (with no sexual involvement and with both roommates having other romantic attachments), living in a tent while traveling in Europe, sharing a dormitory or a fraternity room, or sharing a room with another cohabiting couple. However, the most common pattern was for the girl to move into the boy's room (or vice versa) in an apartment or house which he was sharing with several other males (one of whom might also have a girl living in). Graduate student pairs are more likely to live alone in an apartment or a house; freshman couples are more likely to share a dormitory room. Very few couples shared their bedroom with a third person.

In the majority of cases, living quarters had not been obtained initially with living together in mind (although many men arrange to have a single room in order to allow privacy for any potential entertaining). Living arrangements were not usually jointly arranged until the second year of a relationship. However, even then, couples were hesitant to arrange for a single joint living situation, and planning simply involved ensuring that the potential apartment-mates were willing to have a girl share the premises. Practically all girls also maintained a room in the dormitory or sorority or in an apartment with other girls. Most went back once a day for a few hours to visit, get messages or mail, exchange clothes, shower, or study. Maintaining a separate residence precludes having to explain to parents, ensures a place to live if the relationship is not working well, helps maintain contact with female friends, serves as a convenient place to study, and provides often necessary storage space (the boy's room being too small to hold both sets of belongings).

In about half of the relationships, the couple spent seven nights a week together. In the remaining half, the girl returned to her own room one or two nights a week in order to see her friends and to allow him time with his friends. It should be noted at this point that spending the night together, even in the same bed, need not imply a full sexual relationship. Aside from the instance of the non-emotionally involved coed roommates, there were couples who had lived together for more than three months without intercourse because they did not yet feel ready for this experience (these were usually virgin women). The irony of this is the frequency with which the older generation refuses to accept that this could be true, or if it is, insists that the male must be a "queer."

There was a wide range in amount of time spent together. The majority reported being together about 16-17 hours a day on weekdays (5 P.M. to 8 A.M. plus lunch). Most couples shared at least two meals a day, although occasionally dinner was eaten separately because of the inconvenience involved in having an extra person at dinner or because her parents had already paid for her meals on campus and funds were tight. There was practically no instance of total pooling of finances in these relationships, although the couple normally shared food and entertainment expenses. Usually the girl paid her way and maintained her own separate finances, either because the couple could not afford otherwise or as a matter of principle. When there were chores involved, the couple generally did them together (e.g., shopping or laundry), although there was a tendency for the girl to assume responsibility for cooking and cleaning. There was a wide range in the degree to which they shared activities (e.g., classes, study, or hobbies) or spent time with others. The tendency was to share the majority of activities, to have many mutual friends, and to spend much of their time with others as opposed to time only with one another.

Why Students Live Together

There are three aspects to the question of why students are now living together: the circumstances existing at the particular institution, the broader societal reasons, and the personal motivations of the specific students.

Changes in dormitory regulations and the slow demise of *in loco parentis* have greatly facilitated the development of the new pattern. If one goes back to earlier issues of the campus newspaper (*Cornell Daily Sun,* 1962, 1963, 1964), one notes that in 1962, a graduate student was indefinitely suspended from the University for living with a woman in his apartment, and in 1964, a male student was reprimanded for staying overnight at a local hotel with a non-University female. Sexual morality was considered a legitimate concern of the University faculty and "overnight unchaperoned mixed company" was considered by the Faculty Council on Student Conduct to be a violation of sexual morality. (*Cornell Daily Sun,* 1962, p. 2)

Today, Cornell students are free to live in much the same way that non-students who are living and working in the outside world are free to live: they are likely to be residing in a structure which also houses persons of the opposite sex (many of the dorms are now coed, with men and women segregated by floors, wings or suites, although there is experimentation with men and women living on the same corridor); if they are sophomores or beyond, they are free to elect to live off campus; and they may entertain someone of the opposite sex in their room at any time during the 24-hour day. Official policy still prohibits "continuous residence" with someone of the opposite sex in the dormitory setting, but this is difficult to police.

These changes in curfew and dormitory policy must be seen as a reflection of broader social changes: a change in the status of women which makes it difficult to justify different regulations for men and for women, youth's increasing demand that they no longer be treated as children, a questioning of the rigid sexual mores which have traditionally governed people's lives, a greater willingness to grant individuals the right to select their own life style, and the increasing availability of contraception and abortion services.

When students are asked to hypothesize why cohabitation has become more common and more open, they mention youth's search for meaningful relations with others and the consequent rejection of the superficial "dating game"; the loneliness of a large university and the emotional satisfaction that comes from having someone to sleep with who cares about you; the widespread questioning of the institution of marriage and the desire to try out a relationship before there is any, if ever, consideration of permanency; the desire on the part of many to postpone commitment until there is some certainty that individual growth will be compatible with growth of the relationship; the fact that young people mature earlier and yet must wait so long until marriage is feasible; and the fact that the university community provides both sanction and feasibility for such a relationship to develop. Given peer group support, ample opportunity, a human need to love and be loved, and a disposition to question the traditional way, it seems only natural that couples should wish to live together if they enjoy being together. One might almost better ask: Why do students choose *not* to live together?

When one asks students why they personally become involved in a cohabitation relationship, one finds a mixture of enjoying being together and expediency (e.g., too far to drive her home at night, easier to stay than to get up and go back at midnight, less expensive, someone else living with one's roommate, or partner was sick and needed someone to care for him). On occasion, curiosity about what it would be like to live with the opposite sex was involved, and sometimes "to test out the relationship" was mentioned, but it was rarely such a purposeful act.

In fact, living together was seldom the result of a considered decision, at least initially. (Cf. Ryder, Kafka and Olson's concept of "unquestioned beginnings" which they suggest characterize much of courtship in our society.) Most relationships involved a gradual (and sometimes not so gradual) drifting into staying together. The general pattern was to stay over one night; in several weeks, if all was well, to stay for the weekend; in another few weeks to add a week night; in another few weeks, a second week night, and so forth. In half the relationships the couple had begun staying together four or more nights a week by the end of four months of dating.

If and when a decision with conscious deliberation was made, it was usually precipitated by some external force (e.g., need to make plans for the summer or next fall, graduation, unexpected pregnancy, or a necessary housing or room change). Until this time, there was only a mutual, often unspoken, recognition of the desire to be together—a natural progression of the relationship.

Nature of the Relationship

When asked to indicate the nature of the relationship at the time they began living together four or more nights per week, about half checked that they "had a strong, affectionate relationship, not dating others" (i.e., "going steady"—although they resisted this term). Another large group indicated that they "had a strong affectionate relationship but were also open to other relationships." Only a few indicated tentative engagement; even fewer stated that they were just "friends." See Table 1.

It is interesting to note that the above is very similar to answers given by all 86 questionnaire respondents when asked what kind of relationship they felt should exist before college-aged students cohabit (see Table 2). One is impressed by the fact that cohabitation is more frequently associated with the "going steady" stage of a relationship than with engagement, even tentative engagement.

The initial commitment to the relationship varied greatly. Some saw it strictly as temporary (e.g., "while traveling," "he was planning to leave Ithaca," or "he was already committed to someone else") and a few, at the other extreme, definitely planned "marriage in the future when it was more

Table 1. Nature of Relationship When Couple First Started Living Together for at Least Four Nights per Week, as Reported by 29 Upperclass Female Students for 35 Cohabitation-Relationships

Nature of Relationship	Number of Relationships
1. Formally engaged	1
2. Tentatively engaged (contemplating marriage)	3
3. Strong, affectionate relationship; not dating others ("going steady")	17
4. Strong, affectionate relationship; open to other dating relationships	12
5. Friends	1
6. Other ("met and immediately started living together")	1
Total	35

convenient." But the vast majority entered it either with a "let's see" attitude (i.e., to test the relationship—to stay together as long as it was mutually satisfying), or—a somewhat more definite commitment—planned to do all they "could to develop a lasting relationship, but future marriage was not definite."

This raises some question about the label "unmarried marrieds" which has often been applied in the popular literature to unmarried cohabitation. Most of the undergraduate couples did not consider themselves married in any sense of the word. Not only did they not consider themselves married, they rarely considered marriage as a viable alternative to their present cohabitation. When asked, "Did you consider the possibility of getting married instead?" a frequent response was "Heavens no!" Marriage might be seen as a possibility for the future, but the distant future. The future seemed too indefinite to plan that far ahead, they needed more time to grow and develop before considering marriage, and it was financially impractical. Moreover, marriage appeared to have some negative connotations for many of these students—it was seen as limiting their freedom and their growth (cf. the period of youth as discussed by Keniston in *Young Radicals*), and they feared falling into the traditional roles they associated with being wives, even though over two-thirds of those interviewed said their parents would consider their own marriage "very successful."

Problems Encountered

As with any real relationship, these were not always blissful. It was encouraging that those interviewed seemed very aware of the problem areas and were able to verbalize about them easily.

Table 2. Responses of 86 Upperclass Female Students to "What Kind of Relationship Do You Feel *Should* Prevail Before College-Aged Students Cohabit?"

Nature of Relationship	Percent of Respondents
1. Married	4
2. Formally engaged	—
3. Tentatively engaged (contemplating marriage)	8
4. Strong, affectionate relationship; not dating others ("going steady")	60
5. Strong, affectionate relationship; open to other dating relationships	15
6. Friends	8
7. Other (e.g., "anything acceptable to both parties")	5
Total	100%

Problems could be divided into four major categories: emotional problems, sexual problems, problems with parents, and problems related to the living situation. (In the interviews, no one had experienced problems with the community; thus the question was not included in the questionnaire.)

The major emotional problem (see Table 3) was the tendency to become over-involved and to feel a subsequent loss of identity, lack of opportunity to participate in other activities or be with friends, and an over-dependency on the relationship. On the basis of the available data, one is tempted to hypothesize that how this issue is dealt with and the success with which it is handled are major determinants of the outcome of the relationship. The problem of how to achieve security without giving up the freedom to be oneself, and how to grow together and yet leave enough space so the individuals can grow also, appears central.

Other problems in this category were feelings of being trapped (should break up but afraid to do so), feelings of being used, jealousy of partner's involvement in other activities or relationships, and lack of feeling of belonging (e.g., "When I expect that he will share his money with me now that my parents have cut me off, he reminds me that we are not married"). It should be recognized, however, that although there were a few who indicated that these problems caused them a great deal of trouble, the majority indicated little or no problem. It is also important to note that more than two-thirds indicated no feelings of guilt, and the remainder indicated only a minimal amount. In the interviews, when guilt was stated to be present, it was usually related to having to conceal the relationship from parents or it occurred in those instances where they knew that the relationship could not last.

Sexual problems were common (see Table 3). Only a few indicated "no

Table 3. Extent to Which Emotional, Sexual, and Living Situation Problems Were Experienced in 35 Cohabitation Relationships as Reported by 29 Upperclass Female Students (Categories Are Ordered by Number of Persons Reporting the Problem)

	Number Indicating		Average rating given by those
	No	Some	indicating some
Problem Area	Problem	Problem	problem*

Emotional Problems

1. Overinvolvement (loss of identity, lack of opportunity to participate in other activities or with friends, over-dependency)	14	21	2.7
2. Jealousy of partner's involvement in other activities or relationships	14	15	3.1
3. Feeling of being trapped	18	15	2.9
4. Feeling of being used	19	13	2.6
5. Guilt			
-at beginning of relationship	20	9	3.7
-during relationship	25	5	3.8
-at end of relationship	15	2	4.0
6. Lack of feeling of "belonging" or of being "at home"	22	9	3.4
7. Other "will have to separate for a while after his graduation"	—	1	3.0

Sexual Problems

1. Differing degrees or periods of sexual interest	10	23	3.4
2. Lack of orgasm	11	21	3.6
3. Fear of pregnancy	15	15	3.1
4. Vaginal irritation or discharge after intercourse	17	15	3.4
5. Discomfort of partner during intercourse	18	10	3.7
6. Impotence of partner	23	6	3.0

Problems Related to Living Situation

1. Lack of privacy	15	17	3.4
2. Lack of adequate space	19	13	3.0
3. Did not get along with apartment or housemates	20	6	2.2
4. Lack of sufficient money	26	6	3.3
5. Disagreement over use of money, sharing of money, etc.	27	4	3.5

*Respondents were asked to rate each problem from 1 to 5, with 1: great deal of problem, 5: no problem (no other points defined). The last category (5: no problem) has been separated because it may be qualitatively different from the other rating categories. Average ratings are therefore based on ratings from 1 to 4; thus, the lower the average rating the greater the problem for those experiencing it.

problem" in this area. Differing degrees or periods of sexual interest, lack of orgasm, fear of pregnancy, vaginal irritations, feelings of sexual inhibition, and less satisfaction with sex as the relationship deteriorated were the more frequently mentioned problems. However, in spite of problems, over three-fourths of the respondents rated the relationship as sexually satisfying. Practically all used contraception (over 80 percent used either the pill or the diaphragm), with about two-thirds of these having started contraception before or at the time of the first intercourse in the cohabitaion relationship.

A major problem area was parents. More than one-fourth indicated that parents had caused "some" or "many" problems: parental disapproval of the boy, fear of discovery, guilt because they were deceiving or hurting their parents, rejection by or ultimatums from parents, and most frequently, sadness at not being able to share this important part of their lives with their parents. Because of fear of disapproval or unpleasant repercussions, more than two-thirds had tried to conceal the relationship from their parents—by not telling them the whole story, by distorting the truth, and by developing often elaborate schemes to prevent discovery. Almost half of the respondents believed their parents to be unaware of their cohabitation, with the remainder divided equally between those who felt they definitely knew, those who thought they probably knew, and those who were unsure. The boy's parents were much more likely to be aware.

Problems related to the living situation were considered minimal. Lack of privacy, lack of adequate space, lack of sufficient funds or disagreement over money, and friction with apartment mates were all mentioned, with lack of space or privacy and tension with others in the living situation the most common. It should be noted that there was practically no problem experienced as a result of the external community, i.e., landlords, local employers, school administration, neighbors, or contemporaries. In fact, the great majority felt their friends strongly approved of and supported their relationship. In cases where this was not true, it was because friends considered the particular relationship rather than the cohabitation *per se* undesirable.

Benefits

It is important that the problems not be seen as outweighing the values of such relationships. More than half rated their relationship as "very successful," and more than 80 percent checked that it was "both maturing and pleasant." Even in those few cases where the relationship was said to be "painful," they emphasized the personal growth which had occurred, e.g., "I question whether I'd understand myself as well without the hard times." In no case was the experience rated "very unpleasant" or "not at all maturing," and in no case was it considered primarily detrimental to the person involved.

In more than 60 percent of the cases, they would do it over again with the same person, even in those relationships which had broken up at the time of the report.

The benefits seen by the participants included a deeper understanding of themselves and of their needs, expectations, and inadequacies; increased knowledge of what is involved in a relationship and of the complexities of living with someone else; clarification of what they wanted in a marriage; increase in emotional maturity and in self-confidence, e.g., "learned not to commit myself too soon," "learned through breaking up how much strength I have," increased ability to understand and relate to others; emotional security and companionship; and confidence in the possibility for success of the particular relationship, e.g., "because we have coped with problems and come out topside, I have more faith that we will be able to do so again." The main undercurrent in the data was the many ways in which the experience had fostered growth and maturity. All persons interviewed indicated that they would not consider marriage without having lived with the person first, and all—while hesitant to say what others should do—felt the move toward cohabitation could only be seen as a healthy trend.

Outcome of the Relationship

At the time of the questionnaire, one-third of the relationships had dissolved (having lasted an average of four and one-half months from the time they began staying together four or more nights a week), one-third were married or planning to be married, and another third were still in the process of defining the relationship (either were still living together but not yet contemplating marriage, or were still "going together" but not living together—either because the partner was away or they sought more freedom than they had when living together). A somewhat larger portion of those interviewed had broken their relationship, but this may be due to the fact that the interview was later in the academic year. The 23 relationships which were still in process had existed an average of 13 months, with five having continued for two or two and one-half years.

Implications

1. It appears that cohabitation has become an increasingly common aspect of courtship on the campus studied and one could predict that the trend will proliferate.

Although the phenomenon of unmarried persons living together is obviously not a new one, either in this society or others (Berger, 1971), it has certainly not been a common phenomenon among unmarried middle class youth in the United States until quite recently. Some pass it off by saying it is merely a more open expression of what students have been doing sexually on the sly for years, but this suggests a very narrow interpretation of the present situation. The pattern which is currently evolving appears to be primarily concerned with total relationships and only incidentally with the sexual aspects. It is this concern with getting to know another as a whole person and the emphasis on sharing as openly and as completely as possible with that person, which is probably the major new dimension being added to old courtship patterns.

2. There is some question whether cohabitation as now practiced on the college campus fits the concepts of trial marriage, premarital marriage, companionate marriage, or two-stage marriage which some have sought to apply to it (Berger, 1971; Grant, 1968; Karlen, 1969; LeShan, 1971; Mead, 1966). Trial marriage, for instance, tends to imply a level of commitment usually associated with the engagement portion of the courtship continuum which is not characteristic of the campus relationships studied. These students do not in general see themselves as consciously testing or even contemplating a potential marriage, at least not initially. Instead, in most cases, living together seems to be a natural component of a strong, affectionate "dating" relationship—a living out of "going steady"—which may grow in time to be something more, but which in the meantime is to be enjoyed and experienced because it is pleasurable in and of itself.

3. In addition to the question of whether it does in fact lead to healthier marriages or more "fully functioning" persons, there are other intriguing issues. For instance, what is the relationship between commitment to a relationship and identity formation? To what extent must one have developed a strong identity before one can achieve a strong intimate relationship (in Erikson's sense)? What chance is there for a mature, mutual relationship when the individual is still so necessarily focused on his own development? How much commitment to a relationship is necessary for it to have a strong chance of success? Alternately, does early commitment to a relationship hinder identity development? When a person should be at a point of maximum identity development, is it healthy for him to be devoting so much of his energy to the development of a relationship or will this simply accelerate the process? These become very real problems as cohabitation inevitably occurs earlier and becomes increasingly common as a freshman experience.

4. There is a great need to help society adjust to the evolving courtship patterns. Parents in particular tend to see cohabitation as antithetical to all that they consider healthy or moral. They need help if they are to understand and to react without alarm, recrimination, and rejection. Consideration will have to be given to legal implications of the new patterns—some present laws conflict and maybe should be changed, and some new protections for the rights of unmarried participants may be necessary. The professions touched

by the new trends are myriad. Bankers, for instance, as they seek to help parents write wills and set up trust funds, and as they themselves seek to administer these trusts, find themselves confronted with having to understand and interpret the new patterns. Students in particular need more realisic preparation, both at home and in school, and more opportunity for relationship and sex counseling, if they are to cope as responsibly and effectively as possible with the increased freedom and the new pressures. The first step, which most of the adult population has not yet taken, is to acknowledge that the changes are actually occurring and to be willing to entertain the hypothesis that they may indeed be an improvement on the traditional patterns.

References

Ald, Roy. *Sex Off Campus*. New York: Grosset and Dunlap, 1969.

Bauman, Karl E. "Selected Aspects of the Contraceptive Practices of Unmarried University Students." *Medical Aspects of Human Sexuality*, 5 (August 1971): 76–89.

Bell, Robert R., and Jay B. Chaskes. "Premarital Sexual Experience among Coeds, 1958 and 1968." *Journal of Marriage and the Family*, 32 (1970): 81–84.

Berger, Miriam E. "Trial Marriage: Harnessing the Trend Constructively." *The Family Coordinator*, 20 (1971): 38–43.

Bloch, Donald. "Unwed Couples: Do They Live Happily Ever After?" *Redbook*, April 1969, p. 90.

Cannon, Kenneth L., and Richard Long. "Premarital Sexual Behavior in the Sixties." *Journal of Marriage and the Family*, 33 (1971): 36–49.

Christensen, Harold T., and Christina F. Gregg. "Changing Sex Norms in America and Scandinavia." *Journal of Marriage and the Family*, 32 (1970): 616–627.

Coffin, Patricia. "Young Unmarrieds: Theresa Pommett and Charles Walsh, College Grads Living Together." *Look*, January 26, 1971, p. 634.

College and University Business. "Parents OK Strict Rules." December 1968, p. 16.

Cornell Daily Sun, October 9, 1962; October 8, 1963; March 6, 1964.

Crist, Takey. "The Coed as a Gynecological Patient." Mimeographed. Chapel Hill, N.C.: University of North Carolina, 1970.

Davids, Leo. "North American Marriage: 1990." *The Futurist*, October 1971, pp. 190–194.

Esquire. "Room-Mates." September 1967, pp. 94–98.

Fell, Joseph P. "A Psychosocial Analysis of Sex-Policing on Campus." *School and Society*, 98 (1970): 351–354.

Fleming, Thomas, and Alice Fleming. "What Kids Still Don't Know About Sex." *Look*, July 28, 1970, p. 59.

Grant, A. "No Rings Attached: A Look at Premarital Marriage on Campus." *Mademoiselle*, April 1968, p. 208.

Hall, Elizabeth, and Robert A. Poteete. "A Conversation with Robert H. Rimmer about Harrad, Group Marriage, and Other Loving Arrangements." *Psychology Today*, 5 (1972): 57–82.

Herr, Sylvia. "Research Study on Behavioral Pattterns in Sex and Drug Use on College Campus." *Adolescence*, 5 (Spring 1970): 1–16.

Hunt, Morton. "The Future of Marriage." *Playboy*, August 1971, p. 117.

Johnson, Michael P. "Courtship and Commitment: A Study of Cohabitation on a University Campus." Master's thesis. University of Iowa, 1969.

Kaats, Gilbert R., and Keith E. Davis. "The Dynamics of Sexual Behavior of College Students." *Journal of Marriage and the Family*, 32 (1970): 390–399.

Karlen, Arno. "The Unmarried Marrieds on Campus." *New York Times Magazine*, January 26, 1969, p. 29.

Keniston, Kenneth. *Young Radicals*. New York: Harcourt, Brace, and World, 1968.

LeShan, Eda J. *Mates and Roommates: New Styles in Young Marriages*. Public Affairs Pamphlets, No. 468. New York: Public Affairs Pamphlets, 1971.

Lever, Janet, and Pepper Schwartz. "Men and Women at Yale." *Sexual Behavior*, October 1971.

Life. "Coed Dorms: An Intimate Campus Revolution." November 20, 1970, p. 32.

Luckey, Eleanore B., and Gilbert D. Nass. "Comparison of Sexual Attitudes in an International Sample of College Students." *Medical Aspects of Human Sexuality*, 6 (1972): 66–107.

Malcolm, Andrew H. "Sex Goes to College." *Today's Health*, April 1971, pp. 27–29.

McWhirter, William A. "The Arrangement at College." *Life*, May 31, 1968, p. 56.

Mead, Margaret. "A Continuing Dialogue on Marriage: Why Just Living Together Won't Work." *Redbook*, April 1968, p. 44.

Mead, Margaret. "Marriage in Two Steps." *Redbook*, July 1966, p. 48.

Mosher, Donald L., and Herbert F. Cross. "Sex-Guilt and Premarital Sexual Experiences of College Students." *Journal of Consulting and Clinical Psychology*, 36 (February 1971): 27.

Moss, J. Joel, Frank Apolonio, and Margaret Jensen. "The Premarital Dyad During the Sixties." *Journal of Marriage and the Family*, 33 (1971): 50–69.

Newsweek. "Unstructured Relationships: Students Living Together." July 4, 1966, p. 78.

Packard, Vance. *The Sexual Wilderness*. New York: David McKay, 1968.

Peters, Muriel, and William Peters. "How College Students Feel About Love, Sex, and Marriage." *Good Housekeeping Magazine*, June 1970, p. 85.

Reiss, Ira L. "The Sexual Renaissance in America: Summary and Analysis." *Journal of Social Issues*, 22 (April 1966): 123–137.

Rimmer, Robert H. *The Harrad Experiment*. Los Angeles: Sherbourne Press, 1966.

Rockefeller, John D., III. "Youth, Love and Sex: The New Chivalry." *Look*, October 7, 1969, p. 32.

Rollin, Betty. "New Hang-up for Parents: Coed Living." *Look*, September 23, 1969, p. 22.

Ryder, Robert G., John S. Kafka, and David H. Olson. "Separating and Joining Influences in Courtship and Early Marriage." *American Journal of Orthopsychiatry*, 41 (April 1971): 450–464.

Sarrel, Philip M., and Lorna J. Sarrel. "How We Counsel Students on Sex Problems at Yale." *The Osteopathic Physician*, June 1971.

Schrag, Peter. "Posse at Generation Gap: Implications of the Linda LeClair Affair." *Saturday Review*, May 8, 1968, p. 81.

Sheehy, Gail. "Living Together: The Stories of Four Young Couples Who Risk the Strains of Nonmarriage and Why." *Glamour*, February 1, 1969, p. 136.

Smith, Patrick B., and Ko Kimmel. "Student-Parent Reactions to Off-Campus Cohabitation." *Journal of College Student Personnel*, May 1970, pp. 188–193.

Time. "Linda, the Light Housekeeper." April 26, 1968, p. 51.

Whitehurst, Robert. "The Unmarried on Campus." Presented at NCFR Annual Meeting, 1969. Copy available from author, University of Windsor, Windsor, Ontario, Canada.

Whitehurst, Robert. "The Double Standard and Male Dominance in Non-Marital Living Arrangements: A Preliminary Statement." Presented at the American Orthopsychiatric Association Meeting, New York, 1969. Copy available from author, University of Windsor, Windsor, Ontario, Canada.

A psychoanalyst and a psychologist present their impressions of a number of counterculture or "hippie" married couples. Those studied were not patients, but research subjects in a larger study of early marriage. The authors found a consistent tendency for conventional patterns to reappear in the unconventional lives of these couples. Another major finding was a "demystification" of sexuality: These couples were both very active sexually and less awed by sex. Sex for them has more of a natural and less of a romantic flavor than among conventional people.

Notes on Marriages in the Counter Culture

John S. Kafka and Robert G. Ryder

In the course of an extensive study of early marriage (Raush, Goodrich, and Campbell, 1963; Ryder, 1970a, 1970b; Ryder, Kafka, and Olson, 1971), the authors located a small number of couples (less than 1 per cent) who seemed to have serious allegiance to what has been called the counter culture (Roszak, 1969). These and other couples located by a variety of ad hoc means were interviewed in either individual or joint sessions, and in some cases in informal group settings in which some interviewees casually entered or left while the interview was in progress. The interview procedure makes it impossible to arrive at a well-defined figure for sample size, but we estimate that we each spoke with some 40 persons, located mostly on the East and West coasts, especially around Washington, D.C. and San Francisco. Participants were treated more like informants, in the anthropological sense, than like subjects; i.e., we were as interested in reports about other families known to an interviewee as in self-reports. Most participants were in their middle twenties, with a range from the late teens to the late forties.

Reproduced by special permission from *The Journal of Applied Behavioral Science*, 9:2/3, "Notes on Marriages in the Counter Culture," John S. Kafka, M.D., and Robert G. Ryder, Ph.D., pp. 321–330, © 1973, NTL Institute for Applied and Behavioral Science.

The writers wish to acknowledge their debt to the various colleagues who have contributed ideas, information, and critical commentary in the course of completing this paper, particularly to David H. Olson, who has made many substantial and valuable contributions and was closely associated with this project. We wish also to express our thanks to Raymond K. Yang, whose comments on various drafts of this paper have been most helpful.

John S. Kafka, M.D., is a Clinical Professor of Psychiatry and Behavioral Science, George Washington University School of Medicine, Washington, D.C.; Training and Supervising Analyst, Washington Psychoanalytic Institute; Consultant to the Family Development Section, NIMH. Robert G. Ryder is Chief, Section on Family Development, Child Research Branch, NIMH.

There can be little doubt that, as Roszak (1969) has emphasized, the expression "counter culture" refers to a poorly defined, heterogeneous, and changeable set of phenomena; and yet, as Roszak also points out, it is a set of phenomena with a slippery but insistent reality. In the present study, couples were included only if they explicitly intended to avoid the "hangups" of conventional marriage, to maximize intimacy, minimize utilitarian aspects of a relationship (cf. Cuber and Harroff, 1965), and to eschew possessiveness and loyalty to conventional roles. The importance of money was generally minimized. Boundaries, as in separating what is inside or outside marriage, or inside one's living quarters, were deemphasized. Geographical mobility seemed high. Most participants, but not all, were comfortable with drug use. Many participants, but by no means all, presented a manifestly "hippie" appearance in their clothing and hair styles.

All participants shared one anomaly in terms of a thoroughgoing counterculture orientation: They were all legally married, and were primarily involved in dyadic relationships.*

This group of couples, and the others described by them, seemed to manifest several notable tendencies:

1. Although there was substantial overt unconventionality, there was also a consistent tendency toward a sometimes covert "return of the conventional."

2. Although sexual activity was a prominent aspect of their lives, there is a sense in which sexuality was given a reduced role; one contemporary way of putting it is that sexuality was "demystified."

3. The "demystification" of sexuality was related to the tendency of some couples to confront emotional tension and sometimes go out of their way to create it.

4. Finally, a psychology of plenty, as it were, may have led some couples to altered affectional and sexual patterns.

Return of the Conventional

John and Sally† lived downtown in a small flat. Sally and her family were somewhat more affluent and better educated than was John. He was a poet, which is to say he generally slept during the day, spent the evening with his

---

*Although nondyadic relationships occurred in this group, none were primarily nondyadic, and there were no "multilateral" marriages of the sort described by Constantine and Constantine (1970).

†Case material is presented to illustrate the writers' impressions rather than to provide evidence for them. Any given "case" may include a selection of material from several actual couples, and is in all instances disguised to protect their identities.

wife, and stayed up all night writing and playing with the couple's six-month-old baby. Sally had a regular office job with a major insurance company and provided the family's sole source of income. Certainly this is not a conventional middle class couple, even setting aside the fact that they lived downtown rather than in the suburbs. Husbands usually have higher socioeconomic status than wives, wives usually provide more baby care than husbands, and of course the husband usually works for money while the wife stays home. There was even a role reversal in the skills John and Sally attributed to each other, with Sally seen as having practical, instrumental abilities and John as being good with feelings and emotional matters. Yet there is a sense in which all this overt unconventionality did not prevent the emergence of conventional sex roles. John was not a male housewife. He was a poet (or a guru), i.e., the performer of a highly valued activity. Sally was not seen as the head, or the mainstay, of the family, but as the performer of meaningless work, i.e., earning money at a "straight" job. Again, John was not just the enactor of a socio-emotional role; John was the socio-emotional *expert*, while Sally performed the *merely instrumental* activities. In short, to the extent that sex-role conventionality means that the husband has the higher family status and performs more valued activities, this couple and others like them were quite conventional.

There were other ways in which unintended conventionality occurred gradually: John and Sally eventually rented a house in the suburbs, which they shared with several other people. John took a part-time job in the records section of a local hospital and supplemented his income by occasionally stealing his friends' records. They bought a Volkswagen bus. For one reason and another, the several companions moved out of the house. Sally became pregnant again and was forced to leave her job. At this point in time they thus became a nuclear family living alone in the suburbs, with the wife staying home and the husband wondering how he could earn enough money to make the house and car payments.

Conventional patterns sometimes appeared suddenly and surprisingly, and caused interpersonal problems, most notably in the case of jealousy. Sometimes the wife, but more often the husband, was an articulate advocate of nonpossessiveness, including sexual nonpossessiveness. John and Sally boasted that they put a great deal of energy into honestly sharing their feelings and beliefs with each other. It turned out that this "sharing" largely consisted of John's telling his wife about the various women he would like to sleep with and advocating a permissive attitude toward sexual sharing. Jealousy, however, emerged abruptly and intensely when Sally told her husband that she had been putting his ideas into practice.

Two serious qualifications must be made with regard to the unexpected appearance of jealousy. First, there do appear to be couples in which serious jealousy simply does not occur, or is resolved to their apparent satisfaction. Second, while jealousy is in itself a conventional enough feeling, the attitude taken toward it by this sample is not. One would expect, in a conventional marriage, that John would be jealous and that Sally would be seen as misbehaving. If she persisted, Sally might be perceived as having a "problem." In our sample, however, it was the jealousy, not the sexual behavior, that was likely to be seen as the source of marital difficulty. It was John who was seen as having the problem, and who was faced with the task of somehow dealing with his unpleasant feelings. There was no question of Sally's right to sleep with whomever she wished.

Connotative Changes in Sexuality

One assumed feature of the counter culture that has received much public attention has been not only a permissive, but an open and forward, attitude toward sexual behavior and related matters. Those who believe we are in the midst of a sexual revolution commonly perceive the counter culture to be in the revolutionary vanguard. Marcuse (1969) speaks of this process in terms of "desublimation" and suggests that overt and blatant sexuality has a political effect, subverting not only conventional sexuality but also the psychic defensive structures that help to support contemporary political forms. It is perhaps in such a context that one is to understand newspaper reports of pornography in which performers insist on being identified by their correct (and well-known) family names, and such publications as "Zap Comix," in which obscenity and violence are played for laughs, in a comic book format.

One would expect that those who live in the context of overt and "desublimated" or "demystified" sexuality would not esteem sexual behavior in quite the same way as people in a more conventional context, and such seems to have been the case in our sample.

Harrison (1965) has suggested that technological innovations alter our experience of awe. Vast mountain ranges and oceans, for example, are seen in a more matter-of-fact way since the invention of the airplane. The uncanny effect that may have accompanied certain bodily movements is experienced no more by those who have grown up used to riding in elevators. We would suggest that a similar process has attenuated a certain "awesomeness" that used to accompany the reality and the fantasy of sexual behavior for persons like those in our sample.

Participants appeared to be more sexually involved than conventional persons, but to esteem it less highly, at least in the sense that sexuality was not the object of a reverential or fearful attitude. Nor did couples' social lives revolve around sex in the way that seems true for those couples who have

been referred to as "swingers" (Bartell, 1971; Denfield and Gordon, 1970).*
Awe and related feelings seemed to be found more in connection with mystical belief systems, drug use, and other similar ways of altering one's experiences.

Approaching Tension

Many persons in this group seemed to feel almost an obligation to approach and face up to tension. The stance taken *vis-à-vis* jealousy is related
to this, in that there was more tendency to deal with the jealousy as such than
to terminate it by ending extramarital sexuality. For example, Donald and
Connie joined together to help one of Connie's girl friends. When Connie discovered that Donald's "helping" included sexual intercourse, she became
furious. She "yelled and threw things." The extramarital sexuality continued,
but Connie claimed to have largely mastered her jealousy and found pleasurable excitement in her husband's sexual sharing.

George and Betty traveled around the country a great deal. They used to
hitchhike and seemed to enjoy the adventure of not knowing whom they
would meet on the road. After their baby was born, they acquired a small
van for their travels. They emphasized that at the beginning of each trip they
would be quite uncertain whether they would be coming back, or coming
back together, and they seemed to enjoy the thrill of not knowing what would
become of them.

Susan lived alone, and was therefore not really part of this sample; but
her attitude toward her way of living is illustrative of its positive evaluation
of tension. Susan felt guilty about living alone, because it was comfortable
for her. She could be with people when she enjoyed it and avoid them when
she wished, and thereby avoid the possibility of being caught in a difficult
interpersonal situation. She therefore feared that her behavior was a "cop-
out," and that it would prevent her from "growing."

On a more public level, encounter groups and related activities appear to
be popular in the alternative culture. In political confrontations (other than
racial ones), the more dangerous barricades, as it were, tend to be peopled by
individuals from the counter culture. Even the valued ability to remain "cool"
is often shorthand for the ability to remain comfortable in a situation of
potentially disabling stress.

A conceptual connection between the tendency to approach tension and
the "demystification" of sexuality is possible. Lichtenstein (1970) suggests
that the problem of "how to affrm human beings in the emotional conviction
of their existence" is central to the "alienation of our youth." Although he

---

*Young children of these couples also tended to be exposed to open and matter-of-
fact sexuality, with consequences that are as yet unclear.

states that "sexuality is . . . the most basic way . . . to experience an affirmation of the reality of . . . existence," he adds that "in the course of ontogenesis, other methods, as yet poorly understood, of feeling affirmed . . . develop. . . ." We wish to suggest that in couples like those in our sample, the self-confirmatory function of overtly sexual experience may be altered and perhaps diminished, to be replaced in part by a search for drug-related and other ecstatic experiences, and a general valuing of tension and intensity as such. That is, tension and intensity as such are valued because they serve the need for self-confirmatory experience.

A Psychology of Plenty

The idea of limited resources—of scarcity—seemed alien to many of the people we considered. Husbanding one's resources, saving up for the distant future, or in general denying oneself in the present for the sake of one's own long-term benefit—these were not popular ideas. Though one orientation toward the future was expressed in the saying, which seemed to achieve popularity for a while, that: "When you are sailing on the Lusitania, you might as well go first class," there was a concomitant orientation to the effect that satisfaction of one's wants would be readily available in the foreseeable future. In financial terms there was realistic support for this view in the form of money from parents, welfare checks, and in the discovery claimed by some couples that they could be comfortable on $100 or $200 a month. One couple calculated that in order to be self-supporting they needed to work for money on no more than one day out of thirteen.*

A psychology of plenty seemed if anything to be more accepted in social rather than in material terms. At one time, people like those in our group seemed to believe, with some apparent accuracy, that they could wander into certain neighborhoods in almost any major city, or hitchhike across the country, and feel assured of being befriended and treated as comrades by nominal strangers. If not love, at least warmth, friendliness, and comradeship were felt to be available on any street corner. This rosy world view was not so widely held in our sample as it once was, or at least it was not held in such an extreme form. But it was still believed that for a prudent and "together" person, companionship is plentiful and easily available. Sexual satisfaction was also seen by many persons as plentifully available with a minimum of effort.

To summarize, a psychology of plenty in terms of goods and services was supported by a dramatic attenuation of felt needs. A psychology of plenty in social terms was supported by social arrangements which in effect partially

---

*Compare the centrality of money and money problems among conventional couples suggested by Mitchell, Bullard, and Mudd (1962).

abrogated conventional boundaries between friends and strangers, and also between spouses and nonspouses.

Plentiful social resources were seen by some as making clinging and possessiveness irrelevant. It was one explanation offered for reduced jealousy in the face of extramarital sexuality or affection. In at least quasi-psychoanalytic terminology, one aspect of this point of view is that an anal-genital basis for object relations was partially supplanted by an oral-genital one; i.e., affectional ties became less controlled and more diffuse. Some participants explained it as the replacement of a "capitalist" model of relationships by a communitarian model. Still another quasi-psychoanalytic description of this change might be in terms of the formation of relationships less similar to an oedipal model, in which gratification is primarily dependent on one particular person, and more like a sibling model, in which many "siblings" may have some functional equivalence.*

Although it has been noted that the retention of pregenital capabilities may be adaptive (Kris, 1952; Novey, 1955; Weissman, 1966, 1967), the basic psychoanalytic position nevertheless traces a hierarchical and more or less linear development of object relations. Object choices progress from anaclitic to nonanaclitic, from part to whole object, from pregenital to genital phases, and from pre-oedipal to oedipal (or part oedipal); and each shift along this developmental scale represents a partial supplanting of primitive characteristics by more advanced ones. Some of the persons we have interviewed would regard any hierarchical scheme as restrictive, and might suggest that in a situation of plentiful resources "supplanting" one kind of relationship with another might be senseless self-denial—one can have both.†

Whether on this kind of basis or some other, it did seem to be true that in some of our couples polymorphous perverse relationship aspects seemed to be tolerated or even valued in a de-differentiation of the usual developmental phases.

Overview

The several aspects of ideology and living patterns upon which we have commented fit together with a certain degree of consistency. The idea of plentiful resources supports and is in turn supported by a sharing orientation, which some of our participants would call communitarian. That aspect of sharing which is affectional or sexual directly creates bountiful resources (cf. Slater, 1970, ch. 4). It also tends to remove from sexuality a certain tinge of

---

*We are deliberately refraining from discussing defensive, including counterphobic, considerations.

†Though the "plentiful resources" ethos may be in some conflict with hierarchical formulations, it is perhaps more in harmony with less linear formulations, such as Lichtenstein's (1970).

awe, a certain transcendental quality.* Perhaps this more matter-of-fact atti-tude toward sexuality leaves unfulfilled a need for self-affirmation, which may contribute to a high evaluation of tension and intensity in general. This in turn relates not only to drug use and "up front" interpersonal relationships but also to a confrontational political attitude, which again may contribute to openness and bluntness in some aspects of sexuality.

But there are flaws in this ideological–behavioral configuration, even apart from the degree to which it may oversimplify an extremely hetero-geneous and complex set of phenomena. It is not true that the people in our sample were so confident of gratification that they eschewed all arrange-ments that might bring them security. They did, after all, get legally married, and their marriages did tend to include a "return of the conventional," in the form of conventional sex-role attitudes that were masked by overt sex-role reversals, in an occasional drift back into concerns with middle class economic security, and in the disvalued but real appearance of jealousy. One possible view, which we sometimes heard, is that these aspects merely repre-sented unfinished business: Heightened awareness will gradually diminish sex-role bias; the disvaluation of jealousy and increased appreciation of the availability of affection and sexuality will gradually eliminate jealousy. An alternative view might be that the character structure of people in our society does not support, for example, radically nonpossessive affection. It may also be that our society is simply not dependably enough bountiful, and is getting less so, and that the mutual relationship between sharing and ample re-sources is in the direction of less sharing, leading to less plentiful resources, and so on.† Obviously we do not know which if any of these interpretations have any validity. We do not even know whether our small set of couples is representative of some significant portion of the vague entity called the counter culture, or whether it only illustrates aberrant and ephemeral pheno-mena, although we lean toward the former view. We do believe, however, that the ideologies, attitudes, and life styles observed in these couples pro-vide useful and suggestive information about alternative patterns of close personal relationships—and some idea of the complications which such changes might encounter.

References

Bartell, B. G. *Group Sex: A Scientist's Eyewitness Report on the American Way of Swinging.* New York: Peter H. Wyden, 1971.

*For a more extended consideration of the implications of this kind of affect, see Kafka (1969, 1971).

†One is reminded in this context of the words of Mack the Knife, the pertinence of which is emphasized in a different but not unrelated context by Smith (1972): *Erst kommt das Fressen, dann kommt die Morale.*

Constantine, L., and J. Constantine. "Where Is Marriage Going?" *The Futurist*, 4 (1970): 44–46.

Cuber, J. F., and P. B. Harroff. *The Significant Americans: A Study of Sexual Behavior among the Affluent*. New York: Appleton-Century, 1965.

Denfield, D., and M. Gordon. "The Sociology of Mate Swapping: Or the Family that Swings Together Clings Together." *Journal of Sex Research*, 6 (1970): 85–100.

Harrison, J. B. "A Reconsideration of Freud's 'A Disturbance of Memory on the Acropolis' in Relation to Identity Disturbance." *Journal of the American Psychoanalytic Association*, 13 (1965): 518–527.

Kafka, J. S. "The Body as Transitional Object: A Psychoanalytic Study of a Self-Mutilating Patient." *British Journal of Medical Psychology*, 42 (1969): 207–212.

Kafka, J. S. "Ambiguity for Individuation: A Critique and Reformulation of Double-bind Theory." *Archives of General Psychiatry*, 25 (1971): 232–239.

Kris, E. *Psychoanalytic Explorations in Art*. New York: International Universities Press, 1952.

Lichtenstein, H. "Changing Implications of the Concept of Psychosexual Development: An Inquiry Concerning the Validity of Classical Psychoanalytic Assumptions Concerning Sexuality." *Journal of the American Psychoanalytic Association*, 18 (1970): 300–318.

Marcuse, H. *An Essay on Liberation*. Boston: Beacon Press, 1969.

Mitchell, H. E., J. W. Bullard, and E. H. Mudd. "Areas of Marital Conflict in Successfully and Unsuccessfully Functioning Families." *Journal of Health and Human Behavior*, 3 (1962): 88–93.

Novey, S. "Some Philosophical Speculations about the Concept of the Genital Character." *International Journal of Psychoanalysis*, 36 (1955): 88–94.

Raush, H. L., D. W. Goodrich, and J. D. Campbell. "Adaptation to the First Years of Marriage." *Psychiatry*, 26 (1963): 368–380.

Roszak, T. *The Making of a Counter Culture*. New York: Doubleday, 1969.

Ryder, R. G. "Dimensions of Early Marriage." *Family Process*, 9 (1970): 51–68.

Ryder, R. G. "A Topography of Early Marriage." *Family Process*, 9 (1970): 385–402.

Ryder, R. G., J. S. Kafka, and D. H. Olson. "Separating and Joining Influences in Courtship and Early Marriage." *American Journal of Orthopsychiatry*, 41 (1971): 450–464.

Slater, P. E. *The Pursuit of Loneliness: American Culture at the Breaking Point*. Boston: Beacon Press, 1970.

Smith, M. B. "Ethical Implications of Population Policies: A Psychologist's View." *American Psychologist*, 27 (1972): 11–15.

Weissman, P. "Psychological Concomitants of Ego Functioning in Creativity." *International Journal of Psychoanalysis*, 49 (1966): 464–469.

Weissman, P. "Theoretical Considerations of Ego Regression and Ego Functions in Creativity." *The Psychoanalytic Quarterly*, 36 (1967): 37–50.

One of the most famous sentences in world literature is the one with which Tolstoy opened Anna Karenina: *"Happy families are all alike, but each unhappy famly is unhappy in its own way." This article suggests that Tolstoy was wrong: there are at least five ways that marriages can be happy, or at least not unhappy. Some marriages may thrive on constant arguments, some on the dead embers of past love, some on convenient partnerships that never had much passion in them, while some achieve the great or total involvement that corresponds most closely to the romantic ideal of the happy marriage.*

Five Types of Marriage

John F. Cuber and Peggy B. Harroff

The qualitative aspects of enduring marital relationships vary enormously. The variations described to us were by no means random or clearly individualized, however. Five distinct life styles showed up repeatedly and the pairs within each of them were remarkably similar in the ways in which they lived together, found sexual expression, reared children, and made their way in the outside world.

The following classification is based on the interview materials of those people whose marriages had already lasted ten years or more and who said that they had never seriously considered divorce or separation. While 360 of the men and women had been married ten or more years to the same spouse, exclusion of those who reported that they had considered divorce reduced the number to 211. The discussion in this chapter is, then, based on 211 interviews: 107 men and 104 women.

The descriptions which our interviewees gave us took into account how they had behaved and also how they felt about their actions past and present. Examination of the important features of their lives revealed five recurring configurations of male-female life, each with a central theme—some prominent distinguishing psychological feature which gave each type its singularity. It is these preeminent characteristics which suggested the names for the relationship: the *Conflict-Habituated*, the *Devitalized*, the *Passive-Congenial*, the *Vital*, and the *Total*.

The Conflict-Habituated

We begin with the conflict-habituated not because it is the most prevalent, but because the overt behavior patterns in it are so readily observed and because it presents some arresting contradictions. In this association there is

From John F. Cuber and Peggy B. Harroff, "Five Kinds of Relationships," in *Sex and the Significant Americans* (Baltimore: Penguin, 1965), pp. 43–65.

much tension and conflict—although it is largely controlled. At worst, there is some private quarreling, nagging, and "throwing up the past" of which members of the immediate family, and more rarely close friends and relatives, have some awareness. At best, the couple is discreet and polite, genteel about it in the company of others—but after a few drinks at the cocktail party the verbal barbs begin to fly. The intermittent conflict is rarely concealed from the children, though we were often assured otherwise. "Oh, they're at it again—but they always are," says the high-school son. There is private acknowledgment by both husband and wife as a rule that incompatibility is pervasive, that conflict is ever-potential, and that an atmosphere of tension permeates the togetherness.

An illustrative case concerns a physician of fifty, married for twenty-five years to the same woman, with two college-graduate children promisingly established in their own professions.

> You know, it's funny; we have fought from the time we were in high school together. As I look back at it, I can't remember specific quarrels; it's more like a running guerrilla fight with intermediate periods, sometimes quite long, of pretty good fun and some damn good sex. In fact, if it hadn't been for the sex, we wouldn't have been married so quickly. Well, anyway, this has been going on ever since. . . . It's hard to know what it is we fight about most of the time. You name it and we'll fight about it. It's sometimes something I've said that she remembers differently, sometimes a decision—like what kind of car to buy or what to give the kids for Christmas. With regard to politics, and religion, and morals—oh, boy! You know, outside of the welfare of the kids—and that's just abstract—we don't really agree about anything. . . . At different times we take opposite sides—not deliberately; it just comes out that way.
>
> Now these fights get pretty damned colorful. You called them arguments a little while ago—I have to correct you—they're brawls. There's never a bit of physical violence—at least not directed to each other—but the verbal gunfire gets pretty thick. Why, we've said things to each other that neither of us would think of saying in the hearing of anybody else. . . .
>
> Of course we don't settle any of the issues. It's sort of a matter of principle *not* to. Because somebody would have to give in then and lose face for the next encounter. . . .
>
> When I tell you this in this way, I feel a little foolish about it. I wouldn't tolerate such a condition in any other relationship in my life—and yet here I do and always have. . . .
>
> No—we never have considered a divorce or separation or anything so clear-cut. I realize that other people do, and I can't say that it has never occurred to either of us, but we've never considered it seriously.
>
> A number of times there has been a crisis, like the time I was in the automobile accident, and the time she almost died in childbirth, and then I guess we really showed that we do care about each other. But as soon as the crisis is over, it's business as usual.

There is a subtle valence in these conflict-habituated relationships. It is easily missed in casual observation. So central is the necessity for channeling conflict and bridling hostility that these considerations come to preoccupy much of the interaction. Some psychiatrists have gone so far as to suggest that it is precisely the deep need to do psychological battle with one another which constitutes the cohesive factor insuring continuity of the marriage. Possibly so. But even from a surface point of view, the overt and manifest fact of habituated attention to handling tension, keeping it chained, and concealing it, is clearly seen as a dominant life force. And it can, and does for some, last for a whole lifetime.

The Devitalized

The key to the devitalized mode is the clear discrepancy between middle-aged reality and the earlier years. These people usually characterized themselves as having been "deeply in love" during the early years, as having spent a great deal of time together, having enjoyed sex, and most importantly of all, having had a close identification with one another. The present picture, with some variation from case to case, is in clear contrast—little time is spent together, sexual relationships are far less satisfying qualitatively or quantitatively, and interests and activities are not shared, at least not in the deeper and meaningful way they once were. Most of their time together now is "duty time"—entertaining together, planning and sharing activities with children, and participating in various kinds of required commuity responsibilities. They do as a rule retain, in addition to a genuine and mutual interest in the welfare of their children, a shared attention to their joint property and the husband's career. But even in the latter case the interest is contrasting. Despite a common dependency on his success and the benefits which flow therefrom, there is typically very little sharing of the intrinsic aspects of career—simply an acknowledgment of their mutual dependency on the fruits.

Two rather distinct subtypes of the devitalized take shape by the middle years. The following reflections of two housewives in their late forties illustrate both the common and the distinguishing features:

> Judging by the way it was when we were first married—say the first five years or so—things are pretty matter-of-fact now—even dull. They're dull between us, I mean. The children are a lot of fun, keep us pretty busy, and there are lots of outside things—you know, like Little League and the P.T.A. and the Swim Club, and even the company parties aren't always so bad. But I mean where Bob and I are concerned —if you followed us around, you'd wonder why we ever got *married*. We take each other for granted. We laugh at the same things sometimes, but we don't really laugh together—the way we used to. But, as he said to me the other night—with one or two under the belt, I think—"You know, you're still a little fun now and then." . . .

Now, I don't say this to complain, not in the least. There's a cycle to life. There are things you do in high school. And different things you do in college. Then you're a young adult. And then you're middle-aged. That's where we are now. . . . I'll admit that I do yearn for the old days when sex was a big thing and going out was fun and I hung on to every thing he said about his work and his ideas as if they were coming from a genius or something. But then you get the children and other responsibilities. I have the home and Bob has a tremendous burden of responsibility at the office. . . . He's completely responsible for setting up the new branch now. . . . You have to adjust to these things and we both try to gracefully. . . . Anniversaries though do sometimes remind you kind of hard. . . .

The other kind of hindsight from a woman in a devitalized relationship is much less accepting and quiescent:

I know I'm fighting it. I ought to accept that it has to be like this, but I don't like it, and I'd do almost anything to bring back the exciting way of living we had at first. Most of my friends think I'm some kind of a sentimental romantic or something—they tell me to act my age—but I do know some people—not very darn many—who are our age and even older, who still have the same kind of excitement about them and each other that we had when we were all in college. I've seen some of them at parties and other places—the way they look at each other, the little touches as they go by. One couple has grandchildren and you'd think they were honeymooners. I don't think it's just sex either—I think they are just part of each other's lives—and then when I think of us and the numb way we sort of stagger through the weekly routine, I could scream. And I've even thought of doing some pretty desperate things to try to build some joy and excitement into my life. I've given up on Phil. He's too content with his balance sheets and the kids' report cards and the new house we're going to build next year. He keeps saying he has everything in life that any man could want. What do you *do?*

Regardless of the gracefulness of the acceptance, or the lack thereof, the common plight prevails: on the subjective, emotional dimension, the relationship has become a void. The original zest is gone. There is typically little overt tension or conflict, but the interplay between the pair has become apathetic, lifeless. No serious threat to the continuity of the marriage is generally acknowledged, however. It is intended, usually by both, that it continue indefinitely despite its numbness. Continuity and relative freedom from open conflict are fostered in part because of the comforts of the "habit cage." Continuity is further insured by the absence of any engaging alternative, "all things considered." It is also reinforced, sometimes rather decisively, by legal and ecclesiastical requirements and expectations. These people quickly explain that "there are other things in life" which are worthy of sustained human effort.

This kind of relationship is exceedingly common. Persons in this circumstance frequently make comparisons with other pairs they know, many of whom are similar to themselves. This fosters the comforting judgment that "marriage is like this—except for a few oddballs or pretenders who claim otherwise."

While these relationships lack visible vitality, the participants assure us that there is "something there." There are occasional periods of sharing at least something—if only memory. Even formalities can have meanings. Anniversaries can be celebrated, if a little grimly, for what they once commemorated. As one man said, "Tomorrow we are celebrating the anniversary of our anniversary." Even clearly substandard sexual expression is said by some to be better than nothing, or better than a clandestine substitute. A "good man" or a "good mother for the kids" may "with a little affection and occasional attention now and then, get you by." Many believe that the devitalized mode is the appropriate mode in which a man and woman should be content to live in the middle years and later.

The Passive-Congenial

The passive-congenial mode has a great deal in common with the devitalized, the essential difference being that the passivity which pervades the association has been there from the start. The devitalized have a more exciting set of memories; the passive-congenials give little evidence that they had ever hoped for anything much different from what they are currently experiencing.

There is therefore little suggestion of disillusionment or compulsion to make believe to anyone. Existing modes of association are comfortably adequate—no stronger words fit the facts as they related them to us. There is little conflict, although some admit that they tiptoe rather gingerly over and around a residue of subtle resentments and frustrations. In their better moods they remind themselves (and each other) that "there are many common interests" which they both enjoy. "We both like classical music." "We agree completely on religious and political matters." "We both love the country and our quaint exurban neighbors." "We are both lawyers."

The wife of a prominent attorney, who has been living in the passive-congenial mode for thirty years, put her description this way:

> We have both always tried to be calm and sensible about major life decisions, to think things out thoroughly and in perspective. Len and I knew each other since high school but didn't start to date until college. When he asked me to marry him, I took a long time to decide whether he was the right man for me and I went into his family background, because I wasn't just marrying him; I was choosing a father for my children. We decided together not to get married until he was established, so that we would not have to live in dingy little apartments like

some of our friends who got married right out of college. This prudence has stood us in good stead too. Life has moved ahead for us with remarkable orderliness and we are deeply grateful for the foresight we had. . . .

When the children were little, we scheduled time together with them, although since they're grown, the demands of the office are getting pretty heavy. Len brings home a bulging briefcase almost every night and more often than not the light is still on in his study after I retire. But we've got a lot to show for his devoted effort. . . .

I don't like all this discussion about sex—even in the better magazines. I hope your study will help to put it in its proper perspective. I expected to perform sex in marriage, but both before and since, I'm willing to admit that it's a much overrated activity. Now and then, perhaps it's better. I am fortunate, I guess, because my husband has never been demanding about it, before marriage or since. It's just not that important to either of us. . . .

My time is very full these days, with the chairmanship of the Cancer Drive, and the Executive Board of the (state) P.T.A. I feel a little funny about that with my children already grown, but there are the grandchildren coming along. And besides so many of my friends are in the organizations, and it's so much like a home-coming.

People make their way into the passive-congenial mode by two quite different routes—by default and by intention. Perhaps in most instances they arrive at this way of living and feeling by drift. There is so little which they have cared about deeply in each other that a passive-congenial mode is a deliberately intended arrangement for two people whose interests and creative energies are directed elsewhere than toward the pairing—into careers, or in the case of women, into children or community activities. They say they know this and want it this way. These people simply do not wish to invest their total emotional involvement and creative effort in the male-female relationship.

The passive-congenial life style fits societal needs quite well also, and this is an important consideration. The man of practical affairs, in business, government service, or the professions—quite obviously needs "to have things peaceful at home" and to have a minimum of distraction as he pursues his important work. He may feel both love and gratitude toward the wife who fits this mode.

A strong case was made for the passive congenial by a dedicated physician:

I don't know why everyone seems to make so much about men and women and marriage. Of course, I'm married and if anything happened to my wife, I'd get married again. I think it's the proper way to live. It's convenient, orderly, and solves a lot of problems. But there are other things in life. I spent nearly ten years preparing for the practice of my profession. The biggest thing to me is the practice of that profession, to be of assistance to my patients and their families. I spend

twelve hours a day at it. And I'll bet if you talked with my wife, you
wouldn't get any of that "trapped housewife" stuff from her either. Now
that the children are grown, she finds a lot of useful and necessary work
to do in this community. She works as hard as I do.

The passive-congenial mode facilitates the achievement of other goals too.
It enables people who desire a considerable amount of personal independence
and freedom to realize it with a minimum of inconvenience from or to the
spouse. And it certainly spares the participants in it from the need to give a
great deal of personal attention to "adjusting to the spouse's needs." The
passive-congenial menage is thus a mood as well as a mode.

Our descriptions of the devitalized and the passive-congenials have been
similar because these two modes are much alike in their overt characteristics.
The participants' evaluations of their *present situations* are likewise largely
the same—the accent on "other things," the emphasis on civic and professional responsibilities, the importance of property, children, and reputation.
The essential difference lies in their diverse histories and often in their feelings of contentment with their current lives. The passive-congenials had from
the start a life pattern and a set of expectations essentially consistent with
what they are now experiencing. When the devitalized reflect, however, when
they juxtapose history against present reality, they often see the barren
gullies in their lives left by the erosions of earlier satisfactions. Some of the
devitalized are resentful and disillusioned; others, calling themselves "mature
about it," have emerged with reasonable acceptance of their existing devitalized modes. Still others are clearly ambivalent, "I wish life would be
more exciting, but I should have known it couldn't last. In a way, it's calm
and quiet and reassuring this way, but there are times when I get very ill at
ease—sometimes downright mad. Does it *have* to be like this?"

The passive-congenials do not find it necessary to speculate in this fashion.
Their anticipations were realistic and perhaps even causative of their current
marital situation. In any event, their passivity is not jarred when teased by
memory.

The Vital

In extreme contrast to the three foregoing is the vital relationship. The vital
pair can easily be overlooked as they move through their worlds of work,
recreation, and family activities. They do the same things, publicly at least;
and when talking for public consumption say the same things—they are
proud of their homes, love their children, gripe about their jobs, while being
quite proud of their career accomplishments. But when the close, intimate,
confidential, empathic look is taken, the essence of the vital relationship be-

comes clear: the mates are intensely bound together psychologically in important life matters. Their sharing and their togetherness is genuine. It provides the life essence for both man and woman.

> The things we do together aren't fun intrinsically—the ecstasy comes from being *together in the doing*. Take her out of the picture and I wouldn't give a damn for the boat, the lake, or any of the fun that goes on out there.

The presence of the mate is indispensable to the feelings of satisfaction which the activity provides. The activities shared by the vital pairs may involve almost anything: hobbies, careers, community service. Anything—so long as it is closely shared.

It is hard to escape the word *vitality*—exciting mutuality of feelings and participation together in important life segments. The clue that the relationship is vital (rather than merely expressing the joint activity) derives from the feeling that it is important. An activity is flat and uninteresting if the spouse is not a part of it.

Other valued things are readily sacrificed in order to enhance life within the vital relationship.

> I cheerfully, and that's putting it mildly, passed up two good promotions because one of them would have required some traveling and the other would have taken evening and weekend time—and that's when Pat and I *live*. The hours with her (after twenty-two years of marriage) are what I live for. You should meet her. . . .

People in the vital relationship for the most part know that they are a minority and that their life styles are incomprehensible to most of their associates.

> Most of our friends think we moved out to the country for the kids; well—the kids *are* crazy about it, but the fact of the matter is, we moved out for ourselves—just to get away from all the annoyances and interferences of other people—our friends actually. We like this kind of life—where we can have almost all of our time together. . . . We've been married for over twenty years and the most enjoyable thing either of us does—well, outside of the intimate things—is to sit and talk by the hour. That's why we built that imposing fireplace—and the hi-fi here in the corner. . . . Now that Ed is getting older, that twenty-seven-mile drive morning and night from the office is a real burden, but he does it cheerfully so we can have our long uninterrupted hours together. . . . The children respect this too. They don't invade our privacy any more than they can help—the same as we vacate the living room when Ellen brings in a date, she tries not to intrude on us. . . . Being the specialized kind of lawyer he is, I can't share much in his work, but that doesn't bother either of us. The *big* part of our lives is completely mutual. . . .

Her husband's testimony validated hers. And we talked to dozens of other couples like them, too. They find their central satisfaction in the life they live with and through each other. It consumes their interest and dominates their thoughts and actions. All else is subordinate and secondary.

This does not mean that people in vital relationships lose their separate identities, that they may not upon occasion be rivalrous or competitive with one another, or that conflict may not occur. They differ fundamentally from the conflict-habituated, however, in that when conflict does occur, it results from matters that are important to them, such as which college a daughter or son is to attend; it is devoid of the trivial "who said what first and when" and "I can't forget when you. . . ." A further difference is that people to whom the relationship is vital tend to settle disagreements quickly and seek to avoid conflict, whereas the conflict-habituated look forward to conflict and appear to operate by a tacit rule that no conflict is ever to be truly terminated and that the spouse must never be considered right. The two kinds of conflict are thus radically different. To confuse them is to miss an important differentiation.

The Total

The total relationship is like the vital relationship with the important addition that it is more multifacted. The points of vital meshing are more numerous—in some cases all of the important life foci are vitally shared. In one such marriage the husband is an internationally known scientist. For thirty years his wife has been his "friend, mistress, and partner." He still goes home at noon whenever possible, at considerable inconvenience, to have a quiet lunch and spend a conversational hour or so with his wife. They refer to these conversations as "our little seminars." They feel comfortable with each other and with their four grown children. The children (now in their late twenties) say that they enjoy visits with their parents as much as they do with friends of their own age.

There is practically no pretense between persons in the total relationship or between them and the world outside. There are few areas of tension, because the items of difference which have arisen over the years have been settled as they arose. There often *were* serious differences of opinion but they were handled, sometimes by compromise, sometimes by one or the other yielding; but these outcomes were of secondary importance because the primary consideration was not who was right or who was wrong, only how the problem could be resolved without tarnishing the relationship. When faced with differences, they can and do dispose of the difficulties without losing their feeling of unity or their sense of vitality and centrality of their relationship. This is the mainspring.

The various parts of the total relationship are reinforcing, as we learned from this consulting engineer who is frequently sent abroad by his corporation.

> She keeps my files and scrapbooks up to date. . . . I invariably take her with me to conferences around the world. Her femininity, easy charm and wit are invaluable assets to me. I know it's conventional to say that a man's wife is responsible for his success and I also know that it's often not true. But in my case I gladly acknowledge that it's not only true, but she's indispensable to me. But she'd go along with me even if there was nothing for her to do because we just enjoy each other's company—deeply. You know, the best part of a vacation is not *what* we do, but that we do it together. We plan it and reminisce about it and weave it into our work and other play all the time.

The wife's account is substantially the same except that her testimony demonstrates more clearly the genuineness of her "help."

> It seems to me that Bert exaggerates my help. It's not so much that I only want to help him; it's more that I want to do those things anyway. We do them together, even though we may not be in each other's presence at the time. I don't really know what I do for him and what I do for me.

This kind of relationship is rare, in marriage or out, but it does exist and can endure. We occasionally found relationships so total that all aspects of life were mutually shared and enthusiastically participated in. It is as if neither spouse has, or has had, a truly private existence.

The customary purpose of a classification such as this one is to facilitate understanding of similarities and differences among the cases classified. In this instance enduring marriage is the common condition. The differentiating features are the dissimilar forces which make for the integration of the pair within each of the types. It is not necessarily the purpose of a classification to make possible a clear-cut sorting of all cases into one or another of the designated categories. All cannot be so precisely pigeon-holed; there often are borderline cases. Furthermore, two observers with equal access to the facts may sometimes disagree on which side of the line an unclear case should be placed. If the classification is a useful one, however, placement should *as a rule* be clear and relatively easy. The case is only relative because making an accurate classification of a given relationship requires the possession of amounts and kinds of information which one rarely has about persons other than himself. Superficial knowledge of public or professional behavior is not enough. And even in his own case, one may, for reasons of ego, find it difficult to be totally forthright.

A further caution. The typology concerns relationships, not personalities. A clearly vital person may be living in a passive-congenial or devitalized relationship and expressing his vitality in some other aspect of his life—career being an important preoccupation for many. Or, possibly either or both of the spouses may have a vital relationship—sometimes extending over many years—with someone of the opposite sex outside of the marriage.

Nor are the five types to be interpreted as *degrees* of marital happiness or adjustment. Persons in all five are currently adjusted and most say that they are content, if not happy. Rather, the five types represent *different kinds of adjustment* and *different conceptions of marriage*. This is an important concept which must be emphasized if one is to understand the personal meanings which these people attach to the conditions of their marital experience.

Neither are the five types necessarily stages in a cycle of initial bliss and later disillusionment. Many pairings started in the passive-congenial stage; in fact, quite often people intentionally enter into a marriage for the acknowledged purpose of living this kind of relationship. To many the simple amenities of the "habit cage" are not disillusionments or even disappointments, but rather are sensible life expectations which provide an altogether comfortable and rational way of having a "home base" for their lives. And many of the conflict-habituated told of courtship histories essentially like their marriages.

While each of these types tends to persist, there *may* be movement from one type to another as circumstances and life perspectives change. This movement may go in any direction from any point, and a given couple may change categories more than once. Such changes are relatively *in*frequent however, and the important point is that relationship types tend to persist over relatively long periods.

The fundamental nature of these contexts may be illustrated by examining the impact of some common conditions on persons of each type.

Infidelity, for example, occurs in most of the five types, the total relationship being the exception. But it occurs for quite different reasons. In the conflict-habituated it seems frequently to be only another outlet for hostility. The call girl and the woman picked up in a bar are more than just available women; they are symbols of resentment of the wife. This is not always so, but reported to us often enough to be worth noting. Infidelity among the passive-congenial, on the other hand, is typically in line with the stereotype of the middle-aged man who "strays out of sheer boredom with the uneventful, deadly prose" of his private life. And the devitalized man or woman frequently is trying for an hour or a year to recapture the lost mood. But the vital are sometimes adulterous too; some are simply emancipated—almost bohemian. To some of them sexual aggrandizement is an accepted fact of life. Frequently the infidelity is condoned by the partner and in some instances even provides an indirect (through empathy) kind of gratification. The act of infidelity in such cases is not construed as disloyalty or as a threat to continuity, but rather as a kind of basic human right which the loved one ought to be permitted to have—and which the other perhaps wants also for himself.

Divorce and separation are found in all five of the types, but the reasons, when viewed realistically and outside of the simplitudes of legalistic and ecclesiastical fiction, are highly individual and highly variable. For example, a couple may move from a vital relationship to divorce because for them the alternative of a devitalized relationship is unendurable. They can conceive of marriage only as a vital, meaningful, fulfilling, and preoccupying interaction. The "disvitality" of any other marriage form is abhorrent to them and takes on "the hypocrisy of living a public lie." We have accounts of marriages which were unquestionably vital or total for a period of years but which were dissolved. In some respects relationships of this type are more readily disrupted, because these people have become adjusted to such a rich and deep sharing that evidences of breach, which a person in another type of marriage might consider quite normal, become unbearable.

> I know a lot of close friendships occur between men and women married to someone else, and that they're not always adulterous. But I know Betty—and anyway, I personally believe they eventually do become so, but I can't be sure about that. Anyway, when Betty found her self-expression was furthered by longer and longer meetings and conversations with Joe, and I detected little insincerities, not serious at first, you understand, creeping into the things we did together, it was like the little leak in the great dike. It didn't take very long. We weren't melodramatic about it, but it was soon clear to both of us that we were no longer the kind of pair we once were, so why pretend. The whole thing can go to hell fast—and after almost twenty years!

Husbands in other types of relationships would probably not even have detected any disloyalty on the part of this wife. And even if they had, they would tend to conclude that "you don't break up a home just because she has a passing interest in some glamorous writer."

The divorce which occurs in the passive-congenial marriage follows a different sequence. One of the couple, typically a person capable of more vitality in his or her married life than the existing relationship provides, comes into contact with a person with whom he gradually (or suddenly) unfolds a new dimension to adult living. What he had considered to be a rational and sensible and "adult" relationship can suddenly appear in contrast to be stultifying, shallow, and an altogether disheartening way to live out the remaining years. He is left with "no conceivable alternative but to move out." Typically, he does not do so impulsively or without a more or less stubborn attempt to stifle his "romanticism" and listen to well-documented advice to the effect that he should act maturely and "leave the romantic yearning to the kids for whom it is intended." Very often he is convinced and turns his back on his "new hope"—but not always.

Whether examining marriages for the satisfactions and fulfillments they have brought or for the frustrations and pain, the overriding influence of life style—or as we have here called it, relationship type—is of the essence. Such a viewpoint helps the observer, and probably the participant, to understand some of the apparent enigmas about men and women in marriage—why infidelities destroy some marriages and not others; why conflict plays so large a role for some couples and is so negligible for others; why some seemingly well-suited and harmoniously adjusted spouses seek divorce while others with provocations galore remain solidly together; why affections, sexual expression, recreation, almost everything observable about men and women is so radically different from pair to pair. All of these are not merely different objectively; they are perceived differently by the pairs, are differently reacted to, and differently attended to.

If nothing else, this chapter has demonstrated that realistic understanding of marital relationships requires use of concepts which are carefully based on perceptive factual knowledge. Unfortunately, the language by which relationships between men and women are conventionally expressed tends to lead toward serious and pervasive deceptions which in turn encourage erroneous inferences. Thus, we tend to assume that enduring marriage is somehow synonymous with happy marriage or at least with something comfortably called adjustment. The deception springs from lumping together such dissimilar modes of thought and action as the conflict-habituated, the passive-congenial, and the vital. To know that a marriage has endured, or for that matter has been dissolved, tells one close to nothing about the kinds of experiences, fulfillments, and frustrations which have made up the lives of the people involved. Even to know, for example, that infidelity has occurred, without knowledge of circumstances, feelings, and other essences, results in an illusion of knowledge which masks far more than it describes.

To understand a given marriage, let alone what is called "marriage in general," is realistically possible only in terms of particular sets of experiences, meanings, hopes, and intentions. This chapter has described in broad outline five manifest and recurring configurations among the Significant Americans.

4

Children and Parents

Introduction

Social scientists have looked at parent-child relations under the heading of "socialization"—a process by which new generations replace their elders. Children are born, socialized, take their place in the social order until they die; new children are born, and the process is repeated. Like a long-run play performed by a succession of different actors, the system itself remains the same.

The obedient child, in this conception, is the forerunner of the good citizen. The parents are cast in the role of upholders of social order and civilization itself.

A few observers have seen the fallacy in this idealization of parenthood. In 1858 Herbert Spencer noted:

> The current assumption respecting family government, as respecting national government, is that the virtues are with the rulers and the vices with the ruled. Judging by educational theories, men and women are entirely transfigured in their relations to offspring. The citizens we do business with, the people we meet in the world, we know to be very imperfect creatures. In the daily scandals, in the quarrels of friends, in bankruptcy disclosures, in lawsuits, in police reports, we have constantly thrust before us the pervading selfishness, dishonesty, brutality. Yet when we criticize nursery management and canvass the misbehavior of juveniles, we habitually take for granted that these culpable persons are free from moral delinquency in the treatment of boys and girls. (p. 87)

Concepts of socialization also imply images of what children are like. Two images of the child have prevailed in Western culture. One is the child as angel, all sweetness and innocence, to be protected from the sexuality and workaday concerns of the adult world. This image has always coexisted with actual conditions of great brutality and neglect of children. The opposing image is found in both Calvinistic Protestantism and early psychoanalysis: it is the child as devil, imp of darkness, seething cauldron of murderous and sexual impulses, a beast who must be tamed. This image has been forcefully portrayed in such literary works as *Lord of the Flies, The Bad Seed,* and others.

Both images of the child share the assumption that socialization is something done to the child, that he learns to be reasonable, moral, and competent from the outside, as a result of adult guidance. This is also the position of sociological functionalism and Freudian theories. It suggests as a model for human socialization the child being weaned or toilet trained— precisely those aspects of childrearing in which child and parent are most likely to be embroiled in a battle for control of the child's impulses. The concept of socialization as the control of impulses overlooks, however, the intellectual aspects of the process, and the active, creative part played by the child himself. The model child for theories of socialization need not be the child on the potty chair, but the child learning his native language and the elementary nature of the physical world.

The creative side of human growth has been most forcefully stated and experimentally documented in the work of Jean Piaget. According to this view the child is an active participant in the attainment of logical and moral competence, rather than the passive recipient of rules and rewards from the outside. The infant banging his cup, throwing toys out of his crib, or fitting objects into each other is actually performing experiments in physics, learning about the nature of matter. Later, when he learns to communicate in words, he will also learn the rules of logic and morality. As Roger Brown writes:

> The mature persons with whom a child interacts behave in accordance with such systems of norms or rules as are called logic, mathematics, language, morality, aesthetics . . . and so on. For the most part these systems have not been explicitly formulated by the adults whose behavior is governed by them and they will not be explicitly formulated by the child who acquires them. This process is not a simple "passing over" of the systems from one generation to another. What each child extracts at a given age is a function of his idiosyncratic experience and of his present intellectual capabilities. The systems governing the child change as he grows older and they need not, in the end, simply reproduce the rules that prevail in his society. The outcome can be unique and sometimes revolutionary. (1965, p. 193)

Child Abuse

If the prevailing views of parenthood overestimate the parents' role as teacher, they underestimate the potential for parental irrationality. Everyone has read of some of the more spectacular incidents of child abuse in the papers. One's first reaction to such incidents is to define them as extreme acts, mercifully rare, carried out by deranged, bizarre, or otherwise disreputable people. In other words, a phenomenon quite apart from the normal life of society.

Researchers who studied the problem also approached it this way at first. But in time they saw that they were dealing with the tip of an iceberg: The part above water was easy to see and identify, the tens of thousands of children severely battered or killed yearly in the United States. But it was hard to identify the waterline, i.e., the line at the "milder" end of the continuum that did not encompass the rest of "normal society."

> Physical punishment is an accepted form of reprimand in our society. A rigid definition for a battered child, therefore, cannot be determined. ... (State Dept. Social Welfare, Kansas, 1965)

In one of the leading studies on the battered child syndrome (Steele and Pollack, 1968, p. 104) the sample consisted of parents of infants and children under three who had been significantly abused by their parents, short of direct murder. Although these children had come to the attention of hospitals, doctors, or the police, their parents seemed a cross section of the population. Such attributes as social class, occupation, IQ, or urban-rural residence did not set them apart. Neither did the researchers find any particular psychopathology or character type. What they did find was a pattern of childrearing which exaggerated the normal. They conclude:

> There seems to be an unbroken spectrum of parental action towards children ranging from the breaking of bones and the fracturing of skulls through severe bruising, through severe spanking and on to mild "reminder" pats on the bottom. To be aware of this, one has only to look at the families of one's friends and neighbors, to look and listen to the parent-child interactions at the playground and the supermarket, or even to recall how one raised one's own children or how one was raised oneself. The amount of yelling, scolding, slapping, punching, hitting, and yanking acted out by parents on very small children is almost shocking. Hence, we have felt that in dealing with the abused child we are not observing an isolated, unique phenomenon, but only the extreme form of what we would call a pattern or style of childrearing quite prevalent in our culture. (Steele and Pollack, 1968, p. 104)

The problem is not that parents are sadists. The nuclear family, especially in its more isolated version, gives parents nearly absolute power over children at the same time that it makes parenthood more burdensome. Jules Henry states the problem succinctly as follows:

> Pinched off alone in one's own house, shielded from critical eyes, one can be as irrational as one pleases with one's children as long as severe damage does not attract the attention of the police.
> ... There is minimal *social regulation* of parent-child relations in our culture; this is, above all, what makes lethal child care practices possible. In a primitive culture . . . or in large households, where many people can see what a mother is doing and where deviation looses critical, interested tongues, it is impossible for a parent to do as he or she pleases with his children. In a literal sense, the baby is often not even one's own in such societies, but belongs to a lineage, clan, or household— a community—having a real investment in the baby. (1963, p. 332)

Evidence on the effects of nuclear family isolation were found in a cross-cultural study of childrearing (Minturn, Lambert, et al., 1964). In comparing mothers and children in six cultures, this study found that the households in a New England suburb called Orchardtown were much more isolated than in the five other, more primitive societies. It also found that, in general, mothers in isolated households tended to be more hostile to children than mothers in households where other women were around. Further, the Orchardtown mothers entertained a host of beliefs, which they put into practice, concerning children's needs for much sleep and outdoor play, for independence and settling fights by themselves, which were absent in the other cultures, and which the investigators felt were best explained by the mothers' needs for relief from the unremitting burdens of child care.

The psychological process of parents' setting up rules supposedly for the benefit of the children, but which are actually based on their own needs or on other circumstances, has been labeled mystification by R. D. Laing (1967). Starting with the study of schizophrenics and their families, Laing came to the conclusion that there is a "politics of experience" in every family, normal as well as schizophrenic. At issue is a political or power struggle over whose experience is to be validated, or defined as real. For example, parents may promise a child a trip to an amusement park, and then, finding that for some reason it is inconvenient to go, may say to the child, "You don't really want to go there anyway." Similarly, "bedtime problems" may be defined as a conflict of two perceptions of reality: the child's that he isn't sleepy, and the adult's perception that the child really needs his sleep and, besides, we need some peace and quiet around here.

The realities of modern parenthood, especially motherhood, are considerably less idyllic than the myth portrays them. The woman who has invested the most in the culturally prescribed maternal role is most likely to be devastated by the natural course of the maternal role: the adulthood of her children. The transition to the role of parent is usually experienced as a life crisis. Even "good" mothers may be overwhelmed at times by the relentless demands of young children, and be horrified by the rage their children are capable of stirring up in them. For battering parents, the myth that children are supposed to be fulfilling and gratifying has dangerous effects; these parents blame their own children for not living up to the mythical standards they suppose other children meet.

Yet the power of the parent is limited. Jane Loevinger (1959) argues that in spite of the physical power of the parent over the child, no parent can ensure that the child will learn precisely what the parent wants him to learn. Even the professional knowledge of the psychiatrist or the child-development expert does not help; the parent-child relationship inevitably involves a conflict of interest and impulse.

The Case for Parental Relief from Isolation

If the mythology of the nuclear family tends to place child-beaters out in the moral limbo reserved for sex fiends and other "degenerates," while denying the danger to children from ordinary parents, it also exaggerates in an opposite but perhaps equal direction another threat to children, that of "maternal deprivation."

The first studies of children placed in institutions early in life revealed many cases of irreparable emotional, intellectual, and in some cases, physical damage. The concept of maternal deprivation passed into the popular lore on childrearing to mean that any separation from the mother must have devastating effects on the child. All separations, no matter how long they lasted, for what reasons, and without regard to what happened to the child in the interim, tended to be lumped together. One of the consequences has been large-scale inattention, especially by psychoanalytically oriented child-rearing specialists, to the possibilities of enriching children's lives through day care centers, supervised playgrounds, and similar institutions which relieve the strain of both parenthood and childhood.

Changing Concepts of Childhood and Adulthood

There is a tendency to think that the concept of childhood and the relations between parents and children are universal and unchanging. Yet the historical evidence suggests that there have been profound changes in the conceptions of childhood and adulthood, in the psychological relations between children and parents, and in the stages of the life span. In pre-industrial times, as noted earlier, differences between parents and children were not emphasized. Children were seen as little adults. In our own era, the concepts of childhood and adulthood that have prevailed for several centuries may be in process of changing again.

The increasing pace of social change has made one generation's knowledge and perspectives irrelevant for the next. Margaret Mead (1970) has noted that for the first time we are living in a society in which adults can no longer serve as models for the futures of their children. Like the children of immigrants, young people more in touch with current social change must lead the way for the parents. The central problem of socialization today is not how can society ensure that the culture and skills of the older generation will be passed on to the children, but rather, how can the burden of obsolescent knowledge be kept from interfering with necessary changes? How can children be taught in a way that will not close their minds against further knowledge? How, in sum, can human beings remain childlike all their lives in their curiosity and openness to new experience?

References

Brown, R. W. *Social Psychology*. New York: Free Press, 1965.

Casebook and Proceedings Seminar on the Battered Child Syndrome. Topeka, Kansas: State Department of Social Welfare, Jan. 21, 1965.

Henry, J. *Culture Against Man*. New York: Random House, 1963.

Laing, R. D. *The Politics of Experience*. New York: Ballantine, 1967.

Loevinger, Jane. "Patterns of Childbearing as Theories of Learning." *Journal of Abnormal and Social Psychology*, 59 (1959): 148–150.

Mead, Margaret. *Culture and Commitment*. New York: Doubleday, 1970.

Minturn, L., and W. W. Lambert, et al., *Mothers of Six Cultures*. New York: Wiley, 1964.

Spencer, H. *Essays on Education*. 1858. Reprint, New York: Dalton, 1946.

Steele, B. F., and A. Pollack. "A Psychiatric Study of Parents Who Abuse Infants and Small Children." In *The Battered Child*, edited by R. E. Helfer and C. H. Kempe. Chicago: University of Chicago Press, 1968.

Chapter **8**

Childhood

Several articles in this part argue that our society tends to exaggerate the in-competence of children and sees more discontinuity between adults and children than really exists. It is important, however, to distinguish among children of different ages. Evidence suggests that the period between five to seven years marks a major transition from "primitive," "pre-logical," and "unrealistic" thinking to more adultlike mental processes. In this article, Anna Freud spells out the essential aspects of the young—pre-five-year-old—child's thoughts and feelings, with special reference to legal cases in which such children may be involved. She observes that far from sharing adult concerns and interests, young children are often in direct conflict with them. For example, they have no conception of blood ties; hence a foster parent who raised a child may be perceived as the real parent, while the biological parent seems a stranger to the child. She argues that young children need to have legal representation as persons in their own right, inde-pendently of adults.

The Child as a Person in His Own Right
Anna Freud

Children are presumed by law to be incomplete beings during the whole of their immaturity. Their utter inability to fulfill their own basic needs, or even to maintain life without extraneous help, justifies their being auto-matically assigned by birth certificate to their biological parents or, where this natural relationship fails to function, by later court proceedings to parent substitutes. Responsibility for the child, for his survival, for his physi-cal and mental growth, for his eventual adaptation to community standards

Reprinted by permission of Quadrangle/The New York Times Book Co. "The Child As a Person in His Own Right," by Anna Freud, from *The Psychoanalytic Study of the Child*, vol. 27, pp. 621–625. Copyright © 1973 by Ruth S. Eissler, Anna Freud, Mari-anne Kris, and Albert J. Solnit.

thus passes from the jurisdiction of the State to that of the designated adults to whom the child, in his turn, is responsible for his behavior, his misdemeanors, etc.

This state of affairs on the legal side is matched on the psychological side by a number of tenets, some of old standing, some new, such as the following:

that a child's mental reliance on the adult world is as long-lived as his physical dependency;

that each child's development proceeds in response to the environmental influences to which he is exposed;

that his emotional, intellectual, and moral capacities unfold, not in a void, but within his human relationships;

that his social reactions are determined by them;

that conflicts arise in the child in the first instance with the parental demands and prohibitions before they are internalized and may provide the base for later pathology.

There are, by now, many pediatricians, nurses, health visitors, social workers, probation officers, nursery school workers, school teachers, and child therapists who agree with these findings and conclude from them that no child should be approached, assessed, treated, nursed, taught, corrected, etc., without the parental influences being taken into account, and that without knowledge of their impact neither the child's developmental successes and failures nor his adjustments and maladjustments will be seen in their true light.

However, valuable as these insights are if placed within the general context of psychoanalytic child psychology, if used as guides on their own they are misleading and highlight one side of child development while they obscure another. Some workers within the services for children have learned the lesson of environmental influence too well and consequently err by viewing the child as a mere adjunct to the adult world, as a passive recipient of parental impact. They tend to ignore that children interact with the latter on the strength of their individual innate givens, and that it is this interaction, not mere response, which accounts for the countless variations in resulting characters and personalities as well as for the marked differences between siblings in spite of their growing up in the same family, etc. To see children too one-sidedly as mirroring their backgrounds blinds the observer to the vital characteristics of their own specific nature on which their own specific developmental needs are based.

There are a number of respects, such as the following, in which the mental makeup of children differs from that of the parent generation:

Unlike adults, whose psychic functioning proceeds on more or less fixed lines, children *change* constantly: from one state of growth to another; with regard to their understanding of events, their tolerance for frustration, their demands on motherly or fatherly care for stimulation, support, guidance, and restraint, or, according to the degree in which their personalities mature, for increasing freedom from control and for independence. Since, due to these changes, none of their needs remains stable, what serves their developmental interests on one level may be detrimental to progression on another.

Unlike adults, who measure the passing of *time* by clock and calendar, children have their own built-in time sense, based on the urgency of their instinctual and emotional needs. This results in their marked intolerance for postponement of gratification or for frustration, a heightened sensitivity to the length of separations, a shortening of the periods for remaining attached to absent parent figures, etc.

Unlike adults, whose reasonable mind is able to see occurrences in their true perspective, young children experience events in an *egocentric* manner, i.e., as happening solely with reference to their own persons. Thus, they may experience the mere move from one house or location to another as a grievous loss, imposed on them; the birth of a sibling, as an act of parental hostility; emotional preoccupation or illness of a parent, as rejection; death of a parent, as intentional abandonment, etc.

Unlike adults, who are able to deal with the vagaries of life via ego functions such as reason and intellect, immature children are governed in much of their functioning by the primitive parts of their minds, i.e., the *irrational id*. Consequently, they respond to any threat to their emotional security with fantastic anxieties, denial or distortion of reality, reversal or displacement of feelings, i.e., with reactions which are no help for coping but put them at the mercy of events.

Unlike adults, who are capable of maintaining positive emotional ties with a number of different individuals, unrelated or even hostile to each other, children are constitutionally unable to do so. They will freely love more than one adult only if the individuals in question feel positively to one another. Failing this, they become prey to severe and crippling *loyalty conflicts*.

Unlike adults, children have no psychological conception of relationship by blood-tie, whereas in the adult the fact of having engendered, borne, or given birth to a child produces an understandable sense of proprietorship and possessiveness, which underlies the frequent reconsiderations of consent to adoption, the claiming of offsprings after initial abandonment, etc. These considerations carry no weight with the children, who are emotionally unaware of the events leading to their births. What registers in their minds are the day-to-day interchanges with the adults who take care of them and who, on the strength of these, become the parent figures to whom they are attached.

It is due to these differences between the adult and the childish mind that children, more often than not, do not react according to expectation. As the discrepancies described are not common knowledge, decisions about a child's custody or placement may proceed wholly on the basis of adult reasoning, regardless of what this means in terms of the child's own emotional language.

Thus, it is not only with regard to *timing* that courts and welfare agencies are out of step with the children's own requirements. Following an order for *placement,* a young child may be removed from a known environment to an unknown one, with the adults oblivious of the hazards this implies for the child's still shaky sense of orientation. Following *adoption,* the inevitable change of name, which seems merely incidental to the adults, may have repercussions on the child's sense of identity, which is insecure at best. *Returned* to a biological parent after having been fostered, the child may face the traumatic task, not appreciated by the adults, of transferring emotional allegiance from a familiar and trusted adult to an unfamiliar stranger. Following *divorce,* with custody assigned to one parent, children are expected to concur peacefully with the court's decision, disregarding the fact that they are the prey of their own distorting and unsettling interpretations of the breakup; that they blame the mother for removing the father because of his alleged cruel, male demands on her; that boys fear the same fate awaiting them unless they inhibit their masculinity; that they blame whichever parent they live with and punish him or her by being disobedient; or that they blame themselves for the defection of the absent parent and become dejected and withdrawn. Following *visiting rights* allotted to the absent parent, the child is expected to relate positively to him, regardless of the fact that relations to a parent do not thrive naturally if restricted to prescribed days and hours and, even if they should do so, are interfered with by the child's conflict of loyalty between warring partners. When a child's residence is being divided evenly between the *two parents,* it may not be realized that this prevents both adults from exerting normal parental influence.

What is fair to the adults, their standards and their interests in all these instances, may be far from being in the best interests of the children concerned, or even the least detrimental alternative for them.

What emerges from the foregoing is that children are not adults in miniature but beings per se, different from their elders in their mental nature, their functioning, their evaluation of events, and their reactions to them. It follows from this that children, far from sharing the adults' concerns, are frequently put in direct conflict with them: their needs may contrast with those of their biological parents, their foster parents, or the social agencies concerned with them. For this reason, their rights cannot be represented

adequately by the advocates of either the adult claimant or the adult de-
fendant. They need party status in any court proceeding concerned with
their fate, i.e., to be represented, independently of the adults, as persons in
their own right.

It goes without saying that their own advocates need to be knowledgeable about the specific characteristics which govern any child's specific needs
for more or less unhampered growth and development.

*About a decade ago, Philippe Ariès put forth evidence showing that childhood
as a separate stage of life, requiring special institutions, is an invention of modern
times. In medieval society, as soon as the child could live without constant care
and supervision, he belonged to adult society. Ariès' findings produced surprise
and even disbelief, yet he had only rediscovered for Western society what anthropologists had found in many non-Western cultures: Adults and children participate in the same social world of work and play. No aspect of adult behavior is
hidden from children. In this article, the author discusses the causes and consequences of the modern conception of childhood.*

The Great Change in Children | *J. H. Plumb*

Within the family circle the affections binding parents and children seem
so natural that one assumes these relationships are a part of our humanity.
Certainly some aspects are. Mothers protect, look after, and feed children.
One can see the biological urge of motherhood at work whenever one glances
at animals or even birds. But once one moves away from this biological
fact, one moves into a world of change, of varying social attitudes of remarkable diversity. And certainly our own attitudes toward children not
only differ widely from our fathers' and grandfathers' but differ immensely
once we push back into the early nineteenth century and beyond. The world
that we think proper to children—fairy stories, games, toys, special books
for learning, even the idea of childhood itself— is a European invention of
the past four hundred years. The very words we use for young males—boy,
garçon, Knabe—were until the seventeenth century used indiscriminately to

From J. H. Plumb, "Children: The Victims of Time," from *In the Light of History*
(London: Allen Lane/The Penguin Press, 1972), pp. 153–166. Copyright © J. H.
Plumb, 1971, 1972.

mean a male in a dependent position and could refer to men of thirty, forty, or fifty. There was no special word for a young male between the ages of seven and sixteen; the word "child" expressed kinship, not an age state.

About the ancient world's attitude toward children we know next to nothing, though we are somewhat better informed about the training and education of youths in Greece, and especially in Sparta. For classical China the situation is similar: deep reverence for parents, particularly the father, was insisted upon, but we know very little of what was thought of childhood as a state. The common pattern of attitudes toward children among most primitive peoples, and there are discernible relics of this pattern in most advanced societies, is this: they are regarded as infants until seven years of age; little differentiation is made between the sexes, indeed, they are often dressed alike; at seven infancy goes and the boys begin to follow men's activities—herding cattle, hunting for food, working on the farm. Usually they are not men in two important aspects, the making of love and the making of war.

The entry into full manhood is customarily marked by intricate ritual, almost always painful. Spartan boys were viciously flogged, Arabian boys were circumcised without anesthetic. Nuer boys had their foreheads incised to the bone. The boys undergoing this operation were regarded as being of the same tribal age. They remained "classmates" for the rest of their lives, although their actual ages might vary by as much as four or five years. Most of them, however, would be unaware of their own precise age—indeed, this is true of the majority of men and women in medieval Europe. Often their ages would be associated with a village event, sometimes fairly decisely, but often in the vaguest way: a child of "about seven" could be any age from five to nine. Precision of age is a remarkably modern phenomenon; most societies until modern times simply grouped the young into blocks—infants, noninitiate boys or girls, and the like—in which age was irrelevant.

Again, it is very rare to find children depicted as children before the beginnings of the modern world, at the time of the Renaissance. In Chinese paintings, as in medieval manuscripts, they are usually shown as small adults, wearing the clothes, often having the expressions, of men and women. The Greeks paid little attention to childhood as a special state, and there are no Grecian statutes of children. It is true that in the late Roman Empire there is the hint of a change. There are a few remarkable heads of young boys, ten or twelve years of age, very lifelike and obviously individual portraits; most of these seem to come from funerary monuments. They display a quite extraordinary sense of age, of the young and growing child, which was not to be found again in Western art until Renaissance times. And there was Cupid, who fluttered in and out of frescoes, who as Eros was sculptured again and again during Hellenistic times. He is the ancestor of the naked *putti* that flit through the pictures of so many European artists from

the fifteenth to the nineteenth century, mischievous, impudent, and sentimental. But Eros was a stylized symbol, not a child. Similarly, toward the
close of the Middle Ages, angels appear in illustrated manuscripts, singing
and playing musical instruments, and they are quite obviously neither infants nor adults, but children. Yet they, too, like Cupid, fulfill a special function. And they do not lead to the portrayal of actual children. One has only
to look at the church monuments of Elizabethan England to see how distant
the concept was of childhood as a separate state. There lined up behind the
father are three or four little men, all dressed like himself in the formal
clothes of the age, and behind his wife kneels a group of little girls wearing
the habits of women. Only infants are clothed differently. They are shown
either tightly bound in their swaddling clothes or dressed in the long robes
worn by both girls and boys alike until they were "about seven."

Fortunately, enough records survive for us to be able to state with confidence that pictorial representation is but a reflection of a social attitude.
And we can trace the slow evolution of our modern concepts of childhood
over the past four hundred years. The journey, though slow, was immense—
the development of a separate world of childhood. This seems so natural to
us that it is difficult to conceive of any other.

First, we must remember that infants died more often than they lived. "All
mine die," said Montaigne casually, as a gardener might speak of his cab-
bages. And until they had reached the end of infancy, between the ages of
five and seven, they scarcely counted. A character in Molière, when talking
of children, says, "I don't count the little one." Men and women of the sixteenth and seventeenth centuries would not have regarded the exposure of
children by the Spartans, Romans, and Chinese as callous. Indeed, it is likely
that the poor of Renaissance Europe treated unwanted infants with a similar
brutality. Life was too harsh to bother overmuch about an infant who probably would not survive anyway. At that time the attitude was much nearer to
the instinct of an animal—immense concern while the infant lived to feed
it and protect it, indifference after it was dead, and death was expected.

A new sensitivity toward infant mortality can be discerned near the end of
the sixteenth century, when dead children began to be represented on their
parents' tombs. The fact that they were dead, not living, children is made
grimly clear. They either have skulls in their hands, or kneel upon one, or
have one hanging above their head, and even tiny infants are depicted, still
in their swaddling clothes, which indicates that they were probably younger
than two years of age. Children, even babies, were ceasing to be anonymous;
yet if this was the beginning, the dawn of a new attitude toward childhood,
its fulfillment was still far in the future.

Certainly there was no separate world of childhood. Children shared the
same games with adults, the same toys, the same fairy stories. They lived

their lives together, never apart. The coarse village festivals depicted by Bruegel, showing men and women besotted with drink, groping for each other with unbridled lust, have children eating and drinking with the adults. Even in the soberer pictures of wedding feasts and dances the children are enjoying themselves alongside their elders, doing the same things. Nor need we rely on paintings, alone, for we have a wonderfully detailed record of the childhood of Louis XIII. His physician kept a diary, recording each day what the young dauphin did. From this, we can perceive how his father, Henry IV, and the court treated him. It gives one an insight into aristocratic attitudes toward childhood, and into middle-class attitudes as well, for we have corroborative sources, though none so rich, for this period just before some of the most momentous changes in adults' attitudes toward children were about to take place.

Like the peasant children painted by Bruegel, the young prince was involved in adult life to an outstanding degree. At four Louis was taking part in adult ballets, once stark-naked as Cupid; at five he enjoyed hugely a farce about adultery; at seven he began to go to the theatre often. He started gambling at the same age; indeed, he was playing crambo at three. By seven he was also learning to ride and shoot and hunt. He relished blue stories, as well as fairy stories, with a group of courtiers of all ages: fairy stories did not belong exclusively to children; courtiers, particularly the ladies, loved them. Similarly, the games he played—Hide-and-seek, Fiddle-de-dee, Blindman's Bluff—were all played with adults and adolescents as well as with his child companions.

Although the adult and childhood world intermixed intimately, there were some differences, particularly before the age of seven. The dauphin when very young played with dolls, rode a hobbyhorse, and rushed about the palace with his toy windmill; these were specifically the activities of infants. Before he was breeched, he was often dressed up as a girl. More surprising, however, was the amount of open sexuality permitted. The dauphin and his sister were stripped and placed naked in the king's bed, and when the children played sexually with each other, Henry IV and the court were hugely amused. The queen, a pious and rather austere woman, thought nothing of seizing his genitals in the presence of the court, and the dauphin often displayed himself, to the amusement of his staid middle-aged governess. He acquired the facts of life as soon as he could talk. At seven, however, all was changed. He was severely reprimanded for playing sexually with a girl his own age, and the need for modesty was constantly impressed upon him. The importance of this very detailed evidence from the dauphin's doctor, who saw nothing odd in it, stresses that the world of children and the world of adults were deeply involved. Children, even infants, were not thought of as requiring a special environment, special entertainments, special clothes; nor was it considered necessary to keep them apart from the sophistications and ribaldries of adult life. There were, however, some distinctions: actions that could be permitted, even joked about, in very young chidlren had to stop as soon as they left infancy and became young adults.

In some ways the court was old-fashioned, for by 1600 there was growing up a new conception of childhood. This has been developed by the School-men of the fifteenth century, and adopted and adapted by the educationalists of the Renaissance, especially Erasmus, Vives, and Mosellanus. It became the stock in trade of the Jesuits, who were to dominate the education of the aristocracy and the richer middle class of seventeenth-century Europe. This new attitude was based on the concepts that childhood was innocent and that it was the duty of adults to preserve this innocence. The child, surely, was a prey to passion and to irrationality, but just as innocence could be preserved, so passions could be repressed. The protected child could be guided by remorseless effort into the world of rational behavior; innocence could be transmogrified into adult morality. So even while the dauphin was playing with his naked sister to the ribald amusement of the court, the Jesuits were purging schoolbooks of indecencies and the religious at Port Royal were editing Terence so that he might be read at school. In many educational establishments discipline was becoming extremely stringent and the dangers of childish sexuality legislated against—boys were no longer put two or three to a bed, and there was a steady separation both of the sexes and of age groups. Parallel with this developed the cult of the Infant Jesus, which symbolized childish innocence. One of the most common devotional prints of the seventeenth century showed Christ summoning the little children to his knee. Increasingly, the child became an object of respect, a special creature with a different nature and different needs, which required separation and protection from the adult world. By 1700 for a child of middle-class family to be outwardly licentious would have been deeply shocking, to have been allowed to gamble for money at six would have appeared outrageous. By then, too, the child possessed his own literature, books carefully pruned of adult sophistication or broad humor, but also especially written for the young mind. The period between seven and adolescence was becoming a world of its own.

In the eighteenth century this new vision of childhood became the accepted social attitude of the affluent classes. Among the poor the old attitudes lingered on—poverty bred proximity, and so forced adults and children to share the same world. In villages and in slums children and adults still played games together, listened to the same stories, lived lives much more closely bound together, lives that could not be separated.

Nor was it only in the areas of manners and morals that changes took place in the lives of children between 1600 and 1800. This period also witnessed a revolution in the attitude toward the education of children—and many of the assumptions that we regard almost as belonging to human nature itself were adopted during this time. For example, everyone assumes that the processes of a literate education should develop with the developing child: reading should begin about four or five, writing follow, and then gradually, more sophisticated subjects should be added and become more complex as the child grows. Education now is tied almost inflexibly to the calendar age of children. In the modern world, at least in Europe and America, a class of children at a school will all be nearly the same age—a few months, perhaps, on either side of the average, but rarely as much as a year.

As with manners and morals, there were for a very long time two worlds of education: one belonging essentially to the Middle Ages, which persisted among backward people for a long time; and the other, basically our own, which took centuries to achieve its final organization and definition. The medieval child usually learned his letters with the local priest or a monk from a nearby monastery, more rarely in the singing schools attached to cathedrals, but the age at which he started his primary education would be dictated by his personal circumstances. Often, a boy would not start to learn Latin, without which all but the most basic learning was impossible, until he was in his teens, sometimes even twenty or older, simply because his economic situation prevented it. In the seventeenth century Girardon, the French sculptor, worked at home until he was sixteen; when his father, prosperous at last, sent him off to begin his studies. Still not unusual in Girardon's day, this practice had been customary in the fifteenth century, when old men, young men, adolescents, and children could all be found sitting in the same classroom, learning the same lessons. They turned up for classes, but no one cared about the rest of their lives. Sometimes, as we learn from Thomas Platter's story of his school days in the early sixteenth century, groups of students ranging in age from the early twenties to a mere ten would wander in search of learning from France to Germany and back again. A young boy would be bound to an older boy, beg for him, be beaten by him, and might occasionally be taught by him, but always he would be fed and protected. Occasional jobs would enable them to attend classes and lectures; but usually they begged, and education proceeded by fits and starts. They lived like hippies and wandered like gypsies, begging, stealing, fighting; yet they were always hungry for books, for that learning that would open the doors of the professions. Platter was nineteen before he could read fluently, but within three years his hunger for learning led him to master Latin, Greek, and Hebrew. And in the end he became rector of Basel's most famous school.

Even in Platter's day, however, times were changing. The late Middle Ages witnessed the proliferation of colleges, particularly at Oxford and Cambridge and the University of Paris. Students entered the university at an early age—usually at fifteen, sometimes as young as twelve, though there was, of course, no bar to the very mature. Residence in colleges fixed them in one place, and parents could be certain that their sons would be subject to discipline, sent regularly to lectures and classes, and protected from the excesses of drink, the temptations of fornication, and the dangers of gambling. College rules became very strict; obedience was insisted upon, and whipping frequent for delinquency. Inexorably a world of learning, quite separate from the adult world, indeed, carefully protected from it, was created. In the sixteenth and seventeenth centuries all Etonians were taught in one large room. The boys were divided up into groups in accordance with the progress of their studies, and the usher and master would go from group to group. At this time few grammar schools or *lycées* had more than one master and one usher.

This system began to change at the end of the eighteenth century, and by the early part of the nineteenth century a new system had been established. Schoolrooms were divided up or added, boys of the same age were moved steadily from class to class, and as the numbers swelled, fees grew and so did the number of masters employed. Yet much of the adult world lingered on, even in the boarding schools, which were becoming increasingly popular in England. We know that at Eton, Harrow, Rugby, and elsewhere there was drinking, smoking, fighting with local boys, a great deal of gambling, and a considerable amount of surreptitious wenching. But reform went relentlessly on, creating a separate world of childhood and early youth. Even the leisure and amusements of schoolboys were differentiated. Organized team-games replaced casual, personal sporting activity; innocence was insisted upon and incessantly preached about; sex before entry into the adult world came to be regarded as a social crime; literature was even more carefully censored—the headmaster of Harrow in the mid-century would not allow the reading of any novel, for fear it would corrupt the reader; naturally gambling was forbidden and alcohol banned. Even food became different—far plainer than adult food and dominated by milk and suet puddings, which you may still hear an old-fashioned Englishman dismiss as nursery food. And school clothes changed, too. In the seventeenth century two ribbons at each shoulder marked a child's dress, otherwise it was the same as an adult's. In the eighteenth century children were frequently clothed in semifancy dress—sailor's costume, the kilt and bonnet of the Scottish Highlander, Vandyke dress for special occasions—rather as if society were searching for difference. Greater freedom was permitted to the child, and children were allowed trousers long before adults would wear them. But gradually, two basically separate forms of costume for children and adults evolved. By the early twentieth century boys between infancy and puberty wore short trousers, and their clothes were always far drabber than adults'—confined to grays and blues and blacks. At school children were clamped into uniforms as socially distinct as those of soldiers or prisoners.

In the European upper classes children in the nineteenth century were even excluded from adult society *in the home*. The children were forbidden most of the house and lived in day and night nurseries with nurses, governesses, or tutors, visiting the rest of the house and their parents only for very short periods. Indeed, the difference between the life of a sixteenth- and a late-nineteenth-century child is so vast as to be almost incomprehensible. Three centuries had created a private world for children.

Although this new attitude toward children developed in the middle classes, it seeped down into society as time passed. The pictures of working-class children of Victorian London or Paris show them still dressed as adults, usually in their parents' worn-out and cut-down clothes, and we now know that they participated in every form of adult life—indeed, they physically had no escape from it. But as affluence spread, the working class, too, was caught up in the system of mass education, and working-class children began to have a separate world forced upon them. Social legislation also took a hand. In the nineteenth and twentieth centuries children were excluded from public houses, forbidden to gamble or buy tobacco, and their sexual lives were regulated by the concept of the "age of consent"; for it was assumed that they would be innocent, and prefer innocence, unless a corrupt society forced sex upon them. So by World War I, speaking broadly, there were three ages—infancy, which had been shortened to the age of four or five; childhood, which ran from the end of infancy to late puberty for the lower classes and to early manhood for the rest; and adulthood. And no child anywhere in the Western world was expected to share the tastes, the appetites, the social life, of an adult.

And then the revolutionary change came. The change from medieval to modern had taken more than three centuries, but the revolution that frightens modern society is scarcely a decade old. To understand it, one must know why children had gradually been separated from the adult world, and their lives and education carefully regulated. The short answer is social need: after 1500 the Western world grew ever more complex, demanding more skilled and trained men for commerce and the professions. And for these activities boys rather than girls were needed, which is why attitudes toward the young male changed most of all. Also, the great empires—the French, the British, the Spanish, and the Dutch—required men with the habit of authority. The proconsuls of empire had to be stamped with the image of a gentleman, aware of obligations as well as privileges. Discipline, best enforced by regular schooling, proved the most efficacious mold for the colonial bureaucrat.

But society is never still, and even as the new attitudes toward childhood were becoming fully fledged, there were countermovements in social structure that were to make even profounder changes. Science and technology invaded more and more of economic and social life. From 1880 onward they increasingly dominated the activities of Western society. Their growth demanded a longer and longer education. Before World War I sixteen or seventeen was a not unusual age for a middle-class boy to leave school either in America or Europe. After World War II huge segments of the population, female as well as male, remained in the educational system to twenty-one and beyond, and the number increases every few years. Such a vast social change must necessarily have affected our attitudes toward childhood and youth, but there were other complex social forces at work as well. The great European powers lost their empires. Their need for conformity to a middle-class pattern weakened. America filled up, became urban, and its accepted social images of youth became blurred and confused at the same time. The whole purpose of education, other than the learning of crafts and skills, became entangled in debate. Add to this the psychoanalytical attacks on the Victorian concept of childish innocence, and the social confusion about how to treat childhood is easy to comprehend.

There were other muddying factors. The middle classes grew much richer, and the pressures on their children toward economic and social goals eased, too. They were pressurized neither to be Christian gentlemen nor Horatio Algers. And yet in spite of a myriad of warning signs that attitudes toward children needed to be changed, the attitudes belonging to an earlier and simpler world were still enforced. Children were not allowed to drink; parents and educators insisted on old patterns of overt deference and unquestioning obedience. Behavior, clothes, and hair styles had to conform to archaic standards; juvenile reading was still censored; sex was regarded as belonging to the adult world and certainly not to be practiced by those being educated. Repression, conformity, discipline, and exclusion were until lately the historically bred attitudes of most educationalists and parents.

Kept out of the adult world, the adolescents naturally created a world of their own choosing—one that incorporated their own music, their own morals, their own clothes, and their own literature. And they, of course, began naturally to capture the minds and imagination of the children who, though younger in age, nevertheless lived with them in the same basic educational territory. In consequence, during the past few years the period between infancy and adolescence has been sharply reduced, and may be reduced even further in the future.

Social movements and tensions in the adult world can be adjusted by politics, but adolescents and children have no such mechanism for their conflicts with the exclusive world of adults. And so the result has been, and must be, rebellion. That rebellion, however, is not due to the mistakes or difficulties of the last few years. Rarely do we look far enough into the past for the roots of our present problems. This revolution of youth has been building up for decades because we forced the growing child into a repressive and artificial world—a prison, indeed, that was the end product of four centuries of Western history, of that gradual exclusion of the maturing child from the world of adults. We can now look back with longing to the late medieval world, when, crude and simple as it was, men, women, and children lived their lives together, shared the same morals as well as the same games, the same excesses as well as the same austerities. In essence, youth today is rebelling against four centuries of repression and exploitation.

We tend to think of the emotional lives of families as private dramas where family members express their individual personalities. But even the most isolated nuclear family behind the closed doors of the family home is still not immune to outside influence. In our beliefs and feelings about what it means to be a man, a woman, a child, a parent, we are also products of the place, time, and social group in which we live. Furthermore, the demands and prescriptions we respond to are not always in accord with each other, but may be contradictory. In this article, the author describes the cultural contradictions that beset American families, particularly the middle class families who spawned the dissenting youth of the 1960's.

Growing Up Confused: Cultural Crisis and Individual Character | *Richard Flacks*

It is not too great an oversimplification to say that the central, unifying theme of American culture has always been that cluster of values Max Weber called the "Protestant Ethic." In particular, Americans agreed that the meaning of life was given by one's work, that personal fulfillment and social responsibility required that males be fully engaged in a vocation, and that virtue was measured in terms of success in an occupation. The most valued work was entrepreneurial activity; the most valued model was the rational, thrifty, hard-working, self-denying, risk-taking entrepreneur.

From Richard Flacks, *Youth and Social Change* (Chicago: Markham Publishing Company, 1971), pp. 20–34. Reprinted by permission of Rand McNally College Publishing Company.

Undoubtedly, the vitality of these values was important in the phenomenal growth of the American technological and economic system in the nineteenth century. In a period when accumulation and production were society's central problems, it was fortunate that the average man was highly motivated to produce, to work hard, and to save—in short, to resist temptations that might divert him from doing his part in building the country. It was also fortunate that aspirations for monetary success could be fulfilled by many, while many others could believe that their failure lay in themselves—in their own inability to achieve the cultural ideal—rather than in the ideal itself.

In the American ideal women were not regarded as virtuous if *they* sought independence and success in the world of work. Instead, they were valued if they supported their husbands' capacity to be single-mindedly devoted to work, if they themselves were skilled at producing a self-sufficient household, and if they raised their male children to be independent, self-reliant, self-denying, and achievement-oriented individuals.

Given the entrepreneurial opportunities, the open frontier, and the evident dynamism of American life, it is not surprising that most American young people who were socialized into this cultural framework accepted it with enthusiasm. Boys were eager to become men in the image of their fathers—although encouraged by their fathers and mothers, they were profoundly eager to surpass their fathers' achievements in work and status.

Observers agree that this cultural framework has been severely eroded or at least modified by what has happened in America in the twentieth century. What, in brief outline, happened?

1. An economic system organized around problems of capital accumulation and the need for saving, entrepreneurship, and self-reliance—a system of free market and individual competition—has been replaced by an economic system organized around problems of distribution and the need for spending, interdependence, bureaucratic management, planning, and large-scale organization.

2. As a consequence, work is now coordinated by massive private and public bureaucratic organizations, and work achievement is defined not in entrepreneurial terms, but in terms of successful fulfillment of a career within a bureaucratic or professional hierarchy.

3. These developments have permitted and been required by a tremendous technological leap. Consequently, a vast array of commodities for individual consumption is produced. On the one hand, this situation required that men consume; on the other hand, it obviated the sense of the need to save, postpone gratification, and be self-denying that had been justified by scarcity.

As a result of these massive changes—from individual entrepreneurship to large corporate organization, from free market competition to bureaucratic coordination and planning, from accumulation and scarcity to consumption and affluence—the vitality of the "Protestant Ethic" has declined. Throughout society during the past sixty years, more and more people have felt less committed to the entrepreneurial character and its virtues. Increasingly, self-worth and worth in the eyes of others is organized as much by one's style of life and one's consumption patterns as by one's occupational status as such. Furthermore, although instrumental and rational activity is still highly valued, all observers report that there has been a relaxation on prohibitions against expressiveness and hedonism. Indeed, a society in which the consumption of goods has become a fundamental problem requires that men cease to be ascetic and self-denying and abandon many of the guilts that they experience when they express their impulses.

By the middle of the twentieth century, the American society was qualitatively different from the society that had given birth to the cultural framework of capitalism. The family firm had been superseded by the giant corporation, the free market by the "welfare-warfare" state, and the entrepreneur by the manager and the bureaucrat. Technology had created a superabundant economy in which the traditional virtues of thrift, self-denial and living by the sweat of one's brow seemed not only absurd, but actually dangerous to prosperity. Technology seemed to promise not only an abundance of goods, but a world in which hard physical labor could be eliminated.

Yet, despite the need for new values and a new cultural framework, a cultural transformation was not occurring. Politicians, teachers, and preachers continued to give lip-service to the Protestant Ethic, while the mass media, without announcing the fact, purveyed an increasingly blatant hedonism. Many of the classic symptoms of "anomie" were widespread. Breakdown was widely evident, but new values were not.

I suppose that the best indication of the coherence of a culture is the degree to which parents can transmit a sense of it to their offspring with clarity and effectiveness. Cultural breakdown has reached the point of no return when the process of socialization no longer provides the new generation with coherent reasons to be enthusiastic about becoming adult members of the society. Perhaps the best way I can illustrate what I mean by cultural instability and breakdown is to discuss the American middle-class family as it seemed to most observers to be functioning by mid-twentieth century. An examination of family patterns and childrearing not only illuminates the cultural crisis, but also provides some clues to the sources of youthful discontent.

When you read what follows, remember that I am not criticizing American *parents* for faulty childrearing practices. On the contrary, the main point I am trying to make is that parental confusion is virtually inevitable in a society in which the culture is breaking down. Moreover, the outcomes of that confusion should not be labeled "pathological," in my opinion. On the contrary. When parents raise their children in a manner that causes them to have significant problems of "adjustment," if anything, this is a "healthy" circumstance. I am arguing that the basic source of socially patterned maladjustment is a culture that no longer enables a person to find coherent meaning in his life. The maladjustment of youth offers one of the few hopes that new meanings can be found—that a new culture can be created.

The family, of course, is the primary institution for the inculcation of basic values and molding of culturally appropriate character structures. All observers agree that the American family, particularly the white, "middle class" family, has undergone a substantial transformation over the past several decades—a transformation that both reflects and contributes to the cultural crisis in the society at large.

A major structural change in the middle class family has been its "reduction"—that is, the erosion of close ties to relatives outside the nuclear family unit. Dissolution of extended family bonds is highly functional in a society based on technological development because it permits people to be relatively free of emotional and economic ties to "homes" and "relatives" and enables them to move freely in response to changing occupational requirements, and to take advantage of opportunities for career advancement wherever and whenever they become available. Since the nuclear family is expected to establish a self-contained household, it becomes a highly efficient mechanism for absorbing a vast array of consumer goods—each small family unit seeks to purchase the house, car, furnishings, appliances, and other commodities that will ensure its independence. (On the other hand, an extended family complex living contiguously probably would share many such goods, thereby reducing the need for each household in the network to buy its own.) Thus, in a structural sense the nuclear middle class family meshes nicely with the economy's demand for a mobile labor force and an actively consuming public.

In the typical middle class family, the father works away from home while the mother spends virtually all her time at home rearing the children. Authority—in principle—is shared by the parents (a marked change from the patriarchal structure of the past), but clearly, it is exercised far more intensively and continuously by the mother than by the father. Ideally, the mother (if she is modern) is less concerned with efforts to repress and restrict the expressive, impulsive behavior of her children than she was in the past, just as she is less likely to emphasize obedient, submissive behavior as desirable. Instead, she is expected to facilitate the child's desires to explore, to test the environment, and to encourage self-reliant and autonomous behavior.

What is now "good" is not so much the obedient, quiet, clean, cautious child, but rather the child who acquires verbal and motor skills early, who is precocious in his understanding, who can do things for himself, and who relates well to strangers and to other children. Mother attempts to instill such qualities by use of so-called "psychological" techniques of discipline—giving and withdrawing her love. She tries to avoid the traditional, more "physical" forms of punishment, trying instead to convey a nondomineering attitude, nurturing nonauthoritarian style. Father, relatively a part of the background, strives for a generally warm, nonauthoritarian and supportive approach.

This mode of childrearing has become ascendant in American culture in this century, especially in the last three decades. It relies, then, on a high degree of exclusive dependence on the mother coupled with strong demands on the child for cognitive mastery and a will to strive and achieve. Research suggests that this family situation is a superior one for generating precisely those characteristics that enable successful participation in a culture that stresses individual achievement, formal education, rationality, and flexibility. The culturally desired outcome of this family (and my emphasis here is on *male* character) is a child who achieves masculine identity and independence by fulfilling his mother's expectations that he will be independent and striving, whose guilt and anxiety is focused on achievement of internal standards of excellence, who enjoys testing and is capable of being tested, and who is able to handle sexual, aggressive, and other impulses and emotions by expressing them at the appropriate times and places while not letting them seriously interfere with his capacity for work, rational action, and self-reliance. Thus, impulses are not denied (as the traditional Protestant Ethic demanded) but managed. This process is greatly facilitated by the delicately balanced combination of demand and freedom, dependence and independence, and mothering and autonomy that ideally characterizes the suburban family.

How often such an "ideal" outcome actually results from this family situation is questionable. Although the mother-centered nuclear family meshes nicely with crucial *official values* embodied in the educational and occupational system, it appears to be highly vulnerable to a variety of severe contradictions that occur in the course of actual day-to-day life in the society. These contradictions are readily derivable from the general crisis of the culture I have been trying to sketch.

Parental Value Conflict and Confusion

Undoubtedly, parents experience a great deal of strain when they permit freedom and encourage autonomy on the part of their children. One source of such strain is the difference between the comparatively strict atmosphere in which most middle class parents were raised and the atmosphere they try to create in their own homes. Another is that many parents continue to be emotionally committed to the traditional virtues of cleanliness, obedience, emotional control, and the like. Undoubtedly, then, many mothers and fathers are quite inconsistent with respect to discipline and demands; sometimes they punish their children for infraction of their rules and at other times they do not; sometimes they insist on traditional "good habits" while sometimes they are more relaxed. Frequently such parental inconsistency may result in what has been called "absorption" of the child's personality. Rather than molding a flexible, striving, self-sufficient character, the result is a character who fears failure *and* success, experiences deep anxiety about his acceptance by others, finds it difficult to establish his own autonomy, and is, consequently, far more driven toward conformity and "security" than toward independence and personal achievement. Indeed, some social critics have argued that this "other-directed" character type is becoming ascendant and that the achievement-oriented, "inner-directed" type is fading. Whether or not this is true, it seems plain that parental confusion over the nature of discipline and virtue is widespread and seriously undermines cultural goals rooted in achievement motivation.

Many parents are clearly committed to providing opportunities for free expression and autonomy for their children. They favor a life of fulfillment, experiential richness, and less self-denial. They may desire such a life for *themselves,* but find it difficult to consistently and wholeheartedly treat their children in this manner. Clearly, parents in a small nuclear family revolving around the mother as the exclusive childcare specialist must expend a tremendous investment of patience and energy, especially if they exercise permissiveness. To permit children to wander, experiment, and test requires constant vigilance to protect their physical safety. To provide children intellectual stimulation and sensory variety requires intensive involvement in the quality of their activities. But if parents are to provide the quantities of time, energy, and patience required to achieve these goals they must limit their *own* recreation and pursuits and get enough sleep so that they will have sufficient energy and patience to allow their offspring to be the central focus of attention whenever the children are awake and around. Undoubtedly, this is a source of strain even for parents with articulate commitment to "liberated" values—perhaps especially for them, since they themselves want freedom, autonomy, and the like. This conflict between the demands of childrearing and the personal needs of the parents constitutes another source of parental inconsistency that undermines the "ideal" character of the modern middle class family.

A third source of parental confusion is the conflict between effort and indulgence. Typical middle class parents expect their offspring to strive and achieve and to understand the necessity for self-discipline and effort in attaining goals. Very often, however, such families have surplus incomes and try to provide their children with a sense of being well taken care of. Indeed, in many families, parents indulge their children in order to demonstrate their love and care. Many fathers assuage the guilt they feel because of their absence from the home by showering their children with presents; many rationalize their own self-sacrifice by averring that anything that frees their kids from suffering is worthwhile. In any case, such parental indulgence (which is undoubtedly functional for the consumer goods sector of the economy) tends to weaken the offsprings' sense of necessity for self-discipline, sacrifice, and toil. Indeed, many children of affluence sense that as heirs of their parents' material property, they are likely to have some degree of permanent lifelong economic security. Under these circumstances, effort and achievement lose much of their motivational potency and moral meaning. This is especially so if fathers suggest to their sons (which they often do) that they can afford to enjoy life in ways that previous generations could not.

Thus, it seems plausible that incoherence and confusion are virtually inevitably features of the modern middle class family and the suburban style of life. As we shall see, the consequences for the general culture and for the youths who will inherit it contribute to the sense of crisis.

Maternal Ambivalence

In addition to such value confusion, there are other sources of childrearing imbalance and parental inconsistency. One of the most significant is the ambivalence and discontent that many women experience as they try to play the new maternal roles dictated by the family structure and childraising ideology we have been depicting. These discontents revolve around the fact that the woman who becomes a mother is expected to be a full-time mother and housewife in a situation in which she is highly isolated from adult social relations and must perform tasks that are menial and meaningless. She is expected to accept this role even though her formal education before marriage and motherhood has made her qualified to perform other roles and despite her aspirations for independence and self-fulfillment. Understandably, such a women finds it difficult to narrow her interests to the world of her three-year-old child and even more difficult not to feel guilty because she is discontent and hostile to her children and to her husband.

The ways in which women have adapted to this situation are diverse. Most adaptations that have been recorded, however, have been condemned as culturally dysfunctional and/or psychologically damaging to the child. For instance, there is the smothering, overprotective mother (whose protectiveness is said to be a screen for her unconscious hostility toward the child); the "seductive" mother (who becomes extremely close to her son as a displacement for her more general interpersonal and sexual frustrations); the mother who subtly, and often unconsciously, denigrates her husband to her children as an expression of her jealous resentment of his privilege and his abandonment of her; the mother who attempts to live vicariously through her children (hoping that they will achieve goals that she herself has been blocked from achieving); and the working mother (who, according to some child-rearing experts, intensifies the child's fears of separation and abandonment).

All of these compensations are seen as damaging to the child's ability to manage and overcome his dependence on the mother, prolonging that dependency or forcing him to identify with her (instead of with the father) and weakening the male child's ability to accept culturally approved definitions of masculine identity. All of these patterns may weaken achievement motivation and damage the child's capacity for self-reliance.

Although many psychologists characterize such maternal behavior as "neurotic," a sociological perspective emphasizes the fact that such behavior is *socially determined—it is built into the maternal role* as it is now structured, especially considering the manner in which young women have been socialized and the increasing cultural support for the equality of women. More specifically, the discontent of middle class mothers is an inevitable consequence of the fact that they are forced into roles that do not match their aspirations and self-conceptions—aspirations and self-conceptions they have been taught are their right. Such a fundamental contradiction in women's roles is a further consequence and determinant of the general cultural crisis.

Paternal Ambivalence

The paternal role contains its own built-in contradictions. This is so because fathers, as effective models of adult achievement, self-reliance, and rationality that they are expected to be, must be available for the psychological benefit of their children. At the same time, the middle class male who is striving or is already successful is likely to have a range of responsibilities and commitments outside the home. The highly career-oriented father may be available to his children hardly at all, partly from "necessity" and partly because he finds that life in the family is mundane when compared with life outside the home, where the responsibility and the power he can command are exciting.

Other fathers experience considerable regret and discontent with their work; they have ended up in positions that do not fulfill their earlier aspirations, they find their work unfulfilling or morally dubious, and they find work itself increasingly onerous. Many such fathers undoubtedly communicate their self-doubts and their skepticism to their sons. Still other men experience themselves as failures—as impotent and second rate in their work. The family, for them, becomes an arena for the exercise of power, aggression and self-importance which they cannot find elsewhere.

Like contradictions in the mothers' role, such paternal ambivalence is derived from fundamental cultural contradictions. These contradictions revolve around cultural demands for continuous striving and simultaneous demands for endless consumption—demands that men be dedicated careerists and, at the same time, good fathers, and that they compartmentalize the public and private worlds, reserving personal warmth, intimacy, and expressiveness for the latter.

A second source of strain for the middle class male is that the cultural measure of his worth (as well as his own sense of self-esteem) is based on his occupational success, but that success is a limitless goal on the one hand and is denied most men on the other. To the extent that the male accepts the cultural definition of his value, his self-esteem suffers. This inadequacy is communicated to his children; to the extent that he rejects the cultural standard, he communicates to his children a certain skepticism about the cultural framework.

As a result the developing child is exposed to another source of confusion. To the extent that the father embodies any of these contradictions, he is lacking in his effectiveness as a model, and since the typical suburban family is nuclear and isolated, the male child finds few alternatives to serve as effective models.

The Pace of Social Change

A final source of parental confusion derives from the sense perhaps shared by most people in the culture—that the world in which children will be adults will be substantially different from the world in which they are children, in ways that are considerably obscure. Parents generally conceive of themselves—perhaps more than at any time in history—as inadequate models for their children because they are already obsolete. In this situation, the parental tone of voice lacks conviction, parental guidance has overtones of fatuousness, and parental authority is undermined by the parents' own lack of confidence. This particular source of cultural incoherence may not be directly related to the structure of the nuclear family itself, but it is a rather obvious consequence of a culture that values technological change and development as one of its central priorities. Presumably, a childrearing program that emphasizes independence, flexibility, and openmindedness meshes with a culture that values change. But as we have seen, such virtues are more easily espoused than instilled in a culture that places such heavy reliance on isolated and morally confused mothers and fathers to implement such a program.

It should not be hard to envision from our depiction of the built-in "strains" associated with the middle class nuclear family some idea of the consequences for young people. Briefly, such a family situation is likely to generate considerable confusion over values, goals, roles, and aspirations for the youth who experience it. More specifically, we can suggest that the "new" family is likely to impart a number of dispositions and personality "trends" in its offspring—traits or potentialities that predispose such youth to be restless with, skeptical of, or alienated from certain crucial aspects of conventional culture and, consequently, ready for certain kinds of cultural change.

A listing of some hypotheses concerning certain tendencies that the middle class family situation seems to generate in its offspring follows (I term them hypotheses, which await persuasive empirical tests, because for the most part, there is little direct evidence that these tendencies are clearly linked to childhood socialization):

1. Confusion and restlessness with conventional definitions of success. Such feelings would derive from the types of paternal ambivalence we have described, from the psychological distance of the father's work role from those of his sons', from the parental value confusions we have called attention to, and from the pattern of maternal domination. Even youths who have strong motivations to achieve and who may act these out in school would be likely to entertain doubts about whether material success, status-striving and careerism constitute appropriate avenues for expressing their desires to "do well." But neither conventional parents nor the conventional culture provide very many clues about how one can achieve in ways other than the economic. The consequences of this combination of predispositions to question material success coupled with predispositions to achieve include profound indecisiveness about vocation (what Erik Erikson has called "role confusion"), vague yearnings for recognition and fame, and a restless search for alternative vocations and life styles.

2. Restlessness under conditions of imposed discipline. These derive from such features of the family as parental indulgence and permissiveness and are related to feelings of discontent with conventional definitions of vocation and achievement. Some consequences are discontent with classroom drill and learning situations requiring rote memorization; tendencies to feel bored and restless when concentration is required; avoidance of school subjects requiring discipline and attention to detail; and a generalized resistance to tasks that do not appear to be personally rewarding or are set without

reference to goals determined by the self. These feelings are accompanied by intense desires for immediate experience, often coupled with guilt.

3. Restlessness with conditions of arbitrary or coercive authority. Such feelings might derive from expectations developed in the family for authority structures based on egalitarianism—expectations derived from parental fostering of participation, independence and autonomy and parental refusal to use physical punishment or coercion. Children raised in this way, we can speculate, may grow to expect that authority *outside* the family will be similarly responsive, democratic, nonpunitive and permissive. A consequence of such dispositions and expectations about authority is the tendency to be unusually trusting of teachers and other adults, but vociferously and unusually upset, angry and rebellious when such authority figures betray expectations that they will be egalitarian, democratic, and so forth. Or one might expect such children to be capable of more active expression of opposition and resistance to authority when it appears arbitrary, more skeptical of its claims in general, more likely to ask embarrassing questions, and more ready to systematically test the limits of its tolerance.

4. Discomfort with conventional sex-role definitions. Boys who have ambivalent fathers or who tend to identify with their mothers and have accepting, nonpunitive parents are likely to define masculinity in ways that are quite untraditional. They are likely to be less motivated for dominance, less physically aggressive and tough, less physically competitive, and more emotionally expressive and aesthetically inclined. Presumably, many girls raised in these ways are likely to be less submissive, more assertive, and more self-assured and independent. Insofar as parents continue to expect conventional sex-role performance on the part of their children—and insofar as such performance is expected by the schools and by peers—confusion and feelings of inadequacy can be the result.

Speculation on the kinds of traits, dispositions, and feelings that might be expected to be patterned outcomes of the family structure and childrearing practices we have been discussing could go on indefinitely, but the main line of our argument should be clear: certain major changes in social structure and economy have had a direct impact on the structure of the family, especially in the "middle class." These changes have also had a profound impact on the values and practices of parents. The result is a mixed one: on the one hand, the "new" family appears eminently suitable as an instrument for creating the "right" kinds of people for technological society; on the other hand, inherent in the same family situation are tendencies to generate profound feelings of dislocation and discontent with established values, institutions and roles. Thus, the American family, especially the middle class, suburban

American family with its confusions and ambivalences, reflects the general crisis of American culture. At the same time, it contributes to that crisis by generating in the next generation aspirations, expectations, and impulses that are not compatible with established norms and institutionalized patterns. It creates the psychic grounds for new identities in a society that provides no models, roles, or life styles around which such new identities can crystallize.

The middle class family is *necessary* in advanced industrial capitalism. Nevertheless, it *necessarily* creates many youths who have trouble accepting the society. When the key institutions of socialization inherently generate tendencies toward nonconformity, there surely is a cultural crisis. This seems to be the situation that has developed in the United States during the last three decades, as families have had to come to grips with a cultural framework that no longer fits social reality.

Meanwhile, a similar pattern of incoherence is played out in all the other institutions responsible for socialization and cultural indoctrination. In the schools, the media and the churches, such contradictory values as self-denial and self-expression, discipline and indulgence, and striving and being are preached, dramatized, fostered, and practiced all at once. On the one hand, television and magazines advocate hedonism, consumption, and living it up, while schools and churches continue, uneasily, to embody the Protestant Ethic. The economy demands discipline and self-control in order to *make* a living and spending and self-indulgence as a *way* of living. Political leaders tend to espouse the old virtues, while pop culture celebrities systematically flout them. Incentives to strive, compete, and become disciplined are systematically undermined by affluence, but all institutionalized means to be creative and productive (as in high-level professional work) continue to be linked with demands to be competitive, striving and self-denying. An incredible number and variety of means are provided for hedonistic pursuit and sensuality, yet all such experience is heavily laden with guilt, is often defined as illegal or immoral, is prohibited to minors, or is so highly commercialized as to lose its authentically expressive character.

The incoherence of the general culture thus interacts with the confusion of the individual family. It seems probable that virtually all American youth experience cultural incoherence and "anomie" as an integral feature of their growing up. The argument we are making, however, would lead us to predict that the youth who experience this situation most acutely are those for whom conventional values have been most weakened or irrelevant.

Bibliographical Notes

1. The "decline" of the "Protestant Ethic" has been discussed in many ways by people. Weber's classic definition of the culture of capitalism ap-

pears, of course, in his *The Protestant Ethic and the Spirit of Capitalism* (New York: Scribner's, 1958). Joseph Schumpeter prophesied the decilne of entrepreneurial values in *Capitalism, Socialism and Democracy* (New York: Harper, 1942). An influential work describing changes in the American character was David Riesman's *The Lonely Crowd* (New York: Doubleday-Anchor, 1953). Seymour Martin Lipset and Leo Lowenthal, *Culture and Social Character* (Glencoe, Ill.: Free Press, 1961) contains important commentary on Riesman's work, especially an essay by Talcott Parsons and Winston White.

2. My discussion of the American middle class family is heavily indebted to the following: Kenneth Keniston, *The Uncommitted* (New York: Harcourt, Brace and World, 1962); Riesman, *The Lonely Crowd*; A. W. Green, "The Middle Class Male Child and Neurosis," *American Sociological Review*, 11 (1946): 31–41; Talcott Parsons and Robert F. Bales, *Family, Socialization and Interaction Process* (Glencoe, Ill.: Free Press, 1955); Daniel Miller and Guy Swanson, *The Changing American Parent* (New York: Wiley, 1958); Betty Friedan, *The Feminine Mystique* (New York: Norton, 1963); David C. McClelland, *The Achieving Society* (Princeton, N.J.: Van Nostrand, 1961); and Philip Slater, *The Pursuit of Loneliness* (Boston: Beacon, 1970). In addition, I have relied on impressions gathered from my research on families of activist and nonactivist students and from my own experience as a parent.

Chapter 9

The Parental Mystique

This article questions many of the assumptions about the mother-child rela-tionship that have been made by social scientists, clinicians, and the public which has accepted the doctrines of the "experts." The child development literature has idealized the mother-child relationship by assuming that only the biological mother is capable of providing the emotional satisfaction and stimulation neces-sary for personality and intellectual development. Further, it assumes that dire consequences must follow from any separation of the child from its mother, even if only for part of the day. By focusing on the dangers of maternal deprivation, the prevailing assumptions overlook the harmful potential of ordinary family life when mothers and children are isolated from the rest of society.

The Acceptance of the Concept of the Maternal Role by Behavioral Scientists: Its Effects on Women

Rochelle Paul Wortis

> The maternal "instinct" is a comfortable male myth; a woman can only give freely if she is in a position where she does not feel deprived her-self. (Gail, 1968)

The purpose of this review is to reexamine critically the importance of the concept of "mothering" and to suggest that much of the evidence employed in psychological studies of the importance of the mother for the development of infants and children is based on assumptions that are scientifically inade-

From "The Acceptance of the Concept of the Maternal Role by Behavioral Scientists: Its Effect on Women" by Rochelle Paul Wortis, Ph.D., *The American Journal of Ortho-psychiatry*, 41, no. 5 (1971), pp. 733–746. Copyright © 1971, the American Ortho-psychiatric Association, Inc. Reproduced by permission.

quate. Furthermore, modern psychology, with its emphasis on individual advancement, individual achievement, and individual development, has encouraged the isolation of the adult woman, particularly the mother, and the domestication and subordination of females in society.

I am here challenging a concept that has for generations been viewed as a biological and social necessity. It is important, however, to discuss some of the contradictions inherent in our system of child-rearing that have overwhelming negative, oppressive effects on half the population (women) and on all infants who develop in the environment of the nuclear family, with its prevailing emphasis on the mother-infant socialization process.

There are four basic questions to bear in mind when reading the literature on mother-infant interaction:

1. Is it a biological fact that, in the human species, the mother is the most capable person to socialize the infant?

2. Is it a biological fact that the human newborn seeks out the mother (rather than the father) or a female (rather than a male) as the figure to which it naturally relates best, needs most, and attaches itself to socially?

3. Socially, what criteria should we employ to define whether it is beneficial for the infant to form a strong bond of attachment to one woman?

4. Is it beneficial for the mother to assume the principal responsibility for the care and socialization of the young child?

We must begin with the understanding that we all have a strong prejudice about the need for "mothering" because we were all mothered. In a society such as ours, in which mothering is the principal mode of rearing children, any variant pattern that occurs (such as "multiple mothering," infants being raised by their fathers, or group rearing of infants) is considered abnormal. Participants in such variant patterns are constantly reminded of the "fact" that what they are doing is an exceptional alternative, a poor substitute for the "normal" pattern. This implies that they could never equal or improve upon the norm.

Margaret Mead has long been questioning the provincialism of studies of mother-infant interaction by Western psychologists and psychiatrists. In particular, Mead criticized the emphasis on the exclusive mother-infant bond. She emphasized that the conscious care of the infant is a cultural, not a biological invention. Therefore, whether or not the mother is the principal figure in the developing child's environment is a socio-cultural question and not a biological one. According to Mead (1962), diversified kinds of attachment relationships have been successful in other cultures. In our society, on the other hand, the vast majority of women are conditioned to expect that the child-rearing function will be their major individual responsibility.

Attachment

The "Attachment Function," as defined and elaborated by John Bowlby (1969), is a dual process through which the infant develops a strong psychobiological need to maintain proximity with the mother while the mother has a strong psychobiological need to maintain proximity with the infant. Attachment behavior usually begins to appear at around four to six months and, during the first year of life, a strong affectional bond develops (Ainsworth, 1969; Bowlby, 1969). An "autonomous propensity" by the mother and infant to develop attachment toward each other is assumed by Bowlby's theory. This aspect of the theory will be discussed later in this paper.

The primacy of the mother-infant attachment bond is contradicted by Schaffer and Emerson's (1964) study of attachment. They described three different stages in the development of attachment behavior: an "asocial" stage, in which the infant actively seeks optimal stimulation from *all* aspects of the environment; a "presocial" stage, in which the infant indiscriminately seeks proximity to objects that give it satisfaction; and, finally, a "social" stage, in which attachments to specific individuals occur. Schaffer and Emerson concluded that:

> To focus one's enquiry on the child's relationship with the mother alone would therefore give a misleading impression of the attachment function. . . . In certain societies multiple object relationships are the norm from the first year on: the relevant stimuli which evoke attachment behaviour are offered by a number of individuals and not exclusively one person, and a much more diversified system of attachments is thus fostered in the infant. (pp. 70–71)

That there is no evidence for the assumption that attachments must be confined to only one object, the mother, nor that all other attachments are subsidiary to the mother-infant bond, was one of the findings of their study. They concluded that:

> Whom an infant chooses as his attachment object and how many objects he selects depends, we believe, primarily on the nature of the social setting in which he is reared and not on some intrinsic characteristic of the attachment function itself. (p. 71)

Finally, Schaffer and Emerson suggested that while the mother tends to be present in the child's environment for most of the time, this does not guarantee that she will provide the quantity and quality of stimulation necessary for optimal development of the infant. A recent experimental-observational study by Kotelchuck (1971), one of the few studies on father-infant interaction, demonstrated that one-to-two-year-old infants are equally attached to their fathers and mothers. Furthermore, the strength of attachment to fathers correlated with the degree to which the fathers cared for their children during their development.

Separation

The principal argument used to encourage women to devote their constant attention to newborns is based on the suggested deleterious effects of mother-child separation (the "Bowlby-" (1951) or "Spitz-hypothesis" (Spitz, 1945; Spitz and Wolf, 1946)). Most of the studies of mother-child separation have been based, however, not on normal separation of infants from their parents, but on institutionalized children. Because of the physical and social sterility of many hospitals and orphanages, these children often suffered from inadequate environmental and human stimulation (Casler, 1961; Yarrow, 1961). The mother-child separation studies have not provided an adequate history of "the reasons which led to the children studied being uprooted from their homes or about the conditions in which they lived before this happened," according to Barbara Wootten:

> One can hardly assume that the boys and girls found in a Children's Home constitute a fair sample of the child population generally: something unusual either in themselves or their environment must have happened to account for their being deprived of ordinary family life. (1959, p. 146)

Yarrow's review (1961) of studies published between 1937 and 1955 concluded that most of the studies of institutionalized infants selected subjects who were already under treatment for emotional or personality disturbances. Furthermore, they were lacking in data on the early conditions of maternal care. In addition, Yarrow wrote,

> The dramatic character of these changes [i.e., reactions of infants to separation from the mother] has overshadowed the significant fact that a substantial portion of the children in each study did not show severe reactions to separation. (p. 474)

Casler (1961) concluded that

> None of the clinical or institutional studies ostensibly supporting the "Spitz-Ribble hypothesis" really does so, simply because none is able to demonstrate that probable causes of the adverse effects of institutionalization, other than maternal deprivation, are inoperative. (p. 12)

Casler further described several studies in which institutionalized babies showed no ill effects. Pinneau, who published several articles (1950, 1955a, 1955b) dissecting methodological inadequacies of the Spitz and Ribble studies, concluded that

> It may well be that the burden of blame for the uncritical acceptance of his work does not rest with Spitz, who has published his results as he sees them, but rather with those who have acclaimed his work, and whose research training should enable them to make a critical evaluation of such research reports. (1955b, p. 462)

Positive alternatives to traumatic separation of infant and mother have not been sufficiently discussed in the psychological literature. In fact, there seems to have occurred a dangerously unscientific extrapolation of assumptions from studies of institutionalized infants to the much more common situation in which infants leave their homes for part of the day, are cared for by other responsible individuals, and are returned again to their homes. As a result, women are taught to believe that infants require their undivided attention during the first two or three years of life, at least. The way our society is structured, this attitude functions to confine the woman physically (to her home) and socially (to her family unit). Neil O'Connor observed:

> There is some danger that by analyzing one source of emotional disturbance, such as mother-child separation, the interaction of the society and the family may be neglected, and the family considered as if it were an isolated unit, which alone determines the behaviour of individuals in all their social relations. (1956, p. 188)

On this matter, Margaret Mead wrote:

> At present, the specific biological situation of the continuing relationship of the child to its biological mother and its need for care by human beings are being hopelessly confused in the growing insistence that child and biological mother, or mother surrogate, must never be separated, that all separation, even for a few days, is inevitably damaging, and that if long enough it does irreversible damage. This . . . is a new and subtle form of antifeminism in which men—under the guise of exalting the importance of maternity—are tying women more tightly to their children than has been thought necessary since the invention of bottle feeding and baby carriages. Actually, anthropological evidence gives no support at present to the value of such an accentuation of the tie between mother and child. . . . On the contrary, cross-cultural studies suggest that adjustment is most facilitated if the child is cared for by many warm friendly people. (1954, p. 477)

Finally, returning to the experience of natural separation between parents and children, none of the studies of children of working mothers has demonstrated systematic differences between children who are home all the time and children whose mothers work (Yarrow et al., 1962; Yudkin and Holme, 1969). However, because the Bowlby-Spitz hypothesis has had such a profound impact on child-rearing practice, legislators, employers and educators have refused to provide sufficient adequate free child-care for working women (Yudkin and Holme, 1969). Consequently, working women are usually forced to find their own, individual solutions to the child-care problem. Even in "dual-career" families (families in which the mother and father both have professional careers), the men and women tend to accept as inevitable that women should take on the major responsibility for the organization of child-care and the household in addition to their career responsibilities (Rapoport and Rapoport, 1969). The consequence is that the women in such families carry the strain of both career and family problems. Apparently this is a major problem in Eastern European socialist countries as well as in Western society (Rapoport and Rapoport, 1969; Yudkin and Holme, 1969).

The excellent reviews mentioned above, on the subject of separation and institutionalization, share in criticizing overgeneralizations that have been drawn from separation studies. Several reviewers (Casler, 1961; Yarrow, 1961) attempted to analyze the objective variables that the mothering function provides for the healthy growth and emotional security of the developing infant. However, none has sufficiently questioned the concept that the mother must be the one who does the mothering. Yudkin and Holme wrote:

> Most of the literature, however, tends to stress the value of the exclusive mother-child relationship and to ignore the possibility, or even the need, for its dilution. This is to attempt to justify a particular, local and almost certainly, temporary, economic and cultural pattern as an eternal biological law. This can only do a disservice to both the mothers and the children. (1969, p. 138)

Naturalism and Instinct Theory

The assumption that the biological mother must be the major responsible adult in the infant's life is intimately related to the theory that women have an instinct to mother. The assumption is based on observations, from the earliest recorded history, that confirm that women are usually the ones who nurture and raise children, specifically their own children.[*] It remains an assumption, or hypothesis, however, that what we observe and describe naturalistically is what is biologically correct or socially optimal. John Stuart Mill wrote:

> The unnatural generally means only uncustomary, and . . . everything which is usual appears natural. The subjection of women to men being a universal custom, any departure from it quite naturally appears unnatural. (quoted in Millett, 1970, p. 94)

In the words of one reviewer,

---

[*]An entertaining and informative article by Una Stannard (1970) attempts to document that "Women have the babies, but men have the maternal instinct." In her historical paper, Stannard reminds us that the major books and manuals telling women how to be good mothers have been written by men.

> While most of us will continue to believe in the importance of mother-
> ing during infancy, we must recognize that this belief has more the
> characteristics of a faith and less the basis of demonstrated fact. (Erik-
> sen, quoted in Casler, 1961, p. 9)

Ethology, the study of animals in their natural environments, has had a
strong influence on recent practice in human developmental psychology.
Bowlby has been one of the principal protagonists in the trend to return to
naturalistic observations of human and animal behavior:

> Until recent years, most of the knowledge available about mother-infant
> interaction in humans was either anecdotal or else a result of recon-
> structions based on data derived from older subjects. In the past decade,
> however, enquiries have been begun which have as their aim the sys-
> tematic descriptive and casual study of what actually occurs during a
> baby's interaction with the humans who care for him. (1951, p. xiii)

However, ethologists, carrying out descriptive studies of behavior, have not
approached their observational tasks bias-free. The discipline of ethology
has long been linked with instinct theory, which attributes the organization
of complex patterns of species-typical behavior to hypothetical, pre-formed
biological models (Lorenz, 1935; Tinbergen, 1951). On the human level,
instinct theory emphasizes the biological pre-destination of psychological
characteristics:

> The Freudian view of man's nature starts from the assumption that he
> is really a nonsocial or even an antisocial creature. His primary needs
> are not social but individual and biological. This means that society is
> not essential to man but is something outside his nature, an external
> force to whose distorting pressures he is victim. (Birch, 1953, p. 96)

Critics of instinct theory have stressed its neglect of the social and developmental history of the organisms being observed and its failure to view the
organism as one that both affects and is affected by the biosocial environment in which it develops (Lehrman, 1953; Schneirla, 1956). Bowlby's
theory of attachment behavior (Ainsworth, 1969; Bowlby, 1969) is an inter-
actionist one. However, it assumes that there are certain features of the environment that the infant is biologically structured to be particularly sensitive to. The theory assumes that the environment of the newborn is optimal,
and that the infant is biologically predisposed to adapt to it. As summarized
by Ainsworth,

> Ethologists hold that those aspects of the genetic code which regulate the
> development of attachment of infant to mother are adapted to an en-
> vironment in which it is a well-nigh universal experience that it is the
> mother (rather than some biologically inappropriate object) who will
> be present under conditions which facilitate the infant's becoming at-
> tached to her. (1969, pp. 995–996)

Such a theory is conservative because it neglects the enormous range of sociocultural environments into which newborn infants are thrust and idealizes the mother-infant couple, which, as Orlansky (1949) pointed out long ago, is "one conforming to an ideal-typical norm held by Western psychiatrists" (p. 15).

It is frequently argued that the human female, like other mammals, is biologically best equipped to respond to the needs of a newborn because of her long period of biological, hormonal and psychological priming during pregnancy. It has been suggested, for instance, that in the period immediately after birth, mothers may be particularly sensitive to the needs of their babies (Bowlby, 1969). This may indeed be true. However, it is also true that a woman who has just had her first child, and who has not previously handled, fed, or cared for an infant, has great difficulty in the first days of the baby's life in establishing feeding, whether it be by breast or bottle. New mothers often have to be told how to hold the baby, burp it, bathe it, and dress it. Of course, most women learn how to care for their infants quite efficiently within a short period of time, through practice and determination.

Recent studies have demonstrated that infants play an active role, even in the first weeks of life, in getting their needs satisfied. There is now extensive literature on the way in which the infant actively initiates social interaction and is capable of modifying the behavior of the adult who cares for it (Bell, 1971; Thomas et al., 1963). This means that the infant helps the adult to develop appropriate responses that will bring about the satisfaction of its needs. This, in turn, means that, given a socially acceptable alternative, the mother need not be the principal caretaker of her own infant, although many women may still want to enjoy this responsibility.

Most evidence today indicates that the factors that are important for healthy infant and child development are: consistent care; sensitivity of the caretaking adult(s) in responding to the infant's needs; a stable environment, the characteristics of which the growing infant can learn to identify; continuity of experience within the infant's environment; and physical and intellectual stimulation, love, and affection. "There is no clear evidence," Yarrow (1961) wrote, "that multiple mothering, without associated deprivation or stress, results in personality damage." And Mead wrote,

> The problem remains of how to separate the necessary protection of a child who has been isolated in an exclusive pair relationship with the mother—of a type which cannot be said to be natural at a human level, because it actually does not permit participation by the father, care of the dependent older siblings, and ties with the three-generation family, all of which are human experiences—from advocacy of the artificial perpetuation or intensification or creation of such conditions of exclusive mother-child dependence. (1962, p. 58)

Unlike other reviewers (Herzog, 1960; Myrdal and Klein, 1968; Yudkin and Holme, 1969) who advocate reforms for women that would alleviate the strains of dual or triple careers, while basically accepting the assumption that only women can perform the mothering function, I would like to emphasize that it is scientifically unacceptable to advocate the natural superiority of women as child-rearers and socializers of children when there have been so few studies of the effects of male-infant or father-infant interaction on the subsequent development of the child.

The acceptance of the concept of mothering by social scientists reflects their own satisfaction with the status quo. The inability of social scientists to explore or to advocate alternatives to current child-rearing practices is due to their biased conception of what should be studied and to their unwillingness to advocate social change. As Myrdal and Klein recognized,

> The sentimental cult of domestic virtues is the cheapest method at society's disposal of keeping women quiet without seriously considering their grievances or improving their position. It has been successfully used to this day, and has helped to perpetuate some dilemmas of home-making women by telling them on the one hand that they are devoted to the most sacred duty, while on the other hand keeping them on a level of unpaid drudgery. (1968, p. 145)

The time has come to evaluate more critically the ways in which the home and the single mothering figure *fail* to provide the kind of environment that is optimally stimulating or satisfying to the growing infant.

Mothers' Feelings and the Needs of Women

A young housewife writes:

> I feel it should be more widely recognized that it is the very nature of a mother's position, in our society, to avenge her own frustrations on a small, helpless child; whether this takes the form of tyranny, or of a smothering affection that asks the child to be a substitute for all she has missed. (Gail, 1968, p. 153)

It is important to recognize that many young mothers have ambivalent feelings about the responsibility of motherhood. Hannah Gavron's survey of women in London showed that

> The majority of wives, both working-class and middle-class, appear from the discussion of their own views on home and work to be essentially on the horns of a dilemma. They want to work, feel curiously functionless when not working, but at the same time they sense their great responsibilities toward the children. In both groups those who were at home gave the children as their main reason for being there. (1968, p. 122)

My own experience, studying the development of feeding behavior in infants, corroborates this. I studied mature, healthy, full-term babies, all the products of normal pregnancies and deliveries. The mothers were not tense or unhappy women with unusual medical or psychological histories. Yet, many of the women expressed the same conflicts: boredom, sense of isolation being home alone with the baby, desire to be able to get back to work, and doubts about finding adequate child-care facilities should they have the opportunity of getting employment. Most of the women, whether they wanted to work or not, had the feeling that it would be wrong to go out to work because it might somehow endanger the infant's well-being. The study of Yarrow and her colleagues demonstrated that "Mothers who prefer to work but out of a sense of 'duty' do not work report the most problems in child rearing" (1962, p. 122).

The negative effects of too intensive a relationship developing between mother and child, leading to a clinical pattern of "overprotection," are discussed by Myrdal and Klein (1968). Herzog gives passing mention to the fact that "it is no secret that some mothers are not loving, and some who are do not want to devote themselves exclusively to infant or child care" (1960, p. 18). A recent book on child-rearing restates the problem:

> The role in which most contemporary theorists of child development cast the mother makes it hard for her and hard for her children. What's more, the evidence indicates that she has been *mis*cast. No matter how seriously she takes the demand on her for omnipotence, and no matter how omnipotent the performance she turns out, there is no guarantee that the act will come off. All too often the child fails to reflect the best parents' most studious try for perfection. (Chess, Thomas, and Birch, 1965, p. 14)

We must now turn our attention to the home. We are taught that the best environment for the growth and development of a healthy child is provided within the individual home. The home environment, however, is socially sterile because mobility, outside stimulation, exchange of ideas and socially productive relationships are severely limited there:

> The isolated woman at home may well be kept "in touch" with events, but she feels that the events are not in touch with her, that they happen without her participation. The wealth of information which is brought to her without any effort on her part does not lose its vicariousness. It increases rather than allays her sense of isolation and of being left out. (Myrdal and Klein, 1968, p. 148)

Yudkin and Holme discuss the effects of the physical and social isolation of small families in which:

A large number of children are tied almost exclusively to their mothers for the first five years of life, having little opportunity to meet any other people or to develop the beginnings of social relationships, let alone to explore the world outside their own home, until the sudden and dramatic beginning of their school life. Such isolation is obviously likely to increase the closeness and intensity of the relationship between the mother and her young children and may well have an effect on the type of adult personality that results, but whether the effect is good or bad is another matter. (1969, pp. 137–138)

An English housewife wrote:

Housework is housework, whoever does it. It is a waste socially, psychologically, and even economically, to put me in a position where my only means of expressing loyalty to [the baby] is by shopping, dishwashing and sweeping floors. I have trained for teaching literature to university students; it would be far more satisfying to guide a nursery class with Carl in it than it is to feel too harassed by irrelevant jobs to pay his development much attention. (Gail, 1968, p. 148)

The home, therefore, is physically restrictive and, for many women, is felt to be socially restrictive as well. In the home, one's economic and personal tensions and problems are most pronounced. These factors have a profound effect on the mother and child confined to the home, and are a principal influence on the physical, intellectual, and social development of children coming from different social class backgrounds. Bruner's recent review (1970) of studies dealing with the cognitive development of children from different social class backgrounds is rich in examples of the complex way in which feelings of powerlessness by the mother are conveyed to the children and affect the children's ability to cope with their environment.

Current studies of mother-child interaction in the United States, comparing children of working-class mothers with children of middle-class mothers, have ostensibly demonstrated the "cognitive superiority" of the latter. The conclusions of such research are that working-class mothers have to be taught to behave like middle-class mothers. The form of implementation recently adopted to help these women and their children, is to teach working-class women how to provide optimal maternal stimulation to the child within the home environment. However, no programs are implemented to provide working-class women with the advantages of class privilege that middle-class women enjoy, since it is beyond the power of the behavioral scientist to effect such changes in the social and economic status of the people concerned (*How Harvard Rules Women* (1970), pp. 66–74). Hunt's (1971) recommendation that parent-child centers become the focus of intervention programs by professionals to teach "competence" to poverty mothers and their children was aptly criticized by Gordon, who wrote:

> Hunt is proposing a strategy that, like most formal education, essentially seeks to upgrade black and poor people by identifying all those things that are "wrong" with them, and changing those units. Such a strategy, with its implied criticism and its prescription for the adoption of goals and values of the oppressors, should hardly be imposed upon a group by outsiders, no matter how well intentioned. More effective programs of assistance are likely to come from among the people themselves. (1971, p. 41)

One might add that the people, in this case working-class mothers, might feel that other individuals should be involved in the process of child-rearing and that the responsibility for the socialization of children should not rest on the mothers alone.

In the past and present, day-care programs for children have been officially encouraged during periods of economic strain, when women's labor was necessary for production. Neither economics nor women's needs to get out of the home, however, are sufficient justification for child-care centers. Good day-care programs are a necessity for infants and children because they encourage the development of cooperative social interaction during a period of life in which, in modern Western society, children receive insufficient experience with other trusting, loving, dependable children and adults. In the words of two day-care workers:

> It is well documented that attitudes toward work, race, sex (including male/female roles), initiative, and cooperation are formed during the first five years of life. It follows that we need to be seriously concerned with what happens inside the day care center.
>
> What goes on between the child and the environment (whether it's a home or a day care center) affects the kind of capacities that the child will have as an adult. The ability to feel deeply and be sensitive toward other people, the ability to trust oneself and use one's initiative, the ability to solve problems in a creative and collective way—these all can be given their foundation or stifled in the first five years.
>
> By the age of 4 children are taking in the idea that a woman's place is in the home. Three- and four-year-old children are already learning that it's better to be white. They are learning to follow directions and rules without asking why. They are learning how to deny their own feelings and needs in order to win approval from adults.
>
> These are examples of learning that most commonly result from early childhood experiences. These are elements of the invisible curriculum that usually forms the child's environment in our society. (Gross and Macewan, 1970, pp. 27–28)

Recognizing the social needs of mothers and infants, some investigators have begun to encourage entry into day nurseries at much earlier ages than is customary. While these efforts were, at first, strongly criticized by workers in the field, the findings were very encouraging: assessments made at thirty months showed that children from lower-class families who were enrolled in a day-care center from about one year of age did not differ from home-reared children in the strength of attachment to their mothers. Likewise, mothers of day-care infants did not show any differences from home-mothers in intensity of attachment to their infants. The study (Caldwell et al., 1970) showed that, while the home-reared group declined in developmental quotient at thirty months, the day-care infants increased in developmental level.

I am convinced that new studies will continue to demonstrate that stable, loving, stimulating group environments can produce healthy, affectionate, bright youngsters, and that, quite early in life, infants can spend a good part of their day away from their homes and parents without adverse consequences. The problem ahead of us is to analyze the relationship between the nuclear family and the functioning of society, and to study and create the conditions under which the home ceases to confine the woman and the child to social and productive isolation. The fact is that, in modern Western society, no other institutions offer the adult the comfort, the emotional security, the loyalty, and the emotional dependability that the modern family provides. Even saying this, it is necessary to recognize the converse, that for many children and women, the modern family is a prison, breeding repression, unequal relationships and authoritarian conformity.* I am cautious, however, not to suggest that we overthrow the family and substitute other institutions as alternative child-rearers. To do this would be impossible at this stage because of the already mentioned positive value of the family, and because we have not consciously experimented sufficiently with alternatives that could successfully replace it.

Discussion

The creation of alternative life styles, work patterns, or economic change, cannot be successfully imposed on people or prescribed for them without their cooperation. The creation of any alternative processes, when it involves major changes from historical precedent, is a political problem as well as an educational or psycho-social one. For people to attempt alternatives within this society, they must feel the necessity for change and feel that they are not alone in their efforts to create it. People do not attempt to create even small changes in their lives if they lack the confidence or the ability or the power to make them work. In short, programs that would produce the conscious

---

*The evolution of the family and its relationship to societal structure has been the basis for a good deal of study and renewed analysis (Gordon, 1970; Mitchell, 1966; Reich, 1962).

articulation of goals and criteria for positive social change cannot be undertaken without the initiative of the people who are going to be involved.

Acting on the basis of the common sense of oppression experienced by women in society, the women's liberation movement has begun to analyze the relationship between some transitional and long-range goals which, if won, would significantly change women's status in society. The women's liberation movement will not be satisfied, for example, with equality with men if that equality is defined simply in terms of employment opportunity or work status; in present society, that would mean that they give up one oppressive situation (subjugation in the home) to step into another oppressive situation (exploitation at work). Nonetheless, in order for women to participate in efforts to create more meaningful and rewarding work experiences, they must acheive the transitional goal of shared work with men in the home around the housekeeping and child-rearing functions. This means that ways have to be found in which men can begin to take a more active part in home life and in emotional and social interaction with infants. The encouragement of male participation in early childhood socialization requires, for its success, the transformation of existing social and educational institutions because men today are not prepared to assume major shares of responsibility either in homemaking or in child-rearing. As Sweden has already done, sex-role stereotyping in books (children's and adult's) and in advertising has to be ended in order to discourage traditional practices of sex-differentiated behavior. Paid paternity leaves for men and greater opportunities for fathers to participate in the care of newborns is recognized as essential. Men have to be involved more in early education, from day-care to primary schools. Unless nurseries and schools are staffed by men as well as women, the responsibility for the socialization of children will continue to fall upon women and they will continue to feel that other social responsibilities are not within their domain. This was apparently the experience of women in the kibbutzim in Israel. At the beginning, women were encouraged to share in the heavy work with men, but men were not similarly encouraged to share in the care of children. As a result, women became overburdened with the strain of both kinds of responsibilities and gradually dropped out of the productive branches. A sexual division of labor persists to this day in the kibbutzim. Only women work as nurses and infant's teachers (Spiro, 1965).

For men and women to share in the care of infants while maintaining jobs, then in their capacity as workers, both men and women have to be able to work shorter hours without losing pay. The extra time would be used for child care either at home or in cooperatively organized day care centers at work or in the community. Group day care is considered by the women's liberation movement to be a more progressive alternative to family day care because it removes children and adults from the isolating and non-productive environment of the home, substituting a social environment in which infants and adults may interact with each other in large, unrestrictive spaces with many objects and toys to share. The socialization process, therefore, becomes less individualistic for the children and more cooperative for the adults. It follows that parental control of the organization and staffing of day care centers is essential. The new, radical generation of parents do not want dumping grounds for their children, but rather centers of exciting educational activity and play in which children and adults share collectively in the process of growing up. Dissatisfied with the racist, sexist, and middle-class-biased education that children receive in public schools, the radical day care movement wants day care that is organized and controlled by the people in their communities who wish to create a more democratic, equalitarian society for their children (Gross and Macewan, 1970).

A final word needs to be said about alternatives to the nuclear family, in particular the new movement toward communalism. Seen in the most positive of perspectives, a small percentage of the American population is attempting to establish stable communal living arrangements as a way of socializing productive relationships in the living place. Cooking, shopping, cleaning, child care, and social relationships are being shared by all who live together.

The rennaissance of communalism can be seen to develop out of the women's liberation philosophy. The women's liberation movement helped to convince women that their oppression did not develop from their internal inadequacies, but was the natural outgrowth of problems inherent in the structure of our society. By forming social and political bonds as a group, rather than as individual women, it has been possible for women to experience new and better forms of social relationships and to begin successfully to create some of the changes necessary before all women can, in fact, be liberated. Breaking down alienating forms of social relationships can be seen to be a first step in the process of transforming society. A recent paper on "The Liberation of Children" (Babcox, 1970) concludes:

"If we want to change society we can begin by changing the kind of people we are and the kind of children we raise. People who are more loving, more concerned about each other, more secure and less competitive will have attitudes that are contrary to the ones on which our society is based, and while the creation of new attitudes is not in itself a revolution, perhaps it helps create the preconditions."

References

Ainsworth, M. "Object Relations, Dependency, and Attachment: A Theoretical Review of the Infant-Mother Relationship. *Child Development*, 40 (1969): 969–1025.

Babcox, D. "The Liberation of Children." *Up From Under*, 1 (1970): 43–46.

Bell, R. "Stimulus Control of Parent or Caretaker Behavior by Offspring." *Developmental Psychology*, 4 (1971): 63–72.

Birch, H. "Psychology and Culture." In *Basic Problems in Psychiatry*, edited by J. Wortis. New York: Grune & Stratton, 1953.

Bowlby, J. *Maternal Care and Mental Health*, Geneva: World Health Organization, 1951.

Bowlby, J. Foreword to *Determinants of Infant Behaviour*, edited by B. Foss. London: Methuen & Co., 1961.

Bowlby, J. *Attachment*. Attachment and Loss, vol. I. London: The Hogarth Press and the Institute of Psychoanalysis, 1969.

Bruner, J. "Poverty and Childhood." Paper presented at Merrill-Palmer Institute, Detroit, 1970.

Caldwell, B., et al. "Infant Day Care and Attachment." *American Journal of Orthopsychiatry*, 30 (1970): 397–412.

Casler, L. "Maternal Deprivation: A Critical Review of the Literature." Monograph. *Soc. Res. Child Development*, 26 (1961), no. 2, ser. #80:1–64.

Chess, S., A. Thomas, and H. Birch. *Your Child Is A Person*. New York: Viking Press, 1965.

Gail, S. "The Housewife." In *Work*, edited by R. Fraser. London: Penguin Books, 1968.

Gavron, H. *The Captive Wife*. London: Penguin Books, 1968 (first published by Routledge & Kegan Paul, London, 1966).

Gordon, L. *Families*. Boston: New England Free Press, 1970.

Gordon, L. "Parent and Child Centers: Their Basis in the Behavioral and Educational Sciences. An Invited Critique." *American Journal of Orthopsychiatry*, 41 (1971): 39–42.

Gross, L., and Macewan, P. "On Day Care." Baltimore: *Women: A Journal of Liberation*, 1 (1970), no. 2:26–29.

Herzog, E. *Children of Working Mothers*. Washington, D.C.: U.S. Dept. of Health, Education and Welfare, Children's Bureau, 1960.

How Harvard Rules Women. "The Arrogance of Social Science Research: Manipulating the Lives of Black Women and Their Infants." Boston: New England Free Press, 1970.

Hunt, J. McV. "Parent and Child Centers: Their Basis in the Behavioral and Educational Sciences." *American Journal of Orthopsychiatry*, 41 (1971): 13–38.

Kotelchuck, M. "The Nature of the Child's Tie to the Father." Unpublished Ph.D. thesis, Harvard University, 1971.

Lehrman, D. "A Critique of Konrad Lorenz's Theory of Instinctive Behavior." *Q. Rev. Biol.*, 28 (1953): 337–363.

Lorenz, K. 1935. "Companionship in Bird Life." In *Instinctive Behavior*, edited by C. Schiller. New York: International Universities Press, 1957.

Mead, M. "Some Theoretical Considerations on the Problem of Mother-Child Separation." *American Journal of Orthopsychiatry*, 24 (1954): 471–483.

Mead, M. "A Cultural Anthropologist's Approach to Maternal Deprivation." In *Deprivation of Maternal Care. A Reassessment of Its Effects*. Public Health Papers, #14. Geneva: World Health Organization, 1962.

Millett, K. *Sexual Politics*. New York: Doubleday, 1970.

Mitchell, J. "Women: The Longest Revolution." *New Left Review*, 40 (Nov.-Dec. 1966) (available as a pamphlet from New England Free Press, Boston).

Myrdal, A., and Klein, V. *Women's Two Roles*. 2nd ed. London: Routledge and Kegan Paul, 1968.

O'Connor, N. "The Evidence for the Permanently Disturbing Effects of Mother-Child Separation." *Acta Psychol.*, 12 (1956): 174–191.

Orlansky, H. "Infant Care and Personality." *Psychological Bulletin*, 46 (1949): 1–48.

Pinneau, S. "A Critique on the Articles by Margaret Ribble." *Child Development*, 21 (1950): 203–228.

Pinneau, S. "A Critique on the Articles by Margaret Ribble." *Child Development*, *Psychological Bulletin*, 52 (1955): 429–452.

Pinneau, S. "Reply to Dr. Spitz." *Psychological Bulletin*, 52 (1955): 459–462.

Rapoport, R., and Rapoport, R. N. "The Dual Career Family: A Variant Pattern and Social Change." *Human Relations*, 22 (1969): 3–30.

Reich, W. *The Sexual Revolution*. 3rd ed. New York: The Noonday Press (Farrar, Straus and Giroux), 1962.

Schaffer, H., and Emerson, P. "The Development of Social Attachments in Infancy." Monograph. *Soc. Res. Child Development*, 29 (1964), no. 3, ser. #94.

Schneirla, T. "Interrelationships of the 'Innate' and the 'Acquired' in Instinctive Behavior." In *L'Instinct Dans le Comportement des Animaux et de l'Homme*, edited by P. Grasse. Paris: Masson et Cie, 1956.

Spiro, M. *Children of the Kibbutz*. New York: Schocken Books (first published by Harvard Universities Press, 1958).

Spitz, R. "Hospitalism: An Inquiry into Early Childhood." Part I. *Psychoanal. Stud. Child*, 1 (1945): 53–74.

Spitz, R., and Wolf, K. "Anaclitic Depression: An Inquiry into the Genesis of Psychiatric Conditions in Early Childhood." Part II. *Psychoanal. Stud. Child*, 2 (1946): 313–342.

Stannard, U. "Adam's Rib, or the Woman Within." *Transaction*, 8 (1970): 24–35.

Thomas, A., et al. *Behavioral Individuality in Early Childhood*. New York: New York University Press, 1963.

Tinbergen, N. *The Study of Instinct*. Oxford: Clarendon Press, 1951.

Wootten, B. *Social Science and Social Pathology*. London: Allen and Unwin, 1959.

Yarrow, L. "Maternal Deprivation: Toward an Empirical and Conceptual Revaluation." *Psychological Bulletin*, 58 (1961): 459–490.

Yarrow, M., et al. "Child-rearing in Families of Working and Non-working Mothers." *Sociometry*, 25 (1962): 122–140.

Yudkin, S. and Holme, A. *Working Mothers and Their Children*. London: Sphere Books, 1969 (first published by Michael Joseph, London, 1963).

We tend to think of parenthood as a universal experience, based on tendencies inherent in the human psyche. Yet as this article shows, parenthood is profoundly influenced by social and historical circumstances. The trait that most distinguishes modern parents, particularly middle class ones, from their ancestors, is their tremendous sense of personal responsibility for every aspect of the child's development. In the past, when infant mortality rates were high and contraception rare or unknown, parents felt their children's destinies were in the hands of fate. Personality was believed to be hereditary, rather than something to be shaped by parents. The author traces the emergence of the concept of parental responsibility in the childbearing literature of the last century, culminating in the Freudian writings, which taught parents that every action and every word of theirs had a lasting influence on the child's mind. Ironically, the author notes, advice that was intended to reassure parents often ended up giving terrifying accounts of pitfalls they had never imagined and setting the impossible goal of raising perfectly un-neurotic, happy, successful children.

Freud and the Concept of Parental Guilt

Catherine Storr

Is there any other occupation in the world on which almost everyone is prepared to embark without training, without experience, and without any more specialized knowledge than is provided by having been, so to speak, at the receiving end a good many years before? An occupation, too, which will affect the health and happiness if not the actual survival of one or more people? Which has such a slow gestation that it is necessary for years to pass before it is possible to assess the measure of success or failure attributable to the different measures taken? I am referring, of course, to the job of being a parent, which most of us undertake so light-heartedly, and which, for most of us again, turns out so different from anything we had expected. Our surprise takes innumerable and varied forms, some pleasant, some disagreeable; but what seems to me a comparatively new phenomenon in the history of parenthood is the very prevalent modern feature of parental guilt.

I am not suggesting that the teachings of Freud are solely responsible for this. As it is possible to see from myth, from fable, from history, from fiction and from philosophical writings, guilt has been present in the parent-child relationship since man first began to record the events of his life and his reactions to them. But it is, on the whole, guilt felt for wrongs consciously committed, or, as in the case of Oedipus, for an offense perpetrated under a mis-

From Catherine Storr, "Freud and the Concept of Parental Guilt," from *Freud: The Man, His World, His Influence*, Jonathan Miller, editor, pp. 98–110. Reprinted by permission of Little, Brown and Company, Inc., and Weidenfeld Publishers, Ltd. Copyright © 1972 by George Weidenfeld and Nicolson, Ltd.

apprehension. In general the attitude is one of robust commonsense. Parents who treated their children right were not disappointed in them. The incidence of wicked children born to good parents in the literature of Western Europe is singularly low; the only example which springs instantly to mind is that of Goneril and Regan, and even here it's arguable that Lear was one of those irrational, impetuous characters who so easily alienate their children by demands for extravagant demonstrations of affection. I can't help also suspecting that he was the kind of father who makes a terrific fuss of the new baby, comparing it with the older children to their disadvantage because they are old enough to pit their wills against his and the youngest child is not. Much commoner is the picture of the romanticized child, the innocent, suffering under the ministrations of cruel adults, like so many of the young in Dickens's novels; sometimes these adults are the actual parents, like Mr. Dombey, Mr. Gradgrind, more often step-parents, like Mr. Murdstone, guardians, masters—even, in *Great Expectations*, a sister. How the child preserves his innocence in the face of depravity, his sensitivity and his ideals when surrounded by mentors who have neither, is not fully explained in terms which would satisfy modern psychologists. Something may be attributed to his having had, in early childhood, the experience of security and love; David Copperfield has spent his first years with his loving, if silly, mother and the devoted Peggoty, Pip has had the support of his sister's husband Joe, Florence Dombey had her mother, and little Paul had Florence, to give them values less totally materialistic than those held by their father. But there was, up to the middle or end of the nineteenth century, also a belief in the genetic transmission of what we should now consider acquired characteristics. Little aristocrats, stolen at birth by gypsies, remained apart from their foster brothers and sisters, not only by virtue of their delicate skins and their finely formed limbs, but also by an innate sensibility of feeling and a superior refinement of taste. Little peasants, on the other hand, might be brought up almost on a par with the sons of gentlemen, but they never lost a certain uncouthness which effectually prevented their ever being mistaken for children who had been gently born; Heathcliffe (although it is true his adoption into the Earnshaw household was in early childhood, not in infancy) is the prime example of the character whose rough, animal nature resists all attempts at civilization, while Jane, in *Jane Eyre*, demonstrates the power of an inborn delicacy of feeling to survive coarsening and brutalizing surroundings.

The belief that you can't make a silk purse out of a sow's ear was, however, not applicable to the more usual situation in which parents or guardians brought up children of their own kind; and here it has always been recognized that the children's development depends on what treatment has been given him in his early years. Apart from the isolated case of Lear, the good characters in Shakespeare's plays have good children, the bad usually, though not always, have children who are also bad. The convention continues unchallenged until the nineteenth century, when some of the great Victorian novelists recognized that it was possible for parents who were not absolutely wicked, but who suffered from the more venial and human failings of pride, stupidity, weakness, to mismanage the rearing of their children with disastrous results. Dickens's Steerforth has been ruined by his mother's pride, George Osborne by his father's ambition, Becky Sharp by the atmosphere of squalor and deceit occasioned by her parents' lack of integrity; and in Mrs. Gaskell's *Wives and Daughters*, the beautiful but flawed Cynthia says sadly, 'Oh Molly, you don't know how I was neglected just at a time when I wanted friends most. Mamma does not know: it is not in her to know what I might have been if only I had fallen into good hands,' and on another occasion, 'Oh how good you are, Molly! I wonder if I had been brought up like you whether I should have been as good.' The context makes it clear that by 'brought up like you' she means 'loved as you have been.'

But implied in all these and in other fictional relationships is consciousness. The parents of unsatisfactory children have committed their sins of omission or of commission if not deliberately, at least without consideration of the child's side of the question. The rights of parents were still absolute; they had the power to direct the habits, the thoughts, the feelings, the destinies of their children. A child was a possession as a slave was a possession. A well disposed, kindly owner of slaves, secure in his superior judgment, does not suffer from guilt in his relations with those inferior beings. Nor did our ancestors in relation to their children.

Towards the end of the nineteenth century, however, the structure of family life changed. Medicine, with Pasteur's discovery of the bacterial carriage of infection, with Lister's use of antiseptics, and the subsequent introduction of the aseptic technique in surgery and obstetrics, took a sudden and dramatic step forwards. One of the earliest consequences was the drop in infant mortality. Once it had been established that it was no longer necessary to accept every child that God could send in order to be able to rear three or four to maturity, birth control, though of a fairly primitive kind, had come to stay. The element of choice having been introduced, less responsibility could be laid on Fate, God or the Devil for the outcome, and more taken by the parents; as Adam discovered to his cost, choice involves responsibility and with responsibility goes potential guilt. Parents could now choose not only how many children they had but also the spacing between births, so that jealousy, sibling rivalry, even ill-health became problems which they might themselves, however unwittingly, have created. More than this, the field over which their anxieties, their hopes and their fears were dispersed became very much narrowed, and often one or other sex was represented by only one of their children, so that the only boy or the only girl in a family of three or four had to carry all the parents' ambitions. The pathetically anxious desire to do everything right by each member of a small family inevitably—since the swing of faith from established religion towards science as the savior of the human race had already begun—led to the creation of a discipline in what had previously been regarded as an almost instinctive activity, that of child-rearing. It was felt that parents could not now afford to make mistakes. It was a complete change from the attitude at the beginning of the century, exemplified by Jane Austen's cool comment on the large family of Musgraves who appear in *Persuasion*. 'The real circumstances of this pathetic piece of family history were, that the Musgraves had had the ill-fortune of a very troublesome hopeless son, and the good fortune to lose him before he reached his twentieth year.'

One more factor now, in our own century, enters into the pattern of family life, and this is the loss, in this country and in America, of the domestic servant class. The dwindling of domestic help in middle-class households began during the First World War, accelerated in the 1920s and 1930s, and ended in 1940 with a total drying up of supply. It is interesting to note that up to 1914 it was assumed to be the right of all but the very poorest families to have some help in the house; the Micawber's 'orflin' is even lodged near the King's Bench prison when Mr. Micawber and his family are imprisoned for debt, Trollope's most indigent clergy have some 'little maid of all work' to assist their hard-working wives, and the children in E. Nesbit's stories, though more often than not the family is hardpressed to make ends meet, rely on a girl who cooks them uneatable puddings or, at worst, a full-time visiting daily char. The change affected the middle-class family most; the really affluent could still afford to engage nurses and governesses as they had always done, and the working classes felt no difference since these mothers had always had to care for their own families. It was now the turn of the middle-class mother to keep an eye on her babies while she washed, cooked and ironed; and since these mothers were often from the professional and intellectual classes—were also often themselves professional women—it was second nature to them to look for guidance in this new task by reading. They wanted instruction not only in the physical care of infants, but also in the education of the child's mind. So it was now that the teaching of Freud really came into its own; it had been, as it were, waiting in the wings, enthusiastically adopted by a few, but not yet generally accepted by the lay public. Children in the 1920s were mostly brought up in the old-fashioned way; parents were less repressive than their parents had been, but their word was still conventionally law, however much the children rebelled in private. But with the advent of the domestic revolution, with the increasing popularity of psychology as a 'science', with the gradual surrendering of religious belief, which had before provided reassurance for those who wanted a moral code, with the vogue for psychoanalysis, spread partly by the influx of Continental analysts to Britain and the United States, and partly by the enthusiastic adoption of its practice and thinking as a universal panacea in the latter country, the general awareness and acceptance of the teaching of Freud and of his followers was incalculably increased. The enthusiasm was—and virtually still is—confined to the said middle classes, and has only slowly permeated the general public's attitude towards the treatment and education of children; in Britain certainly there is an unwillingness to adopt new attitudes where old ones can still be seen to operate without obvious disaster, and Freud's psychodynamic theory of the human mind is still no more a part of the way of thinking of the man in the street than is the consciousness of Pasteur's discovery of bacteria. Dreams are still interpreted as if they were tea leaves, and the baby's dummy picked up off the railway carriage floor and stuffed back into the infant's mouth. The middle-class mother has, however, been for decades acutely aware of the danger of 'germs', and is now as conscious of invisible threats to her child's psyche; it has always been this class, I suspect, which has had the time, the energy and the interest to consider and to put into practice new approaches to the familiar and the traditional.

It was not until the end of the 1920s, when Freud's writings had been known in his own country for nearly thirty years, and in translation in Britain for more than half that time, that books on child care and child development, written for the general public and not for the specialist, had begun to show traces of Freud's influence. It is interesting to consider the changes which appear in various handbooks of advice for mothers, beginning before the Freudian era, and continuing up to the present day. Mr. Pye Chavasse, in *Advice to a Mother,* written some time in the late 1830s, confines his advice almost entirely to the physical aspects of child care; much of what he gives is today unexceptionable. Nor perhaps would one quarrel with his remarks on 'the well-being of the child'. 'A child should be happy; he must, in every way, be made happy; everything ought to be done to conduce to his happiness, to give him joy, gladness and pleasure. . . . Love! let love be his pole star.' And later, when dealing with the problem of peevishness, 'If he be in a cross humour, take no notice of it, but divert his attention to some pleasing object. This may be done without spoiling him. Do not combat bad temper with bad temper—noise with noise. Be firm, be kind, be gentle, be loving, speak quietly, smile tenderly and embrace him fondly, but *insist on implicit obedience* [author's italics] and you will have, with God's blessing, a happy child' (Chavasse, 1896).

Sound sense; advice which, one would think, cannot lead a parent much astray; but it takes for granted the absolute supremacy of the parent and, except for the rather ambiguous clause about God's blessing, the inevitability of a happy result following on judicious action. It also assumes the total self-possession of the parent, a point I'd like to return to later. Eighty years later the attitude has not materially altered. *The Mothercraft Manual* by Mabel Liddiard, a disciple of the Truby King school, is again mainly concerned with the child's physical well-being, and implies the same belief that as long as the parent follows instructions both she and the child can hardly go wrong. There is, however, a shift of emphasis; now it is not the child's happiness which is of the first importance, but the necessity for strict training from the earliest days. In feeding, for instance, whereas Mr. Pye Chavasse recommends gradually reaching the optimum interval between feeds of 'about four hours', Nurse Liddiard insists that 'whatever intervals are decided upon, these must be adhered to strictly. . . . Many mothers and nurses think it cruel to wake a baby for a feed and so live in a constant muddle as to meals, rest, outings, etc. This is a mistaken kindness, the baby and mother should live by the clock' (Liddiard, 1936). (More than one of my acquaintances who reared babies in the 1920s and 1930s have told me how they used to sit through their child's frantically hungry yells, waiting till the clock told them that the four hours was exactly up and that they might pacify him.) On toilet training also there is little difference, though Mr. Chavasse is again the less peremptory. 'A babe of three months and upwards ought to be held out at least a dozen times during the twenty-four hours. If such a plan were adopted, diapers might be dispensed with at the end of three months—a great advantage. The babe would be inducted into clean habits, a blessing to himself, and a comfort to all around. . . . A DIRTY CHILD IS THE MOTHER'S DISGRACE' [author's capitals]. This is Mr. Chavasse. Miss Liddiard begins the training even earlier. 'From the third day the nurse should have a small chamber . . . on her knee, and the baby should be held with the back against the nurse's chest. . . . Many nurses train their babies so that they have no soiled napkins after the first week or so, and very few wet ones. . . . Make the child understand that this is a serious business, and do not give him toys to amuse him while sitting on the chamber.' Later, 'As the child grows older a time must be fixed for an attempt at the action of the bowels. The best time is immediately after breakfast. Always insist on their trying to pass urine just before going for a walk; this saves much inconvenience while out.' It is clear that the adults' convenience is the primary consideration. Mother, you could say, is still always right.

But this state of affairs was already doomed. Susan Isaacs published *The Nursery Years* in 1929, only six years after the first appearance of Miss Liddiard's manual, and here already the rights of the child are seen in a very different light. 'So with his training in cleanliness and regular habits of bowel and bladder. We need to be gentle here too, not putting our own standards too rigidly high, nor making our own immediate convenience the first consideration.' She does recommend the mother 'to give the infant an opportunity of regular habits from the earliest days, by putting him on a vessel after each feed' but goes on to say that we shouldn't expect a child to be too docile: '. . . Indeed there are many grounds for feeling distressed about the too-clean and too-docile child even in these earliest days; for he may suffer, in ways that lead to mental illness, under the strain of accepting adult standards too early' (Isaacs, 1936). I find this especially interesting, not only because it is the first indication that the child may be regarded as a separate and autonomous being, whose function may be something more than that of fitting in perfectly with his parents' wishes, but also because it seems probable that this threat of possible insanity at some future date is the age-old one of madness and impotence which was used—and probably unfortunately in some circles still is—to discourage masturbation; but here we have the guilt transferred from the child to the parent. Next, after a gap of sixteen years, is the best-seller, *Baby and Child Care.* Sensible Dr. Benjamin Spock, writing in the United States, where the knowledge and practice of psychological precepts has always been far ahead of that in Britain, tells us that 'some psychologists think that early training is harmful in certain cases at least . . .' (Spock, 1946) and advises leaving any training until the baby can sit up— 'around seven to nine months'. The whole section on toilet training is anti-disciplinarian. Spock's great contribution to social medicine seems to me, here as elsewhere in his book, to be his ability to combine the comparatively new views on child-psychology with sound common sense. He points out that a 'trained' baby of a few months is not in any normal sense trained; it is only the mother who is trained to have a pot ready at the appropriate moment. He emphasizes the desirability of cooperation between parent and child in this and other matters of adapting to social norms, and, as a final comment on Miss Liddiard's 'serious business' remark, has allowed his illustrator—in my copy at least—to show an unworried infant sitting on 'the vessel' with a teddy bear on the floor within reach.

Finally, by 1957, Dr. Winnicott, in *The Child and the Family,* presents an approach which has, presumably, completely integrated the Freudian attitudes. There is no longer any suggestion that the baby should be trained, nor even that it might be 'convenient' for the mother to train herself to avoid dirty nappies. Instead the passing of urine or of a motion have become important emotional experiences which the mother must share with the baby.

> Perhaps someone told you to hold your baby out regularly after feeds from the start, with the idea of getting in a bit of training at the earliest possible moment. If you do this you should know that what you are doing is trying to save yourself the bother of dirty napkins. And there is a lot to be said for this. But the baby is not anywhere near being able to be trained yet. If you never allow for his or her own development in these matters, you interfere with the beginnings of a natural process.

Also you are missing good things. For instance if you wait you will sooner or later discover that the baby, lying over there in the cot, finds a way of letting you know that a motion has been passed; and soon you will even get an inkling that there is going to be a motion. You are now at the beginning of a new relationship with the baby . . . as if he said, 'I think I am going to want to pass a motion; are you interested?' and you (without exactly saying so) answer, 'yes,' and you let him know that if you are interested this is not because you are frightened that he will make a mess, and not because you feel you ought to be teaching him how to be clean. If you are interested it is because you love your baby in the way that mothers do, so that whatever is important to the baby is also important to you. . . . Because what you do is based on the simple fact of your love you soon become able to distinguish between the times when you are helping your baby to be rid of bad things and the times when you are receiving gifts. (Winnicott, 1957)

Before leaving this comparative study, it might be interesting to look at the changes which took place over this period of more than a hundred years regarding that tender subject, the child and sex. Mr. Pye Chevasse ignores the subject completely; perhaps he felt it not suitable for the mothers who would read his book. Miss Liddiard admits that teaching on the subject of mastur- bation has changed during her professional life, and that it is now regarded 'only . . . as a bad habit and one which usually disappears as intelligence and interest in life appear.' She adds: 'The habit itself should be ignored as much as possible and just spoken of as a thing not done by nice people.' Three years after this comment, which appears in a late edition of *The Mothercraft Manual*, published in 1936, Susan Isaacs writes, 'This is but another expres- sion of the intense inner conflict of the child's feelings towards his parents . . . just because it is bound up with the most hidden issues of the child's emo- tional life, we must go very slowly in dealing with it. . . . For the child *always* [author's italics] feels ashamed and distressed about it.' Later she writes, 'If the habit persists, and is more than an occasional thing—for this will happen sometimes even with children of excellent parents in the happiest home— then all that remains to us as parents is to ask the advice of a specialist in psychological medicine.' Even the best parents, then, may find that they are responsible for having perpetuated a habit which must be discouraged, though Mrs. Isaacs's recommendation—'Our main task is very definitely to avoid strengthening the fear and guilt . . . for these rivet the child but more firmly in the habit' may seem too indefinite, not to say negative, to help a parent already anxious to cope with the 'ashamed and distressed' child. Winnicott is more explicit about the symptom—if it is still possible to apply this epithet to a universal phenomenon—but not much more precise in his guidance for the mother.

> Masturbation is either normal or healthy or else it is a symptom of a disorder of emotional development. . . . Perhaps the most common disorder of masturbation is its suppression, or its disappearance from a child's repertoire of self-managed defenses against intolerable anxiety or sense of deprivation or loss. . . . Ordinary masturbation is no more than an employment of natural resources for satisfaction as an insurance against frustration and consequent anger, hate, or fear. Compulsive masturbation simply implies that the underlying anxieties to be dealt with are excessive. Perhaps the infant needs feeding at shorter intervals, or he needs more mothering; or he needs to be able to know that someone is always at hand, or his mother is so anxious that she ought to allow him more quiet lying in a pram and less contact with her. . . . It must be recognized, however, that in rare cases compulsive masturbation is continuous and is so exhausting that it has to be stopped by repressive measures, simply in order to give the child some relief from his or her own symptom. (Winnicott, 1957)

I should like to add to this A. S. Neill's remark: 'A child left to touch its genitals has every chance of growing up with a sincere happy attitude to sex' (Neill, 1940).

These passages illustrate the change which has come about during the last century and a half in the place of the child in adult society. In 1840 the child was to be tenderly cared for, loved and made happy; his needs are seen as being entirely on an immediate and practical level, he is to adapt himself to the established adult conventions as quickly as possible—'implicit obedience; A DIRTY CHILD IS THE MOTHER'S DISGRACE'. The expert, whether it is Mr. Pye Chavasse or Dr. Truby King, can give detailed and precise instructions to the novice mother which will enable her to do what is right by her baby; there is less difference between these two writers separated by nearly a century, than between the later of the two and her successor, writing only sixteen years afterwards. Now the picture is a different one; now every aspect of the child's development, physical or emotional, is seen not only at its face value, but also for the symbolic part it plays in the child's psyche. This can be explained to the uninitiated reader, but to tell her how to cope with it is a more difficult matter. Spock solved this problem by preferring the old-fashioned method of giving factual, commonsense advice, which nevertheless incorporates a certain amount of the less controversial psychological theory; in consequence he is limited, but as many present-day parents would gratefully agree, practical. Dr. Winnicott, however, is more concerned to give parents a true understanding of the growing child and of the mother-child relationship; and because he is far too sensitive and perceptive not to recognize the dangers of writing, so that people can read, about what is basically felt without the need of words, he is constantly at pains to reassure the mother that 'mothering', the right sort of care of babies and children, is 'natural'. He specifically states that he is writing not to instruct, but to 'draw attention to the immense contribution to the individual and to society which the ordinary good mother . . . makes at the beginning, and which she does *simply through being devoted to her infant*' [author's italics].

The trouble is, however, that, as Dr. Winnicott would probably agree, no mother is devoted all the time. Mr. Chavasse is not the only writer on child-care who seems to believe that a mother has only to learn what is the right course of action in given circumstances for her to follow it. In fact, anyone who has been personally concerned in the bringing up of children knows that there are occasions when all the knowledge in the world will not ensure the mother's doing the 'right' thing, because at that particular moment she isn't in a frame of mind to care; she, like the child, can be overcome by frustration and anger—and guilt—and the relief of her feelings comes even before the consideration of what may be best for the child. Years ago a cartoon showed a mother furiously addressing her toddler with the words, 'I don't know what I'm doing to your complexes, but I do know that you're ruining mine!' And this is where the concept of the unconscious and of psychodynamics which we owe to Freud has tipped the balance against the probability of present-day parents feeling confidence in themselves as parents. The suggestion that every action and every word is making a lasting impression on the infant's mind, the consequences of which will not appear for years, and may be quite opposite to what was intended, is enough to alarm all but the very brash. It is especially inhibiting to the anxious tyro, who had hoped, by consulting what has been written by experts, to learn how to avoid the worst mistakes; what he gets instead is a terrifying account of pitfalls he hadn't ever imagined. The trouble is that when Freud's ideas first began to be adopted in the practice of child care it was optimistically assumed by many that a set of principles could be drawn up which would ensure the psychic health of the children whose parents observed them. Parents were encouraged to believe that if they tried hard enough they could save their children from evil by analytic thought, rather as earlier generations of babies had been saved by baptism. What was not allowed for was not only the complexity of the human mind, but also the frailty of the parent. Since no child turns out ideally, and there are bound to be moments when it is clear that a child is unhappy and resentful, or ashamed and angry, or shows other disturbing traits, there are bound also to be moments when parents wonder where to apportion the blame. Before the advent of Freudian teaching, parents may sometimes have blamed themselves for mistakes which, looking back, they recognized, but much more often they blamed the child; either he was ungrateful, or obstinate, or had chosen bad company, or all three. Today's parents, warned in advance of the primary importance of their influence on the child's development, have no such convenient scapegoats. They must blame themselves for everything that goes wrong. The nineteenth-century mother, turning to the pages of Mr. Pye Chavasse to discover why her child is not clean and dry at the age of six months, can regret that she has not been sufficiently insistent on that 'implicit obedience' and can redouble her efforts without a qualm. The modern mother, whose baby screams at the sight of the pot and is unwilling to part with his motions, finds in Dr. Winnicott's text that she has failed in her job; worse than that, the implication that a good mother knows how and when to do the right thing because 'you love your baby in the way that mothers do', suggests that if she has done the 'wrong' thing it is because she is an unnatural, unloving, 'bad' mother. Later, when the child has night terrors, balks at going to school, is finicky about food, tells lies, is quarrelsome, jealous, rebellious—in short, shows any of the innumerable symptoms of normal childhood, the parents' confidence in their own judgment, even in their own feelings, is gravely undermined. They meant to do so well. The believed everything was going as it should, and now it appears that their good intentions have simply led them along the proverbial downward road, and, which increases their guilt still more, taken the child with them.

Anna Freud, writing later than any author quoted above, has summed up the effects of psychoanalytic thought on the theory of child rearing as follows:

> On the other hand, it did not take more than one or two decades of such [psychoanalytic] work before a number of analytic authors ventured beyond the boundaries of fact finding and began to apply the new knowledge to the upbringing of children. The therapeutic analyses of adult neurotics left no doubt about the detrimental influence of many parental and environmental attitudes and actions such as dishonesty in sexual matters, unrealistically high moral standards, overstrictness or overindulgence, frustrations, punishments, or seductive behaviour. . . .
> The sequence of these extrapolations is well known by now. Thus, at a time when psychoanalysts laid great emphasis on the seductive influence of sharing the parents' bed and the traumatic consequences of witnessing parental intercourse, parents were warned against bodily intimacy with their children and against performing the sexual act in the presence of even their youngest infants. When it was proved in the analyses of adults that the withholding of sexual knowledge was responsible for many intellectual inhibitions, full sexual enlightenment at an early age was advocated. When hysterical symptoms, frigidity, impotence, etc., were traced back to prohibitions and the subsequent repressions of sex in childhood, psychoanalytic upbringing put on its program a lenient and permissive attitude towards the manifestations of infantile, pregenital sexuality. When the new instinct theory gave aggression the status of a basic drive, tolerance was extended also to the child's early and violent hostilities, his death wishes against parents and siblings, etc. When anxiety was recognized as playing a central part in symptom

formation, every effort was made to lessen the children's fear of parental authority. When guilt was shown to correspond to the tension between the inner agencies, this was followed by the ban on all educational measures likely to produce a severe super-ego. . . . Finally, in our own time, when analytic investigations have turned to earliest events in the first year of life and highlighted their importance, these specific insights are being translated into new and in some respects revolutionary techniques of infant care. . . .

. . . Some of the pieces of advice given to parents over the years were consistent with each other; others were contradictory and mutually exclusive. . . . Above all to rid the child of anxiety proved an impossible task. Parents did their best to reduce the children's fear of them, merely to find that they were increasing guilt feelings, i.e., fears of the child's own conscience. Where, in its turn, the severity of the super-ego was reduced, children produced the deepest of all anxieties, i.e., the fear of human beings who feel unprotected against the pressure of their drives.

In short, in spite of many partial advances, psychoanalytic education did not succeed in becoming the preventive measure that it had set out to be. It is true that the children who grew up under its influence were in some respects different from earlier generations, but they were not freer from anxiety or from conflicts, and therefore not less exposed to neurotic or other mental illnesses. (Freud, 1966)

Of course all the mistakes and disappointments of the last forty years should not be laid at the door of Sigmund Freud. I hope I have succeeded in drawing attention to the other factors which contributed to make the recent generations of parents particularly susceptible to attacks on self-confidence in their relations with their children. If we, in this century, were not so much addicted to the belief that there must be a 'science' of everything, including of that unpredictable, barely charted area of human behaviour, we should not have fallen so readily into the snare of supposing that we might be able to rear new human beings superior in psychic health to their forefathers. What was not taken into account by Freud's many disciples, who, like St. Paul, St. Augustine and other organizing secretaries who succeeded another great Jewish prophet, was that the disclosure of a revelation, whether it is that infants have sexual feelings or that all men are brothers, cannot subsequently be translated into a book of rules which will transmute human nature and bring about a millennium. The foundation of the early Christian Church, the drawing up of the Athanasian creed, the threat of punishments, the establishment of dogma, led to the activities of the Inquisition and to massacre on religious grounds, and not to the spread of brotherly love. In the same way, the organization of the rules which were supposed to help parents to rear psychically sound offspring also proved to lead to unexpected and often unwelcome results; and where rules are only partially formulated, and the parent is merely warned of the dangers, but told that his natural instincts will guide him aright, the effect is comparable to that of showing a lone sailor a chart of the currents and winds on the ocean on which he is sailing, but telling him at the same time that his best compass is within his own head. The truth is that most of us learn not so much from theory as by experience; and also that children respond not to what their parents know, but to what they are. The father who has not come to terms with his own aggressive instincts cannot, by carefully adopted attitudes, reconcile his child in turn to his fantasies of destruction; the anxious mother is unlikely to produce an anxiety-free child. I don't mean by this that there is nothing we can do to make ourselves better parents, nor that there are not many invaluable vistas of insight opened up by Freud's work. But I do believe that, partly from a misunderstanding of the application of that work, we have lost confidence in ourselves to an unnecessary degree. Perhaps it is time that we lowered our standards a little. Instead of trying to rear a generation of perfectly un-neurotic, well-integrated, fearless, sexually uninhibited children, we might recognize that such people have never existed. We might remember that, just as we do not expect to give birth to children who are never physically ill, so we might allow our children the common failings of humanity, but hope that we could give them the psychic resilience, the security of being assessed as individuals—which involves hate as well as love—which would enable them to fight for survival; even when this involves a struggle against ourselves.

References

Chavasse, Pye Henry. *Advice to a Mother*. 14th ed. London, 1896.
Freud, Anna. *Normality and Pathology in Children*. London, 1966.
Isaacs, Susan. *The Nursery Years*. 5th ed. London, 1936.
Liddiard, Mabel. *The Mothercraft Manual*. 10th ed. London, 1936.
Neill, A. S. *The Problem Family*. London, 1940.
Spock, Benjamin. *Baby and Child Care*. New York, 1946.
Winnicott, D. W. *The Child, the Family and the Outside World*. London, 1957.

The myths surrounding motherhood, such as the "maternal instinct" and "anatomy is destiny," have obscured real conflicts of interest between men, women, and children. As the author of this article points out, our male-oriented culture has held childbearing and childrearing in low esteem, despite rhetoric to the contrary. The rejection of the feminine mystique by the women's liberation movement raises an interesting question: Who is going to have and care for children? Citing survey and other evidence, the author finds that the women most interested in childrearing are conservative, anti-women's liberationists, who are also dependent, fearful, risk-avoiding, resistant to change, and low in curiosity and flexibility. The author suggests that a more desirable outcome would be for both men and women to participate in the care of their children, without losing their own occupational identities and skills. She suggests some policy changes which would make such participation possible.

Who Wants the Children? | *Bernice E. Lott*

As a woman, a psychologist, and a feminist, I have paid a great deal of attention to the ever increasing numbers of statements being made about the experiences and problems of women. The most widely articulated argument stresses the need for liberation from culturally imposed rules that are restrictively narrow and unresponsive to the challenges and opportunities of contemporary life. Such voices for liberation have already been responsible for some real social changes, and they have also succeeded, as the earlier feminist movement did not, in pushing into relatively clear focus some very serious and fundamental questions about the actual and potential relationships among men, among women, between the sexes, and between parents and their children.

Among these questions are, I believe, the following:

1. What are the relative contributions of biology and socialization to the development of those characteristics that have traditionally defined "masculine" and "feminine" personality? What are the relationships among genetically determined sex, anatomically apparent sex, and culturally defined gender (cf. Money, 1970)?

2. If the overlap between boys and girls in distribution of many physiological and practically all psychological characteristics is found to be potentially so sizable that gender differences (if they are not reinforced by dif-

From Bernice E. Lott, "Who Wants the Children? Some Relationships among Attitudes toward Children, Parents, and the Liberation of Women," *American Psychologist*, July 1973, pp. 573–582. Copyright © 1973 by the American Psychological Association. Reprinted by permission.

ferential socialization) will cease to be a significant component of individual differences, then what cultural changes will follow, especially in regard to sexuality? It appears to me not at all accidental that a heavy subject among educated, contemporary women is "the myth of the vaginal orgasm" (cf. Koedt, 1970; Sherfey, 1970) and that Norman Mailer (1971), stung by the new challenge to men's role, was moved to attempt a serious and personal defense of the masculine stereotype.

3. If the patriarchal family is to go, as the primary breeder of male supremacist attitudes and the Freudian (and pre-Freudian) ideology of female "passivity, masochism, and narcissism" (Millett, 1969), what are the viable, desirable, and/or inevitable alternatives?

4. What is to become of the children who continue to be conceived and born? Which women will want to bear children? (Why is the development of extrafemale alternatives to childbearing so tempting to some [e.g., Atkinson, 1970; Firestone, 1970]?) Who will want to rear the children? Can they be reared, without sacrifice to their potential, by adults intent on living self-fulfilling, liberated lives?

Although the above questions are all ultimately interrelated, this article is only directly concerned with the last group. It appears to me that a significant number of the most forceful spokeswomen for liberation have essentially very little use for children. When spoken of at all, the tendency is to do so coldly and unsympathetically, and to project the view that children are nuisances and a major barrier in one's path toward fulfillment in the larger world outside one's home. The function of child rearing is denigrated and regarded as basically burdensome, noncreative, and in the same category as domestic chores like cleaning and cooking.

Limpus (1970), for example, argued that it is a woman's "relationship to her children," and not to a man, "which prevents her from seriously committing herself to a job" and is thus the major "stunting influence upon her creativity." Kate Millett (1969) accurately noted that it is to the female that "domestic service and attendance upon infants" are assigned while "the rest of human achievement, interest, and ambition" is prescribed for the male. She herself, however, makes no distinction between these two realms of activity and seems even to concur in the judgment that attendance upon infants is among the lowliest of human activities, classing this as an "animal" rather than as a "distinctly human" pursuit. Millett, like Friedrich Engels a century earlier, calls for the education of children to become "a public matter"; child rearing, she writes, "is infinitely better left to the best trained practitioners . . . who have chosen it as a vocation" (p. 126) than to harried and frequently unhappy parents.

In an article debunking the "motherhood myth," Betty Rollin (1970) suggested that "often when the stork flies in, sexuality flies out," and that even if children are "sweet and marvelous to have and rear; the question is whether or not one wants to pay the price for it." The price to be paid is variously described by others but I think nowhere quite so frighteningly as in an essay on marriage and motherhood by Jones (1970), who referred to giving birth as being, for many women, "like a bad trip," and the infant's presence at home is discussed in terms of "the agony" of being awakened in the middle of the night, and so on. After her first child, a mother is seen as "ready for her final demise. Too tired to comprehend or fight, she only staggers and eventually submits" to a second-class existence.

Or consider what Una Stannard (1971) wrote about pregnancy. She very neatly analyzed the manifold negative effects of women's imposed preoccupation with beauty and attractiveness, noting especially what a shaky foundation this provides for self-esteem. But she, herself, appears to fall victim to the very same cultural straitjacket that she dissects so well. How else can one explain the following words from the pen of an active seeker for liberation?

> The pregnant woman is not beautiful. During pregnancy a woman's face may be radiant (and that belief is by and a large a myth too), but what of her body?—the breasts swollen, the nipples brown, the belly distended and shiny with stretch marks, the belly button protruding. . . . However beautiful one may think women are, their beauty leads to the nonbeauty of pregnancy. Woman's body is functional. Since the man does not have to carry a child within him, he is better fittted to keep whatever looks he was born with. . . . (p. 123)

Germaine Greer (1970) would not share this view, but one of her plans (a "dream") is to bear a child in a farmhouse in Italy where the child will remain in the care of a local family. From time to time, Greer and other parents of children being similarly cared for, and their friends, would leave their busy adult lives in the cities and "visit the house as often as they could, to rest and enjoy the children and even work a bit" (p. 232).

Certainly not all of the statements on children within liberation literature are unsympathetic or ambivalent. One can find the expression of very positive sentiments as well (cf. Shaw, 1970), but the more dominant view is that for alert women who desire to move freely within the public world outside their homes, childbearing is burdensome and child rearing is unchallenging, dull, and time consuming.

I believe that such attitudes toward children are not peculiar to proliberation women but, on the contrary, that they are veridical with the feelings of many women and men to whom the names of Millett and Greer are unknown or to whom the concept of "women's liberation" may be frightening, insulting, or a stimulus to anger. Objectively, there can be little doubt that the rearing of children is time and energy consuming. And scores of middle-class

mothers and fathers have very resourcefully found ways of turning themselves away from this task and tuning themselves out. While verbalizing the
value and significance of having children, many parents actively practice
disinterest and laissez-faire under the guise of permissiveness and democracy and make good use of adult escapes like "the job," "the meeting," and
so on. Many of our expectations regarding parenthood are unrealistic, and
we are consequently frustrated when idealized, unreal goals prove largely
unattainable (e.g., the ever smiling, cleanly scrubbed, sweet-smelling baby
of the full-color magazine photographs). Mothers and fathers must certainly
communicate their own ambivalence about child rearing to their children,
who are themselves potential parents. And other social institutions contribute similar cues.

Why should any girl really want to be a mother, for example, after reading in one book after another the same dreary image of mom as a selfless,
limited, mindless, and colorless human being? An analysis of 2,760 stories
appearing in 134 recently published school readers and used in three suburban New Jersey systems, found this composite picture of "mother":

> Not only does she wash, cook, clean, nurse, and find mittens; these
> chores constitute her only happiness. . . . She is perpetually on call, . . .
> available. . . . She is never shown making something of her own or work-
> ing at some task unconnected with domestic duty. Children never hush
> to allow her to concentrate . . . never bring her cups of tea while she
> relaxes with the papers . . . never meet her at the station or the air-
> port. . . . (Women on Words and Images, 1972, p. 40)

It is hardly to be wondered at, then, that children grow up feeling that to
be a mother is not exciting, despite the fact that contrary verbalizations are
consistently reinforced. (That verbal behavior can be learned independently
of other kinds is, of course, not a startling new idea.) Fathers come off
somewhat better in the children's books. They are "where the fun is," but
for them, of course, parenting is what they *sometimes* do, when they choose
to, and when they are not too busy with other things.

What I am suggesting is that there is already a very strong cultural basis
for the rejection of child rearing and that what some within the liberation
movement are doing is simply reflecting this existent bias without having
carefully considered its source. Thus, for example, one finds embedded in
a well-reasoned argument for the abolition of restrictive legislation on abortion and contraception (Sedler, 1971) the view that the woman's biological
capacity to produce children is the "burden" of her sex. It is precisely this
kind of well-meaning and enlightened, now-we-can-admit-it point of view
that having children (and, God forbid, rearing them too) is for the birds,
but literally, which is resoundingly reiterated or subtly present in much
liberation literature. In this respect, I believe, the movement has been vic-

timized and shaped by the very culture it is attempting to shake to its senses and by the same male chauvinist values it is questioning and hoping to change. Despite verbal excesses to the contrary, the actual treatment of women and children within our male-oriented culture provides clear evidence that childbearing and rearing are consistently undervalued and held in generally low esteem. It is as though since men don't do it, it can't be very important! And this very denigration seems to be echoed, on other grounds, by supporters of a new feminism.

Years ago Margaret Mead (1949) noted a fascinating cultural phenomenon: Regardless of the nature of the activity, whether weaving, doll-making, or what have you, when performed by men that activity is valued and honored; when it is "woman's work" the very same pursuit is taken for granted or disdained. It seems to me highly probable that it is *because* childbearing is necessarily a female-only activity (at least at the moment; cf. Gaylin, 1972) and because child rearing, too, has been primarily performed by women that both are accorded so little respect. Even a serious critic of male-dominated societies like Millett (1969) can recognize this point with respect to weaving or fishing, and still end up sharing, with the dominant males, the judgment that child rearing is not so terribly important. This, it seems to me, is powerful testimony to the tenaciousness of our masculine-oriented values.

All of the assumptions and speculations that I have quite freely expressed in the above discussion are clearly in need of empirical investigation. As a very simple first attempt in this direction, it was decided to explore the general relationship between attitudes toward children and two possibly significant variables: the quality of one's own remembered childhood experiences with parents and the extent of agreement with propositions relevant to the movement for women's liberation. To obtain data bearing on these questions, a paper-and-pencil survey instrument was devised, consisting of the following self-report items:*

1. Self-descriptions of gender, marital status, and age; and whether or not, during most of the respondent's childhood, his or her father had lived at home; and whether his or her mother had worked outside the home;

2. Seven adult activities, presented in alphabetical order (art or music, business, child rearing, engineering, politics, research in science, teaching) to be ranked from high (1) to low (7), first in terms of their *value to any society,* then to be ranked in terms of the degree to which they are believed to *require individual creativity,* and lastly to be ranked for the respondent's

*The assistance and collaboration of Albert Lott in designing the reported investigation and of Francis Sporadeo and John McCue in the coding and organizing of the data are gratefully acknowledged.

personal interest in pursuing them. Our focus was only on the position of child rearing relative to the other activities, and its ranking thus constituted a somewhat oblique measure of attitude;

3. Four concepts, presented in the same order for all respondents (your mother; your father; your children, actual or anticipated; and yourself), each on a separate page, to be rated on eight semantic-differential bipolar adjective scales known to be highly loaded with evaluative meaning (bad-good, beautiful-ugly, bitter-sweet, cruel-kind, fragrant-foul, important-unimportant, shallow-deep, warm-cold) intermixed with 10 adjectives taken from a previously developed Liking Scale (Lott, Lott, Reed, and Crow, 1970; complaining, considerate, energetic, happy, insincere, intelligent, intolerant, quarrelsome, self-centered, truthful) which were also presented in bipolar fashion. These eighteen 9-point scales were arranged in alphabetical order and in such a way that positive and negative poles appeared equally on the left- and right-hand sides in random order;

4. Forty-two statements, each concerned with the behavior of men and women in various situations relative to one another (modified and adapted from Kirkpatrick; cf. Shaw and Wright, 1967). This constituted a women's liberation scale. Respondents were instructed to reply to each statement by indicating strong agreement, agreement, disagreement, or strong disagreement. Half of the items were phrased in a pro- and half in an antiliberation direction, and these were randomly arranged to offset response bias. Two illustrative statements are: "17. Only the very exceptional woman is qualified to enter politics" and "39. It is foolish to regard scrubbing floors as more proper for women than mowing the lawn";

5. Five 9-point scales ranging from very much (9) to very little (1) to be used in answering the following questions: How eagerly do you anticipate having children? During your childhood, how much energy did your mother devote to your care and well-being (when not at work)? During your childhood, how much energy did your father devote to your care and well-being (when not at work)? How much information do you have about the Women's Liberation movement? and How much do you agree with the dominant positions taken by the Women's Liberation movement?

Our sample consisted of 109 University of Rhode Island undergraduate men and 133 women, all tested at the same time in an introductory psychology classroom, and 47 additional undergraduate but older women from a special Continuing Education for Women (CEW) program. Each of these three groups, men (M), women (W), and CEW, was subdivided into the following categories descriptive of their *attitudes toward having and rearing children: highly positive:* if they said that they "eagerly anticipated" having children (ratings of 7, 8, or 9) *and* were "personally interested in rearing"

them (ranked this activity first, second, or third relative to the other six);
moderate: if eagerness for having children was rated 4, 5, or 6 *and* personal
interest in rearing was ranked third, fourth, or fifth; *low:* if having children
was not eagerly anticipated (rated 1, 2 or 3) *and* rearing them personally
was ranked in sixth or seventh place; *eager to have but not to rear:* if eagerness was rated 7, 8, or 9 *and* personal interest in rearing was ranked in
fourth place or lower; *inconsistent:* if responses indicated an interest in personally rearing children but not in having them. Respondents falling into
this latter category were omitted from further consideration despite the fact
that realistic motivations for this position can certainly be imagined and
appreciated; their number, however, was so small (8 M, 16 W, 5 CEW)
that removal from the larger group was deemed best. In addition, since only
a small number of subjects fell into the low category, this was combined with
the moderate category for all subsequent data analyses. The number of subjects in each attitudinal category is shown in Table 1, along with other data
which will be discussed below.

Table 1.   Attitudes Toward Having and Rearing Children Related to
Mean Ratings of the "Children" Concept and Mean Scores on the
Women's Liberation Scale

	ATTITUDE		
GROUP	HIGHLY POSITIVE	MODERATE TO LOW	EAGER TO HAVE BUT NOT REAR
Proportion			
Men	.35	.37	.28
Women	.59	.32	.09
CEW	.86	.14	0
Mean rating of "children" concept			
Men	7.64	7.16	7.28
Women	7.91	7.56	7.81
CEW	7.57	7.44	—
Mean score on liberation scale			
Men	18.49	11.63	8.18
Women	20.26	34.39	14.54
CEW	29.21	39.67	—

Note. CEW = undergraduate but older women from a Continuing Education for
Women program. Men, $N = 101$; Women, $N = 117$; CEW, $N = 42$.

As would be expected, men and women differed substantially in the proportions among them who indicated a desire to both personally rear children and an eagerness to have them. Chi-square analyses comparing men

and women ($\chi^2 = 17.34$, $p < .001$), and the young undergraduate women (W) with the older CEW group ($\chi^2 = 6.20$, $p < .02$),* indicated significant differences in both cases. As can be seen in Table 1, the CEW group contains the largest proportion of highly positive respondents, with the younger campus women having the next largest proportion, and the men the smallest. These findings are not surprising, with men traditionally being expected to rank personal involvement in child rearing as of lesser interest to them than a public occupation; to find as many as one-third of our male sample in the highly positive category is more unexpected. As for the difference between the younger women and the CEW group, this may well reflect the fact that the majority of the latter were married and already mothers.

Since attitude toward having and rearing children constituted the major dependent variable of this investigation, it was important to get some indication that the categories into which we divided our respondents were more than just arbitrary and idiosyncratically determined divisions. Subjects categorized as highly positive toward children on the basis of their self-reported eagerness to have and to rear them should be expected to differ from others not so categorized in their responses to the concept of "your children" on the evaluative and likability scales. We therefore compared the highly positive and moderate-low subjects, within each of the groups, M, W, and CEW, on their responses to the 18 bipolar adjectives previously listed. The group averages are shown in Table 1. These data were analyzed by means of a 2 × 3 analysis of variance† and, as predicted, highly positive subjects were found to have made significantly higher ratings of the "children" concept than the moderate-low subjects ($F = 4.00$, $p < .05$).

Having some degree of assurance, then, that our attitudinal categories were true reflections of differences in the way in which our subjects respond to the idea of children, we proceeded to look for other ways in which the highly positive and moderate-low persons could be distinguished in our search for meaningful relationships with these attitudes.

Marital Status and Age

Since the vast majority of the male and female campus sample was single (only 7 men and 5 women were married or divorced), and between 17 and 24 years old (only 7 were older), these variables in no way differentiated between the two major attitudinal groups. Within the small CEW group,

---

*Since no CEW subjects were categorized as eager to have but not to rear, this category was not included in this and all subsequent analyses involving this group.

†The Walker and Lev (1953) technique for unequal cell frequencies was used in this and subsequent analyses of variance.

however, significantly more of the highly positive women were married or divorced (33 out of 36) than was true of the moderate-lows (2 out of 6; $\chi^2 = 8.75, p < .01$). In addition, the CEW group obviously differed sharply from both of the others, M and W, in age (most were over 25) and in the proportion of married persons within it, regardless of attitudinal category.

Father at Home

No relationship was found between desire to have and to rear children and having had a father who lived at home during most of one's childhood, but here again response variability was low. Only 7 M, 4 W, and 4 CEW subjects reported that their fathers had lived apart from them when they were children.*

Working Mother

Although a sizable minority of mothers was reported to have worked either full- or part-time outside the home during our subjects' childhoods (38% M, 28% W, and 52% CEW), this did not relate to attitudinal category. Of interest, however, is the fact that the younger campus women had a significantly smaller proportion of working mothers than did the CEW group ($\chi^2 = 6.94, p < .01$). If one views the CEW women as actually reaching toward self-liberation by studying for a college degree at some considerable personal sacrifice (attending formal classes three hours a day, five days a week, while being wives and mothers), then the greater tendency for them to have had working mothers suggests one way in which such mothers may directly or indirectly influence their daughters. Our finding is quite congruent with reports by others (e.g., Hartley, 1970; Rossi, 1971) that the daughters of working mothers tend to be more assertive, less dependent, and less passive than other girls.

Creativity of Child Rearing

It would be expected that subjects categorized as highly positive in desire to have and to rear children would see the activity of child care as more creative than subjects classified as low or moderate. Here, too, was an opportunity to obtain face validity for our categories. An analysis of variance on rank order of child rearing along the creativity dimension indicated a significant main effect for attitude (high versus moderate-low, $F = 5.92$, $p < .05$). A group's main effect ($F = 3.83, p < .05$) was also found, CEW subjects having ranked child rearing as reliably more creative than

---

*Since the single most common ethnic background of our subjects was Italian Catholic, this indication of family stability is not surprising.

the younger campus women, who, in turn, ranked it as reliably more creative than did the men. Group means are shown in Table 2.

Table 2. Attitude toward Having and Rearing Children Related to Other Variables

GROUP	ATTITUDE	
	HIGHLY POSITIVE	MODERATE TO LOW
Mean rank for creativity of child rearing		
Men	3.43	4.79
Women	3.57	3.57
CEW	2.81	3.50
Mean rank for social value of child rearing		
Men	1.66	2.84
Women	1.80	2.16
CEW	1.78	2.83
Mean score: mother's energy		
Men	7.94	7.32
Women	8.35	7.73
CEW	7.36	6.33
Mean score: father's energy		
Men	6.43	5.73
Women	7.28	6.30
CEW	5.03	3.67

Note. CEW = undergraduate but older women from a Continuing Education for Women program.

Value of Child Rearing to Society

These data, too, also shown in Table 2, were found to distinguish among our attitudinal categories, as we had hoped they would. An analysis of variance of rank given to child rearing on this dimension indicated that highly positive subjects felt that such an activity was significantly more socially valuable than did moderate-low subjects ($F = 9.33, p < .01$).

Mother's and Father's Nurturance

We had speculated that adult desire for parenthood would be a positive reflection of the quality of one's own childhood. This was tested by examining responses to two questions regarding the amount of attention respondents remembered having been devoted to their care and well-being by their mothers and by their fathers (when each was at home). Table 2 presents the relevant group means. On the question regarding mothers, we found significant differences across all three groups (M, W, and CEW), in the predicted direction, between subjects highly motivated to being parents themselves and those not so motivated ($F = 5.73, p < .05$). And, with respect to fathers, too, highly positive subjects differed significantly from moderate-lows, across all subject groups ($F = 5.74, p < .05$). Not only, then, do the adults who look forward to parenthood differ from less child-oriented adults in remembering more nurturant mothers, but they also rated their fathers higher on the amount of care and trouble they remember them taking on their behalf. It is especially interesting, I believe, that this is as true of men as it is of women for both their mothers and their fathers.

Mean ratings of the concepts of "your mother" and "your father" on the 18 bipolar adjective scales did not discriminate between highly positive and moderate-low subjects. We believe this to be due to the difficulty many persons have in breaking the verbal stereotypes learned in connection with parent symbols, but this is an ad hoc speculation requiring further study.

Attitudes Toward Women's Liberation

As would be expected, men and women were found to diverge sharply from one another on this variable. Table 1 presents the mean scores for all of the subgroups on the 42-item women's liberation scale described previously.* It is clear that the men in all three attitudinal categories have less positive views on women's liberation than both the younger campus women and the CEW groups, and that the latter have more positive views than the former ($F = 9.19, p < .01$).

What was not expected, simply because we did not really think about the men in this respect, was that the most child-oriented men, that is, those who were eager both to have and to personally rear children, were more favorable toward women's liberation than either the moderate-low men or the more traditional eager-to-have-but-not-rear group. The extremely low level of agreement with liberation sentiment shown by men in this last group fits conceptually with their highly conventional attitudes toward parenthood: a strong desire to conceive children who will be cared for by their wives. The differences among the men's groups, while considerable, are not statistically reliable. On the other hand, the opposite trend among the women, that is, stronger proliberation views among women who are not much interested in

*Scores were obtained by weighting +2 all responses of strong agreement with pro-liberation propositions or strong disagreement with antiliberation views, weighting +1 responses of agreement with proliberation items or disagreement with antiliberation items, weighting −1 agreement with antiliberation statements and disagreement with proliberation statements, and weighting −2 strong agreement with antiliberation statements or strong disagreement with proliberation statements. Scores, then, could vary from +84 to −84.

rearing children, is a significant one ($t = 3.16$, $p < .01$ for positive versus moderate-low, with W and CEW groups combined).

The validity of the lengthy liberation questionnaire is supported by responses to the simple question (answered along a 9-point scale): "How much do you agree with the dominant positions of the women's liberation movement?" Combining campus women with CEW women, the highly positive child-oriented subjects were found to rate themselves in significantly less agreement than the moderate-low subjects (4.56 versus 5.58, $t = 2.55$, $p < .02$). There was no reliable difference between highly positive and moderate-low men.

The data on attitudes toward liberation suggested that we might profitably examine our subjects by utilizing this variable as a basis for comparison on others. Taking just our larger groups of University of Rhode Island men and women, that is, excluding the CEW women, we separated out that quarter which had obtained the highest proliberation scores (30 women with scores between 79 and 41 [$M = 50.53$]; and 24 men with scores between 62 and 30 [$M = 39.83$] and that quarter which had indicated the least agreement with liberation sentiments (28 women with scores ranging from -33 to $+9$ [$M = -3.68$; and 25 men with scores between -42 and -2 [$M = -16.36$]). For both men and women, separately, the top quarter, or proliberation group, was then compared with the lowest quarter, or anti-liberation group.

The antiliberation men viewed child rearing as less creative, of less value to society, and indicated less personal interest in pursuing this activity than did the proliberation men, but none of these differences are statistically reliable. Only on the 9-point scale question regarding agreement with the liberation movement's dominant positions do the proliberation and the antiliberation men differ significantly (6.60 versus 2.52, $t = 8.16$, $p < .001$). When we compare proliberation with antiliberation women, however (see Table 3), we find significant differences on the following important dimensions. Although proliberation women ranked child rearing as more creative than did antiliberation women, they ranked themselves as less interested in personally engaging in this activity. Proliberation women said that they were far less eager to have children, and they differed also from antiliberation women on our measures of parental nurturance, remembering less care and attention being devoted to them by their mothers as well as by their fathers. Proliberation women, understandably, said that they had more information on the relevant issues and agreed more with the dominant positions of the liberation movement than did the antiliberation women.

The final three comparisons shown in Table 3 provide some provocative new information. While the pro- and antiliberation women did not differ in the adjective ratings made of their mothers, they did differ reliably with respect to their fathers, with the proliberation women evaluating their fathers more poorly. And when we measured the differences between average rating given to mother and that given to father, taking each subject separately, we found further evidence to suggest that proliberation women, in contrast to antiliberation women, had more positive feelings for their mothers than for their fathers.

Table 3.   University of Rhode Island Campus Women Who Are Most and Least in Favor of Women's Liberation Compared on Other Variables

| Measure | Mean score | | t |
	PRO-LIBERA-TION WOMEN	ANTI-LIBERA-TION WOMEN	
Creativity of child rearing[a]	3.30	4.18	2.15*
Personal interest in rearing[a]	3.70	2.57	2.40*
Eagerness to have children	5.33	7.96	3.70**
Mother's energy	7.47	8.61	2.85***
Father's energy	6.10	7.61	2.75**
Information on liberation	5.90	4.39	2.90**
Agreement with liberation movement	6.63	2.68	9.19***
Mother scales	6.90	7.18	ns
Father scales	6.42	7.08	1.74[b]
Mother-father difference	1.43	.83	2.07*

[a] The lower the score the higher the rank.
[b] $p < .05$, one-tailed test.
* $p < .05$.
** $p < .01$.
*** $p < .001$.

Our data, briefly summarized above, may take on added significance when considered together with some findings recently reported by Worell and Worell (1971). The Worells studied a sample of white students at the University of Kentucky and obtained personality correlates of support for and opposition to the women's liberation movement. Using a variety of measures, they found that the "one compelling characteristic" which sets the female supporter off from other American college women is her "very strong desire for autonomy. In comparison both to the opposed women and to college girls in general, she wants to be independent, self-sufficient and free from external control." She was also found to be significantly less authoritarian than women opposed to liberation. The latter, in contrast, emerged as self-protective, fearful of danger, risk avoiding, resistant to change, and low in curiosity and flexibility.

If we consider the pictures of the pro- and antiliberation college women that emerge from the Worells' report and then ask which one would make the better mother, my answer is immediate and unhesitating. On any criterion of competence for motherhood, my choice is for the independent, flexible, and democratically oriented proliberation woman. But who do we find planning to have the children and desiring to rear them? Not those who would make the best mothers, but those with the least desirable characteristics.

When we turn our attention to the male supporter of women's equality we find, according to the Worells' data, a reflective, self-reliant, non-conformist, resourceful, and nonauthoritarian person—a perfect companion for the female supporter of liberation except for one rather intriguing difference. Recall that it is such men in our sample who tend to place a higher value on personally rearing their children than do antiliberation men. Perhaps those men who favor greater freedom and respect for women do not see women's traditional activities as so demeaning and want to share the pleasures of parenthood with their wives. For proliberation women, however, motherhood is too much associated with women's inferior status and is therefore rejected. Will it be the case, then, in view of the very strong pressures to limit population, that the majority of children born to college-educated parents will be reared by the most conservative and change-resistant women in traditional families where it is mother who stays at home and "looks after the kids"?

My negative evaluation of this projection should not, in any sense, suggest that I would prefer a return to the "feminine mystique." What then? I suggest first that what has contributed significantly to the mistreatment and inferior status of women by men, to the whole ugly syndrome of sexism, is the fact of intimate association between women and infants. Many feminist women, sensing this very strongly, have sought to break this tie and to assert that they, like men, are independent of the children. To this end, the old, tired myths surrounding motherhood and biological destiny are being rationally attacked, but we have not yet gone quite far enough. What must also be a part of the postliberation future is the recognition that you do not have to be a woman to be a nurturant rearer of children. (A recently written great line is Besdine, 1971, "One doesn't have to be Jewish, a mother, or even a woman, to be a Jewish mother.") All the known needs of human infants can in the modern world be as easily satisfied by a father as by a mother or by any involved and caring adult. (Nursing mothers satisfy their own needs, primarily.) Mead's (1965) lyrical insistence that "the child whose mother has succeeded in giving it a sense of being valued as a unique individual, entirely for itself . . . is prepared to meet the challenges of living" (p. 18) would be just as valid if the word father, for example, were substituted for "mother."

I believe, therefore, that not only should American industry grant long and leisurely maternity leave, with pay, to new mothers (as is the case in Sweden) but that paternity leave should be granted to fathers as well. With great satisfaction, I recently noted a legal case in New York City, *Danielson* v. *Board of Higher Education*, which involves the issue of leave to fathers for purposes of child care. Plaintiffs are members of the faculties of the City University of New York who are asking that fathers be entitled to the same provisions presently applied only to mothers. Such options for men are being proposed elsewhere, such as at Douglass College (cf. Romer and Secor, 1971).

There is some very good suggestive evidence (cf. Maccoby and Jacklin, 1971) that the major stimulus for nurturant behavior on the part of mammalian mothers is the presence of the infant. Men who are given the opportunity to interact with neonates, which is so rarely the case, might well respond similarly and become deeply involved in that interplay of attachment behaviors which characterizes the best relationship between mother and child. The prenatal tie of a child to its mother is a biological given, but after its birth the tie is social and is culturally prescribed.

For fathers (as well as mothers) to want to be parents, and not just regular "visitors" to their homes, society must provide recognition of the value of such a pursuit and of the importance it attaches to the care and education of children. When President Nixon vetoed a comprehensive nationwide early education program for children and there was only a barely perceptible ripple of protest, and a minimum of critical comment, this made it quite clear how very little our society values its children. As long as child care is viewed as a woman's duty or destiny, it will also be viewed as requiring few or no facilitating social supports. (And for some children, even their mothers are expendable; those who are poor and whose mothers are on welfare can be given cheap custodial care while their mothers provide cheap domestic and other services to those who are more affluent.) We provide little real recognition of the worth of parenthood, and this is primarily, I believe, because we define it as the relationship between two low-status groups, women and children, rather than as the involvement of caring adults in the nurturance and growth of society's most important resource.

Men should be encouraged to train for and work in jobs relevant to children, like preschool and primary education, and nursing. We also need to develop more community-organized and community-operated centers where parents can joyfully and guiltlessly leave their children to the creative attention of other adults who are their neighbors and friends, or trained, informed professionals who know their children and respect them.

Also included in my vision of a postliberation future is the recognition of the dignity of part-time work schedules so that men and women can share in enjoying the earliest years of their children's lives without losing their own adult professional or occupational identities and skills. It is encouraging in this respect to note that a recent report by a Harvard committee "specifically recommends that part-time study and part-time teaching become fully acceptable" (cf. Romer and Secor, 1971). A portion of American industry is already showing its awareness of the advantages of flexible and reduced workweek schedules, and who can doubt that technology, provided with requisite incentives, could soon make the eight-hour day a laughable anachronism? To have men and women equally able to participate in the world of public work, in which we are rewarded by money and status, and to raise the value of what we do privately at home, the world of labor (to borrow from the Marxist lexicon), is to the potential benefit of women and men, and their children.

I return, finally, to one of the questions that began this article, Who will want to rear the children? If we continue to allocate this activity on a strictly sexual basis, if we continue to generally denigrate its significance, and to make it necessary for those who do it to sacrifice their self-esteem and independence and to reduce their potential for other kinds of contributions to their culture, then the answer, I believe, is that those who want to rear the children will be those who are fearful of autonomy and distrustful of their own capacities to function in the larger community. If, however, we come to view child rearing as not incompatible with other creative activities, then such a question will not need to be asked. Many will still decide, for all sorts of personally valid reasons, that parenthood is not for them, but others, remembering their own joyful childhoods, will be eager to participate in such an experience again, as parent now instead of child.

References

Atkinson, T. G. "The Institution of Sexual Intercourse." In *Notes from the Second Year: Women's Liberation*, edited by S. Firestone and A. Koedt. New York: Radical Feminism, 1970.

Besdine, M. "Mrs. Oedipus Has Daughters, Too." *Psychology Today*, 4 (1971): 62.

Firestone, S. *The Dialectic of Sex.* New York: Bantam, 1970.

Gaylin, W. "We Have the Awful Knowledge to Make Exact Copies of Human Beings." *New York Times Magazine*, March 5, 1972, pp. 12–13, 41–49.

Greer, G. *The Female Eunuch.* New York: McGraw-Hill, 1970.

Hartley, R. E. "American Core Culture: Changes and Continuities." In *Sex Roles in Changing Society*, edited by G. H. Seward and R. C. Williamson. New York: Random House, 1970.

Jones, B. "The Dynamics of Marriage and Motherhood." In *Sisterhood Is Powerful*, edited by R. Morgan. New York: Vintage, 1970.

Koedt, A. "The Myth of the Vaginal Orgasm." In *Notes from the Second Year: Women's Liberation*, edited by S. Firestone and A. Koedt. New York: Radical Feminism, 1970.

Limpus, L. "The Liberation of Women: Sexual Repression and the Family." In *The*

Uptight Society, edited by H. Gadlin and B. E. Garskof. Belmont, Calif.: Brooks/Cole, 1970.

Lott, A. J., B. E. Lott, T. Reed, and T. Crow. "Personality Trait Descriptions of Differentially Liked Persons." *Journal of Personality and Social Psychology*, 16 (1970): 284–290.

Maccoby, E. E., and C. N. Jacklin. "Sex Differences and Their Implications for Sex Role." Unpublished manuscript, Stanford University, 1971.

Mailer, N. "The Prisoner of Sex." *Harper's*, March 1971, pp. 41–91.

Mead, M. *Male and Female*. New York: Dell, 1949.

Mead, M., and K. Hyman. *Family*. New York: Macmillan, 1965.

Millett, K. *Sexual Politics*. New York: Doubleday, 1969.

Money, J. "Sexual Dimorphism and Homosexual Gender Identity." *Psychological Bulletin*, 74 (1970): 425–440.

Rollin, B. "Motherhood, Who Needs It? *Look*, September 22, 1970, pp. 15–17.

Romer, K. T., and C. Secor. "The Time Is Here for Women's Liberation." *Annals of the American Academy of Political and Social Science*, 397 (1971): 129–139.

Rossi, A. S. "Changing Sex Roles and Family Development." Unpublished manuscript, Goucher College, 1971.

Sedler, R. A. "The Legal Dimension of Women's Liberation." In *Women's Liberation: Equality, Legality, and Personality*, L. Worell, chm. Symposium presented at the annual meeting of the American Psychological Association, Washington, D.C., September 1971.

Shaw, M. E., and J. M. Wright. *Scales for the Measurement of Attitudes*. New York: McGraw-Hill, 1967.

Shaw, R. "Artists Today: A Conversation." *Women: A Journal of Liberation* (Fall 1970): 38–42.

Sherfey, M. J. "A Theory on Female Sexuality." In *Sisterhood Is Powerful*, edited by R. Morgan. New York: Vintage, 1970.

Stannard, U. "The Mask of Beauty." In *Women in Sexist Society*, edited by V. Gornick and B. K. Moran. New York: Basic Books, 1971.

Walker, H. M., and J. Lev. *Statistical Inference*. New York: Holt, 1953.

Women on Words and Images. *Dick and Jane as Victims*. Princeton, N.J.: Author, P.O. Box 2163, 1972.

Worell, J., and L. Worell. "Supporters and Opposers of Women's Liberation: Some Personality Correlates." In *Women's Liberation: Equality, Legality, and Personality*, L. Worrell, chm. Symposium presented at the annual meeting of the American Psychological Association, Washington, D.C., September 1971.

Alarming numbers of children are admitted to hospitals annually as a result of traumatic injuries for which parents cannot provide plausible explanations. Parents who abuse children are difficult to characterize. They are not necessarily psychotic, inadequate, or disadvantaged, although they may be all of these. Parents who are both abusive and affluent may be able to cover up through private arrangements what the poor reveal in public emergency rooms. Whatever the social and psychological correlates of child abuse, it is a historic phenomenon that is difficult to remedy. Not only does society seem unwilling to invest in protective services or institutional care for children, argues the author, but the perception of children as property or chattel still has strong roots in our society.

Battered Children | *Serapio R. Zalba*

In 1962 a group of doctors in Denver wrote a landmark paper reporting on the "alarming number" of children being admitted to hospitals for traumatic injuries for which the parents could not provide plausible explanations.

One news story in a Cleveland paper, for example, reported that a court hearing had been set "to determine the cause of injuries suffered by an eight-month-old baby hospitalized for a month . . . with two broken arms, a broken left leg, a fingernail missing from his left hand and body scars. . . . The child's mother said he fell forward from an upholstered chair and that his arms apparently caught in the sides of the chair, policewoman reported."

Generally these children are in poor health, with unsatisfactory skin hygiene, multiple soft tissue injuries, deep bruises and malnutrition. An indication of the problem's gravity was provided by Dr. C. Henry Kempe, who cited one day in November 1961 when there were four battered children in Colorado General Hospital alone—two died of central nervous system traumas, and one was released to his home in satisfactory condition but subsequently died "suddenly" in an unexplained manner (a not unusual occurrence). A new term was coined to describe such situations: the "battered child syndrome."

Solving or even managing this problem is not easy. Despite evidence that serious physical assault on children is not rare, incidents are not generally brought to the attention of the authorities. And the authorities have relatively few resources to turn to for help in ameliorating the problem.

To begin with, it is often difficult for agents of societal institutions—physicians, nurses, social workers, teachers, police, prosecutors, judges—as well as concerned relatives and neighbors—to decide when the line has been

From Serapio R. Zalba, "Battered Children," *Transaction* (July/August, 1971), pp. 58–61. Published by permission of Transaction Society. Rutgers University, New Brunswick, New Jersey.

crossed between severe punishment and physical assault or abuse, even though the polar extremes are fairly clear: a mild spanking on the buttocks of a two-year-old child is quite different from the case of abuse that finds its way into a protective agency, where a child may have had scalding water poured on his genitals.

The most extreme cases probably end up in hospitals (when they don't end in the death of the child), especially since the younger children typically seen there are unable to defend themselves by running away from battering or abuse. Yet some studies of nonhospital cases reveal equally serious abuse. Edgar Merrill, an official of the Massachusetts Society for the Prevention of Cruelty to Children (SPCC), gives examples of the kind of cases seen at that agency:

A five-year-old girl went onto her porch though told not to do so; she was kicked into the house, thrown across the room and hit on the face and head with a frying pan.

A nine-month-old boy's eyes were blackened, his fingers, face and neck burned and his skull fractured by his father.

A 13-month-old girl was X-rayed at the hospital; revealed were multiple skull fractures—some old, some new—and marked subdural hematoma.

X-rays on a seven-month-old boy showed healed fractures of one arm, the other one currently broken, healed fractures on both legs and multiple skull fractures.

The physical abuse of a child does not generally occur only once. In fact, in most of the cases in a study by Shirley Nurse the abuse has been going on for one to three years. Indeed, one of the medical indicators that physical injuries may have been inflicted rather than accidental is X-ray evidence of prior, often multiple injuries, such as fractures of the limbs and skull.

In the hospital studies of Elizabeth Elmer and Helen Boardman, the children were very young, over half of them being under one year of age. There was a high mortality rate among them: in 12 of the 56 cases followed up (21 percent) the children died. Of the 46 homicides of infants and preadolescents in Lester Adelson's Cleveland study, 21 were under three years old. In contrast, in the private agency protective service studies reported by Harold Bryant and Edgar Merrill in Massachusetts and James Delsordo in Philadelphia, the children were older, with half of them (in a combined sample of over 260 children) under seven years old, and with no report made of any deaths. The abusers of children were usually their own parents with whom they were currently living—mothers and fathers were identified as the abusers in equal numbers of cases. While there was a great deal of marital and family conflict found in these cases, the non-abusive parent tended to protect the abusive one, supporting his or her denial of having assaulted the child. As a way of hiding the effects of their cruelty, many parents shopped around for medical care—one child under one year of age had been hospitalized three times in three different hospitals. The grim fact is, to quote Adelson: "It is relatively simple to destroy the life of a child in almost absolute secrecy without the necessity of taking any elaborate precautions to ensure the secrecy."

Characteristics of Abusive Parents

In the child abuse cases I have seen or read about, the parents came from the complete range of socioeconomic classes. Many were middle class and self-supporting, with well-kept homes. All, however, could be characterized as highly impulsive, socially isolated and in serious difficulties, with their marriage, with money and so forth.

Irving Kaufman has taken a psychoanalytic view that the physical abuse of children implies a distortion of reality: the child as a target is perceived by the parent in a symbolic or delusional way; he stands for the psychotic portion of himself he wishes to destroy, his own abusive parent or the like. But the vast majority of abusive parents do not fall into any easy psychiatric categories, even though some of the most violent and abusive might be called schizophrenic. In Adelson's study, for example, 17 of the 41 murderers of children were patently mentally ill; that is, they had been hospitalized or had shown profound mental disturbance for some time before the eruption of violence.

The Massachusetts SPCC reported that in 50 percent of the 115 families they studied there was premarital conception. Other studies also point out the typicality of youthful marriages, unwanted pregnancies, illegitimacies and "forced" marriages. How much we can make of this is, however, questionable, since many, if not most, American families share one or another of these characteristics. More important, perhaps, is the finding that parents had themselves been abused and neglected as children. The epidemiological implications are, consequently, rather serious. While the 180 children in the Massachusetts study were generally normal physically, all of them were found to have a seriously impaired relationship with the abusive parent. These children tended to overreact to hostility, were depressive, hyperactive, destructive and fearful. The Philadelphia study characterized the children in their cases as bed wetting, truant, fire setters and withdrawn.

How Many Children Are Being Abused?

It is difficult to assess the number of children being physically abused or battered. For one thing, even the number of abuse cases that actually get reported is not known. For another, figures given by individual protective agencies or hospitals may be typical only for their geographic localities. Reported statistics on referrals to protective agencies generally include cases of both neglect and abuse; no definitive statement of how many of each are involved can be made. Eustace Chesser of England's National Society for the Prevention of Cruelty to Children concluded that between 6 and 7 percent of all children in England are at some time during their life "so neglected or ill-treated or become so maladjusted as to require the protection of community agencies." On the basis of a 1964 study in California, it would appear that a minimum of approximately 20,000 children were in need of protective services in that state alone. The American Public Welfare Association reported that in 1958 approximately 100 cases were referred monthly to the public welfare department in Denver, Colorado, for protective services. Elizabeth Barry Philbrook cited the figure of 250,000 children living outside their own homes in 1960. She indicated that one-third of the children had been moved to at least two or three different foster homes and that protective services were needed in those cases, implying that this would serve a preventive as well as restorative function.

David Gil's reports from a nationwide study on child abuse conducted by Brandeis University for the United States Children's Bureau demonstrate once again the difficulty of determining the actual incidence of child abuse. Gil found that approximately 6,000 cases were reported in 1967. But when a sample of people were asked if they personally know of cases of abuse, their reports, if extrapolated to the total population of the United States, would have indicated an incidence of from two to three million cases *annually*. Gil charges us to be careful in interpreting the findings; it was not possible to determine whether the abuse represented only a slap on the face or something more ominous.

Extrapolation on the basis of the data from California and Colorado produces a conservative estimate of between 200,000 and 250,000 children in the United States needing protective services each year, of which 30,000 to 37,500 may have been badly hurt.

How New Is Child Abuse?

The basic problem of serious child abuse by parents and parent substitutes is not new. Indeed, as Elizabeth Elmer has pointed out, it is only comparatively recently that there has been any community consensus and sanction for recognizing and protecting the rights of children. In much of recorded history, infanticide, child abandonment, maiming as an aid in begging and the selling of children have been common rather than exceptional. It was common to flog children without provocation in colonial times in America in order to "break them of their willfulness" and make them tractable, ostensibly for the good of their souls. Not until the last half of the nineteenth century was the first Society for the Prevention of Cruelty to Children organized in the United States. And it came about as a result of New York City's infamous Mary Ellen case in 1866 which brought out that the American Society for the Prevention of Cruelty to *Animals* was the only agency willing and able to intervene to protect a child suffering from abuse.

As Norris Class points out, early workers in the field of child welfare proceeded on the assumption that physical abuse and neglect were associated almost exclusively with poverty, slums, ignorance, industrial exploitation and immigration. Physical mistreatment was quite open in these sectors, and it was not difficult to introduce admissible and dramatic evidence into the courts in the prosecution of abusive and neglectful parents. But as the conditions they associated with physical neglect and abuse abated, so did its visibility.

During America's intensive romance with psychoanalysis and dynamic psychiatry in the 1920s and 1930s the child welfare people became concerned more with emotional factors and treatment, and greater emphasis were given to permissive, voluntarily sought services, with a consequent confusion about the role of authority and legal sanctions in social services. Acceptable legal evidence of emotional neglect or abuse was and still is more difficult to define or produce than is its physical counterpart. Interest in protective services declined, and the close working relationship between the protective agency and the court deteriorated. On the positive side, however, there was an increase in the public's awareness that prosecution of abusive and neglectful parents does not solve the problems of the victimized children or their families. As the family system came to be seen first as the diagnostic and eventually the treatment unit of reference, we began to pay greater attention to the possibility of treating the parents and attempting to maintain the structural integrity of the family. In child welfare today we still face the basic problem: at what point does the harm of leaving a child in a poor home override the negative consequences of splintering the family by use of foster homes or other placement facilities outside the parental home?

An important factor in providing protective services, and an important value in American society, has been the tradition of parental rights regarding the rearing of children. The intervention of the state in parent-child matters is for the most part invoked reluctantly and carefully. When there is a reasonable question as to parental adequacy, the tendency has been to rule in favor of the parent. This may reflect a "folk wisdom" about the child's need for enduring family ties; however, children are sometimes left in homes that are neglectful and even dangerous.

The relatively recent interest in more aggressive (that is, reaching-out) approaches in social work, greater clarification of the role of authority and accumulated experience and knowledge in work with those persons psychiatrically categorized as character-disordered have brought us to the place where we are better able to consider what we can or should do about the abuse of children.

The Child Abusers

Who are the parents that abuse their children? Are they "normal" people who have overreacted? Or are they a clearly distinguishable group?

The picture that emerges in studies done in hospitals and protective agencies is of a number of different types of abusers. One grouping can be made of abusing parents with personality problems that could be characterized in the following ways: patent psychosis, pervasive anger, depressive passive-aggressive personality and cold, compulsive disciplinarians.

A second grouping consists of parents who are impulsive but generally adequate, with marital conflicts or identity-role crises. In the first group we would expect to find a representative cross section of American families. Findings from a national study by David Gil, however, indicate there are more cases of child abuse among the socioeconomically disadvantaged, especially in broken homes and in large families. But if there is a significantly greater proportion of abuse cases among the disadvantaged populations, it is likely to consist of cases of the second type. The reporting of such cases, and the interventions of protective services with legal sanctions, does not necessarily reflect its pattern of incidence. Police, schools, hospitals and social agencies are more likely to intervene in the lives of lower income families than they would in the lives of the more affluent. Practitioners have not tended to agree with Gil. They do not think there is a social class difference in the incidence rate. They argue that the abused child in a more affluent family will probably be taken to a private physician who will, where necessary, make arrangements to hospitalize the child. The source of injury may not be reported. If the family is poor, the child would probably be taken to the emergency room of the hospital, where the staff is likely to complete a report of suspected abuse.

It is interesting to speculate on why we tend to turn our faces away from much of the child abuse that occurs around us. Kempe and others have pointed out that physicians, teachers, social workers, nurses and others in positions where they might identify cases of abuse are reluctant to do so. They wish to avoid court appearances. They prefer not to confront or estrange patient-families (or clients). And frequently they are less than certain that they are correct in their suspicions. Thus it becomes easy not to "notice" abusive behavior.

There is still another explanation for what appears to be widespread lack of awareness of incidents of child abuse. Is there any mother or father who has not been "provoked" almost to the breaking point by the crying, wheedling, whining child? How many parents have not had moments of concern and self-recrimination after having, in anger, hit their own child much harder than they had expected they would? How many such incidents make a "child abuser" out of a normal parent? There may be a tacit agreement among us not to meddle in each other's private matters unless it is simply impossible to ignore the behavior involved.

All 50 states have attempted to counteract our "know-nothing" tendencies by passing laws regarding the reporting of suspected child abuse: some states provide protection against claims of slander and other defamatory "injuries" against persons in certain professional categories (doctors, for example).

Another interesting speculation can be made on the societal level: why has our society provided so *little* protection for children?

Despite the historical trend toward increased children's rights and protection—the SPCC, child labor laws, the day care movement, Head Start and the *Gault* decision of the Supreme Court—it seems clear that the perception of children as property or chattels has strong roots in our society. Parental rights are still rated high on the scale of values.

Related to the issue of personal versus social control is the question about the extent to which our society is willing to invest in broad social welfare services. Our national willingness to invest heavily in public education in the past few years seems to have lost its impetus. Mental hygiene and correctional reform have likewise lost momentum. The progressive strides of the period starting with Franklin Roosevelt and ending with the first Johnson term of office have slowed almost to a standstill.

We do not seem willing to provide adequate protective services or institutional care for children in need of them. An example of our low priority for such services is the role and status of the child care worker which is quite different in the United States as compared to Scandinavian countries. In those countries the work has been professionalized through training programs that adequately prepare the worker—a preparation that is reflected in his relative income.

In the United States, in contrast, child care work is low status work. Little is invested in professional preparation or in in-service training. And the pay is typically quite poor. The result is that few child care institutions are able to provide the quality of care and treatment that is needed.

It seems obvious that protective services *in the community*—counseling and supervision of parents and children—are called for. But it is also clear that the level of investment in community protective services is also inadequate.

Why, then, is there not *more* child abuse? Major forces work against it: 1) our society stresses the desirability of youth, the "happiness" of childhood and the reliving—with desirable modifications—of our own childhoods through our children; 2) our standard of living has increased, which attenuates the stress of physical survival—one of the sources of family stress that can lead to child abuse; and 3) for better or worse, there is a higher level of screening and surveillance in our highly organized society, where increasing amounts of information about each of us are collected and recorded at schools, hospitals, banks, license bureaus and so forth.

What, then, is to be done about child abuse? We cannot wait for all men and women to become angels to their children. One sensible, concrete proposal has been made to offer preventive mental and social hygiene services at the most obvious points of stress in the family. One such point is reached when a child is born and introduced into the family. This may be especially true for the first child, when husband and wife must now take on the additional roles of father and mother. Assistance for men and women who seem under unusual strain because of this role change might lead to fewer incidents of child abuse.

More effective remedial efforts will await our willingness to spend greater sums of money on community-based health and welfare services. Protective services are under-staffed for the number of cases requiring their help and surveillance. And the alternative child care resources—whether they are institutions or paid individual or group foster homes—require additional resources if they are to be adequate either in terms of the number of children they can handle or in the quality of personnel.

What will we do about this tragic problem, apart from venting our concern for the child, and our rage and disgust toward the abuser? We could try to develop a more sensitive social monitoring network for the early identification of possible abuse cases. But our past efforts in this direction have resulted in only a slight improvement in reporting cases, and these, predictably, came primarily from lower socioeconomic classes and from racial minority groups. We are still, rightly, reluctant to invade the privacy and sanctity of most people's homes. And with the increasing encroachments on our privacy through telephone taps and recording devices, one is reluctant to propose another opportunity for the informers, however "benign" their intentions might be.

There is another part to this terrible dilemma. Neither professionals nor nonprofessionals are likely to report suspected cases of abuse when it is doubtful that such cases will subsequently receive adequate and effective service. Only when they are convinced that involving themselves in these difficult situations will result in positive benefits for the child, and his abuser, will the average citizen be willing to risk reporting cases of suspected child abuse.

Women are rebelling against the notion that child care is their exclusive responsibility, to be carried out with few or no social supports. Two solutions have been proposed to replace the child care services now provided by women: bringing men back into the home to share in the care of young children, and the institutional solution of day care. This article discusses some of the problems involved in setting up day care institutions on a large scale; there is, for example, the danger of setting up large, schoollike bureaucracies for infants and young children. Also, the authors point out certain conflicts of interest among groups who are advocating day care. One limitation of this article is that in pointing out the problems of reform, it fails to emphasize the need for reform in the area of child care services.

Day Care: Patchwork, Realization, or Utopia?

Peggy and Peter Steinfels

Day care is an idea whose time has come. That does not necessarily mean it is a good idea, but simply that it is on the national agenda. It is on the national agenda because it is the common interest of a constellation of forces: government bureaucrats concerned with welfare reform, educators concerned with early child development, women concerned with "liberation." Some of these forces see day care as auguring major adjustments in American life, profound changes, for example, in the form of the family or the status of women. Others conceive of day care as a natural addition to present social institutions, an extension of the school system downward, or a substitution for the haphazard babysitting available to working mothers. But serious contemplation of the implications of day care remains strikingly slight, given the massive proportions of the programs many advocates propose.* The same person who one moment expresses the belief that "our schools are prisons" may the next moment endorse handing over infants to a large, school-like bureaucracy providing "24-hour day care."

It is, of course, a truism by now that reform measures often finish by defeating the reformers. David Rothman's *The Discovery of the Asylum* (1971), which describes the utopian impulses animating the founding fathers of such institutions as asylums, workhouses, orphanages, and prisons, is only

Reprinted by permission from "Day Care: Patchwork, Realization, or Utopia?" by Margaret and Peter Steinfels in *The Family, Communes and Utopian Societies*, Sallie Teselle, editor (New York: Harper & Row, 1971), pp. 42–61.

*Representative Bella Abzug (D., N.Y.), for example, has called for 24-hour childcare centers to be funded at the rate of ten billion dollars annually by the end of the 1970's *(New York Times,* February 23, 1971).

the most recent study to give pause to anyone contemplating a major "progressive" social innovation. If one cannot assume that the future of day care lies along these lines, it is partially because some day-care advocates are all too conscious of the dismal past, even if for many of them it only goes back as far as Headstart. Yet such a wide variety of groups and interests is presently pressing for the expansion of day care and child development services, for an equally wide variety of reasons, that it seems inevitable that someone be disappointed. Chicago's Crisis Committee for Day-Care, for example, represents a broad range of organizations from local day-care centers to private welfare agencies to organizations of the three major religious faiths. The National Ad Hoc Coalition on Child Development manages to encompass both the Family Life Division of the U.S. Catholic Conference and Zero Population Growth.

All these groups seem to agree that services to young children and day care in particular need to be expanded. They provide, on both the local and national level, a large, effective, broad-ranging lobbying force promoting legislation, funding, and administrative implementation. Their vigorous lobbying effort grows out of new perceptions about children, families, pre-school education, women, and welfare, set in relation to what some see as a crisis in family life, child-rearing, and education, others see as a necessary adaptation of basic institutions like the family and schools to a rapidly changing technocratic society, and still others as a golden opportunity for introducing new values into American life.

No set of categories devised to characterize this multitude of motivations and hopes can be sewn together without some overlap here or some sawdust leaking at the seams there; nevertheless, duly noting the danger of oversimplification, we would distinguish three attitudes toward the relationship between day care and the general movement of society.

1. Day care as patchwork. This outlook views day-care services essentially as repairing breakdowns in present social institutions. It is a kind of first aid —for fatherless families, for children needing better care and extra educational assistance, for mothers whom economic or emotional difficulties prevent from providing full-time care for their children. Day care helps to compensate for faults in family structure, educational resources, or the economic system. Goals for day care are thus defined largely by the status quo in "mainstream" society. Day care should bring those disadvantaged in one way or another up to this standard, or keep them from falling below it if hardship strikes the home.

2. Day care as realization. This outlook fundamentally accepts the values and direction of the present society but feels these are far from realized in the status quo. By assuming duties of the home, day care would provide entry

into advanced industrial society for a vast number of previously excluded women. Day care would offer to all children an early educational environment employing the best resources the society has developed, thus equipping the greatest possible number of them for successful entry into a rapidly changing society demanding refined skills. Day care would also buttress certain changes in family structure—its loosening, if not its disappearance altogether—already set in motion by the mobility, individualization, and egalitarianism of modern industrialism. Women and children would be freed from the patriarchal, nuclear household. Society would accept new responsibilities for the care and development of children.

3. Day care as utopia. This outlook views day care as a means of renewing society in a way radically discontinuous with the present. The possibility of changing society by infusing new values into the young has always been part of the utopian inheritance. So, too, has been the potential of women as a reforming force not yet fully integrated into a society largely formed by men. Day care would not maintain the status quo or extend the logic of the society to its full realization, but would in some significant ways attempt to block the present direction of society and start it off in a new one.

Perhaps this triad of views should be considered points on a spectrum rather than sharply distinct alternatives. One could conceive, for instance, of the further realization of advanced industrial society, through the admission of women and the preparation of more children, as a form of "patchwork" on a large scale, even though the patches would be coming to equal or surpass the original garment. On the other hand, the drive toward full realization of the society's logic, whether conceived simply in terms of fulfilling the "American Dream" or more strictly in terms of extending the technical rationality of industrialism into areas which have eluded it, suggests a kind of utopian effort (some might consider it a negative utopia); and it becomes hard to draw a line between those reforms, of the family, for example, which promise the "same" society to the nth degree and those which promise something not only new but basically different. Finally, this triad does not imply some kind of normative hierarchy. Within each category will be found those whose attitudes toward day care is more or less well thought out, or more or less self-serving.

I

The patchwork view, to begin, has dominated the rationale for day care since the establishment of the first "day nurseries" a century ago. That view was reinforced after World War I by the influx of professional social workers into what had been the domain, and a rather flourishing one, too, of amateur "day nursery ladies." Where these amateurs had been unimaginative enough to treat day care as a relatively straightforward response to economic hardship, the professionals regarded the application for day care as an indication of "maladjustment" and a sign of the family's need for extensive casework. It was repeatedly asserted that day care, like patchwork, was only a temporary expedient, with the pious hope that it would be rendered unnecessary by improved family or social conditions.*

If the renewed interest in day care hardly suggests a phenomenon about to disappear, neither does it suggest that the patchwork view has any fewer adherents. They might be divided, however, by what it is they primarily hope to patch: the tax rolls, touched and in some cases strained by never popular welfare costs; the economic duress of poor families, especially the female-headed families who constitute such an imposing percentage of the welfare population; or the emotional and intellectual deprivation of children in such homes.

Day care, it should be understood, has been and continues to be closely connected with welfare. At the local level, the intake procedures and the financing of day care centers have been intertwined with the work of the welfare department. Welfare departments are always under pressure to put recipients to work, and in some cases day care has provided a means of pressuring welfare mothers to take jobs, although the scarcity of day-care space has meant that, in fact, there may have been far more welfare mothers desiring to work but unable to do so because day care was not available than welfare mothers forced to work because it was. At least until the present.

But the expansion of day-care services has been spurred by federally assisted work-training programs for welfare mothers as well as by a growing public realization that the welfare rolls are not filled with "able-bodied men." Day care has become an essential ingredient of welfare reform plans. Whether it will help combine the needs and desires of welfare mothers concerning work and child care so that they truly can better themselves economically, or whether it will be aimed primarily at cutting welfare costs, providing only minimal care so as to assuage consciences uneasy about pressuring mothers of young children to take jobs, is yet to be seen.

Three separate efforts at day-care legislation exemplifiy the great differences which can exist within the patchwork category.

1. The Nixon Administration's welfare reform bill calls for extensive day care facilities within a few years' time. Mothers of school-age children could be obliged to use these and take available jobs or lose all welfare assistance—an aspect of the reform which has disturbed observers familiar with the abuse of work requirements at the local level. Their concern has been

*There is no real history of the over one hundred years of day care in America, a lack we hope will be remedied in a forthcoming book on day care by Peggy Steinfels.

justified by Federal approval of pilot projects in California, Illinois, and New York which would force welfare mothers even of pre-school children either to take jobs or to care for the children of other welfare mothers who are working; a measure, say the critics, raising serious problems of family rights as well as of the quality of care these children might be receiving.

2. Senator Russell Long, chairman of the Senate Finance Committee, has introduced a bill (Child Care Services Act, S. 2003) that would create a Day-Care Corporation to lend money to local groups who wish to provide day care (Senate Committee on Finance, 1971). His bill is thought to stand little chance of passage, but since he is chairman of the Senate Finance Committee other day-care bills will pass through his hands for funding. If his own bill is any indication he seems to favor strong work requirements in exchange for day-care funding, little community control over day-care centers, and a minimum of Federal expenditure, without which there can be no quality day care. While Long's bill has the attractive feature of raising the income level for sliding scale fees and the income tax deduction for child care, the day-care centers would be largely funded by parent-paid fees, almost certainly resulting in custodial centers with minimum standards for staff ratio and programming.

3. The Comprehensive Child Development Program (Title V of the Economic Opportunity Amendments of 1971) emerged from a House-Senate conference reconciliation of bills introduced by Senator Walter Mondale and Representative John Brademas and passed by the Senate and House respectively. The measure, approved by Congress and then vetoed by President Nixon, was meant to fulfill the stated aims of the Administration's welfare reform program by freeing women on relief as well as assisting the "working poor" to move into the economic mainstream. But the bill went beyond work-oriented economic patchwork to offer another justification and organizing concept for day care, namely child development. The first hope was to break the "poverty cycle": if children were given good medical care, sound nutrition, and a stimulating environment in their earliest, most impressionable years, then perhaps widespread retardation, medical problems, and school failure might not handicap the children presently condemned to becoming second- and third-generation welfare recipients (Senate Subcommittee on Children and Youth, 1971; House, 1971).

The intent of the Mondale-Brademas bill was, in fact, a radical departure from previous government attitudes toward early childhood services. The legislation still provided free or subsidized services largely to disadvantaged families (but including the "working poor"), but the bill's language and provisions were concerned with nothing less than providing "every child with a fair and full opportunity to reach his full potential. . . ." In rationale, then, it expressed the realization view of day care as much as the patchwork, suggesting that not only the special cases but the average child as well must be guaranteed superior child care. "The bill is as American as apple pie," declared Senator Alan Cranston during Senate debate (Senate Subcommittee on Children and Youth, 1971, p. 3), comparing the measure with the American tradition of public education. Day care, in this case, becomes not merely a means of repairing anomalies but a next step in the evolution of society.

The fact that Title V was a new departure was firmly admitted, even exaggerated, in the President's veto message, which cited it as grounds for the measure's rejection. "For the Federal Government to plunge headlong financially into supporting child development would commit the vast moral authority of the National Government to the side of communal approaches to child rearing over and against the family-centered approach." By declaring that the need for the comprehensive program had not been demonstrated, that it duplicated in part his own welfare reform efforts, that it was too expensive, that its decentralized local control features left no role for the state governments, and that it might "diminish both parental authority and parental involvement with children," the President signalled his own more strictly patchwork view of day care as an unfortunate but necessary deviation from American norms, a minimal effort associated with the poor and public relief.

Allied to the Mondale-Brademas approach to child care, and similarly straddling the patchwork and realization notions, is the work of numerous educators and psychologists in child development.

Attention to early child development has been part of educational baggage for well over a century (Pestalozzi, Frobel, Montessori) if not longer (Mill, Rousseau). Frobel and Montessori even enjoyed a short-lived popularity in the United States before World War I, but it is only since World War II that such thinking has had a large scale impact here. The work of the Swiss psychologist Jean Piaget and the American psychologists Jerome Bruner and J. McVicker Hunt has had a tremendous influence in pointing out the early and rapid cognitive development of children long before the age of five or six, when they traditionally begin school. From its first day an infant begins to learn, to construct theories, to have expectations about other people's behavior, and by the age of two has, as Noam Chomsky showed, reinvented the basic grammatical and syntactical rules of his language. Such scientific work is the basis for many of the changing attitudes toward children, child-rearing, and pre-school education (e.g., Hechinger, 1966; Pines, 1970).

For a variety of historical and social reasons it has been difficult to put these theories to work. Thinking about the infant and small child has been governed until recently by Freudian analysts; the work of such people as Anna Freud and John Bowlby, with their emphasis on the affective relationship between mother and child, has supported the prevalent American prejudice against the mothers of young children leaving their care to mother substitutes or day-care centers and nursery schools (Caldwell, 1971; Bowlby, 1966; Mead et al., 1967). About the best one was able to do by way of providing for child development in any formal way was to send a child to a nursery school from the age of three, and at that only for a half-day. This was a course almost exclusively open to those who could pay stiff tuition fees, and therefore almost universally closed to the poor.*

Until the early sixties, when Montessori was re-introduced into the United States and some of Piaget's theories began to be circulated, even these nursery schools could be considered little more than play schools. Whatever day-care centers existed operated in much the same way in terms of educational offerings. All this changed radically in the sixties. The beginning of Headstart in 1965 helped more than any other single factor to publicize these child development theories and popularize the importance of early childhood learning.

In addressing its program primarily to what were described as "culturally disadvantaged" children, Headstart inspired a number of programs and techniques especially addressed to the needs of children from deprived environments. From this perspective Headstart has been directed largely to patchwork efforts—to giving children a "head start" in their primary school years, compensating for the apparent inability of public schools to teach, educate, or understand the non-Anglo or non-middle-class child. For the same reasons pre-school education has come to seem an attractive addition to day care. The hope that potential school non-achievers, with the proper intellectual, emotional, and social stimulation, will improve their chances in school is a politically attractive counterbalance to the considerable cost of adding effective education programs to day-care centers.

It is hard to dispute the aims of the patchwork approach to day care. But it is less difficult to wonder whether these aims will be accomplished and to point out the ways in which different patchwork approaches work against one another. To begin with, day care is expensive. The cost per child of full care in a day-care center was estimated at $1,245 a year in 1967 for *minimum* care—that which was "essential to maintaining the health and safety of the child, but with relatively little attention to his developmental needs." A "desirable" program replete with individual developmental activities was estimated at $2,320 per child. In fact, the present makeshift care arranged by working mothers or welfare mothers in work-training programs averages

---

*A recent study of pre-school education by the United States Office of Education suggests that this picture may have changed somewhat. Among children age three and four, the percentage of black children enrolled in pre-school programs (14.4 and 30.9) was slightly higher than the percentage of white children (12.6 and 27.1) (*New York Times*, October 5, 1971).

less than $500 a year in cost, when it is done for remuneration at all (Senate Committee on Finance, 1971, pp. 11–12).

Those who imagine day care as a cheap instrument for getting women off welfare rolls are apt to be disappointed—or else to support extremely minimal care, in which case unconscionable pressures on mothers to surrender child-rearing to institutions they distrust may be the outcome. Such minimal care, of course, runs directly against the intentions of those who see day care as providing a health and education environment presently not available in poor homes. Nor are funds the only question mark.

Jerome Bruner, Director of Harvard's Center for Cognitive Studies, who more than any other scholar and researcher gave the theoretical underpinnings to early childhood education in the U.S., has recently taken a cautious position regarding the present state of developmental studies and their potential for day-care programming. He made special note of the problems that white, middle-class social scientists have in seeing their own theories as culture-bound and therefore subject to some of the criticism that Blacks, Chicanos, and Puerto Ricans have made about Headstart and other compensatory education programs (Office of Economic Opportunity, 1971). In testimoney before the Mondale Committee, Evelyn Moore, Director of the Black Child Development Institute, took a strong critical stance against the research provisions of the Comprehensive Child Development Act on the grounds that past efforts have had little program effect and that they inevitably end—because of language, project design, and white, middle-class perceptions—in demeaning the black child (Senate Subcommittee on Children and Youth, 1971, pp. 366–371). Indeed, scientific respect for cultural pluralism may be hard to attain in developing educational programs for day care. In the same volume in which Jerome Bruner takes a critical look at early childhood studies, Jerome Kagan, his counterpart at Yale, [sic] began an article on "Cognitive Development and Programs for Day Care" with the following observation:

> Most Americans believe that young children should: 1) feel loved and valued by the adults who care for him, develop trust in, and affection and respect for those adults, so that in the future the child will 2) develop an autonomous identity and believe that he can determine his own actions and decide what he alone should believe, 3) be free of fear and anxiety and be able to enjoy life, 4) develop his intellectual capacities to the fullest and perform with competence on those problems society presents to him. (Office of Economic Opportunity, 1971, p. 136)

At first glance such a supposed consensus may seem unexceptionable, although even a casual observer might note a certain middle-class, professional tone to the language (which could simply be accepted as Kagan's way of putting what others might express differently). The fact is that, even in such generalities as these, the problem is greater than one of tone. Though many Americans would agree in theory that their children should develop an "autonomous identity" (it sounds up-to-date, after all), in practice they have something else in mind. And other Americans would not even grant the point in theory. For them children should *not* believe they can determine their own actions or individually decide what to believe. Nor is developing "intellectual capacities to the fullest" necessarily such a clearly held ideal in a situation where other capacities—social, athletic, etc.—may compete for attention. Any reader of Herbert Gans' *Urban Villagers* knows that many Italians, to name one relatively intact ethnic group, think there are community values more important than "autonomous identity." These are not quibbles, for people operating programs can sadly learn that "autonomous identity" translates very differently from culture to culture and class to class.*

Nor is the absence of commonly agreed upon child-rearing values the last difficulty facing day-care programmers. Trained personnel for day-care programs are also in short supply. The day-care provisions foreseen under the 1967 Work Incentive Program foundered on this very point. "Directors and head teachers are so scarce that problems of financing and licensing would seem small next to lack of staff," read one report on the program (Senate Committee on Finance, 1971, p. 14; see also Senate Subcommittee on Children and Youth, 1971, p. 167).

The basic problem faced by the patchwork approach is that in our society quality services, whether in medicine, transportation, or schooling, are more likely to be available to the middle class than to the poor, even when subsidized. The Mondale-Brademas legislation, like the Family Assistance Plan, has attempted to obtain wider support for better services by including the working poor along with the welfare poor in its consideration, and indeed the Mondale bill has received enthusiastic backing from the AFL-CIO. The patchwork use of day care today differs from its earlier version, which asserted that the ideal was always the mother in the home. The new version springs, partially, from a great suspicion that the lower-class family is a defective socializing agent for children. But the fallout from changing attitudes toward work, home, and day care, in combination with the expansion of *quality* services and the change in ideology, may yet, as in so many other cases, limit the poor to the "trickle-down" from the more affluent.

While Headstart has been directed toward patchwork efforts its underlying impetus and that of most early learning research is clearly concerned

---

*For example, the Amalgamated Clothing Workers Union at its Chicago day-care center found that the center's policy of "no corporal punishment for misconduct . . . often raises conflict with the parents, who are more accustomed to responding to misconduct or conflict with a more severe or physical means of punishment" (Senate Subcommittee on Children and Youth, 1971, p. 484).

with the goals of realization, of pushing present tendencies along their logical course, toward equal opportunity for all members of American society to make it through the educational system—a process which has become the single most important standard for judging whether people are employable and prepared to fit into a rapidly evolving technological society. Maya Pines in *Revolution in Learning* realistically assesses the expectation of most preschool educators when she writes:

> The pioneers of early learning want to give every child a chance to develop his capacities to the fullest. Their techniques will increase man's variety, not reduce it. If they succeed, middle-class children will no longer be held back to some comfortable average—and poor children will no longer be crushed before they can learn to learn. Both will be allowed to find their own intellectual identities. Both still come closer to reaching their potential. This should make each human life more interesting, more productive, and more rewarding. (1970, p. 272)

II

We have already seen the tendency of some legislators and educators to treat day care as a normal, not merely a remedial advance in American society. This view of day care as a natural realization of the society's direction also gets support from working women, some industrial and franchise day-care services, and an important segment of the women's liberation movement. At one end of the spectrum marked by this category, working women —some 4.5 million of them have children under six—simply seek a satisfactory solution for a problem which less and less can be handled by family and friends and more and more is viewed as a normal part of economic life. At the other end, futurists imagine our "super-industrialism" logically issuing not only in day care but in "professional parenthood":

> Raising children, after all, requires skills that are by no means universal. We don't let "just anyone" perform brain surgery. . . . Yet we allow virtually anyone . . . to try his or her hand at raising young human beings. . . . the greatest single preserve of the amateur.
>
> As the present system cracks and the super-industrial revolution rolls over us . . . we can expect vociferous demands for an end to parental dilettantism. . . . professional parenthood is certain to be proposed, if only because it fits so perfectly with the society's overall push toward specialization . . . Even now millions of parents, given the opportunity, would happily relinquish their parental responsibilities—and not necessarily through irresponsibility or lack of love. Harried, frenzied, up against a wall, they have come to see themselves as inadequate to the tasks. Given affluence and the existence of specially equipped and licensed professional parents, many of today's parents would not only gladly surrender their children to them, but would look upon it as an act of love, rather than rejection. (Toffler, 1970, pp. 215–216)

Among the more workaday efforts to adjust the demands of child care to the demands of full employment for women are industrial and franchise day-care centers. A few manufacturing and service organizations with a high percentage of women employees have expressed interest in or have actually established day-care centers. Such centers, it is argued, will help provide a stable work force, reduce tardiness and absenteeism, and increase the level of production by insuring working mothers "peace of mind." So far, however, interest—on the part of workers, unions, and the companies themselves —has far outrun action. Many companies are hesitant to expand fringe benefits in the direction of day care. The New York Bell Telephone Company, despite union pressure, has expressed great reluctance to initiate day care for its employees, although it has a 70% staff turnover every year. They cite as reasons cost, lack of adequate space, and the fact that mothers would have to travel during the rush hour with small children. On the other hand, Illinois Bell Telephone has taken a step in assisting its employees by setting up a day-care staff that helps employees find day-care homes in their own neighborhoods. The company gives no financial aid aside from staff expenses toward day care (*New York Times,* 1970; Illinois Bell). Other industries, including KLH in Cambridge, Avco in Boston, and Tioga Sportswear in Fall River, Massachusetts, have opened centers to provide day care for their employees. If these pioneering companies succeed in proving that day care will indeed cut employee turnover, tardiness, and absenteeism and increase production, then it could become as commonplace for a factory to have a day-care center as a cafeteria.

A related development is franchise day care, sometimes referred to as "Kentucky Fried Children." Franchise centers, which must be able to make a profit, are a riskier operation than industrial centers; many observers feel that the future of such operations will depend on the availability of government funds and welfare reform. On the other hand, industrial and franchise day care may end by addressing different population groups, although the result will be the same: easier entry of women into the labor market. Industrial centers will largely serve a population of semi-skilled and skilled "blue-collar women"—telephone operators, factory operators, hospital staff, clerks, etc. Franchise centers are more likely to serve a population of white-collar women—teachers, executives, professionals. They could therefore charge sufficiently high fees, probably stressing in return the "latest" in early-learning techniques for an appreciative middle- and upper-class clientele.

Low-income working women and welfare mothers tend to see quality day care as supportive of their family situation, a means of keeping the family intact and functioning while a mother either becomes a primary or absolutely necessary secondary breadwinner. The feminist movement does not challenge such an outlook, and most feminist literature tries to keep the interests of low-income and welfare women in mind; but feminists' hopes for day care certainly go beyond the income question. For them, day care offers a means of encouraging basic social changes, changes with which low-income and poor women are not necessarily in agreement.

Women's Liberation is, of course, an extremely diverse movement, but the National Organization for Women (NOW) probably represents the broadest consensus. Like other women's liberation groups it has emerged from the general American Left; hence its demands are couched as sharp criticisms of the nation's status quo. Nonetheless, NOW's aims appear more directed at *opening up* the present economic structures to women than at challenging those structures. While NOW has learned from the tactics of black militancy, its philosophical attitude toward U.S. society, if we may draw an analogy to the racial situation, is still more integrationist than separatist or revolutionary. Its thinking tends in the direction of encouraging women to adopt the qualifications and orientation of the male-dominated work ethic. Its three major demands (abortion on demand; free 24-hour day care; equal pay for equal work) are directly related to freeing women from their sex-role occupations and allowing them to participate equally with men in the labor market. It is interesting to note that two of the three demands are concerned with motherhood and only one with the situation at the workplace. Day care is a crucial ingredient in a view of women's liberation which focuses on "integrating" present economic structures. It does not simply propose that women should have equal child-rearing responsibilities with men (which could be accomplished a number of other ways, e.g., a shorter work week); rather it proposes that women should have no greater child-rearing responsibilities than do men *in our present society.* Day care, in effect, would fulfill the functions women presently fill.*

Other feminists like Eva Figes and Shulamith Firestone are more radical in their predictions that present pressures on the family are, and should be, only preliminaries to its total withering away, or at least its transformation into an entirely egalitarian and non-permanent form of companionship.

Shulamith Firestone in *The Dialectic of Sex* has pushed the logic of anatomy-ought-not-to-be-destiny to its extreme conclusions and described

---

*To be exact, a statement of the NOW Task Force on Child Care, "Why Feminists Want Child Care," declares: "NOW believes that the care and welfare of children is incumbent on society *and* parents. We reject the idea that mothers have a special child care role that is not to be shared equally by fathers. Men need the humanizing experiences of nurturance and guidance of another human organism." The concrete proposals in the statement, however, deal only with day care and not at all with enlarging the present child-rearing role of fathers.

the ultimate revolution as one in which the feminist and the cybernetic revolution will have joined to create a new paradise on earth, which would include "1. the freeing of women from the tyranny of their biology by any means available [including artificial reproduction], and the diffusion of the childbearing and childrearing role to the society as a whole, to men and other children as well as women; 2. the economic independence and self-determination of all [including children] and 3. the total integration of women and children into the larger society." In the society which she foresees there would be no necessary sex or economic roles for individuals. Thus the family would become superfluous; children would belong to everyone and be cared for by everyone. Interestingly enough, in the short term Firestone sees day-care centers as they are now constituted as a means of taking pressure off women and thereby undermining their revolutionary consciousness: "Day-care centers buy women off" (Firestone, 1971, pp. 238–240).

Eva Figes in *Patriarchal Attitudes* is equally forthright in her prediction that, one way or the other, marriage will disappear: "Either one goes on liberalizing the divorce laws, until marriage stands exposed as a hollow sham . . . or one takes a short cut and abolishes marriage altogether. . . . Women must be treated as total human beings in their own right. . . . Children must be treated as primarily the property of the state. . . . This means fairly substantial child allowances for all children, and sufficient state and/or industrial nurseries for children" (Figes, 1970, p. 179).

Firestone's and Figes' positions would certainly be labelled "utopian" by most of the public, if harsher language were not employed. Firestone without question, and possibly Figes, and surely many other feminists themselves consider such proposals "radical" and "utopian." But it is just as reasonable to consider them under the "day care as realization" heading: they regard day care as part of a process in which the autonomy and freedom of action of the individual, woman or child, is the overriding goal. Their views seem to be further extensions of an affluent, technologically advanced, production-oriented society which puts relatively little value on contemplation, permanency, tradition, or community.

Some radical feminists, opposed to the family though they may be, nonetheless recognize that its passing would not guarantee a society very different from the one they contest. Linda Gordon, a Marxist feminist, points out that "If it were clever enough . . . the system could survive the destruction of the family."

> The system gave us the vote and equal rights, and it still exploits us all, woman and man. The system could give us equal wages, equal education, and could probably provide day-care centers and jobs for us all. . . .
> In contemporary society men and women could be equal—equally harnessed to the demands of consumption, technology and imperialism.

. . . Child care could be given over to large nurseries and schools (probably still run by women), as well adapted families to the task of brainwashing children. . . . Women could win the freedom to produce children only at will, with partners (or injections) of their choice, and with state-provided facilities for their care, without making themselves whole human beings. (Gordon, 1971, pp. 186–187)

She goes on to comment, "Some of these nightmares may not be so fantastic." In certain strata of society the breakdown of the family is well underway. This development is "objectively revolutionary" but not, the author adds, "entirely desirable . . . nor do we think its outcome predetermined."*

III

It would be unfair, however, to suggest that women's liberation, in looking upon day care as an instrument for modifying the whole family structure, is concerned solely with achieving economic freedom for mothers. According to feminists, the nuclear family is a good place neither for women to spend their lives nor for children to grow up: the nuclear family, one might say, is not healthy for children or other living things. Thus, in concluding that "quality child-care programs are good for children," NOW argues that

Young children need peer relationships, additional adult models, enriched educational programs, particularly true because half of the intellectual development of a child is achieved by age 4. . . . A child socialized by one whose human role is limited, essentially, to motherhood may be proportionately deprived of varied learning experiences. In a circular fashion, the development of children has been intimately influenced by the development of women. (NOW Task Force on Child Care)

Although the rest of the NOW statement reads like that of any parent group demanding the "best for our children," it does introduce a certain utopian element in its suggestion that a generation of children reared outside the grasp of oppressed women would be significantly enriched in learning and experience. And generally an emphasis on the "children's liberation" aspect of day care marks the utopian approach to the issue. Collective child-rearing has been a common feature of utopian schemes throughout history. In the American context it has been seen as one way to mitigate traits thought undesirable in the American character: competitiveness, selfishness, violence, intolerance, acquisitiveness. Such views are current today in the American commune movement—but are not limited to it. One day-care licensing official remarked, in an interview, that he saw day care as a means of creating

---

*These phrases are from Linda Gordon's pamphlet *Families* (Cambridge, Mass., 1970), pp. 23–24. The ending to the pamphlet is essentially the same as that of the article cited, with a few changes in wording.

a cooperative, non-authoritarian society. Children would be changed by their day-care experience, learning to share, to be tolerant . . . and in changing them one would change the society regardless of its political or economic structure.

Other voices of the utopian school are less sanguine about this greening of the children and more conscious of the need to put a special stamp on day care lest it become just another prop of unredeemed society. The Radical Education Project distributes a pamphlet attacking government and industrial day care as a means of "tracking" women into low-paying jobs. "If the need for child care is isolated from other needs, women will be caught in limited reforms that will only add public to private exploitaton." While maintaining women in exploitative jobs, "the day care centers will also train children to be docile, obedient workers that the system needs (Breitbart, p. 7). Another women's liberation document, making a similar case, provides an excellent statement of the utopian attitude. "We think it is a mistake to view day care solely as an issue of women's liberation. We would like to assert that day care centers in which children are raised in groups by men and women could be as important for the liberation of children as [they] would be for the liberation of women. Group child care has a radical potential through its impact on young children" (Women's Center).

Historically, the paper argues, day care has been a function of the need for women in the labor force; if it has emerged slowly in the United States, that is only due to the belief that young children and mothers belong at home. The women's liberation movement is rejecting this latter ideology, but "the movement's present demand parallels the historical attitudes toward day care in its non-child centered approach." The paper accuses the "majority of existing U.S. day care centers" of being "glorified babysitting services," teaching children passivity, programming them through routine, and instructing them in an "invisible curriculum" of attitudes toward work, race, sex roles, competition, and cooperation.

Day care poses the problem of sharply conflicting value systems; and radicals, the paper states, should limit their demands to "space and money" while running their own centers themselves. The precise ways in which the radical center would be different are illustrated with examples concerning sex roles— the treatment of the "housekeeping corner," the presence of men teachers and the like—and the paper concludes: "Although women will benefit from a good day care program, in the final analysis their liberation depends on a total transformation of society. However, the radical restructuring of one institution (child care) can help to transform the society, for the way that children develop is a part of that transformation" (Women's Center).

The Russian and Israeli child-care systems have naturally been of special interest to those who see day care as a means of instilling radically new values. The kibbutzim and children's collectives are seen as evidence not only that group rearing of children and multiple mothering are not psychologically harmful but also that group child care could be a positive and relatively fast means of introducing and reinforcing social change at the same time they provide socialization and intellectual stimulation.

Urie Bronfenbrenner, a student of Russian child-care practices, has supported day care as a means for freeing women—presumably not simply disadvantaged ones—from the isolation and "drudgery" of the nuclear family system. In that regard, Bronfenbrenner does not differ much from the "day care as realization" approach. However, he makes much of the importance of parent participation in day care—male as well as female; and elsewhere Bronfenbrenner has elaborated a new approach toward child-rearing in the United States which reveals sharp differences in emphasis with women's liberation spokeswomen who are primarily concerned with granting mothers economic independence. Bronfenbrenner protests the segregation of children from adult activities and the "real world." He would restructure community, school, and work life to break down the barriers between play, education, and productive work, and between the assigned roles of men and women, of children, employed adults, and the aged. Bronfenbrenner is clearly proposing the family and child-rearing as the fulcrum for shifting American values and institutions in a utopian direction (Bronfenbrenner, 1970, pp. 152–166; New York Times, 1971; White House Conference on Children, 1970).

Bronfenbrenner's proposals do not depend strictly on his study of Soviet child-rearing. But the relevance of the Russian and Israeli examples is a problem in any case. The primary feature of their child-care systems, after all, is that they are only part of a radical, conscious, and planned system for social change within the whole society. They exist in a national and ideological context quite different from anything in the United States.

In general, the utopian approach to day care is far stronger in intention than in program. Government and industrial co-optation is feared; the desire to create a different sort of child is announced, but insofar as the method to this end is described, it seems like rather minor variations on the techniques of other day-care programs. (This is not true of Bronfenbrenner, of course, whose innovations are less within the day care center itself than in the patterns of employment, school, and local community, which he would restyle in order to integrate children with other age groups and with adult activities.) Even the utopian goals are stated rather vaguely. Bettye Caldwell, whose work in Syracuse has convinced her of the vast possibilities of truly early learning in infant day-care centers, has criticized all approaches in this regard.

> With our tradition of valuing rugged individualism, we have been reluctant to say much about the kinds of children we want. Do we want obedient children? Happy children? Adaptive children? Children who

remain faithful to the values of their families? Militant children? Bright children? Group-oriented children? Woodstock and Maypole youth or Peace Corps youth? Eventual adults who can slip from one type to another? . . .

At this moment in history, when we are on the threshold of embarking on a nationwide program of social intervention offered through comprehensive child care, we let ourselves prattle about such things as cost per child, physical facilities, or even community control. And when we begin to think big about what kinds of children we want to have in the next generation, about which human characteristics will stand them in good stead in a world changing so rapidly, we fall back on generalities such as care and protection. (1971, pp. 65–66)

Perhaps what Bettye Caldwell considers a failure of nerve is an understandable modesty before the somewhat awesome task she proposes: thinking big "about what kinds of children we want to have in the next generation." But it is interesting that not even among those who oppose the present direction of society is much of such "thinking big" done.

IV

Day-care services are going to be expanded. If nothing else, the broad range of forces desiring day care practically guarantees Federal funding of some sort. But the same combination of forces may produce unexpected results. Two examples will suffice.

1. A conflict exists between the patchwork outlook, which foresees a large but still limited constituency for day care, and the realization outlook, which foresees day care (and the working mother) as part of the normal pattern of American family life. The former may determine the funding of day care while the latter, increasingly accepted, may determine the demand. The consequence of a demand which far outstrips the supply will be custodial care, or educational care which could easily duplicate the mistakes of the urban school systems.

2. Another possibility is that the "realization" and "utopia" views may be less influential in accomplishing their own aims than in unwittingly reinforcing the ability of some patchworkers to force welfare mothers to leave their children in day care and take jobs against their will. Ironically, the "mother at home" sterotype which women's liberation understandably criticizes has also been an uncertain but nonetheless real protection for welfare mothers against the dictates of local authorities. And if the support given day care by women's liberation, both in its "realization" and "utopia" branches, may prove all too congruent with the aims of the penny-pinching version of patchwork, on the issue of the family it is theoretically at odds with the more generous version of patchwork day care. The latter envisions day care as part

of a welfare reform program with the ultimate end of strengthening the family unit. Women's liberation, on the other hand, has envisioned day care as part of the process of loosening or even dissolving the family unit. Patchwork theorists see day care as a step forward enabling families, especially female-headed ones, to finally take responsibility themselves for their children's upkeep rather than have it be a (poorly borne) state burden. Many "realization" and "utopia" supporters of day care, however, see it at least partially as a transferral of responsibility for children to the state.

One can imagine other conflicts and convergences among the presently united day-care front that may lead to unintended consequences—and one ought to. Those who believe in the great potential of day care would be wise to indulge in a little futurism, speculating on the books to be written twenty years hence chronicling the controversies and disappointments surrounding the national day-care system. For a starter, how about *Day Care and Sex Education?*

References

Bowlby, John. *Maternal Care and Mental Health.* 2nd ed. New York: Schocken, 1966.

Breitbart, Vicki. "Day Care, Who Cares?" Detroit, n.d.

Bronfenbrenner, Urie. *Two Worlds of Childhood.* New York: Russell Sage, 1970.

Caldwell, Bettye M. "A Timid Giant Grows Bolder." *Saturday Review*, February 20, 1971, p. 49.

Figes, Eva. *Patriarchal Attitudes.* New York: Stein and Day, 1970.

Firestone, Shulamith. *The Dialectic of Sex.* New York, Morrow, 1971.

Gordon, Linda. "Functions of the Family." In *Voices from Women's Liberation*, edited by Leslie B. Tanner. New York: New American Library, 1971.

Hechinger, Fred M., ed. *Pre-School Education Today.* New York: Doubleday, 1966.

Illinois Bell Employees' House Organ, n.d.

Mead, Margaret, et al. *Deprivation of Mental Care: A Reassessment of Its Effects.* NOW Task Force, New York, 1967.

New York Times, October 29, 1970.

New York Times, March 28, 1971, interview with Urie Bronfenbrenner.

NOW Task Force on Child Care. "Why Feminists Want Child Care."

Pines, Maya. *Revolution in Learning: The Years from Birth to Six.* New York: Harper & Row, 1970.

Rothman, David. *The Discovery of the Asylum.* Boston: Little, Brown, 1971.

Toffler, Alvin. *Future Shock.* New York: Random House, 1970.

U.S. Congress, Senate Committee on Finance. *Material Related to Child Care Legislation: Description of S. 2003.* 92nd Cong., 1st sess., 1971, pp. 39–47.

U.S. Congress, Senate Subcommittee on Children and Youth. *Comprehensive Child Development Act of 1971: Hearings on S. 1512.* 92nd Cong., 1st sess., 1971, pp. 3–55.

U.S. Congress, House. *H.R. 6748: A Bill to Provide a Comprehensive Child Development Act.* 92nd Cong., 1st sess., 1971.

U.S. Office of Economic Opportunity. *Day Care: Resources for Decisions.* 1971, pp. 91–94.

White House Conference on Children. "Children and Parents: Together in the World." Report of Forum 15, 1970.

Women's Center of New York. "Day Care." Mimeographed.

5

The Politics of Household and Life Style

433

Chapter 12 Out of the Mainstream

Rhona and Robert N. Rapoport
The Dual-Career Family: A Variant Pattern and Social Change

Robert Staples
Towards a Sociology of the Black Family: A Theoretical and
Methodological Assessment

Arlie Russell Hochschild
Communal Life-Styles for the Old

Marvin B. Sussman
Family Systems in the 1970's: Analysis, Policies, and Programs

Introduction

During the 1950s and 1960s, family scholars and the mass media presented an image of the typical, normal or model American family. It included a father, a mother, and two or three children. Middle class, they lived in a single-family home in an area neither rural nor urban. Father was the breadwinner, and mother was a full-time homemaker.

No one denied that many families and individuals fell outside the standard nuclear model. Single persons, one-parent families, two-parent families in which both parents worked, three-generation families, and childless couples abounded. Three- or four-parent families were not uncommon, as one or both divorced spouses remarried. Moreover, many families, neither white nor well-off, varied from the dominant image. White and seemingly middle class families of particular ethnic, cultural, or sexual styles also differed from the model. And the image scarcely reflected the increasing ratio of older people in the post-family part of the life cycle. But like poverty before its "rediscovery" in the middle 1960s, family complexity and variety existed on some dim fringe of semi-awareness.

When noticed, individuals or families departing from the nuclear model were analyzed in a context of pathology. Studies of one-parent families or working mothers, for example, focused on the harmful effects to children of such situations. Couples childless by choice were assumed to possess some basic personality inadequacy. Single persons were similarly interpreted, or else thought to be homosexual. Homosexuals symbolized evil, depravity, and degradation.

As Marvin Sussman notes in his article, "This preoccupation with the model nuclear family pattern and efforts to preserve it at all costs prevented sociologists from describing what was becoming obvious to non-sociological observers of the American scene: a pluralism in family forms existing side by side with members in each form having different problems to solve and issues to face" (Sussman, 1970, p. 42). Curiously, although social scientists have always emphasized the pluralism of American society in terms of ethnic groups, religion, and geographic region, the concept of pluralism had never been applied to the family.

To exclude consideration of these variant family patterns because they do not fit the model of what ought to be is to inform one's theory of the family not with reality, but with ideology. Perhaps the most pernicious outcome of this ideology is the stigmatization of families that do not conform to what is, in effect, a normativist model of the nuclear family decked out in positivist attire. In particular, this ideology stigmatizes the families of the poor and implies that they are the major cause of their own troubles. With respect to the black family, the assumption is that its "pathological" characteristics may be located in the so-called matriarchal form of the family. Yet the research evidence does not support the notion that the matriarchal form of the family causes social pathology. Surely, there is a high correlation between poverty and matriarchy, yet to assume that matriarchy rather than poverty is causing the problems permits the broader society to see itself as relatively unproblematic and to define the family organization within the black community as the source of social pathology.

Changing the Image—Individually

What we are witnessing today is not so much new forms of family living as a new way of looking at alternative family patterns that have been around for a long time. Even the flowering of communal living experiments in America during the late 1960s was not something new under the sun, but rather the revival of an old American tradition. As Rosabeth M. Kanter writes:

> Though many communes are short-lived, there have been a number of utopian communities in the past that lasted considerable periods of time with a relatively stable membership, and there are groups today, such as the Bruderhof, the Hutterites, Cedar Grove, and Koinonia Farm, that have maintained themselves successfully over time. There are over 220 Israeli kibbutzim, the first founded in 1910. Synanon, too, is growing and flourishing, with a stable core of people for whom the community is both permanent home and career, as well as a number of people who come for a short period just to participate in the program of re-education. These communities, being far from temporary, prove that viable utopian communities are indeed possible. Any assessment of such communities thus depends on what the observer chooses to observe —the "failures" or the "successes." (Kanter, 1972, p. 217)

G. R. Taylor argues that the early Christians lived in utopian communal groups, and that the tradition has survived in an underground way for the past two thousand years.

The Challenge of the Communes

Perhaps the most significant impact of the contemporary commune movement may be its challenge to the prevailing nuclear family ideology and imagery. Indeed, as Zablocki (1971, pp. 303–307) points out, the commune movement can be understood in part as a rebellion against the conventional nuclear family: its emotional intensity and instability, the narrowiness of its loyalties, its devotion to material consumption and competitiveness "success." At the same time, nuclear family ideology was challenged on other grounds: Blacks challenged the validity of the white middle class family as a model for all groups in society; the population explosion made singleness, childlessness, and even homosexuality seem to be adaptive responses to a pressing social problem; the women's movement challenged the traditional roles of wife and mother and argued for the validity of singleness, childlessness, unwed motherhood, homosexuality, and even celibacy.

Still, it would be wrong to romanticize alternatives to the nuclear family. Regarding contemporary communes, for example, as the articles in this part show, the gap between ideal and reality is often as large as in ordinary nuclear families. As a number of observers have pointed out, there are many similarities between the goals and ideals of commune members and those of nuclear family members. People marry and join communes to find love, personal fulfillment, and a peaceful haven away from a harsh, impersonal society. Communes fail for reasons similar to those for which individual marriages fail: Communards develop personality clashes, value disagreements, contradictions between individual desires and commitment to the group or family, and difficulties arising from the routine necessities of daily family life.

Can There Be an Ideal?

Is there some ideal form of family—or nonfamily organization—that will unfailingly provide love, security, and personality fulfillment? The answer seems to be no. We now have evidence concerning a variety of family forms: the traditional extended family, which tended to be patriarchal, the nuclear or conjugal family, the mother-child or matrifocal family, and many varieties of communal family. Each offers benefits, but also liabilities. For example, traditional family systems provide lifelong security, but they are often experienced as oppressive by the family members locked into them, especially women and young people.

In part, family life falls short of the ideals ascribed to it because families are not isolated havens set off from the surrounding society. In societies marked by scarcity, insecurity, inequalities of goods and power, anxiety over status, fear, and hatred, family life will bear the stamp of these qualities rather than reverse them. The family, in short, can never be a solution to social problems—in a malfunctioning society it is part of the problem.

Even in a relatively untroubled society, chances are family life will still be problematic, because of the special psychology of close relationships: The family, as one writer has put it, is where you are dealing with life and death voltages. No matter what form the family takes, family life always implies intimacy and commitment. This distinctive intimacy plus the continuing commitment of family life provides the source of both the joy and the torment that are to be found there.

Changing the Image—Institutionally

Surely the internal lives of families constitute difficult emotional environments. But the stress and strain of family is not a dismal certainty, beyond thought and action. The intransigence of the intimate environment suggests a more sweeping strategy of social intervention toward change in the social and physical environments surrounding family life, rather than in the family itself. Despite rhetoric from politicians and others about the sanctity of the family, the institution enjoys little attention in government policy, social planning, and economic support. "Our national rhetoric notwithstanding," concluded the organizer of the White House Conference on Children, "the actual patterns of life in America today are such that children and families come last" (Hess, 1970, p. 10).

Although the White House Conference focused on the needs of economically and socially deprived families, there was recognition of inadequacy in middle class families as well; "the rats are gone but the rat race remains."

Still, most current social planning envisions the conventional nuclear family as the best family form as well as the most prevalent. When housing and urban renewal projects are developed, the women in them are assumed to be mothers who stay home with the children, while father goes off to work, often at a great distance from the home. The housewife is assumed to be fully capable of providing the child care, the domestic administration, the general support and nurturing services the family needs. Emergency services are provided—hospitals, mental health clinics—but socially organized services are considered unnecessary for routine functions. The absence of such services creates strains not only for overburdened nuclear families, but special hardships for families departing from the conventional model—especially single individuals, one-parent families, working mothers, or dual-career families.

The idea of the conventional nuclear family, sufficient unto itself, has been carried too far both as an ideology and as a guide for urban development. Today, it is unrealistic to regard the family as an idyllic retreat from an impersonal society, for several reasons. First, because utopian standards of family interaction, i.e., perfect harmony and happiness, are impossible to achieve and the unrealistic expectation that family life can be perfect imposes even greater strains on family interaction. Second, the emphasis on the family as the major source of human interaction places even further demands on intimate relationships. People require other forms of sociability as escape hatches from the pressures of family life, much as they require the family for its deep and enduring relationships. Third, human beings are nourished not only by friendship, but by a more diffuse and public sociability such as formerly offered by street life in towns and cities and still found sometimes in Europe.

Earlier housing developers and urban planners often included public places for people to meet or merely to engage in the pleasures of people-watching. City planner Charles Abrams has criticized modern planners of suburbs for their insensitivity to this area of human need:

> Suburban development programs . . . have demonstrated little capacity for dealing with the human aspects of community life, and programs like FHA have found little room in their manuals for such commonplace things as meeting and mating, or walking and browsing, or giving people a sense of belonging, or adding something of ourselves to the prepackaged community, or expanding the opportunities for adult education, or providing escape hatches for the sameness of living. (Abrams, 1968, p. 216)

Such humanistic planners as Abrams, Jane Jacobs, and Victor Gruen have envisioned the possibility and desirability of both privacy and a community, where varied social groups, ages, and languages could mix without sacrificing safety, open space, and beauty.

New family values and behavior are beginning to give rise to demands which may implement the vision presented by earlier generations of humanistic planners and architects of space and sociability. The suburban trend is being rejected as both environmentally unsound and socially unacceptable, since it is based on conventional sex roles in conventional nuclear families. Thus, in a discussion of the dual-career family, Rapoport and Rapoport point out some changes in the ecology and organization of domestic life which would relieve some of the strains on that form of the family. Their suggestions hold promise for other forms of the family, including the standard nuclear family as well as the single person:

> To the extent that new complexes of living bring work and family into more easy interplay, as in some of the new towns organized with industry as well as housing in mind, the impediment of the ardous journey to work now placed on women and men, and contributing to their role overloads, will be diminished. If housing developments are oriented in the future to the sharing of domestic care facilities—cleaning, food buying and preparation, child-care, etc.—rather than simply [to the multiplication of] individual living units as seems to be the present tendency, a greater diffusion of the pattern is possible. New mixtures of individualism and communalism may be expected in postindustrial society, with an increase in the latter for the Western countries. (Rapoport and Rapoport, 1969, p. 30)

References

Abrams, Charles. "Housing in the Year 2000." In *Environment and Policy*, edited by W. R. Ewald, Jr. Bloomington: Indiana University Press, 1968.

Hess, Stephen. Letter of Transmittal, *Report to the President, White House Conference on Children*. Washington, D.C. (20402): U.S. Government Printing Office, 1970.

Kanter, Rosabeth M. *Commitment and Community: Communes and Utopias in Sociological Perspective*. Cambridge: Harvard University Press, 1972.

Rapoport, Rhona, and R. N. Rapoport. "The Dual-Career Family: A Variant Pattern and Social Change." *Human Relations,* 22 (1969): 3–30.

Sussman, Marvin B. "Family Systems in the 1970's: Analysis, Policies, and Programs." The Annals of The American Academy of Political and Social Science, vol. 396: The American Academy of Political and Social Science, 1971.

Zablocki, B. *The Joyful Community*. Baltimore: Penguin, 1971.

Chapter 10

Experimental and Utopian Forms of the Family

This report is from what will doubtless ultimately emerge as the most extensive and thoughtful analysis of contemporary communal life in America. The research director and senior author, Bennett Berger, is a sociologist who has recently accepted a professorial position at the University of California, San Diego. Berger is professionally regarded as a rare combination of literary craftsman and sensitive theorist. These qualities are apparent as Berger and his colleagues first make distinctions among types of communes and then pull together general features including tensions, beliefs, and an emerging conception of children as relatively equal human beings. The article is required reading for those interested in understanding the limits and possibilities of communal family structure.

Child-Rearing Practices in the Communal Family

Bennett M. Berger,
Bruce M. Hackett, and
R. Mervyn Millar

Introduction

The report that follows is a schematic summary of more than a thousand pages of field notes and working papers accumulated in a little over a year and a half of field activity by our group. These notes and the summaries of them describe what we have observed in the fourteen communes, urban and rural, which we have studied closely at first hand. These data and, perhaps more importantly, the conclusions which we have drawn from them are supplemented wherever possible by data from the approximately two dozen ad-

From Bennett Berger et al., "Child-Rearing Practices of the Communal Family," excerpts from a progress report to the National Institute of Mental Health, Grant No. 1–R01–MH 16570–01A1–SP to Scientific Analysis Corporation, San Francisco. References cited in the original have been deleted.

ditional communes which we have only visited or studied less closely, and by the more reliable ethnographic literature on communal living which has only very recently begun to appear.

A word is necessary about the organization of the report. Although the major mandate of our study was child-rearing in hippie communes, we discovered very early in our participant-observation that we could not begin to understand the lives of commune children without close attention to the social structure of family life in communes and to the culture (beliefs, religions, ideologies) which envelops the lives of children in them. Our report, then, is concerned not only with the specific character of child-child and child-adult interaction in communal families but with communal life in general, which constitutes the familial and other environmental setting in which and through which the lives of children are made meaningful.

In addition to the child-rearing data per se, therefore, we are reporting other data under the structural headings which bear most directly upon the viability of the communal setting, and therefore upon the role of children. Primary among these are the basic economic arrangements of communal life, the structure of nuclear family units and the character of male-female relations in them, the problems of leadership, authority, and decision-making, recruitment, and ideology.

Two Basic Distinctions

In our initial attempts to make organized sociological sense of our findings thus far, we have found it useful to make two major sets of distinctions: between urban and rural communes, and between what we call "creedal" communes.

We have found the urban-rural distinction useful not only for most of the usual reasons that are invoked to find patterns in any set of sociological data, but for reasons specific to communes themselves. For one thing, urban communes are easier to start—if not to sustain; all it takes is a rented house and a group of willing people. Because they are easier to start, urban communes tend to have a more fluid membership; it is sometimes difficult to tell who is a member, who a visitor, and who a crasher. Around the college, university, and bohemian districts of the San Francisco Bay area, group living is not a very deviant choice for young people, many of whom are poor and in the early stages of breaking away from their parental families. And this fact suggests what also seems true to us: that urban communes represent a less thorough commitment to serious communal experiment than rural communes do, because choosing to live in an urban commune is not so profoundly consequential a choice; it does not necessarily involve isolation from and inaccessibility to one's former milieu, a radical change in the structure of one's daily life, or engagement in unfamiliar forms of work which may require the development of new skills which present a deep challenge to one's very identity.

For reasons like these we believe that rural communes represent a relatively more advanced stage, a purer form, of the "New Age" movement than urban communes do. For this reason, too, a recurrent topic of discussion in urban communes is whether to get some land and move to the country, while rural communes almost never talk about collectively moving back to the city —although individual communards of course do.

The distinction between creedal and noncreedal communes is a more complex one. Creedal communes are those organized around a systematic or otherwise formally elaborated doctrine or creed to which members are either required or eventually expected to adhere: communes of "Jesus Freaks," or ashrams devoted to the teachings of an Indian saint, or crusading communes devoted to the eccentric visions of a self-proclaimed messiah. Creedal communes often have sacred books or other written documents which are regarded as the repository of the beliefs of groups affiliated with a religious leader or movement whose following includes more than a single commune. Some creedal communes, however, do not have constitutive documents or sacred books, but in these communes there are usually one or two central figures whose oral command of doctrine (the ability to "lay down a good rap"), backed by a physical or psychological authority, serves as an embodiment of collective beliefs.

Although in noncreedal communes there is no formal repository of ideology or collective beliefs, there does tend to be a taken-for-granted set of beliefs which is assumed to be widely known and shared by the members, even though constitutional precepts or other written documents are absent. But the distinction between creedal and noncreedal communes is not ideologically hard and fast because there is often very little difference in the content of *what* they believe, and it is this fact, among others, which gives to communes, regardless of whether they are creedal or not, the character of a "movement."

Although much of the hip-communal value system or ideology transcends the distinction between creedal and noncreedal communes, the distinction is an important one for several reasons. For one thing, creedal communes almost by their very nature tend to have a firmer structure of authority (and are occasionally extremely authoritarian) because one of the things a formal creed does is to make explicit the rules of conduct which adherents are expected to observe. Rules against drug use, for example, are almost exclusive to creedal communes. Particularly where the creed is a religious or quasi-religious doctrine, there is frequently a holy man or his chief disciple(s) at hand in whom ultimate authority resides. Members of creedal communes seem on the whole somewhat younger than members of noncreedal communes (a hypothesis we shall look into further when we begin our formal interviewing) perhaps because their tenderer years make them more susceptible to grand cosmologies and charismatic leaders. Because creedal communes are sometimes missionary (while noncreedal ones are rarely or never so) their membership tends to be more open so that at any given time there are likely to be several members or incipient members, who, fresh from the street or responding to the missionary appeal, do not actually know each other or the older members very well. Noncreedal communes, on the other hand, tend to rely on friendship networks as sources of membership, so that members of noncreedal communes tend to know each other very well. Indeed, noncreedal communes may be said in general to rely upon the history of friendship as a source of solidarity which creedal communes try to find in their commitment to doctrine.

It should be borne in mind that these summary statements represent tendencies; our field notes contain examples of exceptions to every one of them. But enough has been said to indicate the reasons for the basic distinctions with which we are working.

What Communards Believe

There exist by now in the literature on the hip-communal subculture several more or less adequate attempts to summarize the values, beliefs, and ideology of this movement (Fred Davis, Bennett Berger, Nathan Adler, Philip Slater, Theodore Roszak, Kenneth Keniston—not to forget Charles Reich), and our own findings have not produced reasons for major argument with them. It should suffice in this summary report to affirm that the ideology is a genuinely "contracultural" (Milton Yinger) or culturally revolutionary one (though not thereby directly threatening in a political sense to established interests) in that its major tenets represent an almost systematic reaction against or disaffirmation of the culture taken for granted by most middle-class Americans of the middle generation.

Thus, they prefer candid, total, effusive, and unrestrained expression of feeling—joy and sensuality, as well as anger and hostility—to the careful, guarded, modulated balances, and instrumental (or manipulative) modes of personal relatedness; "upfrontness" is for them a term of high praise. They want to possess and consume as little as they need rather than as much as they can be induced to want. They affirm the present, the immediate, the *now* over careful future planning and anticipated future gratification. They value the "natural" (for nature is benign—particularly for rural communards), for example, in nudity, organic foods, organic architecture, etc., over the civilized, the synthetic, the contrived. They prefer the colorful and the romantic to the classical, the sober, and the orderly. Their sensibility is given to impulse and spontaneity rather than to calculation and structure. Although they have and recognize leaders, their modes of relationship to each other affirm brotherhood and egalitarianism rather than hierarchy. They prefer the primitive to the sophisticated, transcendent ecstasy to order and security. They prefer invoking mystical and magical forces to scientific ones. Their impulse is to share as much of their lives as they can with the community of their brothers and sisters, sometimes even beyond the point where it threatens those areas of privacy and reserve to which many communards are still at least partially attached. They want to share a mutually dependent communal fate without the obligatory constraints of social bonds; indeed, they depend upon the affirmation by their brothers and sisters of the value of personal expressiveness to enable each of them to exercise an unbounded freedom to do his thing; to engage, above all, in a spiritual search for personal meaning, for health and happiness, for self and selflessness, for transcendence and godhood.

Even so truncatedly sketched in, the foregoing contains the rudiments of a value system, and even if we had the space in this report to elaborate it more fully we would not intend to suggest that it is either unprecedented or logically consistent or consistently practiced or even that it consistently represents noble ideals, difficult but worthy of attainment. Although the contemporary version of the hip-communal ideology contains strong and relatively recent thematic emphasis on elements of Eastern religion and mysticism (much talk of "vibrations" and "flow" and a great deal of meditation and other yogic practice), the history of bohemian movements and religious cults in the West is rich with ideological precedents of this sort.

Like any other value system, moreover, the hip-communal one is replete with logical contradictions and discontinuities between theory and practice. Freedom and communal solidarity can and do cause conflicts, and the balance between privacy and communal sharing is a recurrently thorny problem in several of the communes we have observed. Despite the emphasis on spontaneity and impulse, the apples have to be picked when ripe, the goats have to be milked regularly, the meals have to be cooked and the dishes washed. Despite the benignity of nature, something's got to be done about the flies in the kitchen and the mice in the cupboard. Despite egalitarianism, some communards are deferred to more than others; despite the emphasis on the present and the immediate, wood has to be laid in for the winter, and crops put in for the growing season, and money set aside for the rent or the mortgage and the taxes; despite transcendent ecstasy, the communards have to be discreet about acid or peyote freak-outs in town. And they'll wear clothes when alien eyes will be offended by their nudity.

Like other value systems, finally, the hip-communal version contains as many adaptive responses to circumstance and makings of virtue out of necessity as it contains noble ideals worthy *because* difficult to attain. Perhaps the best things in life *are* free, but that is certainly more convenient for poor people to believe than for rich people; perhaps urban-industrial society will sink into oblivion under the weight of its garbage, its pollution, its racial conflicts, and its individual loneliness and personal estrangement, but that is certainly more convenient for down-home country folk to believe, secure in their possession of the primitive skills it will take to survive the apocalypse, than it is for the urban professional (who may not be able to change a light bulb) to believe. Most people try to make moral capital out of the resources available to them—including, we should add, not only communards but social scientists.

Nevertheless, communal ideology is important because it has serious consequences, as will be made evident below, for the rearing of children and for most other common concerns, for it affects everything from the nursery rhymes which are sung (". . . this little piggy had yogurt . . .") to children to the very conception of what children are: autonomous human beings, equal to adults.

Recruitment

Commune recruitment comes by and large from the pool of middle-class youth in the larger society. Friendship networks in the youth culture, whose members already have some commitment to many of the ideas in the hip belief system, are the major source of new members for communes. In urban, noncreedal communes, it is usually a matter of deciding to share living arrangements with a group of friends or of moving into one previously established by other friends. Given this prior knowledge of many of the people and the ideas they share, as well as the mutual economic interest young, poor people have in sharing their resources for food and housing, such conflicts that do arise are only rarely concerned with major ideological matters, except when interpersonal hostilities are escalated into a moral confrontation (for example, when the suggestion of one member that a Shell No-Pest strip be hung in the kitchen was met with accusations that he was in favor of poisoning nature), or when an occasional major upheaval (for example, a drug bust) provokes a search for blame.

Creedal communes, on the other hand, are usually founded by an individual and a few of his disciples, although they may often expand in terms of friendship networks, like noncreedal ones. While the sources of recruitment are similar, actual induction into creedal communes often has a more formal or ceremonial character, sometimes because the required ideological credentials are more explicit (e.g., abstention from drugs, acceptance of Christ, etc.) and sometimes because they are more at variance (possibly to an extreme extent) with the ideas that even an alienated youth is ready to believe.

In creedal communes, then, there may be books, lectures, encounter groups, initiations, and other rituals that a prospective member may be required to go through in order to achieve one or another stage of membership on his way to fully accredited status. In noncreedal communes, on the other hand, recruitment is much less formalized; in urban places, where turnover tends to be rapid, a new member or couple is likely to be accepted when a room becomes available if he or they are merely friends of friends; and if the prospective member is particularly attractive or compatible, room may be made for him or her. Because turnover tends to be less rapid in rural, noncreedal communes (and because family solidarity tends, therefore, to be stronger), new members are accepted much less easily. Members may be privileged to invite a guest (usually a friend) for a limited peroid, who, if the others like him, may be asked to stay longer, and eventually (if he wishes it) be considered for membership at a commune meeting. In noncreedal communes, then, the difference between transient, guest, extended visitor, probationary member, and member is sometimes difficult to tell: with the excepiton of fully accredited members, the transitions are gradual. While friendship networks account for almost all of the recruitment in noncreedal communes and much of it in creedal ones (proselytization and advertising account for the rest of it in the latter), there is one other source of recruitment that deserves special mention. There is a great deal of mobility—simple moving from place to place—in the hip world, and much of this mobility takes the form of hitchhiking, much of the time with no particular destination in mind. Those who pick up and those who are picked up often strike up quick friendships that lead to an invitation to spend the night. One recurrent form that this takes is for a communard with a vehicle to pick up a woman with or without a baby. He takes her home, where she becomes his old lady. He may leave again a few weeks later, leaving her with the commune as a "member" with an ambiguous status as "his" old lady—although he may not return, or return with another woman.

Another striking phenomenon we have observed is the apparently high incidence in the communes of sons and daughters of career military personnel, an observation which we intend to look into further when we do our formal interviewing.

In our analysis of recruitment to communes, we are currently exploring two interpretive perspectives—one of them, we believe, quite unusual. The first is whether communal development, particularly in its rural manifestations, can be understood as continuous with long-existing social trends, for example, the exodus from the cities, the suburbanization of the past twenty-five years (of which the parents of communards were presumably a part) which expressed, at least partly, the ideology of "togetherness" (much publicized in the late 1940s and 1950s): the suburban family, warm and secure in its domestic enclave full of plenty. Other existing social trends include the increasing diffusion of the encounter movement in middle-class circles, the development of homogeneous communities, represented by retirement communities and apartment developments renting exclusively to youngish "swingles," each of which group comes together on the basis of common problems it has (by virtue of age or some other status attribute) which can be solved collectively but not singly. In this perspective, communes are not nearly so radical a phenomenon as they are commonly thought to be.

The other perspective, of course, is that communes represent a radically discontinuous social trend which is best understood from the standpoint of deviance theory. In support of the first perspective is the fact that joining most communes does not involve a conversion experience for most persons; it is the outcome of an individual's confrontation of available alternatives and situational contingencies, and from that perspective is no more deviant (though statistically less likely) than entrance into business or the professions. In support of the second perspective is the radical divergence in ideology, world view, and personal conduct from those sanctioned by law and custom in the nation represented by Richard Nixon.

There is obvious sense in the latter perspective, but we think that there is much that can be done with the former perspective. There is a sense in which the more serious rural communards, despite their apparently total "rejection" of middle-class, industrial styles of life, may be said to be "conservative" in the sense that this term is sometimes applied to rural or small-town folk who resist the technological incursions of "modernity." Concerned primarily with the creation and sustenance of a relatively self-contained community composed of people they regard as kinsmen, tribesmen, clansmen, they are sometimes distrustful of strangers, intolerant of threats to their solidarity, and suspicious of unfamiliar vibrations. We intend to explore these matters more fully by using our interview data to make inferences about the extent to which the communal phenomenon represents a more or less reluctant and *ad hoc* adaptation for youth without more attractive alternatives, and the extent to which it is a pioneering attempt to re-create or restore some of the lost but nostalgically still-yearned-for rural virtues on a postindustrial basis.

Economic Arrangements

A distinctive normative feature of communal life is the desire for economic independence or self-sufficiency. Rural communes, especially of the non-creedal variety, emphasize agricultural life, and take self-sufficiency ideally to mean that they consume only that which is produced on the land—including not only food, but the making of clothing and shelter from available raw materials. None of the communes we observed have achieved self-sufficiency, but they often interpret this in development terms: it reflects the newness of the commune, the priority of survival, and remains an aim to be achieved at an indefinite future time.

For the present, "unearned" income is crucial to the majority of communes, rural and urban, which we have studied. "Welfare" is a major source of income on which many communes (particularly rural ones) we have seen depend, a fact which serves to enhance the attractiveness of unattached mothers and their babies—in much the same way that in the working-class districts of industrializing England, eighteenth- and early-nineteenth-century mothers with several illegitimate children were regarded as desirable wives because the children were significant more as breadwinners than as mouths to feed. "Crazy" people, with disability income from the state for their craziness, are also a not uncommon phenomenon in communal settings.

Although we have encountered some cynicism toward living on public largesse (it is often regarded as a legitimate rip-off), most communards, like most other welfare recipients, share the dominant society's view of welfare as an ideally temporary, if sometimes necessary, evil; they know they cannot depend upon it permanently, and they know that it makes them vulnerable to the state, when and if it should decide to make trouble for them.

The Department of Agriculture's surplus food program is also an important source of sustenance, particularly in rural places. But although we have been to more than one delicious communal dinner in which the bartered-for freshly caught red snapper was swimming in surplus butter, surplus food distribution is itself too little institutionalized to allow for real dependence upon it. More important as another source of income is a category we call "windfalls," which includes everything from occasional inheritances, birthday checks from parents or grandparents or other unsolicited gifts from relatives and benefactors (communards tend to come from relatively prosperous backgrounds, and the communal movement has occasionally enlisted the support of wealthy benefactors). We suspect that this source of income may be more important than it may appear at first glance, but we will have poor information about it until we have undertaken extensive interviewing of communards (even among persons noted for their upfrontness about all matters, we have so far found relatively little open sharing of information about noncommunal sources of personal income).

Agriculture in rural communes tends to be limited to a well-organized and sometimes extensive garden growing a wide variety of vegetables, and the cultivation of some fruit trees. Animal husbandry, limited mainly to chickens for eggs and goats for milk, is not highly developed, perhaps because it would require levels of technology and "rational" social organization which would threaten the valued "looseness" of communal life at the present time. An expenditure of $10 per month per person for food not provided by the land seems at this writing to be an accurate estimate; $40 per month per person is about the median contribution to the communal treasury expected of each member, but this is an expectation rather than a fact. Some, who can afford it, pay more, and those who have no personal source of income at all may be supported by the group so long as it is economically feasible and so long as he is a valued member in other respects. Communal families also occasionally discuss at meetings whether members should contribute all of their income regardless of what it is, but at one meeting we attended this proposal caused a great deal of controversy and a bitter remark by one member that he would contribute all his income if it were a real family, by which he didn't mean a blood family but a more "together" one.

Much nongrown food is procured through trade rather than purchase; barter arrangements are valued for social as well as economic reasons (as was made clear in the previous year's report), and there is, typically, considerable exchange of vegetables and goat's milk for fish, wool, grain, hardware, and similar commodities. "Gathering" is also a widespread source of food supply in the rural communes we have studied—as in the extensive picking of the rich supply of various wild berries along the northern California coast during what one communard, quoting Keats, referred to as "the season of mists and mellow fruitfulness."

Scavenging is likewise important, although perhaps not primarily as a matter of practical economics; a skilled picker-over of the County Dump in one commune and a cook in another who can obtain and utilize the produce discarded when supermarket vegetable displays are arranged are highly valued people, and ingenious methods for "recycling" a variety of materials find frequent appreciation, though for what seem to us more aesthetic and political reasons than economic ones. Indeed, the motif of "survival" is an important one in the hip setting, and almost anything that contributes to it in what is regarded as a hostile social environment is cause for satisfaction— although this motif is more prevalent among hippies who live in loose-knit "communities" than among those who live in relatively well-established communes. In either case, however, there exists considerable concern for the development of what could be termed a "nongrowth" economic system.

Whereas most rural communes, particularly of the noncreedal variety, see to their economic needs through subsistence farming, barter, welfare, and windfalls, some rural communes and most urban ones, in addition to the latter two, have other sources of income. In a modal urban commune, for example, some members are likely at any given time to be employed in a relatively "straight" job; small-time drug-dealing provides some income in one urban commune we studied closely, and probably in others. But in addition to these, several communes (and near communes), urban and rural, are organized around collective enterprises which are ideologically respectable and remunerative as well: rock bands, "free schools," automobile repair, underground newspapers, and other institutions of the hip community. While not all of these have been a focus of major concern in this research (partly because some of them don't have children, partly because of the ephemeral nature of some, and partly because of the ambiguous status of some of them as communes), it is important to note that the relationships developed out of these enterprises have sometimes served as the basis upon which communes are formed—in which communion itself, rather than the economic enterprise, becomes the central focus.

Moreover, some communes, urban and rural, on which we have done extensive ethnographic work have well-developed "cottage industries" which provide a major source of income. Although there are exceptions, there seems to be some tendency for these communes to be creedal—to adhere to an elaborated system of religious doctrine. The firmer authority structure of these communes may contribute the essential element that makes "industry" possible—namely, a commitment to a relatively regularized and impersonal "devotion to duty." And the enterprises themselves (e.g., a restaurant and an incense factory) bind the members together, require relatively continuous work on behalf of the group, limit outside contacts which may undermine loyalty to the commune, and result in a clearly collective monetary income.

But it is also true that the nature of the work associated with "industry" is accepted at best only ambivalently in the hip world. The avowed and repeatedly voiced ideal is to undertake only those tasks that are intrinsically and not merely instrumentally valued, to eliminate the distinction between work and play, to make work a holy and a personal concern. This is easier to accomplish in rural, agricultural communes, where we have encountered quite explicit attempts to tailor the *pace* of work to what is regarded as an "organic" model: work should be slow, periodic, integrated with, not separated from, other spheres of life such as courtship, play, "visiting," and even philosophical reflection; not, that is to say, "alienated."

One consequence of this morality is actually to enlarge the individual's contribution to collective welfare, precisely because it is viewed as self-serving rather than coerced. In the cottage industries of creedal communes, on the other hand, it is only a strong ideology of "service" that stands between an individual's labors and his sense of doing alienated work.

One of the most potentially important consequences of this approach to work is its application to the status of children. One rural creedal commune has recently been extensively debating a proposal to have children over the age of six join adults in doing the work of the farm; and another creedal commune, this time urban, has actually organized the children around their own cottage industry. The stated rationale for this is that it will both enhance the independence of children and promote the desired integration of work and play. There is a sense in which communards, having rejected middle-class models of "maturity," are faced with having to rethink the definitions of childhood, adulthood, and the relations between them. And there is more than a suggestion (which we are studying more carefully at the present) that this rethinking involves a rejection of the idea of children as incompetent dependents with a special psychology needing special protections and nurturings. Like the big "kids" who are their parents, communal children seem to be just littler kids, less skilled, less experienced, and only perhaps less wise.

Children

The birth of a child—particularly in a rural commune, and especially if the birth is "natural," as many of them are—is often the occasion of a collective celebration of great significance. In the case of the earliest "first-generation" communards, the event can have a virtually constitutional meaning, symbolizing the collective property as a home to its occupants, and the occupants themselves as members of a single family. Natural childbirth is additionally constitutional in the degree to which its clear-cut contrast with the studied impersonality of the hospital setting gives palpable reality to the communards' rejection of those technologies which are seen as depersonalizing of life in general. Since having made this initial observation (mentioned in a previous report), it has been verified again and again in our subsequent field work. (Of course, the dissemination of information about natural childbirth "methods" is itself a technological development that substantially reduces the risks involved, thus permitting the rejection of the "straight" world by communards without great danger.)

In partial contrast, however, to the solidarity-affirming nature of birth ceremonies, communal children tend to be viewed (in rural, urban, creedal, and noncreedal communes alike) as rather independent, self-contained persons—although they participate, to be sure, in the higher cosmic unities (for example, in the widespread belief and slogan that "we are all One"). This is of special interest to us as macrosociologists because the ways in which adults conceptualize and thus "act toward" children vary historically and between social groups, and the hippie "theory of children" is in some respects distinctive.

In viewing the history of how children are conceptualized by adults, social scientists have thus far emphasized the differences between pre-industrial, agricultural, or sometimes lower-class views on the one side, and industrial or middle-class views on the other. In the former view, the status of children is seen as essentially ascribed at birth and rooted in the kinship system. In this view, children are seen as simply small or inadequate versions of their parents, totally subject to traditional or otherwise arbitrary authority. The "modern" industrial, middle-class view, by contrast, tends to treat the child as a distinctive social category: children have their own special psychology, their own special needs, patterned processes of growth often elaborated into ideas about developmental stages which may postpone advent to "full" adulthood well into a person's twenties, and sometimes still later. The task of parents and other "socializers" in this view is to "raise" or "produce" the child (the industrial metaphor is often used) according to scientifically elaborated principles of proper child-management—a process which in many middle-class families results in the differentiation of family roles in a way that transforms a woman-with-child into a full-time child-raiser.

The view that we find prevalent in the hip-communal settings we have studied fits neither of these models with precision. "Young people" are regarded as independent of the family, but not as members of an autonomous category of "children"; instead, their status is likely to be ascribed as that of "person," a development which can be understood as part of an egalitarian ethos, and as complementary to parallel developments in the status of females, from "women" (or even "mothers") to "people," and in the status of men, from being characterized in invidious status terms to being characterized as above all a "human being." Again, "we are all One."

As a practical matter, however, children are not simply independent, autonomous individuals. Age makes an important and understandable difference. Infants and "knee babies" are almost universally in the charge of their mothers, who have primary responsibility for their care. Communards, particularly rural ones, frequently discuss the possibility of "communalizing" even infants—as in the notion of placing infants at an available breast rather than an exclusively parental one, but this proposal seems as yet to be too radical. We have, however, made several observations of what could be called communal child care, for example, collective feedings, bathings, and defecations (this last, a rich scene in which three toddlers in the care of one adult squatted in the woods, chatted amiably about the color, smell, and texture of each other's productions, then under the ecological guidance of the grown-up buried the shit and burned the paper with which they cleaned themselves).

Children aged two to four or slightly older frequently "belong to the commune" in a stronger sense than infants and knee babies do because they are less dependent upon continuous supervision, although even with children of this age the conventional pattern of sharing their care is largely limited to the group of mothers-with-children. This is not to say that young children do not get a lot of fathering; they do; fathers hold the children often, feed them, cuddle them, and may be attentive in other respects. But this depends upon the personal predispositions of the men involved; there are not strong *norms* apparent which *require* the attentiveness of fathers.

But for children older than four or five, the responsibilities of either parents or the other adult communards may be much attenuated. All children are viewed as intrinsically worthy of love and respect *but not necessarily of attention.* As they grow out of primitive physical dependence upon the care of adults, they are treated and tend to behave as just another member of the extended family—including being offered (and taking) an occasional hit on a joint of marijuana as it is passed around the family circle. When problems crop up, children are particularly susceptible to being labeled and understood astrologically, in a manner of speaking, as "cosmic wards" with their own karma or fate and their own problems that they must work out themselves. They are expected to use first names in referring to their parents and other adults (the children themselves have names like "Cloud," "Forest," "Blue Jay," "River," "Sweet Pea," etc.), are seen as the equal of adults (they fall quickly and easily into use of the hip vernacular: far out, outasight, as well as all of the routine four-letter obscenities—there are no "bad words" in the language), and are in more than a few instances drawn into doing adult work. In one setting, the children have, with adult approval, established their own separate residences.

In a previous report we raised the question of whether the variations we observed in the extent to which a child belongs to its parents or to the extended communal family was a variation in types of communes or a sequential development occurring as the child gets older. We are now able to give a fairly conclusive answer: it is a sequential development, but this fact requires a good deal of explication. Insofar as there exists a role for adults in facilitating the development of children, the role is essentially exemplary (charismatic) rather than paternalistic and authoritarian (traditional) or didactic and hortatory ("rational"). In spite of this limitation which learning-through-imitation-of-adults places on the belief that children must "work out their own fate," attempts are seriously made by adults to allow children to grow "naturally," to be autonomous and free. But the single most important belief governing the relation between children and adults is that *the experiences had by children not be fateful or self-implicating for adults;* that adults cannot be legitimately characterized in terms of what they do with or to their children—in rather clear contrast to both pre-industrial and middle-class views in which the behavior of children "reflects upon" their parents, who are in some sense "responsible" for it.

In saying this, some important cautions are in order. First, the great majority of the children we have observed are six or under, and there are numerous communes that are only now beginning to recognize a "schooling" problem; and it may be that in time a distinctive "child psychology" and set of child-management practices will emerge. There may also be important sex differences in the ways adults relate to children; communal ideologies tend to be elaborated by men, and the men are clearly the most mobile sex (from time to time women express some wishes that men would spend more time with the children), and therefore most likely to seek freedom from parental responsibilities—*a freedom that is itself legitimated in part by the view of children as autonomous.*

But the women share this view too, and benefit from its application. One young mother, harried with the care of her two-year-old, said, "What I wanted was a *baby;* but a *kid,* that's something else." That is to say, having "babies" is good because it's natural, organic, earthy, and "beautiful," and besides which babies are wonderful because they represent human potential unspoiled by the corrupting influence of repressive institutions. But "raising" a child involves obligations that they have not "committed" themselves to in the sense that many middle-class mothers, who regard their lives as "settled" and their futures as a working out of what is already implicitly present (home, husband, and children), devote themselves to a full-time job called "child-rearing." But as we have noted, hippies, including communal mothers, tend to regard themselves as "kids," their lives unsettled, their futures uncertain, and they are generally unwilling to sacrifice their own personal questings (for meaning, identity, transcendence, etc.) to full-time devotion to child-rearing. And it is in this context that the hippie "theory of children" seems to us most relevant.

Communards generally tell us that "communes are good for the children" —one of the meanings many of their own parents almost certainly gave to their suburban communities: the setting itself may be said to possess medicinal qualities. In this respect there may be an important continuity between the generations—although communards frequently report that their own childhoods were frustrating experiences of little autonomy and little opportunity to develop "real" skills. In relatively isolated and sometimes bucolic rural communes, of course, it *is* possible to grant children much autonomy without much risk of waywardness, and children do in fact enjoy some of what are probably the real benefits of an inadvertent rather than a compulsory education.

Family Structure and Sexual Relations

Everything we have said about the children of the communes occurs in the context of hippie relationships and family structures, and it is important to understand these, not only because they are the most palpably real aspect of the research scene but because they contain the seeds of the potential futures of the commune movement.

The most important single feature of hip relationships is their fragility. We mean by this not that many of the relationships don't last; quite the contrary. In several of our more stable communes couples have been "together" as long as the commune has existed (two to three years), and sometimes longer. We mean, rather, that there tend to be few if any cultural constraints or structural underpinnings to sustain relationships when and if they become tension-ridden or otherwise unsatisfying. The uncertainty of futures hovers over hip relationships like a probation officer, reminding the parties of the necessary tentativeness of their commitments to each other.

Very few nuclear units, for example, are legally married; neither the men nor the women have the kinds of jobs that bind them to a community; in other respects their investments in the environmental locale or its institutions are minimal. Like many of their parents (whom theorists have suggested have been highly mobile—a hypothesis which we will test in our interviewing), they move around a great deal, getting into and out of "intimate" relations rather quickly through such techniques as spontaneous "encounter" and other forms of "upfrontness." And above and beyond these, there is a very heavy emphasis on "present orientation"—a refusal to *count on* futures as a continuation of present arrangements—and a diffuse desire to remain "kids" themselves in the sense of unencumberedness, a freedom *from* the social ties that constrain one toward instrumental action.

Yet despite the fact of (and the attitudinal adjustment to) the fragility of relationships, there are romantic images also superimposed. Although the fragility of old man-old lady relationships is a fact, communards of all sorts are generally reluctant to believe in a future of serial monogamy. Many communards, particularly the women, hope for an ideal lover or a permanent mate but tend to have not much real expectation that it will happen. Instead, compensatory satisfactions are found in the *image* of the communal family and household, always full of people, where a group of brothers and sisters, friends as kin, spend all or most of their time with each other, working, playing, loving, rapping, "hanging out"—where wedding bells, far from breaking up the old gang, are themselves so rare that they are occasions for regional celebrations of solidarity when they do ring out.

Where it exists, it is the fact of communal solidarity which functions as the strongest support for fragile relations among couples. For when the communal scene is a wholesome and attractive one, as it sometimes is, couples whose relationship is very unstable may elect to stay together in order to share those benefits rather than threaten them by breaking up.

But in spite of the fragility of relationships in a system which defines futures as uncertain and in an ideology emphasizing spontaneity and freedom, heterosexual couples are the backbone of most communes, urban or rural, creedal or not. They seem more stable and dependable as members than single people do, if only because their search for partners is ended, even if that ending is temporary. The temporary character of the relationships is more pronounced in urban communes, both, we believe, because the very presence of couples in rural communes is itself generally evidence of more stable commitment, and because of the higher probability in urban scenes of meeting another man or woman who is ready and willing to enter into a close relationship at little more than a moment's notice.

When a couple has a child, their mobility is reduced somewhat, of course, even when the child is the product of a previous union of either the female or male. But only "somewhat," because of the importance of what we call the "splitting" phenomenon, particularly as it applies to men. We mentioned previously that children (especially very young ones) "belong" to their mothers, and that norms *requiring* paternal solicitude for children are largely absent. What this means is that fathers are "free"—at the very least free to split whenever they are so moved. Since they are not "legally" fathers (even if they biologically are) they have no claims on the child, and since there is generally a strong communal norm *against* invoking the legal constraints of straight society (i.e., calling the police), fathers have no obligation to the child that anyone is willing to enforce. Moreover, no norm takes priority over the individual's (particularly the male's) search for himself, or meaning, or transcendence, and if this search requires father's wandering elsewhere "for a while," there is nothing to prevent it.

One consequence of this family pattern is the frequency of woman-with-child (and without old man) in many of the communes we have studied—although this occurs as often as a result of the woman-with-child arriving on the commune scene that way as it does as a result of her partner "splitting." A situation like this does not typically last a long time in any commune we have studied, although it was present in almost all of them. Even when the women involved say they prefer celibacy, there is some doubt that they actually do. One afternoon in a tepee, three young women (without men) with infants on the breast agreed that they welcomed a respite from men, what with their bodies devoted almost full time to the nursing of infants. Within a week, two of them had new old men and the third had gone back to her old one. Celibacy or near celibacy occurs only in those creedal communes whose doctrines define sexual activity as impure or as a drain on one's physical and spiritual resources for transcendence.

But although celibacy is rare and although couple relations are fragile, this should not be taken to mean that sex is either promiscuous or disordered. At any given time, monogamous coupling is the norm in all the communes we studied closely; in this respect hippies tend to be more traditional than the "swingers" and wife-swappers one reads about in the middle class. Although there are communes whose creed requires group marriage (in the sense that all the adults are regarded as married to all the others, and expected to have sexual relations with each other), we have not studied any of these at first hand. But even in communes where coupling is the norm, there seems to be evidence of a natural drift toward group marriage—although it may still be ideologically disavowed. For one thing, when couples break up in rural communes, it is as likely as not that each will remain on the land; and this occurs frequently in urban communes too. Without a drift toward group marriage, situations like this could and do cause great communal tensions which threaten the survival of the group. Whereas, on the other hand, a not uncommon feature of communes is a situation in which over a long period of time, many of the adults have had sexual relations with each other at one or another point between the lapses of "permanent" coupling. Under these conditions, group marriage can seem like a "natural" emergence rather than unnaturally "forced" by a creed—a natural emergence which, by gradually being made an item of affirmed faith, can conceivably solve some of the problems and ease some of the tensions generated by the fragility of couple relations and the break-ups which are a predictable result of them. Broken-up couples may still "love" each other as kin, under these conditions—even if they find themselves incapable of permanently sharing the same tent, cabin, or bed, an incapacity more likely to be explained astrologically than any other way. (Astrology is used to explain "problems" with respect to children and intimate relations between couples.)*

But the widespread presence of women-with-children as nuclear units in the communes is not merely an artifact of the splitting of men or an expression of the belief of hip parents in the unwisdom of staying together "for the sake of the child." The readiness of hip women to bear the child even of a "one-night stand" is supported by social structures which indicate its "logic." Unlike middle-class women, for example, a hippie female's social status does not depend upon her old man's occupation; she doesn't need him for that. The state is a much better provider than most men who are avail-

---

*We think, indeed, that there is a close relationship between the commune movement, on the one hand, and the complex of stirrings in the middle class which includes the encounter movement, swingers, sensitivity training, and the incipient gestures toward group marriage represented by "wife-swapping." Each represents an attempt to cope with similar problems (e.g., alienation, existential discontents with the prospects or the realities of middle-class life) by groups of people differently situated in the life-career cycle: the communards being mainly college dropouts in their twenties, the others being mainly married couples in their thirties or forties with children and already well into their professional careers with which they may have become disenchanted.

able to her. Having a baby, moreover, helps solve an identity problem by giving her something to do. An infant to care for provides more meaning and security in her life than most men could. And in addition, these women are often very acceptable to communes as new members. They are likely to be seen as potentially less disruptive to ongoing commune life than a single man; they are likely to be seen as more dependable and stable than a single man; and these women provide a fairly stable source of communal income through the welfare payments that most of them receive. From the point of view of the hip mothers, commune living is a logical choice; it solves some of the problems of loneliness—there are always others around; it provides plenty of opportunities for interaction with men—even if they aren't always immediately "available"; instead of having to go out to be picked up, a hip mother can rely on a fairly large number of male visitors passing through the commune, with whom she may establish a liaison. And if she does want to go out, there are usually other members of the family present to look after her child, and other males to act as surrogate fathers.

If these descriptions sound as if they bear some similarity to working-class or lower-class patterns in extended-kin groups, the similarity is not inadvertent, although the correspondence is far from perfect. Communal life tends to be very dense, although most communes do have clearly marked areas of privacy. Most communes of all kinds are typically divided into public or communal areas and private areas. In rural communes, there is usually a communal house where people cook, eat, and engage in other collective activities such as meetings, musicales, entertainment of visitors, and so on. In addition there may be a library, sewing rooms, room for spare clothing, and other needs for whose satisfactions collective solutions are made. But rural communes tend to discourage "living" (i.e., sleeping) in the communal house, except when the commune is crowded with visitors, guests, or new prospective members. Sleeping quarters are private, and one of the first expressive commitments of a new member in a rural commune is building his own house (containing usually a single room)—a tepee, an A frame, a dome, a shack or lean-to—out of available local materials, and ideally out of sight of the nearest other private dwelling.

In urban communes, the kitchen and living room-dining room generally serve as communal areas, whereas the bedrooms are private and "belong to" the couples who sleep in them. Privacy, of course, is more difficult to sustain in urban communes than in rural ones, even though knocking on closed or almost closed bedroom doors before entering is an item of communal good manners.

In urban and rural communes, children tend to sleep in the same room as their parents (or mother), although if space is available older children may sleep in a room of their own or, as in one rural commune, in a separate house. Although a typical item of commune architecture is the use of sleeping lofts both to increase privacy and to make use of unused space above the head but below the roof, children are regularly exposed to sexual activities —as is true in any community where people cannot afford a lot of space. But the less than perfect privacy for sexual and excretory functions—particularly when the commune is crowded with visitors or crashers—although sometimes a source of tension, is not typically a major problem because of the latent communal belief in most places that no normal and honorable functions *need* to be hidden from public view. The high value of upfrontness, the commonness of nudity, the glass on bathroom or outhouse doors (or no doors at all) and the general belief that people are and should be perfectly transparent to each other is not always enough to overcome years of training in shyness, modesty, etc., regarding sexual and excretory functions, but it generally is enough to at least constrain people to regard their remaining shynesses as hang-ups which they should try to overcome in the name of communal sharing of as much as can conceivably be shared.

Nevertheless, even under crowded conditions, communards develop ways of creating private spaces for the activities, such as sex, for which they still require privacy. Thus tapestries will often be tacked up between one mattress and the next or music will constantly be coming from a radio or record player to cover sounds of love-making or private conversations. People sometimes forego sexual activity when conditions are crowded, but we have also seen strong compensatory satisfactions taken from the simple fact of a lot of people just sleeping together.

In the report for 1970 we mentioned that the women's liberation movement would probably not approve of the position of women in most communes. Although this is still largely true, it requires some explication. The fact is that in most communes of all types women tend to do traditional women's work: most of the cooking and cleaning (they are more concerned with tidiness than most men), and, in the rural communes, much of the traditional female farm roles in addition. But it is also true that women share in the general ethos of egalitarianism of most communes. With the exception of those religious communes which have an explicitly "sexist" creed, women can be found doing any but the most physically arduous labors, and in several communes we have studied closely, women do play important leadership roles. But on the whole they are less ideologically forceful than men, and express themselves with generally less authority—although we have encountered important exceptions to this tendency.

Concern over the status of women is more common in urban communes than rural ones (this is true in general of political matters), and female liberation has been a heavy topic of conversation in two urban communes we have studied (along with the male liberation which female liberation is said to bring in its wake). And in one of these communes, there is a distinctly "funky" working-class atmosphere, combining a lot of roughhouse play (ass- and crotch-grabbing, mock-rape, etc.) by both the men and the women, with a fairly equal sexual divsion of labor.

Communal Authority and Decision-making

One important condition of understanding authority and decision-making in hip communes is the fact that the communards are where they are because they have "dropped out" of straight society. One of the things this means is that they are less than enthusiastic and certainly not pious about "democratic" processes in the sense of majority rulings or parliamentary procedure. Freedom for communards, then, inheres not primarily in the democratic model of exercising a voice in the decisions that shape their lives (and then perhaps having to adjust to losing a vote). It lies, rather, in one or the other of two modal forms in the communes we have studied and read about. In one form, nobody is forced to accept a decision even if majority sentiment is in favor of it. In the other form, the individual yields his personal autonomy to a leader, usually authoritarian, whose charisma lies in his command of doctrine which points to The One Correct Way, or in the strength of his personal presence (and the submissiveness of his devotees) which itself manifests what his followers want.

The first form of freedom-authority is characteristic of noncreedal communes, urban and rural, most of which tend to be anarchistic. In these groups (by far the most prevalent on the commune scene) there is no formal authority structure, and although, of course, some people are more influential (heavier) than others, even the most influential typically disavow their authority. "I'm so glad," said one communard at a place like this, "that we don't have to deal with any self-appointed leaders." In these places, routine decisions are usually made by the people with the relevant functional skills to carry out the implied tasks, and this system is made viable by the fact that these communes are typically friendship-based and with a relatively high degree of solidarity. In these groups there is a general reluctance to make any major collective decision or to embark upon any more-than-routine collective enterprise unless there is near unanimity of opinion, or at the very least no strongly felt opposition. This generally results in relatively few important decisions of serious consequence being made—and haphazard enforcement of the few that are, because few if any people have any desire to perform the role of policeman. A typical example is when the persistent troublesomeness of a member or visitor provokes a move to oust him from the commune. Where this occurs, encounter techniques or persuasion are used to attempt to convince the dissenter that what the majority or almost everybody wants is also best for him too, if he would only try to understand the sources of his own dissent or resistance—all so that decisions will not have to be forced upon the unwilling.

But this reluctance to make important decisions does not typically create serious problems for anarchistic noncreedal communes because relative inaction is consistent with the generally quasi-Buddhist-Eastern stance of preferring to stand there than to do something, with their ideology of slow, organic development (particularly in rural places), and with their own dominant, precommunal political *experience* as a minority dissenter, which seems to predispose them to be reluctant to impose a majority view on their dissenting brothers in the commune.

In general, however, this ability of anarchistic communes to get along without formal leadership depends upon the history of friendship which characterizes them, and on the general consensus about the person(s) empowered to speak for the group should such occasions arise. These people are usually the longest-tenured members of the commune, the eldest in years, or the ones regarded as wisest and most serene, and these are frequently the same person(s).

Creedal communes are not necessarily different with respect to the structure of authority and decision-making from noncreedal ones, but they usually are—just as noncreedal communes are not necessarily consensual and informal in their structure of authority and decision-making. (The notorious "Manson Family," for example, is noncreedal but had a charismatic leader in whom all authority resided.) What a creed does for a commune is usually to provide a cosmology, a set of beliefs and a leader and/or his representatives charged with the authority to apply the creed to the contexts in which the commune lives.

It is generally true that the leaders of creedal communes tend to be considerably older than their followers, who themselves tend to be the youngest communards we have seen. This "gap," if you will, often makes it difficult for followers to contest the will of leaders—even when they (the leaders) are not arbitrary or completely authoritarian, because the elders are likely to be in firm command of the official "rap" and its appropriate interpretation in a way that makes it difficult for all but the most ideologically gifted younger people to quarrel with. More often than not, the creed is of an "Eastern" kind, emphasizing the "we are all One" theme, which enables leaders to identify the interests of each with each, and to speak both through and for them. Paradoxically, there is evidence to suggest that despite the firmer structure of authority in creedal communes, there is probably more argument and disagreement in them than in noncreedal ones. For one thing, the leader or guru is sometimes not right there on the communal scene, and this provides occasion for difference in the interpretation of doctrine which cannot immediately be resolved by an authoritative decision. And the doctrine itself is often the source of discrepancies between theory and practice which are absent where, as in noncreedal communes, there is no formal theory to begin with. Moreover, the very existence of formal authority structures can breed jealousies and ambitions for position, which are absent in formally egalitarian settings.

In either situation, however, it is important to remember that formal democratic processes are not salient. Many communards have learned to distrust the "democracy" of the larger political landscape where political choices are "fixed" in advance so that voters' powers can seem merely formal (the Chicago convention of 1968 was a shattering event for most hippies of the Left, and the movement to rural communes sharply accelerated after that event). With their faith in democracy seriously undermined, it is not surprising to see communards turning away from it in the two ways we have reported: either toward leaderlessness and anarchism or toward a mystical authoritarianism in which one's freedom is yielded to a charismatic figure regarded as "knowing the way."

Proposed Work

The bulk of our ethnographic field work is already done. Some of our field workers are still at the communal sites, sensitized to making observations which might replicate or cast doubt on what we have already learned. We have plans to do just a little more field work, in places where we have not been before, where we have reason to believe there are important things to observe that we have not observed in our present sample—for example, in a group-marriage commune. But with respect to our ethnographic research, the major task remaining to be done is a finer systematic coding of our categories in order to make our comparisons of data more rigorous.

The major part of our proposed work involves survey techniques. We are about to begin an interview survey of commune parents and mail questionnaires of their own parents in order to find, most generally speaking, a three-generation perspective on the route from the middle class to communal living. In this respect our plans are still contained in our original research proposal. In the present report, we have indicated several of the questions which we cannot answer by observation but only by eliciting direct information by interview. We have high hopes for the interviews because most of the items in our questionnaires will have been suggested by problems empirically encountered in the field work.

Originally published anonymously in Liberation *magazine, this article is a searching and painfully personal narrative of the organization and troubles of a Berkeley political collective. "We must struggle," concludes the author, "but learn to struggle with compassion." The latter quality was too often lacking as a group of former college students sought to give life to utopian visions of liberated men and women and nonrepressive social relations.*

Wish I Could Give All I Wanted to Give. Wish I Could Live All I Wanted to Live.

Joel Whitebook

Originally, I intended to write a theoretical article discussing the ideological and practical advantages of collective and communal forms of organization.* After personal reflection and discussion with friends, I decided it might be more useful to discuss the firsthand experience I had as a member of COPS Commune in Berkeley.† With the rapid proliferation of collectives and communes nationally, this article may help new groups to choose their direction and avoid many of the difficulties we encountered.

COPS was originally a political collective of twenty to thirty people which had vaguely-defined politics and made minimal demands on its members. After almost a year together, about half of the members felt that we wanted more from a collective. We wanted to move towards communal living, income sharing, larger work commitments, more discipline, more personal support, training in revolutionary skills, and sexual experimentation. Most of us in this subgroup had worked very closely together on the Third World Strike at the University of California—which was our first real experience with protracted confrontation and police terror—and urgently felt the need

From "Wish I Could Give All I Wanted to Give/Wish I Could Live All I Wanted to Live." by Joel Whitebook, *Liberation,* August-September-October 1970, pp. 24–31. Reprinted by permission of *Liberation,* 339 Lafayette Street, New York, New York 10012.

*For a complete discussion of a decentralized organization, see Murray Bookchin's forthcoming book *Post Scarcity Anarchism,* published by Ramparts Press.

†The name "COPS" stands for Committee on Public Safety. Originally the collective was going to work on a community-control-of-police campaign and thought COPS provided an appropriate pun. Later, we tried to shake the name and use Warring Street Commune, but, by that time, the name was too well established and people persisted in using it.

to further integrate our personal, political and social lives, both for support and motivation. The original collective split. Those of us who wanted a more complete organization spent hours in meetings trying to define ourselves and the purposes of this new group. Having drafted a document entitled *Revolutionary Families*, which is surprisingly close to Weatherman's original conception of collectives, we found a vacant fraternity house and moved in on May 1, 1969. We lived there as a commune until June, 1970.

Revolutionary Families was characterized by its simplistic clarity, its use of rhetorical generalities with which nobody could disagree, and its naive certainty. We discussed everything from our eating habits to imperialism. The collective discipline we prescribed for ourselves would not be abhorrent because of our revolutionary consciousness and collective spirit—on the contrary, we would thrive on this true merging of individual and collective interests. We were going to do everything possible to rid ourselves of bourgeois traits and mold ourselves into the best possible revolutionaries. Of course, the problem is that concepts like 'bourgeois' and 'revolutionary' are quite complex, paradoxical and sometimes even self-contradictory.

Throughout our year together we were forever being forced to sort out the infinite dialectical subtleties in the things we had originally taken to be so obvious. Needless to say, our original simple-mindedness caused us all endless torment, guilt and anguish since it was impossible to live up to the personal and communal expectations we had set for ourselves.

Any self-consciously political commune must come to grips with a fundamental theoretical problem which I think is basic in solving most 'practical' problems. Our utopian visions of liberated women, men and social relations are what primarily provide the direction we try to give to communal life. But we obviously do not have the social, economic or political prerequisites for realizing those utopian visions now. The question then arises, how far is it possible to push ourselves towards those ideals given the present conditions, and when does that pushing become self-destructive? In order to pace our personal and collective transformations we must acquire a sense of process and an understanding of given possibilities. If we push too much, we only accomplish counter-productive frustration and guilt; too little, and we are complacent. The general problem constantly manifests itself in questions such as income sharing, privacy, militancy, sexual experimentation. . . .

I would like to make one last point by way of introduction. If I sometimes sound overly critical of our experience in this article, it is neither because of cynicism nor malice, but rather because I want to communicate a sense of the complexity and magnitude of the problems involved. In fact, I would say that the most valuable thing we gained from the experience was just this sort of understanding. The strategic problems of 'smashing the state' are dwarfed next to the problems of getting ourselves together. As one of the first political communes in Berkeley, COPS was highly successful in the effect it had on its members, the services it provided the community and its stimulation of others to form communes.

> The 'hippy,' whose desire to be a 'Man,' a 'rugged individualist,' isn't quite as strong as the average man's, and who, in addition, is excited by the thought of having lots of women accessible to him, rebels against the harshness of a Breadwinner's life and the monotony of one woman. In the name of sharing and co-operation, he forms the commune or tribe, which, for all its togetherness and partly because of it (the commune, being an extended family, is an extended violation of females' rights, privacy and sanity), is no more a community than normal 'society' . . . The most important activity of the commune, the one on which it is based, is gang-banging. The 'hippy' is enticed to the commune mainly by the prospect of all the free pussy—the main commodity to be shared, to be had just for the asking; but blinded by greed, he fails to anticipate all the other men he has to share with, or the jealousies and possessiveness of the pussies themselves.
>
> —Valerie Solanas, *S.C.U.M. Manifesto*

Sex is by far the most explosive and complicated problem to be dealt with. Our experiences and changing views on the subject are illustrative of the way we moved from simplistic to more sophisticated understandings of certain problems. It also illustrates how forces in the movement outside of the house affected the development within the commune. Our year together coincided with the year that Women's Liberation rose to its present prominence.

The problem is basically this: We could all agree that some sort of non-repressive sexuality along the general lines that Marcuse discusses in *Eros and Civilization* is probably the way that liberated individuals will relate to one another. But what does this tell us about our present behavior when we have yet to achieve the political, material or psychological transformations necessary for this sort of sexuality? To take the argument further, as Kate Millett does in *Sexual Politics,** given a general male supremacist framework, abstinence, frigidity and 'puritanism' in general are valid forms of political resistance for women. Thus, as we can see, it is not a simple problem of 'smashing bourgeois morality.'

Prior to moving in together, our discussions of sex remained very vague, equivocal, and generally evasive. They were invariably accompanied by uncomfortable joking. We knew that we wanted our relations to be more 'liberated' and that we were against privatistic monogamy, but we never grappled with what that meant in practice. When we finally moved in, there was an anxious undercurrent of excitement about all the new possibilities. This phase ended in an ill-fated exchange of partners by a group of people

---

*For a full discussion see her chapter on "Sexual Revolution." Although she makes the argument for the Victorian Era, it can well be applied today.

which resulted in several of them getting totally trounced. After the failure of this initial episode, there was a general withdrawal into our well-established, customary sex lives which lasted for quite some time.

Some months later, I came home from the movies late one night and could not wait to go to sleep. When I reached the second floor of the house, I found most of the commune members gathered in a bedroom heatedly discussing monogamy. Although I knew that there was something wrong with the way people were talking about the subject, I could not yet explain what it was. This uncertainty, combined with my own defensiveness about being in a couple, caused everything in me to resist becoming involved in the meeting. But I knew that there was no way to avoid it.

My uneasiness was due, in part, to the way the subject had arisen. Several COPS people, having been severely challenged by a group of Weathermen about monogamy, returned to the house and began pushing the debate. I had always been suspicious of the vulgar way the Weathermen handled the subject of 'smashing monogamy.'

Briefly, these are the main arguments that were raised against monogamy: (1) Previously, when couples had been broken up, it had released new strength and energy in the woman. (2) The two members of a couple make an implicit 'deal' to never question certain fundamental aspects of their lives, for such questioning might undermine their stability and security as a couple. (3) In collective struggle situations, when one member of a couple gets attacked, the other member protects her or him. (4) Rather than sharing their problems with many of the other people in the house, which would serve to communalize private experience, one member of a couple tends to rely solely on the other for help with personal problems. (5) Since a couple is a somewhat self-sufficient unity, they tend to withdraw to their own rooms and thereby privatize space in the house and lessen collective activity. And (6) monogamy is a bourgeois, propertied relationship where one person tries to possess another because of all sorts of inadequacies.

Throughout the argument, I had the feeling that it was not the specific principles of the debate itself that motivated people, but rather a general feeling that we were just not moving fast enough in transforming our personal lives, a fear that we were just still too bourgeois.

It was one of those discussions which confused me so much that I found it excruciatingly uncomfortable to sit through. The confusion resulted, as it always did in highly personal debates, from my inability to distinguish whether I held a position because of its objective truth or because of some subjective, psychological mechanism on my part. (Even now as I write, I do not know whether it is from an understanding of the real situation or from a need to rationalize the way I live my life.)

The discussion went around and around well into the night when one of the women had a flash which I think provided a key to understanding much about the sexual roles and social dynamics of the house. She realized that the men were doing almost all of the talking, and, moreover, that the heated way in which they were talking revealed their tremendous ego-investments in the subject. 'Smashing monogamy,' at least the way we were talking about it, was a male trip. Once this was brought into the open, many of the other women admitted that they had objected to what was going on but had been too intimidated to speak up. They said they were afraid of being bourgeois, unliberated, or whatever you choose to call it.

In retrospect, it had also been the men who had always talked the most about sexual liberation and who had initiated what ill-fated sexual experimentation had actually taken place. It is tempting to attribute this solely to the men's desire to sleep with many women, and this undoubtedly played a part. But I think the explanation is far more insidious than the mere *physical* excitement and satisfaction gained from sexual variety. To be a successful movement male, one has to prove that as well as being intelligent, militant and articulate, he is also sexually liberated; sexual liberation is another arena for movement macho competition. It was not even the desire for the women as sexual objects, must less as human beings, that primarily motivated the men. Rather, it was the need to establish their image among the men, and their position in the social hierarchy of the house.

Disturbed by the passive roles that they had allowed themselves to be forced into, the women decided to hold separate meetings regularly. These meetings continued for quite a while, but I do not think that they ever attained the sense of unity and excitement that all the women had experienced at women's meetings outside of the house. It was soon realized, regardless of their intentions, given the situation of the commune, the women's first loyalties were not to their communal sisters but to the men of the house—whether their own individual man or the men in general. At women's meetings it was always agreed that they would support each other in situations with the men, but as soon as one arose, this promised solidarity failed to materialize. I think that this major shortcoming of COPS can be partially explained by the original composition of the commune which consisted of five couples, two single women and a single man. Nevertheless, I am afraid that it might be a severe problem for any sexually mixed commune.

Reacting through fear and guilt to the women's meetings, the men also began holding meetings. The discussions stayed within safe boundaries that were established very early. It was permissible to discuss all the ways we were insensitive to women, all the sexist prejudices we each had and all the ways we behaved chauvinistically. But we never discussed the ways we related to each other as concrete individuals in any substantive way. At best, we discussed men in general. Our images of ourselves and each other, the competition between us, and our sexual feelings about one another were all *verboten*.

The commune never reached any explicit consensus or position on the questions of monogamy and sex in general. However, I imagine that many of us, having shared the same experience, have reached similar conclusions. The following, therefore, are provisional conclusions that I have reached after a year of communal living. I stress their tentativeness, for one of the lessons of the past year is how rapidly opinions on these subjects can change.

First, I think far too much emphasis is put on sexual practice, often taking it as an end in itself rather than as a means of enriching personal relationships. What sort of sex is performed is irrelevant; what matters is the emotional effect on the people involved. To use social science jargon, it is not the behavior that is important but the attitudes. Sexual practice—whether it be having intercourse with the pet cat or complete abstinence—should only be evaluated in terms of its increasing affection, openness, trust, pleasure, respect and support between those involved.* Just the opposite is now commonly the case. Sexual relationships are evaluated almost entirely in terms of the acts performed—how far they deviate from bourgeois sexual behavior —ignoring the emotional component of the relationship. The essence of bourgeois does not lie in the acts performed but in its dehumanization. The very emphasis on the act is itself a bourgeois perspective. Sexual liberation too often becomes a rationale for practice which is emotionally destructive.

I would like to draw a two-fold conclusion concerning the question of monogamy: We must do everything within our power to transcend it, while simultaneously guarding against the formalistic, destructive way that much of the movement has dealt with the question. There is no doubt that monogamy is an inherently insidious form which ultimately has no redeeming characteristics. It is founded on insecurity, possessiveness and jealousy as well as economic domination. For the woman, it is nothing more than an exchange of her human potential for a chimerical security. Moreover, the relationships of domination which result from this exchange become through the children the source of the slave mentality which infects all our social relations.

The error that is often made with disastrous consequences in dealing with

---

*By not advocating a concrete sexual practice such as homosexuality or group sex, I realize that I might be accused of a liberalism of sorts. It might be argued that my lack of specificity could be used to rationalize complacency about sexual practice. People could retain basically exploitative sexual practice which might satisfy the false emotional needs of their social conditioning. They could therefore maintain that their sexual practice was enhancing their emotional relationship. My only reply is that these needs are false, and the sort of emotional evaluation that I am talking about requires a critical grasp of true needs. I believe that anyone who has a true sense of these emotions could not continue the sort of sexual practice, whether group or individual, that they have been socially taught.

monogamy is to mistake mere form for the essence. Although monogamy may manifest itself in the bed, it primarily exists in the head as a nexus of attitudes. Those socially caused and reinforced attitudes are not transformed simply by ending their contingent manifestations. At the risk of seeming trite, we must deal with the cause of the illness and not its symptoms. To transcend monogamy we must wholeheartedly plunge into its attitudinal basis and not mechanistically rearrange our sleeping habits.

The key to transforming these deformed attitudes is trust and support— human solidarity. Couples must be helped to grow into a part of a larger collectivity rather than being coerced to dissipate into an atomized unit which often lends itself to hustling and being hustled. They must feel they are gaining something rather than losing something. This sort of support requires hours of patient discussion and analysis of the most obscure and fundamental minutiae of our psyches.

Every aspect of our communal life, from the quality of the meals to the productivity of our meetings, followed a surprisingly regular cycle of degeneration and regeneration. To understand this cycle, one must have a sense of the psychological riskiness of living in a commune. There were occasions when entering the front door was such a brutalizing experience that I seriously considered climbing the fire escape to my room to avoid encountering anyone. With tears constantly welled up in my eyes there were weeks on end when I experienced the house as totally hostile 'Otherness.' Given this potential for hostility, it is understandable that everyone wanted to protect themselves and was reluctant to take psychological risks.

Yet, in order to function, a commune requires constant investments of psychic energy and commitment. Withdrawal of the psychic investment by any one person can cause a crisis of confidence which, in turn, sends all the other dominoes tumbling. The primary communal task is maintaining confidence, and this is subject to the vicissitudes of everything from an individual's unconscious to international politics—most factors are far beyond our awareness, much less our control.

Our attempts to hold regular house meetings illustrate many of the difficulties in trying to wrestle commitment from commune members. If nothing else, we were a group of meeting goers, sometimes attending three or four a day. With these heavy schedules, it is understandable that everyone would covet their time. Yet, problems of personal transformation, home economics, communal psychology and house politics required regular meetings. Periodically we would once again decide to hold regular house meetings. We would then explain to each other how essential these meetings were and how each of us had tremendous individual power over their success or failure.

The delicate nature of these commitments and their strong tendency towards dissipation always amazed me. For instance, at one point, we decided to hold meetings at nine o'clock on Sunday morning—'Sunday morning struggle sessions'—and stressed the importance of beginning promptly. Several members were inevitably late, and the consequences of their tardiness went far beyond mere annoyance at the inconvenience. For this coming late was a way of symbolically announcing one's independence from the collectivity; it was a semi-conscious, arrogant way of protecting one's private prerogative. And as an announcement of independence, it had the effect of sending everyone psychologically scurrying to protect their vulnerable Selfs from the awesome collectivity. It might be objected that I am over-psychologizing or belaboring the trivial, but it is precisely these apparently trivial incidents that have repercussions far out of proportion to their seeming unimportance.

There was another side to this problem of withholding commitment, for when any of us did it at some level of consciousness we were each painfully aware of it and of the consequences. Constantly aware of our shortcomings, we suffered from guilt and self-hatred which was often unleashed on our communal sisters and brothers. The more bourgeois someone felt, the more she or he bourgeois-baited others.

For instance, an unobserved, minor infraction of communal ethics, such as doing a poor job in cleaning up the kitchen or failing to put gas in a car after using it, could be the hidden cause of quite violent and personal and political confrontations. Originally motivated by the need for defiance, the offender usually grew to feel that her or his motives and guilt were totally transparent to everyone. In fact, I was always surprised to find out how much harsher the view I had of myself was than the view others had of me. The way to shield oneself from this feeling of transparency was usually to posture—to act "more revolutionary-than-thou." As a result, people often found themselves adamantly advocating absurd positions and viciously impugning things to others that they themselves felt guilty of. We had unbelievably violent debates over everything from whether it was bourgeois to shower in the morning, to the merits of adventuristic acts of militance that none of us had any intention of doing.

The physical objects surrounding us, most of them the left-over trappings of our previous lives as students, were some of the most persistent reminders of our revolutionary shortcomings. On the one hand, we were constantly paring down, but nonetheless always seemed to have too much. On the other hand, keeping things, like hi-fi's and cars, was security for the future; although the house was glutted with them now, after all the commune wasn't going to last forever. But as security objects they also indicated the limitations of our commitment to the collectivity, and how we were still keeping an eye out for ourselves. Again, we fell into all sorts of mind games in trying to vindicate ourselves of the guilt we felt over our possessions.

For example, a car owner was constantly faced with a dilemma. Car upkeep is both time-consuming and costly. A car can be an enormous convenience and most people would like to keep theirs for as long as possible. Yet feelings of anxiety over the condition of a car, no matter how legitimate, were inevitably accompanied by feelings of guilt over being so uptight. When somebody asked to borrow a car, with mixed feelings one always wanted to emphasize the importance of taking care of it. The borrower invariably resented this both as a sign of distrust, often justified, and as an indication that the owner was watching out for herself or himself. Out of this resentment, the borrower might often be semi-purposely irresponsible, and justify it by saying property is bourgeois. This would, in turn, reinforce the owner's anxiety and thereby his dilemma, only to perpetuate the vicious circle even further. This was a pattern that was repeated with most possessions.

One last point before concluding. There were very good reasons to protect yourself. Inter-communal brutality was not only the result of hidden 'psychological' factors. Like any other presently existing social unity, a commune, regardless of how revolutionary it is, is permeated with hierarchy, competition and domination. There are structural incentives which induce psychological violence. There are real things to be won and lost. The collective interest of revolutionaries is not much more harmonious than that of any other social group. And this is the real heartbreaker: After running from the terror of functioning within bourgeois social institutions and finally ending up in the libertarian wing of the movement, I discovered that the dynamics of in-groups and out-groups, of pecking orders and advancing yourself at the expense of yourself as well as others, is—although more confusing because of its political garb—every bit as brutal as was my adolescent peer group, a prototype of bourgeois social barbarism.

The communal hierarchy was calibrated in units of 'revolutionaryness.' To be on top was to be the most revolutionary. There were basically two paths of ascent. If one felt confident enough, one took the direct path, trying to establish oneself in fairly traditional terms of what it means to be revolutionary—disciplined, energetic, militant, self-sacrificial, etc. The indirect path was better suited for the less confident. This path consists in redefining what it means to be revolutionary, usually in more personal and cultural terms.* Of course, these are the two polar positions and there were many

*The discussion of which emphasis or combination of emphases is most *objectively* appropriate at this point in history is a topic for another article, in fact the theoretical article that I decided not to write in order to write the present piece.

combinations between them. Thus on any given issue there was a continuum from the 'hards' to the 'softs.' Regardless of the content of the debate, people usually took the same position on the spectrum. The actual content of a debate always went far beyond the apparent topic being discussed.

For example, a dispute over whether or not we should eat meat and, if so, how often?—the famous meaties-vegies debate—became a cram-packed metaphor for the way each of us saw ourselves and others on the hard-soft continuum. Vegetarianism, or concerns over health foods, was only one symbolic aspect of the whole socio-political *gestalt* which included an emphasis on the inner workings of the commune, on not playing the part of the professional revolutionary, and on the importance of the cultural revolution. A meatie, even the symbology is so consistent, subscribed to a different socio-political totality. Their emphasis was on political work outside the house even to the detriment of our communal togetherness, on being disciplined full-time organizers, and on the co-optable nature of youth culture as opposed to internationalism.

One important political lesson that I have learned from this is that in order to evaluate a position somebody holds, it is necessary to understand the socio-psychological setting in which they hold it. This is not to say that there are not objective canons for judging the validity of a position. It's just that the problem of subjectivity is greater than I had ever imagined; it is extremely important to sort out an advocate's psychological predispositions in order to consider the merits of the position itself.

I do not think that despair need any longer follow from a severe view of movement competitiveness. I just do not think that the Left should delude itself about its humanity nor harbor any illusions about the extent to which it has rid itself of bourgeois remnants. The point is not how malignant movement people are. It is not a question of intentions. It is just that the methods we use to transcend our pasts, pasts that we all know provide no possibility for happiness, are constantly being subverted by the very things they are meant to overcome. But recently there have been very encouraging developments, especially in the more advanced parts of the women's movement. With its critique of movement macho, its grounding of all forms of oppression in sexism and patriarchy rather than mere economics, its critique of the quality of daily life, its decentralized organization and its rejection of elites and leaders, women's liberation holds the promise of a way out of the mire from which there previously seemed to be no exit.

I would like to now return to a question I raised in the introduction, and that is how do we pace our collective and personal transformations? Most of the steps forward, such as communalizing personal property, being risky ventures, require a high degree of confidence and trust. But given the psychological dangers of communal living, it is a wonder that any of these steps are ever taken. Our experience was that there is a great unevenness in people's readiness to move. At any given time, one group of people would be up to taking risks and another would not, while at another time the positions might be exactly reversed. The people who were ready to move felt they were being held back, and those not ready to move felt they were being pushed too hard. To resolve the problem we tried several experiments where only the people who felt ready in a given area moved on their own. Rather than providing a solution, this would usually cause problems of in-groups and out-groups and subtle competition; we were never able to let a subgroup act semi-independently in good faith.

For two reasons, the problem is not a mere question of waiting for a personal sense of readiness. First, we are all, to one degree or another, complacent, and without external provocation would remain unmotivated on certain issues. And, second, if we wait until everybody is ready on a particular issue, we will never move, for everybody will never be simultaneously ready. There are certain issues we are each predisposed never to move on and need the prodding of our sisters and brothers to break out of self-reinforcing systems of rationalization, false needs and false consciousness which all serve to perpetuate our complacency. It simply cannot be done in isolation. The other side of the question of complacency is the danger of destructive coercion. For when we do not understand ourselves in terms of existing in a given set of conditions and possibilities in terms of an unfolding process, we push one another to live up to unattainable, necessarily frustrating, abstract revolutionary ideals. This usually results in immobilizing self-hatred. There are shattered egos scattered all around the country as a result of 'self-criticism' sessions. Right on!

If we cannot wait for everyone to be in the proper headset before we move, then just how do we proceed? The only logical solution of the problem is to be able to move even when some people feel unready, and this presupposes establishing a very special sort of trust, a trust which COPS never attained as a whole, but which existed between certain individuals. This trust consists of a sense that your subjective worldview, the way you see and feel things around you, is shared; an understanding that although you are plagued by remnants from the past, that although you are capable of betraying and crushing one another, you hate yourselves for it and, in a very real sense, you do it unintentionally; of a sense that you share a similar vision and are moving in the same general direction; of a sense that no one person is any more guilty for the shortcomings of the commune than another, for every member has his own area of deficiency which will surface sooner or later; and finally, of a sense that you are all in the same lifeboat on the same angry sea, where everyone or no one will make it. We must struggle, but learn to struggle with compassion.

The author is a sociologist who has conducted major historical research on communes. In this article, she compares major social and cultural features of earlier groups and contemporary communal arrangements. Earlier groups sought to build long-standing utopian communities. Contemporary communes are more anarchic in philosophy and attempt to create utopian family-style intimacy. The high failure rate of individual communes, contends the author, is no sure indication of the failure of the movement.

'Getting It All Together': Some Group Issues in Communes	Rosabeth Moss Kanter

Communes are both an old and a new social form. Some kind of communal living was practiced by a small number of groups in the United States even before its establishment as a nation, and many groups today look to those older traditions for their inspiration. On the other hand, today's communes are new in their large numbers, high visibility, and limited goals. While many communal groups of the past were a response to institutional strains in the society (religious, economic, or political), and sought to become full-fledged alternative communities, today's communes are more often a response to interpersonal and psychological strains in the society, and want to become a new kind of family (Kanter, 1972). Many communes today seek to recreate a romanticized version of the extended family, in a search for intense, intimate, participatory, meaningful, group-based ways of life. In the midst of an advanced technological society seen as isolating, meaningless, fragmented, and machine-like, today's utopians seek a shared life. They desire freedom and the concomitant ability to define their own life conditions. They want to be "together" in all ways that the new counter-culture uses this word: inner peace and self-acceptance; whole person relating to whole person; barriers of ego, property, sex, age disappearing.

The result of today's quest for togetherness is the vast number of experiments in communal living springing up across the country. There are small urban groups sharing living quarters and raising their families together while holding outside jobs. There are rural farming communes combining work

From Rosabeth Moss Kanter, " 'Getting it all Together': Some Group Issues in Communes," *The American Journal of Orthopsychiatry*, 42(4), July 1972. Copyright © the American Orthopsychiatric Association, Inc. Reproduced by permission. An expanded version of the ideas in this article is to be found in Rosabeth Moss Kanter, *Commitment and Community: Communes and Utopias in Sociological Perspective*, (Cambridge: Harvard University Press, 1972).

life and family life under one roof. There are formal organizations with their own business enterprises, like the Bruderhof communities, which manufacture Community Playthings (Zablocki, 1971); and there are loose aggregates of people without even a name for their group. Some communities, like those forming around personal growth and learning centers, may create a total life-style for their members: sleeping, waking, working, playing, loving, eating, even breathing, all guided by the philosophies of the group. Others experiment in more limited ways, several couples, for example, trying group marriage. There are differences in the degree of collectivization—whether the communal group shares only space or also property, money, work, and values. There are differences in ideology—from spiritual groups with a religious philosophy, to *Walden Two* groups modeled after Skinner's utopia governed by experts and scientific experimentation (Kanter, 1972; Newman and Wilhelm, 1970), to self-help communities such as Synanon or Camp Hill Village, to Open Land communes without any intentional qualities, to friendship groups that want nothing more than to share their lives and their children in a richer way. There are also differences in size—from six people in a house in Boston to over 200 in a Bruderhof village.

The extent of the commune movement is vast, but similarly vast are the problems of building viable communities. Today's communal movement represents a reawakening of the search for utopia that has been carried out in America from as early as 1680, when the first religious sects retreated to the wilderness to live in community. But while experiments in communal living have always been part of the American landscape, only a few dozen of these ventures survived for more than a few years. Building community has proven to be difficult, and today's communes fall heir to the difficulties.

Communes of the Past

Previous research (Kanter, 1968, 1972) has uncovered some of the things that distinguished successful communes of the past. In order to learn about the kinds of things that make a commune work, this research compared thirty nineteenth-century American communes—nine that lasted thirty-three years or more (called "successful") with twenty-one that existed less than sixteen years and on the average about four years ("unsuccessful"). Among the communes in the study were the Shakers, Oneida, Amana, Harmony, New Harmony, and Brook Farm. The study asked over 120 questions about the presence or absence of certain social arrangements that build commitment and create a strong group.

Successful nineteenth-century communities built strong commitment to their group through the kinds of sacrifices and investments members made for and in the community, through discouraging extra-group ties and building strong family feeling within the community, through identity change processes for members, and through ideological systems and authority structures that gave meaning and direction to the community.

Long-lived communities tended to require some sacrifices of their members as a test of faith, and full investment of money and property, so that participants had a stake in the fate of the community. They tended to ensure the concentration of loyalty within the community by geographical separation and by discouraging contact with the outside. They spread affection throughout the whole community by discouraging exclusive relationships based on two-person attraction or biological family—through either free love (in which sexual contact with all others was required) or celibacy (in which no one had sexual contact) and separation of biological families with communal child-rearing. These mechanisms aimed at creating an equal share in man-woman and adult-child relationships for everyone. Family feeling was enhanced by selection of a homogeneous group of members; by full communistic sharing of property; by communistic labor in which no jobs were compensated, everyone shared equally in community benefits, jobs were rotated through the membership, and some work was done by the whole community; by regular group contact through meetings (routine decision-making ones and T-group-like sessions); and by rituals emphasizing the communion of the whole. Identity change processes in long-lived communes tended to consist of T-group-like mutual criticism sessions in which issues of commitment and deviance and meeting of community standards were examined, and through stratification systems that accorded deference to those best living up to community norms. Finally, long-lived communes tended to have elaborate ideologies providing purpose and meaning for community life and an ultimate guide and justification for decisions. There tended to be strong central figures, charismatic leaders who symbolized the community's values and who made final decisions for the community and set structural guidelines. That is, while routine decisions might be made by assemblies of the whole or committees with special responsibilities, and while administrative and other work assignments might be rotated and shared, the charismatic leader, as value bearer, still was the ultimate source of authority. Long-lived communities also tended to have fixed daily routines for carrying out tasks and to have personal conduct rules—all deriving from ideology and informing an individual of his responsibilities. Finally, they tended to require ideological conversion for admissions and did not automatically admit all applicants.

What was found, then, was that successful nineteenth-century utopias developed a number of ways of dealing with group relations, property, work, values, and leadership—all of which created an enduring commitment, involving motivation to work, will to continue, fellowship, and cohesion as a group. At the same time that this enabled the successful communities to survive in terms of longevity, such practices also created strong communities in the utopian sense and fulfilled many of the desires impelling people toward community today. The successful groups provided for their members strong feelings of participation, involvement, and belonging to a family group. They built a world centered around sharing—of property, of work, of living space, of feelings, of values. They offered identity and meaning, a value-oriented life of direction and purpose.

Today's Communes

Today's communes* are different from those of the past, however, in that the vast majority of them tend to be small in size, anarchic in philosophy, and seeking family-style intimacy without much else in the way of a utopian platform. There *are* a number that resemble the successful communes of the past—Synanon, the Bruderhof communities on the East Coast, some religiously-oriented groups, a few older, more established communes. But most of the new communes range in size from six to forty people and reject the rigid structuring of group life true of past communes. "Do your own thing" is a pervasive ethic. Yet, despite this ethic, and despite variations in style or ideological orientation, all communes of any size or length of existence share one important issue: creating a group out of a diverse collection of individuals.

The kind of group today's communes wish to build is one that provides the warmth and intimacy of a family. A hippie commune of 50 people in California, for example, called itself "the Lynch family," and all members adopted the last name of the founder. A New Mexico commune at one time called itself The Chosen Family; a New York City group, simply "the family." The Fort Hill community in Roxbury, Massachusetts, reports that it has evolved a family structure, with all members brothers and sisters, and the leader, Mel Lyman, the father at the head of the family.

For some communes, becoming a family means collective child-rearing: shared responsibility for raising children. Children as well as adults, for example, in a Vermont commune, have their own separate rooms, and they consider all the adults in the community their "parents." Other communes are interested in sexual experimentation, in changing the man-woman relationship from monogamy, an exclusive two-person bond, to group marriage, in which many attachments throughout the community are possible and encouraged. The sharing of sexual life and children as well as living space are all attempts to bring people closer together, to liberate women from exclusive domestic responsibility, to free couples from all the weight

*Material on contemporary communes comes from a questionnaire study, field visits and observation of several dozen groups, secondary sources, and personal experience in a commune.

that a two-person bond must bear, and to free parents and children from excessive dependence on one another.

Behind these practices lies the desire to create intense involvement with the communal group as a whole—feelings of connectedness and belonging and the warmth of many attachments.

Creating a Group

While communes seek to become families, they are, at the same time, something different from families; they are groups with their own unique form, something between communities, organizations, families, and friendship groups, and they may contain families in their midst. Certain social and interpersonal issues faced by all human groups affect communes, in particular, because they do not yet have the legal status, wider legitimacy, or institutionalized form that the family has in American society. For example, not only were most of today's commune members socialized from birth to be members of conventional families, and thus not given the skills and experiences to deal with the issues they face as adult commune members, they also may have to unlearn some of the lessons gleaned from growing up in conventional conjugal families.

Each commune must create its own social form from scratch; it must cope afresh with those group issues that are at least partially pre-solved for families or other accepted institutions in our society. Part of the definition of a commune, in fact, is that it is a group that comes together to create for itself its own form. No matter how much a commune participates in the emerging commune culture that is beginning to institutionalize particular patterns of organization and behavior, to some extent each group seeks to create and control its own existence and to do those things that meet its own particular needs in its own way. For example, Zablocki (1971) has pointed out that rural hippie communes may resist even taking advice from others about farming; making their own mistakes is positively valued.

Communes, like other groups, start with certain goals or ideas, sometimes well-defined, sometimes vague. Their social structure comes about through the process of coping with several important group issues, in the context of their ideals. These issues revolve around how the commune becomes a group and comes to define itself with respect to its environment.

Even the most organized nineteenth- and twentieth-century communes did not spring into being full-blown from a blueprint. Instead, they went through periods of anarchy, chaos, non-direction, high turnover, and open boundaries as they struggled to translate global ideals about community into specific behavior. The development of social organization is a step-wise process, and the history of many communes demonstrates this. The Bruderhof are now over fifty years old and well-organized. But in its early years in Germany, the community struggled with issues of developing a group identity and defining the group's boundaries. In fact, during its first summer, the now-traditional, straight-laced, and organized religious group resembled many of today's new communes. It began with no financial resources, an open-door policy (that brought floods of strange characters and curiosity seekers), and no clear notion of how to translate ideology into practice. The numbers of people grew and declined (more in summer, fewer in winter), living conditions were primitive, and the vast majority of members came from urban backgrounds and knew nothing of farming. They rented rather than owned their quarters. But group cohesion was promoted through song and celebration of all events, from picking up stones to hoeing beans. And out of the interaction of the diverse people who came together, group coherence gradually developed. The first crisis dealt with how the group would support itself, finding a task in which cooperation and shared fate would be embodied. Ideological and practical disagreements led to the definition of boundaries: who could become a member and who could not; which characteristics of members would be supported, which changed; what the focus of the group was to be (Arnold, 1964).

Similarly, some of the kibbutzim in their early years also strongly resembled the budding period of today's youth communes. The kibbutz studied by Spiro (1956) grew out of the German youth movement. A number of urban young people migrated to Palestine together, partly out of shared rebellion against their parents and urban life and partly out of a sense of adventure. When they actually found themselves in Palestine, they had little idea of what to do next. An intense, profound emotional experience provided the bond that translated itself gradually into the development of communal institutions. Other kibbutz researchers have indicated that early kibbutzim, like many American hippie communes, went through periods of anarchism and unwillingness to organize or set limits, before growing into the strong communities of today.

The same step-wise development of organization can be seen in the history of American communes of the past. Oneida started as an informal Bible discussion group in Putney, Vermont. Personnel changed, ideas and institutions developed, ideologists grew to explain and justify the practices that members found they preferred. As a group, they finally moved to Oneida, New York, several years later, and created a full-scale, well-organized, long-lasting communal village (Kanter, 1972). For other groups, practices also grew out of daily interactions and circumstances encountered after the initial decision to form a community was made. The extent of a well-defined blueprint varied, but many practices were a result of communal values plus the practical requirements of building a group. Ideology both informed and justified choices. The contemporary Twin Oaks commune is an illuminating example, for it did have a clear blueprint in Skinner's *Walden Two,* the inspiration for its founding. Yet here, too, the first months were without structure or organization. Out of the demands and limits of that situation, systems for group order gradually emerged, and five years later, in 1972, they are still emerging. Many of the formal practices have been borrowed from *Walden Two* or guided by it, but many of the informal ones have grown out of members' interactions while working out their relationships with one another and developing group coherence.

The ideologies and social practices of communes, then, can be seen as more than an outgrowth of utopian values. They are the solutions arrived at in face-to-face interactions and daily life to the crucial issue all new and non-institutionalized social groups face: how to become a group.

Group Issues

The first important issue is admission to the group: how does a person become a member? There are societally-delimited ways of entering a family —through marriage, birth, or legal adoption—but no similar guidelines for joining a commune. In American society, strangers do not knock at the doors of residences, asking to become a member of the family, but they *do* approach communes with this request. Many modern communes began with the wish to be open to all comers, and some still operate on the "open land" concept; anyone can come and stake out a bit of territory on the property. In strong contrast to the successful communities of the past, which required an ideological commitment for membership or had some screening procedure, some modern communes do not even make a member/nonmember distinction; whoever is there at the time "belongs." But as the group begins to define itself, it also begins to define criteria and procedures for membership, an issue that many communes are reluctant to face. Some limit membership by the size of their property, others ask that people come in for probationary periods first; gradually, even some of the more anarchic communes are beginning to control entry. The consequences of failing to control it are sometimes demoralizing for the group, as a resident of Morningstar Ranch said in 1967 about its leader's open admission policy:

> It's not like it used to be. Too many outsiders have been coming up here during the summer—Hell's Angels, tourists, people who come up for the wrong reasons. I don't know if [he's] right, letting everybody in. (Lamott, 1968)

By contrast, the viable communes of the past all had selective entry procedures.

"Getting it all together" is a central group issue—to find sources of cohesion, to create and solidify the bonds holding the group together. I've heard members of urban groups, in particular, ask themselves what it is that makes them a commune. In this there is a searching for the basis of solidarity and a reaching for the specialness of the group as an entity beyond the collection of individuals present. Even brand-new groups of limited duration tend to reach for the blanket that wraps the separate individuals together; this is true even of temporary groups such as encounters (Slater, 1968). In communes, several things may happen to provide sources of cohesion. One is the development of belief in the group's superiority. Nineteenth-century communities had elaborate beliefs of this kind, certain that they were heralding a new age, bringing about the millenium, and that, by contrast, the surrounding society was sinful. The Oneida community felt that contact with the outside was sufficiently contaminating that after visitors left, the whole community joined to clean the buildings in a ritualistic purification. What a sense of membership in their own special group the Oneidans must have had—to scrub away traces of contact with non-Oneidans. The Shakers developed to a high art their condemnation of non-Shakers and of the previous non-Shaker life of Shaker converts. One example is a hymn in which Shakers indicated their great love for other Shakers after first expressing their deep hatred for their biological families:

> Of all the relations that ever I see
> My old fleshly kindred are furthest from me.
> O how ugly they look, how hateful they feel;
> To see them and hate them increases my zeal. (Kanter, 1968)

It is a sociological canon, expressed by theorists from Freud (1962) to Simmel and Coser (1964), that the existence of external enemies heightens in-group cohesion. But the feeling of rejection of the past, past relationships, and attachments outside the group is not only a way to channel hostility and aggression outward and thereby define the group by its love. It grows also out of the tendency of radical groups to seek all the loyalty and affection of members, and to deny that any of them could have ever existed or been happy outside the group. Bittner (1963) has described this as one of the norms that develops in radical movements: all extra-group ties must be suspended.

We can see parallels to the Shakers today in the bitterness with which some communards condemn their parents or, more often, the life that their parents have led. The firm rejection of other ways of life, particularly those representing options once open to commune members, helps reinforce the belief that the commune is, indeed, a special, valuable, worthwhile place. What parents also represent is a set of ties that not all members of the commune share—yet the cohesiveness of the group is dependent in part on elevating that which is shared to a higher moral and emotional place than that which cannot be included in the group or shared by all members. "What we have together is more beautiful than what we have apart" is echoed by many communes. Also recurrent is: "What we have and are *now* is more important and worthwhile than what we may have been separately." In some communes this results in a noticeable lack of interest in members' pasts, and even resentment at talking much about life before the group—in T-group language, the "there and then" rather than the "here and now."

A researcher (Harmer, 1970) at a communal farm in Oregon reports that the ten adults there knew relatively little about each other's backgrounds. ("We accept a person for what he is, not what he was.") Such reasoning is part of the elevation of the group's present existence to a higher moral plane than past or outside lives. Even when these sentiments are not voiced explicitly, even when the group is content with a loose federation of individuals rather than a close-knit entity, there is still an underlying theme in communes. A woman living with her husband in an urban commune that they intend to leave at the end of the school year, still reported to me the awkwardness and uneasiness she experienced when her parents came to visit her in the commune. They were a reminder of her non-communal past, as well as being people with whom she shared something that other commune members could not share. Of course, the issue of outside relations and friends visiting can be dealt with in many ways that enhance rather than detract from the commune's cohesiveness. Some groups take over visitors as the property of the group, no matter whom they have come to visit, and visitors may find themselves overwhelmed by greetings, by curious children, by the desire to find them a place in the life of the whole commune rather than just with those they came to visit. With a friend of mine who is a frequent visitor, I recently visited a West Coast commune where members had small separate dwellings—log cabins, tepees, one-room plastic houses—and did not spend all their time in the communal house that held the kitchen and dining room. It was interesting to notice that my friend tried to get around to *all* the houses and say hello to everyone. In other communes the process of visiting and the role of visitor may become a matter of group policy and decision. Drop City in New Mexico built a special visitors' dome, particularly for parents who wished to visit—in a sense, putting them in their place (Hedgepeth and Stock, 1970).

Belief in the group's specialness is one step away from belief in its superiority, and a big theme in the commune culture is superiority of their way of life over others. One rural commune prides itself on the purity and naturalness of its existence, as opposed to the corruption of the city. A member said, "In the city you don't even know your own *motives*."

Many of these sources of solidarity are dependent on the existence of a wider society—the group becomes special by delimiting who and what it is not, who and what it rejects. But, at the same time, communes struggle with defining what they *are*. At this point the issue of common purpose becomes essential: what are we trying to make happen together? What goal or idea or symbol "gets it all together"? This is a major problem for many modern communes, particularly anarchistically-oriented ones. They tend to come together in the shared rejection of the established society, particularly of its structure, and wish to make no demands on members that would detract from "doing their own thing." This lack of a common purpose has been cited by the members of one now-defunct commune as a reason for its failure:

> We weren't ready to define who we were; we certainly weren't prepared to define who we weren't—it was still just a matter of intuition. We had come together for various reasons—not overtly for a common idea or ideal, but primarily political revolutionaries . . . or just plain hermits who wanted to live in the woods. All of these different people managed to work together side by side for a while, but the fact was that there really was no shared vision.

Defining "who we are" is particularly difficult for urban communes in which members hold outside jobs. It is much easier when members work together in community jobs, as was true of all the nineteenth-century utopian communities. Some urban groups deal with this by trying to find employment as a group.

In the absence of elaborate integrating philosophies, of a sense of destiny or mission such as the religious groups have, or of an essential over-riding goal, many groups develop a sense of purpose by finding shared tasks that represent a common endeavor. Construction seems to be the most important of these, for it leaves the group with a permanent monument to the shared enterprise. The emphasis on building and shaping one's own environment that is so central to the commune movement may have roots here. The end —the actual building—may not be as important for the group's identity as the means by which the buildings came about. I have experienced on many communes an infectious sense of group pride in the self-made buildings, like the gala celebration in the Connecticut Bruderhof community after the construction of new beams in the dining hall.

Rituals and shared symbols also tell a group what it is, particularly those that are unique to it. Ritual was an important part of the life of many communes of the past, especially so for the Shakers. Every evening, each Shaker group gathered to dance, pray, and express the togetherness of the group. Many aspects of the Shaker ceremony resemble encounter group exercises in their use of energetic body movement and emotional outburst; after the ritual, one Shaker reported that the group felt "love enough to eat each other up." The Shakers also had a number of special ceremonies in which spiritual or imaginary events occurred. Some of these centered around spiritual fountains on magic hills near the villages reputedly populated by angels and spirits—but spirits only Shakers could see of course. Among them were such luminaries as Napoleon, George Washington, and Queen Elizabeth. Present day communes often create their own rituals, some with the same special or hidden elements that only group members share. Particularly those groups oriented around religion or mysticism find ritual an abundant source of group feeling. But even creed-less communes develop ritual. One group begins its "family meetings" by sitting in a circle and chanting "om." A number of communes use sensory-awakening or encounter exercises as a kind of ritual. In the community where I lived one summer, we arose around 6:30 and met on a grassy lawn at 7 for T'ai Chi Chuan exercises, a beautiful flowing Chinese moving meditation. For an hour before breakfast we stood in rows and moved together, all following the same pattern.

The desire for the group to become a group sometimes means that members feel a pressure to take pride only in things held in common, rather than those that belong to them separately. This, of course, was an explicit norm of the communistic groups of the last century that held all property in common (including clothes in Oneida), and found that joint ownership was an important source of community feeling. But even in "do your own thing" communes today that maintain a great deal of individual ownership and resist making demands on each other, some people still feel it important to take pride only in that which is shared. In a rural hip commune, I spoke to a woman, a particularly respected member of the commune, who had just finished building a striking-looking one-room, two-level redwood house, with the help of some others in the group. It was very cleverly and artistically created, with windows that were really sculptures, framed with pieces of twisted wood found in the forest. She expressed both great pride and guilt—guilt that she should have such a nice house for her own.

The same push to take pride in what is shared rather than separate often pervades relationships. As several theorists have pointed out, groups are often threatened by exclusive relationships in their midst and desire instead diffusion of affection throughout the group (Coser, 1967; Slater, 1963). Many nineteenth-century communes tended to discourage or eliminate marriage, through free love or group marriage or celibacy (Kanter, 1968). Similarly, some communes today formally adopt systems of group marriage that eliminate separate, exclusive attachments. Others develop informal norms that discourage pairing-off or that exhort couples to continue their relationships with the whole group rather than isolating themselves. Members of a loosely structured, family-type "do your own thing" commune of students report that two members who formed a couple faced hostility from the others. One person said:

> There were subtle hostilities from almost everyone being directed at their partial withdrawal from the rest of us into their own world. It came out in criticisms of their relationship by various people . . . It's true that if you start to get into a heavier-than-usual relationship with anyone, you should have every freedom to let it develop. Living in a commune, however, carries with it a responsibility to maintain a certain amount of awareness of where everyone else is at and how what you are doing is affecting the total group. If we are trying to do anything at all revolutionary and collective, we can't afford to revert to old patterns of looking out only for our own immediate needs.

A group can become a special entity if members value it above other things. It is difficult to maintain outside allegiances in a commune, for there is often pressure from the group to be fully present and involved. Most of what a commune is, after all, is the devotion and energy of those who belong—it *is* the group composed of specific people, and it needs *those* people to be what it is. Some of the nineteenth-century communities solved this problem by eliminating the possibility of conflicting loyalties; they tended to break ties with the surrounding society and move to isolated locations that the average member rarely left. But today, even for rural communities this is rarely feasible, and for urban groups it is impossible. So an important source of interpersonal friction in communes is how involved and present a member is. Meetings in which tensions and hostilities are confronted often revolve around this kind of theme. There is a dilemma here for many present-day groups, for while there may be a group pressure for involvement, there is sometimes an accompanying reluctance to make demands or to create norms that will regulate the individual's involvement—even in such simple matters as doing his share of domestic work. Yet the failure to make such norms explicit undermines the group-ness of many communes and helps lead to their dissolution. The members still feel the weight of group pressure, but there are no clear norms that pull the commune together as a group.

The reluctance to make formal rules is pervasive in the commune movement; communities such as Synanon that *do* have a highly-developed normative structure are viewed by many other communes as autocratic. There is a split among communes around the degree of organization they are willing to create. However, those that fail to organize their work and their decision-making procedures tend to find that work stays undone, some decisions never get made, and group feeling develops only with difficulty. The unwillingness to make decisions or impose order seems to be not only a function of a "do your own thing" ideology but also of a lack of trust in the group. One hip commune reported the difficulties in the group's working together on construction. ("Everything was a hassle, an object for discussion. Even how many hammer blows to use on a nail. Should it be 5 or 7?") Those communes, on the other hand, in which there is enough mutual trust and commitment to the group—often through the sense of shared purpose mentioned earlier—find that they can build organization, and that this enhances rather than detracts from their functioning as a group. In fact, I have found among residents in the very anarchic hip communes a longing for more order and group-ness than they have. A resident of Morningstar made this remark about Tolstoy Farm:

> It's a groovy place. They don't let *everybody* in—just people who really believe in it. They've got some organization there. Everybody knows what he's supposed to be doing. (Lamott, 1968)

Tolstoy Farm, of course, is now almost ten years old, and has a developed structure; there are other more mature communes that have evolved toward building cohesiveness through becoming a well-defined group. Zablocki (1971) documents the shift that many hippie communes have gone through over time, developing organization out of anarchism.

The group issues discussed here are not the only critical ones for communes; authority and decision-making are also important. But much of the identity and cohesion of communes does derive from confronting group issues.

Conclusion

What can be said about the viability of today's commune movement? First, many of today's groups are not looking for the same kind of permanent, stable community that utopians of the past sought, so while it is true that many of today's groups are temporary and subject to much change and turnover of members, it is this kind of temporary system that some communes themselves seek. Their ideologies say that nothing should be forever, that change is part of life. On the other hand, a number of groups do wish to create long-range viable alternative communities, and to these the lessons of the past apply. Those communes that develop common purpose, an integrating philosophy, a structure for leadership and decision-making, and criteria for membership and entrance procedures, organize work and property communally, affirm their bonds through ritual, and work out interpersonal difficulties through regular open confrontation have a better chance of succeeding than those that do not. They will be building commitment and also satisfying their members by creating a strong family-like group. The failure rate of communes is high, but so is the failure rate of small businesses. And no one is suggesting that small business is not a viable organizational form. As the commune movement grows, so do the number of groups that build for themselves what it takes to succeed as a commune. Part of the difference between stable and unstable, anarchistic or organized communes lies in their stage of group development. A strong commune takes time and work to develop.

References

Arnold, E. *Torches Together: The Beginnings and Early Years of the Bruderhof Communities.* Rifton, N.Y.: Plough Publishing, 1964.

Bennett, M. "The Alternative." *The Mother Earth News*, 1 (September 1970): 32–34.

Berger, B., B. Hackett, and R. Millar. "Child-Rearing Practices in the Communal Family." Mimeographed. Progress report to NIMH, 1971.

Bittner, E. "Radicalism and the Organization of Radical Movements." *Amer. Soc. Rev.*, 28 (December 1963): 928–940.

Coser, L. *The Functions of Social Conflict.* New York: Free Press, 1964.

Coser, L. "Greedy Organizations." *European J. Soc.*, 8 (October 1967): 196–215.

Freud, S. *Civilization and Its Discontents.* New York: Norton, 1962.

Harmer, R. "Bedrock." Mimeographed. Boston: Harvard Business School, 1970.

Hedgepeth, W., and Stock, D. *The Alternative: Communal Life in New America.* New York: Macmillan, 1970.

Jones, S. "Communes and Social Change: Thoughts on Communal Living Based on Interviews with Communes in the Boulder-Denver Area." Mimeographed. 1970.

Kanter, R. "Commitment and Social Organization: A Study of Commitment Mechanisms in Utopian Communities." *Amer. Soc. Rev.*, 33 (August 1968): 499–517.

Kanter, R. "Communes." *Psychology Today*, 4 (July 1970): 56–70.

Kanter, R. 1972. *Commitment and Community: Utopias and Communes in Sociological Perspective.* Cambridge: Harvard University Press, 1972.

Lamott, K. "Doing Their Own Thing at Morningstar." *Horizon*, 10 (Spring 1968): 14–19. (Reprinted in *Utopias: Social Ideals and Communal Experiments*, edited by P. Richter. Boston: Holbrook Press.

Newman, K., and Wilhelm, H. "Twin Oaks: The Great Farm Revolution." *The Mother Earth News*, 1 (January 1970): 56–59.

Plath, D. "A Case of Ostracism—and Its Unusual Aftermath." *Transaction*, 5 (January/February 1968): 31–36.

Slater, P. "On Social Regression." *Amer. Soc. Rev.*, 28 (June 1963): 339–364.

Slater, P. *Microcosm: Structural, Psychological, and Religious Evolution in Groups.* New York: Wiley, 1968.

Spiro, M. *Kibbutz: Venture in Utopia.* Cambridge: Harvard University Press, 1956.

Yaswen, G. "Sunrise Hill." *The Modern Utopian*, 4 (Summer-Fall 1970): 4–13.

Zablocki, B. *The Joyful Community.* Baltimore: Penguin, 1971.

Chapter 11

Singleness and Childlessness

The social definition of the single woman has undergone dramatic changes in the twentieth century. In the decades before World War II, being single was regarded as an acceptable choice for a spirited or career-minded woman. Around the middle of the century the "feminine mystique" prevailed, and the single woman was assumed to be a neurotic failure in the search for a husband. The women's liberation movement has revived the earlier concept of singleness as a desirable life style. The present article reviews the changing social situation of the single woman.

The Single Woman in Today's Society: A Reappraisal | *Margaret Adams*

Writing on a theme of major societal significance today—such as the changing role of women—resembles a natural history exercise in which the student starts out to study a particular species, only to find that its ecological status and respondent characteristics have altered beyond recognition. So it is with the topic of single women. This article was planned on the basis of my own life experience as a middle-aged professional single woman, augmented by friends and colleagues of different ages, and reinforced by the model of three maiden aunts who functioned as significant social figures in my English west-country childhood. However, considering the subject more carefully, I realized that these seemingly stable and clearly delineated models are to a large extent an anachronistic figment of a bygone—or at least swiftly passing—social era, and that a fresh definition of what constitutes the single woman today must precede any discussion of her social role.

From "The Single Woman in Today's Society: A Reappraisal" by Margaret Adams, *The American Journal of Orthopsychiatry*, 41, no. 5 (1971), pp. 776–786. Copyright © 1971, the American Orthopsychiatric Association, Inc. Reproduced by permission.

By tradition, the term single has been applied to women who have never been married, and until recently it carried the official, if not de facto, connotation of sexual abstinence. In this way the phenomenon of singleness was the antithesis of marriage, and its clearly defined social status was dependent on marriage being a stable social institution only ruptured by the death of one partner. Today, a different set of variables is needed to identify the single woman category because earlier marriages and easier divorce practices have robbed marriage of its permanence, while easily available and safe contraceptive techniques have made extramarital sex a commonplace. Within this article, then, singleness will apply not only to the numerically restricted group of never-marrieds but will also embrace widows and divorced women who fit other criteria that I am putting forward as the basis for a more relevant concept of singleness by today's social standards.

The primary criterion—or vital prerequisite—of being single is the capacity and opportunity to be economically self-supporting. This basic condition provides the elementary social independence from which most of the other features of singleness derive, and it relates this social status to broader societal issues. Thus the incidence of single women as a defined category within any given society is closely connected with its economic and political system and the roles that devolve on women. A society that engages in periodic bouts of violent warfare will have a surplus of women, so that, unless polygamy is the approved marital pattern, some will be without husbands and have to maintain themselves. In the Middle Ages, for example, lower-class single women found a livelihood on the land, in domestic service, and as alewives or spinners (hence the term spinster) while their upper-class counterparts were absorbed in the religious system as anchorites or nuns (Power, 1926). These arrangements came into being to counteract the decimation and absence of the male population occasioned by the Crusades.

A second essential criterion of singleness is social and psychological autonomy. The single woman's basic lifestyle is emotionally independent of relationships that carry with them long term commitment and a subjugation of personal or individual claims for their maintenance. This means she does not recognize a core relationship with a man as the primary or exclusive source of emotional satisfaction or social identity, neither is she encumbered by direct and statutorily defined dependents such as children. Single women, however, often have to assume some less direct, informal family responsibilities, such as contributing substantially to the financial support of aging, sick, or otherwise needy relatives, taking direct care of them on a temporary or protracted basis, and being available for emotional support and advice at times of crisis. My definition deliberately excludes the many unmarried, divorced, and widowed women who are female heads of families, on the grounds that their situation contains many features not pertinent to the life style of the single woman, and merits a discussion of its own.

The third criterion is a clearly thought through intent to remain single by preference rather than by default of being requested in marriage, either as first venture or following widowhood and divorce. It is important to stress this factor because marriage is invested with such a high premium in American society that very little credence is given to the idea that some women remain unmarried on purpose. Even when the choice seems arbitrarily imposed by a shortage of men, the failure of some personable women to secure a husband may be explained by their selective standards, set so high that they have not been met by the males available. In such cases, it may be inferred that the basic, often unconscious, intention has been realized, though some of these women may be so hitched to the prevailing societal norms as to cherish the belief that they would have liked to have married.

Age is another significant factor and I have selected 30 and upwards as the chronological boundary delimiting the single state, on the grounds that the bulk of unmarried girls in their twenties concentrate their energies on remedying their condition. This assumption is supported by statistics of March 1969, which show the following age distribution (in thousands) for single women—20–24 years, 2850; 25–29 years, 726; 30–34 years, 345; with the three successive decades showing a relatively stable figure between 560 and 600 (Department of Commerce, 1970). Thus we see that in the latter half of the 20 age group, the numbers of single women have declined to nearly a quarter of the figure reported in the 20–24 age group, and that this attenuated number is halved in the next five-year period. On the basis of these figures, one can infer that by 30 most women who are still unmarried are beginning to build up economic independence, an investment in work, and a viable value system that allows them to identify and exploit major sources of personal and social satisfaction in other areas than marriage and family. Even those whose first preference is marriage are compelled to readjust their social sights and relationships because the number of eligible men will have thinned out and their married peers will be caught up in a web of social and domestic activities with which they cannot identify and that do not meet their needs. At this juncture the unmarried woman, if she is not to be plagued by a constant sense of dissatisfaction, must take stock of her situation and carefully evaluate both its negative features and its assets. The remainder of this paper will try to define some of these social issues, and suggest solutions that will enable single women to realize a more viable and socially sanctioned identity.

The problems of unattached women range from the practical mechanics of day-to-day existence, such as a job and living accommodations, to the more subtle but equally vital questions of social role, acceptability, and personal self-esteem. Most of the intangible difficulties stem from one major core disadvantage, namely that single women constitute a clearly defined minority group* that demonstrates a conspicuously deviant pattern of functioning in terms of the dominant value system and the organizational goals of American society.

Although the world population crisis is fast turning the nuclear family into an obsolete and negatively redundant system, the myth of the sanctity of family life still has such a tenacious hold on the American imagination that women who eschew this modus vivendi are subject to a subtle array of social sanctions that erode their self-esteem, distort their relationships and disturb their sense of homeostasis in the shifting world scene. Single women, for example, are still the victims of quite outrageous stereotyping in regard to their ascribed characteristics, and their unmarried status is popularly attributed to personal failings, such as lack of sexual attractiveness (whatever that elusive quality may be), unresolved early psychosexual conflicts, narcissistic unwillingness to be closely committed to another individual, latent lesbianism. These characteristics may often be present, but if being single was not defined in terms of social deviance they would carry a less pathological connotation.

In this connection it is interesting to note the greater frequency with which psychological reasons have been adduced to explain singleness, rather than equally cogent sociological causes. While women today (except for the very poor and uneducated) have access to an increasingly broad repertoire of interesting opportunities in both work and social spheres, these factors are rarely put forward as serious reasons for not being married; if considered at all they are usually dismissed as second-best sublimated options. We have already mentioned the questionable value of the family as a useful social unit, but no one openly commends the decision of the unattached woman not to ally herself with this dinosaurlike social pattern.

Many of the less flattering qualities traditionally associated with unattached women—rigidity, overpreoccupation with minutiae, lack of self-confidence, excessive diffidence, or the overcompensatory quality of brazen hostility—are invariably attributed to poor ego-functioning, but very little thought is given to the extreme social insecurity within which the single woman has to operate. In a society that grants her sex the semblance of protection and economic support in exchange for subordinate obedience to male

*In the age range 30–74, the combined total (in thousands) of single, widowed, and divorced was 10,856, as against 35,279 married women, and in what might be termed the age span of greatest social activity, i.e., between 30 and 54, the unmarried were 4,294 as against 25,218 (Department of Commerce, 1970).

supremacy, the single woman who fends for herself is fair game for any exploitation the male-dominated working world chooses to exact. The fact that *all* women are in a relatively powerless position in most significant spheres of life—as demonstrated by salary differentials, sex discrimination in the more prestigious and powerful professional jobs, and numbers of women holding real executive power (Hedges, 1970)—means that the single ones have to be highly sensitive to potential exploitation and forearmed with defensive tactics. This social predicament is a more likely reason for aggressive behavior towards men than is the more personal psychological explanation of sexual frustration or defensive denial of forbidden wishes. Furthermore, survival in today's highly competitive society demands a high level of self-assertiveness from both sexes; therefore this characteristic in single women must be seen as part of a societal mode of interaction rather than a personal idiosyncracy of sexual status.

The accusation that single women are malicious or lacking in generosity towards each other also requires a sociological as well as psychological interpretation. The emotional frustration that results from any devalued minority status tends to be turned inwards upon the group, rather than outwards to the social forces responsible: this is the same type of defense mechanism manifested by socially respectable members of racial minorities who castigate the social inadequacy of welfare recipients.

This devalued social definition of single women and the distorted self-image of inferiority that it creates can exert a subtly damaging effect on the quality of social relationships with peers, the opposite sex, and married couples. The insidious conviction of being only second best makes it hard for single women to put a proper value on themselves; they tend to approach relationships in an over-diffident, if not apologetic, frame of mind, and perceive them as bestowing something of value on themselves rather than as of reciprocal benefit. In relationships with men this attitude has been particularly destructive, making women over-susceptible to exploitation and often ending in an abandonment that serves to reinforce the latent conviction of failure.

The more aware single woman, who is becoming liberated from this fettering self-concept of inadequacy, still has some residual uncertainity about her own identity, and in her heterosexual relationships is liable to be caught in a double bind of trying to decide what priority in time and emotional energy to devote to serious involvement with a man, while raising anew the question of how sincerely she is committed to the freedom of being single. For the man in question, there is confusion about the woman's newly emerging identity and the ambiguous and unclear goals of the relationship. The old exploitative options of "getting trapped" or "ditching the girl" no longer seem valid, which evokes anxiety—particularly when it involves redefining the beggar maid in more equitable terms.

Friendships with other single women are prone to a similar kind of problem, particularly if both still believe in the inferior status of women and suspect that each is only using the other's companionship and emotional support as a stopgap to ward off loneliness and fill in the time, pending a more rewarding relationship with a man. Further, the overwhelming importance attached to this latter objective introduces a frustration and desperation heightened by the fear that one may succeed, thus abandoning the other to loneliness and a reinforced sense of underachievement. This ambiguous and destructive situation will improve only when marriage or long-term involvement with the other sex is seen as a matter of personal choice and not of social prestige and obligation.

Relationships with married friends are also invested with hazards, although they offer the best scope for the single woman to be herself, because she is not being measured solely for her sexual viability. She may even lose her poor-relation status and be welcomed as someone whose broader range of work experience and more varied social and cultural contacts can introduce a note of novelty into a family situation. To the children, she presents a different facet of the adult world from the familiar one they experience in their own mother and those of their friends. Through this contact the wife is kept aware of roles open to women other than the strictly homemaking one she is momentarily absorbed in; this sort of unobtrusive psychological reinforcement to the fuller personality and identity of the housebound woman is an important liberating factor. For the husband, the relationship with the single friend supplies a fresh dimension to the absorbing model of domesticity with which he and his wife have become saddled, as well as the prospect of other more varied facets of life that both can resume in the future. It also provides opportunity for enjoying additional feminine company in the safe confines of a family friendship.

Here, a comment is needed on the word "safe," which is used deliberately to illustrate another unconscious social and psychological belittlement of the single woman, through its implication of the wife's superior sexual attractiveness, her impregnable sense of security in possession, or implicit reliance on the friend's loyalty. This dilemma of the "friendly threesome," and the under-pull of tensions that sustain the relationship, is rarely acknowledged, while almost universal recognition is given to its more pronounced version, the eternal triangle. If she is not careful, the single woman can often unwittingly find herself in the position of being a stand-in spouse, even to being consigned the future care of the husband should he survive his wife. Such situations are reminiscent of Biblical parables, of tribal customs for ensuring the care of dependent survivors, and even suttees—the common factor to all these practices being the testimentary disposition of socially vulnerable women for society's convenience.

I have been concentrating on the more subtle aspects of personal relationships because these are closely tied to the emerging social identity of women and, being less obtrusive, have been overshadowed by more obvious problems. Up till recently, scope for sexual experience presented a major difficulty for single women because of narrow penalizing sexual mores and the actual danger of becoming pregnant. The development of effective and reliable contraceptive techniques that are within women's control has, to a large extent, removed both these obstacles and provided single women with opportunity for sexual relationships equal to those hitherto available to legally married women and *all* men. This end to the double standard of sexual behavior is having an influence on the quality of sexual relationships in that the activity is developing a more strongly social character with less heavy psychological weighting than when it was precarious and taboo. One result seems to be a tendency for sexual liaisons to be more numerous and frequent, with much shorter-term commitment. (This is also reflected in the divorce rate (Department of Commerce, 1970), an institutionalized version of the same phenomenon.)

In this context I should like to mention the psychological myth that women are more inherently faithful than men in sexual relationships, are inclined to invest more emotion over a longer time span, and feel proportionately traumatized when the relationship terminates. My feeling is that this psychological attribute has been developed over time to rationalize and make bearable a situation into which women were trapped by marriage or recurrent childbearing, and that when these fettering external circumstances open up there will be accompanying internal flexibility and freedom. The freewheeling single woman should be among the first to be emancipated from this misconception and to invest the pejorative term, *promiscuity* (an exclusively female epithet), with the adventurous insouciance evoked by the phrase, *wild oats*. The revelation that women have greater and more sustained capacity for sexual activity than hitherto suspected will add grist to this notion once the prim ideas of monogamous loyalty and irrevocable emotional investment have been exploded (Masters and Johnson, 1966, 1970).

The social relationships of unattached women also present practical difficulties, particularly the question of how to develop a pattern of life that satisfies the need for day-to-day ongoing social intercourse. Apart from a relatively small number of women who have exceptional inner resources of their own or are involved in creative projects that require a good deal of solitary leisure, most single women have to cope with recurrent problems of personal loneliness. To counteract these social lacunae the single woman has to organize a deliberately structured social life for herself and invest a good deal of time and energy in maintaining its momentum.

Establishing a satisfying and stimulating social life bears especially hard on single women when they move to a new community because they have fewer introductory lines of communication than their married counterparts, whose husband and children provide a contact with other families or individuals. Also, as long as single women are regarded as a tiresome surplus, there is a reluctance to co-opt new members of the species into an extant social circle lest they disturb the balance of the sexes. For this same reason, single women are often denied admission to more formal social groups, such as country clubs.

A significant lack in the single woman's life is a congenial, trustworthy, and accessible person to serve as a sounding-board and provide the requisite feedback. To meet this need and to offset potential loneliness many single women are beginning to develop informal, loosely-knit communes of unattached individuals who are not close and intimate friends but operate among each other on the basis of shared needs and reciprocal services. Such a group can provide casual and ad hoc entertainment and an exchange of small but vital homemaking services in times of illness or emergency.

Living accommodation is another problem area for single women, though there has been a substantial development of accommodation suitable for single occupants over the last 40 years. In the 1930s, for example, unmarried professional or white collar women workers frequently had to live at home in the ambiguous role of adult child of the family or in a carefully selected private hotel or woman's residence (often euphemistically termed a "club," as in Muriel Spark's novel, *The Girls of Slender Means*), a bed-sitting room with shared cooking facilities, or, more rarely, a private apartment. Today, efficiency apartments and cooperatives offer a range of independent options. However, the lower salaries earned by women at all levels place an economic bar on their taking advantage of these opportunities (considerable savings are needed to purchase an even modest cooperative) and they are often forced into the compromise of rooming with one or two others in order to meet the rent and maintenance bills. While this may sometimes be a deliberate choice, it is more often an expediency involving a sacrifice of standards —in space or privacy— that diminishes the single woman's social self-sufficiency and autonomy. There is also a subtle prestige factor in that a certain level of social sophistication is associated with having your own menage (vide Helen Gurley Brown!), whereas a household shared by several women has a slightly comic undertone, calling up a residual picture of a college dormitory and adolescence.

Single women are also very vulnerable to harassment and intimidation by unscrupulous landlords, particularly in areas where there is heavy competition for housing, such as the larger cities to which unattached women tend to migrate because of the greater choice of work and social, educational, and cultural opportunities. Where there is a large financial investment at stake, such as purchasing a house in a socially desirable area, single women are liable to encounter prejudice of the same order experienced by blacks, in which realtors operate on the basis of a preconceived stereotype about the applicant rather than on whether the applicant earns enough money to be an effective purchaser, and to maintain the property at the level demanded by the community. All these problems—major and minor—represent an accumulative discrimination that keeps single women in a chronically second-grade living situation, reduces their social status, and saps their individual and corporate self-respect.

If this has been a rather dismal catalogue of complaints about the social condition of single women, I want to end with a brief account of what I consider to be some of the invaluable assets that also attach to this status. My intent in delineating the disadvantages has been to help identify the negative social forces that stand in the way of these assets being fully realized. By making explicit the severe psychological and social devaluation that has settled like an accretion around the concept of singleness, I mean to imply that this attitude is a societal product capable of being changed once its destructive potential is understood. By pointing up the practical difficulties single women face in everyday living, I hope to set in motion ingenious ideas and innovative experiments that will develop more efficient social arrangements to minimize these hazards.

The advantages of being single are two-fold—those that redound directly upon the single woman and those that accrue to the corporate good of society. To start with individual benefits, the unmarried woman has greater freedom to take advantage of the exceptional opportunities for new experiences offered by today's rapidly changing world. This can mean moving to work in a different city, country, or continent; it can mean leaving one type of employment for another. For the well-paid professional woman who has been able to save, this freedom from personal commitment allows her to purchase time and involve herself in some different creative activity such as traveling, writing a book, or continuing her education. Because her psychic energy is not primarily invested in the emotionally absorbing task of maintaining a home, a family, or a partner whose needs have to take precedence, the single woman can be more receptive to fresh experience and new ideas, and is able to develop the heightened capacity for social analysis and commentary so vital in today's swiftly evolving pre-revolutionary society. She also has greater freedom to involve herself in social action and reform movements, including activities that involve a high degree of risk-taking, such as being fired from employment, arrested for civil disobedience or physically assaulted by today's violently repressive process of law and order.

Having examined the social entity of the single woman and the debits and assets of the role she has been allotted in today's society, we must now consider how her societal characteristics relate to the radical women's movement, whether she has a special contribution to make to this dynamic social trend, and what impact its changes will have upon her modus vivendi.

The radical feminist movement has three major goals. First, to help women free themselves from the socially restrictive and psychologically enervating roles into which they have been forced by the exigencies of a male-dominated social system. Second, to demonstrate the connection between the tyranny imposed upon women as a sex and the exploitation of all powerless groups, both of which are an inevitable outcome of a capitalist economy. Third, to tap and channel the constructive social energy of women—currently dissipated in many futile, if not destructive, activities—as a motive force for propelling the basic social changes needed to bring about a more equitable and functional distribution of power.

In brief, the aim of women's liberation is to change the prevailing ideas about women—their rights, their potentialities, their aspirations; to change the social structure that has created and still supports this impotent definition; and to offer women, along with other oppressed groups, the opportunity to assume a more viable and satisfying social role with corresponding different functions and life styles.

How does the single woman fit into this scheme? Two areas immediately suggest themselves: psychological emancipation, and radical redefinition with altered social status and functioning.

The single woman, as we have seen, has been a particular victim of the psychological enslavement to which all women have been subjected. Feminist writing has frequently focused on the plight of married women, emphasizing the psychological seduction that has enmeshed them in the spider-web belief that their domesticated condition represents physical, mental, and cultural fulfillment. Less is said about the other side of the coin by which those outside of marriage are saddled with a sense of deprivation, deficit, and alienation. By defining women as sound, whole, viable beings in their own right the radical movement has restored the single woman's sense of self-esteem and put her into the mainstream of social acceptability and importance. Single women, if they can recognize the assets attaching to their status, are in a position to offer a more sharply defined model for the emerging social identity of their sex and the new societal roles that may devolve upon women.

Because of the stringent necessity to be economically self-supporting, single women have also had to develop a greater sense of personal independence and some practical expertise in fending for themselves in a discriminating economic sphere. Women in the working and professional world have been conspicuously lacking in executive power, but involvement in this masculine arena, even at a lower social level, has given them an intimate familiarity with the habits of the male and the ecology of his power system. Such knowledge can be turned to good diagnostic account when the time comes for invading that system and instituting radical change. This knowledge is shared by all the female work force but the greater investment that single women are likely to have in their work, which is not only their economic mainstay but also a major force in defining their social identity, probably gives them sharper insights. The business executive's indefatigable secretary, the loyal nurse-receptionist who is privy to her doctor-employer's professional commitments, the woman faculty member, if they do not have a domestic male figure on which to exercise these observational skills, become very adept at sizing up the quirks, weaknesses, strengths and Achilles' heels of their male colleagues, much as potential revolutionaries study the characteristics of the regime they plan to overthrow. What may start as an intuitive diversion becomes a self-conscious exercise with important educational significance.

In terms of purposeful intent, single women are also likely to have a greater capacity for hardheaded, clear-thinking judgment because they are not influenced by the same conflicts and ambivalences that necessarily afflict women who are in a relationship of affectionate amity with a husband or long-term equivalent. This is not to say that the radical feminist movement is the work of single women alone, since the facts suggest quite the opposite, but merely that some of the burdens fall more heavily on their married counterparts.

Finally, what effect will radical change have on the small coterie of women I have designated as single? First, they are likely to be rendered obsolete as a specifically defined group, and far from being in a deviant minority may find that their situation has been transformed into the popular norm. This corresponds with the position that is currently predicted and advocated by many radical feminist writers. The threat of overpopulation and diminishing food supply has already begun to rob marriage of its vital rationale—*i.e.*, the procreation of children and maintenance of a stable family setting for their nurturance—and as more attention is focused on the importance of restricting population growth, marriage will come to be seen as a societal liability perpetuating an outmoded dysfunctional social system. Once women become disabused of the notion that marriage and rearing a family represent the most rewarding way of life, and can choose the sort of life they want to lead and where to invest their social energies and skills, there will be a much smaller drift towards this goal. I arbitrarily imposed the lower age limit of 30 on my definition of singleness to highlight its antithetical stance to marriage; when the lure of the latter has receded, singleness may become the more widely sought option and some of the characteristcs and interactive patterns that I have described as pertaining to the present-day single woman may be assumed by women in the younger age bracket.

What effect this change of focus will have on women's social objectives and opportunities remains to be seen, but we can speculate that there will be greater and more visible scope for individuals to develop what Ruth Benedict terms their "congenial responses" instead of the contorted antics preordained by society. Those for whom pursuit of knowledge, exploration of ideas, and wider range of experience have a greater appeal than do close interpersonal relationships will be freer to follow this bent without having to pay lip service to the other, more socially dominating, objective of securing a lifelong male companion. Others for whom emotional involvement has higher priority will be able to rechannel their nurturing and protective impulses into public activities that foster the common weal rather than the private family unit. The diminished few who mate and produce children will be the minority, and their pattern of life will approximate more to that of their working counterparts who are unencumbered by dependents. Day care and other socially contrived family supports will be essential pieces of equipment for child-rearing, as the vacuum cleaner is for housework, and mothers —with or without attendant spouses—will be expected and encouraged to develop a wider sphere of interest than the narrow unit of the family within which most of them are currently confined. This trend has already been set in motion. When it attains its full momentum the more obvious differences between the officially single and officially married woman will be absorbed in a new common life pattern.

References

Hedges, J. "Women Workers and Manpower Demands in the 1970s. In *Women at Work: Monthly Labor Review*. U.S. Department of Labor, Bureau of Labor Statistics. Washington, D.C.: Government Printing Office, 1970.

Masters, W., and Johnson, V. *Human Sexual Response*. Boston: Little, Brown, 1966.

Masters, W., and Johnson, V. *Human Sexual Inadequacy*. Boston: Little, Brown, 1970.

Power, F. "The Position of Women." In *The Legacy of the Middle Ages*, edited by C. Crump and E. Jacob. Oxford: Clarendon Press, 1926.

U.S. Department of Commerce. *Statistical Abstracts of the United States*. Washington, D.C.: Government Printing Office, 1970.

This study explores a population that has been virtually ignored by family research: couples who refuse to assume parental roles even though they are capable of becoming parents. Looking at the motivations and experiences of the childless throws a fascinating light on the phenomenon of parenthood. It reveals the tremendous social pressures behind procreation: There is a norm that married people should have children and should rejoice at having children. The childless have tended to be treated as a deviant group, suffering from physical abnormalities or psychological defects. Yet the population problem and women's liberation are already changing the social definition of childlessness from deviance to a legitimate life style.

Voluntarily Childless Wives: An Exploratory Study

J. E. Veevers

Students of the family have generally tended to accept the dominant cultural values that married couples should have children, and should want to have them. As a result of this value bias, although parenthood (especially voluntary parenthood) has been extensively studied, the phenomenon of childlessness has been virtually ignored (Veevers, 1972a). This selective inattention is unfortunate, for to a large extent the social meanings of parenthood can be comprehensively described and analyzed only in terms of the parallel set of meanings which are assigned to non-parenthood (Veevers, forthcoming). Although sociologists have occasionally discussed the theoretical relevance of voluntary childlessness, and have speculated regarding some empirical aspects of it (Pohlman, 1970), virtually no direct research has been conducted. As a preliminary step towards filling this gap in the sociological study of the family, an exploratory study of voluntarily childless wives was conducted. The present article will not attempt to describe this research in its entirety, but rather will be concerned with brief discussions of four aspects of it: first, the career paths whereby women come to be voluntarily childless; second, the social pressures associated with that decision; third, the symbolic importance attributed to the possibility of adoption; and fourth, the relevance of supportive ideologies relating to concern with feminism, and with population problems.

Selection and Nature of the Sample

Conventional sampling techniques cannot readily be applied to obtain large and representative samples of voluntarily childless couples (Gustavus

From J. E. Veevers, "Voluntarily Childless Wives," *Sociology and Social Research*, (April, 1973), pp. 356–365. Reprinted by permission of *Sociology and Social Research*, University of Southern California, Los Angeles, California 90007.

and Henly, 1971). Only about five per cent of all couples voluntarily forego parenthood (Veevers, 1972b), and this small deviant minority is characterized by attitudes and behaviors which are both socially unacceptable and not readily visible. The present research, which is exploratory in nature, is based on depth interviews with a purposive sample of 52 voluntarily childless wives. Although the utilization of non-random samples without control groups is obviously not the ideal approach, and can yield only suggestive rather than definitive conclusions, in examining some kinds of social behaviors it is often the only alternative to abandoning the inquiry.

In the present study, respondents were solicited by three separate articles appearing in newspapers in Toronto and in London, followed up by advertisements explicitly asking for volunteers. Of the 86 individuals who replied, 52 wives were selected. Three criteria were evoked in these selections. First, the wife must have stated clearly that her childlessness was due to choice rather than to biological accident. Second, she must either have been married for a minimum of five years, or have been of post-menopausal age, or have reported that either she or her husband had been voluntarily sterilized for contraceptive purposes. Third, she must have affirmed that she had never borne a child, and had never assumed the social role of mother.

The interviews, which were unstructured, averaged about four hours in length, and included discussion of the woman's life history, considerable detail concerning her marriage and her husband, and attitudinal and evaluative aspects of her responses to the maternal role. Data are thus available on the characteristics of 104 voluntarily childless husbands and wives, whose demographic and social characteristics may be briefly summarized as follows. The average age of the sample is 29, with a range from 23 to 71 years. All are Caucasian and living in urban areas, most are middle class, and many are upwardly mobile. Although educational experience ranges from grade school to the post doctoral level, most have at least some university experience. With the exception of one housewife, all are either employed full-time or attending university. Most individuals are either atheists or agnostics from Protestant backgrounds, and of the minority who do express some religious preference, almost all are inactive. Most individuals come from stable homes where the mother has been a full-time housewife since her first child was born. The incidence of first born and only children is much higher than would ordinarily be expected.

With the exception of two widowers, all of the subjects in the present research are involved in their first marriage. The average marriage duration is seven years, with a range from three to twenty-five years. Most couples have relatively egalitarian relationships, but still maintain conventional marriages and follow the traditional division of labor. Configurations of marital adjustment cover the entire continuum described by Cuber and Harroff (1966), ranging from conflict-habituated to total relationships, with many wives reporting vital or total relationships with their husbands.

All of the couples agree on the desirability of preventing pregnancy, at least at the present time. Most of the wives had never been pregnant, but about a fifth had had at least one induced abortion, and most indicate they would seek an abortion if pregnant. More than half of the wives are presently on the pill. About a quarter of the husbands have obtained a vasectomy, and another quarter are seriously considering doing so. Many of the women express positive interest in tubal ligation, but only one, a girl of 23, has actually been sterilized.

The Nature of Childless Careers

In reviewing the processes whereby couples come to define themselves as voluntarily childless, two characteristic career paths are apparent. One route to childlessness involves the formulation by the couple, before they are even married, of a definite and explicitly stated intention never to become involved in parental roles; a second and more common route is less obvious, and involves the prolonged postponement of childbearing until such time as it was no longer considered desirable at all. These two alternatives will be elaborated.

Nearly a third of the wives interviewed entered into their marriages with a childlessness clause clearly stated in their marriage "contract." Although none of these women had a formal written contract in the legal sense of the word, the husband and wife explicitly agreed upon childlessness as a firm condition of marriage. The woman deliberately sought a future mate who, regardless of his other desirable qualities, would agree on this one dimension. Generally the negative decisions regarding the value of children were made during early adolescence, before the possibility of marriage had ever been seriously considered. In contrast, a few of the wives had different or even vaguely positive attitudes towards childbearing until they met their future husbands. During their courtship and engagement, they gradually allowed themselves to be converted to the world view of voluntary childlessness, and by the time of their marriage were quite content to agree to never have children.

More than two thirds of the wives studied remained childless as a result of a series of decisions to postpone having children until some future time, a future which never came. Rather than explicitly rejecting motherhood prior to marriage, they repeatedly deferred procreation until a more convenient time. These temporary postponements provided time during which the evaluations of parenthood were gradually reassessed relative to other goals and possibilities. At the time of their marriages, most wives involved in the postponement model had devoted little serious thought to the question of having children, and had no strong feelings either for or against motherhood. Like conventional couples, they simply assumed that they would have one or two children eventually; unlike conventional couples, they practiced birth control conscientiously and continuously during the early years of marriage.*

Most couples involved in the postponement pattern move through four separate stages in their progression from wanting to not wanting children. The first stage involves postponement for a definite period of time. In this stage, the voluntarily childless are indistinguishable from conventional and conforming couples who will eventually become parents. In most groups, it is not necessarily desirable for the bride to conceive during her honeymoon. It is considered understandable that before starting a family a couple might want to achieve certain goals, such as graduating from school, travelling, buying a house, saving a nest egg, or simply getting adjusted to one another. The degree of specificity varies, but there is a clear commitment to have children as soon as conditions are right.

The second stage of this career involves a shift from postponement for a definite period of time to indefinite postponement. The couple remains committed to the idea of parenthood, but becomes increasingly vague about when the blessed event is going to take place. It may be when they can "afford it," or when "things are going better" or when they "feel more ready."

The third stage in the cycle involves another qualitative change in thinking, in that for the first time there is an open acknowledgment of the possibility that in the end the couple may remain permanently childless. The third stage is a critical one, in that the very fact of openly considering the pros and cons of having children may increase the probability of deciding not to. During this time, they have an opportunity to experience directly the many social, personal, and economic advantages associated with being childless, and at the same time to compare their life styles with those of their peers who are raising children. It seems probable that the social-psychological factors involved in the initial decision to postpone having children may be quite disparate from the social-psychological factors involved in the inclination to remain childless, and to continue with the advantages of a life style to which one has become accustomed. At this stage in the career, the only definite decision is to postpone deciding until some vague and usually unspecified time in the future.

Finally, a fourth stage involves the definite conclusion that the couple are never going to have children, and that childlessness is a permanent rather than a transitory state. Occasionally this involves an explicit decision, usually precipitated by some crisis or change in the environment that focuses atten-

*Whelpton, Campbell, and Patterson report in one study that nearly two out of three newlyweds do not start using contraception before the first conception. See Whelpton, Campbell, and Patterson (1966).

tion on the question of parenthood. However, for most couples, there is never a direct decision made to have or to avoid children. Rather, after a number of years of postponing pregnancy until some future date, they gradually become aware that an implicit decision has been made to forego parenthood. The process involved is one of recognizing an event which has already occurred, rather than of posing a question and then searching or negotiating for an answer. At first, it was "obvious" that "of course" they would eventually have children; now, it is equally "obvious" that they will not. The couple are at a loss to explain exactly how or when the transition came about, but they both agree on their new implicit decision, and they are both contented with its implications.

Childnessness and Informal Sanctions

All of the wives interviewed feel that they are to some extent stigmatized by their unpopular decision to avoid having children, and that there exists an ubiquitous negative stereotype concerning the characteristics of a voluntarily childless woman, including such unfavorable traits as being abnormal, selfish, immoral, irresponsible, immature, unhappy, unfulfilled, and nonfeminine (Veevers, 1972c). In addition, these devaluating opinions are perceived to have behavioral consequences for their interaction with others, and to result in considerable social pressure to become mothers. Some of the sanctions reported are direct and obvious, including explicit and unsolicited comments advocating childbirth and presenting arguments relating to the importance of motherhood. Other pressures are more subtle, and in many cases are perceived to be unintentional. For example, the childless frequently complain that, whereas parents are never required to explain why they chose to have children, they are frequently required to account for their failure to do so.

Childlessness is of course not always a disapproved state. Couples are rewarded, not punished, for remaining childless for the first several months of marriage, and thereby negating the possibility that they were "forced" to get married. After the minimum of nine months has passed, there is a short period of time when the young couple is excused from not assuming all of their responsibilities, or are perceived as having been having intercourse for too short a period of time to guarantee conception. The definition of how long a period of time childbearing may be postponed and still meet with conventional expectations is difficult to determine, and apparently varies considerably from one group to another. In most groups, the first twelve months constitutes an acceptable period of time. After the first year, the pressure gradually but continually increases, reaching a peak during the third and fourth years of marriage. However, once a couple have been married for five or six years there appears to be some diminution of negative responses to them. Several factors are involved in this change: part may be attributable to the increased ability of the childless to avoid those who consistently sanction them; part may be attributable to the increased ability of the childless to cope with negative and hostile responses, making the early years only seem more difficult in retrospect; and part may reflect an actual change in the behavior of others. After five or six years, one's family and friends may give up the possibility of persuading the reluctant couple to procreate or to adopt, and resign themselves to the fact that intervention, at least in this case, is ineffective.

It is noteworthy that although all wives report considerable direct and indirect social pressures to become mothers, most are remarkably well defended against such sanctions. Although on specific occasions they may be either indignant or amused, in most instances they are indifferent to negative responses, and remain inner-directed, drawing constant support and reaffirmation from the consensual validation offered by their husbands. Many strategies are employed which "discredit the discreditors" (Veevers, 1973) and which enable the voluntarily childless to remain relatively impervious to the comments of critics and the wishes of reformers. One such strategy concerns the possibility of adoption.

The Symbolic Importance of Adoption

A recurrent theme in discussions with childless wives is that of adoption. Most wives mention that they have in the past considered adopting a child, and many indicate that they are still considering the possibility at some future date. However, in spite of such positive verbalizations, it is apparent that adoption is not seriously contemplated as a viable alternative, and that their considerations are not likely to result in actually assuming maternal roles. The lack of serious thought about adoption as a real possibility is reflected in the fact that generally they have not considered even such elementary questions as whether they would prefer a boy or a girl, or whether they would prefer an infant or an older child. With few exceptions, none of the couples have made even preliminary inquiries regarding the legal processes involved in adoption. Those few that had made some effort to at least contact a child placement agency had failed to follow through on their initial contact. None had investigated the issue thoroughly enough to have considered the possibility that, should they decide to adopt, a suitable child might not be immediately available to them.

For the voluntarily childless, the importance of the recurrent theme of adoption appears to lie in its symbolic value, rather than in the real possibility of procuring a child by this means and thereby altering one's life style. This symbolic importance is twofold: the reaffirmation of normalcy, and the avoidance of irreversible decisions. A willingness to consider adoption as a possibility communicates to one's self and to others that in spite of being voluntarily childless, one is still a "normal" and "well-adjusted" person who does like children, and who is willing to assume the responsibilities of parenthood. It is an effective mechanism for denying the possibility of considerable psychological differences between parents and non-parents (Veevers, forthcoming), and legitimates the claim of the childless to be just like parents in a number of important respects.

The possibility of adoption at a later date is of symbolic value, in that it prevents the voluntarily childless from being committed to an irreversible state. One of the problems of opting for a postponement model is that eventually one must confront the fact that childbirth cannot be postponed indefinitely. The solution to this dilemma is to include possibility of adoption as a satisfactory "out" should one be needed. The same strategy is employed by many couples who chose sterilization as a means of birth control, but who are not entirely comfortable with the absolute and irreversible solution. The theoretical possibility of adoption is also comforting when faced with the important but unanswerable question of how one will feel about being childless in one's old age.

The Relevance of Supportive Ideologies

The voluntarily childless appear to be in a state of pluralistic ignorance, in that they are unaware of the numbers of other individuals who share their world view. Although the deliberate decision to avoid parenthood is a relatively rare phenomenon, it is not nearly as rare as the childless themselves perceive it to be, especially among urban and well-educated middle class couples. A large proportion of wives indicated that until they read the article and/or advertisement asking for subjects for the present study, they had never seen the topic of voluntary childlessness discussed in the mass media. Many reported that they did not know any other couple who felt as they did about the prospect of parenthood, and many others reported having met only one or two like-minded people during the course of their marriage.

Feelings of uniqueness and of isolation are somewhat mitigated by the explicit agreement of husbands on the appropriateness of foregoing parental roles. However, regardless of how supportive the husband is in his reaffirmation of the legitimacy of childlessness, and how committed he is personally to avoiding fatherhood, because of cultural differences in sex roles he does not share an entirely comparable situation. He may be totally sympathetic, but he has a limited ability to empathize. The childless wife may be generally comfortable with her decision not to have children, and still express the wish that she could discuss her situation with other like-minded women who might have shared similar experiences within the female subculture, and who might provide a model for identification.

It is noteworthy that within the psychological world of the voluntarily childless, existing social movements concerned with population or with feminism have surprisingly little relevance, and provide relatively little intellectual or emotional support. The concern with population problems, especially as manifest in the Zero Population Growth movement, does provide a supportive rationale indicating that one is not necessarily being socially irresponsible and neglectful of one's civic obligations if one does not reproduce. However, although there is a clear statement that procreation is not necessary for all, most ZPG advocates are careful to indicate that it is not procreation *per se* they are opposed to, but rather excessive procreation. The slogan "Stop at Two" asserts that one should have no more than two children, but also implies that one perhaps should have at least one or two. Some of the childless wives are superficially involved in ZPG and sympathetic with its goals, but in all cases this identification is an *ex post facto* consideration, rather than a motivating force, and their satisfaction with being childless is related to concerns other than their contribution to the population crisis.

It is sometimes suggested that an inclination to avoid motherhood is a logical extension of the new feminism. It is difficult to generalize about a social phenomenon as amorphous as the women's liberation movement, a rubric which incorporates many diverse and even contradictory attitudes. However, "A significant feature of the women's liberation movement is that, although its demands have been made on the basis of equity for women, it has not usually been anti-marriage or anti-children (Commission on Population Growth, 1972, p. 68).

In many instances, the ideological statements endorsed by the women's liberation movement are implicitly or explicitly pro-natalist. Motherhood is not perceived as an unfulfilling and unrewarding experience; rather, it is perceived as a positive experience which, although desirable, is not sufficient in and of itself for maximum self-actualization. Considerable concern is expressed with the problems involved in combining successful motherhood with comparable success in other careers. Rather than advising women to give up having children, the new feminist literature advises them to consider other careers in addition to motherhood, and advocates changes in society which would make the motherhood role easier. For example, there is considerable stress on the provision of maternity leaves, on increased involvement of fathers in childcare, on accessibility to adequate day care facilities. Although advocates of the new feminism may provide some support for the idea that motherhood is neither necessary nor sufficient for fulfillment, they do still advocate that normally it will be an important part of that fulfillment. Only a few of the voluntarily childless are at all concerned with women's liberation, and these few apparently came into the movement after their decision was made and their life style was established.

Although none of the voluntarily childless are actively seeking group support for their life style, many would welcome the opportunity to become involved in a truly supportive social movement. The first example of such an association is the National Organization for Nonparenthood (NON) which was formed in California in 1971. Because of the state of pluralistic ignorance which surrounds voluntary childlessness, and because of the inadequacy of demographic and feminist movements in expressing the world view of the childless, such attempts to formulate a counter culture might be expected to be very successful.

Summary

The present research on a purposive sample of 52 voluntarily childless wives is exploratory in nature. Although it is not possible to make definitive statements regarding the nature of childless couples, several tentative conclusions are offered. It is suggested that couples come to be voluntarily childless by a number of diverse paths beginning both before and after marriage, and that considerable diversity might be expected between those who enter marriage only on the condition of a clear childlessness clause in the marriage contract, and those who remain childless after a series of postponements of parenthood. Although considerable social presures are directed towards the childless, most of the individuals involved appear to be very well defended against such sanctions, and the mechanisms of re-defining situations and of protecting themselves are worthy of further study. One such mechanism appears to be the use of the possibility of adoption to deny the status of voluntary childlessness while not seriously threatening the accompanying life style. Finally, it is suggested that existing social movements do not provide much relevant support for the voluntarily childless, and that an explicit counter culture, such as the National Organization for Nonparenthood, might be expected to meet with considerable success.

References

Commission on Population Growth and the American Future, *Report*. Washington, D.C.: Commission on Population Growth and the American Future, 1972.

Cuber, John F., and Peggy B. Harroff. *Sex and the Significant Americans: A Study of Sexual Behavior among the Affluent*. Baltimore: Penguin, 1966.

Gustavus, Susan O., and James R. Henly, Jr. "Correlates of Voluntary Childlessness in a Select Population." *Social Biology*, 18 (September 1971): 277–284.

Pohlman, Edward. "Childlessness: Intentional and Unintentional." *The Journal of Nervous and Mental Disease*, 151 (1970), no. 1: 2–12.

Veevers, J. E. "Voluntary Childlessness: A Neglected Area of Family Study." *The Family Coordinator*, 21 (April 1972).

Veevers, J. E. "Factors in the Incidence of Childlessness in Canada: An Analysis of Census Data." *Social Biology*, 19 (December 1972).

Veevers, J. E. "The Violation of Fertility Mores: Voluntary Childlessness as Deviant Behavior." In *Deviant Behavior and Societal Reaction*, edited by Craig L. Boydell, Carl F. Grindstaff, and Paul C. Whitehead, pp. 571–592. Toronto: Holt, Rinehart and Winston, 1972.

Veevers, J. E. "The Moral Career of Voluntarily Childless Wives: Notes on the Construction and Defense of a Deviant World View." In *Marriage and the Family in Canada*, edited by S. Parvez Wakil. Toronto: Longmans Green, 1973.

Veevers, J. E. "The Social Meanings of Parenthood." *Psychiatry: Journal for the Study of Interpersonal Processes*, forthcoming.

Whelpton, Pascal K., Arthur A. Campbell, and J. E. Patterson. *Fertility and Family Planning in the United States*. Princeton: Princeton University Press, 1966.

The authors, both sociologists, regard theories of homosexuality as inadequate because they concentrate on the individual's psychic predisposition to be homosexual, rather than on situational or normative factors facilitating and governing homosexual behavior. For example, they argue that the male-female difference in promiscuity is better explained by lack of opportunity for stranger meetings by females than an innate interest in love that all females are presumed to have. The article shows how the world of homosexuality is socially organized, and how the individual's capacity to participate in it is learned through experience.

The Social Organization of Homosexuality

Maureen Mileski and Donald J. Black

Social science theories that seek to explain behavior often explain no more than the motivation to behave. Theories about deviant behavior, for instance, typically are theories about the psychological disposition to deviate. Investigators discuss how specific conditions implant these dispositions to deviate, but they usually say little or nothing about the social conditions that must be present before these deviant acts can occur. In fact, most social science seems to assume that people have available to them the means to behave in accordance with their motives. In our view, this assumption frequently is unjustified, and hence these motivational theories are empirically wrong.

"The Social Organization of Homosexuality," by Maureen Mileski and Donald J. Black is reprinted from *Urban Life and Culture*, Vol. 1, No. 2 (July, 1972), pp. 187–199 by permission of the Publisher, Sage Publications, Inc.

It may be that a particular form of behavior thrives in some social settings while it is nearly or totally absent in others, and this difference can be independent of variation in the relevant motivational underlayer.

To elaborate this argument we select the case of homosexuality.* Our approach to homosexuality is an application of a strategy of sociological explanation that applies equally well to conforming behavior—namely, the general study of social organization. A theory of social organization attempts to uncover supraindividual principles and mechanisms according to which social events occur. It is particularly appropriate to apply this strategy to homosexuality since a considerable body of literature has accumulated around the subject which takes for granted that a theory of homosexuality must be a theory of the motivation to engage in the behavior. Often this work follows a psychoanalytic strategy (see, e.g., Bieber et al., 1962). Rather than addressing the problem of homosexual motivation, then, our discussion assumes that the motivation to indulge in homosexual conduct is present in the population at large. This is not an assumption of a population with lively desires to have homosexual relations—an assumption which would be preposterous—but only of the basic psychological conditions necessary for persons to take part in homosexual encounter.† In sum, we make problematic what theories of homosexuality usually assume—the social conditions prerequisite to the behavior—and we assume what other theories usually make problematic.

Another way to word this is that other explanations of deviant behavior are social-psychological, whereas we try to locate the direction that a sociological theory would go. With Durkheim's theory of suicide, some confusion was laid on the field of sociology, especially for inquiry into deviant behavior. He attempted to draft a theory of suicide "disregarding the individual as such, his motives and his ideas"; but, he goes on, "returning to the individual . . .

---

*In part of what follows we draw upon what we learned in an observation study of homosexual social life. Over a period of a year (1966-1967), we visited seven gay bars in a large, a medium-sized, and a small midwestern city, a total of about fifty times. We also attended a number of after-hours homosexual parties. We informally talked with numerous participants. The quotes that follow are derived from our field notes.

†The high rate of homosexual behavior in prisons among persons who are, on the outside, heterosexual lends a great deal of credibility to our assumption. Kinsey, for instance, found no long-term men's correctional institutions with fewer than 60% of the inmates participating in homosexuality, and he found one prison where over 90% of the inmates admitted such experience (cited in Barnes and Teeters, 1959, p. 375). The rate of homosexuality likewise appears high in women's prisons (see Ward and Kassebaum, 1965). Indeed, the assumption of homosexual motivation almost seems justified by the rate of homosexuality in the population at large. Kinsey reports that 37% of the male population has some homosexual experience between the beginning of adolescence and old age, and of those who remain unmarried, 50% have homosexual experience between adolescence and 35 years of age (Kinsey et al., 1948, pp. 623–625).

we shall study how these general causes become individualized so as to produce the homicidal results involved" (Durkheim, 1951, p. 151; compare
Inkeles, 1959, pp. 249–255). Thus he joins an analysis of the social level of
reality with an analysis of the individual level, looking at the impact of one
upon the other. Although his theory of suicide is in this sense social-psychological in deed, it often is taken as a model of explanation that is truly
and wholly sociological. Perhaps we could say, then, that our account of
deviance is Durkheimian in spirit.

A Girl in Indonesia

If the motivation to act in a given manner is assumed in a theory of human
behavior, then the question becomes a matter of what else besides a particular
psychological state must be present before the behavior can occur. In the case
of homosexuality, what besides psychological homosexuals must be present
before homosexual behavior can take place? Simply put, what social
mechanisms make homosexual behavior possible?

To dramatize the importance of the social aspect of homosexuality, it is
helpful to draw on the following personal document written by a girl in
Indonesia to an American lesbian journal (anonymous, 1964):

> You know, we haven't got *any* bars in our whole country, let alone gay
> ones. Gay people, yes: male prostitutes, along the streets dressed up
> like women. But gay women, no. That is, none that I know of, except
> myself. . . . Nobody could tell by my looks that I am different from the
> rest. [And] if the other girls are acting like I am, it's small wonder I
> can't find them.

With existing theory, a social scientist might well infer from the virtual
absence of lesbian behavior in Indonesia that there is an absence of lesbian
motivation in that society. On that basis, he might then seek to discover the
social and psychological factors that contribute to this pattern. He might, for
example, focus upon the process of sex identification, perhaps examining the
family structure to learn what creates women without homosexual motivation. But his search would be misguided. Plumbing the Indonesian personality would not yield the appropriate data to account for the lack of lesbianism there. The absence of behavior of a particular kind does not automatically indicate the absence of particular motives. Correlatively, the presence
of motives does not explain a rate of behavior, though it is routine for social
science to try to advance this explanation. The Indonesian girl is, motivationally, a homosexual, but behaviorally she is not. Her social situation
dooms her to conformity. Or, we could say, the social mechanisms that allow
female homosexuality are absent from Indonesia.

Mechanisms

The presence of specifiable social mechanisms makes it possible for individuals to form homosexual liaisons. These mechanisms appear unevenly across social space. Where mechanisms are available, the rate of homosexuality will be high and without them it will be minimal. These mechanisms appear at two levels of group life: at the level of the community, where the mechanisms are organized territories, and at the level of the face-to-face encounter, where the mechanisms are rules regulating the coming into being of sexual situations. These organized territories and situational rules facilitate homosexual behavior; without them, the world divides into so many isolated cases like that of the girl in Indonesia.

Territories

By now it is well known that there are territories in communities where homosexuals congregate. A growing literature describes these territories (see Leznoff and Westley, 1956; Cory, 1960; Hooker, 1961). Most widely known and most common is the gay bar (see, e.g., Cavan, 1963; Rechy, 1964; Sawyer, 1965; Achilles, 1967). Also common are organized "cruising" or pick-up areas, such as sections of public parks, street corners, bus stations, and movie theaters (Reiss, 1961; Rechy, 1967). Likewise there are numerous public restrooms, sometimes called "tearooms," where rapid but systematically staged homosexual encounters take place (Humphries, 1970). Still other ostensibly conventional settings such as clothing stores, bookstores, steambaths, and gymnasiums occasionally function as homosexual territories. These homosexual territories are by no means obvious to the untrained eye. The newcomer to homosexuality must learn from his fellows the range of opportunities that his home city affords him.

Some urban communities harbor a rich array of these settings; others have very few or none at all. In fact, homosexuals sometimes stratify cities on the basis of the extent and quality of the gay life appearing in each; they speak of cities as "good," "not so good," or "bad," depending upon their offerings for the homosexual. In the larger cities, some of these territories, especially the gay bars, are highly differentiated with respect to the characteristics of their participants. There is, first, specialization according to the behavior of the homosexuals involved. There are, for example, "home territory" gay bars where there is a great deal of sociable behavior among friends and acquaintances (Cavan, 1963), "cruising bars" where pairing off between relative strangers takes place at a higher rate, and what are sometimes called "leather bars" where homosexuals with sado-masochist and fetishist proclivities gather. There may also be specialization according to the various statuses of the homosexuals involved: their social class, race, sex, and age. In smaller cities, there is likely to be a more democratic participation in homosexual facilities, such that there may be a gay bar serving both males and females, rich and poor, old and young. Still other urban communities offer no homosexual territories whatsoever, let alone specialized ones.

It has frequently been noted that the rise of urban centers is accompanied by a decline of the close-knit, intimate community life of the traditional sort. The specialization of behavior found in a large city, however, yields its own kind of community. Namely, in the midst of the heterogeneity, the anonymity, and the fast and changing pace of the urban scene, an individual nonetheless often finds himself in a pocket whose boundaries reach no further than to other individuals very much like himself. The more the specialization and differentiation, the more any given individual can and does deal with others who have like involvements. In the language of Durkheim, social differentiation is a multitude of social colonies, each held together by a mechanical solidarity based upon social likeness. Durkheim understood that this social solidarity based upon similarity was characteristic of occupational groupings within the division of labor, though he did not examine the other varieties of specialization that characterize city life (see Durkheim, 1933, pp. 187–193). Since subcommunities coalesce around single dimensions of behavior, the entire scope of one's life is not bounded by any one of these agglomerations alone. Social networks are grounded in occupational attachment, life styles, or subcultures, recreational activities, neighborhood linkages, ethnic identities, and, we hardly need add, sexual orientations. The gay world is just one among the many worlds of the modern urban configuration.

A small or medium-sized urban center, wherein specialization is high relative to traditional society but low relative to the large metropolis, hangs the individual somewhere between these basic forms of community, providing neither the totalizing integration of primitive likeness nor the cellular purification of specialization.* In these smaller communities, homosexual life tends to be impoverished. By contrast, we would predict that in larger cities, such as New York, Chicago, or Los Angeles, those with a differentiated bouquet of homosexual territories, there will be found more enduring relationships among homosexuals ("marriages"). Under these conditions, homosexuals have the luxury of specialization along such dimensions as sexual leanings, race, and social class, and also the numbers necessary for the formation of solidary dyads (see Helmer, 1966).

In sum, the rate and diversity of homosexuality in a community is in good part conditioned by the number and kinds of territories it tolerates; the ter-

---

*This midpoint—at which there may be, contrastingly, an integration of diversity— is outlined for urban groupings in Sennett (1970, pp. 107–188).

ritories are the setting for encounters between vast numbers of homosexuals who otherwise would likely not meet. Thus, whether a given individual takes part in a homosexual act and, if he does, what kind of homosexual act it is and what kind of relationship he likely has with his partner, tell us more about where he is to be found in social space than it tells us about what is to be found in his mind.

Approaches

Homosexual acts do not automatically arise from the congregation of homosexually oriented persons in one physical setting or territory any more than heterosexual behavior spontaneously occurs when males and females are in proximity. Other mechanisms necessary for the coming into being of homosexuality are located at the level of face-to-face interaction within these territories. The face-to-face encounter is to the territory what the territory is to the community; no more can isolated individual motives create social behavior at one level than at the other.

Notable among these mechanisms are the rules of approach. These rules define the proper sexual advance within the homosexual territory. In most homosexual settings, direct approaches are taboo; they are considered, in the vocabulary of the participants, "fruity." Direct approaches do occur, but in specifiable settings; for example, they occur in highly specialized settings of an orgiastic sort (such as steambaths), in densely populated "cruising" bars, or, interestingly, in assorted nonhomosexual contexts, as when a driver makes an advance upon a passenger-hitchhiker or when a stranger approaches another stranger in a public setting such as a bus station.

Typically, however, no one in an established homosexual territory is likely to be subject to a direct approach with manifest sexual purposes. The process of partner recruitment is in its essentials an interactive one that blurs the line between seducer and seduced. Speaking of the psychology of this process, one homosexual remarked, "Every homosexual wants to be seduced." Through the exchange of a variety of often-used cues (e.g., a request for time, a match, a dance, a short series of interested glances, an ostensibly idle comment, a change of chairs) the level of intimacy is gradually escalated until either one party withdraws or the sexual encounter is actualized. Approaches commonly last a period of minutes and consist of a series of gestures. In one case, for example, a male (A) began to eye another across a table. The latter (B) returned the glances. Shortly thereafter B entered the restroom, and A followed. B returned to his chair at a large, round table (rather like the "piano bar" that is often seen in gay bars), and after a short wait A took a seat nearby. When B drew out a cigarette, A had a match waiting. Conversation ensued, and A asked B to dance; B accepted. Not long after, however,

B excused himself from the general area, and a fuller intimacy was thus gently aborted. The escalation process is fragile, with the exchange of cues by its nature allowing for a graceful exit by either or both parties at any point. In short, the proper and the standard homosexual approach is indirect.

One of the observers once stood in a sexually mixed ring of four to five people when closing hour was approaching, and a gay participant said, for the group to hear, "O.K., X, how about coming home with me tonight?" The question was so out of order that it was simple for the researcher to laugh at its bluntness, as though it were a joke. This response was reinforced by the laughter of the other participants. One homosexual psychologized the matter, and said, "That's not romantic enough." In those homosexual territories which are shorn of romance, approaches are somewhat more direct, but even there one finds a patterned give and take which prefaces the sexual act (Humphries, 1970, pp. 59–80). Usually, however, an interactant has no occasion to react to directness one way or the other, since direct approaches are rare. The point, then, is both that direct approaches empirically are unlikely to occur and that they would fail if they were to occur. There is a rule that approaches be indirect.

The play of the indirect approach has been as little understood by would-be participants as it has been by social science; for example, individuals report having gone with adventuresome intentions to homosexual territories only to have "nothing happen." What occurs in these instances is that the newcomer does not participate in the normative linking of individuals one to another. He falsely assumes that his and others' intentions create social deviance. But the deviance is unavailable to those who do not know its normative arrangement. Were it not for rules of approach, the homosexual territories would be peopled by individuals pursuing their erotic interests as they saw fit. A chaotic situation surely would result. Homosexual territories thus have their own moral organization, and one who visits them oblivious to the structured life therein may find himself a stranger to the social order that surrounds him. On at least two levels, then, social mechanisms feed individuals into homosexuality while their absence or the failure to use them largely immobilizes individuals.

Other Mechanisms

Apart from homosexual territories and approaches, there are other mechanisms in the social organization of homosexuality. There are some mechanisms access to which is limited by forces beyond the control of individuals. For example, aspects of sex or age may be more or less facilitative of homosexuality.

In contemporary American society, it is normatively permissible for two well-acquainted females to display a platonic affection for one another.* In private relations among adult males, contrariwise, intimacy need not be carried far before the behavior is treated as replete with homosexual connotations. The slight caress, word of love, or even kiss on the cheek which the female can legitimately extend to one of her own sex is taboo in the male world. In the male world, such advances are quickly called "queer."†

Not surprisingly, therefore, many females first engage in homosexuality with a friend in an ordinary social setting rather than in an organized homosexual territory. The norms of intimacy framing personal relations between females constitute the mechanism that allows for homosexuality in these instances. Females often have this first sexual experience with another female in a process which lesbians label "turning straight girls." That is to say, their first homosexual experience is a result of escalated intimacies. An excerpt from field notes captures an instance of this:

> "Why doesn't your friend S— ever come to the bars?"
> "She doesn't like to come out in public—she's more discreet than that."
> "How is she able to meet other girls?"
> "Gay girls? Oh, she turns straight ones."
> "How's that?"
> "Oh, you know, she meets a girl, gets up tight with her, then turns her."

Another girl, upon mentioning that she moved to a small town which lacked any gay center for females, was advised "to get busy and start turning straight girls." When both partners are homosexually naive, we might say that these intimacies at some point spill over or drift into homosexuality (see Matza, 1964).

*At this point, we should emphasize that we are speaking only of contemporary American society, though it is expected that other societies will share these characteristics. In Indonesia, however, presumably there is an absence of organized territories for females and these other mechanisms as well.

†These rules of intimacy are specific to particular age groups and, to a lesser extent, are specific to social classes and other kinds of status groups. For example, it is now well known that children and younger adolescents engage in homosexuality at a relatively high rate (Kinsey et al., 1948, pp. 168–172, 623–659). That they conceal their homosexuality from their parents and other adults suggests that they are aware that their behavior is deviant from an adult standpoint. With adulthood comes an abrupt shift to different rules of intimacy. Rather suddenly, most adults cease to be sexually attracted to members of their own sex, an expressed attitude which takes hold and apparently continues for the rest of their lives.

Similarly, rules of intimacy vary across cultures; rates of homosexuality vary accordingly. Among the Nambikwara of Brazil, for example, homosexuality has been permitted to unmarried cross-cousins, even in public places. This practice is called "the loving lie" (Lévi-Strauss, 1963, pp. 306–307). A survey of the ethnographic and historical literature would yield numerous illustrations (see Ford and Beach, 1951, pp. 130–133).

This process cannot so readily happen between males, since intimations of love are typically halted at their first appearance. The first postadolescent contact with homosexuality for a male usually takes the form of a trip to a gay bar or other well-known homosexual territory. The norms of intimacy cast males away from their friends into sometimes jarring encounters with people whom they have never before met:

> The first time it was with this horrible old man. I met him at a burlesque house. . . . I'd heard that was one place to go in Dayton. I picked him up and went to this house with him . He wanted to do it right there in the john at the burlesque house, so I made up some story about having been arrested there. Anyway, it was just awful—I vomited.

The following self-report of a female contrasts with the stranger-stranger relationships among males:

> Love? Yes, I've been in love. It was the first girl. . . . It was really wonderful then. There was another girl after that one, but that relationship wasn't as good as the first. I met the second girl here at the bar.

Until a male becomes involved in private networks of friends and associates, male homosexuality must be pursued in the homosexual marketplace. And even within homosexual friendship groups, sexual intimacy very often is considered taboo and unattractive. Consequently, for many male homosexuals, gay territories play a major role throughout their sexually active lives. For the female homosexual, organized territories are more supplemental than central. In a city which sports twenty gay bars, for instance, only one of these is likely to be claimed by females. In sum, the normative nature of private relations among females allows for a reportedly high rate of lesbianism in the United States even though there is not a high number of public lesbian territories.

There is an interesting consequence of the difference in the social organization of homosexuality among the two sexes. It appears that lesbians are much less "promiscuous" than are male homosexuals; that is to say, females have a much lower rate of "one-night stands." The social mechanisms of lesbianism subvert promiscuity. No matter how much individual lesbians may desire a high turnover of partners, they cannot obtain it without mechanisms for the recurrent meeting of strangers. Where lesbians do have access to bars peopled by relative strangers, on the other hand, it appears that they are quite as likely to carry on numerous ephemeral relationships, just as many males do. The male-female difference in promiscuity has been accounted for by the interest in love that all females are presumed to have (Gagnon and Simon, 1967, pp. 214–215). However, the overall low rate of one-night stands among lesbians probably says at least as much about their social organization as it does about their motivation. In other words, promiscuity, like homosexuality, can be usefully understood as a property of social organization* Patterns of sexual moderation tell us very little about motivational tendencies of the persons involved. Within limits, what is sexually possible predicts sexual behavior patterns.

Concluding Remarks

We have discussed several examples of mechanisms that facilitate homosexual behavior.† The mechanisms fall into two categories, those constituted by rules or norms and those organized according to some other structural property such as physical space or time. What we called the rules of approach and the rules of intimacy, then, are normative mechanisms, while homosexual territories are part of social morphology.

It is important to note that when we consider normative mechanisms we treat rules in terms of how they organize social behavior. This conception of rules as facilitative or ordering devices contrasts though it does not logically conflict with the more usual view of rules as protective devices, mechanisms by which a given social system is maintained (see Ehrlich, 1936, pp. 53–55). Rules both establish social organization and attend the social organization already established. When rules are approached as facilitative devices, nonconformity cannot be understood as an illegitimate means to an end (compare Merton, 1949, ch. 4). Thus, for example, failure to conform to the rules of approach in a homosexual territory is no short-cut to a sexual liaison; rather, only through conformity is it possible to reach one's sexual ends. Obedience to rules, then, sometimes is the only technique available for attain-

---

*When one considers what male homosexuals say as against what they do, it is clear that they are extremely interested in what they call love or enduring relationships. It is more that the organization of male homosexuality is not geared to producing enduring relationships than that the males have no interest in them. Indeed, one homosexual questioned the value of studying anything but the phenomenology of homosexuality: "I don't see how you can study homosexuals. There is nothing about it that you will be able to see that is distinct from the outside, because the most important thing is love. You have to be gay to study it, or you can't know how important love is for gay people." In any event, male homosexuals may not find but nevertheless seek relationships that are based on more than purely physical attraction. As one young man put it when asked why he frequented gay bars, "Well, frankly, I am always looking for a miracle."

†The vocabulary of our approach is related to opportunity theory. The opportunity approach, however, contains a psychological or subjective component. For example, Cloward and Ohlin (1960) join frustration and a desire for upward mobility to opportunity in their interpretation of delinquency. Lofland (1969, pp. 61–173) discusses access to physical sites, objects, and other people as part of the production of a deviant identity. And in the classic statement, Sutherland (1960, ch. 4) considers opportunity from the standpoint of what a potential deviant can learn from others.

ing a particular social outcome.* Rules tell us not only what we may do; they tell us what we can do in the literal sense of what we are able to do. Rules belong to a class of mechanisms that help make social life possible.

At present, there are no theories of homosexual behavior in social science; there are only theories of homosexual motivation. A motivational theory provides an explanation of motivation, and that is all. However primitive and inadequate our own approach may be, we may at least have brought to the fore some of the empirical and logical failings of motivational theories of homosexuality. Beyond that, we have sketched outlines of a theory of behavior, using the case of homosexuality. Social-organizational analysis is just one of many ways to study behavior. To repeat, it seeks to find the supraindividual principles and mechanisms by which social events occur. Although we have dealt with just one type of deviance, our approach is applicable to other forms of deviance and, more importantly, to systems of behavior in general. Neither homosexuality nor any other kind of deviant behavior requires a special form of theory. Perhaps it is because individual-oriented theory has dominated thinking about deviance that it is generally assumed that deviance requires its own special theory, for one may suppose that the motives of men who do what is considered evil are different from the motives of others. There is, however, a grammar of social life that is indifferent to the content of men's minds. An analysis of motivation cannot reveal that larger design; that is the task for the theory of social organization.

References

Achilles, N. "The Development of the Homosexual Bar as an Institution." In *Sexual Deviance*, edited by J. H. Gagnon and W. Simon, pp. 228–244. New York: Harper & Row, 1967.

Anonymous. Letter in *The Ladder: A Lesbian Review* (June 1964), pp. 9–11.

Barnes, H. E., and N. K. Teeters. *New Horizons in Criminology*. Englewood Cliffs, N.J.: Prentice-Hall, 1959.

Bieber, I., et al. *Homosexuality: A Psychoanalytic Study*. New York: Basic Books, 1962.

Cavan, S. "Interaction in Home Territories." *Berkeley Journal of Sociology*, 8 (1963): 17–32.

Cloward, R. A., and L. E. Ohlin. *Delinquency and Opportunity: A Theory of Delinquent Gangs*. New York: Free Press, 1960.

Cory, D. W. *The Homosexual in America*. New York: Castle, 1960.

Durkheim, E. *The Division of Labor in Society*. New York: Macmillan, 1933.

Durkheim, E. *Suicide: A Study in Sociology*. New York: Free Press, 1951.

*Durkheim (1953, pp. 35–37) makes a distinction between moral rules and rules of technique. The violation of a moral rule such as the rule against theft, creates the risk of sanction, a consequence of rule violation that is imposed from without. The violation of rules of technique, such as rules of horticulture, however, destroys the very project one pursues. In Durkheim's terms, then, we are viewing what would normally be considered moral rules as rules of technique.

Durkheim, E. "The Determination of Moral Facts." In *Sociology and Philosophy*, pp. 35–62. New York: Free Press, 1953.

Ehrlich, E. *Fundamental Principles of the Sociology of Law*. Cambridge: Harvard University Press, 1936.

Ford, C. S., and F. A. Beach. *Patterns of Sexual Behavior*. New York: Harper & Row, 1951.

Gagnon, J., and W. Simon. "Femininity in the Lesbian Community." *Social Problems*, 15 (1967): 212–221.

Helmer, W. J. "New York's 'Middle Class' Homosexuals." *Harper's* (March 1966): 87–93.

Hooker, E. "The Homosexual Community." *Proceedings of the Fourteenth International Congress of Applied Psychology*, 2 (1961): 40–59.

Humphries, L. *Tearoom Trade. Impersonal Sex in Public Places*. Chicago: Aldine, 1970.

Inkeles, A. "Personality and Social Structure." In *Sociology Today: Problems and Prospects*, edited by R. K. Merton et al., pp. 249–276. New York: Basic Books, 1959.

Kinsey, A. C., W. B. Pomeroy, and C. E. Martin. *Sexual Behavior in the Human Male*. Philadelphia: W. B. Saunders, 1948.

Lévi-Strauss, C. *Tristes Tropiques*. New York: Atheneum, 1963.

Leznoff, M., and W. A. Westley. "The Homosexual Community." *Social Problems*, 3 (1956): 257–263.

Lofland, J., with L. H. Lofland. *Deviance and Identity*. Englewood Cliffs, N.J.: Prentice-Hall, 1969.

Matza, D. *Delinquency and Drift*. New York: Wiley, 1964.

Merton, R. K. *Social Theory and Social Structure*. New York: Free Press, 1949.

Rechy, J. *City of Night*. New York: Grove, 1964.

Rechy, J. *Numbers*. New York: Grove, 1967.

Reiss, A. J., Jr. "The Social Integration of Queers and Peers." *Social Problems*, 9 (1961): 102–120.

Sawyer, E. "A Study of a Public Lesbian Community." Master's thesis, Washington University, 1965.

Sennett, R. *The Uses of Disorder*. New York: Alfred A. Knopf, 1970.

Sonenschein, D. "The Ethnography of Male Homosexual Relationships." *Journal of Sex Research*, 4 (1968): 69–83.

Sutherland, E. H., and D. R. Cressey. *Principles of Criminology*. Chicago: J. B. Lippincott, 1960.

Ward, D., and G. Kassebaum. *Woman's Prison*. Chicago: Aldine, 1965.

In this article the author argues that the one-parent family is statistically more numerous and psychologically less pathological than generally assumed. He describes the various types of one-parent families and the characteristics of each type.

Parents Without Partners | *E. E. LeMasters*

In thinking about parents it is easy to assume a model of what might be termed "the biological parent team" of mother and father. In this model two parents act as partners in carrying out the parental functions. Furthermore, both of the parents are biological as well as social parents.

What is not realized by many observers, especially by parent critics, is the fact that a considerable proportion of contemporary American parents do not operate under these ideal conditions. These parents include "parents without partners" (mostly divorced or separated women, but including a few men also); widows and widowers with children; unmarried mothers; adoptive parents; step-parents; and, finally, foster parents.

Some of the groups in the list above are amazingly large—Simon, for example, reports that in the 1960s in the United States there were about *seven million* children living with a step-parent. This means that approximately one out of every nine children in modern America is a stepchild.

Mothers Without Fathers

One of the by now familiar parental types in our society is the mother rearing her children alone. As of 1960 about one household out of ten in the United States was headed by a woman. In an earlier, more innocent America, this mother without father was seen as a heroic figure—a brave woman whose husband had died who was struggling to rear her brood by scrubbing floors, taking in family laundry, and so on. This was the brave little widow of an earlier day.

After the end of World War I, as the divorce rate began to climb, this picture—and this woman—underwent a radical change. With the rapid improvement of American medicine, marriages in the early and middle decades of life were no longer broken primarily by death; now the great destroyers of marriages came to be social and psychological, not biological.

With this shift the public's attitude toward the mother with no father by

From E. E. LeMasters, "Parents Without Partners," in *Parents in Modern America* (Homewood: The Dorsey Press, Inc., 1970), pp. 157–174. Reprinted by permission.

her side changed drastically—it became ambivalent. In some cases she might be viewed with sympathy and understanding, if she happened to be your sister or a close friend, but more often she was perceived as a woman of questionable character—either the gay divorcee of the upper social-class levels or the ADC mother living off of the taxpayers at the lower social-class levels. In either case the image was a far cry from that of the heroic little widow of the Victorian era.

Statistically, and otherwise, these mothers without fathers fall into five different categories: divorced, separated, deserted, widowed, and never married. All of these categories overlap, so that some mothers might at some point in their lives occupy all five positions in the list.

Our procedure in discussing these mothers in their parental role will be to identify the generic patterns and problems shared by all of these mothers, and then to look at the relatively unique patterns that cluster about any specific position.

Generic Features of Mothers Without Partners

1. *Poverty.* It has been estimated that while households headed by a woman comprise only about 10 percent of all U.S. households, they constitute about 25 percent of the families in the so-called poverty group in American society.

In the best study yet published on divorced women, Goode found financial stress to be a major complaint. At any given time approximately 40 percent of the divorced husbands in this study were delinquent in their support payments, a pattern that seems to be nationwide.

Poverty is extremely relative, as is deprivation. A divorced woman receiving even $1,000 a month in support payments may have to reduce her standard of living from what it was before her divorce.

The reasons for the financial difficulties of these mothers are not mysterious or difficult to identify. Most American men cannot afford to support two living establishments on a high level. This is one reason why some support payments are delinquent. The man usually gets involved with at least one other woman, and this costs money. Often his new woman is not well off financially and the man may find himself contributing to her support also.

Since a considerable proportion of divorced women are apparently employed at the time of their divorce, they had what is commonly called a two-income family. The mother may continue to work after the father has left the home, but with two living establishments to maintain, two cars, and so on, the financial situation tends to be tight.

In a study of ADC mothers in Boston, it was discovered that these women faced financial crises almost monthly. They coped with these difficult situations by accepting aid from members of their family; by pooling their resources with neighbors and women friends in the same plight; and by occasional aid from a boy friend.

In several counseling cases with divorced women, the writer was impressed with the annoying feature of the relative poverty experienced by these women—one woman didn't have the money to get her television set repaired and this created tension between herself and her children. Another woman, who lived in an area with inadequate bus service, could not afford an automobile. Any person in our society can understand how frustrating problems of this nature can be.

2. *Role conflicts.* Since these women have added the father role to their parental responsibilities, they tend to be either overloaded or in conflict over their various role commitments. The presence of a husband-father provides more flexibility than these women now have—if the mother is ill, or has to work late, the husband may be able to be home with the children.

When these mothers are employed outside of the home, as a sizable proportion are, the work hours usually conflict with those of the school system. Children leave for school too late, get home too early, and have far too many vacations for the employed mother. There are also childhood illnesses that must be coped with.

It is true that the termination of the marriage has reduced or eliminated the mother's role as wife, but she is still a woman in the early decades of life and men will be in the picture sooner or later. Thus she may not be a wife at the moment but she will soon be a girl friend, and the courtship role may be even more demanding than that of wife.

It is the writer's belief, based on numerous interviews with divorced women, that being the head of a household is, for most women, an 18-hour day, seven days a week, and 365 days a year job. It would seem that only the most capable, and the most fortunate, can perform all of the roles involved effectively.

3. *Role shifts.* Since the vast majority of the mothers being discussed here —80 to 90 percent—will eventually remarry, they face the difficult process of taking over the father role and then relinquishing it. This is not easy for most of us; once we have appropriated a role in a family system, it is often difficult to turn it over to somebody else.

Furthermore, these mothers operate in an unusual family system in that, for an indefinite period, they do not have to worry about what the other parent thinks. They are both mother and father for the time being.

This is not entirely true, of course, in the case of the divorced woman, but it seems to be largely true, even for this group. The departed father starts out with the best intentions of "not forgetting my kids," but a variety of factors tend to reduce his parental influence as time goes on. . . .

4. *Public attitudes.* These mothers are operating in deviant family situations, and for the most part the community tends to regard them and their children as deviants. Except for the widow, all of these mothers are viewed with some ambivalence in our society. They receive some sympathy, some respect, and some help, but they are viewed as women who are not "quite right"—they did not sustain their marriage "until death do us part."

The unmarried mother, of course, never had a marriage to sustain and the public has no ambivalence about her; they simply condemn her and that's that.

If these mothers require support from public welfare they will find the community's mixed feelings reflected in their monthly check—the community will not permit them and their children to starve, but it will also not allow them to live at a decent level.

We have now examined some of the generic problems of the one-parent family system, except for the system in which the one parent is a father, which will be looked at later. Now let us analyze the specific features of the subsystems in the one-parent family.

Specific Features of the Subsystems in the One-Parent Family

1. *The divorced mother.* The divorced mother has several advantages over the deserted mother: she at least has had the help of a domestic-relations court in spelling out the financial responsibility of the father, also the legal arrangements for custody. In this sense divorce is a lot less messy than desertion in our society.

The divorced mother is also legally free to associate with other men and to remarry if she finds the right person—advantages the deserted woman does not have.

The divorced father, it seems to us, is not in an enviable position in his role as father. He may be happy not to be married to his children's mother any more but he often hates to be separated from his children. In a sense he still has the responsibility of a father for his minor children but few of the enjoyments of parenthood. To be with his children he has to interact to some degree with his former wife—a process so painful that he was willing to have the marriage terminated.

In an unpublished study of 80 divorced men, one of the most frequent regrets expressed by the men was their frustration and concern about their relationship to their children.

The divorced mother has one parental advantage that she shares with all other parents without partners; she does not have to share the daily parental decisions with a partner who might not agree with her strategy. In the Goode study of divorced women, the mothers seemed to think this was an advantage.

The parental partner can be of great help if the two parents can agree on how their children should be reared, but when this is not the case one parent can probably do a better job going it alone.

2. *The deserted mother*. It has already been indicated that desertions in our society are more messy than divorces. There are two reasons: (1) desertion is more apt to be unilateral with the decision to pull out being made by one party alone; and (2) there is no court supervision of the desertion process —it is unplanned from society's point of view.

The deserted mother is likely to have more severe financial problems than the divorced mother because support payments have not been agreed upon.

Psychologically, desertion is probably more traumatic than divorce, partly because it is more unilateral but also because it is less planned. To the extent that this is true—and we recognize that the evidence on this point is not conclusive—then the deserted mother is handicapped in her parental role by her emotional upheavel or trauma.

This woman also has other problems; she is legally not free to remarry and in a sense not even free to go out with other men since she is technically still a married woman. These feelings, of course, will tend to reflect the social class and the moral subculture of the particular woman.

3. *The separated mother*. If we assume that most marital separations in modern America have been arrived at by mutual agreement, then this mother has certain advantages over the deserted mother. One disadvantage is that her courtship status is ambiguous; another is that she is not free to remarry. Psychologically, the separated mother should reflect patterns similar to those of the divorced mother: her marriage has failed but she has done something about it and now has to plan for her future life.

4. *The widowed mother*. The one big advantage of this parent is the favorable attitude of her family, her friends, and the community toward her. This tends to be reflected in her self-image, thus giving her emotional support. Once she emerges from the period of bereavement, however, she has to face about the same problems as the women discussed previously—she probably will have financial problems; she will have to be father as well as mother. . . .

5. *The unmarried mother*. This is not the place to review the status and problems of the unmarried mother in our society—the literature on this woman is quite voluminous. It only needs to be said here that this mother has all of the problems of the women discussed before plus a few of her own. She is more likely to be a member of a racial minority—one of the extra burdens she has to shoulder. She is also more likely to be on public welfare —a major burden in itself in our society. Her chances for marriage are not as gloomy as some people once thought, but her chances for a successful marriage may be more dubious. . . .

Father-Only Families

It has been estimated that approximately 600,000 U.S. families have only a father present in the home at any given time. This figure seems large but is small compared to the 4 to 5 million American families in which only a mother is present.

There seems to be relatively little research data available on these "father-only" families. Since custody of minor children is awarded to the mother in our divorce courts in 90 to 95 percent of the cases, it seems logical to assume that the bulk of these "fathers without mothers" represent either desertion or the death of the mother.

It seems likely that these fathers do not continue indefinitely to rear their children alone, that the majority of them remarry, in which case they would experience the same problems of role shifts discussed earlier for mothers on their own.

It also seems likely that these men experience role conflicts between their jobs, their social life, and their parental responsibility.

It is doubtful that these solo fathers would suffer from poverty to the extent found among solo mothers—but the writer has no data to cite in support of this statement.

The rat race experienced by mothers rearing families without the help of a father would likely be found among these men also; it simply reflects what might be termed "role overload."

Psychologically, . . . these men probably suffer from the same syndrome found among mothers who have lost their husbands—loneliness, sorrow, perhaps bitterness, often a sense of failure, plus a feeling of being overwhelmed by their almost complete responsibility for their children. About the only effective treatment for feelings of this nature is to find a new partner and get married—the solution most adult Americans rely on for whatever ails them. These fathers are no exception to this statement.

It would appear that these men have a few problems that would be less likely to bother mothers: the physical care of preschool children and the tasks of home management, such as shopping for food and clothes, preparing meals, doing the family laundry, and cleaning the house. Some men become quite adept at this women's work after awhile, but for others a stove or an iron remains a mystery forever. . . .

Is the One-Parent Family Pathological?

Most of us probably assume that the one-parent family is inherently pathological—at least for the children involved. It seems only logical to assume that two parents are better than one—the old adage that two heads are better than one.

In his text on the American family, Bell summarizes several studies that question the assumption that two parents are better than one—judging by the adjustment of the children. This, however, does not say anything about the impact of solo child rearing on the parent, which is the major concern of this book.

If one wishes to debate the number of adults required to socialize children properly the question can be raised: who decided that *two* parents was the proper number? Biologically this is natural enough, but this does not prove its social rightness.

As a matter of fact, a good family sociologist, Farber, has asked the question—"Are two parents enough? . . . In almost every human society *more* than two adults are involved in the socialization of the child."

Farber goes on to point out that in many societies a "third parent," outside of the nuclear family, acts as a sort of "social critic" of the child.

In a recent review of the literature on the one-parent family by Kadushin, the data did not seem sufficient to support the hypothesis that the one-parent family is inherently dysfunctional or pathological. It has been demonstrated by Schorr that the one-parent family is considerably overrepresented in the American poverty population and also on our public welfare rolls. This does not prove, however, that these families are inherently dysfunctional; it merely proves that our economic, political, and social welfare systems are not properly organized to provide an adequate standard of living for the one-parent family. A casual drive through many rural areas in America, especially Appalachia and the rural South, will soon demonstrate to an unbiased observer that the mere presence of *two* parents does not assure a decent standard of living for a family in our society.

To prove that the one-parent family is inherently pathological one would have to demonstrate that the system generates a disproportionate amount of personal disorganization. Kadushin's search of the literature did not reveal enough firm research data to support such a conclusion. This, of course, does not prove that one parent in the home is as good as two—it simply says that the research to date is not adequate to answer the question.

It is obvious to any clinician that the two-parent system has its own pathology—the two parents may be in serious conflict as to how their parental roles should be performed; one parent may be competent but have his (or her) efforts undermined by the incompetent partner; the children may be caught in a "double bind" or crossfire between the two parents; both parents may be competent but simply unable to work together as an effective team in rearing their children; one parent may be more competent than the other but be inhibited in using this competence by the team pattern inherent in the two-parent system.

The writer happens to believe that one *good* parent is enough to rear children adequately or better in our society. It seems to us that enough prominent Americans have been reared by widows or other solo parents to prove the point.

It is interesting to note that adoption agencies are taking another look at the one-parent family and that some agencies are now willing to consider single persons as potential adoptive parents.

Chapter 12

Out of the Mainstream

The term "alternative family pattern" usually brings to mind the much-publicized commune, group marriage, or "swinging" couples. Yet the variant family pattern discussed here—in which husband and wife are committed to careers—may be both more widespread in the future and more of a break with the conventional family that has prevailed until recently. As the studies of communes and swingers show, far-out sexual behavior can coexist with traditional sex role ideologies and a conventional division of labor between the sexes. The commitment of the mother-wife to a career strikes at the heart of this division of labor and is the source of many of the stresses, as well as the rewards, of this family pattern. In this selection, which is a summary of a much longer article, the authors discuss the salient features of the dual-career family and the environmental changes that are needed to reduce the strains it now experiences. They have also published a book entitled Dual-Career Families *(New York: Penguin, 1971).*

The Dual-Career Family: A Variant Pattern and Social Change

Rhona Rapoport and Robert N. Rapoport

There is a trend toward increased participation of women in the work force. Women are doing this not at the expense of marrying but along with it and increasingly expect to combine marriage and career. This is producing, more and more often, the phenomenon of the dual-career family, in which husband and wife are not only companions and equal on different scales of

From *Human Relations*, Rhona Rapoport and Robert N. Rapoport, "The Dual-Career Family: A Variant Pattern and Social Change," 22:1 (January, 1969). © Plenum Publishing Corporation. Reprinted by permission. See also Rapoport and Rapoport, *Dual Career Families* (London: Penguin, 1971), and Rhona Rapoport, Robert N. Rapoport, and Michael Fogarty, *Sex, Career, and Family* (London: Allen & Unwin, Ltd., and Beverly Hills: Sage Publications, Inc., 1971).

evaluation but are both participating on the same evaluative planes. Thus, while there has been a good deal written about "women's two roles," the point of reference of the present paper is not the role of women but the family in relation to its social environment. The dual-career family is one in which both "heads" of the family pursue careers. The implication is not, as with the concept of women's two roles, that men do not also have two roles. Both men and women, in the dual-career family, have both career roles and familial roles, and with the exception of pregnancy and childbirth, there is no assumption that any of the activities are inexorably sex-linked. This is not to say that there are categorically no biologically linked sex differences in the capacities of men and women to perform specific activities, e.g., "mothering." The probability is that there are "overlapping curves" of characteristics such that some men may have more of an attribute (say, nurturance) than some women and, conversely, some women may have more of an attribute (say, mechanical skills) than some men. At the same time more women may turn out to be more nurturant biologically than most men and more men may turn out to be biologically more "mechanical" than most women.

At present there are strongly held socio-cultural beliefs about sex-linked attributes which affect self-conceptions and interaction patterns. Different subsystems within society change at different rates. Within the socio-cultural domains, a very complex interrelationship exists between ideology, social structure, and behavior. In contemporary society, egalitarianism is a dominant ideological theme. This is expressed, for example, in the educational subsystem. Boys and girls at school are taught and compete with one another on a single set of evaluative scales. When they leave school or university, however, the sex differential becomes more marked. It is to be noted that egalitarian education is a tendency, not an actuality. Many graduate women accommodate to the traditional sex-differentiated norms of the postuniversity role systems wihtout apparent strain. Some similarly highly educated women conform to the traditional pattern but show great strain (the "captive wife" syndrome). Ohers extrapolate the egalitarian norms of their educational period into the adult stage, working out new patterns as they go because role models and precedents for equality in the work-family relationships of married couples with children are largely lacking. For the men there would seem to be less discontinuity.

The level of analysis which we have conducted is "microsociological," in that we have concentrated on the small innovating units—the dual-career partnership famil[ies]. Though our study does not attempt to encompass a cross-section of such units so as to estimate the prevalence of each of the patterns observed, we believe that it covers a sufficiently broad range of examples to provide insight into some major contemporary process of change. Because each of the units functions in a larger cultural system of norms and values and in a larger social system of relationships and interactions, the innovating patterns which are attempted may be seen as going "against the grain" of society in various ways. As society itself is changing, the strains outlined in this paper are not presented as permanent or intrinsic in the dual-career family situation but rather [offered as] a matter of contemporary concern. The contemporary concern has policy implications, but looking at the issue more theoretically, we suggest that the analysis of structural sources of stress [is] relevant for social change. In Goode's terms, each couple strikes a series of "role bargains" to reduce or otherwise deal with the strains and dilemmas they experience. Taken all together, these role bargains form new structures, which are more collaborative, in the sense described for postindustrial society as a whole by Trist.

The structures evolved by dual-career families of the type studied are more than of private interest. These are couples who are unusually visible and articulate. They provide models for a wide range of less distinguished members of the society and may be seen in varying degrees as exemplars, or at least "trial balloons," for those who follow. In addition, they tend to participate in more complex and dispersed clusters of relationships.

In the immediate situation, the new behavioral models which are evolved may be evaluated in various ways. Personal satisfaction is a dimension which provides one element of evaluation but which is too diffuse and complex for our current form of analysis. It would involve matching specific personality constellations to the different structural models. For the present, a structural form of analysis is suggested. Structural sources of stress may be detected and the consequent patterns of strain described. Individual differences in capacity to absorb the strains will affect satisfaction, but, as indicated, we do not go to this level here. Within limits, the economic metaphor of a cost-benefit analysis is useful. Each family works out for itself whether the "costs" of pursuing the variant life career of a dual-career family—in any of its various forms—is worth it to them in relation to the "benefits" they derive.

These costs and benefits may be summarized for the couples studied in relation to five structural dimensions of stress:

1. *Role overloads.* Dual-career families benefit in taking on an additional set of occupational roles by the increased family income, the stimulation and personal development afforded the wife, her utilization of her training, the closer relationship between father and the children, and so on. These benefits, which are consistent with the values of postindustrial society, are realized at the cost of taxing the energies of both members through role overloads and possibly restricting of the husband's career participation. The couples generally tend to reduce the overload effect by curtailing nonessential, particularly leisure and social, activities.

2. *Normative dilemmas.* [These] arise through the discontinuities in ideol-

ogy as between educational and adult roles, producing strains. One way of reducing this kind of strain is to extrapolate the earlier role ideals into the later behavior—continuing the wife's career development. This leads to benefits for the woman (and indirectly for the husband) of a sense of integrity, of feeling "true to oneself," as distinct from having to "put the lid on" or to compromise one's ideals or waste one's capacities. This may be accomplished, however, at the "cost" of diverging from the norms and expectations representing the other side of the dilemma—the more traditional female role norms, holding it right and proper for a woman to be at home looking after her family. The strains, both intraphysically and in significant social relationships, are dealt with by various devices of insulation and compartmentalization.

3. *Maintenance of personal identity.* [This] becomes a problem when one departs from the standard patterns of behavior that are institutionally supported in the traditional role structures. Where men and women continue to pursue their personal development through the same rather than different channels of roles with their different norms and sanctions, they may find themselves confronting the issue of how to maintain their distinct identity. The "benefits" of equal participation are in terms of fairness and equity in access to society's valued resources. The "costs" may entail competitive rivalries and their concomitants, interpersonal discord, difficulties in sexual relations, and so on. The couples studied seem to deal with the identity issue by constructing (in their psychic and interpersonal world of reality) a "tension line" which demarcates areas within which they feel they can comfortably function as separate and distinct individuals.

4. *The social network dilemmas.* [These] provide structured sources of strain in reconciling obligations (e.g., in kinship relations) with desires (e.g., in friendship relations) and responsibilities (e.g., in erecting a network of effective service relationships), all in the face of overloads in the work and family role systems. The "benefits" of a fairly decisive limitation on network relationships and concentration of them on gratifying components (e.g., by eliminating unwanted relationships, delegating obligations to service personnel, etc.) may be reckoned in comfort and an enhanced capacity to function and develop in work and family roles. On the other hand, the process of network construction which this tends to represent may lead to feelings of guilt by the individual, and resentment by others, and these must be reckoned among the "costs."

5. *Role cycling.* The husband and wife in the dual-career family are involved in three role systems: the work system of each spouse (except where they are partners, in which case the two work systems are merged) and the family system which they share. Each system makes different demands according to the position of the role in the system, and each role makes different demands on the individual according to phase. The tendency for heavy de-

mands to be made on people in work roles [occurs] when working upward toward senior positions (more than once one actually reaches an established senior role), and within roles shortly after the initial ("honeymoon") period when the new structure of person-in-role is being worked out. In the family, the heaviest strain is at the time of having young children of preschool age. There are different costs and benefits according to what the correspondence is between the peak demands on roles in these three spheres. If the couple arrange their lives so as to have the family role demands "peak" first, they may miss opportunities for career advancement. If they allow the two career role strains to "peak" first, they may pay the costs in family life of the additional strains imposed through fatigue as they are older, and a greater age gap between themselves and their children. If one spouse "peaks" while the other defers heavy involvement, the one that defers may have to pay a price in career development as well as perhaps bear a heavier brunt of family role strains. This is, obviously, an oversimplified picture and many combinations are possible, but the issue of role cycling and the "fits" in the family among the various role cycles is only beginning to be understood.

Finally, we are concerned with indicating briefly what social changes may facilitate diffusion of the dual-career family structure. The policy implications of these considerations are apparent but will not be dealt with in depth here. It is suggested that the dual-career family structure is likely to become more prevalent in our society to the extent that three arenas of change provide compatible arrays of factors to support the diffusion of the pattern:

a.   the arena of work role relationships
b.   the arena of domestic role relationships
c.   the arena of the built environment.

Many occupational groups and organizations are working toward a reduction of the crude forms of discrimination linked to archaic sex role stereotypes. The issue of similarities or differences between men's and women's capacities is increasingly seen as part of the more general issue of individual differences, and the entire range of jobs in the world of work is becoming increasingly open to women on an equal basis with men. However, the capacity of women, particularly married women with children, to grasp the increasingly available opportunities and to exercise to their fullest capacities the available career roles will depend on the degree to which these roles can be made compatible with the demands of women's other roles. Many current ways of organizing the world of work are not intrinsically necessary and yet make participation difficult for women because of being based on "male" assumptions about times of accessibility, etc.

The arena of domestic role relationships, similarly, will provide a set of factors affecting the diffusion of the dual-career pattern. The greater diffusion will depend on the extent to which husbands as well as wives redefine the marital role relationship so as to give explicit recognition to the interconnectedness of domestic and occupational roles. If the pursuit of a career by the wife is to become a possibility for more than the "amazons" of this world, it will depend on men having an attitude more supportive than "it's all right so long as it doesn't affect me." The whole area of child-care seems to be the most important element in this constellation of roles. To the extent that husbands can participate more in child-care and that auxiliary roles and arrangements are developed, the pattern may diffuse more.

The "built environment" can be expected to play an important part in the extent to which the dual-career family becomes more viable and pervasive in the future. This seems to be most relevant in two areas: the journey to work, and the pooling of services in the areas of domestic arrangements. The tendency following the Industrial Revolution to remove the work place as well as the husband from the home is no longer as relevant, given the more agreeable general conditions of work. To the extent that new complexes of living bring work and family into more easy interplay, as in some of the new towns organized with industry as well as housing in mind, the impediment of the arduous journey to work now placed on women and men, and contributing to their role overloads, will be diminished. If housing developments are oriented in the future to the sharing of domestic care facilities—cleaning, food buying and preparation, child-care, etc.—rather than simply [to the multiplication of] individual living units as seems to be the present tendency, a greater diffusion of the pattern is possible. New mixtures of individualism and communalism may be expected in postindustrial society, with an increase in the latter for the Western countries.

The situation, in summary, is that the trend toward cultural norms which are compatible with the dual-career family seems to be well underway. In many instances the mono-career family structure will be chosen for self-expressive rather than traditional reasons. However, where there is the wish to choose the dual-career structure and there are normative conflicts, these are due, in our view, partly to cultural lag and partly to defensive reactions from people in the environment who have not been able to succeed in evolving a dual-career family on a microsociological level. The structural changes which are necessary to fully implement these changes are not yet in effect, particularly in the areas of organization of work, organization of domestic role relationships, and the conception of the built environment.

In conclusion, what is being suggested is that the availability of these facilities [and structural changes] will be important in making it possible for individual families to have a choice of potential arrangements. It is not implied that the dual-career family is advocated as a universal pattern.

During the past decade, there has been a great deal of research and debate about the black family. Most of this research and discussion assumes that the lower class black family is pathological and disorganized. The Moynihan report raised a storm of controversy when it asserted that this malfunctioning family was the cause of the plight of black people in America. Many of Moynihan's critics argued that poverty and racism were the cause of the black family's pathology, rather than the other way around. This paper summarizes and evaluates the recent research literature, and comes to a rather different conclusion. Staples argues that the black family isn't disorganized, and it is only the imposition of white middle class values that makes it seem so.

Towards a Sociology of the Black Family: A Theoretical and Methodological Assessment | *Robert Staples*

In the past ten years interest in the black family has accelerated. The last decade has been the most productive period of research on the black family in history (Somerville, 1970). The emphasis on the problems of poverty and race relations has made the black family a central focus for dealing with these problems and their effects on lower-income and black families. Consequently, research on the black family has transcended the boundaries of family sociology and has become a matter of interest to the public in general and minority groups in particular. Black family research has served as an instrument of public policy and official action in seeking to alleviate the causes of socioeconomic deprivation among Afro-American citizens. For that reason it is important that the findings of research on the black family be evaluated for their relevance in understanding the nature of black family life in contemporary America.

Furthermore, the traditional canons of evaluation shall not be the only evaluative yardstick employed in our assessment of black family research. Another concern shall be the role of the behavioral scientist in formulating public policy, the value structure of social scientists who study the black family and the experiential factor as an influential variable in developing a viable sociology of the black family. The importance of the black family as a field of study and the controversy that frequently surrounds it means that we should address ourselves to all the dimensions involved in order to bring

From Robert Staples, "Toward a Sociology of the Black Family: A Theoretical and Methodological Assessment," *Journal of Marriage and Family*, (February, 1971), pp. 119–135. Reprinted by permission.

some order and understanding out of the complex of contradictory and value-laden notions concerning its role in American society.

The past history of black family research has been characterized by the reiteration of unfounded myths and stereotypes which produce in the public mind the image of black families as a pathological social unit—a system incapable of rearing individuals who can adjust to the demands of a civilized society (Staples, 1969). But the myths perpetuated about the black family are, perhaps, no less important than the myth of a value-free sociology (Gouldner, 1962). While the basic data for sociological research are values (Kolb, 1954), the sociologist theoretically reaches his conclusions objectively (Znaniecki, 1952). In reality, the field of family sociology has a biased value orientation that is reflected in the emphasis on middle-class norms as the barometer of what is regarded as a desirable family structure and behavior (Rodman, 1965). The black family that does not meet the criteria of middle-class family behavior is ipso facto defined as a deviant type which should be studied as a pathological form of social organization.

Using what are presumed to be middle-class "normal" families as measuring rods for black families has stigmatized those Afro-American families. Consequently, research on the black family is predicated on the assumption that it is a malfunctioning unit and the research problem is to assess the etiological determinants of its pathological structure. What is of concern to us is what research on the black family has produced, the reliability and validity of the research instruments used, alternative explanations of black family behavior, and questions that need to be answered in order to understand the nature and function of family life in the black community.

Since this is an analysis of both theory and research on the black family, this writer has organized the various works on the black family into two areas: The Macro-sociological and the Micro-sociological. The macro-sociological works on the black family deal with a total view of the black family, its structure and the component parts of the structure. Frequently, the macro-sociological theories deal with the nature of black family life and its ramifications for individual blacks and American society. In contrast, the micro-sociological studies accept the theories of the macro-sociologists and attempt to test their hypotheses in specific areas of family functioning. Occasionally, micro-sociological studies have no theoretical precepts to guide their research.

Before examining the theory and research on the black family, it is important to note the culture vs. class dichotomy in analyzing black family life. These two levels of analysis characterize most research on the black family and determine the behavioral scientist's views on the black family and the type of action needed to bring it into conformity with the modal white, middle-class, family ideal (Lewis, 1967).

As a separate sub-culture, distinguishable from other lower-class groups, the black family may be depicted as an autonomous social system with mores and folkways that diverge from the larger society. Culture is sometimes defined as ways of acting, thinking and believing (Kroeber and Kluckhohn, 1952). Since these attributes of culture are endemic to persons sharing membership in the black race, it is usually associated with typical life experiences encountered by people who belong to this group—not inherent biological predispositions to act in a particular fashion. While using culture for the analysis of family behavior brings up the question of the determinants of culture, the black historical experience is usually considered the basic cause for the development of a black, lower-class culture (Potter, 1960).

Using class as the primary causal variable for black family behavior dictates that the black family be conceptualized as a slight variant of the lower-class white family. It is the larger concentration of blacks in the lower socio-economic category that confuses what is essentially lower-class behavior with what is labeled a separate black subculture. According to this level of analysis, the economic deprivation of black and white lower-class families makes it difficult to sustain a stable family life due to the lack of economic conditions which are conducive to the maintenance of a stable family life. Eliminating the economic deprivation, consequently, would reveal the primary causes of family disorganization among lower-class blacks (Rodman, 1963).

While this description of the two levels of analysis is probably an over-simplication, and even overstatement of them, it will suffice as an explanation of how most sociologists approach the study of the black family. For the most part, culture or class is used to explain black family disorganization—a conclusion that will be subjected to greater scrutiny later.

Macro-Sociological Theories

It is generally accepted that the precursor of sociological research and theories on the black family was the late black sociologist, E. Franklin Frazier. He began investigating the black family in the twenties and his works are still considered the definitive findings on black family life in America (Frazier, 1932a, 1932b, 1939). As a sociologist, Frazier was primarily interested in race relations as a social process and sought to explain that process through the study of the black family. Through his training in the University of Chicago's social ecology school under the tutelage of Park, Wirth, Burgess and others, Frazier came to believe that race relations proceeded through different stages of development with the final stage being assimilation (Edwards, 1968).

Since it is through the family that the culture of a group is transmitted, Frazier chose this group as the object of his sociological study. Using the natural history approach to the study of black family life, the present condition of this group was explained as the culmination of an evolutionary process, its structure strongly affected by the vestiges of slavery, racism and economic exploitation. The method of enslavement and slavery virtually destroyed the cultural moorings of blacks and prevented any perpetuation of African kinship and family relations. Consequently, the black family developed variegated forms according to the different situations it encountered (Frazier, 1939).

Variations in sex and marital practices, according to Frazier, grew out of the social heritage of slavery and what slavery began, the pattern of racism and economic deprivation continued to impose on the family life of Afro-Americans. The variations that he speaks of are the matriarchal character of the black family whereby black males are marginal, and ineffective, figures in the family constellation; the instability of marital life because the lack of a legal basis for marriage during the period of slavery meant that marriage never acquired the position of a strong institution in black life and casual sex relations were the prevailing norm; and the process of urbanization dissolved the stability of family life that existed among black peasantfolk in an agrarian society (Frazier, 1939).

As have most people who have studied the black family, Frazier sought a solution to the family disorganization that permeated the black community. His solution, of course, was influenced by his loyalty to the Assimilationist ideology of his mentors, Park, Burgess and Wirth (Edwards, 1968, VII-XX). The deducible solution, consequently, was acculturation: that the survival of the Afro-American in American civilization depended on the measure of his success in adopting white culture. Because of their cultural and spatial isolation from whites, blacks have retained a primitive folk culture which is dysfunctional in the modern technological and urban milieu. The problem of the black family, then, is one of acculturation and this is a process that requires time—time measured in human generations rather than years (Frazier, 1939).

It is this conceptualization of the black family that inspires much of the contemporary theory and research on the black family. When dissenters from the pathology concept of the black family criticize much of this research and question the racial views of the people conducting it, the theories of Frazier, and his racial membership, inevitably are brought up to cloud the issue. However, Frazier's (1962) last words on the subject are either not known to many of his supporters, or are conveniently ignored. The fact that the paper was published in a magazine with a predominantly black readership could account for its anonymity.

Just before his death in 1962, Frazier revised his belief in integration and assimilation as a panacea for black Americans. He continued to believe that it was necessary for blacks to be integrated into the economic and social

organization of American life. But integration was only the initial stage in
the resolution of a much greater problem which involves more than individuals. It also involves the organized life of the black community vis-a-vis
the organized life of the white community. Frazier's legacy to the black
scholar was his warning that:

> The African intellectual recognizes what colonialism has done to the
> African, and he sets as his first task the mental, moral and spiritual
> rehabilitation of the African.
> But the American Negro intellectual, seduced by dreams of assimila-
> tion, has never regarded this as his primary task . . .
> It is the responsibility of the Negro intellectual to provide a positive
> identification through history, literature, art, music and the drama.
> The truth of the matter is that for most Negro intellectuals, the inte-
> gration of the Negro means just the opposite, the emptying of his life
> of meaningful content and ridding him of all Negro identification. For
> them, integration and eventual assimilation mean the annihilation of
> the Negro—physically, culturally and spiritually. (Frazier, 1962, p. 16)

In one of the few works on the middle-class black family, Frazier made similar observations: in its enthusiatic efforts to assimilate into the mainstream
of American society, the black middle-class has rejected the organized life
and social heritage of the black community. Although repudiating the black
cultural heritage, they remain stigmatized by their blackness and retreat into
a make-believe world characterized by superficial emulations of middle-
class whites. Middle-class black family life was severely criticized by Frazier
who asserted that divorces and scandals in family and sex behavior did not
result in a loss of status—rather, notoriety adds to one's prestige. Marital life
among this group is portrayed as based upon making a good marriage with a
husband of high social status or a light-skinned wife from an "old" family.
The husband is depicted as playing the role of worshipping his wife and supporting her extravagances and vanities. Many husbands in such positions release their frustrations in extramarital affairs. These couples usually have
very small families and there is not only a deep devotion to their children but
a subservience to them. This fierce devotion to middle-class black children
usually results in spoiling them (Frazier, 1957).

Most of Frazier's studies are limited to pre-World War II black family
life. His research method was the use of case studies and documents whose
content he analyzed and from which he attempted to deduce a pattern of
black family life. The next large-scale theory of the black family was developed by Daniel Moynihan (1965), based largely on census data, and per-
tained to black family life that existed in the sixties. In a sense, Moynihan attempted to statistically confirm Frazier's theory that the black family was
disorganized as a result of slavery, urbanization and economic deprivation.
But he added a new dimension to Frazier's theory, namely that "at the heart

of the deterioration of the fabric of Negro society is the deterioration of the Negro family" (Moynihan, 1965, p. 5). Moynihan attempts to document his major proposition by citing statistics on the dissolution of black marriages, the high rate of black illegitimate births, the prevalance of female-headed households in the black community, and how the deterioration of the black family has led to a shocking increase in welfare dependency (Moynihan, 1965).

This study of the black family, commonly referred to as the "Moynihan Report," generated a largely critical response from members of the black community. It drew a mixed response from the white academic community, some critically supporting most of Moynihan's contentions, others imputing no validity to his assertions (Rainwater and Yancey, 1967). The reasons for the negative reaction to Moynihan's study are manifest. In effect, he made a generalized indictment of all black families. And, although he cited the antecedents of slavery and high unemployment as important variables historically, shifted the burden of black deprivation onto the black family rather than the American social structure.

The "Moynihan Report" assumed a greater importance than other studies on the black family for several reasons. As an official government publication, it implied a shift in the government's position on dealing with the effects of racism and economic deprivation on the black community. However, the Moynihan report did not spell out a plan for action. The conclusion drawn by most people was that whatever his solution, it would focus on strengthening the black family rather than dealing with the more relevant problems of segregation and discrimination. Additionally, the Moynihan report brought to the fore the question of the role of the behavioral scientist in formulating and influencing public policy.

To some observers, Moynihan's dual role as social scientist and government official complicated the issue at hand. When intellectual issues are confined to the academic milieu, they lend themselves to corrections and additions brought forth by the process of scholarly dissent and advice. In the interim the lives of the body politic are not affected, adversely or positively, by research which is in an incomplete state due to faulty methodology or poor logic. On the other hand, research that is quickly translated into the arena of public policy should bind the scholar to the most stringent adherence to the principle of value neutrality and objectivity in formulating conclusions from his research (Rose, 1954).

The problems that accrue from using inadequate research data to reach spurious conclusions are many. Since clear-cut proof of cause and effect relationships are elusive in the study of social relations, it is incumbent upon the behavioral scientist to temper his conclusions with the knowledge of its impact on the subject under investigation. As Rainwater has pointed out:

> If social scientists can move rapidly toward a more precise under-
> standing of the dynamics of the situation of Negro Americans, they have
> an opportunity to make a very major contribution to the society. On the
> other hand, continuing imprecision (intellectual, not quantitative) will
> serve to sustain confusion and stereotypes in public discussion of these
> matters and to delay the development of really effective solutions for
> the injustices Negro Americans now experience and the effect of these
> injustices on the rest of society. (1966a, p. 442)

While some criticisms of the Moynihan Report were politically motivated
and others were visceral reactions, the poor methodology employed forms a
sound basis for rejecting most of Moynihan's conclusions. By basing his
theory of black family disintegration on census data, he made the gross error
of interpreting statistical relationships in cause and effect terms (Ryan,
1965). In effect, many of his findings about the black population are subject
to the fallacy of ecological correlations.

Instead of employing individual correlations where the thing described is
an indivisible unit, a person, many of Moynihan's findings are based on
ecological correlations, i.e., the thing described is the population of a state,
and not a single individual. The variables are percentages, descriptive properties of groups, and not descriptive properties of individuals. There is no way,
for instance, of determining that the illegitimate births in a particular census
tract, which has a large nonwhite population, can be traced directly to the
blacks in that census tract. In other words, variables correlated within groups
may not hold for particular individuals within those groups (Robinson,
1950).

In most cases alternative explanations are available to counteract Moynihan's findings. Instead of accepting as absolute truths the Census Bureau
statistics on illegitimacy rates for whites at about 3 percent, for blacks
at about 22 percent, a 7-to-1 ratio, one could cite the fact that there are
racial differences in reporting illegitimate births; that premarital pregnancies
among whites are more frequently resolved by marriage and the abortion
rate is considerably higher in the white group. Taking such facts into consideration would considerably diminish the illegitimate birth ratio among
whites and blacks and should alter the inferences drawn about the ratio (Hill
and Jaffe, 1967).

A key conclusion of the Moynihan Report is that the breakdown of the
black family has led to the deterioration of the black community. One index
of this deterioration is the increase in welfare dependency. Rather than imputing to family disorganization as the causal factor, one could just as easily
attribute the increase in black welfare recipients to more liberal welfare laws.
Liberal welfare laws and the fact that vast numbers of blacks moved from
rural areas of the South where it is relatively difficult to obtain welfare bene-

fits, to urban regions where it is relatively easier, partly account for the increase of blacks on welfare. Between 1960 and 1968, the numbers of welfare recipients increased by more than 1,600,000 persons, with almost half of that increase taking place in just two urbanized states—New York and California. Since welfare payments in these states are in some cases double the amount paid in the South, the increase in the public assistance cases is chiefly a political phenomenon, not an economic one (Cloward and Piven, 1968).

It is estimated that less than half the people eligible for public assistance are on the welfare rolls and consequently, making more flexible the welfare regulations can augment the number of welfare recipients without a corresponding increase in family disorganization (Carper, 1966).

The major thesis of Moynihan's study is most subject to intellectual criticism: that the fabric of black society is dependent upon the malfunctioning of individual family units in that society. It is this thesis that Moynihan fails to document in any scientifically acceptable fashion. For instance, his correlations between female-headed households and poor academic performance of blacks ignores the substandard conditions of most black ghetto schools and the results that ensue from unequal educational opportunity (Coleman, 1966). By raising the familiar specter of the relationship between the fatherless homes and juvenile delinquency, he overlooks the fact that the children in a fatherless home are frequently relegated to the lowest living standards in our society—a fact that suggests that juvenile delinquency is more a function of poverty rather than paternal absence.

Although Frazier's and Moynihan's studies of black families share certain commonalities, the differences are important. A major difference is the epoch of study and the conclusions reached. Frazier, for instance, would probably take into account black nativist tendencies and its impact on black family structure. He undoubtedly would not seek to place the blame for the black condition on its family structure. Both the Frazier and the Moynihan studies deal with the black family in a structural manner. That is, they deal with its form and the arrangement of roles within the family constellation rather than the behavior that transpires within the structure. It is in the post Moynihan study by Lee Rainwater (1966b) that the dynamic processes that take place are critically examined.

Just as Moynihan attempted to quantify Frazier's suppositions on the black family, Rainwater sought to expand on, and analyze in depth, the black family's role in the "tangle of pathology" which pervades the fabric of the black community. The Rainwater thesis is essentially the same as Moynihan's: that the condition of black family disorganization evolved out of the black man's history of enslavement and racist oppression, and the outcome of the situation has been that black family life itself becomes a major factor in sustaining and perpetuating the oppressive conditions under which black

Americans are forced to live. Or, as Rainwater states the problem: "The victimization process as it operates in families prepares and toughens its members to function in the ghetto world, at the same time that it seriously interferes with their ability to operate in any other world (Rainwater, 1966b, p. 173).

There are some, although minor, distinctions between the Moynihan and Rainwater studies of black family life. Unlike Moynihan, Rainwater does not generalize his findings of massive black family disorganization to the entire black population. He confines his analysis to lower-class black families but relates his belief that other literature on black family life suggests that the findings of his study are not limited to his sample of 10,000 people in the Pruitt-Igoe housing projects in St. Louis.

This assumption of similarity between his lower-class black family and other black families—even other lower-class black families—should not be too readily accepted. One might easily question the selection of families in a housing project as representative of anything but the most deprived and disorganized segment of the black community. Rainwater gives no operational definition of the term lower-class, but the characteristics of his sample give some indication of the population he chose for study. For instance, over half of the households have female heads. One estimate on the basis of 1960 census data is that 33 percent of non-white families earning under $3,000 a year were headed by females (Lefcowitz, 1965). The principal income of the majority of this group comes from public assistance of one kind or another. The question might be raised as to where comparable lower-class black families could be found who are subject to such conditions of poverty.

Nevertheless, the Rainwater proposition is that black family life and racial victimization are interdependent variables. He tries to show the relationship of destructive cultural and interactional patterns in black families to their failure to take advantage of those few opportunities that are available to black slum dwellers. To accomplish this task, he outlines the typical family stage sequence and analyzes the psycho-social implications of growing up in families characterized by this sequence.

Beginning with the formation of heterosexual relations in the ghetto, the pattern of rampant, and casual, sexual relations leads to the premarital pregnancy of many adolescent girls in the black ghetto. According to Rainwater, for females in the black slum a premarital pregnancy is seen as an inevitable consequence of the permissive sex code and behavior that exists in this environment. As he found:

> It is in the easy attitudes toward premarital pregnancy that the matrifocal character of the Negro lower-class appears most clearly. In order to have and raise a family it is simply not necessary, though it may be desirable, to have a man around the house. While the AFDC program

may make it easier to maintain such attitudes in the urban situation, this pattern existed long before the program was initiated and continues in families where support comes from other sources. (Rainwater, 1966b, p. 187)

Although it is generally agreed that an illegitimate child does not confer the same degree of social stigmatization on the black mother or her child as it does for the white mother and child, there is, by no means, unanimity on the existence of casual attitudes toward a premarital pregnancy on the part of the black people involved. At least one other study, for instance, reported that a majority of the black females they had studied who had become pregnant before marriage, stated that they were both unhappy and incredulous when they discovered that they were pregnant. Contrary to Rainwater's opinion that the parents of these girls readily accept the fact of their daughter's premarital pregnancy, the mothers of these girls overwhelmingly had negative attitudes about their daughter's pregnancy (Furstenberg, 1970).

Despite the frequency of premarital sex relations and the high rate of birth out-of-wedlock, most black men and women ultimately enter a marital relationship and live together for indefinite periods of time. Marriage among this group, reports Rainwater, is a tenuous affair. The relationship is entered into with a less than sanguine attitude that it will be a successful arrangement for either party. The Rainwater conclusion is that when marital disruption occurs, it is usually due to sexual dalliance or the inability of the male to provide any economic support for the family. Once the male ceases to bring money into the house the wife withdraws her commitment from him and from the marriage (Rainwater, 1966b).

In this analysis Rainwater is either overgeneralizing from certain typical consequences of the husband's unemployment or ignoring alternative possibilities of the family grouping together as a unit to buttress the effect of the male's temporary job dislocation. It is difficult to accept as a fact of ghetto life that the emotional ties between husband and wife are so tenuous as to be incapable of withstanding the temporary stress caused by the husband's loss of employment. In the opinion of at least one research assistant on this same project (Ladner, n.d.), she did not witness a single case whereby the wife withdrew her support from the husband because he had lost his job. Her analysis of these same black famililes will appear in her forthcoming book on the black woman.

Rainwater also claims that the male role models presented to Afro-American boys are primarily ones which emphasize expressive, affectional techniques for making one's way in the world rather than instrumental, goal-oriented means for achieving the normative objectives of the society. Here, Rainwater is again assuming the ethnocentric level of analysis that pervades his entire study. He is confusing what is essentially a cultural life style with the achievement levels of black people. While adherence to a strict interpretation of the Protestant Ethic may work for members of the white group who are not subject to barriers of race, there is no guarantee that adopting an instrumental technique would augment black achievement, nor does Rainwater present any evidence of same.

The victimization process that takes place in the family, states Rainwater, has its greatest impact on the personality structure of the black child. In the black slum culture, children experience an ever-increasing appreciation of individual shortcomings, and of the impossibility of finding a self-sufficient and gratifying way of living. The parents contribute to the formation of the child's negative self-concept by exposing him to identity labeling as a "bad" person. His subsequent lack of gratification in life only serves to confirm his self-image as an essentially unworthy person (Rainwater, 1966b).

In his analysis of the black personality structure. Rainwater is in accord with other studies on black self-esteem. However, a challenge to this prevailing view has been cogently put forth by a pair of sociologists who undertook a rigorous and systematic review of the literature on the personality formation of black children. After pointing out the theoretical and methodological weakness of much of this research, they concluded that:

> Negroes are less likely to be personally disorganized than their white counterparts since they find themselves part of a solidary group. The solidary group helps one to confront the views and actions of the oppressive majority. . . . The black man can rely upon a group which possesses a rather well articulated ideology which explains (his) lowly position. (McCarthy and Yancey, 1970, p. 34)

In Rainwater's terms, the source of the black child's negative self-esteem is not white discrimination and prejudice but the unstable family and the hostile world of the slum peer group. Although similar identity labeling processes are operative in white lower-class culture, an added factor for the Afro-American is the reality of blackness. In Rainwater's view, black comes to mean membership in a community of persons who think poorly of each other, who attack and manipulate each other, who give each other small comfort in a desperate world (Rainwater, 1966b).

Anyone who has witnessed the incretions in black consciousness and solidarity in the past five years may judge the validity of Rainwater's view for themselves. It must be recognized, however, that Rainwater does not agree with Moynihan that programs should be developed to remediate this family pathology. It is his belief that if black family patterns have been created as adaptations to their socioeconomic situation, it is more logical to change that socioeconomic situation and then depend on black families to make new adaptations as time passes on. Only through the provision of steady jobs and decent incomes are the destructive patterns of black family life likely to change (Rainwater, 1966b).

In assessing the over-all validity of the Rainwater study, it appears that he has made the same mistake as other behaviorial scientists in viewing the culture and the adaptations of the black poor as pathological (Rodman, 1964). The adaptations which the lower-class black family are seen to make to their peculiar circumstances are viewed from a middle-class perspective, and such a perspective easily leads to characterizations of those adaptations as unhealthy, destructive of human potential and physically damaging (Valentine, 1968). The fact that Rainwater used data gathered through participant-observation and open-ended interviews creates certain problems. While this is an eminently respectable research technique, it also lends itself more easily to the subjective bias of the investigator (Bruyn, 1966). The definition of lower-class black family behavior as pathological by a white, middle-class sociologist can cast serious doubt on the validity of such studies.

Characteristic of the middle-class bias in studying black family life is the view of Jessie Bernard (1966a). She ignores income levels as determinant variables in the explanation of family life and formulates the concept of two cultural strands in order to understand black family patterns. These two cultural strands relate to the degree of acculturation wherein the individual has internalized the moral norms of western society as these exist in the United States. One strand is labeled the "acculturated" wherein western norms become an intrinsic part of their personality. This is generally considered the "respectable" strand. The other strand is known as the "externally adapted." Among this group, the norms relating to marriage and the family are only superficially adhered to, not one of internal conviction. This group learns to use and manipulate white culture rather than taking over their norms (Bernard, 1966a).

Such a conceptual level of analyzing black family behavior is of limited value for understanding patterns of black family life. By disregarding the socioeconomic situation of black families, the primary variable that causes the differentiation of black family behavior is not taken into account. This forces the analyst to consider the black family only in relation to external social forces rather than analyzing the distinctive family life style of the black subculture, a subculture with its own values, norms, sanctions, etc. Bernard's level of analysis, then, deals with the acculturation process as it relates to black family life and not to the understanding of black family processes which are subject to other influences.

Just as Bernard dismisses the socioeconomic variable in her analysis of the black family, the theory of Andrew Billingsley (1969) concentrates heavily on economic forces influencing the pattern of black family life. Succinctly,

Billingsley views many manifestations of the black family as a result of the over-representation of black families in the poverty category. The Billingsley position differs from that of Moynihan and Rainwater in that he sees the black family as a strong and resilient institution, both in a historical and contemporary sense.

Whereas this position has a great deal of currency, Billingsley uses middle-class models and norms to support his position. Instead of stressing the fact that black marital and family behavior represent positive functions and values in the social organization of the black community he accepts the negative view of the black family and responds that this negative family phenomonen is a predictable response to repressive forces in the American social structure. For example, he devotes an entire chapter in his book to successful upper-class black families rather than outlining the positive values in much of lower-class family life (Billingsley, 1969).

Even more disappointing is Billingsley's structural study of the black family. Like the studies of yesteryear, he describes the family structure and the arrangement of roles in the family constellation. He does not penetrate the interior of the black family and explore some of the sociodynamic processes that contribute to its character. His is mostly the view of the middle-class sociologist who accepts middle-class norms, concludes that most black families share middle-class value orientations and prescribes action to eliminate poverty to bring disadvantaged black families into conformity with the modal middle-class family (Billingsley, 1969).

Despite its weaknesses, the Billingsley work represents the latest development in the improvement of research and theory on the black family. At least he recognizes that the black family represents a unit of considerable variety and complexity; that many of its constituent features are a misunderstood source of strength in the black community; and that some of its characteristics have been given invidious labels by those whose motives are politically suspect. It is upon such an understanding that we can develop a sociology of the black family.

Micro-Sociological Research

Dyadic Relations

A review of the literature on black dating patterns reveals that very little is known on this subject. The research available shows that black dating behavior is largely an unstructured process, that males and females somehow manage to get together and establish emotional ties to each other (Staples, 1971). On a comparative basis, dating begins earlier for black females; going steady is the most prevalent mode of dating and the least common is double-dating; and black females tend to favor getting married someday more often than black males (Anderson and Himes, 1959; Broderick, 1965).

Courtship in the lower-class group frequently involves gifts and economic support on the part of either partner (Schulz, 1969b). One can discern a dichotomy of economic relationships among lower-class black couples. Either the male is contributing to the economic maintenance of the female partner or attempting to exploit her for financial gain. As an ego-enhancing process, many lower-class black males prefer to see themselves as exploiters, women as the exploited. The man who does not make capital of his relationships with a woman is failing to prove his masculinity (Liebow, 1966).

It is reported that there are almost a million more black women in this country than black men (U.S. Department of Labor, 1969). This shortage of black men means many black women have to take love on male terms and some black men are strongly tempted to take advantage of such a situation and trade love for a living (Bernard, 1966a). In the dating context in which the male's primary motivation is sexual conquest and the female's primary motivation is courtship, the shortage of black males has cancelled any advantage of the black female. For, if she refuses his sexual access, there are always others who will not. Consequently much dating behavior in the black community is, in reality, sexual behavior (Staples, 1971).

In his study on premarital sexual standards, Reiss (1964) found that blacks had a more permissive premarital sex code than whites; that black males are the most permissive race-sex group, while white females are the most restrictive. Among women and whites, sexual permissiveness is more likely to be controlled by such influences as church attendance, beliefs in romantic love, etc., while among men and blacks, such influences are not so great. Blacks were more likely to require affection as a basis for sex relations and were less inclined to accept kissing and petting without affection.

The reasons for the difference between black and white sexual behavior are not clearly known (Staples, 1967b). It is generally assumed that the greater sexual permissiveness of Afro-Americans can be traced to the historical experience of slavery. During the era of black enslavement, the sexual impulse was released from the restraints imposed by kinship groups in Africa. The indiscriminate mating of black slaves by the slave-owning class led to the severance of the nexus between sex and marriage. Along with the lack of a puritan tradition in matters relating to sex, the expressive function of black religion, the shortage of black males, a permissive premarital sex code has prevailed in all segments of the black community (Frazier, 1961).

The little research done on this subject has confirmed the greater prevalence of premarital coitus in the black culture. In general, black females have higher rates of premarital coitus and premarital pregnancy than do whites.

But their rates are significantly affected by social class membership—if educational levels are accepted as measurements of social class in the black population (Gebhard *et al.*, 1958).

Racial differences in patterns of sexual behavior are very similar to sex role differences. Only socialization by the parents appears to be more directly responsible for sex role differences, while cultural values are more influential in racial differences. While the family is usually the primary mediator of cultural values, there seems to be a greater amount of peer group socialization among blacks and lower-class whites. This fact is confirmed by Hammond and Ladner, who report that:

> It appears that among adolescents the most important socializing influences are conversations of peers, and adults; observations of these groups; and actual participation in or imitation of the acts themselves. There is no sequential ordering of these influences. The child may observe a sexual act, engage in it, and later hear conversations about it. What may have been imitative play then comes to have a new conceptual meaning for him. The point should be stressed, however, that most of these children are exposed to sex at such an early age that they have not had the opportunity to formulate convictions which would sustain them against sexual involvement. (1969, p. 46)

In trying to explain the results of the permissive premarital sexual behavior of blacks, Rainwater (1966a) has noted that the meaning and function of sexual relations in the black community are difficult to assess since the issues are too subtle and ramified to be captured in the traditional categories of sex research. Even so, he has concluded at one point that the competitive and exploitative attitudes on the part of black dating partners make sexual relations a tense and uncertain matter as far as gratification goes (Rainwater, 1966c). Elsewhere he has reported that black women receive more sexual satisfaction in marriage and are more aggressive partners during coitus than white women (Rainwater, 1964).

If any conclusions can be drawn about black sexual behavior vis-a-vis white sexual behavior, it is that they are converging into a single standard of permissiveness with affection (Pope and Knudsen, 1965). Much of the racial difference in sexual practice can be accounted for by the pretend rules of whites, what Kroeber once called the trick of professing one thing and doing another. According to him the reason for this gap between standards and behavior is that it is better to have standards and fall short of them than to not have them (Kroeber, 1958, p. 272).

Although problems are encountered during the courtship period, more blacks eventually marry than do whites (Bernard, 1966a). These marriages, however, can not be characterized as mutually gratifying arrangements. According to Blood and Wolfe (1969), black wives are less satisfied with the love aspect of their marriage than white wives. Among lower-class black wives, they discovered that the majority would not marry if they had to do it over. Black husbands were rated low as providers; they did not satisfy their wives' need for understanding and communication was poor between black husbands and wives.

Not suprisingly, we find that the black divorce rate is higher than for whites. While the differential divorce rate is only slightly higher the difference in separations is very great (Staples, 1967a; Udry, 1966). Obviously economic factors have some influence here since divorce costs are a heavy burden under any circumstances. Also, there is a significant association between residence patterns and family stability. Among Afro-Americans family stability decreases as the size of the place of residence increases (Mercer, 1967).

Of all the groups studied by Bernard (1966b), she found that black males were less likely to have been married only once and to have their wives living with them. Only 52.2 percent of black males had such stable marriages. Although the probabilities of a stable marriage are greater for white men than for non-white men, the differences between them decreased as income, schooling and job level rise.

The major factor attributed to the high rate of marital instability among Afro-Americans is the husband's or wife's employment status. Aldous (1969) reports that when the wife is employed outside the home and shares the provider function, the husband may become unsure of his status in the family and withdraw from family tasks and decisions. Therefore, women who are in greatest need of husbands who will assist in performing household functions are less likely to have such husbands. The problem, then, is to provide not just employment but employment at a wage that allows the male to be the major provider for the family. Parker and Kleiner (1969) discovered that deviance in the black male family role performance was related to generalized feelings of failure and hopelessness in the black male. These same males who perceived themselves as low achievers with little hope of success are more inclined to believe that they are failing in their family performance. Another contributing factor to black marital instability is the lack of a close unit kin network in lower-class black communities. This deprives married couples of resources available for confident relationships or persons who have any commitment to whether or not the husband and wife stay together (Rainwater and Swartz, 1965; Feagin, 1969).

Rather than attempting to analyze the causes of marital instability among blacks, a more fruitful approach might be to concentrate on the institution of marriage itself and the factors in the social structure which make marriage such a tentative condition. The odds on any marriage being a success are not too great. If we take into account the marriages that end in divorce, annulment and desertion, almost half of the marriages in America are failures. Add to the figure the morbidity marriage, where a man and woman may continue living together just for appearances or convenience, we find that, as Goode has stated, "Most people in all cultures will achieve at best a life of quiet desperation in their family relations" (Goode, 1962, p. 380).

Although interracial marriages in this country are still few, changes in the racial climate of this country have also produced an increase in marriages across the color line (Heer, 1966). Most of these marriages involve spouses from the same social class (Pavela, 1964). When intermarriages involved members of different social classes, there was a pronounced tendency for black women to marry up rather than to marry down. The wives of black men usually had a higher educational level than their husbands, whether white or black, reflecting the generally lower level of education for black males (Bernard, 1966c).

The Myth of the Black Matriarchy

A unique feature of most theory and research on the black family is some discussion of its notorious matriarchal structure. It was Frazier (1939) who first suggested that because of the system of slavery, the black male's function was biological rather than sociological or economical. The only source of family continuity was through the female and there was a heavy reliance of the black child on his mother. This pattern, according to Frazier, together with the continued post-slavery subordination of the black male to a menial and subservient status, has made the female the dominant person in the black family.

Rather than seeing the peculiar role of black women in the family as a sign of the strength and resiliency of the black family, Frazier's successors (Moynihan, 1965; Rainwater, 1966b; Clark, 1965) chose to attribute many of the problems black American encounter to the female-headed households in the black community. The Moynihan Report (1965), in particular, attempted to document that the absence of the father figure in the black family would lead to a host of pathologies in the next generation of black children. He noted that in 1960, 21 percent of black families were headed by women, as compared with nine percent among white families, and that children from such homes do more poorly in school, drop out earlier and have higher delinquency rates.

The black matriarchy and the problems it generates has been too easily accepted as a valid fact by most behavioral scientists. And the number of dissenters are too few (Hyman and Reed, 1969; Josephson, 1969; Staples, 1970) in light of the tenuous underpinnings of the matriarchy theory. The term matriarchy, denotatively, is a misnomer when only applied to a minority of black families in the United States. A genuine matriarchy is a society in which some, if not all, of the legal powers relating to the ordering and governing of the family are lodged in women rather than men (Mead, 1949). If this definition is accepted, the view of most historians is that men reign dominant in all society; no matriarchy (i.e., a society ruled by women) is known to exist (Goode, 1964).

Considering this fact, how do Moynihan and others justify referring to black families as matriarchal in structure? The Moynihan (1965) rationale is based primarily on the census figures which show that the father is absent in less than a quarter of all black families in the nation. His other evidence presented on the existence of a black matriarchy is in the nature of learned opinions or generalizations. Rainwater (1966b) limited his generalizations about female-dominated families to the lower-class black community. He cites 1960 census data that show that among urban blacks with incomes under $3,000, 47 percent of the families with children have female heads. However, in the same census, one finds that in the comparable white stratum, 38 percent of the families have female heads, a difference of only nine percentage points.

While it is an irrefutable fact that female-headed households are more common among blacks, the question might be raised as to how much more frequent does the situation have to be for this label of matriarchy to be endemic to black family life. Another factor behind the matriarchy theory is the fact that even in male-headed black households, the wife has an inordinate influence on family tasks and decisions. The only empirical evidence on the husband's subordination to the wife in decision-making is presented in the Blood and Wolfe (1960) study of 103 black wives and 554 white wives in Detroit.

In the Blood and Wolfe (1960) study, they found that the black wife was dominant, as measured by the criterion of decision-making, in almost half of the families; the husband, in only 19 percent; and in 38 percent of the families, both had equal power. They did not, however, interpret these findings as proof of a black matriarchy. Rather, they stated that black wives assumed the decision-making role only because it was thrust upon them. Since only women were interviewed it is also possible that they were inclined to inflate their own power when reporting on who made decisions in the family (King, 1969; Ballweg, 1969).

At any rate, making decisions that black men cannot or refuse to make is not a valid measure of the power a black woman has in the family. The chances are that few decisions are made by the wife that he actively opposes. A possible reason for his deference to her in certain decisions is that black wives usually have more formal education than their husbands (Bernard, 1966c) and are better equipped to make those decisions. Frequently, she is more familiar with the machinations of white bureaucracies since contacts with the white world have been more available to black women than to black men.

Moreover, in a secondary analysis of three existing surveys, Hyman and Reed (1969) reported that the actual white pattern (of female influence) is almost identical to that for black families; that women's influence exceeds that of men in a number of instances. Even in the area of politics, where male dominance has long been assumed, white and black children are more likely to side with the mother when parents disagree on a party choice. The authors conclude that the concept of a culturally linked black-white difference in family organization needs to be critically re-examined.

Although the debate rages on as to the role of black women in the family, whatever that role may be has evolved out of the struggle for black survival in American society. The black woman has assumed an important position in this survival action. She has developed her personality and sense of responsibility out of the necessary role adjustments required to withstand the oppressive odds against her family's survival in an admittedly racist society. While the white role models for females may conform to the desires of male chauvinists, they may be antithetical to the goals of black liberation. The black woman's flexibility in adopting her role has, historically, proven an asset to the survival of black people and it is through this past performance that she can demand a new set of definitions and a recognition of herself as a citizen, companion and confidant, not a matriarchal villain (Larue, 1970).

Parental Roles and Socialization Processes

The dyadic structure of the black family subsequently expands to encompass not only spousal roles but the roles of children as well. Child-bearing rates among blacks are usually higher than white fertility rates although in the last few years there has been a somewhat larger absolute decline in black fertility rates than in white rates. Nevertheless, in 1967 black fertility was still 30 percent higher than white—25.4 births per thousand population compared to 16.7 (Hill and Jaffe, 1967).

In some quarters, the fertility differential between blacks and whites is seen as evidence of a widening tangle of pathology among lower-income blacks—a pathology which has become internalized, is self-perpetuating, and has produced in zoological tenements of the urban ghetto a state of biological anarchy (White, 1964). Such an analysis has generated a plethora of suggestions on how to stem the tide of black babies being imposed on the heavily burdened ecological structure and public assistance resources. These suggestions range from subtle exhortations to the poor to be more "responsible" to advocating the compulsory sterilization of mothers of out-of-wedlock children (Hill and Jaffe, 1967).

Upon reexamining the patterns of black fertility behavior in greater detail, a far different picture emerges—one of considerable underlying aspiration for family limitation and upward mobility (Rainwater, 1964; Beasley *et al.*, 1966). Almost all of the difference in white and non-white total fertility can be accounted for by differences in their socioeconomic status. For instance, the 1960 census revealed that blacks with four years of high school education have about the same number of children as whites with the same amount of education while those with four years of college have fewer than whites of an equivalent background. Moreover, the discrepancy is considerably less in the occupation and income categories above the poverty level. We find, for instance, that while black mothers aged forty-five to forty-nine with incomes below $2,000 have one third more children than comparable whites, in the income brackets above $3,000 the difference is cut in half (Hill and Jaffe, 1967).

Although the high fertility rate of blacks appears to be more a function of the low socioeconomic status of blacks than any other factor, there can be little doubt about the importance of motherhood to the black woman. To the black female, motherhood signifies maturity and the fulfillment of one's function as a woman. Among black women, children tend to be regarded as a value in themselves, whether born in wedlock or not. This attitude may have its roots in the black historical experience, when the status and value of slave women largely depended upon their breeding capacity. Among plantation blacks, for example, the assertion that a woman could not have children constituted a slur (Johnson, 1934).

There is some evidence that the maternal role is more highly valued than wifehood among black women. The Bell (1967) study of 202 black mothers in the Philadelphia area showed that although the lower-class black male considered his marital and parental roles of little importance, the lower-class black woman believed the role of mother to be of high significance to her. Furthermore, she saw marriage as potentially dangerous because of the possibility that economic resources which could be used for taking care of their children might be squandered by the husband.

The family role performance of the black male has been alternatively described as deriving from a normative conformity to a subculturally distinct family situation (Frazier, 1939; Moynihan, 1965) or as a painful adjustment to social conditions of discrimination and a high probability of failure (Liebow, 1967; Hannerz, 1969; Schulz, 1969). Whatever the source of his role failure, the research literature indicates that the black male is not adequately carrying out his parental role function (Aldous, 1969; Blood and Wolfe, 1969).

Both Liebow (1967) and Schulz (1969a) used the participant-observer technique to study intensively the family role performance of lower-class black males. In general, they found that the role of the father in the black family is highly dependent on the male's ability to earn a living and his willingness to share that living with his family. He learns to resort to unstable family behavior as a direct response to the failures (unemployment, low income, uninteresting jobs, discrimination, etc.) that he meets in life. The empirical verification of the Liebow and Schulz position is found in the Parker and Kleiner (1969) findings that discrepancies in the black male's family role performance are related to relatively low self-evaluations of his achievements and probability of success in goal striving, as well as relatively higher discrepancies between achievement and aspiration.

While these studies reflect a sympathetic view of the black male's difficulty in meeting the normative expectations for husband and father, it has been noted that in the attempt by these investigators to disprove that blacks are lazy, irresponsible, apathetic, etc., they deny any validity to the values and attitudes blacks express in their marital and family relationships. By asserting that the only difference between Afro-American males and other American males is that they are black and live under adverse social conditions, they ignore the existence of a unique black culture with its own beliefs, attitudes, and rituals which constitute a life style that gives every culture its own distinctive character (Davidson, 1969).

Considering the problems faced by many black families, it is understandable that the socialization of children would reflect the consequences of living in a poverty-stricken culture. Like so many other reports on the black family, child-rearing practices are seen as undesirable according to middle-class norms. Past research indicates that the frequent employment of the mother creates special problems in the socialization of the black child, especially if we accept as valid the findings that black husbands/fathers do not help out their wives in the home (Blood and Wolfe, 1969). According to several studies, lower-class black children are trained to be of little bother to their parents and are expected to mature early (Davis and Dollard, 1940; Kardiner and Ovesey, 1951; Rainwater, 1966b). These same children are liberated earlier for productive activity, and children freed for work and economic independence are also liberated from parental control. Thus, a great deal of socialization takes place within the peer group context rather than in the family environment (Ausubel and Ausubel, 1963).

Some of the child-rearing practices of black parents are common to all lower-class groups and may be attributed to the tensions and stresses associated with lower-class life, which repercuss in the parent-child relationship as well as the husband-wife relationship. Almost twenty-five years ago, Davis and Havighurst (1946) found that differences in child-rearing practices between middle-class and lower-class blacks were similar to those between middle-class and lower-class whites. In addition to the social class differences, they found that blacks are more permissive than whites in the feeding and weaning of their children, but are much more rigorous than whites in toilet training.

Her methods of child rearing cannot be attributed solely to the black mother's employment outside the home. In Blau's (1964) study of mothers interviewed during confinement in the hospital, she discovered that class for class, fewer black mothers than white mothers had been exposed to articles on child rearing. The reason given for this phenomenon was the low number of blacks in the middle-class strata. Although they are more often favorable toward child-rearing experts, the new member of the black middle-class has fewer opportunities than her white counterpart for exposure to and assimilation of middle-class modes of child rearing within her color group.

In another investigation of class differences in the socialization practices of black mothers in the context of their child-rearing goals, Kamii and Radin (1967) concluded that middle- and lower-class black mothers do not differ fundamentally in their goals but they differ considerably in their socialization practices. Middle-class black mothers were more likely to gratify their child's socio-emotional needs, to reward the child for desirable behavior and to use reasoning along with physical punishment to influence the child's behavior more often than lower-class black mothers.

As the primary socializing agent in American society, the family must see that the child receives material and emotional support and that he is motivated to acquire the educational and occupational skills necessary for achieving socially acceptable goals. In a society where the opportunities for reaching these objectives are distributed differentially on the basis of racial distinctions, the black family has a dual socialization role: to inculcate the appropriate motivational elements in the black child for goal striving and to prepare him for the harsh vicissitudes of ghetto life. The socialization process must be compatible with the requirements of survival for those Afro-Americans that exist outside the pale of American justice and equal opportunity.

Towards a Sociology of the Black Family

In an overall assessment of theories and research on black family life, their value is diminished by the weak methodology employed; the superficial analysis that ensues from the use of poor research designs; biased and low samples; and inadequate research instruments. While data must be theory oriented and theory must be confirmed by data collection (Merton, 1959), the inferences drawn from data to theory on the black family are unjustified on the basis of the research evidence presented by most investigators of black family life. Much research on black family patterns seems to have been based on preconceived notions about the pathological character and malfunctioning of the black family—notions that frequently derive from the use of white, middle-class models as an evaluative measure for families subject to an entirely different set of social forces which determine its structure and dynamics (Rodman, 1959).

The fact must be accepted that the black family cannot be explained by the use of normative social science models. For the most part sociology has been a normative science operating with implicit equilibrium models. What this means is that the traditional approach to the study of black family life has been to define the consequences of their family behavior on the basis of standards of the white community, and not only the white community in general, but white, middle-class people in particular. Rather than using a more objective approach and accepting the fact that black families are different and one must understand the way in which they live and try to understand their values and standards—other values and standards—white values and standards have been imposed on the study of black family life. The result has been that the black family continues to be defined as a pathological unit whose unique way of functioning sustains the conditions of its oppression.

This brings us, then, to the question of whether the white social scientist, who does not have the background of black family experience, can adequately interpret what happens in the black family milieu. While the intrusion of such a question may appear inappropriate, or unnecessary, in a discussion of behavioral science research, it nevertheless is being posed in academic circles—and for fairly good reasons. Ideally, sociologists are committed to the pursuit of truth, the objective study of human relationships (Rose, 1954). While the white sociologist may not consciously, or intentionally, assume a point of view based on his racial membership, the problem develops that when studying the black family, he must investigate a group of which he is not an intimate part. He is a member of a racist society, participates in racist institutions, and develops a view of black people partially derived from these relationships (Davidson, 1969). As Marx once stated, "The ideas of a society are of necessity the ideas of its ruling class" (Marx, 1904, pp. 11–12). This statement, although intended to explain the ideology of ruling classes, may also be applied to the dominant racial group in a society.

However, there is no definitive evidence of a racial polarization of theory and research on the black family. The purveyors of the pathology view have belonged to both racial groups, as well as the defenders of the black family. The difference most likely arises from adherence to middle-class ideology and values rather than a value-free approach to the study of black family life. A problem remains that much of what we know is a mere oversimplication of popular stereotypes about black family life which serve to inculcate in the public mind a host of useless and invalidated generalizations—and there is much that we need to know that has not yet been explored.

The void in our knowledge of black family life consists of such phenomena as the dynamic processes of family interaction in the black community. As previously mentioned, past research on the black family has focused on its structural features, not its interactional processes. Additionally, most research on the black family has been confined to certain regions of the country. Since regions may constitute autonomous cultural groups, it may be difficult to generalize the findings on black families in one region of the country to all Afro-Americans. For instance, is it not possible that Southern blacks may have developed a more distinct pattern of family life since they are more spatially and culturally isolated from white, middle-class norms (Gillin, 1955)?

Very little is known about the middle and later years of black families. It has been suggested that the early age of blacks at the onset of procreation means that the family hardly has time to recover from the economic drain of raising one generation before it must turn to the problem of supporting a growing set of grandchildren, followed by the problem of supporting declining parents (Fischer et al., 1968). Others have also noted that the black grandmother is a very supportive element in the rearing of children. It is assumed that she takes on this importance because the men are absent from the household (Rainwater, 1966b; Frazier, 1939).

A very important area of neglect is middle-class patterns of black family life. If we want to ascertain the economic variables that impinge on black family life, a fruitful approach would be to investigate variations within the black community. This would allow us to isolate those features of the black family related to socioeconomic factors and to analyze the role of culture in patterning black family behavior. Previous theorists have not paid that much attention to middle-class black families. Frazier (1957) concluded that the old black bourgeoisie had stable families but that the new members of the black middle-class retained elements of their folk culture and were exaggerated Americans. Moynihan (1965) claimed that middle-class black families would eventually be caught in the tangle of pathology because of their close proximity to the black lower-class.

Ultimately, as sociologists, we must define our role in American society. Are we to accept the socially defined reality, the value structure, of this society and give it an academic validity through our theories and research? Or, are we going to accept the challenge, and continue the tradition, of a humanistic, value-free, discipline as put forth by the founding fathers of sociology? Can we continue to conduct research which serves the purpose of validating a certain life style ordered along racial and class lines and which denigrates attributes which do not conform to that life style.

If we were to look at black family life styles objectively, we would find that its culture is not a poor imitation of its white counterpart but a fully developed life style of its own. Whether its distinctive cultural patterns are due to its African past, alienation from white society, or economic deprivation is not important. What matters is how it is integrated into black family life and whether it is related to the black condition in American society. This writer submits that black family culture and social achievement are largely independent of one another.

As an example of the positive aspects of black family subculture, we can, briefly, examine the culture linkage between sexual attitudes and behavior and out-of-wedlock children. The greater sexual permissiveness of black people more accurately reflects the absence of a double standard of sexual conduct among that group. It is not that white people have high moral standards, but the fact that white women lack the same sexual freedom as white men that accounts for most sexual chastity that still exists among this group. Although this writer knows of no published study comparing the proportion of black males with white males who have engaged in premarital sex relations, the results of his unpublished research revealed that there is no difference—almost all of the bi-racial males reported a premarital sexual experience. The white males in the group, however, were much more likely to have a double standard of sexual conduct. Among blacks, the lack of a double standard means that members of this group can engage in a meaningful sexual relationship rather than participating in sex role conflicts, or developing neurotic feelings of guilt over the question of premarital sex. As a result, sex relations—both before and after marriage—have a much more positive meaning in the black community.

The greater sexual freedom of blacks is linked to the attitudes toward out-of-wedlock children. The normative expectation that one will engage in premarital sex relations alerts most blacks to the possibility that an illegitimate child may result from such a prenuptial relationship. While the belief that blacks are not troubled by illegitimacy is untrue, the illegitimate black child is not stigmatized by the conditions of his birth. Children have a value independent of the legitimacy of their conception. In essence there is no such thing as an illegitimate child in the black community. All children are legitimate and have a value to their families and their community. There are only children without fathers, and these children may incur special problems because of the national oppression of women in this society. Sociologists might best study the facts of deprivation and the varied responses rather than the dysfunctional aspects of illegal parenthood in the black community.

In summation, it can be said that in the understanding of black family life there remain questions to be answered and answers to be questioned. What we know from past research is that the black family has evolved a unique structure and style to cope with the circumstances that it has confronted. In order to build a sociology of the black family, we must ascertain the norms and values that animate the process of family interaction and how that process is related to the forces that have shaped it and its various expressions in American life. This is the task before us and how we can fulfill it is not clear (MacWhorter, 1969). In this summary and analysis of theory and research on the black family in the past decade, one fact seems certain: that we cannot develop a viable sociology of the black family that is based on the myths and stereotypes that pervade the research of past years.

References

Aldous, Joan. "Wives' Employment Status and Lower-Class Men as Husbands: Support for the Moynihan Thesis." *Journal of Marriage and the Family*, 31 (August 1969): 469–476.

Anderson, Charles S., and Joseph Himes. "Dating Values and Norms on a Negro College Campus." *Marriage and Family Living*, 21 (April 1959): 227–229.

Ausubel, David, and Pearl Ausubel. "Ego Development among Segregated Negro Children." In *Education in Depressed Areas*, edited by A. Harry Passow. New York: Teachers College Press, 1963.

Ballweg, John A. "Husband-Wife Response Similarities on Evaluative and Non-evaluative Survey Questions." *Public Opinion Quarterly*, 33 (Summer 1969): 249–254.

Beasley, Joseph D., *et al.* "Attitudes and Knowledge Relevant to Family Planning among New Orleans Negro Females." *American Journal of Public Health*, 56 (November 1966): 1847–1857.

Bell, Robert. "The Relative Importance of Mother and Wife Roles among Negro Lower-Class Women." Paper presented at the Groves Conference on Marriage and the Family, San Juan, Puerto Rico, April 1967.

Bernard, Jessie. *Marriage and Family among Negroes*. Englewood Cliffs, N.J.: Prentice-Hall, 1966.

Bernard, Jessie. "Marital Stability and Patterns of Status Variables." *Journal of Marriage and the Family*, 28 (November 1966): 421–439.

Bernard, Jessie. "Note on Educational Homogamy in Negro-White and White-Negro Marriages." *Journal of Marriage and the Family*, 28 (August 1966): 274–276.

Billingsley, Andrew. *Black Families in White America*. Englewood Cliffs, N.J.: Prentice-Hall, 1969.

Blau, Zena Smith. "Exposure to Child-Rearing Experts: A Structural Interpretation of Class-Color Differences." *American Journal of Sociology*, 69 (May 1964): 596–608.

Blood, Robert, and Donald Wolfe. *Husbands and Wives*. New York: The Free Press, 1960.

Blood, Robert, and Donald Wolfe. "Negro-White Differences in Blue-Collar Marriages in a Northern Metropolis." *Social Forces*, 48 (September 1969): 59–63.

Broderick, Carlfred. "Social Heterosexual Development among Urban Negroes and Whites." *Journal of Marriage and the Family*, 27 (May 1965): 200–203.

Bruyn, Severyn. *The Human Perspective in Sociology: The Methodology of Participant-Observation*. Englewood Cliffs, N.J.: Prentice-Hall, 1966.

Carper, Laura. "The Negro Family and the Moynihan Report." *Dissent*, 13 (March-April 1966): 133–140.

Clark, Kenneth. *Dark Ghetto*. New York: Harper and Row, 1965.

Cloward, Bernard, and Frances Fox Piven. "Migration, Politics, and Welfare." *Saturday Review* (November 1968): 31–35.

Coleman, James. *Equality of Educational Opportunity*. United States Department of Health, Education and Welfare, Office of Education, 1966.

Davidson, Douglas. "Black Culture and Liberal Sociology." *Berkeley Journal of Sociology*, 15 (1969): 164–183.

Davis, Allison, and John Dollard. *Children of Bondage: The Personality Develop-

ment of Negro Youth in the Urban South. Washington, D.C.: American Council on Education, 1940.

Davis, Allison, and Robert Havighust. "Social Class and Color Differences in Child Rearing." *American Sociological Review,* 21 (December 1946): 710–714.

Edwards, G. Franklin, ed. *E. Franklin Frazier on Race Relations.* Chicago: University of Chicago Press, 1968.

Feagin, Joel. "The Kinship Ties of Negro Urbanites." *Social Science Quarterly,* 49 (December 1969): 660–665.

Fischer, Ann, *et al.* "The Occurrence of the Extended Family at the Origin of the Family of Procreation: A Developmental Approach to Negro Family Structure." *Journal of Marriage and the Family,* 30 (May 1968): 290–300.

Frazier, E. Franklin. *The Free Negro Family.* Nashville: Fisk University Press, 1932.

Frazier, E. Franklin. *The Negro Family in Chicago.* Chicago: University of Chicago Press, 1932.

Frazier, E. Franklin. *The Negro Family in the United States.* Chicago: University of Chicago Press, 1939.

Frazier, E. Franklin. *Black Bourgeoisie.* Glencoe, Illinois: The Free Press, 1957.

Frazier, E. Franklin. "Negro Sex Life of the African and American." In *The Encyclopedia of Sexual Behavior,* edited by Albert Ellis and Albert Arbanel. New York: Hawthorne Books, 1961.

Frazier, E. Franklin. "The Failure of the Negro Intellectual." *Negro Digest,* 30 (Summer 1962): 214–222.

Furstenberg, Frank F. "Premarital Pregnancy among Black Teenagers." *Transaction,* 7 (May 1970): 52–53.

Gebhard, Paul, *et al. Pregnancy, Birth and Abortion.* New York: Harper and Brothers, 1958.

Gillin, John. "National and Regional Cultural Values in the United States." *Social Forces,* 34 (December 1955): 107–113.

Goode, William. *World Revolution and Family Patterns.* Glencoe, Illinois: The Free Press, 1962.

Goode, William. *The Family.* Englewood Cliffs, N.J.: Prentice-Hall, 1964.

Gouldner, Alvin W. "Anti-Minotaur: The Myth of a Value-Free Sociology." *Social Problems,* 9 (Winter 1962): 199–213.

Hammond, Boone, and Joyce Ladner. "Socialization into Sexual Behavior in a Negro Slum Ghetto." In *The Individual, Sex and Society,* edited by Carlfred Broderick and Jessie Bernard, pp. 41–52. Baltimore: John Hopkins Press, 1969.

Hannerz, U. "Roots of Black Manhood." *Transaction* (October 1969): 13–21.

Heer, David. "Negro-White Marriage in the United States." *Journal of Marriage and the Family,* 28 (August 1966): 262–273.

Hill, Adelaide Cromwell, and Frederick S. Jaffe. "Negro Fertility and Family Size Preferences: Implications for Programming of Health and Social Services." In *The Negro American,* edited by Talcott Parsons and Kenneth B. Clark. Boston: Beacon Press, 1967.

Hyman, Herbert H., and John Shelton Reed. "Black Matriarchy Reconsidered: Evidence from Secondary Analysis of Sample Surveys." *Public Opinion Quarterly,* 33 (Fall 1969): 346–354.

Johnson, Charles S. *Shadow of the Plantation.* Chicago: University of Chicago Press, 1934.

Josephson, Eric. "The Matriarchy: Myth and Reality." *The Family Coordinator,* 18 (October 1969): 268–276.

Kamii, Constance, and Norma Radin. "Class Differences in the Socialization Practices of Negro Mothers." *Journal of Marriage and the Family,* 29 (May 1967): 302–312.

Kardiner, Abram, and Lionel Ovesey. *The Mark of Oppression.* New York: W. W. Norton, 1951.

King, Karl. "Adolescent Perception of Power Structure in the Negro Family." *Journal of Marriage and the Family,* 31 (November 1969): 751–755.

Kolb, William L. "The Impingement of Moral Values on Sociology." *Social Problems*, 2 (October 1954): 66–70.

Kroeber, Alfred, and Clyde Kluckhohn. "Culture: A Critical Review of Concepts and Definitions." *Papers of Peabody Museum of American Archaeology and Ethnology*, 47 (1952): 3–223.

Kunz, Phillip R., and Merlin B. Brinkerhoff. "Differential Childlessness by Color: The Destruction of a Cultural Belief." *Journal of Marriage and Family*, 31 (November 1969): 713–719.

Ladner, Joyce. Personal communication, n.d.

Larue, Linda. "The Black Movement and Women's Liberation." *The Black Scholar*, 1 (May 1970): 36–42.

Lefcowitz, Myron J. "Poverty and Negro-White Family Structure." Agenda Paper for White House Planning Session on Race, November 1965.

Lewis, Hylan. "Culture, Class and Family Life among Low-Income Urban Negroes." In *Employment, Race and Poverty*, edited by Arthur Ross and Herbert Hill. New York: Harcourt, Brace and World, 1967.

Liebow, Elliot. *Tally's Corner*. Boston: Little, Brown, 1966.

MacWhorter, Gerald. "The Ideology of Black Social Science." *The Black Scholar*, 1 (December 1969): 28–35.

McCarthy, John D., and William L. Yancey. "Uncle Tom and Mr. Charlie: A Review of the Negro American's Self-esteem." *American Journal of Sociology* (November 1970).

Marx, Karl. *A Contribution to the Critique of Political Economy*. Chicago: C. H. Kerr, 1904.

Mead, Margaret. *Male and Female*. New York: William Morrow and Company, 1949.

Mercer, Charles V. "Interrelations among Family Stability, Family Composition, Residence and Race." *Journal of Marriage and the Family*, 29 (August 1967): 456–460.

Merton, Robert K. "Introduction: Notes on Problem-Finding in Sociology." In *Sociology Today*, edited by Robert K. Merton, *et al.* New York: Basic Books, 1959.

Moynihan, Daniel P. *The Negro Family: The Case for National Action*. Office of Policy Planning and Research, United States Department of Labor, 1965.

Parker, Seymour, and Robert J. Kleiner. "Social and Psychological Dimensions of the Family Role Performance of the Negro Male." *Journal of Marriage and the Family*, 31 (August 1969): 500–506.

Pavela, Todd H. "An Exploratory Study of Negro-White Intermarriage in Indiana." *Journal of Marriage and the Family*, 26 (May 1964): 209–214.

Pope, Hallowell, and Dean D. Knudsen. "Premarital Sexual Norms, the Family and Social Change." *Journal of Marriage and Family*, 27 (August 1965): 314–323.

Potter, David M. *People of Plenty*. Chicago: University of Chicago Press, 1960.

Rainwater, Lee. *Family Design: Marital Sexuality, Family Size and Contraception*. Chicago: Aldine, 1964.

Rainwater, Lee. "Marital Stability and Patterns of Status Variables: A Comment." *Journal of Marriage and the Family*, 28 (November 1966): 442–446.

Rainwater, Lee. "Crucible of Identity: The Lower-Class Negro Family." *Daedalus*, 95 (Winter 1966): 172–216.

Rainwater, Lee. "Some Aspects of Lower-Class Sexual Behavior." *The Journal of Social Issues*, 22 (April 1966): 96–108.

Rainwater, Lee. *Behind Ghetto Walls: Negro Families in a Federal Slum*. Chicago: Aldine, 1970.

Rainwater, Lee, and Marc J. Swartz. *The Working Class World: Identity, World View, Social Relations and Family Behavior Magazines*. Social Research, Inc., 1965.

Rainwater, Lee, and William Yancey. *The Moynihan Report and the Politics of Controversy*. Cambridge: M.I.T. Press, 1967.

Reiss, Ira L. "Premarital Sexual Permissiveness among Negroes and Whites." *American Sociological Review*, 29 (October 1964): 688–698.

Robinson, William S. "Ecological Correlation and the Behavior of Individuals." *American Sociological Review*, 15 (June 1950): 351–357.

Rodman, Hyman. "On Understanding Lower Class Behavior." *Social and Economic Studies*, 8 (December 1959).

Rodman, Hyman. "The Lower-Class Value Stretch." *Social Forces*, 41 (December 1963): 205–215.

Rodman, Hyman. "Middle-Class Misconceptions about Lower-Class Families." In *Blue-Collar World: Studies of the American Worker*, edited by Arthur B. Shostak and William Gomberg. Englewood Cliffs, N.J.: Prentice-Hall, 1964.

Rodman, Hyman. "The Textbook World of Family Sociology." *Social Problems*, 12 (Spring 1965): 445–457.

Rose, Arnold. "The Social Responsibility of the Social Scientist." *Social Problems*, 1 (January 1954): 85–90.

Ryan, William. "Savage Discovery: The Moynihan Report." *The Nation*, 201 (November 1965): 380–384.

Schulz, David. "Variations in the Father Role in Complete Families of the Negro Lower-Class." *Social Science Quarterly*, 49 (December 1969): 651–659.

Schulz, David. *Coming Up Black: Patterns of Ghetto Socialization*. Englewood Cliffs, N.J.: Prentice-Hall, 1969.

Somerville, Rose. "Contemporary Family Materials—Black Family Patterns." *The Family Coordinator*, 19 (July 1970): 279–285.

Staples, Robert. *The Lower-Income Negro Family in Saint Paul*. Saint Paul: The Urban League, 1967.

Staples, Robert. "Mystique of Black Sexuality." *Liberator*, 7 (March 1967): 8–11.

Staples, Robert. "Research on the Negro Family: A Source for Family Practitioners." *The Family Coordinator*, 18 (July 1969): 202–210.

Staples, Robert. "The Myth of the Black Matriarchy." *The Black Scholar* (January-February 1970): 9–16.

Staples, Robert. *The Black Family: Essays and Studies*. Belmont: Wadsworth, 1971.

Udry, Richard J. "Marital Instability by Race, Sex, Education, and Occupation Using 1960 Census Data." *American Journal of Sociology*, 72 (September 1966): 203–209.

United States Department of Labor. *The Social and Economic Status of Negroes in the United States*. CBLS Report No. 375, Current Population Reports, Series P-23, No. 29, 1969.

Valentine, Charles A. *Culture and Poverty*. Chicago: University of Chicago Press, 1968.

White, Theodore H. *The Making of the President*. New York: Atheneum, 1964.

Willie, Charles V., ed. *The Family Life of Black People*. Columbus, Ohio: Charles V. Merrill, 1970.

Znaniecki, Florian. "Should Sociologists Be Also Philosophers of Values?" *Sociology and Social Research*, 37 (November-December 1952): 79–84.

"Old age," writes the author, a Berkeley sociologist, "is the minority group almost everyone joins." As humans age in American society they are likely to be treated as outsiders. As a result, the aged are increasingly clustering together for mutual support or simply to enjoy themselves. A now familiar but significant phenomenon has taken place in the last decade—towns and communities and apartment buildings populated solely by 60-, 70-, and 80-year-olds who fix their own meals, pay their own rent, shop for themselves, and help each other out, all outside of institutions. The author examines an "old-age commune" and analyzes developing life styles for the old.

Communal Life-Styles for the Old | *Arlie Russell Hochschild*

Merrill Court is a small apartment building near the shore of San Francisco Bay, and the home of 43 people. As persons over the age of 62 they are called, by the public housing authorities who built the project, "senior citizens." Most of the residents are conservative, fundamentalist widows (37 of the 43 are women) from the Midwest and Southwest and as such they might not seem likely candidates for "communal living" or "alternatives to the nuclear family." Nonetheless their social life together is, in many ways, communal and it suggests an alternative way of life for many other older people as well.

The main theory over the last ten years in the field of aging has been the theory of disengagement. According to this theory, as the older person grows older, he or she tends to reduce social ties to the outside world. The few remaining ties are characterized by less and less emotional investment, and the individual becomes increasingly "de-socialized" and self-centered. This study is a negative case study of that theory—a study of engagement, in some cases re-engagement. It suggests that whether or not an older person disengages, socially if not psychologically, depends among other things on the social milieu. Socially isolated older people are, it suggests, more likely to disengage than are those supported by a community of appropriate peers. Had these 43 people not signed up for this low-cost housing that put them together by chance, the probability is good that they too would have become isolated and disengaged, something which other studies have documented for their counterparts in "normal" settings.

From Arlie Russell Hochschild, *The Unexpected Community*, © 1973. By permission of Prentice-Hall, Inc., Englewood Cliffs, New Jersey.

Rural Ways in Urban Settings

Merrill Court is a strange mixture of old and new, of a vanishing Okie culture and a new blue-collar life-style, of rural ways in urban settings, of small-town community in mass society, of people oriented toward the young in an age-separated subculture. These internal immigrants to the working-class neighborhoods of West Coast cities and suburbs perceive their new environment through rural and small-town eyes. One woman who had gone shopping at a department store observed "all those lovely dresses, all stacked like cordwood." A favorite saying when one was about to retire was, "Guess I'll go to bed with the chickens tonight." They would give directions to the new hamburger joint or hobby shop by describing its relationship to a small stream or big tree. What remained of the old custom of a funeral wake took place at a new funeral parlor with neon signs and printed notices.

The communal life which developed in Merrill Court may have had nothing to do with rural ways in an urban setting. Had the widows stayed on the farms and in the small towns they came from, they might have been active in community life there. Those who had been involved in community life before remained active and, with the exception of a few, those who previously had not, became active.

For whatever reason, the widows built themselves an order out of ambiguity, a set of obligations to the outside and to one another where few had existed before. It is possible to relax in old age, to consider one's social debts paid, and to feel that constraints that do not weigh on the far side of the grave should not weigh on the near side either. But in Merrill Court, the watchfulness of social life, the Protestant stress on industry, thrift and activity added up to an ethos of keeping one's "boots on," not simply as individuals but as a community.

Forming the Community

"There wasn't nothin' before we got the coffee machine. I mean we didn't share nothin' before Mrs. Bitford's daughter brought over the machine and we sort of had our first occasion, you might say."

There were about six people at the first gathering around the coffee machine in the recreation room. As people came downstairs from their apartments to fetch their mail, they looked into the recreation room, found a cluster of people sitting down drinking coffee, and some joined in. A few weeks later the recreation director "joined in" for the morning coffee and, as she tells it, the community had its start at this point.

Half a year later Merrill Court was a beehive of activity: meetings of a service club; bowling; morning workshop; Bible study classes twice a week;

other classes with frequently changing subjects; monthly birthday parties; holiday parties; and visits to four nearby nursing homes. Members donated cakes, pies and soft drinks to bring to the nursing home, and a five-piece band, including a washtub bass, played for the "old folks" there. The band also entertained at a nearby recreation center for a group of Vietnam veterans. During afternoon band practice, the women sewed and embroidered pillow cases, aprons and yarn dolls. They made wastebaskets out of discarded paper towel rolls, wove rugs from strips of old Wonder Bread wrappers, and Easter hats out of old Clorox bottles, all to be sold at the annual bazaar. They made placemats to be used at the nursing home, totebags to be donated to "our boys in Vietnam," Christmas cards to be cut out for the Hillcrest Junior Women's Club, rag dolls to be sent to the orphanage, place cards to be written out for the bowling league banquet, recipes to be written out for the recipe book that was to go on sale next month, and thank you and condolence cards.

Social Patterns

The social arrangements that took root early in the history of Merrill Court later assumed a life of their own. They were designed, as if on purpose, to assure an "on-going" community. If we were to visually diagram the community, it would look like a social circle on which there are centripetal and centrifugal pressures. The formal role system, centered in the circle, pulled people toward it by giving them work and rewards, and this process went on mainly "downstairs," in the recreation room. At the same time, informal loyalty networks fluctuated toward and away from the circle. They became clear mainly "upstairs," where the apartments were located. Relatives and outsiders pulled the individual away from the circle downstairs and network upstairs, although they were occasionally pulled inside both.

Downstairs

Both work and play were somebody's responsibility to organize. The Merrill Court Service Club, to which most of the residents and a half-dozen nonresidents belonged, set up committees and chairmanships that split the jobs many ways. There was a group of permanent elected officials: the president, vice-president, treasurer, secretary and birthday chairman, in addition to the recreation director. Each activity also had a chairman, and each chairman was in charge of a group of volunteers. Some officers were rotated during the year. Only four club members did not chair some activity between 1965 and 1968; and at any time about a third were in charge of something.

Friendship Networks

Shadowing the formal circle was an informal network of friendships that formed over a cup of coffee in the upstairs apartments. The physical appearance of the apartments told something about the network. Inside, each apartment had a living room, kitchen, bedroom and porch. The apartments were unfurnished when the women moved in and as one remarked, "We fixed 'em up just the way we wanted. I got this new lamp over to Sears, and my daughter and I bought these new scatter rugs. Felt just like a new bride."

For the most part, the apartments were furnished in a remarkably similar way. Many had American flag stickers outside their doors. Inside, each had a large couch with a floral design, which sometimes doubled as a hide-a-bed where a grandchild might sleep for a weekend. Often a chair, a clock or picture came from the old home and provided a material link to the past. Most had large stuffed chairs, bowls of homemade artificial flowers, a Bible and porcelain knickknacks neatly arranged on a table. (When the group was invited to my own apartment for tea, one woman suggested sympathetically that we "had not quite moved in yet" because the apartment seemed bare by comparison.) By the window were potted plants, often grown from a neighbor's slip. A plant might be identified as "Abbie's ivy" or "Ernestine's African violet."

Photographs, usually out of date, of pink-cheeked children and grandchildren decorated the walls. Less frequently there was a photo of a deceased husband and less frequently still, a photo of a parent. On the living room table or nearby there was usually a photograph album containing pictures of relatives and pictures of the woman herself on a recent visit "back east." Many of the photographs in the album were arranged in the same way. Pictures of children came first and, of those, children with the most children appeared first and childless children at the end.

The refrigerator almost always told a special story. One contained homemade butter made by the cousin of a woman on the second floor; berry jam made by the woman three doors down; corn bought downstairs in the recreation room, brought in by someone's son who worked in a corn-canning factory; homemade Swedish rolls to be given to a daughter when she came to visit; two dozen eggs to be used in cooking, most of which would be given away; as well as bread and fruit, more than enough for one person. Most of the women had once cooked for large families, and Emma, who raised eight children back in Oklahoma, habitually baked about eight times as much corn bread as she could eat. She made the rounds of apartments on her floor distributing the extra bread. The others who also cooked in quantities reciprocated, also gratuitously, with other kinds of food. It was an informal division of labor although no one thought of it that way.

Most neighbors were also friends, and friendships, as well as information about them, were mainly confined to each floor. All but four had their *best* friends on the same floor and only a few had a next-best friend on another floor. The more one had friends outside the building, the more one had friends on other floors within the building. The wider one's social radius outside the building, the wider it was inside the building as well.

Neighboring

Apart from the gratification of friendship, neighboring did a number of things for the community. It was a way of relaying information or misinformation about others. Often the information relayed upstairs influenced social arrangements downstairs. For example, according to one widow,

> The Bitfords had a tiff with Irma upstairs here, and a lot of tales went around. They weren't true, not a one, about Irma, but then people didn't come downstairs as much. Mattie used to come down, and Marie and Mr. Ball and they don't so much now, only once and again, because of Irma being there. All on account of that tiff.

Often people seated themselves downstairs as they were situated upstairs, neighbor and friend next to neighbor and friend, and a disagreement upstairs filtered downstairs. For example, when opinion was divided and feelings ran high on the issue of whether to store the club's $900 in a cigar box under the treasurer's bed or in the bank, the gossip, formerly confined to upstairs, invaded the public arena downstairs.

Relaying information this way meant that without directly asking, people knew a lot about one another. It was safe to assume that what you did was known about by at least one network of neighbors and their friends. Even the one social isolate on the third floor, Velma, was known about, and her comings and goings were talked about and judged. Talk about other people was a means of social control and it operated, as it does elsewhere, through parables; what was told of another was a message to one's self.

Not all social control was verbal. Since all apartment living rooms faced out on a common walkway that led to a central elevator, each tenant could be seen coming and going; and by how he or she was dressed, one could accurately guess his or her activities. Since each resident knew the visiting habits of her neighbors, anything unusual was immediately spotted. One day when I was knocking on the door of a resident, her neighbor came out:

> I don't know where she is, it couldn't be the doctor's, she goes to the doctor's on Tuesdays; it couldn't be shopping, she shopped yesterday with her daughter. I don't think she's downstairs, she says she's worked enough today. Maybe she's visiting Abbie. They neighbor a lot. Try the second floor.

Neighboring is also a way to detect sickness or death. As Ernestine related, "This morning I looked to see if Judson's curtains were open. That's how we do on this floor, when we get up we open our curtains just a bit, so others walking by outside know that everything's all right. And if the curtains aren't drawn by mid-morning, we knock to see." Mattie perpetually refused to open her curtains in the morning and kept them close to the wall by placing potted plants against them so that "a man won't get in." This excluded her from the checking-up system and disconcerted the other residents.

The widows in good health took it upon themselves to care for one or two in poor health. Delia saw after Grandma Goodman who was not well enough to go down and get her mail and shop, and Ernestine helped Little Floyd and Mrs. Blackwell who could not see well enough to cook their own meals. Irma took care of Mr. Cooper and she called his son when Mr. Cooper "took sick." Even those who had not adopted someone to help often looked after a neighbor's potted plants while they were visiting kin, lent kitchen utensils and took phone messages. One woman wrote letters for those who "wrote a poor hand."

Some of the caretaking was reciprocal, but most was not. Three people helped take care of Little Floyd, but since he was blind he could do little in return. Delia fixed his meals, Ernestine laundered his clothes, and Irma shopped for his food. When Little Floyd died fairly suddenly, he was missed perhaps more than others who died during those three years, especially by his caretakers. Ernestine remarked sadly, "I liked helping out the poor old fella. He would appreciate the tiniest thing. And never a complaint."

Sometimes people paid one another for favors. For example, Freda took in sewing for a small sum. When she was paid for lining a coat, she normally mentioned the purpose for which the money would be spent (for example, bus fare for a visit to relatives in Montana), perhaps to reduce the commercial aspect of the exchange. Delia was paid by the Housing Authority for cleaning and cooking for Grandma Goodman, a disabled woman on her floor; and as she repeatedly mentioned to Grandma Goodman, she spent the money on high school class rings for her three grandchildren. In one case, the Housing Authority paid a granddaughter for helping her grandmother with housework. In another case, a disabled woman paid for domestic help from her social security checks.

The "Poor Dear" Hierarchy

Within the formal social circle there was a status hierarchy based on the distribution of honor, particularly through holding offices in the service club. Additionally, there was a parallel informal status hierarchy based on the distribution of luck. "Luck" as the residents defined it, is not entirely luck. Health and life expectancy, for example, are often considered "luck," but an upper-class person can expect to live ten years longer than a lower-class person. The widows of Merrill Court, however, were drawn from the same social class and they saw the differences among themselves as matters of luck.

She who had good health won honor. She who lost the fewest loved ones through death won honor, and she who was close to her children won honor. Those who fell short of any of these criteria were often referred to as "poor dears."

The "poor dear" system operated like a set of valves through which a sense of superiority ran in only one direction. Someone who was a "poor dear" in the eyes of another seldom called that other person a "poor dear" in return. Rather, the "poor dear" would turn to someone less fortunate, perhaps to buttress a sense of her own achieved or ascribed superiority. Thus, the hierarchy honored residents at the top and pitied "poor dears" at the bottom, creating a number of informally recognized status distinctions among those who, in the eyes of the outside society, were social equals.

The distinctions made by residents of Merrill Court are only part of a larger old-age status hierarchy based on things other than luck. At the monthly meetings of the countywide Senior Citizens Forum, to which Merrill Court sent two representatives, the term "poor dear" often arose with reference to old people. It was "we senior citizens who are politically involved versus those 'poor dears' who are active in recreation." Those active in recreation, however, did not accept a subordinate position relative to the politically active. On the other hand, they did not refer to the political activists as "poor dears." Within the politically active group there were those who espoused general causes, such as getting out an anti-pollution bill, and those who espoused causes related only to old age, such as raising social security benefits or improving medical benefits. Those in politics and recreation referred to the passive card players and newspaper readers as "poor dears." Uninvolved old people in good health referred to those in poor health as "poor dears," and those in poor health but living in independent housing referred to those in nursing homes as "poor dears." Within the nursing home there was a distinction between those who were ambulatory and those who were not. Among those who were not ambulatory there was a distinction between those who could enjoy food and those who could not. Almost everyone, it seemed, had a "poor dear."

At Merrill Court, the main distinction was between people like themselves and people in nursing homes. Returning from one of the monthly trips to a nearby nursing home, one resident commented:

> There was an old woman in a wheel chair there with a dolly in her arms. I leaned over to look at the dolly. I didn't touch it, well, maybe I just brushed it. She snatched it away, and said "Don't take my dolly." They're pathetic, some of them, the poor dears.

Even within the building, those who were in poor health, were alienated from their children, or were aging rapidly were considered "poor dears." It was lucky to be young and unlucky to be old. There was more than a 20-year age span between the youngest and oldest in the community. When one of the younger women, Delia, age 69, was drinking coffee with Grandma Goodman, age 79, they compared ages. Grandma Goodman dwelt on the subject and finished the conversation by citing the case of Mrs. Blackwell, who was 89 and still in reasonably good health. Another remarked about her 70th birthday:

> I just couldn't imagine myself being 70. Seventy is old! That's what Daisy said too. She's 80 you know. It was her 70th that got her. No one likes to be put aside, you know. Laid away. Put on the shelf you might say. No sir.

She had an ailment that prevented her from bowling or lifting her flower pots, but she compared her health to that of Daisy, and found her own health a source of luck.

Old people compare themselves not to the young but to other old people. Often the residents referred to the aged back in Oklahoma, Texas and Arkansas with pity in their voices:

> Back in Oklahoma, why they toss the old people away like old shoes. My old friends was all livin' together in one part of town and they hardly budged the whole day. Just sat out on their porch and chewed the fat. Sometimes they didn't even do that. Mostly they didn't have no nice housing, and nothin' social was goin' on. People here don't know what luck they've fallen into.

They also compared their lot to that of other older people in the area. As one resident said:

> Some of my friends live in La Casa [another housing project]. I suppose because they have to, you know. And I tried to get them to come bowling with me, but they wouldn't have a thing to do with it. "Those senior citizens, that's old folks stuff." Wouldn't have a thing to do with it. I tried to tell them we was pretty spry, but they wouldn't listen. They just go their own way. They don't think we have fun.

On the whole, the widows disassociated themselves from the status of "old person," and accepted its "minority" characteristics. The "poor dears" in the nursing home were often referred to as childlike: "They are easily hurt, you know. They get upset at the slightest thing and they like things to be the way they've always been. Just like kids." Occasionally, a widow would talk about Merrill Court itself in this vein, presumably excluding herself: "We're just like a bunch of kids here sometimes. All the sparring that goes on, even with church folk. And people get so hurt, so touchy. You'd think we were babies sometimes."

If the widows accepted the stereotypes of old age, they did not add the "poor dear" when referring to themselves. But younger outsiders did. To the junior employees in the Recreation and Parks Department, the young doctors who treated them at the county hospital, the middle-aged welfare workers and the young bank tellers, the residents of Merrill Court, and old people like them, were "poor dears."

Perhaps in old age there is a premium on finishing life off with the feeling of being a "have." But during old age, one also occupies a low social position. The way the old look for luck differences among themselves reflects the pattern found at the bottom of other social, racial and gender hierarchies. To find oneself lucky within an ill-fated category is to gain the semblance of high status when society withholds it from others in the category. The way old people feel above and condescend to other old people may be linked to the fact that the young feel above and condescend to them. The luck hierarchy does not stop with the old.

The Sibling Bond

There were rivalries and differences in Merrill Court, but neither alienation nor isolation. A club member who stayed up in her apartment during club meetings more often did it out of spite than indifference. More obvious were the many small, quiet favors, keeping an eye out for a friend and sharing a good laugh.

There was something special about this community, not so much because it was an old-age subculture, but because the subculture was founded on a particular kind of relationship—the sibling bond. Most residents of Merrill Court are social siblings. The customs of exchanging cups of coffee, lunches, potted plants and curtain checking suggest reciprocity. Upstairs, one widow usually visited as much as she was visited. In deciding who visits whom, they often remarked, "Well, I came over last time. You come over this time." They traded, in even measure, slips from house plants, kitchen utensils and food of all sorts. They watched one another's apartments when someone was away on a visit, and they called and took calls for one another.

There are hints of the parent-child bond in this system, but protectors picked their dependents voluntarily and resented taking care of people they did not volunteer to help. For example, one protector of "Little Floyd" complained about a crippled club member, a nonresident:

> It wasn't considerate of Rose to expect us to take care of her. She can't climb in and out of the bus very well and she walks so slow. The rest of us wanted to see the museum. It's not nice to say, but I didn't want to miss the museum waiting for her to walk with us. Why doesn't her son take her on trips?

The widows were not only equals among themselves, they also were remarkably similar. They all wanted more or less the same things and could give more or less the same things. They all wanted to *receive* Mother's Day cards. No one in the building *sent* Mother's Day cards. And what they did was to compare Mother's Day cards. Although there was some division of labor, there was little difference in labor performed. All knew how to bake bread and can peaches, but no one knew how to fix faucets. They all knew about "the old days" but few among them could explain what was going on with youth these days. They all had ailments but no one there could cure them. They all needed rides to the shopping center, but no one among them needed riders.

Their similar functions meant that when they did exchange services, it was usually the same kinds of services they themselves could perform. For example, two neighbors might exchange corn bread for jam, but both knew how to make both corn bread and jam. If one neighbor made corn bread for five people in one day, one of the recipients would also make corn bread for the same people two weeks later. Each specialized within a specialization, and over the long run the widows made and exchanged the same goods.

Hence the "side-by-sideness," the "in the same boat" quality of their relations. They noticed the same things about the world and their eyes caught the same items in a department store. They noticed the same features in the urban landscape—the pastor's home, the Baptist church, the nursing homes, the funeral parlors, the places that used to be. They did not notice, as an adolescent might, the gas stations and hamburger joints.

As a result, they were good listeners for each other. It was common for someone to walk into the recreation room and launch into the details of the latest episode of a mid-afternoon television drama ("It seems that the baby is not by artificial insemination but really Frank's child, and the doctor is trying to convince her to tell. . ."). The speaker could safely assume that her listeners also knew the details. Since they shared many experiences, a physical ailment, a death, a description of the past, an "old age joke" could be explained, understood and enjoyed. They talked together about their children much as their children, together, talked about them. Each shared with social siblings one side of the prototypical parent-child bond.

This similarity opened up the possibility of comparison and rivalry, as the "poor dear" hierarchy suggests. Whether the widows cooperated in collecting money for flowers, or competed for prestigious offices in the service club, bowling trophies or front seats in the bus, their functions were similar, their status roughly equal, and their relations in the best and worst sense, "profane."

Not all groups of old people form this sibling bond. Although we might expect subcultures to arise in nursing homes, certain hospital wards or convalescent hospitals, the likes of Merrill Court is rare. It is not enough to put fairly healthy, socially similar old people together. There is clearly something different between institutions and public housing apartments. Perhaps what counts is the kind of relationships that institutions foster. The resident of an institution is "a patient." Like a child, he has his meals served to him, his water glass filled, his bed made, his blinds adjusted by the "mother-nurse." He cannot return the service. Although he often shares a room or a floor with "brother" patients, both siblings have a nonreciprocal relationship to attendants or nurses. Even the research on the institutionalized focuses on the relation between patient and attendant, not between patient and patient. If there is a strong parent-child bond, it may overwhelm any potential sibling solidarity. If the old in institutions meet as equals, it is not as independent equals. The patient's relation to other patients is like the relation between *real*, young siblings, which may exaggerate rather than forestall narcissistic withdrawal.

The widows of Merrill Court took care of themselves, fixed their own meals, paid their own rent, shopped for their own food, and made their own beds; and they did these things for others. Their sisterhood rests on adult autonomy. This is what people at Merrill Court have and people in institutions do not.

The Sibling Bond and Age-Stratification

The sibling bond is delicate and emerges only when conditions are ripe. Rapid currents of social change lead to age-stratification, which, in turn, ripens conditions for the sibling bond. Tied to his fellows by sibling bonds, an individual is cemented side by side into an age stratum with which he shares the same rewards, wants, abilities and failings.

French sociologist Emile Durkheim, in his book *The Division of Labor*, describes two forms of social solidarity. In organic solidarity there is a division of labor, complementary dependence and differences among people. In mechanical solidarity there is no division of labor, self-sufficiency and similarity among people. Modern American society as a whole is based on organic solidarity, not only in the economic but in the social, emotional and intellectual spheres.

Different age strata within the general society, however, are more bound by mechanical solidarity. This is important both for the individual and the society. Although division of labor, complementary dependence and differences among people describe society's network of relations as a whole, they do not adequately describe relations among particular individuals. An individual's complementary dependence may be with people he does not know or meet—such as the person who grows and cans the food he eats, or lays the bricks for his house. And in his most intimate relations, an individual may also have complementary relations (either equal or unequal) with his spouse and children. But in between the most and least intimate bonds is a range in which there are many sibling relationships which form the basis of mechanical solidarity.

In fact, many everyday relations are with people similar and equal to oneself. Relations between colleague and colleague, student and student, friend and friend, relations within a wives' group or "the guys at the bar," the teenage gang or army buddies are often forms of the sibling bond. These ties are often back-up relations, social insurance policies for the times when the complementary bonds of parent and child, husband and wife, student and teacher, boy friend and girl friend fail, falter or normally change.

From an individual's viewpoint, some periods of life, such as adolescence and old age, are better for forming sibling bonds than are other periods. Both just before starting a family and after raising one, before entering the economy and after leaving it, an individual is open to, and needs, these back-up relationships. It is these stages that are problematic, and it is these stages that, with longer education and earlier retirement, now last longer.

From society's point of view, the sibling bond allows more flexibility in relations between generations by forging solidarity within generations and divisions between them. This divides society into age layers that are relatively independent of one another, so that changes in one age layer need not be retarded by conditions in another. The institution that has bound the generations together—the family—is in this respect on the decline. As it declines, the sibling bond emerges, filling in and enhancing social flexibility, especially in those social strata where social change is most pronounced. The resulting social flexibility does not guarantee "good" changes, and continuity is partly sacrificed to fads and a cult of newness. But whether desirable or not, this flexibility is partly due to and partly causes the growing importance of the sibling bond.

The times are ripe for the sibling bond, and for old-age communities such as Merrill Court. In the social life of old people the problem is not the sibling bond versus the parent-child bond. Rather, the question is how the one bond complements the other. The sisterhood at Merrill Court is no substitute for love of children and contact with them; but it offers a full, meaningful life independent of them.

The Minority Group Almost Everyone Joins

Isolation is not randomly distributed across the class hierarchy; there is more of it at the bottom. It is commonly said that old age is a leveler, that it affects the rich in the same way it affects the poor. It doesn't. The rich fare better in old age even as they fared better in youth. The poorer you are, the shorter your life expectancy, the poorer your health and health care, the lower your morale generally, the more likely you are to "feel" old regardless of your actual age, the less likely you are to join clubs or associations, the less active you are and the more isolated, even from children. Irving Rosow's study of 1,200 people over 62 living in Cleveland found that roughly 40 percent of the working class but only 16 percent of the middle class had fewer than four good friends. Another study of 6,000 white working-class men and women showed that of those over 65 with incomes under $3,000, a full third did not visit or speak to a friend or neighbor during the preceding week. The rock-bottom poor are isolated, but they are not the only ones.

The isolation of old people is linked to other problems. The old are poor and poverty itself is a problem. The old are unemployed and unemployment, in this society, is itself a problem. The old lack community and the lack of community is itself a problem. There is some connection between these three elements. Removed from the economy, the old have been cast out of the social networks that revolve around work. Lacking work, they are pushed down the social ladder. Being poor, they have fewer social ties. Poverty reinforces isolation. To eliminate enforced isolation, we have to eliminate poverty, for the two go together. The social life of Merrill Court residents, who had modest but not desperately low incomes, is an exception to the general link between social class and isolation.

Even if every old person were in a Merrill Court, the problem of old age would not be solved. But, allowing every old person the possibility of such an arrangement could be part of the solution. The basic problem far exceeds the limits of tinkering with housing arrangements. It is not enough to try to foster friendships among the old. Even to do that, it is not enough to set up bingo tables in the lobbies of decrepit hotels or to hand out name cards to the sitters on park benches. This would simply put a better face on poverty, a cheerful face on old age as it now is, at not much social cost.

Merrill Court is not set in any island of ideal social conditions; it is essentially an adjustment to bad social conditions. For the lives of old people to change fundamentally, those *conditions* must change. In the meantime, Merrill Court is a start. It is a good example of what can be done to reduce isolation. I do not know if similar communities would have emerged in larger apartment houses or housing tracts rather than in a small apartment house, with the married rather than the widowed, with rich rather than poor residents, with people having a little in common rather than a lot, with the very old person rather than the younger old person. Only trying will tell.

Merrill Court may be a forecast of what is to come. A survey of 105 University of California students in 1968 suggested that few parents of these students and few of the students themselves expect to be living with their families when they are old. Nearly seven out of ten (69 percent) reported that "under no circumstances" would they want their aged parents to live with them, and only 3 percent expected to be living with their own children when they are old. A full 28 percent expected to be living with *other* old people, and an additional 12 percent expected to be "living alone or with other old people."

Future communities of old people may be more middle class and more oriented toward leisure. Less than 10 percent of the students expected to be working when they passed 65. A great many expected to be "enjoying life," by which they meant studying, meditating, practicing hobbies, playing at sports and traveling.

But some things about future communities may be the same. As I have suggested throughout this book, communal solidarity can renew the social contact the old have with life. For old roles that are gone, new ones are available. If the world watches them less for being old, they watch one another more. Lacking responsibilities to the young, the old take on responsibilities toward one another. Moreover, in a society that raises an eyebrow at those who do not "act their age," the subculture encourages the old to dance, to sing, to flirt and to joke. They talk frankly about death in a way less common between the old and young. They show one another how to be, and trade solutions to problems they have not faced before.

Old age is the minority group almost everyone joins. But it is a forgotten minority group from which many old people dissociate themselves. A community such as Merrill Court counters this disaffiliation. In the wake of the declining family, it fosters a "we" feeling, and a nascent "old-age consciousness." In the long run, this may be the most important contribution an old-age community makes.

Although historians, sociologists, and political scientists have often analyzed and emphasized the diversity of American society—along racial, ethnic, social class, rural and urban lines—sociologists of the family have usually ignored the plurality of family forms. The moral dominance of the nuclear family engendered a false appearance of societal reality overemphasizing the traditional nuclear family. In this article the author, a well-known family sociologist, makes a case for the pluralism of American family life as a social fact and a basis for public policy.

Family Systems in the 1970's: Analysis, Policies, and Programs | *Marvin B. Sussman*

When confronted with a suggested subject like "Strengthening the Home and Family," one might be tempted to respond with the usual rhetoric of "what ought to be"—the "For God, country, and Yale" gambit, plus motherhood and, to be safe, a quick reference to the women's liberation movement. But this is contrary to my self-concept. I am much more comfortable in analyzing "what is," and my recommendations for action have a decidedly pragmatic, if not existentialist, flavor. My ideological position is that all behavioral science research faces the ultimate test of salience by the power of its explanation and usefulness to the solution of the problems of the human condition.* The basic issue is, How can the quality of life be improved for individuals of varying capabilities, motivations, and ambitions who live in pluralistic societies with extensive differentiation and complexity in occupations, organizations, associations, and family forms?

Having stated a capsulated version of my philosophical posture, I will proceed to dissect the social, political, and academic developments which sustain a particular perspective on the social system commonly identified as a family. This analysis, while particularly oriented toward the American scene, is by no means restricted, since similar developments and social movements are to be found in transitional and complex societies.

There are two main sections of this paper. The first covers theoretical formulations and research, which provide a perspective for looking at the family as a group and its linkages with nonfamily organizations and institutions in the 1970's. Included are:

*See Sussman (1966) for a statement of this position.

1. variant family forms
2. structural properties of kin family systems
3. major tasks and functions: family-organizational linkages
4. kin network as a mediating-linking system
5. internal role structure: accommodations to exigencies of the 1970's.

The second section deals with practical applications, needed policies, programs, and strategies for increasing the level of competence of human service systems to meet the expectations, capabilities, interests, and aspirations of members of variant family forms found in pluralistic societies.

Variant Family Forms

Ethnic historians and race-relation sociologists and psychologists have long emphasized the pluralistic characteristic of United States society. Over the years there has been quibbling in academic halls over whether a melting pot was cooking an amalgam composed of ethnic and cultural distillates called "American," or whether this society was persisting as a salad bowl with its shapes and hues of ethnic, religious, and racial identities. The argument is by no means over, but the salad bowl adherents are winning out in this decade.

Surprisingly, this notion of pluralism, or variability and differentiation of groups, did not take hold among students of the family. This may be a sensitive area which supports the rhetoric of "what ought to be"—an ideal family form according to some preordained, and often religiously sanctioned, set of values. The power and pervasiveness of this belief in the ideal family have resulted in the formulation of research questions which do not capture empirical descriptions of what family systems are actually like in the real world. Forms that vary from the traditional nuclear family of husband, wife, and children living in neolocal residence with the male as breadwinner and female as homemaker have been viewed as deviant. Research in the 1950's and 1960's on the working mother of the single-parent or dual-work family was mainly concerned with the deleterious effects of such gainful employment upon children. The implications were that women should be "in the home where the good Lord intended them to be," and in the case of the single parent, to marry or remarry as soon as possible. Very little attention was accorded to the meaning and significance for women of working, the circumstances under which women took jobs, or the implications for the reallocation of roles within the dual-career family (Rapoport and Rapoport, 1969).

This preoccupation with the model nuclear family pattern and effort to preserve it at all costs prevented sociologists from describing what was becoming most obvious to non-sociological observers of the American scene: a pluralism in family forms existing side by side with members in each of these forms having different problems to solve and issues to face. Moreover, few individuals over a lifetime remain in a single type of family structure, although the majority have some experience in the traditional nuclear family.

Traditional Family Structures

The most prominent traditional types of family structures now existing, and variations on these structures, are:*

1. Nuclear family—husband, wife, and offspring living in a common household.
   a. Single career
   b. Dual career
      1) Wife's career continuous
      2) Wife's career interrupted
2. Nuclear dyad—husband and wife alone: childless, or no children living at home.
   a. Single career
   b. Dual career
      1) Wife's career continuous
      2) Wife's career interrupted
3. Single-parent family—one head, as a consequence of divorce, abandonment, or separation (with financial aid rarely coming from the second parent), and usually including pre-school and/or school-age children.
   a. Career
   b. Non-career
4. Single adult living alone.
5. Three-generation family—may characterize any variant of family forms 1, 2, or 3 living in a common household.
6. Middle-aged or elderly couple—husband as provider, wife at home (children have been "launched" into college, career, or marriage).
7. Kin network—nuclear households or unmarried members living in close geographical proximity and operating within a reciprocal system of exchange of goods and services.
8. "Second-career" family—the wife enters the work force when the children are in school or have left the parental home.

Emerging experimental structures which have an effect on children include:

---

*An analysis of variant family forms is found in Sussman et al. (1970). Margaret P. Brooks, Research Associate, Institute on the Family and the Bureaucratic Society, has suggested a modification of the original typography, which is incorporated in this presentation.

1. Commune family
   a. Household of more than one monogamous couple with children, sharing common facilities, resources, and experiences; socialization of the child is a group activity.
   b. Household of adults and offspring—a "group marriage" known as one family—where all individuals are "married" to each other and all are "parents" to the children. Usually develops a status system with leaders believed to have charisma.
2. Unmarried parent and child family—usually mother and child, where marriage is not desired or possible.
3. Unmarried couple and child family—usually a common-law type of marriage with the child their biological issue or informally adopted.

The implications of variant family forms for legislation, policy, and programs to help families are obvious. No single policy, legislative act, or program will be equally supportive of all types of family structures. There will be more discussion on this topic later.

The problem of strengthening variant family forms is complicated by such intervening variables as the stage in the life cycle and the socio-economic status of the family. When a traditional nuclear family becomes a single-parent one, the problems created by this transition and the mechanisms for handling them will vary according to the cause(s) which induced this change: whether the new single parent has small children, yet requires gainful employment (or training), or whether the parent is middle-aged with grown children and requires resocialization into a career or new uses of leisure. Consequently, the age composition, size, and socio-economic status of each family undergoing this structural transition will create issues and problems for the human service systems of the society.

It is becoming increasingly common for individuals over the life cycle to move from one family form to another, either because of design or circumstances. Consider the following case: For the first five years of his life, Craig lived in a three-generation rural household with his siblings, grandparents, and a number of aunts, uncles, and cousins. During this time he had many parent surrogates and adult role models; one in particular was his grandfather. Near his fifth birthday, his parents and two siblings left the farm and migrated to a city about one hundred miles away. His father found a job as an unskilled factory worker. The income was insufficient to support the family, so when Craig entered primary school his mother took a job as saleswoman at a downtown department store. Three years later the father, who could not "make it," deserted. Financially the family was secure, because Craig's mother proved to be a competent businesswoman and was soon promoted to the position of department manager. Two years after the father left, a divorce was granted; a year later, the mother married a widower with two children.

It is unnecessary to continue the family life career of Craig to illustrate that over a period of six or seven years he lived in four variant forms of the traditional nuclear (intact) family: the three-generation household, dual-work, single-parent, and remarried. Each of these forms presented different issues and problems for Craig, his parents, and his siblings. These involved changes in interaction patterns, the role system and socialization patterns within the family, and modifications of the linkage of the family with non-family groups and organizations.

Possible explanations of the causes of variant family forms, or at least their greater visibility and increased incidence, are varied and speculative (Sussman, forthcoming a).

1. Traditional institutions have reached the limits of their capabilities to absorb and embrace the adherents of the "new culture." One alternative for members of the "establishment" who hope to continue societal control is to further recognize pluralism by increasing the options for individuals and families of different forms, especially where these forms are characteristic of certain disenfranchised and deprived minorities.

2. A different and somewhat contrary explanation states that powerful elites feel comfortable about their ability to control large-scale change and at the same time perceive tolerance of non-conformity and deviance to be politically salient. Variant behavior and structures become increasingly overt as the more frequent, minor, negative sanctions are removed.

3. American society is in the beginning of a social revolution. It is at a stage when old-order institutions are being attacked, and experimental family forms like communes represent opposition and confrontation with the old culture's way of life. The thrust of some social revolutionaries is to create new forms of the family based on ideologies and arrangements which accommodate the differential capabilities, aspirations, motivations, and needs of its members.

Structural Properties of Kin Family Systems

A plethora of research by family sociologists during the past two decades has established the pervasiveness of a kin family network in urban environments built upon principles of exchange and reciprocity.* This network embraces numerous family forms. The delay until the early 1950's in recognizing this network was due, in part, to conceptualizations which emphasized

---

*For a review of research supporting this view and presentation of empirical data, see Sussman and Burchinal, 1962, 1968, 1970.

that social mobility was the most characteristic feature of complex bureaucratic societies. According to this view, the nuclear family, consisting of a married couple and their minor children, appeared to be the unit best suited to meet the normative demands of the economic system—to move where there was the best opportunity for higher income with parallel improvements in social status, prestige, and power.* The functionality of the nuclear family is still maintained by a large number of investigators. For them, the unit is treated as coterminus with the entire institution of the family today in the American milieu. Talcott Parsons considers it to be a completely integrated unit which has survived by virtue of its superior adaptability. It can bend and reshape its structure according to the needs and demands of more powerful bureaucracies. This view is reinforced by law, policies, and programs which label the nuclear family as the unit which has corporate responsibility for its affiliated members.

At the same time, however, social scientists have been aware that all possible social interactions are not exhausted by contractual arrangements between bureaucratic organizations and discrete units such as the nuclear family. In urban as well as rural settings, nuclear families living in separate households are functionally related so as to form kin family networks. These extensions of the family remain viable through a system of unequal exchanges of services and financial aid which, in goals, norms, and values, vie with other primary and bureaucratic systems for the loyalty of those who are participants. Trust, expected reciprocity, and being able to "count on" the kin member are the most sailent characteristics of this system.

Studies of middle-class and working-class urban families reveal visitation among members with financial aid, advice, and child care as primary modalities. These studies reveal extensive intrafamily and interfamily relationships in a continuous state of change and with differential influence on the behavior of the actors. Linkages are forged or rendered inoperative on the basis of intra-network values. Network relationships are by no means stable; conflict as well as cooperation exists. There is an ongoing struggle among family units in each network for the achievement of in-group goals, as they attempt to meet their own needs and to achieve desired rewards. When shared goals cannot be identified among component units, disintegration of the kin network may result.

A study of family units at differing generational levels revealed cultural factors to be highly influential in assuring family continuity (Hill, 1971; Sussman, 1965). Notable among these were differences in the socio-economic cultural background of marriage mates; the types of courtship and

---

*A theoretical formulation which goes contrary to the theme of dominance of the economic system over the family is found in Sussman and Cogswell (forthcoming).

wedding ceremony that preceded the formation of a family unit; differences in child-rearing philosophy and practice; and the extent to which a help pattern was developed between parents and their married children. Proximity of residence was found to be another factor in determining the influence of those mentioned above, as it was utilized by the family to forge closer links or, alternatively, to lessen tensions.

Major Tasks and Functions: Family-Organizational Linkages

In the 1970's, as in the past, all types of families function with varied degrees of proficiency as facilitating, mediating, and confronting systems for their members, who have differing aspirations, capabilities, and potentials. Families adapt and influence behavior of their members and outsiders simultaneously. They adjust to complex urban life and at the same time modify the development, structure, and activities of contemporary social institutions and organizations. Because of variations in form, families differ in their adaptation and in their efforts to mitigate the demands of nonfamily groups and to influence the behavior of outside organizations such as the school, welfare agency, or factory. Consequently, the main tasks of families are: (1) to develop their capacities to socialize children, (2) to enhance the competence of their members to cope with the demands of the organizations in which they must function, (3) to utilize these organizations, (4) to provide an environment for the development of identities and affectional response; and (5) to create satisfactions and a mentally healthy environment intrinsic to the well-being of a family (Sussman et al., 1970).

In complex societies, there exist many alternative patterns for meeting contingencies. In the urban setting, a great variety of jobs, schools, residences, and facilities are available to family members, with the largest number of options available to the higher social classes and elites.* For some families, especially those of the middle and upper classes, the problem is sometimes too many choices, or "option glut."† For ethnic and racial groups, such as Mexican Americans, blacks, Puerto Ricans, Appalachian whites, there is option scarcity often coupled with pressure to limit or take away existing alternatives. As children acquire additional skills through informal and formal training systems, the potential range of options increases. "Enlightened" elites as well as social reformers recognize the differences in

---

*See working papers of the Cross-National Family Studies Project, Marvin B. Sussman, principal investigator, Case Western Reserve University, and "Policy, Family and Constraints," paper presented at Groves Conference on Marriage and the Family, April, 1970.

†This is the reverse of too few options and was suggested by Robert Rapoport of the Human Resources Centre, Tavistock Institute of Human Relations, London.

option availability when they work to expand the available options for more and more people in such life sectors as education, leisure, welfare, and work (Sussman, forthcoming b).

Although the number of options available to an individual varies according to his class, and ethnic and racial status, some families of every background seem able to enhance the capacity of their members to choose from available options and to perform competently in new roles and within a variety of organizations. Other families seem less able to do so, producing instead various manifestations of individual and familial malfunctioning. We know that the way in which community, social, welfare, and educational systems support or constrain the child and his family has some impact upon the development of competence in the use of options. Moreover, in modern societies the growing needs and demands for social, educational, and welfare services, as well as preventive and therapeutic health care, are extending beyond the capacities of even potential professional and paraprofessional manpower. As a result, the family—as a social unit with caretaking, therapeutic, socializing, expediting, and handling activities—is a vital and sometimes unrecognized partner of bureaucratic service organizations having health, welfare, and rehabilitative objectives.* Thus, the competency of the family unit in managing these societal relationships is an increasingly important issue.

In summary, the salient prerequisites for individual and family survival are competence in using bureaucratic organizations, the family's success in developing these management capabilities, and the family members' uses of options within a framework of satisfaction for self and concern over the welfare of others. Families which "make it" are those which have become aware of and use options and develop successful linkages with nonfamily organizations. The family, being a relatively small group of individuals usually intimately related to one another, forms a closed system. As a rule it does not join with other, non-kin families to develop an organization similar to existing institutional bureacracies that are most resistant to outside influences and change. As a consequence, it and its larger kin network play their most significant societal role as a mediator between its members and bureaucratic organizations, as it provides socialization and competence in coping with the normative demands of bureaucratic systems. Mediation, if it is perceived as successful, has to involve action which results in compromise without an undue loss of position, integrity, or power by participants. It involves a reciprocal process of being able to influence as well as being influenced.

A party to any transaction which is shorn of its strength and power to act on behalf of its members cannot maintain its integrity. It becomes subordi-

---

*For a fuller explanation of this notion, see Sussman (forthcoming c).

nate. Any unit—family, group, or organization—must provide sufficient support and success in transactions so that its members believe it is worthwhile to maintain over time.

The Kin Network Influence

The kin network and its member families may assist in individual adaptation to the larger society and in some instances influence organizational policy and practices. Education, for example, implies learning new roles as well as new knowledge. Much of the socialization in the student role is actually achieved in the family setting; although the latter takes place in the school, the family often exercises considerable influence over its performance. The educational program of the school takes cognizance of the social class of the families it serves, their patterns of socialization, and home environmental conditions. It must cater to these as well as to the needs and demands expressed by its pupils. (Haug and Sussman, 1969).

All families are not equally prepared to perform this mediating function. Research has revealed that the extent to which they are able to perform it depends upon their location and activity in the kin network, life-cycle stage, and experience with organizations. The community status of a family is affected by its kin connections. The position and attitudes of member units of the kin group also affect such matters as family planning, family size, and sponsorship in achieving educational and occupational objectives. This network can be an opportunity structure insofar as it accepts the priorities of the bureaucratic society and has the socio-economic resources to deal with it. Middle-class and upper-class families tend to have the most advantageous linkages through kin for purposes of mobility, and the greatest competency in using the network to achieve individual and family goals. Lower-class families, however, may consider that the intrinsic advantages of familism take precedence over those of increased mobility. The unskilled enjoy little security in the larger social sphere, a condition which encourages dependency upon kin for services which support economic as well as emotional ends. Thus, family cohesiveness, persistence, and continuity are not necessarily coincident with the effectiveness of the family unit in coping with the larger society.

It is apparent that the resources of some families leave them at a disadvantage in those transactions which take place outside of primary groups. In the mediation process, the bureaucracy may rely on the professional expert as its representative. He has been formally socialized for this role and is permitted, through his mandate for public service, to go beyond organizational goals and to concern himself in part with public or primary group needs (Litwak and Meyer, 1965, 1966, 1967). Nevertheless, primarily he supports the more extensive concerns of the bureaucratic institutions with which he is associated. He is likely to possess more resources to be used in the bargaining transaction than are available to the representative of the primary groups, and he is under constraints to mediate in the best interests of his employing organization.

Functionaries of bureaucratic organizations often co-opt primary group members in the mediation process. Even when families or their representatives are given a "piece of the action" through mediation, the degree of shift in their superordinate/subordinate power relationship is determined by the linkers from the bureaucratic organization. The experiences of black families with programs sponsored by Aid to Families with Dependent Children and the Office of Economic Opportunity provide examples.

If primary groups are going to influence the mediation process and are to have any effect on the policies and programs of organizations and, more importantly, maintain the integrity of their own internal structure, then they must socialize their members into the means for coping with mediating relationships of this character. The goals and functions of both the primary group and bureaucratic organization must be understood, and a competence developed in dealing with the complexities of their interaction.

The kin network may be a veritable gold mine for linkers with mediating skills and connections in different life sectors. Initial findings from a pilot study of a barrio in Puerto Rico indicate that members of the kin network and *compadre* system take on "specialist linker roles." If a family member needs a loan, is in trouble with the police, requires a social security number, wants a job, needs to obtain a driver's license, or wants to make a trip to the mainland, he goes to an "expert" kin or *compadre* family member, if such is not present in his household. This individual links the family with the bureaucratic organization and frequently may educate the help-seeker into the use of options as well as socialize him into mediating and handling skills and new roles required by the bureaucratic structure (Cross-National Family Research Project).

Internal Role Structure: Accommodations to Exigencies of the 1970's

A detailed analysis of changes in the internal system of the family in the 1970's would fill a monograph-length manuscript. Our objectives here are simply to illustrate modifications in role relationships and task allocations within families, and to raise some questions of issues and problems of these families without providing definitive answers. The dual-career family will be used to demonstrate the kinds of changes occurring in the interaction system.

Accurate statistics on the incidence and prevalence of this family form are not available. However, analysis of census data since 1948 on mothers who were or are currently employed gives some measure of prevalence and incidence rates. From 1948 to 1969 the percentage of mothers in the labor force with children less than six years old increased from 13 to 30, and mothers with children aged six to seventeen increased from 31 to 51. Nonwhite groups had a disproportionate number of mothers who were sixteen years or over and were gainfully employed during this same period. In March, 1969, of the 9.8 million mothers in the work force, 1.2 million were nonwhite; 64 percent of the nonwhites compared to 47 percent of the whites had children six to seventeen years of age; 44 percent compared to 27 percent had children under age six; 52 percent compared to 33 percent had no children under age 3. These figures suggest the necessity for a large proportion of nonwhite mothers with small children to enter the labor market.*

As married women continued to enter and re-enter the labor force during the 1960's, the dual-career family became more accepted in contemporary American life. In March, 1969, the proportion of families in which the husband and someone else worked was almost 52 percent. That "someone else" was far more likely to be the wife than a son or daughter.† The proportion of multi-worker families among nonwhites was 11 percent higher than among whites.

The amount of the husband's income is directly related to the decision of many women to go into gainful employment. In families with both parents present, mothers with children over six years but under seventeen are more likely to enter the labor market with each increasing year of age of the youngest child. It appears that mothers with younger children are not markedly influenced to go into gainful employment in proportion to the husband's income.‡

In addition to the need or desire for income, there are other reasons why women enter the labor force; for example, aspirations for a career, boredom at home, and a labor shortage in certain occupations. Regardless of the reasons for women increasingly entering gainful employment, the adults of such families do have responsibilities for the socialization of their children and for providing the youngsters with love, attention, and affection.

Earning money is one source of power, and a woman's working usually means re-allocation of roles and tasks within the family. If, as in better

*Source: U.S. Department of Labor, Bureau of Labor Statistics. Table titled, "Labor Force Participation Rates of Mothers (Husband Present), by Race and Age of Children, March 1969." From statistics to be included in *Profiles of Children*, chartbook of the White House Conference on Children and Youth, 1970.

†*Ibid.* Table titled, "Employment Status of Family Head and Labor Force Status of Wife and Other Family Members, by Color, March 1969."

‡Table titled, "Labor Force Participation Rates and Percent Distribution of Mothers (Husband Present) by Income of Husband in 1968 and Age of Children, March 1969."

educated groups, the woman is pursuing a highly skilled or professional career line, the family has more problems regarding mobility and child management than other family types. How does one handle problems arising from differential success of the husband or wife? If a decision is made to move, what adjustment is required in the career change of the marital partner? (The nonmonetary factors affecting job mobility are discussed in Sussman and Cogswell (forthcoming).) What are the special problems of having children? Do dual-employment parents have more guilt feelings than traditional parents about neglect of their children? Does working provide new options, with consequences such as a reduction in fertility? What do such families require in the form of educational, counseling, social and other supportive services and conveniences, which will enable them to pursue their careers successfully and meet their emotional, physical, and social needs and those of their children? What new uses of social and physical space are now required to enhance the functioning of this newly established major family form? What "built-in environments" can be created which will provide the uses of living space most conducive for the self-fulfillment of individual aspirations and needs? (A fuller analysis of this concept will be found in Sussman, 1970.)

For each of the variant family forms, a similar set of questions can be raised—with answers to be found within a framework which recognizes multiple problems and suggests solutions, policies, and programs tailored to fit the life style of that form. Such an approach demands an acceptance of pluralism in structure, belief, and action.

Recommendations for Support of Marriage and Families

In the 1960's, the increased variability in family forms has become more visible. Diversity is based on the right of individual Americans to live in any family form they feel will increase their options of self-fulfillment and help them achieve a desired quality of life. This may be a measure of this society's modernity. An enduringly pluralistic society must recognize that individuals of different capabilities and motivations may find self-fulfillment in any one of the family forms currently in existence in American society.

The type of family structure will affect socialization processes and outcomes. It is assumed that a society is interested in supporting those family structures which foster healthy physiological, emotional, and social growth of children. We are generally aware of the desirable conditions for character and personality development in the traditional nuclear family, but we have little knowledge of the positive qualities inherent in the environmental conditions of variant and experimental family forms.

It cannot be overemphasized that members of each family type have needs, problems, capabilities, and aspirations; some they share with members of other family types and some are limited to their own family form. The major task is to use our advanced technology and scientific discoveries to support all family forms by harnessing and re-allocating the resources on nonfamily groups and organizations to improve conditions for children, parents, and other related kin. To accomplish this we must build policies, structures, and environments around people rather than fit people into mass-produced formal systems and unimaginatively created physical, social, and interactional space.

Government agencies such as Housing and Urban Development, Office of Economic Opportunity, and Statistical Reporting Service can institute this approach by examining their on-going programs and exploring the possibilities of rearranging their policies and activities in order to meet the needs and aspirations of variant as well as traditional family forms. The essential approach of a unified agency program would be a "client-centered" one, in which conditions and environments (communities) are designed around families, rather than trying to fit families and their members into social and physical space on the economic principle of least cost and on narrowly conceived professional expertise.

The need is to abandon the traditional model of superordinate/subordinate interaction in providing services for families. In the 1970's, there are increasingly notable exceptions to traditional types of programming, where members of the family have been viewed as subordinate and in need of being "acted upon" by more knowledgeable and powerful professionals who have organized themselves into intellectual elites. One such international program is within the Home Economics Service of the Nutrition Division of the Food and Agricultural Organization of the United Nations. The "Planning for Better Family Living" program (PBFL) is a family-focused population program developed within FAO to reach rural families. Under this descriptive title is subsumed a multi-faceted educational program operating within theoretical constructs and tested methods used in field programs of FAO, where the objective is to provide families with an increasing number of options suited to members of different aspirations, capabilities, and motivations. Within the context of this varied program there will be extensive population-planning education, together with other services geared to needs of the varying recipient populations.*

"Layered Model" Abandoned

One salient feature of this program is that the traditional "layered model" of research and action, where the researcher and programmer are dominant and manipulative, is being abandoned. On the premises that action without

*The author is under contract with FAO to assist in the research activities of this project.

research into needs is folly and that research into human problems without action is stupidity, the developers of this program are involving the families themselves from the very beginning. Commencing in countries in East Africa and then in other nations which request this program, the focus is on learning by doing, and changing behavior and values by reciprocal socialization. Student and teacher. novice and agent. will operate within a situation which fosters reciprocity in decision-making and mutuality in exchange of knowledge and the giving of self. Family members will be encouraged to become full participants in the research and teaching processes. and will be considered as integral members of the team in achieving the objectives of PBFL.

Although it may be true that the majority of children find optimal conditions for effective socialization and character development in the traditional nuclear household. it is also necessary in a pluralistic society that governmental agencies supplying supportive services to families remove restrictions that prohibit services to children and their families simply because the style of their lives is labeled deviant. This is equally true whether the life style is forced by conditions beyond their control or in an attempt to devise new forms of family living. new patterns of socialization, and new ways of earning a living.

On the scientific level. further active assistance may be offered through research grants. demonstration programs. economic maintenance. or long-term loans for projects designed to investigate living and working processes in varied family forms. focusing on the implications of these structural systems for all aspects of the development of children. Such research and demonstrations must be thoroughly reviewed and evaluated. and mechanisms must be created for the communication and exchange of ideas among participants.

Forum 14 of the 1970 White House Conference on Children issued a strong recommendation to:

> ESTABLISH A PEOPLE-ORIENTED. NATIONAL INSTITUTE FOR THE FAMILY FOR ACTION, ADVOCACY, IMPLEMENTATION, LEGISLATION, AND RESEARCH.
>
> Recognizing that the family is the dominant socializing agent and the primary interface between the individual and society, its central position must be considered by the White House Conference on Children in making recommendations for improving the well-being of our nation's children.
>
> It is vital that children living in all types of family structures, including single-parent, traditional, dual-work, and commune, have equally available options for self-fulfillment.
>
> Present human service systems tend to fragment and undermine the family. All such delivery systems should be redirected to provide services and support through and to the family as a unit with recognition of the different needs, strengths and weaknesses of varying family forms.

Therefore, we recommend that an Institute for the Family be established by the Congress as a quasi-public organization. The process for its operation should be assured by establishing a trust fund through a per capita assessment drawn from federal taxes.

This Institute should have a broadly representative Board of Directors and be adequately staffed for carrying out its functions. These functions are to:

1. Serve as an advocate for families and children.

2. Provide the mechanisms for assuring follow-up and implementation of the White House Conference recommendations at all levels.

3. Develop and support demonstration, action, research, and evaluation programs which focus on building new environments for families and children; reorder existing services and programs to fit around desires and aspirations of families, and to involve families in their development and implementation.

4. Examine existing legislation for its effects on variant family forms.

5. Take action against legislation, regulations, and practices which are punitive to children because of their discriminatory policies against the integrity of families or variant forms of parenting.

6. Provide technical assistance to state and local programs for families and children. (Sussman et al., 1970, p. 6)

This institute is much needed and the proposed program of services for families and children is long overdue. Finally, all recommendations for improving the quality of life for families are strictly academic, unless there is a re-allocation of societal resources buttressed by government policies and programs which will provide an adequate guaranteed annual income for all families. With such an economic base, the way would be paved for the complementary activities of supplying more adequate education, food, housing, and the material amenities of living. In order to provide a greater number of real or meaningful options for an increasing proportion of all families, basic survival resources are essential. Only then can programs of family life education, including elements of family planning, home management, nutrition, maternal and child care, growth and development, interpersonal competence, and socialization make any sense.

Questions and Answers

Q: I am concerned with urban renewal, which was fleetingly referred to when HUD was mentioned. I was afraid Dr. Sussman would come to the end of his speech without making any reference to a guaranteed family income or to something like a negative income situation. Since he did refer to it briefly at the very end, I would like to ask him if he would comment more fully on the guaranteed family income and family income tax?

A: I support guaranteed family income. I think all the other programs of uplift don't take on much significance unless there is the economic means of life. I just got back from abroad, meeting with people from what we call the "developing countries" of the world, and saw the programs of providing nutrients, and improving interaction within the family—all far removed from reality because of the basically deprived economic conditions.

When I served years ago on a number of grant-giving agencies, we got in an application for a grant which was going to provide a population a very small sample of what I call the "dancing girl treatment services." It was to provide them ten different kinds of services, "nails on wheels," psychiatric care, home visitation, television, all sorts of support services. (I think support services are important within their context.) The research project was going to demonstrate that if you provided all these services you could increase the longevity of the relatively aged population. One of my colleagues who was more quantitatively oriented than I—he runs a big center at the University of Michigan—figured out that this research project was going to cost fifteen thousand dollars per year for each person that was going to be helped and studied.

He said, "What would my Congressman say if he saw this application?" I in my devilish way made the crass suggestion, "Why don't we give them each six thousand dollars and save the government nine thousand dollars per head, and then study the consequences of this?"

I think that if you were to begin to shift around the economic resources, reallocate them, you would begin to see confidence develop in many ways— that often the program does not require the heavy hand of the professional.

Q: If I understand one of your main points correctly, it seems to me that it is quite revolutionary, so I want to make sure I understand it correctly. If two homosexuals adopt a child or two lesbians adopt a child, or if a hippie commune raises children, are you saying that these families are to be treated in a kind of value-free way by the government, and that they are to be dealt with simply as families?

Are you saying that the general attitude toward such families is to be ignored by the governmental agencies? If you are saying this, how do you expect this to happen, as long as society has the attitudes it has toward these activities and this type of family?

A: That is a great question to ask. I won't hedge on it. I think a pluralistic society like ours—and I think it is a great one—has to survive on its tolerance, on allowing people to make their own decisions as to what is best for them.

I happened to look a little bit into the communes. It has become very fashionable to study them; I am not studying communes, but I did take what seems to be a high-powered forum committee out to New Mexico. I decided not to meet in Washington or Philadelphia—too much tradition there —but to take them out to the West, where these communes were. I think even the monsignor on our committee was quite impressed by the honest efforts of the young people to find themselves in a new form of family life, if you will.

I guess I'll have to say that I would go for this kind of toleration. This doesn't necessarily mean that I would choose to live in one of these groups; I am too old, anyway, and I need not tell you what my preferences are. But I think I would stick by their right to do this, and I would fight for the prevention of hoeing them down, of eliminating them. I don't know what the consequences to children are. I think we ought to find out. We certainly have not done so great a job with our children in the traditional manner.

Q: I'd like to ask Mr. Sussman how planning for an improved family through the use of our technological and economic capacity will avoid the problems of social unrest? As Mr. Cutler illustrated in his discussion of the "J" curve, when one is shown something better, his satisfaction with his present state will diminish rapidly and his unrest will be increased.

A: I don't know whether my own work would enable me to handle the global issue you raised. I mentioned using science and technology because I am working with a group which is trying to create new kinds of environment, in terms of physical and social space which you can actually build—what I call a built-in environment—that would meet different problems which now exist. Let me give you a very commonplace example.

There are some family forms that need the kind of housing in which there is a large space, you might call it community space. You can, using the technology we have, at the same cost as you build the very conventional, unimaginative, what we call "plantation estates"—public housing—begin to work it out. We have computer systems that we can feed data into and give you exactly what it would cost to develop an imaginative environment for a family—a large family, if you will.

Or, if you have a family that doesn't want this, or wants the option of not eating in the sterile kitchen we built for them, but of perhaps eating as a group, you could find out what the cost would be, in housing projects for those of middle income or working-class income, to provide the different options of living. When I talk about built-in environments, I am thinking that some of the fundamental unhappiness, the alienation and frustration, comes about from being unmotivated in the usual sterile environments. I would begin there.

I am not sure I can answer your question. I could handle the big problems of unrest, but I have a feeling that the unrest begins in the monotony, the being constrained, the being forced, the being pushed, and not having much to say about what is happening to you. How many people who develop new institutions, or new communities, really pay attention to the people whom they are going to help?

Q: I am with the Philadelphia Bar Association. I was very intrigued with the answer that you gave a moment ago and I was thinking about it. Let me share my thoughts with you.

How is it possible, in a society with a system of private ownership, of private property, as your society is, with laws relating to adultery, fornication, sodomy, and the like on the one hand, and laws relating to the devolution of property upon death and such things as wills acts and intestate acts on the other—how is it possible, with these things on the books as they are, and with the Supreme Court holding, as it did just a few days ago, that an illegitimate child cannot succeed to the property rights of a deceased parent —how is it possible to work it all out? With these things built so strongly into the superstructure of this society, would it not be impossible, without changing the concept of property and the meaning of property and the way property is distributed, to have these forms that you just have spoken about become viable entities within a pluralistic society?

A: This is an excellent observation and question. I think some of the existing legislation structures are being put to the test; they are constantly being put to the test. I just finished a study of inheritance in the family and what it does or doesn't do to the family. I am hoping that as a consequence of this study, with a whole set of recommendations, there may be some reform in the probate process itself and in some of the legislation governing inheritance of property.

I raised these very questions with the people living in the communes. These matters ought to be studied so we can see what the impacts are. I am not convinced as you are that changes cannot be brought about. I see vast changes in divorce laws in this country. I see vast changes in abortion laws in this country. I suspect that it takes the legal system several hundred years to catch up with the world, but it finally does.

Q: I would like to ask a practical question about the low-income individuals living in public housing. How can you expect these people to live on an income of $138 a month and pay a rent of $74? What good are your ideas if people don't have enough to eat?

A: You are perfectly right. I am with you, and I think this is where the basic income, the guaranteed income, is necessary—modifying the social security system. Some efforts are being made to do this. It is one of the essential problems for a minority of people. There are many people who live with relatives, but I am not saying this is a substitute for having an adequate income. I think anything that the professional suggests or recommends, any of these human service systems of providing a better life, has to have the economic base.

I would almost say that each of the forums in the White House Conference came up with the central theme of a reallocation of resources to provide these minimum levels of life for the underprivileged, the aged, and all the groups that we have labeled as deviant. I think that anything else is a sort of trimming on the cake.

Q: As a parent, I am concerned about family disruption in the urban environment. I have children in the Philadelphia public school system and I am in the Home and School Association and I have observed the problems in the urban area up close. It is my observation that much of the disruptive behavior of young people in the urban environment can be linked to families that for a variety of reasons have given up on the management of their children.

You referred to the concept of child management, which I thought was fundamental. The children as a result of this abandonment are relying on their own devices. This results in a great deal of anti-social behavior on the part of groups sometimes characterized as gangs, and in a great many other problems produced by the present urban environment.

A: Maybe we have to work on the resocialization of parents. I don't think much has been done here. We have tended in much of the effort to "socialize" children, to get the reciprocation of socialization. I think that perhaps even the way we look at it is part of the problem. It is not simply parents shaping and forming children to conform with a growth process involving both. A lot of it has to do with the in-puts the child gets from his parent group, and in school. We find in studying very poor ghetto families that children are much more effective as socialization agents for their parents, because of the exposure to new experiences, new knowledge, and the like.

I wanted, too, to be a sort of devil's advocate in answering the question about disruption. I always felt that a little disruption is very good, that it preconditions for change—makes you begin to think. Many of us have been "shook up" in the last few years by disruptions and we have begun to examine our own cherished hypotheses as a consequence of this.

So, I don't know whether you are talking about blood-thirsty eating or the kind of disruption that one has to learn how to live with in a complex society, which may be part of the training of the child in handling confrontation— I should say (which I did not stress in this paper), in becoming fairly proficient at confrontation. As a matter of fact, I think families might be able to get a better "handle" on the society by helping their children learn skills, and also by confronting injustice rather than accepting it.

You are asking a very direct question because you are bothered by disruption and you are saying, How can we get these parents to do something about it? I am simplifying a very complex question, but I shall ask you to think with me: Who are these parents? What are some of the other hang-ups they have? What other problems are they having—in their marriages? in making a living? What do they know about population control? Maybe they have too many children to pay much attention to any one of them. There are a lot of things like that about which I can't say, "I'll go in there and preach to them, and I'll get them to do this or that." You just can't do it.

References

Cross-National Family Research Project, Caguas, Puerto Rico, working document. Institute on the Family and Bureaucratic Society. Cleveland: Case Western Reserve University.

Haug, Marie, and Marvin B. Sussman. "Professional Autonomy and the Revolt of the Client." *Social Problems*, 17 (Fall 1969): 153–161.

Hill, Reuben. *Family Development Over Three Generations*. Cambridge: Harvard University Press, 1971.

Litwak, Eugene, and Henry J. Meyer. "Administrative Styles and Community Linkages of Public Schools." In *Schools in a Changing Society*, edited by A. J. Reiss, pp. 45–97. New York: Free Press, 1965.

Litwak, Eugene, and Henry J. Meyer. "A Balance Theory of Coordination Between Bureaucratic Organizations and Community Primary Groups." *Administrative Science Quarterly*, 11 (June 1966): 31–58.

Litwak, Eugene, and Henry J. Meyer. "The School and the Family: Linking Organizations and External Primary Groups." In *The Uses of Sociology*, edited by Paul Lazarsfeld, W. Sewell, and H. Wilensky, pp. 522–543. New York: Basic Books, 1967.

Rapoport, Rhona, and Robert N. Rapoport. "The Dual-Career Family." *Human Relations*, 20 (February 1969), no. 1: 3–30.

Sussman, Marvin B. "Relationships of Adult Children with Their Parents in the United States." In *Family, Intergenerational Relationships, and Social Structures*, edited by Ethel Shanas and Gordon Streib, pp. 62–92. Englewood Cliffs, N.J.: Prentice-Hall, 1965.

Sussman, Marvin B. "The Sociologist as a Tool of Social Action." In *Sociology in Action*, edited by Arthur B. Shostak, pp. 3–14. Homewood, Ill.: Dorsey Press, 1966.

Sussman, Marvin B. "A Prospectus: Construction of Built-In Environments—Housing and Services." Institute on the Family and Bureaucratic Society, Case Western Reserve University, 1970.

Sussman, Marvin B. "The Family." In *Encyclopedia of Social Work*. New York: National Association of Social Workers, forthcoming.

Sussman, Marvin B. "Competence and Options: A Theoretical Essay, Implications for Nutritional Research." In *Proceedings of NICHD-PAHO Conference on Assessment of Tests of Behavior from Studies of Nutrition in the Western Hemisphere*, edited by David Kallen. Forthcoming.

Sussman, Marvin B. "Family, Kinship, and Bureaucracy." In *Social Change and Human Change*, edited by Angus Campbell and Philip Converse. New York: Russell Sage, forthcoming.

Sussman, Marvin B., and Lee G. Burchinal. "Kin Family Network: Unheralded Structure in Current Conceptualizations of Family Functioning." *Marriage and Family Living*, 24 (August 1962): 231–240.

Sussman, Marvin B., and Lee G. Burchinal. "Adaptive, Directive and Integrative Behavior." *Family Process*, 7 (September 1968): 244–249.

Sussman, Marvin B., and Lee G. Burchinal. "The Urban Kin Network in the Formulation of Family Theory." In *Families in East and West*, edited by Reuben Hill and René König, pp. 481–503. Paris: Mouton, 1970.

Sussman, Marvin B., and Betty E. Cogswell. "Family Influences on Job Movement." *Human Relations*, forthcoming.

Sussman, Marvin B., et al. "Changing Families in a Changing Society." White House Conference on Children, Forum 14 Report. Washington, D.C.: Government Printing Office, 1971.